REPORTING WORLD WAR II

Reporting World War II

American Journalism 1938–1946

THE LIBRARY OF AMERICA

Some of the material in this volume is reprinted with permission of the
holders of copyright and publications rights. Acknowledgments can be
found on page 832. Cartography on pages 795–811 © Richard Natkiel,
1995, 2001.

Text design by Bruce Campbell.

Distributed to the trade in the United States
by Penguin Putnam Inc.
and in Canada by Penguin Books Canada Ltd.

Library of Congress Catalog Number: 00–067284
For cataloging information, see end of Index.
ISBN: 1–931082–05–7

This one-volume selection is drawn from *Reporting World War II,*
a two-volume hardcover set published by
The Library of America in 1995.

Manufactured in the United States of America

Contents

ix

Preface

By Stephen E. Ambrose

IT WAS the greatest event of the twentieth century. It changed everything. It was also the best reported war, ever. The men and women who covered the war told Americans who was winning, and why, and who did the fighting, and how. Over the radio and in newspapers, magazines, and books. They created images for us that are more vivid than anything seen on the television. The members of the Armed Services they reported on, the GIs, the Navy, the Air Force, the Marines, the Coast Guard, were our parents, or our children. They were part of a great generation. So too were the reporters. Their names thunder like cannon—Edward R. Murrow, William Shirer, A. J. Liebling, Ernie Pyle, Larry Lesueur, John Steinbeck, Margaret Bourke-White, Bill Mauldin, Martha Gellhorn, James Agee, John Hersey, and so many others. They set the standard and remain the touchstones for all war reporting.

This volume is the best of the best. It contains accounts of most major events of the war, from the Munich Conference in 1938 to Hiroshima in 1945. Through them we follow the course of the conflict in stories about the leaders and, even more, the ordinary people caught up in the carnage, the disasters, and the triumphs. Many of the stories reprinted here are American classics, in their own way fit to stand beside Mark Twain on the shelf. And some of them did more than report on what was happening—they caused people to change their minds and thus played a role in making history. One example is Edward R. Murrow's September 1940 broadcast from London during the Blitz. People wondered, Can they take it? Murrow convinced them that they could and that America should be supporting Britain in the war effort. Another is the series of stories, beginning in June 1942 and culminating in a November 1944 report on Auschwitz, that alerted Americans to Hitler's extermination camps and the systematic murder of Europe's Jews. It made us all the more determined to continue the war until we had smashed, completely, the Nazi regime.

The reporters told of what they saw and learned. They refused to glorify America or to repeat a propaganda line — here the contrast with German and Japanese reporters could not be greater. In this volume, for example, we must confront Ted Nakashima's account of the American internment camps for Japanese-Americans, or Roi Ottley's reporting on African-Americans and their segregation in the armed forces of a nation committed to destroying the world's worst racist. Or we follow General Joseph Stilwell in his retreat through Burma in Jack Belden's account. We are forced to face the cost of victory. It is there in Helen Lawrenson's story of the Merchant Marine and the Battle of the Atlantic, in John Steinbeck's story of the men going into the Salerno invasion, in Robert Sherrod's accounts of the Marines at Tarawa and of the first three days at Iwo Jima, in Homer Bigart's report on San Pietro, in Ernie Pyle's story of Omaha Beach, in Tom Lea's on Peleliu, in Martha Gellhorn's on the Battle of the Bulge. There are many others. Throughout we are reminded of what was at stake, perhaps most of all in Edward R. Murrow's broadcast in April 1945 from Buchenwald.

This is not a history of the war. It was much too big and far too important to be covered in a single volume. Nor is it a history of the men and women who fought it, or how or why. But it is an account of the people caught up in the maelstrom. Ordinary people from all walks of life, most of all the soldiers, marines, sailors, and airmen who did the fighting. Nearly every family in America had a father or a son or a husband in the service, and each family wanted to know about what it was like for them. Obviously in armed forces of more than twelve million men it was impossible to tell each experience, but the reporters — at least the best of them — knew that what was happening to the junior officers and the enlisted men in whatever theater, in whatever battle, was their assignment.

Not all the reporters knew this. Ernest Hemingway, for example, a correspondent for *Collier's* magazine and one of the world's most famous writers, did not. When he sat down to write, he was the only person in view. His dispatches to *Collier's* were about what he saw and did. "Never can I describe to you the emotions I felt," he opened his August 1944 report from liberated Paris, before going on to three columns about how he felt.

Ernie Pyle didn't see the war that way, which is why his reports are widely read a half century later, and Hemingway's World War II journalism isn't. Everyone already knew that Hemingway was brave, foolish, and sentimental. What they wanted to know was what the GIs were doing. That was what Pyle wrote about, as did the majority of his fellow reporters.

Of all the men and women whose writings have lasted and are here reprinted, two stand out in this regard. One is Ernie Pyle. His reporting, whether from Tunisia in February–May 1943, or from the Italian campaign in January 1944, or from Omaha Beach in June 1944, or from the Battle of Normandy in July–August 1944, was always concerned with the ordinary soldier, especially the infantryman. Who he was, how he fought, how he suffered, how he endured. In 1945 he went to the Pacific, where he covered the invasion of Okinawa. There he was asked by another reporter, Milton Chase, what his reaction to Japanese dead was. Pyle said dead men were all alike to him, and it made him feel sick to look at one. The next day, he was killed by Japanese machine-gun fire. Evan Wylie told the story.

The other favorite of the men of the war was Bill Mauldin. His cartoons caught the essence of combat for the infantry and life in the war zone exactly. Nearly every GI identified with his characters, Willie and Joe.

Pyle rarely wrote about the generals or the statesmen. Mauldin almost never drew cartoons about them. Pyle and Mauldin covered the war as it was, where it was. Through Pyle's writing and Mauldin's cartoons we get to feel and see what it was like. That they are featured in this book is the mark of what a superb job the editors of The Library of America did in selecting what to reprint from the vast coverage of the war.

Helena, Montana
October 2000

Introduction

By Samuel Hynes

OF ALL America's wars, World War II was the one reported most fully and directly, and in the most memorable words. In other wars, and police actions, and interventions, reporters were kept from the front by mistrustful generals, muffled by censors, and misled by rear-area dispatches and faked body-counts. The Second World War was different. Perhaps that was because it was our most democratic war, the only American war in which a universal draft really worked, men from every social class went to fight, and almost nobody wanted to be exempt. Every American family was involved in the war in some way—a son or a father in uniform, a daughter in a munitions factory, a wife building ships. It was Everybody's War. And because it was, its vast story had to be told, and told vastly. And told by persons who were present. There could be no substitute for eyewitness writing about the war—the kind of war writing that this book contains, and celebrates.

The problem for reporters was to get there, all the way into the war, to see what soldiers see and so break through the limitation that the reporter's job implies—of being only a visitor to war, a noncombatant, an observer, a civilian who is just in the way when the serious business of battle is going on. "You can't see much of a battle," the reporter Vincent Tubbs complained from a beachhead on New Britain, "even if it's just up the road from you"; and so he set off up that road, hitchhiking and walking through the jungle straight into the middle of his piece of the war, so he could tell his readers back in Baltimore what war was really like.

Other reporters immersed themselves in their wars in other ways: they flew on bombing raids over Berlin, dug in with Marines on Guadalcanal, hit the beach at Peleliu, waded ashore at Omaha Beach, parachuted into Germany, sailed on ships that fought in the great battles of Midway and Okinawa. They were bombed by Germans in the London Blitz and by Americans in the Normandy invasion, and torpedoed off Africa by a German submarine. And they took their casualties: killed by a sniper, wounded by mortar fire, dead in plane crashes. They became veterans, like any rifleman or paratrooper or ordinary seaman; and they despised those journalists who weren't, the "press association reporters who waited for [communiqués] back at rear headquarters."

The men and women who filed these dispatches were not historians: they didn't have the information, or the objectivity that distance confers, or the time; they didn't know, when they wrote, what the enemy would do, or which side would win this battle, or this war. Their stories are immediate, limited, and to be continued. The best term for what these reporters were and did is *witness*, in two of that word's meanings: *witness* as the person who sees, and the *witness* that is that person's testimony. One of Ernie Pyle's dispatches is headlined: "What a Tank Battle Looks Like"; every good piece of war reporting could carry a similar line: What a Sinking Aircraft Carrier Looks Like, What a Retreat Through a Jungle Looks Like, What a Kamikaze Attack Looks Like, What a Landing in Normandy Looks Like, What Buchenwald Looks Like.

There's more to it than that, of course; war reporting is more than a matter of looking. All the senses enter in: the sound of battle, the touch of jungle heat, the taste of rations, the smell of death. And the emotions, too: how it feels to be shelled, to fly through anti-aircraft fire, to lie in the sand of a beach under attack, to freeze in a winter foxhole; what fear feels like. War is unimaginable to the back-home reader in his easy chair; it's unlike any experience he could possibly have. The war correspondent must be that reader's imagination, and will be, if he's good, if he's *there*.

The stories they tell are not Big-Picture stories—nobody who is in a battle sees the whole action; war is all foreground when you're in it. But what good war reporting lacks in range it more than makes up for in details, which are what reality is made of. In London, while the bombs of the Blitz fall, milk is delivered to doorsteps every morning; as American troops withdraw from Bataan to the island of Corregidor an earthquake tosses the sea; Stilwell's troops retreating through Burma are joined by three tiny Indian children, a little girl and two even smaller boys whom she holds by the hands; in a ruined house in the Italian village of San Pietro a reporter finds an American baseball glove; during the Battle of the Bulge children at the edge of the fighting go on sledding down their favorite hill. History doesn't give you such curious particulars.

There is not much of the Glory of War in these reports: armies retreat, whole units surrender, bombs fall on the wrong troops, great ships sink, and men die, and die, and die. Not much Heroism, either, not the Hollywood/John Wayne kind, only men and women doing their jobs, and wishing, most of them, that they were back home. Reporters name them, in litanies of ordinary American names and home towns that are a characteristic part of the story: Captain Phelan of Waurika, Oklahoma, Corporal Vaglia of the Bronx, Private Schempp of Pittsburgh, Sergeant Peele of Robstown, Texas, who fought in the battle of San Pietro; McKinney, Seng, Kountzman, Jarrett, Lynnton, Montague, Parsons, Waltz, Watkins, Lanning, Castle, Roads, Mitlick, Larson, Vincent— all killed at Tarawa, and buried together there. That naming of men, the living and the dead, seems right: these soldiers and Marines were the men who fought the war and won it. Heroes don't win wars now, if they ever did; ordinary soldiers do, and their ordinary names should be recorded.

"Remember," Edward R. Murrow warned his radio audience from London in 1940, "this is not the last war"—by which he meant that the war that had just begun in Europe would be different from the *First* World War (which every adult in 1940 remembered well). And indeed it was different: the world's biggest war ever, a war that would cover the earth and kill perhaps sixty million people (most of them civilians), that would destroy cities and ravage countries, nearly annihilate the Jews of Europe, and end with the explosion of a bomb that would change the way the whole world thought about warfare, and about the fragility of life. It was, in a German general's phrase, "total war," war in which every place was a possible battlefield and every living creature a possible casualty.

To cover that world-circling war entirely, reporters would have to cover the earth, and be present at the great battles that have become our myths of that war: the Battle of Britain, Bataan, Guadalcanal, El Alamein, Salerno, D-Day, Bastogne, Iwo Jima. And the small battles too, the fighting for a village, for a narrow island beach, for a bridge, a stone wall. Given the vastness of the assignment, they did well: they were where the fighting was, whenever it was possible to be there.

Sometimes it wasn't possible. There are the *other* stories, the narratives that were beyond any correspondent's range: the war crimes of the Japanese in China and in their prisoner of war camps, the German atrocities in Russia, life in Leningrad and Stalingrad under siege, death in the concentration camps, death in Hiroshima and Nagasaki. These stories could not be told as they occurred; they had to be reported first as rumors of horrors, and only later as horrors seen, when reporters old in war experience witnessed what total war could be, what human beings were capable of doing to other human beings.

Two reporters have a special place in this book of war because they were special to the men who fought. Bill Mauldin was an infantryman in the Italian campaign before he turned to recording the war in cartoons. His drawings make Willie and Joe, his ordinary foot soldiers, as real as rain, as real as mud. Mauldin's drawings are often funny, with the bitter-ironic humor of the troops, but his written text is not. The words in *Up Front* are a description and a defense of men like Willie and Joe, the common dogfaces. Mauldin knew these men and loved their unheroic, cynical courage, and old soldiers love Mauldin; he got as close as anyone could to the realities of the World War II infantry war.

Ernie Pyle was never a soldier as Bill Mauldin was, but he lived with soldiers, shared their discomforts, and grieved for their deaths, and he chased the war with them when it moved, always trying to be where the troops were. Pyle covered the war first in North Africa, crossed to Sicily and then to Italy when the Allies advanced, landed on the beach at Normandy and shared in the liberation of Paris before moving on to the Pacific for the last great battle of the war at Okinawa, where he was killed by a sniper on the little offshore island of Ie Shima. I was on Okinawa then, and I remember how quickly the word spread: "Ernie Pyle is dead. They killed Ernie Pyle." Someone important had died—a guy none of us had ever seen but who was one of us, who was our voice.

In Pyle's pocket when he died was his last piece, written just before he landed on the island where he died. It is not so much a dispatch as a meditation on the end of the war and the monstrous infinity of the dead, addressed to his readers at home who will never have to witness such sights:

> These are the things you at home need not even try to understand. To you at home they are columns of figures, or he is a near one who went away and just didn't come back. You didn't see him lying so grotesque and pasty beside the gravel road in France.
> We saw him, saw him by the multiple thousands. That's the difference . . .

It was a difference that Pyle tried to bridge with his words. So did the other writers in this book. That, they assumed, was their job—to make "you at home" see, really *see*, the war that they saw: not glorious, not heroic, just the way it was, if you were there.

Princeton, New Jersey
November 2000

"It's All Over"

by William L. Shirer

MUNICH, *September 30*

It's all over. At twelve thirty this morning—thirty minutes after midnight—Hitler, Mussolini, Chamberlain, and Daladier signed a pact turning over Sudetenland to Germany. The German occupation begins tomorrow, Saturday, October 1, and will be completed by October 10. Thus the two "democracies" even assent to letting Hitler get by with his Sportpalast boast that he would get his Sudetenland by October 1. He gets everything he wanted, except that he has to wait a few days longer for *all* of it. His waiting ten short days has saved the peace of Europe—a curious commentary on this sick, decadent continent.

So far as I've been able to observe during these last, strangely unreal twenty-four hours, Daladier and Chamberlain never pressed for a single concession from Hitler. They never got together alone once and made no effort to present some kind of common "democratic" front to the two Cæsars. Hitler met Mussolini early yesterday morning at Kufstein and they made their plans. Daladier and Chamberlain arrived by separate planes and didn't even deem it useful to lunch together yesterday to map out their strategy, though the two dictators did.

Czechoslovakia, which is asked to make all the sacrifices so that Europe may have peace, was not consulted here at any stage of the talks. Their two representatives, Dr. Mastny, the intelligent and honest Czech Minister in Berlin, and a Dr. Masaryk of the Prague Foreign Office, were told at one thirty a.m. that Czechoslovakia would *have* to accept, told not by Hitler, but by Chamberlain and Daladier! Their protests, we hear, were practically laughed off by the elder statesman. Chamberlain, looking more like some bird—like the black vultures I've seen over the Parsi dead in Bombay—looked particularly pleased with himself when he returned to the Regina Palace Hotel after the signing early this morning, though he was a bit sleepy, *pleasantly* sleepy.

Daladier, on the other hand, looked a completely beaten and broken man. He came over to the Regina to say good-bye to Chamberlain. A bunch of us were waiting as he came down the stairs. Someone asked, or started to ask: "*Monsieur le President*, are you satisfied with the agreement? . . ." He turned as if to say something, but he was too tired and defeated and the words did not come out and he stumbled out the door in silence. The French say he fears to return to Paris, thinks a hostile mob will get him. Can only hope they're right. For France has sacrificed her whole Continental position and lost her main prop in eastern Europe. For France this day has been disastrous.

How different Hitler at two this morning! After being blocked from the Führerhaus all evening, I finally broke in just as he was leaving. Followed by Göring, Ribbentrop, Goebbels, Hess, and Keitel, he brushed past me like the conqueror he is this morning. I noticed his swagger. The tic was gone! As for Mussolini, he pulled out early, cocky as a rooster.

Incidentally, I've been badly scooped this night. Max Jordan of NBC got on the air a full hour ahead of me with the *text* of the agreement—one of the worst beatings I've ever taken. Because of his company's special position in Germany, he was allowed exclusive use of Hitler's radio studio in the Führerhaus, where the conference has been taking place. Wiegand, who also was in the house, tells me Max cornered Sir Horace Wilson of the British delegation as he stepped out of the conference room, procured an English text from him, rushed to the Führer's studio, and in a few moments was on the air. Unable to use this studio on the spot, I stayed close to the only other outlet, the studio of the Munich station, and arranged with several English and American friends to get me the document, if possible immediately after the meeting itself, if not from one of the delegations. Demaree Bess was first to arrive with a copy, but, alas, we were late. New York kindly phoned about two thirty this morning to tell me not to mind—damned decent of them. Actually at eleven thirty p.m.

I had gone on the air announcing that an agreement had been reached. I gave them all the essential details of the accord, stating that the occupation would begin Saturday, that it would be completed in ten days, et cetera. But I should have greatly liked to have had the official text first. Fortunately for CBS, Ed Murrow in London was the first to flash the official news to America that the agreement had been signed thirty minutes after midnight. He picked it up from the Munich radio station in the midst of a talk.

LATER.—Chamberlain, apparently realizing his diplomatic annihilation, has pulled a very clever face-saving stunt. He saw Hitler again this morning before leaving and afterwards a joint communiqué was issued. Essential part: "We regard the agreement signed last night and the Anglo-German naval accord as symbolic of the desire of our two peoples never to go to war with one another again." And a final paragraph saying they will consult about further questions which may concern the two countries and are "determined to continue our efforts to remove possible sources of difference and thus to contribute to the assurance of peace in Europe."

LATER. *On Train, Munich—Berlin.*—Most of the leading German editors on the train and tossing down the champagne and not trying to disguise any more their elation over Hitler's terrific victory over Britain and France. On the diner Halfeld of the *Hamburger Fremdenblatt*, Otto Kriegk of the *Nachtausgabe*, Dr. Boehmer, the foreign press chief of the Propaganda Ministry, gloating over it, buying out all the champagne in the diner, gloating, boasting, bragging. . . . When a German feels big he feels *big*. Shall have two hours in Berlin this evening to get my army passes and a bath and then off by night train to Passau to go into Sudetenland with the German army—a sad assignment for me.

Berlin Diary, 1941

Aufenthalt in Rosenheim

by Vincent Sheean

THE CAR broke down not far beyond Siegsdorf on the Reichs-autobahn to Munich—the great Reichsautobahn which is the most beautiful of all German motor roads, since it leads to the home of the Führer. It broke down, precisely, alongside the Chiemsee within sight of the fantastic isle where Ludwig II, another mad South German, built his absurd imitation Versailles. There was no traffic on the road at that hour of the night and four and a half hours passed before a mechanic could be routed out of bed at the nearest town and brought to tow us in.

He towed us in to Rosenheim, a comfortable Bavarian town of something like twenty thousand inhabitants. The car was in a dreadful state, it appeared, all of the teeth having disappeared from its tooth-wheel—I translate literally from the German, with no knowledge of the true English equivalents of such terms—and another could not be obtained nearer than Cologne. So here I sit in Rosenheim, day after day, waiting for a tooth-wheel.

The enforced stay in Rosenheim is not without interest. The place is notable, among other things, for having been the birthplace of the General Field Marshal Hermann Göring, and a place so sanctified cannot be altogether forgotten by Nazi solicitude. As I wander about the streets of the town, over the arcaded footwalks and beneath the tall, narrow oriels which the good Baedeker tells me are characteristic of this region, I observe a variety of edifying phenomena unmentioned in the guidebook. For example, the displays of names, photographs and other material on a glassed-in bulletin board entitled "The Jews Are Our Misfortune" (*Die Juden sind un- ser Unglück*). Such bulletin boards are at present no less characteristic of the region, I imagine, than arcaded footwalks and tall, narrow oriels.

4

The chief part of the bulletin board is taken up with typewritten lists of "racial comrades" (*Volksgenossen*) who have committed the crime of buying something from the Jews. These lists are headed "They bought from Jews." There are two such lists, the one obviously a sort of annex to the first, of slightly more recent date. The lists give full names and addresses of such treacherous "racial comrades," but do not specify what was the object bought from Jews. In one corner of the bulletin board there is a group of eight or nine snapshots of such unfaithful Aryans, labeled also "They bought from Jews," and presumably made just as the guilty purchases were about to be taken home. One of these shows an old woman with a market basket; another shows a young man on a bicycle with a package under his arm.

In the center of the bulletin board there is a list headed "Jewish businesses in Rosenheim." This contains only nine names, four of which have subsequently been crossed out in red crayon. You can imagine for yourself what the crossing out in red crayon signifies.

Every inch of the bulletin board is taken up by material of great interest. For instance, here in the upper right-hand corner is a photograph of three men in evening dress smiling in a group at (obviously) a banquet of some sort. Two of them are shaking hands. The caption on this photograph says: "Jewish Instigators of the Satanic Hatred of Germans" (*Judenhetzer des Satanisches Deutschhass*). Underneath this it specifies the three men: "The physicist Albert Einstein—Rabbi Stephen Wise, a Führer of Zionism—Fiorello LaGuardia, the mayor of the Jewish world-metropolis, New York." Next to this is a peculiarly unesthetic photograph of Mr. LaGuardia, chosen for grotesque effect; he has his mouth wide open and his head thrown back, arms and legs all flailing about in every direction. This picture is entitled: "A Singer of Obscene Couplets? No. The Half-Jew Mayor of the Jewish World Metropolis, New York." Two other photographs show members of the Munich Social Democratic Party of the days just after the War, but are chosen with the utmost skill so as to make these gentlemen look as much as possible like the Nazi idea of a Jewish criminal conspirator.

Press clippings are distributed in any free space there may

be on the board. One clipping narrates the "provocative" deed of a Jewish woman who, on buying some apples in a market, complained of their quality and was then set upon by the Aryan women there present and "taught a lesson." Another discusses the crime of purchasing goods from Jews. A third tells of a Jewish merchant named Hess, who, on being asked what his name really was, replied with criminal impudence, "the same as the Führer's—Stellvertreter" (usurper).

Running across the top of this bulletin board is the text of the decree issued by General Field Marshal Hermann Göring last April, making it a crime punishable by imprisonment and fines to deal with a Jew in business, to represent Jews in the law courts, or to take the place of Jews in running a business.

How, actually, can such things be? The thought torments every hour one spends in Germany. Not that prejudice and cruelty are at all unusual in human nature: we see them everywhere. But how can the German nation, this mighty and splendid nation, have sunk so low as to build a whole system on prejudice, construct a philosophy out of inhumanity? How can the ordinary, friendly, good-natured people one sees in the streets and the beer gardens and shops, the clear-eyed German people, accept such twisted and darkened and hideous nonsense as being a rule of life? Similarly, how do they accept the frightful lies their newspapers and radio gave them every day, a few weeks ago, about Czechoslovakia and "Czech atrocities"? How can they believe, as they do believe, that all non-Fascist countries are controlled by the Jews in a sense of sheer hatred for Germany? How can they join with such alacrity in the whole Nazi rigmarole of salutes and "Heil Hitlers!" and "Sieg Heils!" and the rest of it?

In the restaurants where I eat, while waiting for the tooth-wheel for the car, I see all the usual types of southern German. They are not physically so beautiful and strong as the types one sees in, say, Saxony, but they have their share of the national gifts in that direction. They come and go with "Heil Hitlers" on their lips, their right hands pawing the air—old men and young, women and children, doing their part in this mad dance which must in the end be a dance of death. They do not seem to be aware that it is a dance of death. "Our

Führer never wanted war, so we knew there would be no war"—that is what several of them have said to me lately, in Rosenheim. "We were not afraid," they say, "because we knew the Führer would not make war." They laugh at the photographs they see of frantic war precautions in London, Paris and Prague; the pictures of Hyde Park dug up to make refuges against air bombing are regarded as particularly humorous.

How was this done? A people like the Germans, heirs to an immense and irreplaceable culture, cannot be all fools. We know that the life of the modern mind would be crippled—would hardly go on at all—in any country if it were not for the contributions made to it by German genius. Then how can the direct heirs and products of this superior culture behave so like gangster children?

We are thrown back on the explanation offered by Prince Bülow, who had had ample opportunities to know his people. He said (it comes somewhere in his memoirs, but I have no copy here in Rosenheim to quote) that God had so enriched the German people with many gifts that he had in the end to take something away from them. The something which he took away, and without which they have floundered so foolishly through epoch after epoch, was a political sense. They have almost everything else, but in everything that has to do with politics they are the prey of tribal instinct, extreme suggestibility, sheeplike obedience and a total lack of humor or imagination. In short, they have no political sense of any kind, and were made not to rule but to be ruled.

Well, there may be something in that theory. I prefer to believe a related but dissimilar explanation of my own—that the political sense is not totally absent from the Germans, but is still extremely immature. Germany came late to political unity and is untrained in the ways of adult thinking. The war of 1914–18 left it with an assortment of grievances and a desperate sense of humiliation. Immature in the one immense department of human activity—immature for the *polis*—the German is, individually and in the aggregate, such a powerful part of the human body that his political adolescence can only be a time of grave danger for all the rest of us. These gentle, kindly, cultivated people, the clear-eyed, loyal, decent people, are the most easily deluded in the world, politically speaking— and, being deluded, are terrible in their strength.

I remember something I saw along the road in Czechoslovakia the other day. It was the day after the Reichswehr had occupied the "third zone" awarded to them by Neville Chamberlain: the zone which extended beyond Carlsbad to Buchau in old Bohemia. We were driving along towards Prague in the car (which then had its tooth-wheel relatively intact) when we passed a Reichswehr staff car drawn up beside the road. Half in and half out of it were two very brave and elegant young fellows in gray. They had a pair of binoculars which they were passing back and forth as they gazed across the valley in the fading day towards the hills beyond— towards the Czechoslovak line of fortifications. They were laughing. Laughing, that is, in their youth and strength and in the power of their great delusion, that the world belongs to them. It would have done no good whatever to stop and tell them what a disastrous delusion that is, and what certain ruin it must bring upon the Germany they love. They believe it: "Heil Hitler!" and "Sieg Heil!" for a while yet.

Well, the tooth-wheel will probably come tomorrow, and I can move on out of Rosenheim and these melancholy reflections. There is some slight, cold comfort in the thought that Germany's value to the human spirit is untouched by these terrifying phenomena of her political adolescence, and that when the torture of the coming years is over their lies and obfuscations will perish too. As the cynical Direktor says in the first speech of Goethe's prologue: "I know how to propitiate the spirit of the people"— *Ich weiss, wie man den Geist des Volks versöhnt.*

The New Republic, December 7, 1938

Last Warsaw Fort Yields to Germans

by Otto D. Tolischus

WITH THE GERMAN ARMY, Before Warsaw, Poland, Sept. 28 —The German campaign in Poland came to an end today when the fortress of Modlin followed Warsaw in surrendering unconditionally at 7 o'clock this morning. At the same time the bulk of the German Army had returned to the western side of the German-Russian demarcation line, which army circles regard as the new Reich border.

With that surrender of the last fort defending the city, Germany has attained her war aims in the East, namely, the partition of Poland, in exactly four weeks. She is already at work organizing the newly won territory in order to enhance its agricultural and industrial resources.

Again Chancellor Hitler has proved himself the "Mehrer" or aggrandizer, of the Reich. To his political triumph he has added an unprecedented military triumph as well.

But German Army quarters are perfectly well aware that this new aggrandizement has been obtained at a high price that is not measured by German casualties, which are comparatively small, but by the fact that, in place of weak Poland, Germany has again put powerful Russia on her eastern flank. Army circles are so aware of this new situation that they frankly declare:

"Germany must now be stronger than ever, not only to win the conflict with France and Britain but also to prepare for the inevitable dispute with Soviet Russia that must come some day."

In fact that is the consolation the German Army offers the conquered foe remaining on the German side of the demarcation line who still fear National Socialist Germany less than they do Bolshevist Russia.

The final dramatic scenes of Warsaw's and Modlin's surrender were witnessed by this writer together with a group of other foreign correspondents who arrived at the German front line on the edge of the capital yesterday afternoon to find Warsaw in flames and Modlin still being bombed and shelled to pieces.

We stood at the same spot on the Warsaw-Modlin road where General Werner von Fritsch fell and where a Polish army officer with a white flag had appeared a few hours earlier to offer the surrender of the city.

Around us stood German troops in their first line positions and there also lay the Polish dead. In front of us, some 250 yards away, stood the Polish advance guards in the shelter of a gateway, guns in hands, silently and suspiciously watching every move on their enemy's front.

Where they stood began the sea of houses that was Warsaw. Dense columns of smoke rose high above the Polish capital, which the evening sun painted with a rosy glow that turned blood red.

Behind us, in the background, was Modlin, where fighting still continued and which was just being shelled and bombed by a German air attack. The roar of cannon, the bursting of bombs could be heard plainly to be followed a little later by the roar of the engines of the attacking planes. Appropriately enough, Modlin was overhung by sinister-looking storm clouds into which the evening sun put enough reflected light to convert them into an Autumnal background for the columns of smoke and dust rising from the bursting bombs.

When we arrived at the front line firing had ceased, but the Germans still watched enemy movements as closely as did the Poles. For only today, after the "stop firing order" had been sounded for 9:30 in the morning, some misunderstanding arose as a result of which the Poles resumed fire with rifles, grenades, mine throwers and machine guns about 11 A.M. The Germans replied with artillery until a few more houses went up in flames.

What most interested veterans of former wars in our party, however, was the fact that despite motorization and other mechanical improvements on the war machine, modern warfare had really changed little and that its quintessence as represented by the front line, was still mud holes.

The mud i.   happily for their occupants were dry   ., dugouts about five yards
apart manned as .   .: or two men armed with rifles
and hand grenades, wiiiè machine guns were posted at strategic points. Behind this first line were deeper trenches manned
by larger but still remarkably small troop contingents with
rifles, machine guns and mine throwers. After that, for a long
distance, came nothing—at least so far as the eye could
detect.

In fact, the closer one gets to the front line, the emptier
the landscape appears. All outward activity, the mile-long
transports and the marching troops, can be seen only far behind the front, usually out of range of artillery fire. But this
emptiness behind the front is merely modern camouflage,
and any flare-up of serious fighting soon converts innocent-
looking woods and peaceful-looking houses into fire-spitting
infernos.

The present positions, which will be maintained until all
preparations are completed for the German occupation of
Warsaw tomorrow, were not established until Sunday. They
were so recent and had been under such heavy fire that dead
Polish soldiers still lay where they had fallen amid dead horses
and abandoned equipment. In the pathetic inertness of their
sprawling bodies, they somehow, perhaps because of their
surroundings, looked more like inanimate objects than bodies
that once were living men, and in the growing darkness their
faces began to resemble those of mummies. If war robs death
of its majesty, nature compensates by covering up some of the
gruesomeness, enabling active men to keep sane.

A weapon more modern even than firearms, propaganda,
was also being used right at the front line. A large poster
displayed by the Germans announced in Polish:

"Poles! Come to us. We will not hurt you. We will give you
bread."

As explained by German staff officers, Warsaw was first
treated as an open city and only military objectives were
bombed or shelled. Then, however, General Czuma, commander of the defense, restored the old Warsaw forts, such as
Modlin, the last to hold out, and established defense lines
around the city. Whereupon the German Army command an-

nounced it would treat Warsaw as a fortress and shell and bomb it.

But this threat failed to weaken the city's defense. The Germans then offered a truce to evacuate diplomats and the civilian population and called for a Polish representative to appear at a designated point to negotiate.

After this the Germans sent airplanes over Warsaw, throwing millions of leaflets calling on the city to surrender, promising soldiers would be sent home instead of being made war prisoners, and that in view of their brave defense, officers would be permitted to keep their swords. The appeal to the officers was considered especially important because, in the German view, the backbone of the defense consisted of officers who had left their surrendering troops outside and had rallied within Warsaw in regiments consisting for the most part of officers only.

When that failed, two truces were arranged—one for evacuating foreign diplomats, who arrived in Koenigsberg, East Prussia, recently, and another for evacuating sixty-two Soviet diplomats after the Russian occupation of Eastern Poland.

Only then, according to German officers, did the real bombardment start. The forts, and especially the old citadel, were heavily bombed and shelled, as were the barracks, airport and such inferior points as parks where troop concentrations had been observed. As a result, many buildings also were damaged, including, it is understood, the former royal palace. A Polish truce officer, as well as others from Warsaw, asserted that, in fact, a large part of the city is merely "heaps of ruins."

Finally, late Tuesday night a Polish officer bearing a white flag appeared at the German front line and asked for a truce to evacuate the civilian population and the wounded. This was refused and the final unconditional surrender was announced early yesterday morning.

Shortly before midnight last night another Polish officer, a major, appeared at Army Corps Headquarters, where he was cordially received, to arrange for the surrender of Modlin. He carried a letter from General Rommel, commander of the Polish Army around Warsaw, ordering the commander of Modlin to give up.

Accompanied by a group of German officers and announced by a trumpet signal, the Polish major was taken to the Polish front line before Modlin at 1 A.M. A white banner held up on two sticks by two German soldiers was illuminated by a powerful searchlight supplied by a portable dynamo. In conjunction with the bright moonlight, this rather romantic scene was reminiscent of former rather than present-day war practices.

The German demand was surrender by 6 A.M., to be announced by a white flag over the Modlin citadel. When the flag failed to appear promptly the bombing and artillery bombardment of Modlin was resumed and could be heard plainly at our headquarters. Only then the last Polish center of resistance excepting an isolated band on the peninsula of Hela, near Danzig, gave up. The white flag floated over Modlin. The last shot in the German-Polish War had been fired at 7 o'clock this morning.

Today German heavy artillery and munitions trains already are moving westward again, carrying Polish flags and eagles as trophies and bearing on trucks and caissons short inscriptions such as:

"To hell with Poland and England" or "Warsaw-Paris express."

Details of how General von Fritsch was killed in action just before the Polish-German War came to an end were learned here at the front today.

According to this account, General von Fritsch had helped in front-line observation posts throughout the campaign and did so again last Friday in a major reconnoissance attack undertaken with infantry, artillery and bombers to test out the Polish line's strength. Suddenly from a house where no enemy previously was observed, the Poles started a heavy machine-gun fire. A bullet hit General von Fritsch in the thigh and severed an artery. A lieutenant accompanying him tried to bind up the wound but the general merely said:

"Please do not bother!"

These were his last words. Two minutes later he was dead. Despite a heavy fire, the lieutenant carried the body of his commander to the rear.

The New York Times, September 29, 1939

Paris Postscript

by A. J. Liebling

I

ON SATURDAY, May 11th, the day after the Germans invaded Holland and Belgium, I had a letter from Jean-Pierre, a corporal in one of the two French armored divisions, which were created after the Polish campaign. They were good divisions, and Jean-Pierre had no way of knowing that the Germans had six times as many. "The real rough-house is about to begin," he wrote. "So much the better! It will be like bursting an abscess." Jean-Pierre, whose parents were my oldest friends in France, was a strong, quiet boy who in civil life had been a draughtsman in an automobile factory. He liked to play ice hockey and collect marine algae. He had not wanted a soft job in a factory during the war because he did not want to be considered a coward.

On the same morning I had a telephone conversation with another friend of mine, Captain de Sombreuil, who had just arrived from Alsace on furlough. Upon reaching the Gare de l'Est, he had learned that all furloughs were cancelled, so he was going back by the next train. He called me up to say that he wouldn't be able to go to the races at Auteuil with me as he had planned. "It's good that it's starting at last," he said. "We can beat the Boches and have it over with by autumn."

In the afternoon I went to Auteuil alone. I watched a horse belonging to Senator Hennessy, the cognac man, win the Prix Wild Monarch for three-year-old hurdlers. The track was crowded with people whose main preoccupations seemed to be the new three-year-olds and the new fashions being worn by the women. That day the Germans were taking Arnhem and Maastricht in Holland and attacking Rotterdam with parachutists. Nobody worried much. Everyone was eager principally to know whether French troops had yet made contact with the enemy. "The Boches have business with somebody their own size now!" they said pugnaciously. "They will see we are not Poles or Norwegians!" It was conceivable, of course, that the Germans would win a few victories, but it would be a long war, like the last one. All France, hypnotized by 1918, still thought in terms of concentrated artillery preparations, followed by short advances and then, probably, by counterattacks. Even if the Allied troops should fail to save Holland, they would join the Belgians in holding the supposedly magnificent fortified line of the Albert Canal. At worst, the armies could fall back to the Franco-Belgian frontier, where, the newspapers had been proclaiming since September, there was a defensive system practically as strong as the Maginot Line. Confidence was a duty. The advertising department of the Magasins du Louvre discovered another duty for France. The store's slogan was "Madame, it is your duty to be elegant!" "They shall not pass" was considered *vieux jeu* and hysterical. The optimistic do-nothingism of the Chamberlain and Daladier regimes was, for millions of people, the new patriotism. Ten days before the war began in May, Alfred Duff Cooper told the Paris American Club, "We have found a new way to make war—without sacrificing human lives."

The news of the break-through at Sedan, which reached Paris on the fifth day of the offensive, was, for a few Parisians who were both pessimistic and analytical, the beginning of fear. But it happened so quickly, so casually, as presented in the communiqués, that the unreflective didn't take it seriously. The Belgian refugees began to arrive in Paris a few days after the fighting started. The great, sleek cars of the de-luxe refugees came first. The bicycle refugees arrived soon after. Slick-haired, sullen young men wearing pullover sweaters shot out of the darkness with terrifying, silent speed. They had the air of conquerors rather than of fugitives. Many of them undoubtedly were German spies. Ordinary destitute refugees arrived later by train and as extra riders on trucks. Nothing else happened at first to change the daily life of the town.

Tuesday evening, May 14th, I climbed the hill of Montmartre to the Rue Gabrielle to visit Jean-Pierre's parents. Henri,

Jean-Pierre's father, had long limbs and sad eyes; he combined the frame of a high jumper and the mustaches of a
Napoleonic grenadier. He was a good Catholic, and by birth
and training he belonged to the wealthier bourgeoisie. By
temperament, which he had never been allowed to indulge,
he was a bohemian. A long struggle to succeed in business,
which he secretly detested, had ended in a defeat just short of
total. When war was declared, he was working for a firm of
textile stylists whose customers were chiefly foreign mills.
Since September, business had fallen off drastically and Henri
had had nothing to do except drop in once in a while to keep
up the firm's desultory correspondence. Henri spoke English,
German, and Dutch in addition to French, and sometimes
sang in a deep voice which sounded like a good but slightly
flawed 'cello. He often said that he was happy to be living, at
last, high on Montmartre, just under Sacré-Cœur. His wife,
Eglée, would never have permitted him to live there for any
reason less compelling than poverty. Eglée, before her marriage to Henri, had been a buyer in a department store. Recently she had devised a muslin money belt for soldiers to
wear under their shirts. She worked an average of sixteen
hours a day, making the belts with a frantic dexterity, but
about once a fortnight she got so exhausted that she had to
stay in bed for two or three days. She had placed the belts in
several of the department stores, but her profit was small.
Eglée and Henri were both about sixty years old. For thirty-
five years Henri had pretended to like trade in order to hold
his wife's respect, and Eglée had pretended to loathe trade in
order to hold Henri's affection. Neither had succeeded in de-
ceiving the other. He brooded, she scolded, he drank a little,
they quarrelled incessantly, and they loved each other more
than any two people I have ever known.

As I came into their apartment Tuesday night, Eglée was
saying she felt sure Jean-Pierre was dead. Henri said that was
nonsense. She said he was an unfeeling parent. Henri became
angry and silent. Then he said that often, when he was at
Verdun, Eglée had not heard from him for a week at a time.
She said that Henri was always talking about Verdun and be-
littling "Jean-Pierre's war." "To think that after these years of
preparing to avoid the old mistakes," Henri said, "the Ger-

mans are now eighty miles from us. If they get to Paris, it's all over." Eglée said he was a defeatist to mention such an eventuality. He said, "I am not a defeatist. I am an old soldier and also an old travelling man, and I know how near they are to Paris." I tried to console him by saying that the Dutch, at any rate, were fighting better than anyone had expected. Henri had cousins in Holland. Eglée said the Dutch were Boches and would before long prove it.

The next morning there was a radio announcement that the Dutch had surrendered in Europe but were going to continue the war in the East Indies. In the afternoon, some of the American correspondents, including myself, went to the Netherlands Legation to meet Mynheer Van Kleffens, the Netherlands Minister for Foreign Affairs, who had arrived from London to explain the Dutch decision. Van Kleffens, accompanied by the Netherlands Minister to France and the Netherlands Minister for National Defence, received us and the journalists of other neutral countries in the Legation garden. While we were talking, sadly and quietly, among the trees, the French were losing the war. On that Wednesday, May 15th, the Germans made the deep incision which a few days later was to split the Allied armies. The Foreign Minister, a blond, long-faced man, had a pet phrase which he repeated many times, as a man does when he is too tired to think of new forms for his thought. "The Germans tried this," he would say, recounting some particular method of the German attack, and then he would add, "It failed." "It failed," he would say, and again, "It failed"—until you thought he was talking of a long, victorious Dutch resistance—and then finally, "But to fight longer was hopeless." "We will fight on" was another recurrent phrase. When we asked him whether the Dutch had any planes left to fight with, he said, "No. We had fifty bombers. The last one flew off and dropped its last bomb and never returned."

Holland, with one-tenth the population of Germany but with several times the wealth per capita, had presented fifty bombers against five thousand. It had been comfortable to believe in neutrality, and cheap. Norway, with the fourth largest merchant marine in the world, had not built the few good light cruisers and destroyers which might have barred the

weak German navy from its ports. France herself had econo-
mized on the Maginot Line, had decided it was too expensive
to extend the fortifications from Luxembourg to the sea. The
democracies had all been comfortable and fond of money.
Thinking of the United States, I was uneasy.

The first panic of the war hit Paris Thursday, May 16th. It
affected, however, only the most highly sensitized layers of
the population: the correspondents, the American and British
war-charity workers, and the French politicians. In Paris, because of censorship, news of disaster always arrived unofficially
and twenty-four hours late. On the evening of the cata-
strophic May 15th, even the neurotic clientele of the Ritz and
Crillon bars had been calm. But on Thursday people began
telling you about Germans at Meaux and south of Soissons,
points the Germans didn't actually reach until over three
weeks later. There was a run on the Paris branch of the Guaranty Trust Company by American depositors. I lunched in a
little restaurant I frequently went to on the Rue Ste.-Anne,
and after the meal, M. Bisque, the proprietor, suggested that
we go to the Gare du Nord to see the refugees. M. Bisque
cried easily. Like most fine cooks, he was emotional and a
heavy drinker. He had a long nose like a woodcock and a
mustache which had been steamed over cookpots until it
hung lifeless from his lip. Since my arrival in France in October he had taken me periodically on his buying trips to the
markets so that I could see the Germans weren't starving
Paris. On these trips we would carry a number of baskets and,
as we filled one after another with oysters, artichokes, or
pheasants, we would leave them at a series of bars where we
stopped for a drink of apple brandy. The theory was that
when we had completed our round of the markets we would
circle back on our course, picking up the baskets, and thus
avoid a lot of useless carrying. It worked all right when we
could remember the bars where we had left the various
things, but sometimes we couldn't, and on such occasions M.
Bisque would cry that *restauration* was a cursed *métier*, and
that if the government would permit he would take up his old
rifle and leave for the front. But they would have to let him
wear horizon blue; he could not stand the sight of khaki be-

cause it reminded him of the English. "They say the English are very brave at sea," he would say, winking slowly, "but who knows? We don't see them, eh?"

The trip to the Gare du Nord was solemn. M. Bisque dragged me to see various mothers sitting on rolls of bedding and surrounded by miauling children; his eyes would water, and he would offer a child a two-franc piece, and then haul me to the buffet, where he would fortify himself with a glass of Beaujolais. At the buffet I remember meeting a red-bearded gnome of a colonial soldier who kept referring to himself as "a real porpoise." "Porpoise" was the traditional Army term for a colonial infantryman. "A real porpoise," the soldier repeated dreamily, "an old porpoise, and believe me, Monsieur, the Germans need *somebody* to bust their snouts for them." He had two complete sets of decorations, one from the old war and one from the new. He was going north to rejoin his regiment and he was full of fight and red wine.

Saturday morning I had another note from Jean-Pierre. He enclosed a bit of steel from a Dornier shot down near him. "How I am still alive I have not time to write to you," he said, "but chance sometimes manages things well." The letter produced the same effect on me as news of a great victory. I called up Henri. He and Eglée had had a letter too.

On Saturday, May 18th, I went to a press conference held by the Ministry of Information, which had just organized an Anglo-American press section, with quarters in a vast, rococo ballroom at the Hôtel Continental called the Salle des Fêtes. Pierre Comert, chief of the section, held conferences for the correspondents at six every evening, when he would discuss the day's developments from the government's point of view. This evening he announced that Paul Reynaud had taken over the Ministry of National Defence. He also announced that Reynaud had recalled Marshal Pétain from Spain to advise him. General Weygand had already arrived from Syria and it was understood that he would take over the high command in a few days. The two great names, in conjunction, were expected to raise national morale. The two old men, however, were military opposites. Pétain, cautious at sixty, when he had defended Verdun, was at eighty-four incapable of conceiving any operation bolder than an orderly retreat. Weygand believed in unremitting attack. One staff officer later told me, "Weygand's ideas are so old-fashioned that they have become modern again. He is just what we need." Strategically, the two men cancelled each other, but politically they were a perfect team. Both were clericals, royalists, and anti-parliamentarians. There is something about very old soldiers like Hindenburg and Pétain that makes democrats trust them. But Pétain was to serve Laval's purpose as Hindenburg had served Hitler's. However, we were cheerful on the evening we heard about the appointments. The German advance was apparently slowing down, and all of us thought that Weygand might arrange a counterattack soon. A week earlier we had been expecting victories. Now we were cheered by a slightly slower tempo of disaster.

There was a hot, heavy pause the next few days. I took long walks on the boulevards, and up and down dull, deserted business streets. The wartime population of Paris had slowly increased from late November until April, as evacuated families returned from the provinces, but since the beginning of the offensive the population had again decreased. All the people who remained in town seemed to concentrate on the boulevards. It gave them comfort to look at one another. They were not yet consciously afraid, however. There were long queues in front of the movie houses, especially those that showed double features. You could get a table at a sidewalk café only with difficulty, and the ones that had girl orchestras did particularly well. One girl orchestra, at the Grande Maxeville, was called the Joyous Wings and its bandstand and instruments had been decorated with blue airplanes. There were no young soldiers in the streets, because no furloughs were being issued.

It is simple now to say, "The war on the Continent was lost on May 15th." But as the days in May passed, people in Paris only gradually came to suspect how disastrous that day had been. There was a time lag between every blow and the effect on public morale. I can't remember exactly when I first became frightened, or when I first began to notice that the shapes of people's faces were changing. There was plenty of

food in Paris. People got thin worrying. I think I noticed first
the thinning faces of the sporting girls in the cafés. Since the
same girls came to the same cafés every night, it was easy
to keep track. Then I became aware that the cheekbones,
the noses, and the jaws of all Paris were becoming more
prominent.

There was no immediate danger in Paris unless the Germans bombed it, and when the news was in any degree encouraging I did not think of bombing at all. When the news
was bad I thought of bombing with apprehension. It helped
me understand why troops in a winning army are frequently
brave and on the losing side aren't. We heard anti-aircraft fire
every night now, but there were no air-raid alarms, because
the planes the guns were firing at were reconnaissance planes.
The heaviest shooting would begin in the gray period just
before dawn. You wouldn't really settle down to sleep until
the morning shooting was over, and you wouldn't wake up
until noon.

On the night of May 21st, after Paul Reynaud announced to
the Senate that the Germans were at Arras and that France
was in danger, I had a *frousse*—a scare—of such extreme
character that it amounted to *le trac*, which means a complete
funk. It was an oppressively hot night, with thunder as well as
anti-aircraft fire, interspersed with noises which sounded like
the detonations of bombs in the suburbs. When I lay on my
bed face down, I couldn't help thinking of a slave turning his
back to the lash, and when I lay on my back I was afraid of
seeing the ceiling fall on me. Afterward I talked to dozens of
other people about that night and they all said they'd suffered
from the same funk. The next morning's papers carried
Weygand's opinion that the situation was not hopeless. This
cheered everybody. It has since been revealed that May 21st,
the day of the great *frousse*, was the day set for the counterattack which might have cracked the Germans. It never came,
and by May 22nd, when we were all beginning to feel encouraged, the opportunity had been missed.

Later that day, word got around among the correspondents
that negotiations were already on for a separate peace and
that if the French didn't sign it the Germans might arrive in
Paris in a few days. This counteracted the effect of the

Weygand message. Still later, I felt encouraged again as I watched a city gardener weed a bed of petunias in the Square Louvois, the tiny park under my hotel window. Surely, I thought, if the old man believed the Germans were coming in, he would not be bothering with the petunias.

The greatest encouragement I got during those sad weeks came from Jean-Pierre. Shortly after the Reynaud speech, I went up the hill to Montmartre to take some flowers to Jean-Pierre's mother. For once, Henri and Eglée were smiling at the same time. "You should have been here early this morning for a good surprise!" Henri shouted. "At five there was a knock at our door." "And who do you suppose it was?" his wife cried, taking over the narrative. "Suzette?" I demanded, naming their married daughter, who lived in Grenoble. I was sure that it had been Jean-Pierre, but I wanted to prolong Eglée's pleasure. "No," Eglée announced happily. "It was Jean-Pierre. He was magnificent. He looked like a cowboy." "He came with his *adjudant*," Henri broke in, "to get engine parts they needed for tanks. The boy has no rest, you know," he said proudly. "When the division goes into action he fights. When they are in reserve and the other fellows rest, he is head of a repair section. He is a magician with engines. And his morale is good! He says that the first days were hard, but that now they know they can beat the Boche." "On the first day of the battle, Jean-Pierre's general was arrested," Eglée said, with a sort of pride. "What *canaille*! Jean said it was fantastic what a traitor the general turned out to be. And there were German spies in French officers' uniforms!" "They met a regiment of artillery without officers," Henri said, "but completely! 'So much the better,' the artillerists said. 'They were traitors anyway. But where in the name of God are we supposed to go?' Fifteen German bombers appeared over Jean-Pierre's unit. 'We're in for it,' he said to himself. But the boy was lucky. The Germans had dropped their bombs elsewhere. Then Jean-Pierre's unit met German tanks. He says our fellows rode right over them. 'There may be a great many of them,' he said, 'but we are better than they are. Our guns penetrate them but they do not penetrate us. As for the spy problem, we have solved that. We simply shoot all officers we do not know.' Jean-Pierre and the *adjudant* stayed for breakfast. Then they had to go away."

Although I knew that an individual soldier had no chance to understand a military situation as a whole, Jean-Pierre's optimism raised my spirits considerably. I believe fully the details of the encounter with the German tanks. Jean-Pierre was of that peculiar race of engine-lovers who cannot lie about the performance of a mechanical thing.

When I returned to my hotel, I passed along Jean-Pierre's confident report to Toutou, the hotel's cashier, with whom I often discussed the war. She was a patriot but a congenital pessimist. All the employees slept on the top floor of the hotel, and as soon as Toutou had read of the German parachutists in Holland she had bought a revolver and cartridges. "If one lands on the roof, I'll pop him!" she had said. "Or perhaps as he descends past my window!"

In each week of disaster there was an Indian summer of optimism. On the third Sunday after the offensive started, I had dinner with Henri and Eglée. We teased one another about our forebodings a fortnight earlier. "Do you remember how sure you were that the Germans would be here momentarily?" Eglée said to me. "And how you were certain that Jean-Pierre was no longer alive?" Henri asked Eglée. "It seems a year ago," I said sincerely. "I must admit that the French have their heart well hooked on. Any other people would have caved in after such a blow. I wonder where Weygand will make the counterattack." "In Luxembourg, in my opinion," Henri said. "If he made the counterattack too far to the west he would not catch enough Boches. A good wide turning movement, and you will see—the whole band of them will have to scramble off. They will be on the other side of the Albert Canal again in a week."

We talked and listened to the radio, and, as usual, I stayed for tea, then for supper, and then for the final news bulletin broadcast at eleven-thirty. The bulletins earlier in the day had been dull. But something in the speaker's voice this time warned us, as soon as he commenced, that the news was bad. We began to get sad before he had said anything important. Then he said, "Whatever the result of the battle in Flanders, the high command has made provision that the enemy will not profit strategically by its result." "What can he mean?" Eglée asked. "He means that they are preparing to embark that army for England," Henri said. "Unless the enemy captures the army, his victory is tactical but not strategical." "But why must they embark?" Eglée asked. "I do not know," Henri said almost savagely. That was the day—though none of us knew it—that King Leopold told his Ministers he was going to give up. Eglée began to cry. "Now they are coming to Paris," she said, "now they are coming to Paris."

The New Yorker, August 3, 1940

The Beginning of the End

by Virginia Cowles

TRY TO THINK in terms of million. Try to think of noise and confusion, of the thick smell of petrol, of the scraping of automobile gears, of shouts, wails, curses, tears. Try to think of a hot sun and underneath it an unbroken stream of humanity flowing southwards from Paris, and you have a picture of the gigantic civilian exodus that presaged the German advance.

I had seen refugees before. I had seen them wending their way along the roads of Spain and Czechoslovakia; straggling across the Polish-Roumanian frontier, trudging down the icy paths of Finland. But I had never seen anything like this. This was the first *mechanized* evacuation in history. There were some people in carts, some on foot and some on bicycles. But for the most part everyone was in a car.

Those cars, lurching, groaning, backfiring, represented a Noah's Ark of vehicles. Anything that had four wheels and an engine was pressed into service, no matter what the state of decrepitude; there were taxi-cabs, ice-trucks, bakery vans, perfume wagons, sports roadsters and Paris buses, all of them packed with human beings. I even saw a hearse loaded with children. They crawled along the roads two and three abreast, sometimes cutting across the fields and straddling the ditches. Tom and I caught up with the stream a mile or so outside Paris on the Paris-Dourdan-Chartres road and in the next three hours covered only nine miles.

We saw terrible sights. All along the way cars that had run out of petrol or broken down, were pushed into the fields. Old people, too tired or ill to walk any farther, were lying on the ground under the merciless glare of the sun. We saw one old woman propped up in the ditch with the family clustered around trying to pour some wine down her throat. Often the stream of traffic was held up by cars that stalled and refused to move again. One car ran out of petrol halfway up a hill. It was a bakery van, driven by a woman. Everyone shouted and honked their horns, while she stood in the middle of the road with her four children around her begging someone to give her some petrol. No one had any to spare. Finally, three men climbed out of a truck and in spite of her agonized protests, shoved the car into the ditch. It fell with a crash. The rear axle broke and the household possessions piled on top sprawled across the field. She screamed out a frenzy of abuse, then flung herself on the ground and sobbed. Once again the procession moved on.

In that world of terror, panic and confusion, it was difficult to believe that these were the citizens of Paris, citizens whose forefathers had fought for their freedom like tigers and stormed the Bastille with their bare hands. For the first time, I began to understand what had happened to France. Morale was a question of faith; faith in your cause, faith in your goal, but above all else, faith in your leaders. How could these people have faith in leaders who had abandoned them? Leaders who had given them no directions, no information, no reassurances; who neither had arranged for their evacuation nor called on them to stay at their places and fight for Paris until the last? If this was an example of French leadership, no wonder France was doomed. Everywhere the machinery seemed to have broken down. The dam had begun to crumble and hysteria, a trickle at first, had grown into a torrent.

Even the military roads were overrun with panic-stricken civilians. Tom was an officially accredited war correspondent, so he swung off on to one of them. Although the entrance was patrolled by gendarmes, who demanded our credentials, there was no one to keep traffic from streaming in at the intersections and a mile or so farther on we once again found civilian cars moving along two or three abreast. At one point an artillery unit on its way up to the new front southeast of Paris was blocked by a furniture truck stalled across the road. The driver, with perspiration pouring down his face was trying to crank the car while the soldiers yelled and cursed at him. One of them paced angrily up and down, saying "Filthy civilians. Filthy, filthy civilians." At last, the truck got started again and the unit moved past. Another time, a procession of ambulances, with gongs clanging frantically, were held up by congestion on the outskirts of a village for over an hour. The drivers swore loudly but it had little effect; I wondered what was happening to the poor devils inside.

The only military units that succeeded in getting a clear berth were the tanks. Once we looked back to see two powerful fifteen-ton monsters thundering up behind us. They were travelling about forty miles an hour and the effect was remarkable. People gave one look and pulled in to the ditches. They went rolling by, the great treads tearing up the earth and throwing pieces of dirt into the air like a fountain. After them came a number of fast-moving lorries and a string of soldiers on motor-cycles with machine-guns attached to the side-cars. They all seemed in excellent spirits: one of the tanks was gaily marked in chalk *"La Petite Marie,"* and the trucks and guns were draped with flowers. Two of the motor-cyclists shouted at us, asking if we had any cigarettes. Tom told me to throw them a couple of packages. They were so pleased they signalled us to follow them, escorted us past the long string of civilian cars to the middle of the convoy and placed us firmly between the two tanks. For the next ten or fifteen minutes we roared along at forty miles an hour. Unfortunately, eight or nine miles down the road they turned off, the motor-cyclists waved good-bye and blew us kisses, and once again we found ourselves caught up in the slow-moving procession of evacuees.

It was nearly nine o'clock now and we had covered little more than twenty miles. "I wonder if we'll make it," said Tom, looking at his watch. When we had left Paris at five o'clock there were already reports that the Germans were circling around on both sides of the capital to cut off the roads in the rear. Tom had a military map and we decided to try the cross-country lanes. Some of them were scarcely more than footpaths but we could at least average ten or twelve miles an hour, which was a great improvement. It was getting so dark it was difficult to see and twice we barely avoided running over people with no lights on their bicycles. Suddenly the sky lit up with a flash and we heard a far-away rumble. It was the first gunfire I had heard all day. "Something's creeping up on us," said Tom. "Still, if we keep on like this, I think we'll be all right."

We drove along the twisting lane for five or six miles. It was a relief to be in the open countryside away from the suffocating smell of petrol, but the road was so black the driving was a strain. Tom had some food in the back of the car and we decided to stop and have something to eat. He was in favour of finding a haystack to lean against, but the next few miles of country were barren and rocky. At last we saw a clump of trees outlined in the darkness. It seemed the best we could do, so we pulled over to the side of the road. The car gave a violent lurch and careened into a six-foot ditch. Only the right wheels were gripping the road. The left side was flat against the earth. We were suspended at such a sharp angle we had difficulty in forcing the upper door, but at last succeeded in climbing out.

The rumble of guns seemed to be louder and the flashes against the sky more frequent. "*Boches* or no *Boches*," said Tom, "it looks as though we're going to linger here a while. Let's pick out a place to eat, then I'll see if I can find someone to give us a hand."

But even here we were frustrated. The field was soaking wet. There was one miserable haystack in the middle of it, damp and soggy. We went back to the road and paced up and down for ten or fifteen minutes, wondering if anyone would pass. It was getting cold and I began to shiver. After having cursed the traffic for hours, it was slightly ironical to find ourselves longing for the sight of a human being.

Tom finally started back to the last village, several miles away, and I climbed back into the car (which was like going down a toboggan slide) to try and get warm. It was a beautiful night. The sky was clear and starry, and the only noise to break the quiet was the drone of crickets and the spasmodic thunder of guns. I wondered how far the Germans had got. Funny to think that people in America probably knew more than we did as to what was going on.

It was nearly midnight when Tom got back again. He had tried a dozen farmhouses but everyone was in bed. At last (with the help of a hundred-franc note) he had extracted a promise from one of the farmers to come at dawn with a team of horses and pull us out.

That was seven precious hours away, but it was the best he could do. As an American citizen, I was in no danger, but if Tom were captured, it meant an internment camp for the rest of the war. He appeared completely unruffled, however, and commented with characteristic English calmness: "Well, there's nothing to be done about it. Now, let's eat. God, I'm hungry."

We sat by the roadside, drinking wine and munching bread and cheese; then we got out all the coats and sweaters we could find, wrapped them round us, and climbed back into the car. The angle was so uncomfortable I slept only by fits and starts, expecting momentarily to be awakened by the noise of German tanks. Luckily, no such startling developments took place. The farmer kept his promise and shortly after five o'clock appeared with two, large, fat, white horses who pulled the car out as easily as though it had been a perambulator. Once again we started on our way.

We stopped at the next village—I can't remember the name of it—to get some coffee. The first sight that greeted us was half a dozen British Tommies lined up on the crooked cobble-stone street, the corporal standing in front of them, bawling them out for some misdemeanour. They were large, beefy-looking men that might have stepped out of a page from *Punch*. When the corporal dismissed them they grinned sheepishly and made a few jokes behind his back. Tom asked one of them where the officers were billeted, and I went into the café to try to get some of the grime off my clothes. In spite of the early hour there was a buzz of activity inside. Several people were sitting around, and a radio was blaring loudly. The announcer was saying something about the "heroic resistance of our troops." An old man made a gesture of disbelief and muttered something I couldn't hear. The woman with him replied angrily, her harsh voice echoing through the café: *"Ne dites pas ça. Il faut espèrer."*

I asked the waitress if there was any coffee, but she regarded me in mild surprise and replied that the refugees had gone through the village like a swarm of locusts. "Everywhere," she said, "they have stripped the countryside bare."

It took me some time to get clean again, and when I came out I found Tom waiting for me with two officers, wearing the insignia of the Royal Engineers. They offered to give us breakfast and led us down the street to the mess. They seemed to know little more than we did; they told us they had just received orders to move up to a new position. Most of them had been in France for the last five or six months and pressed us eagerly with questions about England. French morale may have been shaky, but there was nothing downhearted about this group. "You don't think people at home will be discouraged by this setback, do you?" 'Setback!' That was a good one, I thought. When we climbed into the car again they all clustered around and one of them said: "Well, so long. See you in Cologne next Christmas!"

We did the next hundred miles to Tours in about five hours. We had learned the trick now and kept entirely to the country lanes which, rough though they were, were fairly clear of refugees. It was only when we got within ten miles of Tours and were forced back on the main road again that the trickle once again became a mighty stream. Added to this, Tom's radiator began leaking. The water boiled up and clouds of steam began pouring out of the front. It took us nearly an hour to get into the city. The great bridge over the Loire looked like a long thin breadcrust swarming with ants.

Finally at one-thirty, with Tom's car gasping and heaving, we drew up before the Hotel de l'Univers. The first person I saw was Knickerbocker, just coming out of the door.

"My God! How did you get here?"

"You're always asking me that."

"But where've you come from?"

"Paris."

"Paris! But the Germans went into Paris hours ago. When did you leave?"

I told him.

"They were in the Bois de Boulogne last night. You must have rubbed shoulders with them on the way out. Probably you just didn't recognize them," he added with a grin. "All soldiers look grey in the dark."

*   *   *

Tours was bedlam. The French High Command had announced that the River Loire was to be the next line of defence and all sorts of wild rumors were circulating: first, that
the German Air Force had threatened to obliterate the town;
and, second, that German motor-cycle units had reached Le
Mans only thirty miles away, and were likely to come thundering through the streets at any moment now. The Government had already left for Bordeaux and the refugees who had
scrambled into Tours in a panic were now trying to scramble
out again in still more of a panic. I ran into Eddie Ward of the
B.B.C., who told me that *Press Wireless*, the only means of
communication with the outside world (all cables to England
were sent via America at eightpence a word) was still functioning, and that he and the *Reuter* staff were remaining another day. As it was my only chance to file a story, I decided
to stay too. Eddie said *Reuter's* could probably provide me
with a bed and he would give me a place in his car to Bordeaux in the morning.

There were a good many speculations about Winston
Churchill's conversation with Reynaud and Weygand three
days before; he was believed to have urged the French, if
the worst came to the worst, to continue the war from
North Africa. Although it had been announced in London
that complete agreement had been reached, "as to the
measures to be taken to meet the developments in the war
situation," most of the journalists were pessimistic about
the prospects of France's continuation of the fight. French
officials seemed in a state of moral collapse; even the censorship appeared to have broken down, but no one complained about that. Up till this time despatches had been
censored so rigidly it was impossible to give any indication
of the situation. Now, quite suddenly, everyone could say
what they liked. I wrote a long piece about the panic and
confusion along the road from Paris and not a word was
cut. Gordon Waterfield sent a story suggesting that France
was threatened with a defeat similar to that of 1870 and the
next morning Harold King sent an even more pessimistic
cable. Gordon told me later that when these despatches
reached London the censors were so surprised they held

them up for a considerable time while they found out from higher authorities whether it was really true that France was in such a bad way.

Eddie drove me over to *Reuter's* headquarters, a large, handsome edifice about a mile from the centre of the town. The house had been taken on a six months' lease to the tune of forty thousand francs and, as it turned out, was occupied exactly forty-eight hours. I spent the night there, which seemed an odd interlude. From a world of dirt and discomfort I suddenly found myself plunged into a Hollywood bedroom, decorated with mirrors and chintz, a thick white rug and a pale green telephone. That evening eight of us dined at a table with candles glowing and silver gleaming. We had turtle soup, tournedos with sauce *Bearnaise*, fresh vegetables and a wonderful cherry pie. The world might be turning upside down, but it was difficult to realize it.

The house was run by a charming, middle-aged couple— a caretaker and his wife. The latter, plump and motherly, was also taut and defiant; she refused to let bad news alarm her and clung ferociously to the belief that France would rally in the end. "If there were more people like her," said Eddie, "there wouldn't be an end. But, unfortunately, there aren't."

I spent that afternoon writing my story for the *Sunday Times*. About seven o'clock the wail of sirens hooted through the town and a few minutes later I heard the drone of bombers. I tried to ignore it and went on typing. Suddenly I heard a shriek from the drawing-room. I ran downstairs and found the eight- and nine-year-old children of the caretakers jumping up and down with joy. *"Nous avons vu les Boches!"* Then they both leaned far out of the window, pointing towards the sky. You could just make out a few small specks circling overhead. I wished I could get as enthusiastic over an air raid; in spite of all the talk about sparing children the terrors of bombardment, they seemed to be the only ones who really enjoyed it.

I was surprised that their mother didn't order them into a shelter, but I learned later she was disdainful of people who took cover. The next morning when the German planes came over again, several bombs fell near us, shaking the house violently. Eddie and I went down to the kitchen. She gave us an enquiring look.

"You're not afraid of the *Boches*, are you?"

"Oh, no," said Eddie weakly. "I thought perhaps you might have an extra cup of coffee."

"Oh, certainly." Her face brightened. "I don't like to see people afraid of the *Boches*. They're all filthy bullies and cowards. My husband was in the last war and he said whenever they came up against equal numbers they turned and ran. They're all the same. There's nothing to be afraid of."

"Nothing," I agreed, my heart still pounding uncertainly. Eddie gave me a sour look.

We left shortly after lunch for Bordeaux. There were six of us: Gordon Waterfield, Harold King, Courtenay Young, Joan Slocombe (the pretty nineteen-year-old daughter of George Slocombe of the *Sunday Express*), Eddie and myself. Gordon had a Ford roadster and Eddie a Citroen, with an R.A.F. number plate, which he had picked up somewhere between Brussels and Tours. They had been wise enough to do a good deal of shopping and it took over half an hour to load up the cars with blankets, sleeping-bags, cooking utensils and stores of food—not to mention typewriters, luggage, office files, a camping tent and a collapsible canoe.

Just before we started off, Courtenay Young and I hurried down to the *Press Wireless* office to send a final despatch. On the way back I heard someone call to me and looked around to see the little Egyptian with whom I had travelled to Paris. His hair was streaming round his face, his clothes were caked with mud, and he looked more agitated than ever. He had had a terrible time. He had found his house deserted, and his children gone; he hadn't yet discovered what had happened to them. He had left Paris only twenty-four hours before and had actually seen the Germans entering the city through the Aubervilliers Gate. Motor-cycle units had passed as close as two hundred yards from where he was standing. He said the occupation had come as a shock to many of the people and the scenes of despair were unbelievable. Men and women wept openly in the street. "Some of them went almost crazy," he gasped. "I saw one woman pull out a revolver and shoot her dog, then set fire to her house."

The Egyptian was on his way to Bordeaux. He was in such a rush he couldn't stop to tell me more and I never learned the story of how he had managed to escape from Paris.

Looking for Trouble, 1941

"Revengeful, Triumphant Hate"

by William L. Shirer

PARIS, *June 21*

On the exact spot in the little clearing in the Forest of Compiègne where at five a.m. on November 11, 1918, the armistice which ended the World War was signed, Adolf Hitler today handed *his* armistice terms to France. To make German revenge complete, the meeting of the German and French plenipotentiaries took place in Marshal Foch's private car, in which Foch laid down the armistice terms to Germany twenty-two years ago. Even the same table in the rickety old *wagon-lit* car was used. And through the windows we saw Hitler occupying the very seat on which Foch had sat at that table when he dictated the other armistice.

The humiliation of France, of the French, was complete. And yet in the preamble to the armistice terms Hitler told the French that he had not chosen this spot at Compiègne out of revenge; merely to right an old wrong. From the demeanour of the French delegates I gathered that they did not appreciate the difference.

The German terms we do not know yet. The preamble says the general basis for them is: (1) to prevent a resumption of the fighting; (2) to offer Germany complete guarantees for her continuation of the war against Britain; (3) to create the foundations for a peace, the basis of which is to be the reparation of an injustice inflicted upon Germany by force. The third point seems to mean: revenge for the defeat of 1918.

Kerker for NBC and I for CBS in a joint half-hour broadcast early this evening described today's amazing scene as best we could. It made, I think, a good broadcast.

The armistice negotiations began at three fifteen p.m. A warm June sun beat down on the great elm and pine trees, and cast pleasant shadows on the wooded avenues as Hitler, with the German plenipotentiaries at his side, appeared. He alighted from his car in front of the French monument to Alsace-Lorraine which stands at the end of an avenue about two hundred yards from the clearing where the armistice car waits on exactly the same spot it occupied twenty-two years ago.

The Alsace-Lorraine statue, I noted, was covered with German war flags so that you could not see its sculptured work nor read its inscription. But I had seen it some years before—the large sword representing the sword of the Allies, and its point sticking into a large, limp eagle, representing the old Empire of the Kaiser. And the inscription underneath in French saying: "TO THE HEROIC SOLDIERS OF FRANCE . . . DEFENDERS OF THE COUNTRY AND OF RIGHT . . . GLORIOUS LIBERATORS OF ALSACE-LORRAINE."

Through my glasses I saw the Führer stop, glance at the monument, observe the Reich flags with their big Swastikas in the centre. Then he strode slowly towards us, towards the little clearing in the woods. I observed his face. It was grave, solemn, yet brimming with revenge. There was also in it, as in his springy step, a note of the triumphant conqueror, the defier of the world. There was something else, difficult to describe, in his expression, a sort of scornful, inner joy at being present at this great reversal of fate—a reversal he himself had wrought.

Now he reaches the little opening in the woods. He pauses and looks slowly around. The clearing is in the form of a circle some two hundred yards in diameter and laid out like a park. Cypress trees line it all round—and behind them, the great elms and oaks of the forest. This has been one of France's national shrines for twenty-two years. From a discreet position on the perimeter of the circle we watch.

Hitler pauses, and gazes slowly around. In a group just behind him are the other German plenipotentiaries: Göring, grasping his field-marshal's baton in one hand. He wears the sky-blue uniform of the air force. All the Germans are in uniform, Hitler in a double-breasted grey uniform, with the Iron Cross hanging from his left breast pocket. Next to Göring are the two German army chiefs—General Keitel, chief of the Supreme Command, and General von Brauchitsch, commander-in-chief of the German army. Both are just approaching sixty, but look younger, especially Keitel, who has a dapper appearance with his cap slightly cocked on one side.

Then there is Erich Raeder, Grand Admiral of the German Fleet, in his blue naval uniform and the invariable upturned collar which German naval officers usually wear. There are two non-military men in Hitler's suite—his Foreign Minister, Joachim von Ribbentrop, in the field-grey uniform of the Foreign Office; and Rudolf Hess, Hitler's deputy, in a grey party uniform.

The time is now three eighteen p.m. Hitler's personal flag is run up on a small standard in the centre of the opening.

Also in the centre is a great granite block which stands some three feet above the ground. Hitler, followed by the others, walks slowly over to it, steps up, and reads the inscription engraved in great high letters on that block. It says: "HERE ON THE ELEVENTH OF NOVEMBER 1918 SUCCUMBED THE CRIMINAL PRIDE OF THE GERMAN EMPIRE . . . VANQUISHED BY THE FREE PEOPLES WHICH IT TRIED TO ENSLAVE."

Hitler reads it and Göring reads it. They all read it, standing there in the June sun and the silence. I look for the expression on Hitler's face. I am but fifty yards from him and see him through my glasses as though he were directly in front of me. I have seen that face many times at the great moments of his life. But today! It is afire with scorn, anger, hate, revenge, triumph. He steps off the monument and contrives to make even this gesture a masterpiece of contempt. He glances back at it, contemptuous, angry—angry, you almost feel, because he cannot wipe out the awful, provoking lettering with one sweep of his high Prussian boot. He glances slowly around the clearing, and now, as his eyes meet ours, you grasp the depth of his hatred. But there is triumph there too—revengeful, triumphant hate. Suddenly, as though his face were not giving quite complete expression to his feelings, he throws his whole body into harmony with his mood. He swiftly snaps his hands on his hips, arches his shoulders, plants his feet wide apart. It is a magnificent gesture of defiance, of burning contempt for this place now and all that it

has stood for in the twenty-two years since it witnessed the
humbling of the German Empire.

Finally Hitler leads his party over to another granite stone,
a smaller one fifty yards to one side. Here it was that the
railroad car in which the German plenipotentiaries stayed during the 1918 armistice was placed—from November 8 to 11.
Hitler merely glances at the inscription, which reads: "The
German Plenipotentiaries." The stone itself, I notice, is set
between a pair of rusty old railroad tracks, the ones on which
the German car stood twenty-two years ago. Off to one side
along the edge of the clearing is a large statue in white stone
of Marshal Foch as he looked when he stepped out of the
armistice car on the morning of November 11, 1918. Hitler
skips it; does not appear to see it.

It is now three twenty-three p.m. and the Germans stride
over to the armistice car. For a moment or two they stand in
the sunlight outside the car, chatting. Then Hitler steps up
into the car, followed by the others. We can see nicely
through the car windows. Hitler takes the place occupied by
Marshal Foch when the 1918 armistice terms were signed.
The others spread themselves around him. Four chairs on
the opposite side of the table from Hitler remain empty. The
French have not yet appeared. But we do not wait long. Exactly at three thirty p.m. they alight from a car. They have
flown up from Bordeaux to a near-by landing field. They
too glance at the Alsace-Lorraine memorial, but it's a swift
glance. Then they walk down the avenue flanked by three
German officers. We see them now as they come into the
sunlight of the clearing.

General Huntziger, wearing a bleached khaki uniform, Air
General Bergeret and Vice-Admiral Le Luc, both in dark blue
uniforms, and then, almost buried in the uniforms, M. Noël,
French Ambassador to Poland. The German guard of honour,
drawn up at the entrance to the clearing, snaps to attention for
the French as they pass, but it does not present arms.

It is a grave hour in the life of France. The Frenchmen keep
their eyes straight ahead. Their faces are solemn, drawn. They
are the picture of tragic dignity.

They walk stiffly to the car, where they are met by two
German officers, Lieutenant-General Tippelskirch, Quarter-

master General, and Colonel Thomas, chief of the Führer's headquarters. The Germans salute. The French salute. The atmosphere is what Europeans call "correct." There are salutes, but no handshakes.

Now we get our picture through the dusty windows of that old *wagon-lit* car. Hitler and the other German leaders rise as the French enter the drawing-room. Hitler gives the Nazi salute, the arm raised. Ribbentrop and Hess do the same. I cannot see M. Noël to notice whether he salutes or not.

Hitler, as far as we can see through the windows, does not say a word to the French or to anybody else. He nods to General Keitel at his side. We see General Keitel adjusting his papers. Then he starts to read. He is reading the preamble to the German armistice terms. The French sit there with marble-like faces and listen intently. Hitler and Göring glance at the green table-top.

The reading of the preamble lasts but a few minutes. Hitler, we soon observe, has no intention of remaining very long, of listening to the reading of the armistice terms themselves. At three forty-two p.m., twelve minutes after the French arrive, we see Hitler stand up, salute stiffly, and then stride out of the drawing-room, followed by Göring, Brauchitsch, Raeder, Hess, and Ribbentrop. The French, like figures of stone, remain at the green-topped table. General Keitel remains with them. He starts to read them the detailed conditions of the armistice.

Hitler and his aides stride down the avenue towards the Alsace-Lorraine monument, where their cars are waiting. As they pass the guard of honour, the German band strikes up the two national anthems, *Deutschland, Deutschland über Alles* and the *Horst Wessel* song. The whole ceremony in which Hitler has reached a new pinnacle in his meteoric career and Germany avenged the 1918 defeat is over in a quarter of an hour.

Berlin Diary, 1941

Can They Take It?

by Edward R. Murrow

SEPTEMBER 10, 1940—10:30 P.M.

This is London. And the raid which started about seven hours ago is still in progress. Larry LeSueur and I have spent the last three hours driving about the streets of London and visiting air-raid shelters. We found that like everything else in this world the kind of protection you get from the bombs on London tonight depends on how much money you have. On the other hand, the most expensive dwelling places here do not necessarily provide the best shelters, but certainly they are the most comfortable.

We looked in on a renowned Mayfair hotel tonight and found many old dowagers and retired colonels settling back on the overstuffed settees in the lobby. It wasn't the sort of protection I'd seek from a direct hit from a half-ton bomb, but if you were a retired colonel and his lady you might feel that the risk was worth it because you would at least be bombed with the right sort of people, and you could always get a drink if you were a resident of the hotel. If you were the sort of person I saw sunk in the padding of this Mayfair mansion you'd be calling for a drink of Scotch and soda pretty often—enough to keep those fine uniformed waiters on the move.

Only a couple of blocks away we pushed aside the canvas curtain of a trench cut out of a lawn of a London park. Inside were half a hundred people, some of them stretched out on the hard wooden benches. The rest huddled over in their overcoats and blankets. Dimmed electric lights glowed on the whitewashed walls and the cannonade of antiaircraft and reverberation of the big stuff the Germans were dropping rattled the dust boards under foot at intervals. You couldn't buy a drink there. One woman was saying sleepily that it was funny how often you read about people being killed inside a

40

shelter. Nobody seemed to listen. Then over to the famous cellar of a world-famous hotel, two floors underground. On upholstered chairs and lounges there was a cosmopolitan crowd. But there wasn't any sparkling cocktail conversation. They sat, some of them with their mouths open. One of them snored. King Zog was over in a far corner on a chair, the porter told me. The woman sleeping on the only cot in the shelter was one of the many sisters of the former King of Albania.

The number of planes engaged tonight seems to be about the same as last night. Searchlight activity has been constant, but there has been little gunfire in the center of London. The bombs have been coming down at about the same rate as last night. It is impossible to get any estimate of the damage. Darkness prevents observation of details. The streets have been deserted save for a few clanging fire engines during the last four or five hours. The zooming planes have been high again tonight, so high that the searchlights can't reach them. The bombing sounds as though it was separated pretty evenly over the metropolitan district. In certain areas there are no electric lights.

Once I saw *The Damnation of Faust* presented in the open air at Salzburg. London reminds me of that tonight, only the stage is so much larger. Once tonight an antiaircraft battery opened fire just as I drove past. It lifted me from the seat and a hot wind swept over the car. It was impossible to see. When I drove on, the streets of London reminded me of a ghost town in Nevada—not a soul to be seen. A week ago there would have been people standing on the corner, shouting for taxis. Tonight there were no people and no taxis. Earlier today there were trucks delivering mattresses to many office buildings. People are now sleeping on those mattresses, or at least they are trying to sleep. The coffee stalls, where taxi drivers and truck drivers have their four-in-the-morning tea, are empty.

As I entered this building half an hour ago one man was asking another if he had a good book. He was offered a mystery story, something about a woman who murdered her husband. And as he stumbled sleepily down the corridor, the lender said, "Hope it doesn't keep you awake."

And so London is waiting for dawn. We ought to get the "all-clear" in about another two hours. Then those big German bombers that have been lumbering and mumbling about overhead all night will have to go home.

SEPTEMBER 11, 1940

The air raid is still on. I shall speak rather softly, because three or four people are sleeping on mattresses on the floor of this studio.

The latest official figures for today's air war list at least ninety German planes down, with a loss of seventeen British fighters.

It is now 4:15 in the morning in London. There will be piles of empty shell casings around London's antiaircraft batteries when dawn breaks about an hour from now. All night, for more than eight hours, the guns have been flashing. The blue of an autumn sky has been pockmarked with the small red burst of exploding antiaircraft shells. Never in the long history of this old city beside the Thames has there been such a night as this. But tonight the sound of gunfire has been more constant than the bestial grunt of bombs.

Several hours of observation from a rooftop in central London has convinced me that the bombing of the central and western portion of the city has been less severe than during last night, and tomorrow's official communiqué will confirm that impression. The number of German planes engaged has probably been about the same—something more than a hundred. Most of the bombings have been over near the river. Judging from the height of the shell bursts, the Germans have been bombing from a somewhat lower altitude tonight. They cruise at about the same height, but when they start their bombing runs, the bursts appear lower down. A few fires have been started, but most of them are believed to be under control.

These London gunners, who have spent the better part of a year sitting around doing nothing, are working tonight. There's a battery not far from where I live. They're working in their shirt sleeves, laughing and cursing as they slam the shells into their guns. The spotters and detectors swing slowly around in their reclining carriage. The lens of the night glasses look like the eyes of an overgrown owl in the orange-blue light that belches from the muzzle of the gun. They're working without searchlights tonight. The moon is so bright that the beam of the light is lost a few hundred feet off the ground. Someone should paint the chimney pots and gables of London as they're silhouetted in the flashing flame of the guns, when the world seems upside down.

Walking down the street a few minutes ago, shrapnel stuttered and stammered on the rooftops and from underground came the sound of singing, and the song was *My Blue Heaven*.

Here's a story of a policeman, his whistle, and a time bomb. It's a true story. I saw it. If the story lacks literary merit, put it down to the fact that composition is not easy when your windows are being rattled by gunfire and bombs. In the central district of London a bomb fell. It didn't explode. The area was roped off. People living in the area were evacuated—moved out of the buildings. I happened to be walking in that particular district and talked my way just inside the police cordon. Peering fearfully around the corner of a stout building, I beheld a policeman standing at an intersection, about thirty yards from where that unexploded bomb lay. He was a big policeman—his feet were wide apart, tin hat pushed well back on his head, chin strap between his teeth, left hand hooked in his belt at the back. That policeman's right hand snapped up from the wrist. Something glinted in the sunlight and dropped back into his hand. Again that slow, easy flick of the wrist. And I saw he had taken his whistle off the chain, was tossing it idly in the air and catching it as it fell. It was an effortless, mechanical sort of business. He stood like a statue, just tossing that silver whistle and catching it. I've seen cops at home perform something of the same operation with a night stick on a warm spring day. If that bomb had gone off, the bobby would have been a dead man, the whistle would have fallen to the pavement.

After watching him for perhaps two minutes I withdrew, convinced that it would have been impossible for me to catch that whistle in a washtub. What the policeman was doing there, I don't know. He may be there still.

These delayed-action bombs create special problems. If a

bomb explodes in a business district, it may do considerable damage, but demolition and repair work can be started at once. Offices and shops that have escaped damage can carry on. But a delayed-action bomb can paralyze the area for a considerable time. If a bomb explodes on a railway line, only a few hours may be required to effect repairs; but a time bomb on a right of way is more difficult to deal with. Anyone can fill in a bomb crater, but experts are required to handle the ones that don't explode.

I know of a case where there was an unexploded bomb between the rails. The local superintendent organized a volunteer crew to take a freight train over it. But when the freight arrived, the regular crew refused to hand it over to the volunteers. They said the locals could have the bomb, but they'd take the train through. They did and, luckily, the bomb didn't explode.

Military medals are getting rather meaningless in this war. So many acts of heroism are being performed by men who were just doing their daily job. And now at 4:20 in the morning we're just waiting for the "all-clear."

This Is London, 1941

"This Dreadful Masterpiece"

by Ernie Pyle

LONDON (by wireless)—Some day when peace has returned to this odd world I want to come to London again and stand on a certain balcony on a moonlit night and look down upon the peaceful silver curve of the Thames with its dark bridges.

And standing there, I want to tell somebody who has never seen it how London looked on a certain night in the holiday season of the year 1940.

For on that night this old, old city—even though I must bite my tongue in shame for saying it—was the most beautiful sight I have ever seen.

It was a night when London was ringed and stabbed with fire.

*   *   *

They came just after dark, and somehow I could sense from the quick, bitter firing of the guns that there was to be no monkey business this night.

Shortly after the sirens wailed I could hear the Germans grinding overhead. In my room, with its black curtains drawn across the windows, you could feel the shake from the guns. You could hear the boom, crump, crump, crump, of heavy bombs at their work of tearing buildings apart. They were not too far away.

Half an hour after the firing started I gathered a couple of friends and went to a high, darkened balcony that gave us a view of one-third of the entire circle of London.

As we stepped out onto the balcony a vast inner excitement came over all of us—an excitement that had neither fear nor horror in it, because it was too full of awe.

You have all seen big fires, but I doubt if you have ever seen the whole horizon of a city lined with great fires—scores of them, perhaps hundreds.

There was something inspiring in the savagery of it.

The closest fires were near enough for us to hear the crackling flames and the yells of firemen. Little fires grew into big ones even as we watched. Big ones died down under the firemen's valor only to break out again later.

About every two minutes a new wave of planes would be over. The motors seemed to grind rather than roar, and to have an angry pulsation like a bee buzzing in blind fury.

The bombs did not make a constant overwhelming din as in those terrible days of last September. They were intermittent—sometimes a few seconds apart, sometimes a minute or more.

Their sound was sharp, nearby, and soft and muffled, far away. They were everywhere over London.

Into the dark, shadowed spaces below us, as we watched, whole batches of incendiary bombs fell. We saw two dozen go off in two seconds. They flashed terrifically, then quickly simmered down to pinpoints of dazzling white, burning ferociously.

These white pinpoints would go out one by one as the unseen heroes of the moment smothered them with sand. But also, as we watched, other pinpoints would burn on and pretty soon a yellow flame would leap up from the white center. They had done their work—another building was on fire.

The greatest of all the fires was directly in front of us. Flames seemed to whip hundreds of feet into the air. Pinkish-white smoke ballooned upward in a great cloud, and out of this cloud there gradually took shape—so faintly at first that we weren't sure we saw correctly—the gigantic dome and spires of St. Paul's Cathedral.

St. Paul's was surrounded by fire, but it came through. It stood there in its enormous proportions—growing slowly clearer and clearer, the way objects take shape at dawn. It was like a picture of some miraculous figure that appears before peace-hungry soldiers on a battlefield.

The streets below us were semi-illuminated from the glow.

Immediately above the fires the sky was red and angry, and overhead, making a ceiling in the vast heavens, there was a cloud of smoke all in pink. Up in that pink shrouding there were tiny, brilliant specks of flashing light—anti-aircraft shells bursting. After the flash you could hear the sound.

Up there, too, the barrage balloons were standing out as clearly as if it were daytime, but now they were pink instead of silver. And now and then through a hole in that pink shroud there twinkled incongruously a permanent, genuine star—the old-fashioned kind that has always been there.

Below us the Thames grew lighter, and all around below were the shadows—the dark shadows of buildings and bridges that formed the base of this dreadful masterpiece.

Later on I borrowed a tin hat and went out among the fires. That was exciting too, but the thing I shall always remember above all the other things in my life is the monstrous loveliness of that one single view of London on a holiday night—London stabbed with great fires, shaken by explosions, its dark regions along the Thames sparkling with the pinpoints of white-hot bombs, all of it roofed over with a ceiling of pink that held bursting shells, balloons, flares and the grind of vicious engines. And in yourself the excitement and anticipation and wonder in your soul that this could be happening at all.

These things all went together to make the most hateful, most beautiful single scene I have ever known.

Scripps-Howard wire copy, December 30, 1940

Under Fire

by Robert St. John

No one agreed about how many people the German bombers killed in Patras, but they surely did a job. A Greek hospital ship with tremendous red crosses painted all over its sides got a direct hit. It was listing badly and before long would go to the bottom. Someone said it was the last hospital ship the Greeks had. The rest were already at the bottom, some of them still weighted down with the bodies of their wounded passengers who hadn't had a chance when the planes came over. The hospital ship in Patras harbor had been full of wounded too. Some said the flimsy wooden boat had been turned into a morgue for at least two hundred soldiers. Others put the casualties lower than that. But the worst job the planes did was on hundreds of refugees.

The people of Patras had had a hunch, like the people of Corfu. Only the Patras hunch came too late. The hunch was that life wasn't going to be pleasant much longer in Patras and they had better get moving. And so they had flocked down to the water front. It had been a well-organized exodus. They were all going away in flat-bottomed barges towed by a large ship. They brought their most precious and their most essential possessions down to the water front with them. They loaded them onto the barges until there was hardly room for the human freight. They were about ready to shove off when the planes came.

Of course it was a stupid mistake. They never should have tried to get away in daylight. Some of them managed to hide between the blocks of concrete on the quay, but most of them just huddled down on the barges, burying their heads in the blankets and mattresses and tin kettles and baby cribs and all the other stuff they wanted so much to save. They tried to play ostrich, but bullets from a machine gun in an airplane can hit people just as well and kill them just as dead even if

48

their heads are buried. That was what happened. The planes dropped some bombs and then they used their machine guns. No one ever counted the bodies exactly. The estimates varied greatly. Anyway at least seventy were killed.

After the planes went away and the dead and the wounded were removed the rest of the people of Patras lost all interest in going places on barges. They fled from the water front. They never wanted to see that water front again. And that was why it was that when we shook hands with the skipper and his crew they weren't paying much attention to us. There was a lot of stuff to look over on those barges. Stuff no one was interested in any more, because most of it belonged to people who were dead now. I saw Shorty's eyes brighten as he stood in the middle of one of the barges holding up a silk dress you could have bought in Klein's, New York, for about ninety-eight cents. He was holding it up at arm's length and admiring it and probably trying to decide whether it would go around his wife's figure. Other members of the crew of the *Spiradon* had their eyes on frying pans and blankets and flashlights. We thought it was a rather sordid scene, because a lot of that stuff was covered with the blood of the people who had owned it, and it didn't seem right for anyone to be touching it. At least not until the blood was dry.

We went straight from the water front to the office of the *État Major*. Up there we ran onto a Greek lieutenant who had once been in Detroit. He said he thought we would be wise to get out of Patras immediately. The Germans were just across the Gulf of Corinth and they might come over with a landing party any hour now. It was about a hundred and fifty miles along the gulf to Athens, but there wasn't any motor traffic moving along the highway. Too dangerous. Too many planes overhead all the time. However, there was a train leaving at four o'clock in the afternoon. He helped us buy tickets so that we would be sure to have places. It might be, he said, the last train that would ever leave Patras.

We were walking back into town when the sirens went off again. We decided to ignore them, but it was the old story again. The natives started shouting at us and pointing up into the air where the planes were. When we just smiled and tried to keep going, angry gendarmes came running after us.

"This thing is getting damned monotonous," Hill grumbled.

"Yes," I said with some sincere bitterness, "it's like a phonograph when the needle gets stuck in a groove and keeps playing the same bars of music over and over again until you think you'll go crazy unless someone shuts the machine off."

But you can't argue with a gendarme if he's got a rifle in his hand, and we were forced up the street to an air-raid shelter. Over the door it said in English as well as Greek, "Built with funds contributed from America." I grinned when I read that sign. The greatest nation in the world had helped the Greeks. Never let it be said that we hadn't. I had seen the proof with my own eyes. We had gone to their help when they were attacked by all the forces of evil. When vast mechanized armies rolled down from the north, America had stood behind little Greece. We had contributed funds to build an air-raid shelter. And I suppose America would have been hurt if she could have seen the Greeks pouring into that shelter without paying a bit of attention to the sign or giving a thought to the great generosity of the United States.

There were more people trying to get in than the place would hold. Gendarmes barked and cursed. The planes came closer. The gendarmes looked nervously over their shoulders and then put their knees in people's backs and pushed. But there was a wall at the far end of this shelter built in the side of a hill, and the people between the door and the back wall were already packed in there so tightly that it was difficult for any of them to breathe. But the gendarmes kept on pushing, and a woman whose head was inside the shelter but whose broad backside stuck out began to scream her fear of being hit in the rear. It wasn't a pleasant scene, because human beings were acting like terrified animals. The lower the planes came and the more bombs they dropped around the city, the more these people were metamorphized into animals, bent only on self-preservation.

Hill and I finally turned away in disgust and sat down a few yards from the entrance to the shelter. When that raid was over we wandered down into the messed-up city and found a café where we couldn't get any food but where we could set up typewriters on a dirty marble-topped table and pretend

that we were right on a dead line and that a telegraph operator with a wire open to New York was sitting beside us waiting to flash our news to America. It was all make-believe, of
course, because the lieutenant at army headquarters had just
laughed when we asked about communications. The only
communication center left in Greece, as far as he knew, was at
Athens. And there was no way to telephone to Athens. We'd
have to wait until we got there. But since we were going to
take a train at four o'clock for Athens we pounded our typewriters and told about the people who had died like rats on
the quay of Patras and the wounded soldiers who were given
their *coup de grâce* as they lay on the hospital ship.

We talked several times about Mike and White and Atherton. We were worried, because we had asked a lot of people
around town already about them and no one had seen them.
Anything might have happened, but our guess was that they
had fallen into the hands of the Axis when they hit Preveza.

Then Atherton walked into the café. He had blood all over
his shirt. Dark, clotted blood. Almost black. His face had
tragedy written all over it. He was limping badly. He tried to
smile when he saw us. We knew he was glad to see us. And we
were damned glad to see him. But he couldn't smile. He just
said two words, and then we all sat down and didn't say anything else for quite a while. The two words turned something
to stone down inside of me. I guess Hill felt the same way
too.

All Atherton said was, "Mike's dead." Then we knew where
the blood had come from. We didn't ask any questions. We
didn't know yet how Mike had died. But we knew he had
died with his head on Atherton's chest. We knew that because
we knew Atherton and we knew he felt about Mike just like
we did. Mike was sixty years old and he was a tough little
fisherman with big gnarled hands like boxing gloves that
mashed your hand when he grabbed it. And Mike wasn't the
kind of a person you'd invite into your home for a cocktail
party. But Mike was worth most of the people I had ever met
at cocktail parties all thrown in together. We had lived with
Mike for days out there on the Adriatic and we knew that
Mike was a real man, with an honest, open heart. But a heart
that wasn't beating any more now.

"Bombed?" Hill finally asked.

"Yes," Atherton replied. "Killed outright. A Stuka dropped something that got him in the head. Mike never knew what hit him."

We finally got some weak tea by arguing with the café owner. Then the story gradually came out. White and Atherton and Mike had started out from Casopi about the same time we started from Corfu. They had found out about Preveza, and so they went right by it. The trouble began when all the gasoline they had leaked out of the fuel can. They hailed a Greek mine sweeper, which took them aboard and towed the *Makedonka* on behind. But the mine sweeper went so fast that the towline broke, and the *Makedonka* capsized, with everything in it. Then the Greek ship, as it got near Patras, was dive-bombed by those same planes we had been hiding from under the concrete blocks. That was when Mike got it. And at the same time a piece of shrapnel had buried itself in Atherton's right knee, so that it was difficult for him to walk now. White had come through the whole thing without a scratch, and now he was looking around town for communications.

A little before four o'clock we all went down to get on the train that was going to take us to Athens, but the railroad men said it had been canceled. They didn't think there would be any more trains to Athens. Things were getting bad. The Germans were sweeping down from the north. Nobody seemed to be able to stop them. They would probably be here in Patras soon. Thousands of people wanted to get out of Patras. Who were we anyway? Were we any better than the people of Patras? This was their town, their railroad. Even if a train did come along, we couldn't get on it anyway. If a train did run, the people of Patras would be given first chance, but there were thousands of them, and there probably wouldn't be any train anyway.

Of course those railroad men were right. But still, you've got to think of yourself when the sky is always full of planes, and people are being killed all around you. You've got to go Nietzsche and look out for your own skin. We spent all the rest of the afternoon and all evening watching the highway to Athens for some sign of transportation and chasing to different army headquarters trying to get some help.

Late in the night we were ushered into the "Great Presence." I guess he was a general. He had enough gold braid on his uniform for all the officers at West Point. You never would have known a war was going on and that right now Greek soldiers were fleeing like frightened rabbits from the German motorized army all over the country and leaving the poor Anzacs to hold what was left of battle lines. We could tell from the fragments of conversation while he conferred with his aides and kept us waiting that they were being just as petty and bureaucratic as ever about a thousand little details that didn't matter a bit now. Greece was falling, but how many carbon copies did the general want his orderly to make of this letter?

Finally he turned to us. So we wanted transportation, did we? Of course we should have it! An army truck was leaving for Athens soon. We had his permission to go on it. No, we didn't need any papers or passes. Just tell the officers out in the anteroom that the general said we were to go on the truck to Athens. We went out and told the officers. They looked puzzled. They talked to other officers. Then they told us the truck had left two hours ago. They were sorry, but that was the last truck going to Athens. There wouldn't be any more. Not tonight or tomorrow either. Maybe later in the week, if—if nothing happened. We asked to see the general again. They told us they were sorry, but the general had gone off to dinner and he wouldn't be back tonight.

Dinner? We decided that we'd like some dinner too, but the food supply of Patras apparently was reserved for generals and people like that. We couldn't find any anywhere. Then Atherton remembered that once when he was down in Greece before the war he had stopped in Patras and had met an engineer who lived at the Cecil Hotel, and so we went to the Cecil. The place had been badly wrecked by bombs, but we crawled through the debris and got up to the engineer's quarters.

In some ways going into the engineer's rooms at the Cecil was just like finding the Monastery of Saint Nicholas on top of the island of Leukas. As soon as we got inside and shut the door we were in another world. Outside, most of Patras was in ruins. There was hardly a building in town with its four walls still standing. But here in a little room in a bomb-damaged hotel a man who spoke four or five other languages as fluently as he did his own was sitting in front of a fireplace listening to soft orchestra music on a radio and reading, of all things, one of Lamb's essays. He had water boiling on a little alcohol stove and he asked us, with that tone you associate with English parlors, how we would like our tea, with milk or lemon?

I wanted to say, "You don't have a sirloin steak hidden away anywhere, do you?" But I didn't, because the engineer was Atherton's friend, not mine. So we sat and drank tea, and when he brought out some English cookies I guess all of us acted as if we had never seen cookies before and thought the thing to do was to make a sandwich of half a dozen and jam them all in our mouths at one time. But the Greek engineer pretended not to notice. Soon he and Atherton were talking about Lamb and mid-Victorian poetry and then about Nietzsche. And that's how we got around finally to that ir-relevant subject of the war, which was being fought almost outside this man's windows.

He said the people of Patras hoped to be occupied by the Germans because they didn't have any feelings about the Ger-mans. They hated the Italians and they'd fight until hell froze over if they were just fighting the Italians. But not many Greeks wanted to fight the Germans. It wasn't that they were any more afraid of the Germans. Not that. It was simply that they had no quarrel with the Germans. Germany was a long way off geographically. Also the Greeks had a great admira-tion for German thoroughness and German discipline and the German way of life.

"You don't mean the Nazi way of life, do you?" Atherton asked, disgustedly.

The engineer said he did. He talked for an hour about how wise Hitler had been in setting up an economic scheme that wasn't based on gold, and then he expounded a lot of other pro-Nazi arguments.

Atherton answered him, point by point. But he failed to convert the engineer.

I began to understand why Greece was falling so quickly. The country must be lacking in unity of thought and unity of

purpose just as much as France and a lot of other countries
had been.

While Atherton and the engineer went on talking I looked
over the hundreds of books that jammed the little hotel
room. The engineer was very catholic in his tastes. He had
read everything from Sinclair Lewis to the Koran, but he
seemed to specialize in the field dominated by Nietzsche. Perhaps that was the clue to why he thought as he did.

After many hours had been idled away we got down to
basic things. We told the engineer we had to find some way to
get out of Patras, and quickly. He picked up a telephone and
called a friend. It seemed strange to have a telephone operating. It was the first telephone we had seen in use in nearly
three weeks. We asked, while he was waiting for his number,
"Can we get Athens on your phone?" He shook his head. He
asked his friend, who was a railroad executive, about trains,
and he found out that at five o'clock in the morning a long
train would be loaded at the Patras station and would set out
at once with Greek soldiers for Corinth, about a hundred and
twenty miles down the gulf and only a short distance from
Athens. It was supposed to be a military secret, but if we went
down to the station before the train came in there wasn't any
reason why we couldn't smuggle ourselves aboard.

We were at the depot at four-thirty. The place was jammed
with soldiers and civilians. If the arrival of this train was a
strict military secret, the Greek army surely let a lot of people
in on its secrets. About five o'clock the train pulled in. Ten
coaches, old, dirty, some with broken windows. But it was a
train and it had a locomotive that ran, and it was headed toward Athens and communications and maybe safety for a
while. We fought just as viciously and as much like hungry
animals as all the rest of the people. It was dark, and no one
could tell that we were foreigners. The only way not to be
mistaken for foreigners there in the dark was to fight for a
foothold on that train just the way the Greeks were doing
themselves.

We made out rather well, in spite of Atherton's game leg.
We found two seats facing each other with only one place
taken. White and Hill and I took those three places. Atherton
got a seat across the aisle. We sat there in the dark grinning

over our good luck and listening to the noise of battle going on out on the platform. The cursing and fighting was being done with a vehemence that might have terrified enemy troops if it had been directed against them. Finally the train got started. There were about seven hundred men aboard, which you'd agree was a lot for ten cars if you knew the size of those Greek coaches.

The sun came up in a burst of red splendor as we were being shunted around the railroad yards. Finally we really got under way. Hill and I spread a map on our legs and studied the route. The tracks followed the very edge of the Gulf of Corinth all the way. We couldn't see the other shore of the gulf at Patras, but we knew that the Germans were in possession over there, just out of sight. The map showed that the farther we went the more the gulf narrowed down, until it ended at Corinth in nothing but a canal. A trainman came through, and we asked him when we would get to Corinth. He said, "With luck, in about fifteen hours." That meant we were going to average exactly eight miles an hour.

The train was full, and we weren't scheduled to make any stops, but every time we hit a town, which was every few miles, we stopped anyway. The engineer couldn't help it. Soldiers, when they saw the train coming, swarmed onto the tracks, waving their arms. Some of them hadn't thrown away their guns yet, so they waved them too. When the engineer put on his brakes rather than mow down a whole Greek regiment, the panicky soldiers clamored to get aboard. Now they were fighting just like the soldiers at Patras. Finally the train started up. Men were hanging onto the steps and some were even sitting on the roofs of the cars. The train looked like a ship covered with barnacles. That same thing happened at each town. Then we began to realize why it was going to take fifteen hours to go a hundred and twenty miles. Fifteen hours would get us into Corinth just after dusk. We would be going along the edge of the gulf all day long. Each hour we would be getting nearer to German territory, because of the way the gulf narrowed down. We thought of all those things as we stared out the window.

That trip in peacetime must be the most delightful, the most scenic in the whole world. The cliffs are high. They drop straight down from the tracks to the sea. A drop of several hundred feet. And at the bottom there's the smooth blue water of the gulf. The map showed that we would never be out of sight of that smooth blue water.

"It's going to be a lovely trip," Hill said.

I knew what he meant, and so did the others. Any minute now German planes might come over from the other shore and pay us a call. After all, our train was a natural for a plane. The men on the roof and the men hanging onto the platforms were living advertisements that this was a troop train. And there was nothing to stop a plane from flying right alongside the train and giving us all guns.

Those were the things we were all thinking, and then I thought, what a hell of a seat I chose! Right next to the window on the gulf side of the car!

"It looks like today's the day," White said.

The rest of us pretended we didn't understand.

"I mean today's the day we'll probably really get it," White went on grimly.

"Well, as long as we can't do anything about it, let's play poker," Hill suggested.

We put a typewriter on our knees, and the three of us tried not to think of what we might soon see out the window. We didn't have any chips or any money, but Hill got out the black notebook in which for more than a year he had been entering material for newspaper stories, magazine articles, and the book that every newspaperman is going to write some day. We didn't play long, but we were playing for high stakes, and Russell had some astronomical figures chalked up in his book. Astronomical if you knew what newspapermen's salaries are. Later we tried to remember who owed whom how much, but those poker winnings were destined never to be paid.

I remember I had just lost a pot and was looking out the window while Hill was making another entry in his notebook. I was facing toward the rear of the train. We were in the next to the last car. The first thing I saw was the wing of the plane. The men in that last car could have reached out and touched it, it was so close. But no one did, because just then the plane's machine gun started to bark out its nasty message.

I never saw men move so quickly. And so instinctively. No

one had ever told us what to do if we were riding in a train
and an airplane started machine-gunning us. But we knew
without any lessons.

White and Hill were next to the aisle, and they fell onto the
floor first. Then a lot of fellows from the other side of the car
fell on top of them. I was last man. The plane was just about
opposite our window when we all got settled there in the
aisle. I kept thinking, what a target I am with my head buried
but with my tail sticking right up in the air!

The rattle of the machine gun lasted for about seven seconds. That was long enough for the pilot to go the whole
length of the train and give every one of the cars a good dose
of lead. Then the plane roared off to make a big circle and
come back again.

About that time the train stopped with a jerk. Windows on
the far side were thrown open. Hundreds of Greek soldiers
dived through them. I saw Atherton go out head first.

White was quite a way under me, but I could hear him
hollering, "I've been shot. I've been shot."

By the time the plane had lined up for its next visit there
wasn't anyone left in the car but the three of us. Hill and I
tried to carry White out before we got a second blasting. But
he was heavy. His right thigh was useless. There were three
bicycles on the vestibule of the car. We were having our
troubles. We were both standing up, with White's arms
around our shoulders, when the car got its second dose.
Somehow the sprinkle of bullets missed us that time.

While the plane was circling around again we got White
under the train. It was impossible to follow the Greek soldiers
up into the woods, because the hill leading away from the
tracks was so steep and White was so heavy.

By the time the Messerschmitt came back for its third visi-
tation the three of us were hugging the gravel and ties under
the car.

White was cursing a blue streak. "Why the God-damned
hell doesn't someone fire at him? The son-of-a-bitching bastard! The God-damned Nazi whore!"

But White's other opinions were drowned out by a roar
that almost split our heads open. The pilot had dropped a

heavy bomb on the right of way a couple of hundred yards behind the train.

Gravel and pieces of ties and rails were flying through the air. There wouldn't be any more trains following us now. There was nothing but a big excavation where the roadbed had been.

I guess we all held our breath for the next second or two. If the pilot dropped a bomb like that on the train, it wouldn't save us to be hiding underneath. I clawed the gravel and gritted my teeth. White was just groaning now. Hill hadn't said a word since the show began.

Now the plane was alongside the train. Now the machine gun began to bark again. Now we could hear the bullets tearing through the windows and the wooden sides of the car. One bullet ripped through a tie just behind us. Another sailed over our heads so close we could feel the heat from it. But the plane was past us now. It was working on the cars up ahead. Now we could breathe again. We could swallow. We could wet our dry lips. We could lift our faces up from the cinders and gravel.

When the plane went off that last time we knew we were safe, because we remembered that a machine-gun belt only has twenty seconds of fire in it, and we surely must have had twenty seconds of punishment by this time.

But just then the engineer got panicky and started off with a roar of steam. Hill and I rolled White out between the wheels just in time.

How many men were killed and how many were wounded inside the cars we never knew, because we never saw that train again.

But the right of way was sprinkled with men who had jumped or been shot off the tops of the cars and with others who had dragged themselves out of the cars and then had collapsed.

Anyway, after the train left we had a problem of what to do with White. He was in great pain. We finally ripped a shutter off a house near the tracks and used that for a stretcher. Then we carried him up the steep hillside to a highway. There wasn't any traffic moving, just as the military people had said.

But Hill and I walked in opposite directions down the road and finally one of us found a broken-down R.A.F. truck. The driver said yes, he'd take us all in to Corinth if we could help him get the truck going. It took about an hour.

Hundreds of Greek soldiers from the train were still up in the woods, some of them in the tops of trees and others hiding under rocks. A lot of them were screaming like mad. We never could figure out why.

A short distance down the road we picked up half a dozen Greeks who had been wounded. Some had shattered legs or arms, and some had machine-gun bullets through their heads or shoulders and were in bad shape, but the worst victim of all was a man nearly fifty years old who kept screaming for his mother. He just lay on top of the truck screaming the word "Mother." When a British ambulance went by we stopped it and asked the driver to look at this man, because his screams were driving us almost crazy. We helped undress the fellow, but the ambulance driver couldn't find a mark on him anywhere. Still, nothing would make him stop screaming. We figured out that he had probably fallen from the top of one of the cars and had had a brain concussion.

On the way into Corinth my right leg felt as if it were asleep and I kept pounding it. Finally I had Hill pull it a few times to loosen the cramped muscles. Since it didn't seem to do any good, I just tried to forget it. Somehow I never thought about being shot. I guess I was too damned tired to think. And besides, things kept happening to keep a man from thinking very much. Like the return visit of that damned Nazi plane. We were about half an hour along the road when someone yelled, "Christ! Here he comes!"

There were no trees along the road, but there was a thicket off in a field. The R.A.F. driver jumped out and started across the field. He yelled at us to follow him. All the Greeks on the truck who could move by themselves went off into the thicket with the driver. But there were two Greek soldiers wounded so badly they couldn't get out of the truck. And then there was White. He was still lying on the shutter. The shutter was on top of a lot of cans of gas. The truck had no top. There was nothing at all between White and the sky. We looked at the plane. It was coming lower and lower. We tried to lift the shutter.

White yelled, "I can't stand the pain, being moved like that. Leave me here."

We didn't like the idea of running off and leaving White lying there on top of the open truck. It didn't seem right. So we buried our heads in some blankets that the other wounded men had left behind and waited. It's crazy how you always want to hide your head. Especially crazy for a newspaperman, who ought to keep his eyes open and see all he can. The plane made a hell of a noise as it came down. Finally it seemed that the landing wheels must be almost touching our backs. As I lay there waiting for something to happen I thought, I wonder whether he'll just drop a bomb or whether he'll play with that God-damned machine gun again. But he didn't do either.

After he disappeared in the clouds the R.A.F. driver and the Greeks came back and we started off again. The driver told me to stand on the running board because he had something he wanted to say. He had to shout so that I could hear him above the noise the truck was making. He said, "Listen, my dear fellow, bravery's a fine thing, but only when there's some sense to it. You and your friends were just sticking your necks out for no good reason. If it happens again you may not be so lucky. Next time you hide with the rest of us. You can't save the wounded men from getting hit just by staying with them. You might as well save yourselves if you can't save them."

Then he told all of us to keep a sharp lookout because he thought the plane would be following us all the way to Corinth. We should hammer on the roof of the cab to warn him if we saw it again. It was only about ten minutes before we did see it. It was coming right down at us again. We all ran into a field. All except White and the poor Greeks who couldn't move either. I saw White pull his coat over his head as we left.

There weren't any trees in the field this time, and we just crouched behind a stone wall. The driver said it was a good safe hide-out. But I didn't feel at all right inside. I could see the truck through a hole in the wall. White and the other wounded men looked as if they were dead already. I was sorry

I had left them in spite of all the driver had said. The driver was right, but I felt mean and selfish. I felt that I'd always be ashamed of running away like that, even though I couldn't have done anybody any good by staying on top of the truck. The R.A.F. driver was right beside me. He pulled out his service pistol and got it ready for use. We were only a few feet from the truck. If the plane skimmed over it again the way it had done last time, a good marksman could plant a bullet where it might hurt. I remembered the automatic that King Peter's bodyguard had given us. I yanked it out of my pocket. I know I couldn't have hit the broad side of a barn then, because I was shaking all over, but it gave me some strength to tighten my fingers around the little gun.

The plane didn't come down so low this time. The pilot seemed to be losing interest in the truck. In a few more minutes we were on our way again.

That R.A.F. driver was really a fine person. He tried so hard not to jostle White around when the road got rough, because every time we did hit a bump Leigh screamed in pain. I guess the driver winced as much as the rest of us did when he heard those screams. We kept giving White drinks of cognac to dull the pain. Halfway to Corinth another truck was waiting for our truck. They switched the gasoline cans, and we transferred all our wounded men. The first truck driver said he had to turn around now and go back to Patras. We shook hands and wished him luck. I had a strange feeling that he was in for trouble. That's why I pumped his hand so hard and said, "Happy sailing! You've probably saved a couple of lives today. We're damned grateful. Hope you can save your own on the way back."

He just grinned and said, "What the hell?" and then he was off. Somehow I felt he was going to get it before he ever reached Patras.

From the Land of Silent People, 1942

The Way of Subjects

by Otto D. Tolischus

Early August. According to announcements in the press, the Education Ministry, "after painstaking study of one year," had finally completed an elaborate booklet which was represented as the new Bible of the Japanese people. It was entitled *The Way of Subjects*, and was supposed to contain the new ethical code of the Japanese nation. As such, it was now being distributed to all schools and adult organizations for the education and guidance of all Japanese, and especially their youth.

It was a startling document, which I cabled to New York at considerable length. It contained all that the most rabid jingos had been saying, but it was much more elaborate, and systematized, and dogmatic, and authoritative, and fantastic. Under the general motto "Back to the Japanese Spirit," it proclaimed a war of extermination against "European and American thought," the essence of which was declared to be "individualism, liberalism, utilitarianism, and materialism." These evils, said the booklet, had deeply penetrated various strata of Japan's national life, had subverted the traditional Japanese spirit, had undermined the foundation of the Empire, and had thereby imperiled the great tasks confronting the Empire.

These tasks, it explained, had been imposed on Japan by the gods of creation, and especially by the Sun Goddess, from the beginning of the world, and had been crystallized in concrete form by Emperor Jimmu at the founding of the Empire in the Hakko Ichiu principle, which called for the extension of the "Capital." In conformity with this principle, the booklet declared, Japan had the holy mission to rescue East Asia from the evil influences of Europe and America, and to extend the "Capital" until the "whole universe be

63

placed under one roof," that is, under Japanese Imperial Rule, as again decreed in the recent Imperial Rescript on the Axis alliance.

This divine mission, the booklet continued, had been obstructed by the American and European Powers, especially by the United States, Great Britain, and France, who, by "outrageous acts . . . unpardonable in the eyes of God and man," had spread their dominion over the colored races, had killed and enslaved Asiatics, Negroes, and American Indians, and had plotted to keep Japan down by limiting Japan's armament, which is "absolutely necessary for propelling the development of her national destiny."

However, the leaflet continued, with the outbreak of the "Manchurian Affair," which was a "violent outburst of Japanese national life long suppressed," things began to change, for Japan started the construction of a new world order based on the moral principles laid down by the gods, in which all nations are to be allotted each its own proper place. But in order to achieve this lofty goal, it declared, the Japanese people must construct a "highly geared and centralized defense state" and strengthen "a total national war framework." For "a nation without defense is one that belongs to a visionary world." And in order to create such a defense state, the booklet concluded, the Japanese people must cast out from their midst all that they had learned from the West, return to the ancient Japanese ways, abandon all private and selfish interests, and uniting in loyalty and filial piety around the Imperial Throne, obey the Emperor, who "rules and reigns His state with a solemn mind of serving the gods."

"Japan," said the booklet, "is the fountain source of the Yamato race, Manchukuo is its reservoir, and East Asia is its paddy field." And in line with the Tanaka memorial, it declared that the China conflict was merely a "steppingstone" toward the reconstruction of the world in which the "evils of European and American influences that have led China astray," would be eliminated from East Asia, and the world "united as one" on the basis of the moral principles propounded by Japan, which, in turn, are predicated on Japanese world rule. World history, it said, is ever changing, and nations rise and fall. But Japan, born of the gods and ruled over by a line of Emperors unbroken for ages eternal, had been steadily rising to her present eminence and prosperity "through accretion, heap by heap, particle by particle."

"Japan," the booklet proclaimed, "today is facing the moment to achieve unprecedentedly great enterprises amid the severest and most intense disturbances that have ever been recorded in the annals of the world. The China Affair is a holy task . . . to propagate the ideals of the Empire-founding throughout East Asia and also the world over."

And lest, in their addiction to "European and American thought," the subjects should have forgotten the divine origin of this mission and their duty to obey, the booklet recapitulated as eternal verities the ancient legends of Shinto mythology, from the birth of the gods and the Japanese islands to Jimmu and his Hakko Ichiu principle, illustrating at the same time how this mission and this principle had been observed and propagated in Imperial Rescripts through the ages to the present day.

There was Matsuoka's "peerless polity" and its "holy mission" in a nutshell, expounded in an official document prepared by Japanese scholars and issued by the Government for the education and preparation of the nation. Steeped in darkest obscurantism that was exceeded only by its arrogance, it surpassed even Hitler's *Mein Kampf* in its sweeping program of world conquest.

However, this new "Bible" was merely the official summary and endorsement of a development which had been going on in Japan for the last decade in the name of the "Showa Restoration," through which the old Samurai were wreaking posthumous vengeance for the Meiji Restoration that overthrew their rule. And Meiji's hapless grandson, a Westernized intellectual himself, was forced to forswear all that his grandfather had stood for, except only the expansion policy.

When Meiji came to power, and Japan was opened up to Western thought and progress, and constitutional government and a parliamentary Cabinet system were established, the young Emperor took an Imperial Oath in which he pledged himself, his posterity, and the nation to the following:

> Old unworthy ways and customs shall be destroyed and the people shall walk along the highway of Heaven and earth. . . .
>
> Knowledge shall be sought among the nations of the world and the Empire shall be led up to the zenith of prosperity.

Later, he issued the famous Imperial Rescript on Education, which up to now had been the guide and inspiration of Japan's intellectual life, in which he instructed his people, among other things: "Pursue learning and cultivate arts, and thereby develop intellectual faculties and perfect moral powers."

Gradually, and in the face of much remaining Samurai opposition and obstruction, these principles were put into effect. The old ways, and especially the Shinto religion, were not entirely abandoned, but they were gradually modified. The constitution still took cognizance of them by specifying that "the Empire of Japan shall be reigned over and governed by a line of Emperors unbroken for ages eternal," and that "the Emperor is sacred and inviolable." But it went no further. Shinto was disestablished as a state religion, and was on the way to becoming a patriotic sentiment and ceremony. Japan sought knowledge among the nations of the world and quickly became Westernized. She was beginning to develop learning and intellectual faculties, and was on the road to the zenith of prosperity. Up to 1931.

Then came the "Manchuria Incident" and the "turning point of the world," through which the descendants of the Samurai plunged the country into war and hoisted themselves into the saddle. Ever since then, using the "Showa Restoration" as a slogan, they had been putting back the clock, not only in matters economic, but more especially in the matter of intellect, of knowledge, and of learning. The ways of Meiji were decried as "un-Japanese," and the "old unworthy customs" proclaimed to be the true Nipponism to which the nation must return. Liberal statesmen were assassinated, parliamentary rule liquidated, the constitution undermined, liberalism and Westernism castigated, and schools and colleges purged of liberal and Western thought and teachers. Nationalism was paired with obscuranticism, and the old Shinto myths, which had always served as a basis of official Japanese history but which enlightened Japanese had come to regard as of merely historic interest to be subjected to higher criticism, were once again installed as the literal, fundamental, and only truth, which scholars disputed at their peril. "Nipponism" became Shinto and Shinto became "Nipponism," and both became words to conjure with; and the only learning of standing was learning in the art of war. It was, therefore, only fitting that in presenting their new-old doctrines, the authors of the new "Bible" should have falsified the Meiji rescript by suppressing, according to the translation by the *Japan Times Advertiser*, the injunction "to develop intellectual faculties."

August 3. A remarkable Shinto ceremony was staged at Hakone, a hot-springs resort, at dawn today by a group of generals, Cabinet Ministers, college professors, lawyers, writers, and other prominent figures in the military, political, educational, and literary circles of Japan, under the auspices of the I.R.A.A. and the supervision of Prince and Princess Kanin of the Imperial family. After worshiping the ancestral gods, they ran in silence, and naked except for a loincloth around their waists, to a stream, waded in knee-deep, and throwing their arms skyward, began to shout "Ei-oh-ei-oh!" until their shouts echoed and re-echoed through the hills. This, it was explained, was a physical exercise practiced by the gods of old in what is known as the Misogi rite. "Misogi aims to lead people to a stage where nothingness prevails," explained General Kuniaki Koiso, former Overseas Minister, "but I don't believe I have reached there yet." But the purpose of this special observance was far removed from "nothingness," for it was staged to harden the participants in the propagation of the Hakko Ichiu principle.

Likewise, solemn Shinto memorial services were held at the Idzumo Grand Shrine for Joseph Warren Teets Mason, American newspaperman and Shinto expert, whose ashes had been brought back to Japan at his request. A temporary altar, draped with white cloth, had been set up at one end of the shrine, above which hung a photograph of Mason. Underneath the photograph reposed the ashes, also wrapped in white cloth. Two sacred Sakaki trees, presented by the *Nichi Nichi*, stood on either side of the altar, and on the right side were vases filled with flowers. The priests, clad in white robes, with black headdresses, offered silent prayers, whereupon offerings of products of the earth and water were brought in and placed on the altar, including sake, fruit, vegetables, seaweed, and uncooked rice.

Tokyo Record, 1943

Valhalla in Transition

by Howard K. Smith

A FRIEND of mine who worked in one told me that when you walk through those big German warehouses the propaganda films used to like to show brimming with food supplies of all kinds, the echo of your footsteps frightens you it is so loud and thundery. They're almost empty now. No caravans of trucks and freight cars unload on their platforms for storage any more. The system of food supplying has become much simpler. It is called the "farmhouse-to-mouth" method. What Germans eat today is what was dug right up from the good earth yesterday, so to speak. It didn't go anywhere to be stored because it couldn't; else markets would sell out mornings in one hour instead of two and Alois Hitler's little restaurant and hundreds like it would have to cut serving time from two hours to one, or not serve at all, which happens sometimes anyhow. Shops are clean and empty, except for a few new bottles of chemical sauces with fancy names nobody has ever seen before. Only the windows outside are full. Full of empty cardboard boxes of *Keks*, which is German for cakes, and wine-bottles filled with water. Willi Loerke's grocery shop next to my house has a big cardboard advertisement for Mumm's champagne in the window, with a pretty girl in a short dress holding up a glass of champagne. Once, before Willie was called up to go East, I asked him why he left that sign in the window when he didn't have any champagne to sell; he said it was because it took up lots of room, the girl was pretty and cheerful, and there wasn't much else to put in windows any more except the sign saying "No more potatoes today," and empty boxes of *Keks*. I like the way Germans try and keep up appearances somehow in spite of everything. It reminds me of the way old, aristocratic, southern families in America used to paint the shabby cuffs of their negro butlers' suits with black ink so the lining would not show over their wrists while serving, when friends from the North came to dinner. The little dairy goods shop around the corner from my house has in its window a row of milk bottles which are seven-eighths full with white salt to look like milk. Inside there is three gallons of milk a day, which sometimes lasts two hours when not too many customers come early. Half-pint to a customer while it lasts, and it is so thin it is blue rather than white. Cigarette shops have good windows too, with all kinds of variegated boxes of "Aristons," "Murattis," "Kemals" named after Camels, and a cigarette that used to be called the "Times," but which for patriotic reasons has been changed, at little printing cost, now to the "Timms." The boxes are empty and a sign in the window says they are only for decorations— *Nus Attrapen*. On the shut front door there is a different sign almost every day of the week. The manager, who is a friend of mine, showed me all the signs he keeps under the counter: closed for repairs, or for taking inventory, or for redecoration, or for lunch, or just plain sold-out which he means by all the others, but uses them from time to time "just for variety's sake." On Tauentzienstrasse, one shopkeeper solved the appearances problem by putting no empty boxes at all in the window, but a big profile photograph of Hitler with a gilt swastika above it and below it, in gold letters, "We Thank Our Fuehrer!" The local Nazi party chief thought it was a crack at the leader and made him change his decoration and put some *Attrapen* in the window. The man didn't really mean it to be a gag, he was just trying to be patriotic. But even appearances are beginning to go now. Berlin is really beginning to look the part of a city-at-war. I should like to stroll down Unter den Linden and beyond with my officer friend now. That, however, is impossible because a Bolshevik shot both his legs off east of Kiev. If they hadn't cut off Bus line number one, due to the petrol shortage, we could ride down, or we could take a taxi, if we could find one. It would be mean, but I would like to point out how buildings are getting grey and dirty, and how the paint is peeling, and lots of things. It would be mean, but it is high time somebody broke the Nazi monopoly of being mean.

Do you know Berlin? If you do, maybe you'd like to know

what that grand old city looks like now that it has become the capital of all Europe, Valhalla on earth, with—as Dr. Goebbels wrote last autumn—the highest standard of living on the continent. The highest except for the only two countries not yet blessed by being Newly Ordered—Sweden and Switzerland. That's really not a fair statement, but unfairness is another Nazi monopoly that's begging to be cracked. Take those big, ornate drinking places on the main drag: Café Unter den Linden and Kranzler's. The stuffing is popping out of the upholstery of their overstuffed chairs now. The cigarette girl in one of them, who has nothing else to do now, told me she spent a week recently just sewing up gaps in the upholstery. She couldn't get any thread, but string from wrapping packages will do until the war is over. Not the string from German packages which is made of paper and snaps when you draw it hard with a needle, but string from packages from Switzerland which you can get sometimes. Food there is not appetizing. It is generally a foul-smelling hunk of fish called *Kabeljau* on the menu, covered with a gummy yellow sauce called *Senftunke*. Frankly, it smells like an open garbage pail on Monday morning. Service also is not what it used to be, mainly because there are only three waiters and all are over seventy. They had been retired but, when the young men were called up in June, they had to be called back to work ten hours a day, lumbago or no lumbago. The Café Unter den Linden had a fine, big awning which could be stretched out like a marquee over tables on the sidewalk, in summer time, but the hinges on it got rusty and nobody could be found to fix them, and so rain water was caught in the folds of the awning and ate holes in it. Café Schoen across the street has no troubles about maintaining front. A couple of British fire-bombs solved that seven months ago. The fire-bombs destroyed the upper floors of the building and scaffolding was set up all around it to repair it, but the Russian war came and all the workers were called up so the scaffolding just stays up and hides the whole front of the building. There is lots of scaffolding along Unter den Linden, hiding the fronts of buildings nobody is any longer working on.

All the embassies on that big street, the Russian, the American, and the French, are empty now and closed up. When the

Nazis closed the Russian embassy, they put a big white streamer fifty yards long across the face of the building with black skulls and cross-bones on either end of the streamer, and in the middle the words: "Beware! This building is Being Fumigated!" People snickered. The Nazis removed the hammer and sickle on the door, but forgot the one on the top of the building in the centre, and it is still there. Most of the big tourists' agencies on Unter den Linden are still open but business is not rushing. Tourists these days wear steel helmets and don't buy tickets. Only the Russian agency, Intourist, and the American Express Company were closed. Intourist was later reopened as an "Anti-Komintern" bookshop and in the window is a magic lantern which shows snapshots of ugly Russian soldiers all day long. Above the screen is a sign saying, "BEASTS are looking at you!" The Russian soldiers are very ugly and might be ugly German soldiers, or ugly British or American soldiers but for their uniforms. Or, did you ever look at your own face in the mirror after you haven't shaved or slept for three days and have just had a fight? In the window of the American Express Company, which has been closed since early autumn, the employees—Germans all—took a last bitter crack at the Nazis for making them lose decent-paying jobs by sticking in a poster saying, "Visit Mediæval Germany." But the Nazis are not subtle, so they didn't get it and left the sign in the otherwise empty window. Even the big florist's shop, Blumen-Schmidt, on the main street, is empty. I went in there once in November to buy some flowers for Jack Fleischer's birthday—a hell of a present for a man to give a man, but there wasn't any schnaps—and when I saw how it was I told the salesgirl, my God, *et tu?* She said, yes, she was sorry, but Udet had just been killed and every time there is a state funeral they clean out not only the shop but also the hothouses. A little later I went back, but it was still empty and the salesgirl was sorry but Moelders had just been killed. I suppose if I had gone back later, she would have said, sorry, but von Reichenau, then sorry, but Todt, and so on. Luck never changes, it continues being good.

Turning off Unter den Linden to the left down the government street, Wilhelmstrasse, you can see the only freshly painted building in Berlin: Ribbentrop's ugly yellow palace, with ugly yellow snakes wrapped symbolically around spheres, that look like the world, on its front pillars. He has just had it remodelled. All the rest of the buildings are getting dirty, even Dr. Goebbels' formerly snow-white propaganda palace. After six o'clock, you can't walk on the side of the street where the Fuehrer's house is located. A cordon of policemen make you cross the street, for they are afraid of bombs after dark, even when the Fuehrer is not at home. The Fuehrer's yellow-brown chancellery is still the same except that the enormous bronze doors on its front have been removed and melted down for the arms industry and replaced with big, brown wooden doors. The last building on the street before you turn is where the New York *Herald-Tribune* office was until the *Tribune*'s correspondent, Ralph Barnes, was kicked out for saying German-Russian relations were not so cordial and might lead to an eventual conflict. Every time I pass the place, I remember that last night I spent with him in his office before he caught the train, drinking cognac because he was very sad about being thrown out; Berlin was a good spot then. Ralph was killed in Greece. He would have liked seeing Berlin as it is now.

Turning down Leipziger Strasse in the direction of Dr. Goebbels' fancy, new press club, you pass a whole block filled with nothing but Wertheims' gigantic department store. There used to be an enormous animated map of Russia in the big central show-window, showing the progress of the Germans each day. After Rostov, it was diplomatically removed and replaced with *Attrapen*. Inside, it looks like a rummage depot. It used to be run by Jews and filled with fine things, but since the Jews were the cause of all Germany's misfortunes, it is now owned by pure Aryans and empty except for trash. Half the big cage-like lifts are out of order until after the war.

At the end of Leipziger Strasse is Potsdamer Platz, a busy, German Piccadilly Circus; second to the Friedrichstrasse railway station it is the best place in Berlin to go to if you just want to look at a lot of people in a big hurry. On Potsdamer Platz is a big building called the Pschorr Haus, whose state I have always kept a close watch on because it is *the* typical, average, big *buergerliche* Berlin restaurant. Inside, it is now dingy and dirty, and so much bad fish has been served on its white wooden tables that the whole place smells like bad fish. People from the Potsdamer railway station next door sit at its tables and sip chemical lemonade and barley coffee between trains, as the Pschorr breweries, which own the big restaurant, are no longer making very much beer. I have a menu from the Pschorr Haus somebody gave me dated November, 1916, and on it are nineteen different meat dishes to choose from. Today, also after two years of war, there are only two meat dishes on the menu, one of which is struck through with a pencil mark along the strategy of the Kaiserhof Hotel. The other is generally two little sausages of uncertain contents, each about the size of a cigar butt. Before the meat they give you a chalky, red, warm liquid called tomato soup, but which a good-natured waiter-friend of mine always called: *Ee-gay Farben Nummer zwei null-eex!* all of which means, "Dye trust formula number 20-X." With the meat you get four or five yellow potatoes with black blotches on them. One of the Pschorr Haus' vast windows on the ground floor was broken up by a bomb recently, but since nobody could be found to fix it, the management simply stuck a flattened out cardboard box in the hole, which exudes the odour of bad fish out on the street.

Potsdamer Strasse, which runs from the Pschorr Haus down past the big Sports Palace where Hitler speaks when he comes to Berlin from the front, used to be a busy shopping centre. It is now a row of derelict shops, all closed for different reasons, and their windows dirty and exhibiting pictures which little boys drew in the dirt on the window with their thumbs. The "Fruit Bar" which used to sell fruit drinks is empty because there is no more fruit, and the wood-block letters that form its name on the front are cracking and falling from their white background, leaving dirty stains where the letters were. Many shops are empty because they no longer have things to sell. Some are, as they say, closed for repairs but no repairs are going on. Some are places which had been run for their middle-aged owners who were called up, by wives and daughters who are now also called up into the munitions factories. Farther down the street are the beginnings of a massive structure, behind a big board fence, which was to be the "German Tourists Centre." All tourist agencies in town were to have offices in it. It was being constructed by Professor Albert Speer, Hitler's little dictator for architecture. But Speer's workers had to be called up when the Russian drain on man-power began, and work had to be stopped. Now Speer, too, has been called to the East to take the job of Dr. Todt who died. Thus Potsdamer Strasse is a long monument to the Russian campaign, dead except for the people trudging in thousands down it. It is too bad that the Tourists' Centre could not be finished, for German Tourists deserve a monument of some sort: they've done thorough work this decade.

To the left of Potsdamer Strasse and parallel with it lie the railway tracks from the Potsdamer station. Across them is a huge, long viaduct for the electric, and from it, evenings, you get the best picture of industry and activity in all Berlin, looking down on a maze of criss-crossing railway tracks and a forest of semaphores with engines and trains puffing up and down. It is very smoky and looks good from that height. The reason I mention it is that the three easternmost lines are always filled with long trains and each coach is clearly marked with a red cross on a white circle; hospital trains unloading maimed Germans from the Eastern front to be taken to hospitals in Berlin. One night late, when I was going home on the electric and the train passed over these coaches, a wizened old *buerger*, drunk as a coot, nudged me and pointed to them and said: "From France we got silk stockings. From Russia we got this. Damn Russians must not have any silk stockings, what?" He was lucky he picked on me to say this to, or he would have had his hangover in Alexander Platz prison the next morning. There are other cynical Berliners who say, however, that the coaches are not unloading anybody; that they're just left there on the sidings to discourage the British from dropping bombs on the Potsdamer station. But I've seen them unloading.

If you turn off Potsdamer Strasse to the right just before you get to the Sports Palace and walk about a mile, you run smack into the *elegante Viertel* of Berlin, the West End. They say the Unter den Linden section lives by day, and the West End lives by night. In peace-time it's a gay, brilliantly lighted neighbourhood speckled with dozens of cinemas, theatres

and variety houses, and hundreds of little hole-in-the-wall
bars. Its geographical and spiritual centre is Kurfuerstendamm, a long boulevard which extends from the big Memorial Church to the Berlin lakes. It is also the Bond Street, with
fine shops, of Berlin—in peace-time. In war Kurfuerstendamm reminds me of a beautiful woman who became the
mistress of a wealthy man and who, after too much loving and
living has now become a jaded, gaudy female who daubs her
face with too much artificial colour in order to hide the deep-
ening lines in it. Her jewels are the thousand and one bars
and night-spots. They were once neat-looking little places,
cubist in decoration and with bright-coloured stucco fronts.
Now, the paint is peeling, the stucco is cracking and falling
off in blobs, like the polish from paste pearls and the gilt from
brass rings. Most of them have closed. The rest of them stay
open only certain nights a week. This is all since the Russian
war began, since the supplies of French Cognac, Dutch Bols
gin, and good Polish Vodka have been exhausted. As they no
longer have any of the ingredients for staple cocktails, they
have struck these off the menu and instituted a "standard"
cocktail. It is called by different names, and by names of varying fantasy, in different bars: "razzle-dazzle," "Hollywood"
(pronounced Holy-Voot cuck-tell; this was before America
became an out-and-out enemy), or "Extase." But the mixture
is always the same, when it is there—a shot of some kind of
raw, stomach-searing alcohol with a generous dilution of
thick, sweet grenadine syrup. Or, if you are lucky, you can get
a bottle of this year's Moselle.

Dancing is strictly forbidden by law everywhere for the duration of the Russian war. Nevertheless, a few joints maintain
"hostesses" who sit and drink with Tired Party Men. As the
best of their profession have been drawn off eastward for the
entertainment of officers, those who remain are a bit on the
seedy side. For one thing, gowns are being worn shorter this
season; it is impossible to buy new gowns and so the girls
simply had to chop off the worn edges of their old ones and
put in new hems, higher up. Physical appearance is not so
good for the obvious reason that they are remainders of a
flock that was never very promising in Germany. Prostitution,
itself, is a moribund profession. They tell me there are still a

few places, one on Kanonier Strasse near the Wilhelmstrasse
and one on Giesebrecht Strasse in the West End, which is said
to be run by the foreign office for the comfort of minor visiting diplomats, especially the Japanese. And you can, they say,
be approached on the streets if you try very hard, but you
must try very hard. But generally, the fact that there are more
than twice as many women as men in Berlin, has made in-
roads into the profession. Regarding the general subject of
pornography, those who like to make facile generalizations
about the immutability of human nature may find a trace of
interesting support in this: one of the first Nazi measures, and
one of their best, was the banning of all pornographic picture
magazines, in 1933. Since the war, under the heading of
"Art," pornographic picture magazines have appeared in le-
gions. Be they called as they may—the "Faith and Beauty"
magazine, "The Dance," "Modern Photography"—they all
contain nothing but photos of naked women and all boil
down to the same old pornographic fare of pre-Nazi days.
Sales, I'm told, are terrific.

War seems to have some causal relation with pornography.
Through it one old portrait painter, who has roomy studios
on Unter den Linden, has gained fame in Berlin. He was once
Kaiser Wilhelm's court-artist, by special appointment, but,
since the war, and Hitler, he had not been doing so well on
sales. So, to make money, he hit on the idea of painting a
series of tantalizing nudes and allowing the public in to see
them for a fee. On his front door today there hangs a sign
advertising for all to see: "Sensation! Vast Canvas of Turkish
Harem including eight beautiful nudes, life-sized. Admission:
fifty pfennigs." Inside you can see, among natural-size portraits of Bismarck, Hindenburg and Hitler, the Sensation with
its swarthy, shapely nudes reclining on velvet-covered divans.
The Nazis have never objected, not even on racial grounds.
The cheap "art shops" of Friedrichstrasse, just off Unter den
Linden, have their windows jammed with fine looking maids
in undress and attract a goodly public at all hours of the day.

A handful of truly popular spots are (not my tastes, but
those of Germans):

The Golden Horse-shoe. Main attractions: among the
hostesses is the only negress in Berlin. A ring in the centre of

the floor around which lady customers ride a horse to music and show their legs above the knees in so doing, while male *buerger* shout with glee. The ladies or their men pay fifty pfennigs for a slow trot, seventy-five pfennigs for a good gallop.

St. Pauli's Bar. Here labours a hostess who has lost not only a husband in the war, but two of them! She thinks the war is a personal frame-up against her. The façade of the joint formerly consisted of the porcelain inlaid flags of every nation in the world. One by one the flags had to be painted over for political reasons, and now the façade is a checkerboard half of grey splotches and half of flags.

Walterchen der Seelensorger, which means, Little Walter, the Soul-comforter. This is a small dance-hall near the Stettiner station area in working-class Berlin, where the famous proprietor, "Walterchen," mates middle-aged bachelors and widowers with middle-aged spinsters and widows—a sort of public matrimonial bureau where rheumatic old gentlemen can rejuvenate their chivalry, and women who have forgotten can once again learn to be coy. Very amusing. Walterchen's trademark is a red heart with an arrow through it.

Die Neue Welt; the "New World"—a vast multi-roomed beerhall in the East End of Berlin. Once the most profitable amusement concern in Berlin, the *Neue Welt* is now closed most of the time for lack of beer. It is interesting if you like to see the German proletariat at play; also because the Gestapo keeps close check on the clientele, and you're likely to be arrested if you happen not to have an identification card to show them when they ask you. It is the only place in Berlin where plain-clothes men have ever cornered me and made me show my passport to prove I was not a parachute trooper or a Jew enjoying illegal fun.

The X Bar. This is the liveliest spot in town. That is not its real name, but since I want to tell some of its secrets, I had best not be too specific. It was my favourite spot when the blues got me and I had to go night-lifing or bust, because it has a good orchestra which defies Nazi propriety and plays American music, and also because the manager, who is a friend, still has a secret stock of Scotch whisky. As it is also a favourite spot for big-shot Nazis, the band doesn't play

American jazz bluntly; it sandwiches it in between opening and closing chords from some German number, salving the consciences of the Nazi visitors who might otherwise be reminded that what they are listening to was written by a racial inferior. On a Saturday night, after police hours, the manager shoos everybody out except a couple of friends and the policeman on the beat, gets his private bottle of Johnnie Walker from under the kitchen sink, and we take off our coats and smoke cigars he got from someone in the Foreign Office and drink and talk until three or four in the morning. After that, the manager used to wrap up a couple of big bottles of beer in the morning's *Lokal-Anzeiger* and we would go off to my apartment to mellow up on beer, have an early morning breakfast and get the first B.B.C. news. The manager never admitted it, but I think his bar has some special pull with the government, by which he gets pretty good liquor stocks for himself and for friends. The Foreign Office boys often take their foreign guests there. I first saw P. G. Wodehouse there. The place needs a coat of paint badly, but it's a good place when you need a change of atmosphere so much you would pop without it.

Theatres and show-houses out in the West End are packed overfull every night. People haven't anything else to spend their money on, so even the worst show in town is a sell-out every night. The big variety houses, the Scala and the Wintergarten, are having a hard time finding enough talent to fill their bills, as narrowed by a whole sheaf of Nazi decrees since the beginning of the war. Fortune-tellers, crystal gazers and all kinds of stage soothsayers used to be popular with German audiences, but when Hess flew to Scotland, Goebbels banned them all for ever from German showhouses because it was said that one of these affected Hess' decision to go. Another big favourite were funny-men who specialized in shady political jokes, but these too were forbidden by Goebbels after a while. Favourite music was American jazz and blues songs, but the dictator of German *Kultur* unofficially informed producers this well also was poisoned. The Scala used to draw entirely on foreign talent, showing a Spanish bill one month and an American one the next, and so on, but the war has rather rigorously limited the nationalities available or desirable, from the point of view of the authorities. Just about all that is left is acrobatics and juggling, which become tiresome; but they take people's minds off war, and that is what people pay for.

Cinemas are not as popular, principally for the reason that they do not take people's minds off war. Once the Nazi film dictators made the mistake of affording a very visible measure of what the public think of their propaganda films by opening a second-rate comedy called the "Gas Man" at the Gloria-Palast on Kurfuerstendamm, while fifty yards away at the Ufa-Palast an extra, super-colossal one hundred and fifty per cent war film, "Bomber Wing Luetzov," was playing. The medio-cre comedy played to packed houses at every presentation, while the war film showed to a half-empty theatre. Unfortu-nately, even mediocre comedies have become rarities as war and propaganda films increase in number. The latter can be exhaustively described by a five-letter word. They're lousy. Especially the pure-war films. Take the one called "Stukas." It was a monotonous film about a bunch of obstreperous ado-lescents who dive-bombed things and people. They bombed everything and everybody. That was all the whole film was— just one bombing after another. Finally the hero got bored with bombing and lost interest in life. So they took him off to Bayreuth music festival, where he listened to a few lines of Wagnerian music; his soul began to breathe again, he got vi-sions of the Fuehrer and of guns blazing away, so he impo-litely left right in the middle of the first act and dashed back and started bombing things again, with the old gusto.

News-reels which last almost as long as feature-films, used to be very popular with Germans, until the Russian war. Since then Germans have developed a bad case of nerves and don't like news-reels any more. Too many of them can visualize sons, fathers and cousins whom they have lost, in those dra-matic explosions on the screen. Once they showed a big fat Nazi bomber with white teeth painted on it to make it look like a shark, opening up its belly and issuing a school of bombs, twenty or thirty of them, one after another. All over the audience you could hear women sucking their breath in through their teeth as though cold shivers were running up and down their spines. People began writing letters to the

Propaganda Ministry complaining and begging for a change of fare. The bombardment of complaints finally induced the Ministry to allow a sequence of peaceful shots about the home front—harvesting grain, intimate shots of a cement factory at work, a film interview with Franz Lehar, the composer, etc.—before the war films. Then Goebbels began receiving letters expressing thanks, but asking for more home-front sequences and fewer war ones, especially to leave out the shots of dead-bodies on battlefields.

(The Germans do not allow their people to see American films, but the big shots sneak peeps at most of our best while nobody is looking. I tried to creep unnoticed into a showing of "Gone With the Wind" one afternoon in the Propaganda Ministry, but was promptly ordered out because this was a private "study" presentation for German film actors and producers. Some we were allowed to see in private showings, however, "Ninotchka," "Pinocchio" and others.)

In a word, films are trashy just like everything else. The advertisement posters in the subway stations are attractive and full of colour, just like those empty cigarette boxes in my tobacco shop window, but the films themselves are pure trash. I never thought it was possible for a country to go so universally trashy so quickly.

The only things that are not trash are their guns, which are handsome and horrifying. Of these you see many, many more in Berlin now than you used to, on top of buildings and on open fields in the suburbs. The biggest and handsomest ones are within two hundred yards of the Theatre Centre on Kurfuerstendamm, in the big Tiergarten. They are anti-aircraft cannon mounted on a tower which, itself, looks like a fantastic monstrosity from a lost world, or another planet. It is huge and positively frightening just to look at (Nazis like to hear it described this way; they are specialists in fright-propaganda. But the world has now advanced beyond the stage of being frightened in any decisive way by anything the Nazi do or create.) It is an enormous, square clod of cement a hundred feet high, about five or six storeys. It is painted green so as not to be too visible among the trees from above. On each of its corners is a long, powerful gun, pointed at the sky. They are fired by remote control from another, similar tower about a hundred yards farther on in the wood, on which there is a big "ear" resembling a fishing net, big as a big bomb crater. You should hear these monsters in action during an air-raid. In my apartment half a mile away it sounds as though all four guns were levelled right at my window. I had never been in an air-raid cellar in Germany until the night last summer when they were first used in an air-raid (it took two years of incessant day and night work to finish the construction of the towers). For the first time, I confess I got the jitters. My windows rattled as though they would shatter and the floor underneath never stopped quaking as all four guns blasted away at the sky in unison for awhile, then began firing in rotation, an endless barrage which a soldier who fought in France told me was more nerve-racking and harder on the ear-drums than anything he had been in at the front. I didn't mind bombs, I accepted each one as a personal favour from the Tommies. But I couldn't take the guns. Also, I found after ten minutes that I couldn't stay in the cellar, for the neighbours had grown bitter against America and Americans, and made it unpleasant. So I stuffed cotton in my ears and sat in my hall.

They are building more towers like these in other parts of Berlin. They have converted the old Reichstag building into one, reinforcing its top corners and mounting guns on them. The Nazis expect lots of fireworks before the show is over; and they know what effect fireworks have on their people, so they are working night and day to prepare Berlin defences.

They have undertaken the most gigantic camouflage scheme ever known, covering up big spots which are conspicuous from the air all over the city. The most conspicuous thing is the "East-West Axis," a five-miles long, hundred-yards broad street which runs from the Brandenburg Gate in the centre of the town out to Adolf Hitler Platz where my office in the radio studio is situated. Last spring, they began covering the whole street with a vast canopy of wire netting mottled with strips of green gauze to make the thoroughfare indistinguishable from the trees of the Tiergarten alongside it. Lamp-posts were covered with green gauze to look like little trees. The big Victory Pillar, a monument to the Franco-Prussian War, in the middle of the Street was covered with netting and the shiny golden angel of Triumph on top which looked like a lighted beacon on a moonlight night was tarnished with dull bronze so that it would not reflect light. At the end of the axis, the radio station was covered in green, too, and straight over the centre of the building a strip of grey netting was laid to look, from the air, like an asphalt street. With Nazi thoroughness they even covered over a whole big lake in West Berlin with green netting and ran another grey, artificial roadway diagonally across it. It was all very nice and very clever. Until the first winds of winter came, straight from the steppes of Russia, like most German misfortunes these days. The first gale ripped yawning holes in the camouflage and blew the false trees off the lamp-posts and hung them, shapeless lumps of gauze and wire, in the branches of the Tiergarten trees. Now the Nazis are having to re-do the whole thing at great expense.

In the past year, Berlin has become probably the best defended city against air-raids in the whole world. I doubt if London can have as many batteries around and in it as Berlin has. I've stood on top of the tall Columbus House on Potsdamer Platz on clear nights and watched the British approaching. As they came closer more and more searchlights fingered the sky, and pin-pricks of light from exploding shells in the air increased from dozens to hundreds. Once, on one small arc of the horizon I counted seventy-five beams of light moving in the sky. Seventy-five searchlights; many, many hundreds of guns on this small sector. There must be many, many thousands of guns all around Berlin. An officer on one of the Flak batteries in the Berlin area once told me that the whole area has been armed far beyond the point of saturation; a real waste of guns has occurred. I asked him the reason for this extravagance, and he said that while the German people were among the worst informed people in the world, the German leadership was certainly the best informed leadership, regarding its own people, in the world. The extravagance is for the sake of morale. The German people simply couldn't take it, and the Nazis were afraid to have them subjected to anything like the London Blitz, he said. I believe him. I have heard it from many Germans, and I've seen enough for myself to confirm it. You can see it in them on the streets today more clearly than ever. They simply could not take it, if it came.

To see Berlin, you take a walk. To see the people you take a subway. You also smell them. There is not enough time nor enough coaches, for coaches to be properly cleaned and ventilated every day, so the odour of stale sweat from bodies that work hard, and have only a cube of soap big as a penny box of matches to wash with for a month, lingers in their interiors and is reinforced quantitatively until it changes for the worse qualitatively as time and war proceed. In summer, it is asphyxiating and this is no figure of speech. Dozens of people, whose stomachs and bodies are not strong anyhow faint in them every day. Sometimes you just have to get out at some station halfway to your destination to take a breath of fresh air between trains.

People's faces are pale, unhealthily white as flour, except for red rings around their tired, lifeless eyes. One would tend to get accustomed to their faces after awhile and think them normal and natural but for the fact that soldiers ride the subway trains too, and one notices the marked contrast between young men who eat food with vitamins in it and live out of doors part of the time, and the ununiformed millions who get no vitamins and work in shops and factories from ten to twelve hours a day. From lack of vitamins in food, teeth are decaying fast and obviously. My dentist said they are decaying all at once almost like cubes of sugar dissolving in water. Dentists are severely overworked as most of them must spend half their time working for the army, and take care of a doubled private practice in the rest of the time. They have raised prices tremendously to discourage the growing number of patients; he said they simply had to do this. This winter there has been the most severe epidemic of colds in Berlin in many winters, and doctors predict it will get worse each year and probably assume dangerous proportions if something cannot be done about food and clothing, especially shoes, which are wearing out fast.

Weary, and not good in health, Berliners are also, and consequently, ill-humoured. That is an understatement; they have become downright "ornery." All lines in faces point downwards. I can recommend no more effective remedy for a chance fit of good humour than a ten-station ride on a Berlin tube train. If the packed train suddenly lurches forward and pushes your elbow against the back of the man standing in front of you, it is the occasion for a violent, ten-minute battle of words, in which the whole coach-load of humanity feels called upon to take part zealously as if their lives hung on the outcome. They never fight; they just threaten (*"Ich zeige dich an, junger Mann!"*—That's the magic phrase these days: "I'll have you arrested, you imprudent young man," that and "I have a friend who's high up in the Party and *he* will tell you a thing or two!" They're like children threatening to call my Dad, who's bigger'n yours). Berliners have always been notorious grousers. They always complained about anything and everything. But it was a good-natured kind of grousing you could laugh at. What has happened in the past year is something new and different. It is not funny; it is downright morbid, the way people with pale, weary, dead-pan faces which a moment ago were in expressionless stupor can flash in an instant into flaming, apoplectic fury, and scream insults at one another over some triviality or an imaginary wrong. You could watch people's natures change as the war proceeded; you could clearly watch bitterness grow as the end of the war appeared to recede from sight just as you watch a weed grow. It has been depressing to watch and it leaves a bad taste in your mouth. Partly it's the jitters and partly it's a national inferiority complex. But mostly, it is because people are sick; just plain sick in body and mind.

It may be just an impression, but it seems to me that the sickness has hit the little middle-classes hardest. Take those little family parties I've been to time and again where middle-class people, bred on middle-class Respectability, used to play *Skat* all evening and maybe open up a bottle or two of cool wine for refreshment. Recently, I've been to several, and the whole atmosphere has changed. They do not play *Skat* any more at all. They round up all the old half-filled bottles of anything alcoholic they can find (this was before the December Drouth set in with a vengeance), and just drink. They do not drink for the mild pleasure of drinking, not to enjoy the flavour of what they drink nor its subtle effects. They drink to get soused, completely and unmitigatedly; to get rollicking, loud and obstreperous, pouring down wine, beer, sweet liqueur and raw *Ersatz* cognac all in an evening. The general

atmosphere is that of a cheap, dock-side dive. I'm not trying
to make a moral judgment, but there are grounds for making
a social one. The atmosphere is one of decay. And that atmosphere seems thickest among just those strata of Germany's
population which have always formed the basis of German
society, the *Kleinbuergertum* (lower middle classes). Any type
or form of society exists because broad sections of the people
have an interest in it existing. In Germany, the petty middle-
classes are the ones who have always had an interest in *Bourgeois* society being maintained. They brought Hitler to power
in the hope of maintaining their society against the air-tight
caste of privilege maintained by the classes above them. Now,
it seems to me that the little middle-classes are losing interest,
and drowning their disappointment in alcoholic lethe, or
lethe of any other sort. Superstition has grown apace. There
has been a wave of morbid interest in all sorts of quack sci-
ences and plain superstitions, phrenology, astrology, all kinds
of fortune-telling. I am sure one reason Goebbels banned all
soothsayers from the German stage was that they were becoming too influential among the people. I am always inevitably reminded by these things of another society where a
man named Rasputin gained influence and power in a higher
circle but for the same reason, shortly before that society collapsed. People who are either unwilling to admit they know
what is wrong with them, or are unable to do anything about
it—i.e. get rid of Hitler—are seeking escape in *Ersatz* directions. That is psychological, but it has its physical complement. People who are suffering from nothing else but the
inevitable effects of bad nourishment, are inventing fancy
names for their ailments and buying the patent-medicine
houses out of wares. Outside the armaments industry, the
only business which is making big money in Germany is the
patent-medicine industry. Every woman carries a full pill-box
of some kind along with her almost empty vanity compact,
and no man's meal is complete without some sort of coloured
lozenge for the belly. A substance known as *Okasa* for sexual
potency has become almost a German national institution.
Young girls welch boxes of *Pervitin* from air-force officers to
reinforce energy that should be natural. The general atmo-

sphere smells strangely like that of an opium dive I once visited in New Orleans many years ago.

If I had to describe Hitler's Reich in one figure, I would compare it with a fine looking fat apple with a tight, red, shiny skin, which was rotten in the core. The strong, polished hull is the army and the Gestapo, which has become the main constituent of the Nazi Party. It is a strong, very strong cover. The rotten inside is *the whole fabric of Nazi society.*

This is a serious statement to make. I sincerely believe that a journalist who consciously misinforms his people and allies about the state of the enemy in time of war for the sake of sensation is the second lowest type of criminal (the lowest type being anyone who makes profits out of arms production). I have always sought to avoid underestimating the strength of the Nazis. I refer to the internal strength of the Nazi system, which this book concerns itself with alone, not the military strength. But, with these self-imposed restrictions in mind, I am sure of what I say: Nazi society is rotten from top to bottom and in all its tissues, save the strong hermetically closed hull. The people are sick of it. The general theory of society denoted by the name *Fascism*, of which Nazism is a form, has had its flare of popularity in Europe, and so far as popular following is concerned, its day is over. It will never again be an attracting force as it was before the world discovered its meaning.

In Denmark, the Nazis are opposed to parliamentary elections being held because they know that elections would result, as certainly as sunrise, in the Danish people throwing out the three measly Danish Nazis who are in Parliament. In Norway and Holland, the Nazis do not dare even to support a planned "plebiscite" for fear of the evidence it would give of how dead their philosophy truly is. As an idea, Nazism is dead as a door-nail. As for the German people, they are attached to the Nazis like the man who unexpectedly found himself holding on to a lion's tail, and kept right on holding on, not because he enjoyed the lion's proximity, but because he was scared speechless at what might happen if he let go. Or like the little boys who were having a fine ride on a toboggan until it hit a slippery place and started zipping down curves on one runner; they were scared to jump off and it got more impossible every second. Don't get me wrong. I don't mean only that the German people are afraid of the Gestapo and that all they are waiting for is for someone to weaken the Gestapo, and then they will revolt. Though the Gestapo is certainly a big element in the fear complex, it is not the biggest. The main reason the Germans cling to the lion's tail is that they are terrorized by the nightmare of what will happen to them if they fail to win the war, of what their long-suffering enemies will do to them; of what the tortured people of their enslaved nations, Czechoslovakia, Poland, France, will do when there is no longer a Gestapo to hold them down. The German people are not convinced Nazis, not five per cent of them; they are a people frightened stiff at what fate will befall them if they do not win the mess the Nazis have got them into. Take note of the new tone of Nazi propaganda of late. For two years Goebbels blew the shiny, gilded horn of how beautiful Victory was going to be, in order to urge his people on to battle. Suddenly in autumn, the tone changed to that of what will happen to Germany if Germany *fails* to win. If you read the dispatches from Berlin by American correspondents at that time, you will recall that famous editorial written by Goebbels and published in *Das Reich* entitled, "When, or How?" In that leader, for the first time, Goebbels admitted to Germany and the world that conditions had grown extremely bad inside Germany, and he ended by warning his people that however miserable things might be now, they would pale beside what would happen to Germany if Germany lost the war. This tune is now being played long and much in the German press. In all its forms, the incitement of Fear in the hearts of Germans, is the only strong weapon in Goebbels' armoury since Dr. Dietrich played hell with the others.

People in the outside world who know the Nazi system only from photographs and films; from dramatic shots of its fine military machine and the steely, resolute faces of its leaders, would be amazed at what a queer, creaky makeshift it is behind its handsome, uniform exterior. It is not only that the people who support those stony-faced leaders are timid, frightened and low-spirited. It is also, the government, the administration of those people and their affairs. In *The House that Hitler Built*, Stephen Roberts drew as nearly perfect a picture of that strange complicated mechanism as it was in peace time, as it is possible for a human to draw. But even that capable author would be bluffed by the thousand queer, ill-shaped accretions that have been added illogically to it and the contraptions that have been subtracted illogically from it since the beginning of the war. It looks roughly like a Rube Goldberg invention, inspired by a nightmare, but it is more complicated and less logical. And there are no A, B, C directions under it to show how it works. The men who work it have no idea how it works, themselves. The old, experienced, semi-intelligent bureaucrats who made the old contraption function wheezingly in peace, have been drained off to the war machine where their experience can be used more valuably. The new, screwier contraption is operated haltingly by inexperienced little men who do not like their jobs and know nothing about them. The I.Q. of the personnel in the whole civil administration machine has dropped from an average of a fifteen-year-old to that of a ten-year-old.

For example, it is strictly against the law for any foreigner to remain in Germany more than a month without a stamp in his passport called by the formidable name of *Aufenthaltser-laubnis*, a residence permit. But nowadays, between the time you apply for one and the time you get it, a year generally passes; you break the law for eleven months because nobody knows what to do with your application once you've filled it out. Most foreigners never get one at all. But that is one of the more efficient departments. My charwoman's sister, who worked in a hospital, disappeared once. Together my charwoman and I tried every police and Gestapo agency in town to find out about her, but nobody knew anything, or what to do to find out anything. Thirteen months later, it was discovered she was killed in a motor car accident in central Berlin, and the record of it had simply got stalled in the bureau drawer of some little official who didn't know which of eleven different departments he should have passed it on to. He tried three of six possible departments, but they didn't know what to do with it.

Nobody knows who is *zustaendig* (responsible) for anything. When I complained to the Propaganda Ministry about being refused trips to the war-front, I was told the Ministry had nothing to do with the matter, that I should see the radio people. I went to the radio people who were not *zustaendig* for such matters and who sent me to the censors. The Foreign Office censor knew nothing about it and told me to see the High Command censor who told me to see the Propaganda Ministry censor, who told me to go back to the Propaganda Ministry itself and complain there. Ultimately, Dr. Froelich, in the Ministry, showed an uncommon sense of the state of affairs and shrugged his shoulders and told me neither he, nor anybody else, had the least idea who the responsible official was, or which the responsible department. I was simply banned from trips to the front by nobody for no reason, but no one could do anything about it. When I was finally banned from the air, I went to the American embassy and asked the proper officer to protest to the Nazi authorities. He smiled and said: "It has become hopeless to protest to the Nazis about anything. Not only because of their ill-will towards Americans, but also because they frankly do not know which department any particular protest should be delivered to." He told me the whole Nazi civil government is in a state of un- believable chaos. Hitler no longer pays the slightest attention to the civil side of German life, and his underlings have fol- lowed the transition of his interests to the purely military side of things. Nobody of any consequence has any interest in the government of the German people, and it has become hope- lessly confused and chaotic, and, in its innards, irremediably constipated. It is, in short, going to hell in a hurry.

For a land ridden by laws, Germany has become the most lawless land on earth. Law means nothing; the password to- day is *Beziehungen*, which means good relations with a party big-shot, influence, pull, jerk. You can threaten someone on the subway with getting the law on him, but when you threaten a bureaucrat or a grocer who doesn't give you full rations, you must threaten that you have *Beziehungen* who will fix him. If you have no pull you can get no goods or service, no matter how strong the law is on your side. If you have got *Beziehungen* you can get anything, any commodity which has disappeared from the shops, or any service, no

matter how many laws there are against it—and there are
hundreds, against everything—written down in the law books.
Law has lost all meaning. We know cheap, corrupt, courthouse politics in localities in America all too well. But Germany
is one great big nation of nothing but cheap, corrupt, courthouse politics, ruled by a single party whose leaders are mostly
fanatical ascetics, but whose several million underlings are as
buyable as postcards. For a half-pound of coffee I have rewritten whole German law books in my favour.

In the field of economics Germany is corrupt and rotten
too. The state is allegedly national "Socialist," but for a socialist state it maintains the finest, fattest crop of unadulter-
ated plutocrats you ever dreamed of. Half of them are the old
plutocracy, the old families who grew rich on guns and
chemicals; half of them are the new plutocracy of higher up
Nazis who had not a pfennig ten years ago, but who got in
the elevator of financial success on the ground floor in 1933,
after its shaft was greased by Nazi victory, and shot straight
up to the top, like Ley the contraceptive king, and Goering
the steel king. The German people are not as conscious of
their money classes as other people are, for the Nazis
shrewdly do not allow their newspapers to publish society
pages, which make American and British people conscious of
their plutocracies. Dividends are, of course, limited to six per
cent. But there is no law against watering stock; against giving
two six per cents to a shareholder instead of one six per cent,
when business is good, as it is today.

The big red apple is rotten and worm-eaten. If and when it
is ever pierced, it will stink to high heaven. But the hull is very
red and shiny. And it is very strong. And the worms inside
who thrive and grow fat on the fruit, like it that way. And the
people of Germany are afraid that no matter how rotten it is
inside, it is better than being gobbled up by the birds outside.

Only one element has been left out of the picture. It is one
of the most important elements of the German population. It,
alone of the civil population is not demoralized; it is enthusiastic and keeps crying for more of the same. It remains, due
to the many favours shown it, the most enthusiastic supporter
of Adolf Hitler. I mean the German Youth; the little boys and

girls. I neglected it, because one no longer sees much of it in Berlin. Most of the little boys and girls have been shipped off to nice boys' and girls' towns in Eastern Germany to get out of the air-raid areas. Hitler is very particular about them.

They are not disappointed with Nazism. Hitler has done well by them, materially and psychologically. His colourful, shallow civilization appeals to them. They enjoy, as children will, its dramatic brutality. Too little attention has been given to the little boys and girls who are growing to maturity in Germany now. For nine years now, their malleable little minds have been systematically warped. They are growing up in a mental plaster-cast, and they like it with its accompaniment of drums, trumpets and uniforms and flags. They are enthusiastic; the biggest hauls in the Winter Relief collections are always made by the Hitler Youth and the *Bund Deutscher Maedel*, the League of German Girls. I have never seen so completely military a German as the little seven-year-old boy who knocked on my door one day and, when I had opened it, snapped to rigid attention, shot his arm high and shouted at me a falsetto "Heil Hitler!" after which he asked me in the clipped sentences of a military command would I donate twenty pfennings to "support the Fuehrer and the Fatherland in this, our life-and-death struggle."

Of all the Germans, they have been most closely guarded in their camps in Eastern Germany against the effects of the Transition. The Fuehrer is still struggling to keep the other side of war a secret from them. With the exception of the soldiers, if it comes to starving, the Youth will be the last to suffer. For Hitler has plans for them, the *Herrenvolk*-in-being.

The little creatures in their brown shirts and short black trousers could be amusing if they were not so dangerous. They are dangerous; more so than a cholera epidemic. There is, so far as I know, no demoralization in their favoured ranks. They love the whole show, and are just aching to get big enough to get into the fight themselves. Frankly, I am more afraid, more terrorized, at watching a squad of these little boys, their tender faces screwed in frowns to ape their idolized leaders, on the streets of Berlin, than I am at seeing a panzer brigade of grown-up fighters speeding across the city. The grown-ups we only have to fight; but we shall have to live under the children who are being trained for their role. They are being trained every day and every hour of the day in their little barracks in Eastern Germany right now. What children of other nations read about, and thrill at, as a record of the past—feudal knighthood—they are reading about and thrilling at in the communiqués of their own High Command every day, embellished by specially trained authors-for-children. Their toys for seven years before the war have been miniature tanks, aeroplanes and guns that actually shoot, and though latest developments have robbed them of their more realistic toys, the insidious training, with cardboard war-games, has continued. Hitler Youth training, drilling and study used to be something which took place after school, extra curricula activities. Now Hitler has decreed it shall be a part of the curriculum: mornings must be given to studying the Nazi version of history and other subjects, and afternoons to Hitler Youth activity. If a boy is a good Hitler Youth, he passes, no matter what he knows about anything else. If he has not been a good, vigorous Hitler Youth, he cannot even enter a secondary school, regardless of how intelligent he is or what talent he has. That is another degree of that year of progress, 1941.

These are the elements of Germany who have not been affected by the Transition. They bear watching. If Hitler wins, they will become the gods, not only of Valhalla but of the rest of the world. They will be worse than the present gods. Hitler got most of his present Gestapo while it was on the verge of becoming adult, or after it became adult. These he has had from birth. If you think the present Gestapo is brutal, just wait until these little tykes—bred on insolence and on their innate superiority to all else in the world, and inspired by the great deeds of the "War of German Liberation," as it will be called—grow up and become the rulers of Victorious Germany and the World. In a sense, this is a war to stop little twelve-year-old Hans and Fritz. We are fighting not so much for the present as for the future. If they win, woe betide, not us so much as our children!

Last Train from Berlin, 1942

"The Worst News That I Have Encountered in the Last 20 Years"

by Robert Hagy

PITTSBURGH, PA.

The strangest development here involved America Firsters assembled in Soldiers' and Sailors' Memorial Hall in Oakland Civic Center, three miles from downtown Pittsburgh. Senator Gerald P. Nye, tall, dark, handsome North Dakotan, spoke to 2500 rank-and-filers (capacity) from a hall-wide platform above which Lincoln's Gettysburg Address is spread in huge dark letters against a dirty buff background. I was assigned to cover it for the *Post Gazette*, and just a few minutes before leaving the office, flashes and bulletins came over the AP wire on the Hawaii and Manila attacks.

I arrived at the Hall at 3:00 p.m., the time the meeting was scheduled to start, and found Nye in a two-by-four room backstage ready to go on with the local officials of the Firsters. I shoved the pasted-up news at him. Irene Castle Mc-Laughlin, still trim wife of the dancer killed in World War I, another speaker, and Pittsburgh Chairman John B. Gordon, clustered around the Senator to read. It was the first they had heard of the war and Nye's first reaction was: "It sounds terribly fishy to me. Can't we have some details? Is it sabotage or is it open attack? I'm amazed that the President should announce an attack without giving details." Cool as a cucumber, he went on to compare the announcement with the first news of the *Greer* incident, which he termed very misleading.

I asked him what effect the Jap war should have on America First, whether it would disband. He replied: "If Congress were to declare war, I'm sure that every America Firster would be cooperative and support his government in the winning of that war in every possible way . . . but I should not expect them to disband even if Congress declared

94

war." Nye and the others then paraded on to the platform as if nothing had happened.

Although the news had come over the radio, apparently nobody in the audience knew anything, and the meeting went on just like any other America First meeting with emphasis on denouncing Roosevelt as a warmonger. Mrs. McLaughlin expressed concern for America's wives and mothers, her voice catching as she referred to Vernon Castle's not coming back; dabbed a tear from her eye as she sat down.

The next speaker was ruddy, ruralish Charlie Sipes, Pennsylvania State Senator, locally famed as a historian. Routine America First stuff until, in the midst of an attack on Roosevelt for trying "to make everything Russian appealing to the U.S.," he cried: "In fact, the chief warmonger in the U.S., to my way of thinking, is the President of the U.S.!" While the hall, decked in red-white-and-blue balcony bunting and "Defend America First" signs, was still full of roaring approval, a white-haired, heavy-set man stood up from an aisle seat well to the rear. The man, although nobody knew him and he was in mufti, was Colonel Enrique Urrutia Jr., Chief of the Second Military Area (Pittsburgh District of Third Corps Area) of the Organized Reserve. "Can this meeting be called after what has happened in the last few hours?" Colonel Urrutia—an infantryman 31 years in the Army—burst out, livid with incredulity and indignation. "Do you know that Japan has attacked Manila, that Japan has attacked Hawaii?"

Apparently the crowd took him for a plain crackpot heckler. They booed, yelled "Throw him out" and "Warmonger." Several men near Urrutia converged toward him. According to Lieutenant George Pischke, in command of a detail of ten policemen assigned to keep down disturbances which usually mark America First meetings here, the committee's blue-badged ushers "tried to manhandle" the colonel. Cops were in quick though, and Lieutenant Pischke escorted Urrutia out of the hall (through a blizzard of "warmonger" shrieks and reaching women's hands) at the latter's own request. "I came to listen," he told me in the lobby, purple with rage. "I thought this was a patriots' meeting, but this is a traitors' meeting." Inside Sipes, a cool hand, tried to restore calm, said soothingly, "Don't be too hard on this poor bombastic man.

He's only a mouthpiece for F.D.R." Then Sipes went on with his speech.

A couple of other people addressed the crowd. Finally came Nye. Still no word from leaders about the war. Nye started at about 4:45 p.m. For nearly three quarters of an hour he went through his isolationist routine. "Who's war is this?" he demanded at one point (referring to war in Europe). "Roosevelt's," chorused the rank-and-filers. "My friends," said Nye callously, "are betting 20 to 1 that if we don't stop in our tracks now, we'll be in before Great Britain gets in." Howls of laughter. A few minutes after this, I was called to the telephone. The city desk had a bulletin on Japan's declaration of war and asked me to get it to Nye. On a piece of copy paper I printed in pencil: "The Japanese Imperial Government at Tokyo today at 4:00 p.m. announced a state of war with the U.S. and Great Britain." I walked out on the platform and put it on the rostrum before Nye. He glanced at it, read it, never batted an eye, went on with his speech . . .

For 15 minutes more, Nye continued his routine, "I woke up one morning to find that we had 50 ships less, that the President had given them away despite laws forbidding it." "Treason," yelled some. "Impeach him," yelled others. Finally, at 5:45 p.m., more than two and a half hours after the meeting started, Nye paused and said: "I have before me the worst news that I have encountered in the last 20 years. I don't know exactly how to report it to you; but I will report it to you just as a newspaperman gave it to me." Slowly he read the note. An excited murmur swept through the packed hall. Nye continued: "I can't somehow believe this. I can't come to any conclusions until I know what this is all about. I want time to find out what's behind it. Previously I heard about bombings in Hawaii. Somehow, I couldn't quite believe that, but in the light of this later news, I must, although there's been many funny things before. I remember the morning of the attack on the destroyer *Greer*. The President went on the radio and said the attack on the *Greer* was without provocation; but I tell you the *Greer* shot first. That was the incident the President said was unprovoked—and that's cheating."

With that, he disposed of the new war, but more or less upset and flushed in the face, he didn't do much more than flounder through five or six more minutes of stuff about America's prime duty being to preserve democracy lest "victor and vanquished alike fall" and communism "grow in the ruins." Loud applause. "Keep your chins up," said Senator Nye and sat down. Benediction, a couple of announcements and the meeting was over.

Plowing through his fanatical followers, I gave Nye a third piece of intelligence—that Roosevelt had called a 9:00 p.m. meeting of the Cabinet and Congressional leaders. I knew he was scheduled to talk tonight at the First Baptist Church (pastor of which is pacifist) and I asked him if he intended to fly to Washington. Flustered, grim-lipped, rosy-faced, sweating, he muttered, "I must, I must try . . ." and strode quickly out of the hall talking to somebody about plane reservations. . . . Whether he couldn't get a plane or what, he nevertheless ended up keeping the church appointment, announcing he would take the train to Washington later tonight. At church, before 600 people, he was grim, bitter, defeated. "I had hoped for long that at least the involvement of my country in this terrible foreign slaughter would be left more largely to our own determination."

Then he reviewed events leading up to the war, accusing Roosevelt of "doing his utmost to promote trouble with Japan." Inferring that we were already at war with Germany, he declared: "I am not one to say my country is prepared to fight a war on one front, let alone two." When several people laughed at a reference (out of habit?) to "bloody Joe Stalin," Nye said coldly: "I am not making a humorous speech." But on the Jap attack he said: "Here is a challenge. There isn't much America can do but move forward with American lives, American blood and American wealth to the protection of our people and possessions in the Pacific."

Leaving the church, another *Post-Gazette* reporter caught him, asked what course he would prescribe for the nation. Finally he gave in completely, the fight gone out of him except for enough to make one more crack at Roosevelt. "We have been maneuvered into this by the President," he said, "but the only thing now is to declare war and to jump into it with everything we have and bring it to a victorious conclusion."

War Comes to the U.S.—Dec. 7, 1941: The First 30 Hours, 1942

President's War Message

WASHINGTON, *Dec. 8.*—*Following is the text of President Roosevelt's war message as he delivered it to Congress:*
Mr. Vice-President, Mr. Speaker, members of the Senate and of the House of Representatives:

Yesterday, Dec. 7, 1941—a date which will live in infamy—the United States of America was suddenly and deliberately attacked by naval and air forces of the Empire of Japan.

The United States was at peace with that nation, and at the solicitation of Japan, was still in conversation with its government and its Emperor looking toward the maintenance of peace in the Pacific.

Indeed, one hour after Japanese air squadrons had commenced bombing in the American island of Oahu, the Japanese Ambassador to the United States and his colleague delivered to our Secretary of State a formal reply to a recent American message. While this reply stated that it seemed useless to continue the existing diplomatic negotiations, it contained no threat or hint of war or armed attack.

It will be recorded that the distance of Hawaii from Japan makes it obvious that the attack was deliberately planned many days or even weeks ago. During the intervening time the Japanese government has deliberately sought to deceive the United States by false statements and expressions of hope for continued peace.

The attack yesterday on the Hawaiian Islands has caused severe damage to American naval and military forces. I regret to tell you that many American lives have been lost. In addition, American ships have been reported torpedoed on the high seas between San Francisco and Honolulu.

Yesterday the Japanese government also launched an attack against Malaya.

Last night Japanese forces attacked Hongkong.

Last night Japanese forces attacked Guam.

Last night Japanese forces attacked the Philippine Islands.

Last night the Japanese attacked Wake Island.

And this morning the Japanese attacked Midway Island.

Japan has, therefore, undertaken a surprise offensive extending throughout the Pacific area. The facts of yesterday and today speak for themselves. The people of the United States have already formed their opinions and well understand the implications to the very life and safety of our nation.

As Commander in Chief of the Army and Navy I have directed that all measures be taken for our defense.

Always will our whole nation remember the character of the onslaught against us.

No matter how long it may take us to overcome this premeditated invasion, the American people in their righteous might will win through to absolute victory.

I believe I interpret the will of the Congress and of the people when I assert that we will not only defend ourselves to the uttermost but will make it very certain that this form of treachery shall never again endanger us.

Hostilities exist. There is no blinking at the fact that our people, our territory and our interests are in grave danger.

With confidence in our armed forces—with the unbounding determination of our people—we will gain the inevitable triumph—so help us God.

I ask that the Congress declare that since the unprovoked and dastardly attack by Japan on Sunday, Dec. 7, 1941, a state of war has existed between the United States and the Japanese Empire.

New York *Herald Tribune*, December 9, 1941

War Hits Manila

by Melville Jacoby

10 a.m., December 8

Manila has not yet digested the fact of war. Toy vendors are on the streets with newspaper extras, fully equipped soldiers are appearing, women in hotel lobbies are collecting children at their sides. Taxi drivers comment: "Not serious—not the Japanese Government's doings—only the Japanese military's mistake in Hawaii."

MacArthur's headquarters were the grimmest place at dawn this morning when the staff was aroused to face war and send troops to battle stations. Extra guards arrived at 9 a.m. as officers began donning helmets, grabbing cups of coffee and sandwiches. Newsmen were deluging the army press office with questions. Admiral Hart's headquarters were quiet. Air Force headquarters were the scene of most bustling, with helmeted men poring over maps and occasionally peering out windows to the sky.

There has been no air alarm in Manila, but it is expected by the minute. Rumors are flying everywhere. It is nearly impossible to get an operator for phone calls. High Commissioner Sayre's office is blocked off by military police. The whole thing has burst here like a bombshell, though the military had been alert over the week-end.

There is no censorship as yet: the voluntary basis is adhered to. Attacks and defense have not yet taken a definite pattern. The Davao bombing, however, signalizes the possibility of a blitz landing. The Bangkok's radio silence and lack of reports are leaving Manila cut off from news of action anywhere else in the Far East.

War feeling hit the populace about noon when there were runs on banks, grocery stores, gas stations. All taxis and garage cars were taken by the military, clogging transport systems. Our own planes overhead are drawing thousands of eyes now: they didn't earlier this morning. The High Commissioner's office is still holding hurried meetings while Mrs. Sayre's Emergency Sewing Circle called off this morning's session.

In downtown buildings, basement shelters are being put together. Building managers found an acute shortage of sandbags after Quezon's palace had bought the last remaining 20,000 to reinforce the Malacanang shelter. There was a frantic rush this morning to tape all shop windows.

Philippine Scouts, equipped with new packs and uniforms, riding in special orange busses, rounded up the majority of Jap nationals. In surprise raids they took 500 Nips from the Yokohama Specie Bank. At the Nippon Bazaar in the center of Manila, soldiers found twelve Japs barricaded inside. They broke down the glass doors, captured the twelve, found a thirteenth hiding under the counter.

11 p.m.

Sporadic reports are still making it difficult to analyze the Pacific picture, while the slowness of communications is obscuring even the Philippine situation.

The Japanese blitz strategy of thinning forces, striking simultaneously, is sure evidence of German coaching. So far the Japanese are hitting only strategic points, such as airfields. The Japanese bombing fits in with the fact that they improved accuracy immeasurably during the last three weeks of Chungking's bombing season, either by a new bombsight or tactics.

The fact that the U.S. communique this evening quotes "sanguinary losses on both sides" after the heaviest raids on Clark Field at 1:30 this afternoon, explodes the old myth that you can knock Japanese planes out of the air with toothpicks.

Manila tonight is quiet, blacked out, waiting. The war atmosphere, entirely lacking until noon, is finally setting in.

December 9

The appearance of ack-acks on the parkways, wardens, Red Crossers, brought real live war to Manila. The Filipino and American populace is getting the first taste of war, far behind even the Chinese children in Chungking, who can distinguish bomber and pursuit sounds, and know the difference between the flash of ack-acks and searchlights. In a few more days, however, the locals will become veterans and automatically go to cover instead of watching the "show."

Bleary-eyed Americans are still jovial. It is odd to see horse-drawn carriages with Americans in front of the swank Manila Hotel, while all taxis are requisitioned for military usage. Gas stations are closed temporarily following yesterday's rush. There is a terrific run on groceries and other supplies, especially food concentrates, bandages, iodine, flashlights, kotex. Many stores have bare shelves. All Japanese shops are closed while the Chinese shopkeepers are identifying their stores with home-made labels reading "Chinese."

Optimistic signs of the formerly lax Civilian Emergency Administration are the air wardens helping to direct traffic and to avoid panic, cooperating under "advice" from MacArthur's headquarters. Though people are still numbed by the actual Jap attack, they are slowly coming out with grim determination. The smoothness of the Japanese air tactics is amazing. Obviously the Japanese are planning to cripple our striking power, then invade according to blitz plans.

Although it is foolish to draw over-early conclusions, the continual daily and nightly exchange visits between Hart, Sayre and MacArthur point out the seriousness of Manila's position. Hart and MacArthur are in closest cooperation. When Hart left MacArthur's office this morning, MacArthur escorted him arm in arm to his car. Hart commented on the large passageway under the old wall in MacArthur's office, joked that it is better than anything he has to go to during raids.

December 11

Manila this evening was very tense in the blackout, the city faintly outlined in the glow from smoldering fires started in the noontime raid. It is real war now. The U.S. Army and Navy are meeting the enemy face to face, both in Manila and elsewhere as the Battle of the Philippines begins. It is not a matter of individual heroism, but a life and death struggle quickly drawing cooperation from all.

The hour-long noon raid heralded the first popping of ack-

acks over the city. The Japs are using fast, heavily-armed, two-seater pursuit jobs, attempting to draw off our fighters so that the white-winged droning bombers can come in. The bombers are kept high by ack-ack, but the thudding bombs sent Manilans scampering.

Ambulances and red-and-white flagged Red Cross cars were racing over the city after the raid, carrying casualties. Rescue workers began to show their stuff: the Filipinos were good and spirited. An interesting side-note was talking to already stubbled, bearded, grimy Yank soldiers at undisclosed posts, who saw their own comrades go down and commented: "I'd like another crack at those low-flying bastards. Write my mother I'm a hero. I'll stay here. I'll stick it out."

A grizzled, gangling corporal pulled a small piece of shrapnel from his pocket, remarking: "We sold 'em this stuff and now they're giving it back."

December 18

The same sunrise is glowing and the same sun sets over Manila Bay after a fortnight, but everything else is changed. Blackouts and daylight-saving time are changing routines. People are in bed very early, rise at dawn. Government office hours are seven to one, the most important offices getting their basements ready to work through raids.

Manila no longer looks like a Florida resort, the men in white sharkskin, the women gaily decked. Men are in checked suits, women in slacks with uncoiffured hair. Correspondents have long since shed coats and ties. Uniforms are now commonplace. Many civilian men are organized in a people's army, packing .45's, helmets and gas masks. Some women are appearing in Red Cross uniforms with gas masks on their shoulders. Other civilians are wearing a variety of armbands, such as Press, Air Warden.

The transportation problem is working out with a few taxis released by the military. Hitch-hiking is now popular for the first time in Manila's history. Horse-drawn *calesas* are disappearing, carrying evacuees over the countryside. Cycling is suddenly popular but many shops carry only Jap bikes. Everything in Manila is now on a cash basis, ending the signing of chits, which is a very old custom in the Orient.

Hotels and big buildings are swarming with women and children, moved from their homes. People eat on the hotel's lawn before the blackout, while the Army and Navy Club eats after dark, not seeing their food.

Groceries are now open with well-stocked shelves, while stores and hotels, short-handed at first, now report job hunters. Movies are open but with very small attendance. Downtown eating places are crowded with Filipino men whose womenfolk have gone to the country.

There are pup-tent encampments over the city and military patrols everywhere. Relief workers bring sandwiches and coffee to soldiers at gun stations and camps. The Red Cross has opened eight emergency hospitals with plenty of volunteer doctors. Regular hospitals are on a wartime basis, storing supplies, caring for bomb victims. Blood banks have been set up via donors, ranging from a Spanish priest to Austrian refugees. Filipinos are volunteering the services of 16,000 women for making bandages. Cattle-owners are offering their stock, one rancher having given 10,000 head.

Evacuation is still underway. Blackouts are very complete, and no one is allowed in the street after 7:30. The few bars still open draw a mixed crowd. Blackout life is systemized to early dinners. Afterwards there is usually some group singing. People wind bandages and gossip, then go to bed after laying their clothes where they can be most easily reached.

December 22

The first week of war, red flares were shooting up from all sectors, many near to military objectives. One pilot flying at night remarked that he could almost see his way to certain landing fields by following the rockets. There was frequent gunfire as the authorities rounded up most of the flare-shooters.

Manila nights are now quiet: only rarely does one see flashing lights. It is generally considered that the rockets were used to create fear and panic. Though a few Japanese nationalists shot flares, the majority were touched off by uneducated natives who did not realize what they were doing. One said a Japanese gave him a peso, knew nothing else.

Fifth-column stories are numerous yet very difficult to

check. It is known that fifth columnists snipped air alarm wires and continue to snip telephone wires, but activities to date are minor. Authorities are placing a very strong guard at all vital points. Saboteurs recently trying to fire shots at oil tanks were unsuccessful. A typical wild rumor was last week's search of the High Commissioner's premises, even under the beds, for an asserted but non-existent parachutist.

During the first few days, enemy roundups were routine, as the lists had been previously prepared. Japanese consular officials were confined to their homes under guard. Other Japanese internees include bankers, businessmen, newsmen, fishermen, etc. Their knapsacks, containing tinned goods, money and clothing, showed that they were ready. A considerable number, hearing the war news on the radio, piled into taxis and cars and drove to concentration camps, giving themselves up. The majority of Japanese women insisted on accompanying their husbands and bringing their children.

The internees are deprived of radio and writing materials. All phone lines to the concentration camps are cut and the inmates are not allowed to contact anyone, even the guards keeping their distance. The women are given good treatment and allowed to go marketing under guard. The swank Nippon Club is filled with internees, the tennis courts being covered with their washing, and children at play. Internees get two meals a day: soup with vegetables, a little meat and rice.

December 26

Manila is definitely an open city despite Tokyo's radio claim that it is heavily fortified. There are no uniforms on the streets, no rush of tanks, army trucks, no military police guards at night. The Jap bombers are not meeting a single anti-aircraft burst and are calmly crisscrossing above the city, picking objectives as if in practice flights similar to Chungking.

A glance from any window shows great spirals of black smoke as the destruction of everything of military value, including oils, is completed. Even Cavite Base is finished. Last night there was faint singing by a few Christmas carolers, blending with the sharp explosions. Flames from all sides shot a hundred feet into the air, lighting the city.

Military offices of the nearby barracks are ghostly empty after convoys of cheering soldiers left for the front, waving their arms in the "V" sign. The local Filipinos' morale is still good. They are not showing fear and are holding up better than most Americans, although everyone is on edge.

December 28

The bombings to date are severe but not exactly indiscriminate, as reported. A number of Manila's most historic churches, convents, hospitals and newspaper offices lay in the path of the bombing, which was most unfortunate. It is difficult, however, to say that the Japanese intended to destroy Santo Thomas University and Santo Domingo Church. Should Jap bombers really begin indiscriminate bombing in the future, it will be mass murder. No U.S. planes have neared Manila since it was officially declared an open city.

The bombers were lower in today's bombing than the previous 4,000 feet, sometimes making several passes at targets. You can easily hear the crackle sound of the bombs falling in mid-air and see the sun glint on them. The bombing looked like an air review as the big, silver twin-engined planes were circling in the same direction, crossing the bay, banking off at the piers, coming down in a set line over the piers and the walled city to the Pasig River at regular intervals, occasionally letting off a few rounds of machine-gun fire for intimidation purposes.

Groups of fire-fighters have been working the past 36 hours, sweaty, wet and tired, but chins up. The areas of the Walled City that were damaged were large, partly from direct hits of large bombs but more from the fires swept by the strong winds of the past two days. The damage done to churches created resentment, and it was pitiful to watch firemen take off their hats when entering the churches to fight the blazes which soared 100 feet, crackling around the figures of Christ and Mary. Some of the statuary was removed and carefully placed in the streets, the crowds standing at a distance respectfully, though the figures might be next to a basket of eggs or books. Spanish priests and a few nuns were present. The rest, evacuated previously, were disturbed when unable to remove the sacraments. It is pathetic to see the beginning look of tragedy in the faces of women hauling a few belongings and bedding from homes endangered by fire.

History in the Writing, 1945

"Prepare to Abandon Ship"

by Cecil Brown

DECEMBER 11, 5:00:16 a.m.

Here's the eyewitness story of how the *Prince of Wales* and
the *Repulse* ended their careers in the South China Sea, fifty
miles from the Malaya coast and a hundred and fifty miles
north of Singapore.

I was aboard the *Repulse* and with hundreds of others
escaped. Then, swimming in thick oil, I saw the *Prince of
Wales* lay over on her side like a tired war horse and slide
beneath the waters. I kept a diary from the time the first
Japanese high level bombing started at 11:15 until 12:31 when
Captain William Tennant, skipper of the *Repulse* and Senior
British Captain afloat, shouted through the ship's communi-
cations system, "All hands on deck, prepare to abandon ship.
May God be with you."

I jumped twenty feet to the water from the up end of the
side of the *Repulse* and smashed my stop watch at thirty-five
and a half minutes after twelve. The sinking of the *Repulse* and
the *Prince of Wales* was carried out by a combination of high
level bombing and torpedo attacks with consummate skill and
the greatest daring. I was standing on the flag deck slightly
forward amidships when nine Jap bombers approached at ten
thousand feet strung in a line, clearly visible in the brilliant
sunlit sky. They flew directly over our ship and our anti-aircraft
guns were screaming constantly.

Just when the planes were passing over, one bomb hit the
water beside where I was standing, so close to the ship that
we were drenched from the water spout. Simultaneously another struck the *Repulse* on the catapult desk, penetrating the
ship and exploding below in a marine's mess and hangar. Our
planes were subsequently unable to take off. At 11:27 fire is
raging below, and most strenuous efforts are under way to

control it. All gun crews are replenishing their ammunition and are very cool and cracking jokes. There are a couple of jagged holes in the funnel near where I am standing.

It's obvious the Japs flew over the length of the ship, each dropping three bombs so that twenty-seven bombs fell around us at first in their attack. Brilliant red flashes are spouting from our guns' wells. The *Prince of Wales* is half a mile away. Destroyers are at various distances throwing everything they have into the air. A splash about two miles off our port beam may be anti-aircraft but we are uncertain. At 11:40 the *Prince of Wales* seems to be hit. She's reduced her speed. Now they're coming to attack us. The communications system shouts "stand by for barrage." All our guns are going. We are twisting and snaking violently to avoid torpedoes. The Japs are coming in low, one by one in single waves. They're easy to spot. Amid the roar from the guns aboard the *Repulse* and the pom-poms of anti-aircraft fire, we are signalled, "We've a man overboard."

Two Jap aircraft are approaching us. I see more of them coming with the naked eye. I again count nine. They're torpedo bombers and are circling us about a mile and half or two miles away. 11:45—now there seems to me more bombers but they are circling like vultures at about one thousand feet altitude. The guns are deafening. The smell of cordite is almost suffocating and explosions are ear shattering and the flashes blinding. The officer beside me yells, "Here comes a tin fish."

A Jap torpedo bomber is heading directly for us, two hundred yards above the water. At 11:48 he's less than five hundred distant, plowing onward. A torpedo drops and he banks sharply and his whole side is exposed to our guns but instead of driving away he's making a graceful dive toward the water. He hits and immediately bursts into flame in a gigantic splash of orange against the deep blue sky and the robins-egg blue water. Other planes are coming, sweeping low in an amazing suicide effort to sink the *Repulse*.

Their daring is astonishing, coming so close you can make out the pilot's outline. One coming in at 11:48 to our starboard just dropped a torpedo. A moment later I hear shouts of joy indicating that he was brought down but I didn't see that. We also claim we brought down two high level bombers previously but I didn't see these crash. At least at the moment I have no recollection of seeing them.

At 12:01 another wave of torpedo bombers is approaching. They are being met with everything we've got except our fourteen inchers. Beside me the signal officer flashes word from Captain Tennant to the *Prince of Wales*. "We eluded all torpedos this second attack." It's fascinating to watch our tracer bullets speeding toward the Jap bombers. 12:03: we've just shot down another torpedo bomber who is about four hundred yards away and we shot it out. All of its motors are afire and disintegrating pieces of the fuselage are flying about. Now it disappears over the surface of the water into scrap. The brilliant orange from the fire against this blue sky is so close it's startling. All the men are cheering at the sight. It's so close it seems you could almost reach out and touch the remains of this Jap bomber.

At 12:15 the *Wales* seems to be stopped definitely. I've been too busy to watch the attacks against her but she seems in utmost difficulty. Her guns are firing constantly and we are both twisting. One moment the *Wales* is at our starboard, the next it's at our port. I'm not watching the destroyers but they have not been subjected to air attacks. The Japs are throwing everything recklessly against the two capital ships.

There's fire aboard us, it's not out. I just saw some firemen and fire control parties. The calmness of the crews is amazing. I have constantly roved from one side of the flag deck to the other during the heavy firing and attacks and the cool precision of all hands has seemed unreal and unnatural. Even when they are handing up shells for the service guns, each shell is handed over with a joke. I never saw such happiness on men's faces. This is the first time these gun crews have been in action in this war and they are having the time of their lives. 12:20: I see ten bombers approaching us from a distance. It's impossible to determine whether this will be a high level attack or another torpedo bomber attack. "Stand by for barrage" comes over the ship's communication system.

One plane is circling around, it's now at three or four hundred yards approaching us from the port side. It's coming closer, head on, and I see a torpedo drop. It's streaking for us. A watcher shouts, "Stand by for torpedo" and the tin fish is streaking directly for us. Some one says: "This one got us." The torpedo struck the side on which I was standing about twenty yards astern of my position. It felt like the ship had crashed into a well-rooted dock. It threw me four feet across the deck but I did not fall and I did not feel any explosion. Just a very great jar. Almost immediately it seemed we began to list and less than a minute later there was another jar of the same kind and the same force, except that it was almost precisely the same spot on the starboard side.

After the first torpedo, the communication system coolly announced: "Blow up your life belts." I was in this process when the second torpedo struck and the settling ship and the crazy angle were so apparent I didn't continue blowing my belt.

That the *Repulse* was doomed was immediately apparent. The communication system announced, "Prepare to abandon ship. May God be with you." Without undue rush we all started streaming down ladders, hurrying but not pushing. It was most difficult to realize I must leave the ship. It seemed so incredible that the *Repulse* could or should go down. But the *Repulse* was fast heeling over to port and walking ceased to become a mode of locomotion. I was forced to clamber and scramble in order to reach the side. Men were lying dead around the guns. Some were half hidden by empty shell cases. There was considerable damage all around the ship. Some of the men had been machine gunned. That had been unquestioned fact.

All around me men were stripping off their clothes and their shoes and tossing aside their steel helmets. Some are running alongside the three quarters exposed hull of the ship to reach a spot where they can slide down the side without injuring themselves in the jagged hole in the ship's side. Others are running to reach a point where they have a shorter dive to the water. I am reluctant to leave my new portable typewriter down in my cabin and unwilling to discard my shoes which I had made just a week before. As I go over the side the *Prince of Wales* half a mile away seems to be afire but her guns are still firing the heaviest. It's most obvious she's stopped dead and out of control due to her previous damage.

The air attack against the *Prince of Wales* carried out the same scheme directed against the *Repulse*. The Japs were able to send two British capital ships to the bottom because of first, a determined air torpedo attack and, second, the skill and the efficiency of the Japanese operations. It's apparent that the best guns and crews in the world will be unable to stem a torpedo bombing attack if the attackers are sufficiently determined.

According to the best estimate obtainable, the Japs used in their operations against both the *Wales* and the *Repulse* eighty-six bombers; eighteen high level bombers and approximately twenty-five torpedo bombers against the *Repulse* and probably an equal number against the *Prince of Wales*. In the case of the *Wales*, however, the Japs started the torpedo bombing instead of initial high level bombing. In the first attack, one torpedo hit the *Wales* in the after-part. Some survivors believe the *Wales* was hit twice in the initial attack, then followed two more torpedo attacks, both successful. The final attack on the *Wales* was made by high level bombers around ten thousand feet. When that attack came, the *Wales* was sinking fast and everyone threw himself down on deck.

Most of the guns were unmanageable as a result of the list and the damage. I jumped into the water from the *Repulse* at 12:35. While I was in the water, the *Wales* continued firing for some time. The *Wales* suffered two direct hits by bombs on the deck. Like the attack on the *Repulse*, the Japs flew across the length of the *Wales* in a single line, each bomber dropping a stick. One officer said a child of six could see some of them were going to hit us. During the entire action Admiral Tom Phillips, Commander in Chief of the Far East Fleet, and Captain Leech, Skipper of the *Prince of Wales*, were on the bridge.

While the torpedo bombers were rushing in toward the *Wales*, dropping tin fish and machine gunning the decks, Phillips clambered up on the roof of the bridge and also atop the gun turrets to see better and to direct all phases of the action.

When it was apparent that the *Wales* was badly hit, the Admiral issued an order to the flag officer for the destroyer then lying alongside close by. "Signal to Singapore to send tugs to tow us." Evidently up to that moment, Phillips was not convinced that the *Wales* was sinking. The last order issued by

Phillips came at approximately 1:15. It said, "Blow up your life belts."

Later the ship was under water. Phillips and Leech were the last from the *Wales* to go over the side and they slid into the water together. It's probable that their reluctance to leave the ship until all possible men had left meant their death, since it's most likely they were drawn down by the suction when the *Wales* was on her side and then settled at her stern with her bow rising into the air.

Swimming about a mile away, lying on top of a small stool, I saw the bow of the *Wales*. When Phillips signalled to ask Singapore to send tugs, the *Wales* already had four torpedoes in her. Like the *Repulse*, the *Wales* gun crews were very cool and although many guns were no longer effective the crew stood beside them. When the final high level bombing attack came, only three guns were capable of firing, except the fourteen-inchers which naturally did not go into action. I did not meet Phillips but last week when I visited the *Wales* at the naval base, I had a long talk with Captain Leech. He's a jovial convivial, smiling officer who gave me the impression of the greatest kindliness and ability. The *Wales* carried a complement of seventeen hundred; the *Repulse* twelve hundred and fifty officers and ratings. When the *Wales* sank, the suction was so great it ripped off the life belt of one officer more than fifty feet away. A fortunate feature of the sinking of both the *Repulse* and the *Wales* was that neither blew up.

Since the tide was strong and there was an extremely powerful suction from both ships, it was extremely difficult to make any progress away from the ship in the thick oil. The gentle, quiet manner in which these shell-belching dreadnaughts went to their last resting place without exploding, was a tribute of gratitude from two fine ships for their fine sailors.

From Pearl Harbor into Tokyo, 1945

"Tanks and Cannons Standing
Starkly in the Snow"

by Larry Lesueur

December 16

We divided into two convoys of white-painted Zis limousines. The auto seats were draped with heavy, colorful Bokhara rugs. I was in a car with a censor and two Red Army officers.

A cutting wind arose with the sun as we drove north along the Leningrad Chaussée. The broad snow-covered highway was filled with hundreds of black-coated workers plodding to the trolley lines even at this hour. Their factories were far out on the city's outskirts. Our cars passed through barricade after barricade. They were huge blockhouses of rough-hewn logs with a narrow, easily closed passageway between. They were in no way as ornate as the solid concrete "dragon's teeth" roadblocks the British had set up the year before on the Dover Road during the Battle of Britain. The Russians had just cut down the near-by trees and joined them together in a series of old-fashioned stockades and wooden forts.

As we bounced north along the heavily ice-rutted Leningrad road, we passed scores of stolidly marching peasant women going back to their homes in newly freed settlements. They had their meager belongings piled high on wooden sleds and dragged them along by ropes. Here and there we saw peasants slowly dragging small sleds with only coffins on them.

We were forced to a skidding stop once to make way for a column of rumbling Soviet tanks, white-painted for camouflage against the snow. Then our two cars again took their place in the endless line of wooden sleds loaded down with yellow fodder and ammunition. Their small, sturdy Siberian horses were driven by expressionless Red Army men whose faces were set against the bitter edge of the wind. They were going north, too, toward the front.

115

At the first dynamited bridge we turned off the asphalt onto a snowy wood road. A group of Russian sentries scrutinized our passes and then pulled up a crossbar to allow our cars to pass.

We skidded and spun our wheels through a dark pine forest whose towering trees almost hid the light of the day. Here and there we passed a clearing with battered German tanks and cannons standing starkly in the snow. This was the kind of country the Battle of Moscow had raged in. This was the high-water mark of the German advance. We were about twenty-five miles from the city limits of Moscow. The German failure must have been the greatest disappointment for an invading army in history. Hitler's troops could look down the long, straight road that separated them from the Soviet capital. Emergency bridges had been thrown over the tank traps. Dug to a depth of some fifteen feet by the sweat of the mobilized population during the fall, they were now deep with snow. Ice-glazed barbed wire ran across lakes and fields. It was evident that certain areas had been carefully prepared in advance. The defenses were laid out with mathematical precision in the areas in which invading tanks would have to travel to skirt the thick woods. One of the types of anti-tank obstacles in which the Red Army had placed most faith consisted of six-foot lengths of iron rail bolted together in the shape of a gigantic child's jack. No matter which way a tank approached them, they presented a heavy spike. They were difficult to blow up with artillery fire because they had no flat surfaces to catch the blast.

Then we passed the first burnt-out villages. Their charred ruins marred the fresh whiteness of the snow. The only upright objects were the gaunt and blackened chimneys that stood out forlornly. Some of the wrecked foundations still smoked. I watched peasant women who had dragged their sleds of household goods all the way from Moscow, picking about in the wreckage. They had found they had no place to come home to. The older women were weeping silently.

At the roadside was a small graveyard of neatly lettered crosses. We stopped our cars to examine them. The workmanship of the crosses was excellent. The names and ages of the fallen Germans had been carefully burnt in the fresh wood.

Many had the outline of an iron cross inscribed below their names. It was remarkable how young the men had been. Their recorded ages averaged from nineteen to twenty-three years. The Soviet colonel who rode with us remarked: "We estimated that 85,000 of those young Germans died in their two offensives against Moscow."

On one side where a number of German and Russian tanks were strewn in an open field, like a junk yard, the surrounding forest was devastated as by a hurricane. There were broken branches everywhere and trees lay tumbled like jackstraws on the ground, evidence of the terrific artillery fire and the death struggles of the tanks. The blackened wreckage of the villages was appalling. Here, too, one or two peasant women poked silently in the ruins of their houses, attempting to salvage what they could. There were only charred, smoking embers.

Our small convoy stopped often to give marching troops the right of way. They were marching just as they had in Napoleon's day, slogging through the snow and bitter cold, on foot. Many of the Russian soldiers wore no steel helmets, only their warm sheepskin hats with thick earlaps. Only a few wore white-painted steel helmets over a lighter peaked hat. I could see that the Red Army reserves were short of this equipment, but the Russians seemed to have no shortage of artillery. Gun after gun wheeled past us, the lighter ones pulled by horses, the heavier by tractors. They had been rushed to the front; no time had been lost to paint them white. Still green-painted as they had come from the factory, they jolted past the white-painted broken German guns, shattered at the roadside, their spiked muzzles splayed out like the petals of a flower.

As we proceeded, the gross rumble of artillery became more insistent. We passed an entire brigade of Red Army men who looked as though they had been marching for days. Their faces were black with fatigue. They were dragging their feet in exhaustion. Several times we saw men stumble as they plodded forward and fall unconscious on the snow. The columns never stopped moving, but I saw fellow soldiers pick up their companions and place them, senseless, on passing sleds loaded with hay. I recalled that many of Napoleon's men had frozen to death on the retreat from Moscow and wondered what would be the fate of these exhausted Red Army men, for they had no blankets. I later learned that during the winter the Red Army carried no blankets, but slept in their heavy greatcoats. When they bivouacked for the night at a village which the Germans had leveled by fire, they quickly dug into the fire-softened earth, next to the foundations, and hollowed dugouts of snow and branches. Throwing a tarpaulin over the top and pulling a stove inside with them, they huddled together for warmth and slept like so many Russian bears.

I was surprised to note that even these columns on forced march were clean-shaven. Our escorting colonel said that Soviet officers order their men to shave each day for discipline's sake. I asked how they managed it in sub-zero weather. He explained that they heat snow water and work in pairs, the men shaving one another simultaneously.

I watched the living soldiers pass by the dead at the roadside without a glance, and the dead looked scarcely human. They resembled wax mannequins thrown from a show-window, lying about in grotesque, inhuman postures, arms pointing toward the sky, legs frozen as though they were running. Their faces were bloodless, waxy white. The clean, cold air carried no taint of decomposition. But sometimes the wind brought us a whiff of acrid cordite smoke and the soot of a burnt village.

We finally skidded to a halt in the town of Solnetchno-gorsk. We were numb from the cold as we stiffly clambered out of the cars and walked over to watch a group of Russian civilians digging a large hole in the frozen ground of the village square. A pile of stiff bodies lay alongside the hole. They were Red Army men who had died to free the city. Solnetch-nogorsk, or Sunnyside Hill, had been the first sizable town to be recaptured from the Germans in the astounding winter offensive that saved the capital. It was here that the hitherto invincible blitzkrieg had finally gone into reverse. As we stood shivering in the street, I listened to the Russian officers say: "The city is virtually unharmed, except for a few houses shattered by gunfire. The Germans were surprised in the middle of the night by a Russian outflanking column and they fled, leaving their belongings, and without time for their destruction squads to set fire to the houses."

We were led into a large, one-story frame house, the home of the village druggist. German officers had been quartered here forty-eight hours before. The druggist's wife, Mrs. Garane Bagranov, was a slender, dark, sweet-faced woman, born in Armenia and married to a Russian. She spoke slowly and without emotion.

"Six German medical orderlies were billeted in my house," she said. "They took all the beds, while my daughters and I slept in the kitchen. They didn't molest us because they were afraid of their officers. They went into our drugstore and ransacked it for all the things they could use, like toothbrushes, soap, and perfume. They couldn't read the labels on the drug bottles because they were in Russian, so they threw the bottles on the floor and smashed them. Everything, children's cough medicines, everything. I told them to stop, but they answered: 'We're the bosses here now,' and the breaking of bottles went on. Finally I complained to their officers. They cautioned the men to stop the breakage, but as soon as the officers left the house, the men went back to the drugstore and began smashing things again. They seemed to be mad at the bottles because the labels were in Russian."

Mrs. Bagranov paused and her dark eyes flashed angrily as she thought of the wreckage.

"I ran into the store again," she said, "and told them they must stop. We wouldn't have any medicines left for the winter. But they brushed me aside and went on looking for perfume and broke the bottles they couldn't identify. I went into the street without my coat on and told their officers. Later one of them came in and tacked up a sign. It said that the drugstore was now the property of the German Army. Then the soldiers stopped breaking things.

"After about a week I knew something was happening in front of Moscow. More German soldiers were coming back from the front than were going forward. Then one day the two young Nazi officers I had complained to came into the house and sat at my kitchen table. One of them began to sob. The other rested his head in his hands and began to cry, too.

I knew in my heart what had happened. They were retreating from Moscow. Next night while they were asleep, an officer came bursting in the front door spreading the alarm. The Red Army was coming."

Mrs. Bagranov's voice rose with excitement.

"All of them, officers, soldiers, ran around wildly, throwing their things into bags. Their trucks and motorcycles were making a deafening noise outside. Then a few minutes later all was quiet. I opened the door into the dining-room where they slept. They had all gone. We were free again."

The old grandmother, who had stood silent while her daughter spoke, said in a quaver: "They took all our blankets."

I asked the silver-haired "babushka" what the Germans had done to her.

"Nothing," she said. "They just let me starve. But I had some dried bread hidden under my pillow and I lived on that."

The women went back into the kitchen to prepare supper and I leaned against the warm chimney, trying to get the chill of the long drive out of my bones. We would have given a lot for a drink of vodka, but the censor who had the vodka supply said firmly: "In Russia we never drink vodka unless we eat something with it. You must wait."

Shivering, we waited until the table was set with a hot meal. The food had been requisitioned from the Red Army supplies. There was soup, herring, browned beef, and little Russian cakes. The vodka was served in pitchers. All through the night we toasted the Red Army and Hitler's crushing disappointment. I wisely picked out the bed nearest the chimney, and after I lost count of the toasts in vodka, I threw myself on it and fell asleep. When I awakened next morning, I was still dressed, but someone had kindly thrown a quilt over me. It was still dark when I began to stumble toward the kitchen for water. I heard the sound of weeping. I realized that the arrival of the distinguished guests, the foreign correspondents, in this war-torn village had once more forced the poor old grandmother to suffer almost as much as she had under the Germans. She had been put out to sleep on the ice-cold porch.

At dawn we left to follow the advance of the Red Army. The road wound through forests of dark pines, their boughs sagging under their fluffy white load. Deep in the forest we could see Russian cavalry troops bivouacked for the day. They moved only at night on their raids into the enemy rear. We turned sharply sometimes at strange noises in the somber forests, caused by pine boughs slipping their load of snow. Looking more closely, we could see white-cowled ski soldiers sitting around tiny fires, brewing endless tea and waiting for darkness to fall. They looked like cowled Ku Klux Klansmen in their hide-out.

Here and there the small steppe horses of Russia cropped their fodder noisily in the dark recesses of the woods. The war was hard on horses. All along the roadside their frozen bodies lay in snow-covered blasted chunks. I saw several uncomplaining beasts limping wounded and frightened in the forest. Some of them were lying down in the snow to freeze and die. There was no time to think of wounded horses in this gigantic battle that was deciding the fate of millions of men and women.

Once we passed an entire wood crowded with monstrous lumps of white tanks in hiding, waiting to move up closer to the front under cover of darkness. Some of the Red Army men, woodsmen all, had thrown up neat-looking walls and roofs of rough hewn logs over dugouts as though they planned to stay in this area for a while.

We pushed our car up hills and out of snowdrifts, and once we had to ask the help of a military tractor to get us up the snow-covered side of a steep, ice-glazed slope. German signs were still nailed to the trees, pointing to command posts and field headquarters.

We passed one village in which only half the houses had been burned down. The Red Army men had left the German signs where they stood, as a reminder to themselves and to the inhabitants. It was interesting to note the difference in the German spelling and the Russian for the same towns. In Latin characters the Germans had placed large signs on the sides of peasants' homes, as guides to their own map-readers.

As the sound of artillery grew heavy, we drew up in a clearing in the midst of a heavy forest where, in a wood-cutters' camp, a squad of Russian nurses had set up a casualty clearing station. The buxom, good-natured-looking girls were glad to

see us and collected around our cars. They all carried re-
volvers slung at their hips. We asked the highest-ranking
girl, a cool-eyed blonde with her sheepskin hat thrust back
over her forehead, if her girls were warmly enough clothed.
She smiled. "Warm?" she mocked. Then she began to unbut-
ton her heavy overcoat and conducted our eyes through layer
after layer until she suddenly drew her overcoat together
again with a loud laugh. From my rather unfavorable position
on the wrong side of the car, I could get only a glimpse of
what she was wearing—a heavy overcoat, a fur vest, a heavy
army shirt, and what appeared to be pink heavy underwear. I
wasn't sure. At any rate, we knew now what made the girls
look so plump. It was layer after layer of clothing.

The blonde captain of nurses had already been wounded
twice, once in 1939 during the three-month Japanese border
war and now in this war by the Germans at Lwow.

The nurses were in high spirits over the advance, and when
one of the smiling girls learned we were Americans, she
jumped on the running board of our car as we started forward
and said with fervor: "I always wanted to go to America.
Won't you take me with you?" We all wished we could.

The Red Army telegraph linesmen were busy on every side
as we moved forward. The Germans in their retreat had sawed
down each telegraph pole near its base. Tangled lines were
strewn in a jumble all over the roadside. The linesmen, like
the bridge-builders, were felling the trees themselves, trim-
ming them, and putting up new poles with remarkable speed.

The countryside was changing now from flat forests with
only occasional rises to heavily wooded hills. It grew warmer
and began to snow. The thick flakes muffled everything, even
the bellow of the guns up ahead. On the opposite side of the
road came the wounded on horse-drawn sleds, often with a
nurse sitting alongside, holding down the edges of the wind-
blown blanket. I remembered what the nurses had said:
"To fall down wounded in the snow in this temperature
means death within minutes unless you cover the men with
blankets." I understood the meaning of some of the boxes
mounted on sleds, like small bungalows, that came creaking
by. They were hot-boxes with stoves inside. Lucky men had

been placed inside these to make the trip from the front line to the casualty clearing station.

Once a brigade of youngsters passed us by. They were no more than nineteen or twenty and I knew this would be only their first action. Their pink, boyish faces were full of wonder as they looked at the wounded going the other way, at the wrecked trucks and German spiked guns and the snow sifting around the stiff bodies at the roadside.

On either side of this road of death were untrodden fields, fenced in by small boards with death's-heads painted on them. They were mined areas as yet uncleared. The officer told us that the Germans were strewing thousands of mines in their retreat, and their method was both simple and deadly. Almost no work was needed because the snow concealed the explosives from sight and the ever falling, impersonal flakes disguised all traces.

Once we passed half a dozen German trucks loaded with rubber boats and tens of paddles. The rivers were long since frozen and it was evident how long the Germans had been held up at this one position, until the rivers of autumn were winter-locked by ice.

We came to the rendezvous where we were to interview General Vlasov, commanding the area. We knew he was simply taking over the last German headquarters as he advanced. But although the sign on the unpainted frame house said plainly "German Divisional Headquarters," there was no one inside. General Vlasov had moved forward again to keep up with the advance of his troops.

A few miles more through the snow-covered forest and we came to a tiny settlement with the unusual name of "Burnt Village." Strangely enough, it was one of the few villages the Germans had not gutted. Here the work of salvaging German war equipment was going on hurriedly. Red Army men were busy gathering up rifles and tommy guns from behind houses and in barns and attics and depositing them in piles on the village square. The Germans had retreated from here within the space of hours.

One happy-looking Red Army man was put-putting through the snow on a captured German motorcycle. When I asked him why it made so much noise, he said gleefully: "All German equipment makes a lot of noise. They think it will scare us."

The Germans had not stopped to bury their dead in this village. Green-gray bodies lay rigid in the snow.

We entered the warmth of an old farmhouse which was now the Soviet Divisional Headquarters. The Germans had vacated it so hurriedly that their excellent maps of the area still remained on the walls. General Vlasov, commander of the Solnetchnogorsk front, was somewhere around but couldn't be found just now, they told us. Instead we were asked by a member of his staff if we would like to see a German prisoner who had just been captured. In a few moments he was led in—a fine-looking soldier.

He was Corporal Albert Koehler of Aachen. He was undaunted, even in the presence of all these Soviet officers and foreign correspondents. We were permitted to question him ourselves. He said bravely that he had been captured going back to rescue prisoners, and the Russian officers nodded agreement. He wore the field-gray double-breasted overcoat that has been standard for the Germans in all their campaigns. It was really not much more than a heavy topcoat. His natty garrison hat was of cotton cloth and his boots the serviceable German jackboots, but they were not suitable for this land of snow and ice. We asked Corporal Koehler if he had been cold.

"No," he replied reluctantly, "not until just recently."

We asked him what equipment he had been issued for winter.

"All of us got a scarf to wear under our hats and a pair of gloves.

Someone inquired why he was fighting against the Russians. Koehler looked surprised and said: "I'm a soldier. I go where I am sent."

"Why are you fighting?"

"To make Germany bigger."

"What do you think of the entrance of America into the war?"

"I heard talk of this on December 14, but we were too busy retreating to discuss it at length."

We thanked Corporal Koehler. He clicked his heels and turned to leave, the very model of a German NCO. One of the intelligence officers whispered to me: "He must be a Hitler Youth."

A violet gloom was falling over the snow as the sun sank behind the wooded hills. Red Army men were busy up and down the streets of the little village, removing engines from the abandoned German trucks, searching through wrecked staff cars for valuable papers; other details were counting German machine guns, tommy guns, rifles, and bayonets. Mounds of captured war material were growing on the snow. I walked over to examine some of the German trophies, hoping to pick up a tommy gun for myself, but the Russian sentry, although he knew full well that a civilian could be at the front only on special duty, threatened me menacingly with his bayonet. I knew he was under orders to let no one approach the pile.

At another point I watched three Red Army men dismantle the motor from a huge German troop-carrier. The speed with which they worked in the sub-zero temperature amazed me. I studied them as they worked and heard them curse as wrenches slipped on frozen bolts. I had more or less expected to see kindly, patient peasant soldiers going about their work by rote, but these men were as sharp and as full of comment about the difficulties of their job as any mechanics I ever encountered in an American garage. I could see that the cold was just as hard for them to bear as it was for the German troops, in full retreat a few miles away.

Here, I thought, was a small cross-section of the Red Army—hard-looking, muscular, young men who would obviously fight hard for an officer they respected and who had confidence in one whose technical knowledge they trusted. I realized that the idea they were men whom the Russian High Command could afford to use extravagantly was as ill-founded as the legend that Russian soldiers had to have their bayonets welded to their rifles so that they could not ruin them by chopping wood. One of the most impressive sights among the combat troops that still marched through the darkening village was the well-oiled cleanliness of their arms, not an easy accomplishment under these tough conditions. The single-mindedness of these men could not be confused with mere simplicity, I thought. They were elated with the defeat of the Germans at Moscow, but from their talk I gathered that they would have been just as critical of the conduct of the war if they were losing. Their curiosity about the German machines was boundless. They poked about in the inside of tanks and troop-carriers like boys on a treasure-hunt.

I could see that the Red Army was really a melting-pot army like the American Army. It had none of that look of race which belonged to the armies of Britain and France. Here were light-haired Ukranians, dark-skinned Armenians and Georgians, blue-eyed Russians, white-toothed and flashing-eyed Uzbeks, and blond Cossacks from the Don. These were seasoned troops. Their confidence in their own abilities was written on their faces. Their attitude was that the Germans had lost the capacity to surprise or frighten them.

As I watched, the little knots of soldiers suddenly stiffened and I followed their gaze to where two finely dressed officers approached through the snow. They were General Vlasov and General Korol, the Divisional Political Commissar. Dressed in handsomely cut long overcoats that reached the ankles of their white felt boots, they gave the impression of great height, emphasized by their tall gray astrakhan hats. With a smile they approached us, and automatically we walked toward them, followed by a group of obviously admiring Red Army men. The soldiers had no fear of their commanding officers, but seemed drawn to them as an admiring college boy is drawn to a respected professor.

"*Zdrastviti tovarishchi* (Good day, comrades)," shouted General Vlasov in greeting, and their answer, "*Zdrastviti* General," re-echoed in the snowy street. When it appeared that the general wished to talk to the Americans, the Red Army men withdrew quickly to their work again.

We shook hands with General Vlasov, who looked more like a teacher than a soldier, so tall that his high gray astra-khan hat with the crimson and gold crown made him tower. He wore gold-rimmed spectacles at the tip of his nose. His eyes had a look of bright elation as he told us his men would capture Volokolomsk this very night. "I have sent my ski battalion out to surround the city," he said. "Von Strauss is trying to avoid combat with us. The Germans hold only until they find themselves in danger of being outflanked. Then they'll send their destruction brigades around, armed with

gasoline and torches, to fire every house so we'll have no protection when we come in." Pointing to the west where a faint
red glow was lighting the sky, he said: "Look, we've already
outflanked Volokolomsk."

I asked General Vlasov where he expected the Germans to
hold a line for the winter. He replied: "I am not planning my
offensive on the basis that the Germans will hold somewhere.
I intend to drive them as far as I can."

I persisted in my questioning. "Do you think they'll try to
hold at Smolensk?" At the word "Smolensk" General Vlasov
looked away and repeated: "Smolensk—that's a different
story." I knew then that I must not expect too much of
Russia's first winter offensive.

We bundled ourselves into the cars and General Vlasov cautioned us against losing the road and running into a mined
area. We thanked him, and our cars spun their wheels on the
hard snow.

As the sun went down, the cold became intense. We heard
cracks in the forest, sharp as rifle-shots, as the sap froze in the
trees. Until eleven o'clock we pushed our car up and down
the snowy hills, making room time and again for the forward
movement of sleds and marching troops. The night march of
the troops, concealed in daylight, had begun.

Finally, we reached our former sleeping-quarters at Solnetchnogorsk. The druggist's wife and her daughters were
not surprised at our late arrival. No time was too late for them
to prepare a hot supper. The same well-rounded waitress sent
down from Moscow was there to serve us. I gazed around the
dining-room as I ate. This house on Russia's "Sunnyside
Hill" was not so different from homes I had known in Indiana. Above the old shawl-draped piano was a picture I recognized. It was none other than the "Three Little Pigs." I
wondered how these Walt Disney characters had got this far
east. A guitar hung near the fireplace, and on the mantelpiece
was a gilt ikon of St. Nicholas, patron saint of Russia.

With a Russian delight in lavishness, our hostess set the
table with all the Red Army provender of the night before,
including unopened boxes of candy, one for each of us. As
the atmosphere grew more friendly, a correspondent suggested that he and the pretty waitress take a walk outside in

the snow to see the stars. The Russian colonel shook his head earnestly and said: "The last three men who took a walk in the moonlight here never came back. They were blown up by mines." We went to bed.

For breakfast we had the traditional Russian meal of "kasha," or brown whole-grain barley, with a piece of butter melting atop it. On the table again were the same large boxes of candy. I didn't realize that to the Russians candy at breakfast was no novelty. They ate it instead of sugar, putting a piece in their mouths while they sipped their hot tea.

I took a last look at the church of Solnetchnogorsk as our cars pulled away. It was from the bell-tower of that gold and blue tulip dome that the Germans first announced they could see, through spy glasses, the towers of Moscow.

We were tired, silent, and thoughtful as our cars rolled back along the four-lane Leningrad Highway, along the brief span of ice-rutted pavement that had stretched immutable and unattainable for the conquerors of western Europe.

Twelve Months That Changed the World, 1943

Bataan Nurses

as told to Annalee Jacoby by
Willa L. Hook and Juanita Redmond

CONDITIONS at Hospital No. 1 in Bataan were not too good during the last few weeks we spent there. Patients were flooding in. We increased from 400 to 1,300 cases in two weeks' time. Most were shrapnel wounds for surgery, but nine out of ten patients had malaria or dysentery besides. We were out of quinine. There were hundreds of gas gangrene cases, and all our supply of anti-gas gangrene serum had gone months before. There were no more sulfa drugs.

We were working in wards when bombers came overhead on April 4. We hardly noticed them. Suddenly incendiary bombs dropped. They hit the receiving wards, mess hall, doctors' and officers' quarters, and the steps of the nurses' dormitory, setting fire to all buildings, but luckily not hitting the wards. Several enlisted personnel wandering outside were killed. The patients were terrified, of course, but behaved well. The Japanese prisoners were perhaps the most frightened of all. We were still frightened until two hours later when someone heard the Jap radio in Manila announce that the bombings had been an accident and wouldn't happen again.

The morning of April 7 about 10:30, we were all on duty when another wave of bombers came over. The first bomb hit by the Filipino mess hall and knocked us down before we even knew the planes were overhead. An ammunition truck was passing the hospital entrance. It got a direct hit. The boys on guard at the gate were smothered in the dirt thrown up by the explosion, and shell-shocked.

Convalescent patients picked us up and we began doing dressings for patients hurt by shrapnel. Everything was terror and confusion. Patients, even amputation cases, were falling and rolling out of the triple-decker beds.

Suddenly a chaplain, Father Cummings, came into the ward, threw up his hands for silence, said: "All right, boys, everything's all right. Just stay quietly in bed, or lie still on the floor. Let us pray." The confusion and screams stopped instantly. He began the prayer as a second wave of planes came over. The first bomb hit near the officers' quarters, the next directly in the middle of our hospital ward. The next wave struck the patients' mess just a few yards away. The concussion bounced us 3 ft. off the cement floor and threw us down again. The beds were swaying and tumbling down. Desks were doing a jitterbug. Red flashes of heat burned our eyes. But through it all we could hear Father Cummings' voice in prayer. When the bombs hit the ward everyone had begun to repeat the Lord's Prayer. Father Cummings' clear voice went through to the end. Then he turned quietly and said: "All right, you take over. Put a tourniquet on my arm, would you?" And we saw for the first time that he'd been badly hit by shrapnel.

The next few hours were a nightmare, except for the way everyone behaved. We were afraid to move, but realized we had to get to work. One little Filipino with both legs amputated—he'd never gotten out of bed before by himself—rolled onto the ground and said: "Miss Hook, are you all right, are you all right?" We tried to care first for the patients hurt worst. A great many all over the hospital were bleeding badly. We went to where the bomb had hit the ward and began pulling patients from the crater. I saw Rosemary Hogan, the head ward nurse, and thought for a moment her face had been torn off. She wiped herself with a sheet, smiled and said: "It's nothing, don't bother about me. It's just a nose bleed." But she had three shrapnel wounds.

It would be hard to believe the bravery after that bombing if you hadn't seen it. An enlisted man had risked his life by going directly to the traction wards where patients were tied to beds by ropes fastened to wires through the fractured bones. He thought it was better to hurt the men temporarily than to leave them tied helpless above ground where they'd surely be hit by shrapnel, so he cut all tractions and told the patients: "Get under the bed, Joe." He probably saved a good many lives too.

The triple-decker beds were all tumbled over. We gave first-aid treatments, then baths, and cleaned up the beds until after dark. Afraid the Japanese would be back again the next day, we then moved the patients to another hospital. Even the most serious cases were moved; giving them any chance was better than none. There were only a hundred left the next morning. We worked all the next day making up beds to admit new patients. Suddenly, after dark, we were told we were leaving in 15 minutes—that we should pack only what we could carry in our arms. The Japanese had broken through the line and the Battle of Bataan was over.

The doctors decided collectively to stay with the patients, even doctors who'd been told to come to Corregidor. We left the hospital at 9 that night and got to Corregidor at 3 in the morning. The trip usually took a little over an hour. As we drove down to the docks, the roads were jammed. Soldiers were walking, tired, aimless, frightened. Cars were overturned; there were guns in the road and bodies. Clouds of dust made it hard to breathe. At midnight on the docks we heard they'd burned our hospital to the ground.

Bombers were overhead. We were too tired to care. But as we crossed the water with Corregidor's big guns firing over our heads and shells from somewhere landing close by, the boat suddenly shivered and the whole ocean seemed to rock. We thought a big shell had gone through the water just in front of us—it wasn't until we landed that we found an earthquake had come just as Bataan fell.

We were on a cargo boat. Some went in barges, some helped paddle rafts. But we had an easy trip compared to that of the nurses from hospital No. 2. It was 3 in the morning before they got away—Bataan had begun to fall at 8. They were cut off by a burning ammunition dump and waited for hours with explosions ahead of them and Japs a few kilometers behind.

Corregidor seemed like heaven that night. They fed us and we slept, two to an Army cot. We went to work the following morning. There was constant bombing and shelling—sometimes concussion from a bomb landing outside would knock people down at the opposite end of the tunnel. The Emperor's birthday, April 29, was specially bad. Bombing began at 7:30 in the morning and never stopped. Several men counted over a hundred explosions to a minute. Dive bombers were going after the gun on the hill directly above our heads and the concussion inside was terrific.

The worst night on Corregidor was when a bomb lit outside the tunnel entrance on the China Sea side. A crowd had gone outside for a cigaret and many were sleeping on the ground at the foot of the cliff. When the first shell hit nearby, they all ran for the tunnel, but the iron gate at the entrance was shut and it opened outward. As more shells landed, concussions smashed the men against the gate and twisted off arms and legs. All nurses got up and went back to work— surgery was overflowing until 5:30 in the morning. There were many amputations. Litter bearers worked outside in total darkness, groping about for wounded. One rolled a body onto his litter; when he got inside he saw it had no head.

Through all those weeks on Corregidor everyone was grand. At 6 o'clock one evening after the usual constant bombing and shelling, 21 of us were called into a meeting and told we were leaving Corregidor by plane with 10 lb. of luggage apiece. We don't know how we were selected. The pilot hustled us aboard because we were between Cavite and Corregidor, directly in the range of artillery. On that trip we sometimes almost skimmed the water. There was so much fog over Mindanao that we had to make a forced landing. People on Mindanao were just as courageous as the rest on Corregidor and Bataan. They knew they would be trapped but cheerfully wished us a good trip and happy landings. At dusk we left for Australia.

Life, June 15, 1942

Flight Through the Jungle

by Jack Belden

THE ROAD to India that night was flooded by the ebb-tide of the British Empire. Officials, refugees, soldiers were pushing through the dust in columns and groups, trampling on the grass beside the road, knocking over children, stumbling on wounded, jumping into halted trucks, streaming, swirling, and ebbing westward.

Dark Chin tribal soldiers were marching in single file in long, ragged columns on either side of the road; their rifles were slung any old which way on straps over their shoulders; their faces wore sullen, expressionless looks. Darker Indians, with packs half again as high as themselves balanced on their heads, were marching between them. Women were shuffling along beside them, carrying bundles wrapped in orange cloth. Wives marched with soldiers. Children tottered along after their mothers. Everything was buried in a haze of dust. Human feet shuffled up dust. Mules and horses kicked up dust. Automobiles whirled up great clouds of dust.

Three tiny Indian children were enveloped in a whirlpool of flying sand. They turned their backs to the cruel particles. Little fists wiped at dirty eyes. They opened their eyes, big, black, and round. They stared with hurt, dazed looks at the eddying throngs. One of them, a little girl wearing a white skirt, carried a tiny knapsack over her shoulder. She was prepared for a journey. She took the hands of the two boys and they marched stolidly onward, their heads bent down, looking at the dust raised by their little feet.

On the befouled grass in front of a Buddhist temple, among scattered grains of rice, dirty tin wash-basins, and discarded, blood-stained bandages, Chinese wounded of the 200th Division were wallowing. Chinese convoys were passing and dust was raining down on injured hands, legs, heads.

Swarms of flies were picking at wounds. A Chinese medical officer ran out to Williams.

"Where shall I take them?"

"To India. To Imphal."

But how? How? How is anyone going to get to India?

Gloucesters walking along the road jeered at us: "Where's your trailer, Yank?"

The Americans are sitting in cars on their asses. The British Empire is walking on its feet. On its last feet? . . .

A dirty white pagoda leaned precariously over the road. Filthy British soldiers lay underneath it on the grass, flat on their backs, looking at the sky. Indians wearing white shirts squatted down with purple skirts tucked between their legs. Indians wear no shirts and are bare to their waists. Indians wear pants. Indians wear orange and black checked skirts. Indians are wrapped in green and red blankets. Indians are naked. Indians wear towels around their shoulders. Members of the Burma Rifles wear wide bush hats and are sitting quietly. Chinese soldiers with greasy uniforms move ceaselessly, looking at everything curiously, chattering, chattering, chattering and laughing irreverently.

A woman, squatting, was peeling tomatoes and onions, dropping slices in an iron pot. The pot hung on sticks, suspended over a bonfire. An Indian in a blue striped shirt and dirty yellow shorts, was looking in a mirror under the light of a lantern and squeezing pimples on his face. Americans were digging vigorously with shovels under the wheels of a stuck truck. Sweat came through their thick shirts. They stank.

Bony black skeletons were carrying small iron pots in their hands, begging for water. They begged the Americans for water, the Chin soldiers for water, everyone for water. Everyone had a pot, a canteen, a cup. Everyone was begging every one else for water.

And a little boy sat on the ground, his elbow on his pack, his chin in his hand, staring.

An Indian girl, her Western-style skirt flashing out with a swirl from her willowy hips, ran up to the car.

"Please may I ride in your jeep?"

"Jump in."

Her name was Zeli. She was twenty-five. She was married to an Indian sergeant. She was one of a group of seventy-five refugees to be evacuated by the government. The British officer in charge of their group had disappeared that morning in a car. Everyone was walking.

An Anglo-Indian girl, sensuous and coarse-looking, ran up.

"May I ride in your jeep?"

"Jump in."

She climbed on top of the baggage in the back. Zeli slid down on a blanket and sat between Jones and me.

A nurse of Dr. Seagrave ran up.

"Our truck broke down. Can I . . ."

"Jump in."

The columns of the vanquished halt and lie down. Refugees huddle together sighing audibly. Rude gibes and coarse epithets shoot out of the dark as individual English soldiers plod on. Remarks are tinged with bitter cynicism. Everyone is losing faith in himself. The defeat is producing an enormous impression. Fright, disappointment, apathy flow down over the road. The retreat has turned into a march of escape, of preservation. There are only two thoughts in everybody's mind: Get to India. Keep alive.

Throngs move on.

A British colony is passing away.

The tide of empire recedes on itself and ebbs in the opposite direction.

Shortly after we pitched camp in a small clearing of dank swamp grass at midnight on May 5, a mysterious rumor spread through the soldiers, girls, and servants. It was said that the Americans would take the jeeps—two Americans to each jeep, with appropriate food stocks—and try to break their way through the jungle to the Chindwin River. It was further said that the Indian servants would be paid off and given a bonus. They, the Chinese, and the Seagrave nurses would be given food—not so much as the Americans, for the nurses spoke the Burmese language and could forage for themselves—and would be allowed to find their own trail to India—if that's where they wanted to go—by ox-cart or on foot.

Excited voices. Red, angry faces appearing in the light of jeep lamps. Suggestions. Insinuations. Recriminations.

But shortly after three o'clock, when we rose once more, without water to drink, with only a plate of dry oatmeal to eat, it was seen that we were not separating, that we were all going together. Guilty looks, accusing looks, relaxed into expressions of morose fatigue.

Zeli ran up to my jeep again. "I was kicked off the jeep on which I was riding. Please may I ride with you? I won't take up much room."

"Sure, jump in."

The column came to a halt beside a monastery. A pink haze slowly suffused the grayish-blue sky. Wisps of gray clouds hung suspended over low-lying green hills. Golden mohr and flame trees flashed like brilliant yellow and red lanterns. Ducks cackled. I grew drowsy. My head drooped with fatigue. "Rest on my shoulder," says Zeli. I do so. It is soft, yielding, comforting. I sleep.

At nine thirty in the morning we drew into the small town of Mansi on the edge of the jungle. British civilians as well as soldiers were crowding into it. A tall young Eurasian woman was walking by the side of a fat, middle-aged Englishman. She looked up. Her eyes were full of smoking, passionate fire. I thought: "You are that man's mistress. But he is too old. You don't like him. Why don't you come into the jungle with me?"

Stilwell got out to confer with the town elder. Breedom Case, the missionary, translated. We learned that five thousand refugees had already passed through the town, making for India. The headman was not sure about the road westward to Homalin, on the Chindwin River, but he said it would take four days to get there. After that, eight days down river by raft to Tammu on the India highway.

Stilwell obtained as much information as he could, but it was not much. He grunted now and then as Case translated the elder's words, and every once in a while he said: "Humph!" Finally he looked up, made a beckoning gesture with his arm at the column, shouted: "Turn 'em over," and once more we started, soon entering a forest.

In a little while we came into a clearing. All the jeeps were told to get at the head of the column. We drew up in front of a swaying, bamboo rope bridge. Below it was a deep chasm. We realized that empty jeeps might just barely get across this flimsy bridge; trucks, never. Everyone was ordered to get out of the cars. Dimly we felt that this was the end of the motor journey.

"Everyone come over here into the clearing," called Stilwell. "The Americans on the left. The Seagraves next to them. The Chinese here. British here. Now the Indians."

We formed in a chained circle. American, Englishman, Chinaman, Burman, Indian, Chin, Karen, Kachin, Malaysian, Anglo-Indian, Anglo-Burman, half-breeds from all of Asia. A motley crew.

Generals, colonels, young privates, radioman, mechanic, cook, servant, dishwasher. American preacher, British Quaker, Karen nurse. Men, women, and a dog.

American names: Stilwell, Jones, Gish, Nowakowski, Ferris, McCabe, Laybourn, Lee. From American towns: Winnemucca, Indiana; Thermopolis, Wyoming; Hopbottom, Pennsylvania; Meridian, Oklahoma; Damariscotta, Maine; San Francisco, Detroit, Yonkers, Brooklyn, Honolulu. British names: Davidson-Huston, Dykes, Haight, McDonald, Campbell, Inchboard. From Liverpool; Willaston, Cheshire; Wanstead, London; Little Buckland Nr Broadway Wores. Chinese and Indian names: Chow, Tseng, Singh. Shanghai, Kweilin, Calcutta. Half-breeds: Alexander, Nathan, Phillips. Daughters of Burma: Ruth, Emily, Lucy, Lasi. And a dog named James.

All in a circle.

Zeli and the Anglo-Indian girl stood apart, belonging to no group.

"Who are you?" called the general.

"Refugees."

"All right. Get over there with the Seagrave unit."

Colonel Wyman began to call out the names of the Americans: "Belden. Chesley. Janes. Young. . . ."

General Stilwell stood in the center of the circle glaring at the strange crew surrounding him. He was wearing a light khaki windbreaker, long khaki pants, over a pair of sturdy army boots, the tops of which were wrapped in canvas leggings. On his head was a battered campaign hat. In his mouth an amber cigarette-holder and a burning cigarette. At the same time he was chewing gum. As he glared around, his eyes finally came to rest on the British group.

Two men—Colonel Davidson-Huston and Major Dykes, the members of the British Military Mission who had boarded the last train out of Shwebo only to rejoin us later when the train broke down—were the only ones we recognized. Nine others, all of them filthy, unshaven, emaciated, and tired-looking, none of whom we knew, were also there.

"Where did you come from?" snarled Stilwell. "Just picking up a ride, huh? I don't mind you hopping a ride, if you only come and ask first." He glared at them for a moment, then suddenly shot out a question: "Got any rations?" A few shakes of the head. "All right, stay where you are. Colonel Huston, you will take charge of the British group."

With a quick gesture the General threw away his cigarette, put his hands on his hips, raised his chin in the air, and began to address all of us who were standing around him.

"The bridge ahead can take only jeeps. We will abandon the transport here. We will stay together in one group."

As he said this, a few happy smiles shot around the circle.

"But we must have better discipline," he continued. "We must be careful of the food. We don't know what is ahead. Be careful of what you eat. Eldridge, you will be in charge of the food. Don't use a single can without getting word from me. All food will be pooled. If I catch anyone who has not turned in his food, he will immediately leave the party.

"Keep your weapons and ammunition. When we get to Maingkaing, we plan to build rafts and get to Homalin in eight days. If we do this, we will have to leave some of the food. But if we work the rafts night and day, we should be able to get there in four days. We are going to try to get a radio set up and have food sent down to Homalin from India. Now, I'm not going to monkey with this food business. Eldridge will be in charge of all of it.

"Throw away your baggage right here. Limit yourselves to what you can carry on a four days' march. We can perhaps figure on taking a couple of jeeps to Homalin. But you might as well split up your clothes, and those who have too many give to those who haven't enough. Unfortunately there are no extra shoes, but we'll take it easy and give everyone a chance to get accustomed to walking.

"We may have a few trying days, but we are ahead of the mob and I think we are all set."

When the general finished his speech, the circle soberly broke up. All went to the cars and began sadly to discard those things they couldn't carry.

Out of the medical trucks spill heavy boxes of medicine. They are broken open, small quantities of quinine and emytine taken out.

Up the sides of these trucks clamber the girls. White bodices, yellow sweaters, red skirts, pink brassieres tumble down on the forest floor. Tiny hands hold up rich Mandalay silks. Audible sighs, pathetic glances, a shrug of the shoulders, and the silks join the growing heap.

Quickly the girls discard almost everything they own. What is left is put in small leather cases, wrapped in towels, in sheets. Knots are tied, bundles are formed, feminine arms are placed through cloth loops, the weight of a bundle is tested against a female back.

The men are slower, seek to hold onto more of their things than the girls; for they can carry more. But swiftly the rubbish heap grows. American shaving lotions, tins of powder, underwear, notebooks, overcoats find their way into the grass.

The clearing takes on the appearance of a rummage sale. Everything is a kaleidoscopic, colorful mess. Pink brassieres hang on thorns, Oxford-gray pants lie on top of olive-green car radiators, gray steel helmets tumble in the weeds. Whisky bottles, whose presence heretofore has been unknown, mysteriously appear. Heads are tilted back, the bottles emptied, thrown away. Blankets full of cigarette tins are opened; they are bought and sold, traded for a pair of khaki shorts.

Alexander, Stilwell's Anglo-Indian chauffeur, discards his own clothing, dons a pair of army pants, delicately laces up a pair of puttees, puts on a pair of army boots two sizes too big for him. Everything hangs loose on him. He looks like a vaudeville clown. But he grins proudly at his new outfit.

Soldiers, girls, mechanics rush about with shrill cries, flinging their belongings from the cars, bursting into cases, carrying tin cans of food to the jeeps, picking, choosing, and throwing away what they don't want. The clearing fills up. Bulky belongings thud onto the ground, lighter things rain through the air, catching on the branches of bushes. On the jungle floor, among mattresses and whisky bottles, brown and black girls, white and yellow men wallow. Only the Chinese have nothing to throw away. They begin gathering up discarded clothing, placing it hastily in knapsacks. Someone says we may be able to carry our belongings on the rafts, and a momentary pang of disappointment stirs those who begin to feel they have thrown away things too quickly. John Grindley has laid an expensive camera aside to carry with him. Someone has taken it or it has become lost in the discarded rubbish. There is no need to throw everything away. Blankets are kept. Rolls are made. Those of the Americans appear larger than first thought. Finally people begin to wander off in knots and groups over the bamboo bridge ahead. Food is loaded in the jeeps. Only one man is allowed in a jeep. The last motor ride starts.

Eleven jeeps in all went through the jungle. Ahead of us straggled the other members of our party. I saw two members of the Friends Ambulance Unit walking slowly, half supporting a tiny Burmese nurse. As I drew abreast of them, one called out: "Will you take this girl? She's been sick with malaria. She doesn't weigh much."

"Sure, I'll look after her," I said.

"More likely she'll take care of you," called a voice as I drove off.

I looked at my companion. About her slender waist and legs hung a lavender silk skirt. Around her head was a blue flowered cloth under which two black braids fell down to a brown sweater covering her shoulders. Her skin was dark brown, very smooth and without a blemish. She had a clean, washed, fresh appearance. Her name was Than Shwe.

"It means in English 'a million dollars gold,'" she said simply.

I asked her what she thought of leaving Burma and going to India.

"I like to go very much. I don't mind leaving home."

Her answers were all given in a serious, quiet tone of voice as if she were replying to very important questions. A funny girl, I thought, and reached into my pocket and took out a cigarette. Placing it in my mouth, I tried to light it while at the same time steering the jeep over the bumpy jungle floor.

I felt her hand brush against my lips; she took the cigarette out of my mouth, placed it in her own, lit it, and gravely put it back between my lips.

I was surprised. "I'm sorry," I said, "I didn't know you smoked. Please have a cigarette."

"Don't smoke. I only do this for others," she replied. "I like do favors for others."

Suddenly I had a feeling that I was looking at myself in the movies. A tough sailor, cast up on a foreign shore, wandering into the jungle and finding a simple native girl who performs little favors for him that charm him and make him forget all his civilization. Melodramatic, yes; but a feeling of romantic melancholy stole over me as we wound slowly through that dry, dead jungle.

We came to a steep bank hanging over a creek. Here we learned that we were not to go to our original destination. Crowds of refugees, we were told, had already poured through there and taken all the rafts. Eighty of them had left only the day before. Instead we were to go to a village five miles distant, and there, away from the crowds, build our own rafts.

"There is almost no road ahead," said an officer. "It will be very difficult for the jeeps to get through. Only one man to a car," he said, looking at me and the girl pointedly.

"She's not a man," I said. "And she doesn't weigh more than a fly, and besides she's sick."

"Okay. Everybody in compound-low," called the officer, and we slid down the bank into the stream, crossed it, and came out into a narrow field. Across this field in parallel lines were a series of ridges, so high that it seemed as if the jeeps could not possibly get over them. To attempt to do so, we began roaring around in a circle, getting as far away from the first ridge as possible, then, like a football backfield, breaking formation and rushing in high gear at the ridges at an angle from the side. The jeeps hit the ridges with terrific force, the front wheels bucked over them, and the momentum brought the back wheels onto the top of the ridge, where a quick burst of gas carried them across. This process was repeated several times, and the spectacle of the jeeps roaring in circles and bucking high off the ground, throwing out boxes, and once a driver, looked like a wild West rodeo.

After we had cleared the ridges we headed straight up a bank at a seventy-five-degree angle into a mass of thickets where at first there appeared no path. We broke through the trees and finally came out into a narrow corridor down which our jeeps could go. The roots of innumerable large trees stuck out across the path, making of it a washboard on which we shimmied and shook as in a Coney Island jolt-and-shake car. I saw Than Shwe holding on and biting her lips and I slowed to a pace slower than a walk.

At last we came to a village on the outskirts of which Stilwell had already set up his headquarters in a large house. I picked up Than Shwe and carried her in my arms up the steps and laid her on a shelf which ran around the walls of a room. Then I placed my blanket over her and my water bottle by her side.

"Please come back," she said as I left to go back through the jungle once more and pick up the rest of the food. This time it was not like an adventure; it was plain torture. When I returned, Than Shwe had already gone, having joined the Seagrave unit in a separate camp in the village.

By now we learned that we were not going by raft, but were going to start walking the next day. For Stilwell, having discovered that it would take several days to build rafts, had decided to push straight ahead for Homalin and the Chindwin River.

Because there were no rafts, we had to obtain bearers to carry our food. Although the shutting down of the forestry services and the timber monopolies had thrown a great many casual laborers back into the villages, the hordes of refugees pouring through had temporarily taken an equal number out again, and though the village headman was able to promise us a number of bearers, they were not enough to carry all our food.

We were brooding about this problem when, late that afternoon, a rather unexpected event occurred. Sitting on the grass about the house, we suddenly heard a tinkling of bells and then a herd of twenty mules went clattering down the path, followed by two Chinese drivers, who were beating them with switches and urging them on.

A British forester, who had joined us that day, jumped to his feet, called for some Chinese soldiers and went racing after the mules. A little while later they all were brought back and we simply commandeered them. The Chinese muleteer was on his way to India anyway. He was from Shantung, far away in North China, and we never did fathom what he was doing here at this time and place. But whatever he was doing, his unexpected appearance proved a windfall and immediately cut our transport problem in half.

The general was very pleased. "That's our first stroke of luck," he said.

That night I had a long talk with Stilwell about our position. Briefly, it was this.

Our group consisted of about 115 persons, twenty-one of them women. For purposes of easy handling on the march, the group had been divided into four sections. They were:

1. American—18 officers, 5 enlisted men, and 3 civilians (Lilly, Case, and myself).

2. British—11 officers and men and 2 civilians.

3. Seagrave Unit—2 doctors, 7 British Quaker members of the Friends Ambulance Unit, 19 Kachin, Karen, and Burmese nurses, 2 women refugees, and servants, totaling about 40 persons.

4. Chinese—Brigadier General Tseng and about 15 soldiers.

Furthermore, there were Indian cooks and mechanics, the latter being formed into a pioneer unit with the American group. In addition, there were twenty mules and one dog.

The area we were to traverse was part of a great triangle of jungle, bounded on the east by the Irrawaddy River, on the northwest by the Bramaputra River and the Himalaya Mountains, and on the south by a dry belt tapering off into Shwebo. This area differed in many places. In some sectors there was nothing but an impenetrable forest, a wet jungle, dissected by torrential mountain streams; in other places were plains and a dry dead jungle. In parts of the area were to be found heavy timber such as teak, kanyin, ingyin, and thayet; in other places were palms, giant ferns, banana, mango, and bamboo trees. The level land abounded in elephants. In the whole area were innumerable tribes of monkeys, tailed on one side of the jungle, tailless on the other side. Russel's vipers, hamadryads, and king cobras—all of them poisonous snakes—were also known to be present in fairly large numbers. Villages were scarce and the population sparse.

Our plan was to head west across part of this area to Homalin on the Chindwin River, and to cross the river before the Japanese coming up from the south in gunboats could cut across our path. We originally estimated that it would take us four days to reach the Chindwin, but we were inclined to increase this estimate because we had no certain information concerning the exact distance. Using guides, with Case as an interpreter, we planned to cut across country through the jungle and come out a day's boat ride from Homalin, when we would look over the lay of the land and see if any Japanese were around.

Our chief problem before we started seemed to be food. When our party had originally set out from Shwebo, we had been equipped with thirty days' dry rations for sixty-five people. But during the journey, stray groups fastening on us here and there had increased our numbers to almost double their original total. In addition, in examining the stores that afternoon, Captain Eldridge had discovered that they contained an abnormally large amount of butter and jams, which were useless in the hot jungle. Thus, facing a trip the duration of which was unknown, we appeared to be short on adequate food stocks.

But to make up for this shortcoming, the danger of a direct Japanese move against us seemed to have lessened considerably.

"The chief dangers we now face," Stilwell said to me, "are food, rains, and the clogging of the roads by refugees. If the monsoons don't hold off we may not be able to cross the rivers. And rains will slow us up so that our food may not last us long enough. I suppose that is the chief danger—the combined threat of rain and food shortage. There are also the soldiers behind us who have disintegrated and are shooting up the villages and killing cows and bullocks with machine guns. We may have trouble with them.

"I have no news, but I believe the British may have held the Japs off the Kalewa road to India. As far as we're concerned, the Japs might get on our tails, but I consider that a remote danger.

"If we reach Homalin, we ought to be all right. I'm trying to send a radio asking the British in India to get food down through the hills to Homalin. If they do, why, our troubles will be over."

As he was saying these words, Sergeant Chambers, our radio operator, was trying desperately to contact our headquarters in Chungking. Over and over again the message was repeated: "Get food and bearers to Homalin. . . . Food and bearers to Homalin."

The power was fast failing and still there was no contact. It was our last chance. Tomorrow, before starting the march, we would destroy the radio, for we could not carry it with us.

Chambers sat on the ground, tapping out his message under the light of a jeep lamp. By him stood Lieutenant Colonel Frank Dorn writing out messages in code.

The tap-tapping of the radio instrument went like a refrain through the jungle. "Food and bearers to Homalin. Food and bearers. . . ."

I looked at the general.

"I'm also radioing the British to get police, guides, food, and water on this road. If they don't, there's going to be a catastrophe. Everyone trying to get out and everyone out of hand. Thousands will die."

Retreat with Stilwell, 1943

"Damn the Torpedoes!"

by Helen Lawrenson

A GROUP of sailors are drinking beer at a bar called George's in Greenwich Village. The juke box is playing "Deep in the Heart of Texas," and every time it stops someone puts another nickel in and it starts up again. A little man with curly hair and bushy eyebrows turns and glares fiercely at it.

"Can't that machine play nothing else?" he roars. He looks tough enough and mad enough to eat it, record, needle, and all.

"Stop beating your gums, brother," drawls the tall sailor with the black jersey. "I like it. It's catchy."

"I just come back from Texas," adds a third whose face is a complete pink circle, illumined by twinkling blue eyes and a cherubic grin.

"How was it?"

"Oh, dandy!" says Cherub, sarcastically. "Just dandy. Fine trip for your health. A Nazi tin fish chased us for three days. We never seen a patrol boat nor a plane the whole time. Saw one destroyer going hell-bent for election into Charleston one afternoon about dusk, but we all figured she was trying to get safe home before dark when the subs come out.

"We was carrying fifty thousand barrels of Oklahoma crude and fifty thousand of high-test gasoline. It sure gives you a funny feeling. I thought we'd get it any minute. Man, those nights are killers! You sleep with your clothes on. Well, I don't exactly mean sleep. You lie in bed with your clothes on. All of a sudden the old engines slow down and your heart speeds up. Someone knocks on the door, and you rise right up in your bed and seem to lie there in the air. So it turns out it's only the watch. You settle down again and try to light a cigarette if your hand don't shake too much. Not that you're scared of course. Oh, noooh!"

The others laugh. "Who ain't scared?" growls the little man with the bushy brows. "A torpedo connects with one of them tankers and it's just like lighting a match to cellophane. You ain't got a chance. Boom! and you're in the hero department. Just like that. And the next thing, all the guys you used to know are going around saying, 'Well, he wasn't such a bad guy after all. Poor old Joe Bananas! He lowered the boom on me for ten bucks the last time he was in port and he never did get a chance to pay it back. Let's have a beer to his memory.'"

"Well, let's have a beer anyway," says Slim, in the black jersey. "Here, Cherub, it's on you. You just got paid off. How about springing for another round?"

"Okay," says Cherub. "Might as well spend it now. It don't do you no good when you're floating around in a lifeboat. No kidding, a guy's a sucker to go through nights like that. You can't believe it. The next morning you come out on deck, and the sea's blue and beautiful and the sun's shining. The night before—with the zigzagging and the sub alarms and the lying there in your bunk, scared stiff and waiting—it can't be true. That night can't have happened to *me*. Impossible. This is the same sea I've always sailed, the same kind of a wagon, the same watch. Last night just didn't happen." He takes a drink of beer. "But then the darkness comes again. Yeah—night must fall."

What worried him most, he adds, was a remark made during lifeboat drill just before sailing. "We was practicing and everything goes off pretty good. Then the Inspector, he says, 'Now just in case any of you fellows have to *jump*—remember when you go over the side to pull down on your lifebelt as hard as you can. Cause if you don't when you hit the water it's liable to break your neck.' . . . My God, I thought. Now I got to worry about holding on to my papers and my chocolate bar and my cigarettes and at the same time I got to hold on to my lifebelt so my neck don't get broke!"

"So you have your choice," says Slim, "burn to death, drown, be blown to bits when the torpedo hits the engine room, starve to death in a lifeboat, or get your neck broke when you first jump over the side. Any way you look at it, you're a gone sucker. Only a lame-brained sailor would go for that. You gotta be muscle-bound between the ears to do that for a living. And what for?"

"I'll tell you what for," says Bushy-Brows. "If the rising sun and the swastika and that bundle of wheat ain't gonna be flying over the White House we gotta keep 'em sailing. They gotta have oil and ore and stuff to fight this war, ain't they? And how we gonna get it to 'em if guys like us don't keep on sailing the ships? So that's what for!"

II

This scene is typical of those being enacted every night in the waterfront bars of ports all over the land. Every few days you pick up the papers and there is the same gruesome picture painted over and over again of sudden death that strikes in the night, of seas brilliant with burning oil, of men screaming in agony, dying in the flaming water under the dark, implacable skies. And every night, in some bar in every port, there will be a group of seamen talking it over, naming the names of those who were once their shipmates, cursing the Axis—what some of them refer to as "Hitler, and his saddle-lights Mussolini and Hirohito"—and drinking toasts to one another's good luck.

"I was asleep when the torpedoes hit us—" said John Walsh, wiper, survivor of the Cities Service tanker, *Empire*, torpedoed off Fort Pierce, Florida "—three of them. I rushed up on deck and helped get one of the lifeboats over the side. I saw our captain on a life raft. He and some of the other men were on it. The current was sucking them into the burning oil around the tanker. I last saw the captain going into a sheet of orange flame. Some of the fellows said he screamed. . . . Monroe Reynolds was with me for a while. His eyes were burned. He was screaming that he was going blind. The last time I saw him he jumped into the fiery water. That was his finish, I guess. . . ."

In the first four months of this year over a hundred American merchant ships were attacked by enemy U-boats off our own coasts. About 950 seamen were killed. Despite improvements in the patrol system, the ships are still being sunk. The average during April was five or six a week.

It is a hideous way to die. I knew two men who were lost when the *Pan-Massachusetts* was sunk. One was a little thin man with spectacles, who had been a newspaperman. His name was Fred Fitzgerald. The other was Paddy Flynn, an oiler, whose two sons had already lost their lives in the war. I don't know how Fitz and Paddy died. The *Pan-Mass* carried 100,000 barrels of gasoline, oil, and kerosene. (A barrel is 53 gallons.) Many of the men burned to death as they stood on the deck of the ship; others died struggling in the blazing sea which was on fire for a mile around the tanker.

"The bo'sun was in charge," said George Lamb, survivor of the *Pan-Mass*. "He did everything possible to save the lives of all the men. He cut a raft loose after the men said they were ready. It burst into flames as soon as it hit the water. . . . Although I couldn't swim I decided to go overboard. I figured it was better to drown than to be burned alive. I said, 'Let's go, Ingraham.' He was the steward. He was standing there beside me in his shorts, the skin peeling off his back from the flames. We shook hands. He said, 'Remember me, Red!' I said, 'OK. If I make it, I'll remember you. . . .' He was burned to death. . . ."

On his final trip Fitz wrote a letter to a man I know. In it he said: "No fooling though, it's a queasy feeling to be shadowed by those bastards. One of them tried to decoy us off St. Augustine by flashing 'P,' which means show your lights. The Old Man zigzagged to hell-and-gone, and most of us were kidding each other about the false alarm when the *Pan Amoco* reported sighting a sub at 6 A.M. off Jupiter. (Our incident had occurred at 11:30 the previous night, 60 miles away.) We quit kidding then."

He went on to report an incident on his previous trip: "Just as the moon was going down the second mate happened to make the big circle with his binoculars and spotted a sub in perfect silhouette. The first thing I knew about it was the Ordinary on watch giving me the shake. 'There's a Jerry on our tail,' he said. 'All hands get dressed with lifebelts and stand by.' I got up all right but nothing happened. Later that day the same sub got the *India Arrow* and the *China Arrow*, just a few miles from where we were. What burns you up is no guns. You can't fight the bastards back. Luckily this crate is fast, so we can get going; but on some of them there isn't a damn thing you can do except call the U-boat commander an old meanie — or something! Later it comes as something of a jolt to discover that fellows you once knew and were shipmates with are gone for good. Worse yet, without a fighting chance."

Hundreds of other American seamen have had to stand by and watch enemy subs sink their ships from under them without guns to fight back. "You can't fight submarines with potatoes," as Bo'sun Walter Bruce said when rescued from the tanker *Malay*, torpedoed off the North Carolina coast.

The law to arm the merchant marine was signed by President Roosevelt on November 18, 1941, but most of the ships which have been sunk have been unarmed. A few which *were* armed have fought off submarines and either damaged them or frightened them away.

Guns are being put on the ships now as fast as possible, but some of the ships are so old and broken down that a gun is almost more of a liability than an asset. As one sailor says, "That rust-pot I just come off, they must of got her out of the Smithsonian Institute! Sure, we had a gun on her. But Holy Mackerel! if we'd ever of had to fire it the whole ship would have fallen apart."

At the insistence of the National Maritime Union, special fireproof life-saving suits have been approved by the Maritime Commission and are being purchased by all tanker companies. On many of the ships new types of life rafts are being installed, and lifeboats are now being stocked with medical kits, food concentrates, and blankets.

When the *Lahaina* was sunk, 34 survivors spent ten days in a lifeboat with a capacity of 17. Two of them became half-crazed with hunger and thirst, jumped overboard, and were drowned. A third lost his mind completely, had to be lashed to the bottom of the boat, and died the next day. A fourth died from exposure. Dan James, nineteen-year-old wiper, describes the death of the last man: "It was cold the last night out. I was sleeping under a blanket with Herman. He'd been feeling low for some time. I kept saying to him, 'Give me some of that blanket.' But he wouldn't let loose. Finally I

grabbed it from him. He just lay still. I touched his hand . . .
it was cold . . . he was dead the whole time."

The patrol system is still not adequate, although vastly improved. In a letter to Secretary of the Navy Knox last March,
President Joseph Curran of the National Maritime Union suggested that the large fleets of fishing boats, most of which are
now laid up, be fitted out as patrol boats for the Atlantic
coast, as was done during the last war. The sooner this is
done the better.

There is no doubt about it, the merchant seamen took it on
the chin during the first half of this year—with no guns, no
patrols, antiquated lifebelts, and practically no safety precautions. They were sent out as helpless targets for the subs; but
their morale was as magnificent as it was unheralded. That
precautions are now being taken to protect them doesn't de-
tract from their courage.

All the seamen know what they are facing when they ship
out. Yet they keep on sailing. Remember, they don't have to.
They are in the private merchant marine, and they can quit
any time they want to. Most of them could get good shore
jobs, working in shipyards as riggers and welders and mechanics and what-not, where the chief worry would be the danger
of someone dropping a wrench on their feet. It isn't the
money that keeps them sailing. On the coastwise run, from
New York to Texas, they get a war bonus which works out to
around $2.33 a day, hardly worth risking your life for. Also the
bonus doesn't apply to the Gulf.

As a matter of fact, former seamen who have been working
in shoreside jobs are going back to sea. A few months ago the
National Maritime Union issued a call to former seamen.
Since then over 2,000 ex-sailors have turned up to ship out
again, hundreds of them at the union hall in the port of New
York alone, among them men who have been working as fur-
riers, truck drivers, electricians, office workers, actors, construction workers, miners, painters, and bakers.

Those who have been torpedoed and rescued ship right out
again as soon as they can get out of the hospital. That takes
plenty of nerve, but the merchant seamen have it. They don't
get much publicity, and you seldom hear anyone making

speeches about them. They don't get free passes to the theater or the movies, and no one gives dances for them, with pretty young actresses and debutantes to entertain them. No one ever thinks much about their "morale" or how to keep it up. It was only recently that a bill was passed to give them medals. And because they wear no uniforms they don't even have the satisfaction of having people in the streets and subways look at them with respect when they go by.

It is not that the seamen, themselves, are asking for any special credit or honors. When you mention words like heroism or patriotism to them they look embarrassed. "Listen, brother, there's a war on!" they say. Ashore, they frequently pretend that they are not brave at all. Not long ago I was talking to a man called Windy, who had just come off the Texas run and had been chased by a submarine for three days. "No more of that for me!" he said. "I tell you, any guy who keeps on shipping these days has got bubbles in his think-tank. The only safe run is from St. Louis to Cincinnati. I'm going to get me a shore job. Why commit suicide at my age?" We believed him; and not one of us could blame him. . . . The next day we heard he had shipped out again. He is now on the high seas, en route to India.

Harper's Magazine, July 1942

The Battle of Midway

by Foster Hailey

WHILE our land-based Midway planes and the squadrons from the carriers were attacking the Japanese striking force, the enemy support group, spearheaded by the Hiryu, was streaking eastward.

Our own three carriers, the Hornet and the Enterprise in the lead and to the southward of the Yorktown, were still speeding westward, closing the gap between the two forces.

On the bridge of the Astoria, which was one of the two cruiser escorts for the Yorktown, we were anxiously awaiting the return of the Yorktown's planes. Shortly after 1 P.M. they began to come back, first the fighters, then the dive bombers, all seventeen of them.

The first one had no more than landed on the Yorktown's deck than Admiral Fletcher sent a message to all the ships within visual range:

"One enemy carrier sunk."

The message was broadcast over our loud-speaker system. The kids around the guns cheered like mad.

Up on the bridge, however, the tension was increasing.

Lieutenant Commander "Dave" Davidson, the communications officer, hurrying past on an errand, told me we had been sighted by an enemy scout plane. It had been shot down, but not before it had gotten away a contact report.

"It won't be long now," said Dave, grimly.

It wasn't.

The Yorktown waved off the last of her returning planes and began to launch her reserve fighters. The flag hoist which means enemy planes approaching shot up to her yardarm.

"Stand by to repel attack" went the command booming over our loud speaker, and a moment later, "action starboard."

First visual evidence from the Astoria's bridge of the approaching attack group of eighteen dive bombers was several big splashes to starboard as the enemy bombers began to jettison their loads as our fighters hit them. Then, following the bombs, flaming enemy planes began to fall. In a matter of seconds five twisting columns of smoke marked the death of as many enemy dive bombers.

"They were in three V's of six planes each at about fifteen thousand feet," said Scott (Go Get 'Em) McCuskey, who was up with the Yorktown fighters to protect his carrier, "Adams," his wing man, "and I went at them from a beam approach. They scattered like a bunch of pigeons and we drove right through them. I knocked one out of one side of the V, then went on across and got one on the other side. Adams got another."

The trailing enemy formations, diving under or zooming over the first section, which was the target of the American fighters, continued on toward the Yorktown.

From the Astoria's bridge we saw the end of one Japanese plane. He came diving down out of the fleecy white overcast with a Grumman Wildcat on his tail. He pulled out close to the water and started radical evasive maneuvers.

"Don't let him get away," the marines on the antiaircraft battery just under the bridge were pleading. "Shoot him down."

The Wildcat fighter pilot, as if answering the pleas he couldn't hear, swooped twice at the fleeing enemy plane. After the second pass, it plunged into the sea to explode in a mass of flames.

Say this for the Japanese fliers, though. They kept on coming. Eleven were shot out of the air before they reached dropping distance, but the other seven won their way over the carrier and peeled off.

Every gun in the force was yammering away at the enemy planes as they plummeted, black as hate, out of the white clouds. The whole starboard side of the Yorktown seemed to burst into flame as her gunners poured out red-hot shells at the enemy bombers.

Standing in the port wing of the Astoria's bridge, watching the carrier two thousand yards away, Captain Frank Scanland saw her begin an evasive turn and called to Lieutenant Commander Bill Eaton, the navigator, who always takes the deck during action:

"Better give her twenty-five right, Bill."

The casualness of his tone was so striking I stared in amazement.

The enemy planes were coming down now, one a second, out of the twelve-thousand-foot overcast. I don't know how it is with others, but for me it was like watching a slow-motion picture. It seemed to take minutes for the planes to come down from first sighting to bomb-dropping distance.

The first one down, making a beautiful dive at an angle of about seventy-five degrees, put his bomb on one side of the flight deck, not far from the midships island structure. There was a great flash of fire when it landed. The next one missed, his bomb falling alongside the carrier, throwing a great column of spray in the air. He never pulled out of his dive but flew flaming into the sea.

The air was full of black antiaircraft bursts, through which the first two planes dived unscathed. The third man, however, was hit while still some five thousand feet above the carrier's deck. His plane seemed to hang in the air a moment, then turned a complete somersault. As it straightened out again, the bomb looking almost half as big as the plane, broke loose and started falling. As though running on a wire, it fell straight for the carrier's smokestack. It hit a quarter of the way down the big pipe, penetrating almost to the fireroom before it exploded. Thick black smoke poured out.

Four more made their dives and dropped their bombs, but only one more hit was scored, with an armor-piercing bomb that penetrated the flight deck forward and exploded four decks down.

The Japanese bombers were paying little attention to the cruisers or destroyers. One, however, after dropping his bomb, turned toward the Astoria and gave us one squirt from his machine gun. It was his last one. As he flew past the cruiser at bridge level, the 20-millimeter guns went to work on him. His gunner already was slumped over as he flew past the ship and as he passed the bridge, only fifty feet above the water, he too was hit and sagged down against the side of his cockpit. His plane never came out of its shallow glide, but plunged into the water astern.

The Japanese dive bombers were identified by our gunnery officer as Baugeki '97s. They had long, tapering wings, and long slim fuselages. Red circles were painted on the wing tops. There were two red bands around the fuselage about halfway back. They were painted a mottled brown.

After the bomb went down her stack, the Yorktown slowed to five knots. A great column of black smoke was pouring up amidships, and thinner wisps of smoke could be seen around the forepeak, seeping up from the fire deep in her forward compartments.

Soon her signal searchlight began blinking and to the Astoria came the message: "Send small boat for admiral and staff."

The bombing had knocked out the ship's radio, and the admiral had to be where he could communicate with the other ships and shore stations.

Captain Scanland turned the Astoria to send her across the bow of the slowly moving carrier, and one of our motor sailers was launched, with Lieutenant Willie Isham at the helm, to bring Admiral Fletcher to us.

Pulling under the side of the burning Yorktown, the little boat took a line from the carrier down which the admiral and eight of his staff clambered, including Captain Spencer Lewis, his chief of staff, Commanders Gerry Galpin and Harry Guthrie, Lieutenant Commander Sam Latimer and Lieutenant Harry Smith.

They came aboard dressed in smoke-begrimed coveralls, looking like refugees from a chain gang. Admiral Fletcher moved in with Admiral Smith. His staff set up housekeeping in Captain Scanland's outer cabin, which they dubbed "Boy's Town."

Just as our boat was completing the final trip, two of the Yorktown's dive bombers that had been circling the formation ran out of gas. Seeing the Astoria stopped, they came in and landed alongside. Both pilots set their planes down beautifully in the roughening sea and were out of the cockpits and in their rubber boats without even getting their feet wet. Our small boat picked them up. One of them was Lieutenant

Commander Leslie, who had led the dive-bombing attack on the Akagi.

As the boat was picking up the pilot and radioman gunner of the second plane, a lookout reported a torpedo approaching the ship from dead ahead.

Looking down from the bridge, fifty feet above the water, Lieutenant Commander Davidson said he saw what he also believed was a torpedo passing parallel to the ship and not more than fifteen feet away. It may have been a fish, he said later, since there were no more torpedoes seen, and the destroyers patrolling around the stricken Yorktown made no contacts. If so, it was the biggest, fastest moving one he ever saw. It was running deep, at an estimated speed of forty-five or fifty knots, and leaving a clearly defined wake.

Anxious to get his boat under way, if there were enemy submarines about, Captain Scanland at that moment saw our small boat going back to take aboard the rubber boats the pilots had used.

"Get that damn boat aboard," he roared. "What in hell do they think they are, a salvage crew?"

Aboard the Yorktown, meanwhile, the fire was being brought under control. The smoke from the fire forward had thinned out to only a few small white wisps. Amidships, the black column of smoke pouring up out of the damaged stack had turned from black to brown. The holes in her deck had been repaired. She was picking up speed.

There was a cheer from our cruiser as a new ensign, bright as the morning, was hoisted to the yardarm to replace the smoke-blackened one that had been flying since dawn.

Knowing that the first attack probably would not be the last, Admiral Fletcher had asked for help to protect the stricken carrier, and two cruisers and two destroyers came boiling over the horizon.

The force was now back in cruising formation, the carrier flanked on either side by two cruisers. Ahead and on either side the destroyers patrolled.

"My speed is fifteen knots," the carrier signaled. Then it was seventeen, then eighteen.

There was a momentary scare as a large formation of planes was reported approaching from the southwest. Then they were identified as friendly. Flying high and fast, they passed overhead on a northerly course. Vengeance for the attack on the Yorktown was soon to be had. One of the Yorktown's scout planes finally had located the one undamaged Japanese carrier, the Hiryu, and Admiral Spruance had sent a striking force from the Enterprise to attack.

The American striking group hardly was out of sight when the ominous report, "many bogies bearing 350 degrees" came up from the flag plot. ("Bogies" was the voice code for unidentified aircraft.) That could mean but one thing, another attack. It was 5 o'clock. It had been three hours since the first attack.

Up to flank speed went the destroyers and cruisers, driving to place themselves between the carrier and the incoming enemy planes. The Yorktown, too, could be seen picking up speed. White water was curling away from her bow.

"She's launching fighters," someone on our bridge yelled. Off the patched flight deck the little Wildcats were roaring out to the attack. There was no preliminary circling this time. Straight for the enemy they flew, throttles full out.

Far to the north we saw the first evidence of the attack— the flash of exploding planes. At the same time came the report from the attacking fighters that the enemy planes were torpedo bombers, the Kogekiki '97s.

As they came in visual range, flying about five hundred feet off the water and in a fast, downward glide, every gun that could be brought to bear opened fire. One of the cruisers nearest to the approach was using her main batteries, firing into the water to raise the splashes that could be as deadly for an approaching plane as a direct hit.

The northern sky was black with AA shellbursts, forming a deadly curtain of steel in front of the approaching Japanese formation.

One group of five enemy bombers zoomed up and over the shellbursts, and then spread to attack the cruisers and destroyers. One of our 5-inch guns, firing point-blank at the enemy pilot that had picked the Astoria as his victim, got a direct hit. The enemy bomber blew up in a great flash of flame. Another skidded into the sea, leaving a flaming trail of burning gasoline a quarter of a mile in length.

Two of the Japanese pilots were very brave men. Right through the curtain of antiaircraft fire they flew, straight for the Yorktown. Captain Elliott Buckmaster, on the Yorktown's bridge, saw them and started an evasive turn. The "Mighty Y," lacking her usual speed, couldn't quite make it. The two enemy bombers, flying within a hundred yards of each other, made their drops not over five hundred yards out from their target. The big two-thousand-pound torpedoes, slanting down to the water, porpoised once or twice, then ran straight and true for the American carrier.

A great column of water splashed over the Yorktown's deck at the first explosion, and she shuddered as though she had hit a stone wall. The other hit within seconds, apparently entering through the hole torn by the first explosion, and exploding deep in the ship.

"I can't bear to watch it," said a young ensign who himself was to die two months later in the Solomons, and he turned away, his face set, tears in his eyes.

As the smoke and spray of the two explosions fell away we could see the big carrier heeling ominously to port.

"My God, she's going to capsize," Captain Scanland whispered, incredulously.

She went over fifteen degrees, twenty, twenty-five, thirty. Waves were lapping at the port edge of the thwartship passageways, through which the setting sun was shining.

"What's that signal?" the captain called to a signalman on the deck below as two colored flags could be seen going up to the Yorktown's yardarm. But it was unnecessary to ask again. They could be plainly seen, whipping in the wind. They were HP (hypo love, to use the phonetics of the fleet). They meant, "I'm abandoning ship."

From below decks blue-clad and khaki-clad figures could be seen climbing topside. Soon they were sliding down the lines to the water.

The "Mighty Y" was fighting hard to save herself. As she rocked on the long Pacific swells, she would seem, at times, to regain some of her trim. Then she would lean over again, as though tired of the struggle. The water rushing through the hole in her side apparently had smothered whatever fires the torpedo explosions had set.

All vessels in the area had their small boats over the side, while the destroyers nosed in as close as they could without endangering the swimming men, and started pulling survivors up onto their low decks.

The oil-covered sea was alive with bobbing heads, small rafts and 5-inch shell casings that had slid off the decks, or had been blown off by the force of the torpedo explosions. Unless you looked closely to see they were not leaving a wake, it was difficult to distinguish them from a submarine periscope.

For over an hour the work of rescue went on. Then, convinced there were no more survivors to be picked up, the escort vessels took up their small boats and the force formed up and headed east. One destroyer was left on guard.

As we headed toward the darkening eastern sky the Yorktown was silhouetted against the setting sun. Viewed from broadside her steep list did not show and she looked as battle-worthy as she had that morning.

Pacific Battle Line, 1944

Concentration Camp: U.S. Style

by Ted Nakashima

UNFORTUNATELY in this land of liberty, I was born of Japanese parents; born in Seattle of a mother and father who have been in this country since 1901. Fine parents, who brought up their children in the best American way of life. My mother served with the Volunteer Red Cross Service in the last war—my father, an editor, has spoken and written Americanism for forty years.

Our family is almost typical of the other unfortunates here at the camp. The oldest son, a licensed architect, was educated at the University of Washington, has a master's degree from the Massachusetts Institute of Technology and is a scholarship graduate of the American School of Fine Arts in Fontainebleau, France. He is now in camp in Oregon with his wife and three-months-old child. He had just completed designing a much needed defense housing project at Vancouver, Washington.

The second son is an M.D. He served his internship in a New York hospital, is married and has two fine sons. The folks banked on him, because he was the smartest of us three boys. The army took him a month after he opened his office. He is now a lieutenant in the Medical Corps, somewhere in the South.

I am the third son, the dumbest of the lot, but still smart enough to hold down a job as an architectural draftsman. I have just finished building a new home and had lived in it three weeks. My desk was just cleared of work done for the Army Engineers, another stack of 391 defense houses was waiting (a rush job), when the order came to pack up and leave for this resettlement center called "Camp Harmony."

Mary, the only girl in the family, and her year-old son,

"Butch," are with our parents—interned in the stables of the Livestock Exposition Buildings in Portland.

Now that you can picture our thoroughly American background, let me describe our new home.

The resettlement center is actually a penitentiary—armed guards in towers with spotlights and deadly tommy guns, fifteen feet of barbed-wire fences, everyone confined to quarters at nine, lights out at ten o'clock. The guards are ordered to shoot anyone who approaches within twenty feet of the fences. No one is allowed to take the two-block-long hike to the latrines after nine, under any circumstances.

The apartments, as the army calls them, are two-block-long stables, with windows on one side. Floors are shiplaps on two-by-fours laid directly on the mud, which is everywhere. The stalls are about eighteen by twenty-one feet; some contain families of six or seven persons. Partitions are seven feet high, leaving a four-foot opening above. The rooms aren't too bad, almost fit to live in for a short while.

The food and sanitation problems are the worst. We have had absolutely no fresh meat, vegetables or butter since we came here. Mealtime queues extend for blocks; standing in a rainswept line, feet in the mud, waiting for the scant portions of canned wieners and boiled potatoes, hash for breakfast or canned wieners and beans for dinner. Milk only for the kids. Coffee or tea dosed with saltpeter and stale bread are the adults' staples. Dirty, unwiped dishes, greasy silver, a starchy diet, no butter, no milk, bawling kids, mud, wet mud that stinks when it dries, no vegetables—a sad thing for the people who raised them in such abundance. Memories of a crisp head of lettuce with our special olive oil, vinegar, garlic and cheese dressing.

Today one of the surface sewage-disposal pipes broke and the sewage flowed down the streets. Kids play in the water. Shower baths without hot water. Stinking mud and slops everywhere.

Can this be the same America we left a few weeks ago?

As I write, I can remember our little bathroom—light coral walls. My wife painting them, and the spilled paint in her hair. The open towel shelving and the pretty shower curtains which we put up the day before we left. How sanitary and clean we left it for the airlines pilot and his young wife who are now enjoying the fruits of our labor.

It all seems so futile, struggling, trying to live our old lives under this useless, regimented life. The senselessness of all the inactive manpower. Electricians, plumbers, draftsmen, mechanics, carpenters, painters, farmers—every trade—men who are able and willing to do all they can to lick the Axis. Thousands of men and women in these camps, energetic, quick, alert, eager for hard, constructive work, waiting for the army to do something for us, an army that won't give us butter.

I can't take it! I have 391 defense houses to be drawn. I left a fine American home which we built with our own hands. I left a life, highballs with our American friends on week-ends, a carpenter, laundry-truck driver, architect, airlines pilot—good friends, friends who would swear by us. I don't have enough of that Japanese heritage *"ga-man"*—a code of silent suffering and ability to stand pain.

Oddly enough I still have a bit of faith in army promises of good treatment and Mrs. Roosevelt's pledge of a future worthy of good American citizens. I'm banking another $67 of income tax on the future. Sometimes I want to spend the money I have set aside for income tax on a bit of butter or ice cream or something good that I might have smuggled through the gates, but I can't do it when I think that every dollar I can put into "the fight to lick the Japs," the sooner I will be home again. I must forget my stomach.

What really hurts most is the constant reference to us evacués as "Japs." "Japs" are the guys we are fighting. We're on this side and we want to help.

Why won't America let us?

The New Republic, June 15, 1942

"A Vast Slaughterhouse"

1,000,000 Jews Slain By Nazis, Report Says

LONDON, June 29 (U.P.)—The Germans have massacred more than 1,000,000 Jews since the war began in carrying out Adolf Hitler's proclaimed policy of exterminating the people, spokesmen for the World Jewish Congress charged today.

They said the Nazis had established a "vast slaughterhouse for Jews" in Eastern Europe and that reliable reports showed that 700,000 Jews already had been murdered in Lithuania and Poland, 125,000 in Rumania, 200,000 in Nazi-occupied parts of Russia and 100,000 in the rest of Europe. Thus about one-sixth of the pre-war Jewish population in Europe, estimated at 6,000,000 to 7,000,000 persons, had been wiped out in less than three years.

A report to the congress said that Jews, deported en masse to Central Poland from Germany, Austria, Czechoslovakia and the Netherlands, were being shot by firing squads at the rate of 1,000 daily.

Information received by the Polish Government in London confirmed that the Nazis had executed "several hundred thousand" Jews in Poland and that almost another million were imprisoned in ghettos.

A spokesman said 10,232 persons died in the Warsaw ghetto from hunger, disease, and other causes between April and June last year and that 4,000 children between the ages of 12 and 15 recently were removed from there by the Gestapo to work on slave-labor farms.

The pre-Nazi Jewish population of Germany, totaling about 600,000 persons, was said to have been reduced to a little more than 100,000.

The New York Times, June 30, 1942

Allies Are Urged to Execute Nazis

LONDON, July 1—The Polish Government in London has been urged in a report on the slaughter of 700,000 Jews in German-occupied territories to call on the Allied governments to adopt a policy of retaliation that will force the Germans to cease their killings.

"We believe," the report says, "that Hitler's Germany in time will be punished for all its horrors, crimes and brutality but this is no comfort for the millions menaced with death. We implore the Polish Government, the guardian representative of all the peoples of Poland, to protect them against complete annihilation, to influence the Allied governments to apply similar treatment against Germans and fifth columnists living at present in Allied countries.

"Let all Germans know this, know that punishment will be meted out to Germans in the United States and other countries.

"We realize we ask the Polish Government to do something most difficult and unusual but this is the only way to save millions of Jews from certain destruction."

The report, describing the Jews' ordeal in occupied Poland and German attempts to exterminate the Jewish population, reached London through underground channels. Szmul Zygelbojm, Jewish Socialist leader and member of the Polish National Council in London, received it and vouched for its trustworthiness. He said the sources were absolutely reliable, although the story seemed too terrible and the atrocities too inhuman to be true.

The report is supported by information received by other Jewish circles here and also by the Polish Government. Its figure of 700,000 Jews slain by the Germans since the occupation—one-fifth of the entire Jewish population of Poland—probably includes many who died of maltreatment in concentration camps, of starvation in ghettos or of unbearable conditions of forced labor.

Here are the main items in the report:

From the first day of the German-Soviet occupation of East Poland the Germans began the extermination of Jews. They started in East Galicia last Summer. Males between 14 and 60 were herded into public squares and cemeteries, forced to dig their own graves and then were machine-gunned and hand-grenaded.

Children in orphanages, old persons in almshouses, the sick in hospitals and women were slain in the streets. In many places Jews were rounded up and deported to unrevealed destinations or massacred in near-by woods.

At Lwow 35,000 were slain, at Stanislawow, 15,000; at Tarnopol, 5,000; at Zloctrow, 2000; at Brzezany only 1,700 were left of 18,000. The massacre still continues in Lwow.

Last Fall the slaughter of Jews was extended to the Vilna and Kovno districts. By November 50,000 had been murdered in Vilna and only 12,000 were left. In the two districts the victims of the German slaughter numbered 300,000.

Simultaneously a massacre started in the Slonim district in Eastern Poland. Nine thousand were killed in the town of Slonim, 6,000 in Baranowicze. In Volhynia the killing began in November and in three days 15,000 had been massacred in Rovny County.

In the early Winter the Germans were methodically proceeding with their campaign to exterminate all Jews. They sent special gas chambers on wheels to Western Poland, territories incorporated in the Reich. In the village of Chelmno near Kolo ninety persons at a time were put in the gas chambers. The victims were buried in graves dug by them in near-by Lubarski forest.

About 1,000 gassed daily from the townships of Kolo, Dable, Izbica and others between November, 1941, and March, 1942, as well as 35,000 Jews in Lodz between Jan. 2 and Jan. 9. Two thousand "gypsies" were gassed. They probably were Yugoslav prisoners and terrorists.

In February the murder wave reached the Gouvernement General area in Central Poland, Tarnow, Radom and Lublin. Twenty-five thousand were taken to an unrevealed destination from Lublin. Nothing has been heard of them since. A few were detained in the suburb of Majdanek; the others disappeared. No Jews were left in Lublin.

In Warsaw a "blood bath" was arranged in the ghetto on the night of April 17. Homes were visited by the Gestapo and Jews of all classes were dragged out and killed.

"This shows," the report concludes, "that the criminal German Government is fulfilling Hitler's threat that, whoever wins, all Jews will be murdered."

The New York Times, July 2, 1942

Bond Rally

by E. B. White

DOROTHY LAMOUR left Portland, Maine, at 7:20 on the morning of September 17th, passed through Woodfords at 7:25, Cumberland Center 7:39, Yarmouth Junction 7:49, and two hours later arrived in Augusta, where she parted with one of her handkerchiefs to a gentleman who bought an unusually large war bond. She left Augusta at 1:38 P.M., passed through Waterville at 2:04, Burnham Junction 2:35, Pittsfield 2:49, Newport Junction 3:01, and arrived in Bangor at 3:40, at the top of the afternoon.

Like most river towns, Bangor is a metropolis loved by the heat, and it was hot there under the train shed that afternoon, where a few dozen rubbernecks like myself were waiting to see a screen star in the flesh. The Penobscot flowed white and glassy, past the wharves and warehouses. On a siding a locomotive sighed its great sultry sighs. The reception committee wiped its forehead nervously with its handkerchief and paced up and down at the side of the waiting Buick roadster—which the daily *News,* in an excess of emotion, described as "blood-red." The guard of honor—a handful of soldiers from the air field—lounged informally, and a sergeant with a flash camera arranged himself on top of a baggage truck. In the waiting room a family of three sat in some embarrassment on a bench.

"I feel so silly," said the woman.

"What d'you care?" replied her husband, obviously the ringleader in this strange daylight debauchery. "What d'you care? I like to come down here to the station and see how things act once in a while." The teen-age daughter agreed with her father and backed him to the hilt, against her mother's deep-seated suspicion of the male errant.

Miss Lamour's train pulled in cautiously, stopped, and she

stepped out. There was no pool, no waterfall, no long dark hair falling across the incomparable shoulders, no shadow cast by the moon. Dorothy the saleswoman strode forward in red duvetyn, with a brown fuzzy bow in her upswept hair. She shook hands, posed for a picture, and drove off through the cheering crowd in the blood-red car, up Exchange Street, where that morning I had seen a motley little contingent of inductees shuffling off, almost unnoticed, to the blood-red war.

While Miss Lamour was receiving the press in her rooms at the Penobscot Exchange Hotel I went down to the men's room to get a shine.

"See her?" I asked the porter.

"Yeah, I was standing right next to her at the curb." Then he added, studiously: "I'd say she was about thirty. A nice-looking woman."

"I suppose they're giving her the works, here at the hotel," I said.

"I'll say they are. Took the furniture right out of Cratty's room. Hell, she's got chairs in there that wide."

Having assured myself that Dorothy was being properly cared for, and having brightened my own appearance to some extent, I went out to the Fair Grounds at the other end of town, where a stamp rally was scheduled to take place. The grandstand alongside the race track was already bulging with children, each of whom had bought a dollar's worth of stamps for the privilege of seeing Lamour. The sale of stamps had been brisk during the week. A booth had been maintained in the square, and Madame Zelaine, the local seeress, had personally handed out stamps and taken in the money for the Treasury. And now the grandstand was a lively place, with much yelling and chewing and anticipation. The Boys' Band of the American Legion, on the platform in the infield, was flashy in blue and yellow silks. In the still air, under the hard sun, gleamed the flags and the banners and the drum majorette's knees. When the car bearing the beloved actress appeared at the infield gate and swept to the bandstand the children hollered and whooped in their delight and little boys threw things at one another in the pure pleasure of a bought-and-paid-for outing.

The meeting got down to business with an abruptness which almost caused it to founder. Miss Lamour was introduced, stepped up, shaded her eyes with an orchid, made a short appeal, and before the little girls in the audience had figured out whether her hair was brown or green, she asked everyone to step along to the booth and buy some stamps. This was an unlooked-for development. Presumably most pockets were empty. Nobody made a move and the silence was oppressive. I have an idea that Miss Lamour herself didn't know quite what she was getting into and perhaps hadn't been told, or hadn't taken it in, that the children were already paid-up supporters of the war and that their presence there, inside the gates, was evidence that they had shelled out. It was simply one of those situations—a situation in the hard, uncompromising sunlight.

Miss Lamour, obviously a sincere and diligent patriot, saw that she was in a spot, and the chairman was visibly embarrassed. He and she hurriedly went into a huddle, shameless in the glaring sun. Then she grasped the mike. "Don't tell me business is *this* slow," she said, rather desperately.

Two or three little millionaires, in sheer anguish at seeing a dream person in distress, got up and moved toward the booth. Miss Lamour seized the moment. "Listen," she said, "I've come a long way to see you—don't let me down." (The bothersome question arose in all minds, the question who had come to see whom in this show.)

"Sing something!" hollered a youngster.

But there was undoubtedly something in her contract which prevented that. After another hurried conference the bandleader handed over his baton.

"I've never done this before," said Dorothy, "but I'm willing to try anything." She stepped up in front of the band, the leader got them started, and then gave over. Miss Lamour beat her way doggedly through a rather heavy number. In a long grueling bond-selling tour this was obviously one of the low moments for her. Low for the children too, some of whom, I am sure, had gone into hock up to their ears. It was just poor showmanship. Disillusion in the afternoon. The music ended and the star took a bow.

A couple of Fortresses flew overhead. This was a break.

Miss Lamour pointed up excitedly. "If you think it doesn't cost money to build those things, look at them. That's what you're buying!"

"Sing something!" shouted the tiny heckler.

Some more customers filed awkwardly down to the booth and in a few minutes the meeting was adjourned.

"I figured her hair was going to be down," said a little girl next me, coming out of a trance. Miss Lamour left in the Buick, respectfully encircled by the Army and the Navy, one man from each.

The big meeting was in the evening, after supper, in the Auditorium; and if Bangor had muffed its afternoon show it made up for it by a curiously happy night performance. It is no secret that enormous sums of money have been raised in America through the generous efforts of motion picture stars, and I was eager to be present at such an occasion. This particular brand of rally is a rather odd American phenomenon—that is, the spectacle of a people with homes and future at stake, their own lives threatened and the lives of their sons hanging by a thread, having to goad themselves to meet the challenge by indulging in a fit of actor worship and the veneration of the Hollywood gods. Everywhere in the country people have shown a peculiar willingness to buy bonds under the ægis of a star of the silver screen. Every race of people has of course its national and religious forms and ecstasies, its own way of doing business, its own system of getting results. The Japanese have their Emperor, an idol who is the same as God; the Germans have the State, closely identified with the Führer. Americans warm to a more diffuse allegiance—they have their Abe Lincoln and their Concord Bridge and their Bill of Rights, but these are somewhat intellectual appurtenances. For pure idolatry and the necessary hysteria which must accompany the separation of the individual from his money, they turn to Dorothy Lamour, or Beauty-at-a-Distance. At first glance this might appear to be a rather shabby sort of patriotic expression, but when you think about it, it improves. It may easily be a high form of national ardor after all, since the Hollywood glamour ideal is an ideal which each individual constructs for himself in the darkness and privacy of a motion picture house, after toil. The spell of

Lamour, the sarong, the jungle code, the water lily in the pool
—these tell the frustration of the civilized male, who yearns
in the midst of the vast turmoil and complexities of his amazing little life, with its details and its fussiness, to chuck his
desperate ways for a girl and an island moon—a dream of
amorous felicity and carelessness. To bring this dream into
line, for a national emergency, and adapt it to the exigencies
of federal finance is an American miracle of imposing and
rather jovial proportions. Miss Lamour was introduced as the
"Bond Bombshell"; the water lily had become an orchid from
a florist's shop, symbol of wealth and extravagance.

The Bangor people, about twenty-five hundred of them,
assembled in the hall, which was a sort of overgrown grange
hall. Admission was by bond only, plus the Annie Oakleys.
The big buyers were in the front seats, the small fellows in the
balcony. The notables and the Bombshell and the Dow Field
military band and WLBZ assembled on the platform, a mixed
group of civil and military servants, variously arrayed. Almost
the first thing that happened was the arrival of a contingent of
Navy recruits (about fifty of them) who were to submit to a
public induction under the combined sponsorship of Uncle
Sam and the motion picture industry. They filed down the
center aisle and climbed sheepishly to the platform, a rag-tag-
and-bobtail company in their ready-to-shed citizens' clothes,
sober as bridegrooms and terribly real. This was it, and the
people cheered. Miss Lamour, sensing the arrival of actors
who could not fail to give an authentic performance and who
would never get a retake, stepped deferentially into the wings.
A Navy lieutenant lined up his charges and prepared to give
the oath. On their faces, bothered by the sudden confusion of
lights and the convergence of their personal fates, was a hang-
dog look, a little tearful, a little frightened, a little resolved.
They were just a bunch of gangling boys in a moderately uncomfortable public position, but they seemed like precious
stones. The dust of glamour had shifted imperceptibly from
Miss Lamour and settled on their heads. After they were
sworn in she glided back on to the stage, shook hands, and
gave each her blessing as he shuffled out to gather up his cap
and his change of underwear and disappear into the theater of
war.

The program continued. A Negro quartet sang. Two heroes were produced—a pint-sized radioman who had been wounded in the Coral Sea, a big lumbering Tiger who had flown for Chennault. They were the "had been" contingent. The radioman told, in masterly understatements, about Pearl Harbor on that Sunday morning. The Tiger, a laconic man in shirtsleeves, was interviewed by a small dapper announcer for WLBZ, and when he was asked how it felt to be an American on foreign shores, he choked up, the strength went out of him, and he couldn't answer. He just walked away. After the band had performed, a young Jewish soldier stepped forward and played a violin solo. For him there could be nothing obscure about war aims. It was a war for the right to continue living and the privilege of choosing his own composer when he played his fiddle. He played solidly and well, with a strength which the Army had given his hands and his spirit. The music seemed to advance boldly toward the enemy's lines.

Here, for a Nazi, was assembled in one hall all that was contemptible and stupid—a patriotic gathering without strict control from a central leader, a formless group negligently dressed (even Dottie had neglected to change into evening dress, thereby breaking the hearts of the women in the audience), a group shamelessly lured there by a pretty girl for bait, a Jew in an honored position as artist, Negroes singing through their rich non-Aryan throats, and the whole affair lacking the official seal of the Ministry of Propaganda—a sprawling, goofy American occasion, shapeless as an old hat.

It made me feel very glad to be there. And somewhere during the evening I picked up a strong conviction that our side was going to win. Anyway, the quota was heavily oversubscribed in this vicinity. I would have bargained for a handkerchief if Miss Lamour had had any to spare. It's the ape-man in me probably.

Harper's Magazine, December 1942

Battle of the Ridge

by Richard Tregaskis

MONDAY, *September 7*

This morning Col. Edson told me that he is planning to make an attack on the Jap positions in the Taivu Point area tomorrow. If I wanted to go along, I was to be at a certain embarkation point at 3:45 this afternoon.

It was pelting rain when I arrived. But the Raiders, who seem to love a fight, were in high spirits. I had been assigned by Col. Edson to go with Col. Griffith aboard a tiny Diesel-engined ship which was acting as an auxiliary transport for the occasion. As we stepped aboard, one happy marine said, "This is the battleship *Oregon*, I presume?"

The captain of the little craft was a jovial Portuguese who had formerly been a Tuna captain on the American West Coast. His name, Joaquin S. Theodore. He still spoke in interesting Portuguese constructions, despite his rank as captain of a naval ship.

"We'll have it coffee for everybody in the morning," he said. Kindly, he warned against smoking on deck. "Tal your men I don't like to smoke it on deck," he said.

He wanted to clear away a space in the small ship so that the tight-packed marines might have a little more room. He pointed to a clothes line and said to his first officer, "Whoever this clothes belongs to I want it out of the lines."

The ship was a tiny thing, with only limited supplies of stores. But Capt. Theodore passed out grub and all available cigarettes to the Raiders, and shared his little cabin with Col. Griffith.

As we put out onto a rough sea, the pink-cheeked, hearty Portuguese told me proudly about his two "'lil kids" back home and about the exploits of his ship.

Col. Griffith later went over the plans for our expedition: we are to land our troops to the east of a small village called

Tasimboko, in the Taivu Point area, and advance from that direction on the town. Tasimboko is supposed to be the bivouac of a large group of Jap troops — estimated to number from 1,000 to 3,000. But the Japs are supposed to be lightly armed.

A bombing and strafing attack on Tasimboko, and shelling from the sea, will be timed to fit in with our attack.

Getting to sleep was a terrible job. The ship's steaming hold, full of the noise of the engines, was crammed with marines; no room to sprawl there. Every nook about deck seemed to be filled as well.

Finally I found a spot on the deck, which was partially shielded by a hatchway, and curled around it. But the ship rolled heavily and rain began to fall. I found another spot on the forecastle deck and pulled the edge of a tarpaulin over me. The rain fell more heavily, and the wind grew cold. I stumbled along to the captain's cabin and lay down on the floor in the stuffy room. It was better than sleeping in the rain.

TUESDAY, *September 8*

Despite the hardships of sleeping aboard Capt. Theodore's tiny tub, the Raiders were fresh and ready to go this morning when the time came for us to climb into our boats and shove off for shore.

Just as we were starting, there came a fortunate happenstance: a small convoy of American cargo ships, escorted by warships, passed very close to our own transports. They had no connection with us, and were bound for a different part of Guadalcanal; but the Japs, seeing our ships and the others together, evidently got the impression that a mass assault was coming. And so, fortunately, many of them ran.

But we naturally had no way of knowing this as we dashed for shore in our landing boats. We were ready for a real struggle, and a bit puzzled when there were no shots from shore.

We were more mystified, when, a few minutes after landing, as we were pushing along the trail toward Tasimboko, we found a fine, serviceable 37 mm. field piece, with the latest split-trail, rubber-tired carriage, sitting at the edge of the beach. It was complete with ammunition, and surrounded by Japanese packs, life-preservers, intrenching tools, new shoes, strewn in disorder on the ground.

As we moved along, we found more packs, more shoes, and life-preservers, and fresh-dug slit-trenches and foxholes in the underbrush. We also found another fine 37 mm. gun, which like the other was unmanned. This second gun was pointed toward the west, indicating we had possibly, as we had hoped, surprised the Japs by circumventing their positions and attacking from the east.

Or perhaps this was only the entrance to a trap. The Japs are supposed to excel at such tactics. We moved on cautiously, circled a small pond and crossed a ford in a river, wading in water up to our waists.

Beyond the ford, we passed a pile of clam shells, evidently freshly opened. "I'm thinking they've gone up for breakfast and knocked things off," snapped Col. Edson with his humorless grin. But he did not relax. He moved his troops ahead fast, barked at them when they failed to take proper cover.

We heard the sound of approaching plane motors, then saw our dive-bombers come out of the sky and slant westward. A few seconds later we heard the thud of bombs falling.

There were strafing planes, too, the long-nosed Pursuits flashing overhead, and we could hear their guns rattling as they dived.

We moved along the shore through an overgrown cocoanut grove and in the brakes of underbrush; we found more foxholes, carefully camouflaged with palm leaves, and caches of food and ammunition.

Shortly after eight o'clock, we made our first contact with the Japs. I saw our people running in numerous directions at once, and knew that something had happened. I ran to the beach and saw what the others had seen: a row of Jap landing boats lying on the sand some distance away, and amidst the boats, a small group of men in brown uniforms, looking our way—Japs.

The colonel called "Nick," quietly, and Maj. Nickerson (Floyd W. Nickerson of Spokane, Wash.) anticipated the order. "Open fire?" he said hopefully.

The colonel nodded his head.

"Nick," who is as lean and hard as the colonel, called, "Machine-gun runner." And when the man came up, which was almost immediately, he gave him the order. Within two minutes our machine guns were firing.

"Red Mike" (as the Raiders call their colonel for the obvious reason that he has red hair) is most taciturn. I asked him, at this juncture, what was happening.

"I think we might have caught a few," he snapped. And that was all he said.

Now the Japs were answering our fire. I heard the familiar flat crack of the .25 rifle, and the repetition of sound in long bursts of light machine-gun fire. Others of our men joined in the firing, and it swelled in volume. In the midst of the outburst, we heard the crash of a heavy explosion. I was lying on the ground under a bush, near Red Mike, taking thorough cover.

"Sounds like mortar fire," he said, concisely.

The burst of firing stopped, and there was a lull for a few moments. Red Mike was on his feet immediately, moving ahead. He sent a message up to Maj. Nickerson, who was leading the advance elements of our troops.

"Nick's got to push right on up," he said, low-voiced. Then he was gone, tending to some military business in the rear. A few moments later he was back again, still moving fast. I had found the colonel to be one of the quickest human beings I had ever known.

Rifle and machine-gun fire burst out again, the Jap guns standing out in the chorus like a tenor in a quartet. The bullets were closer this time. I crawled under a wet bush and kept my head down.

A man was hit over to our left. I heard the cry, "Pass the word back for a corpsman," felt the sickening excitement of the moment in the air. Our first casualty.

Then there came another loud crash from ahead, close and loud enough so that the earth shook under us. I was lying next to a private. "Sounds like a 90 mm. mortar," he said.

Now the blasting concussion of the explosion was repeated, and we heard the furry whistle of a shell passing over our heads, heard it explode well to the rear. Was it a mortar or a field piece ahead of us? There was more than a possibility, it seemed, that we had run into a heavy Jap force, equipped with batteries of artillery.

I was more certain of it when the explosion was repeated. Again we heard a second crash a fraction of a moment later, well behind us. Now it seemed evident that these were artillery pieces firing, probably several of them.

The Jap artillery was answered by the lighter-toned firing of our own mortars, and another chorus of rifles and machine guns. The Jap guns crashed again, and then the firing stopped.

A runner came to Col. Red Mike, who was sitting for a brief second in a clump of underbrush. "Nick says to tell you there are people across the stream," he said. A small stream ran parallel to the beach at this point, and that stream marked off our left flank. The Japs apparently were moving through the jungle on the inland side of the stream, planning to cut off our rear. "We can't see 'em yet, but we can hear 'em," said the runner.

The Colonel called Capt. Antonelli. "Tony," he said, "Nick says there's somebody working back across the stream. Take a patrol. Flank 'em if you possibly can."

There was other business for Red Mike: he wanted to check on the exact location of our companies; he got the "walky-talky" into action, sent runners out. He checked on the wounded by making a personal tour. Then he was back in time to get a report from Col. Griffith that a Jap field piece had been captured, unmanned.

"Shall I go with Tony or get the gun?" asked Col. Griffith.

"Go get it, take it down to the water and shoot it," said Red Mike.

Next, Red Mike disappeared into the foliage ahead. Now we were out of the cocoanuts, getting into thicker growth. But the colonel still moved like the wind. I followed and after a struggle found him at our foremost position, talking to Maj. Nickerson.

"I'm trying to locate that firing up ahead," said Nick.

Our planes came in again, and dived and strafed the Jap village ahead of us. The Japs were not firing. We moved ahead.

We passed through a jungle brake which looked just like any other from the outside, but inside we found stacks of cases filled with medical supplies. "Opium," said a marine, but I made note of the labels on some of the boxes and checked later. Most of the boxes contained "Sapo Medicatus," which is a blood-coagulating agent.

The foxholes were growing more numerous as we progressed. They were everywhere, carefully camouflaged with leaves. And caches of supplies were also more numerous; crates of canned meat, sacks of crackers; there were more groups of new field knapsacks, with shoes strapped to them, and scores of gray life-preservers, indicating the Jap troops who had been here were probably freshly landed from boats.

Something moved in the bush ahead and to our left. "There are troops going through there," said the colonel. "Find out who they are."

Seven minutes later, firing burst out again. I flopped into thick cover, and none too soon. A bullet snapped into the underbrush very close behind me. I picked out the sounds of Jap .25's, our automatic rifles and our machine guns. There was a torrent of Jap .25 machine-gun firing from the left.

"The boys got on the other side of us," said the colonel, with one of his wry smiles.

Now came a terrific blast from only a few yards ahead. It was so loud it made my ears ring, and the concussion shook chips of wood on my head from the trees above. We heard the shell whiz just over our heads and burst a few hundred yards to the rear. We knew then that we must be right smack up against the muzzle of a Jap field piece.

The piece fired again, and again, and then there was another outburst of machine-gun fire, ours heavy-toned against the Jap's cracking .25's. Then silence.

Maj. Nickerson came back to tell the colonel that our men had "killed the gunners on a Jap 75. It's only 150 yards ahead," said Nick. "It was covered by machine-gun fire. We got the gun."

But the Japs had more guns. We advanced only a slight distance, and another opened on us, as close as the last had been. At the time I was squatting in a thick jungle brake, a tangle of vines and dwarf trees, but the crash of the firing so close was scary, despite the good cover. Each time the gun went off, one felt the blast of hot air from the muzzle, and twigs rattled down from the trees above. But we knew we were safer here than back where the shells were falling. We could hear the explosions of the shells well behind us.

There was quite a cluster of us in this jungle grove: marines, squatting or sprawling unhappily in the green wet underbrush. Then it began to rain, and the rain came in sheets and torrents. The firing kept on. There were Jap riflemen around us too. (I later found that there had been one not more than fifty feet from us. We found his body. Why he did not fire at us I don't know.)

Nick shouted at the little group in the jungle brake. "Spread out," he said, with the proper blistering expletives. "We lost one squad of the second platoon with one shell. One of those might come in here."

I moved off to the right, to try to get a look ahead, and then moved back to the rear to see what damage the Jap shells were doing. I passed a marine who was lying on his back in a foxhole, his face very gray. His upper torso was wrapped in bandage, and I could see there was no arm where his left arm had been, not even a stump. A 75 shell had done the work.

A runner came back to report to Col. Red Mike, at 10:45, that a second Jap 75 had been put out of action and the crew killed.

It began to look as if we might have tackled a bigger Jap force than we could handle. The colonel was concerned about the Japs who might, he thought, be sneaking around our flank, cutting us off from the beach where we had landed. The colonel called for naval gunfire support.

A group of destroyers which had come down with us swung in close to shore and began to shell Tasimboko. I went out to the beach to watch the yellow flashes and the geysers of smoke and debris rising where the shells hit.

Then I went forward to look for Nick. Firing broke out again, torrents of it; but there were no more of the heavy crashes of artillery fire this time, only rifles and machine guns firing, and most of them, according to the sound, ours.

It had stopped raining. When the firing stopped a great quiet fell on the jungle. And in the quiet, we heard the desperate shouting of a man who was evidently in great trouble. He was shouting something like "Yama, Yama!" as if his life depended on it. Then the voice was smothered up in a fusillade of machine-gun and rifle fire. It was a Jap. But we never found out what he was shouting about.

The tide of our action seemed to be turning. We heard no more artillery and a runner came back from Capt. Antonelli's troops with the happy word, "We solved the problem, took the village." Nick's men sent back word that more Jap 75's had been captured, unmanned.

Appropriately, the clouds were clearing and the sun was coming out. Fresh reinforcements for our troops were landing. But now we did not need them.

We marched on into Tasimboko without any further resistance. We found many more cases of Japanese food and sacks of rice, and ammunition for Jap machine guns, rifles and artillery pieces, totaling more than 500,000 rounds, Col. Griffith estimated. We burned the ammunition and destroyed the village of Tasimboko, including a radio station which the Japs had established there.

Looking over the bodies of the Japs who had been killed (about thirty), we found some interesting items: pictures of Javanese women, American ammunition with labels printed in Dutch. And we found that the gun-sights with the 75's were of English manufacture, and that some of the Japs had been armed with tommy guns. It seemed that some of these soldiers who had run so fast had been veterans of the Jap campaigns in the East Indies, and possibly Malaya too. Perhaps this was the first time they had been surprised. Or perhaps they had heard too much about what happened to the Japs who tried to cross the Tenaru.

Most of the loot we had captured was destroyed. But we transported the medical supplies back to headquarters, and our men helped themselves to large stocks of British cigarettes, bearing a Netherlands East Indies tax stamp.

The sun had set and there was only a faint reddish glow on the clouds over the horizon to light the darkening sky, when, in our transport ships, we reached a point offshore from the Tenaru River. We were heading toward home.

But the day's excitement was not yet over. We got word

that twelve Jap aircraft had been spotted. Our fighter planes were rising into the twilight sky.

The transport went into evasive maneuvers, and, fortunately, the sky grew quickly darker, and was black, except for high streaks of silver gray, when the Japs arrived.

They did not come to Guadalcanal. For once, they picked Tulagi as their target, and we saw cup-shaped bursts of bright white light rising from the direction of the island, just over the horizon rim. We heard the distant thudding of the bombs a few seconds later, and wondered if the Japs would spot our wakes in the dark. But they did not.

WEDNESDAY, *September 9*

Shortly after 12:30 this morning, I heard the others in my tent dashing for the shelter. Maj. Phipps shouted to me to come along, and I heard cannonading coming from the north, but I was too tired to move.

At breakfast this morning, I heard that a small group of Jap destroyers or light cruisers had shelled Tulagi—and hit Capt. Theodore's little ship and set it afire.

Later in the day, I heard that Capt. Theodore had been wounded through the chest in the course of the engagement. But he had beached his little craft, and saved it from sinking, despite his wounds. I am glad to hear that he is expected to live.

This is the second time that I have left a ship in the evening and it has been attacked and lost before morning. This fact gives rise to the thought that my luck has been good, so far.

There were two air-raid alarms today. But the Japs never appeared. It was a quiet afternoon. We sat in Col. Hunt's CP after lunch, talking of the reunion we will have ten years hence, and the tales we'll tell about Guadalcanal, then, and how by that time our imaginations will have magnified our deeds immeasurably, and we will all be heroes.

Col. Hunt told us about some of his narrow escapes in the World War, when he commanded the Sixth Marines. Our casualties were very high, then, he said, and gave the figures. But the fighting at the Tenaru Battle, he said, was about as concentrated and intense as in any engagement of the World War.

Tonight we were awakened, just before midnight, by the sound of heavy firing in the jungles. There were machine guns, rifles and, occasionally, the crash of a mortar.

We lay awake and listened. And then cannonading started, to the north. We went to the dugout, and I sat on the sand-bagged entrance with Maj. Phipps. The guns, we knew, were big ones, because of their heavy tone and the brightness of the flashes against the sky. But Bill Phipps was sure they were firing in the Tulagi area, not off our shore. He had measured the interval between the time of the flash and the time the related boom of the gun reached us. That interval, he said, was ninety seconds. Multiply the 90 by 1,100, the number of feet sound travel in a second, and you get 99,000 feet, or about twenty miles. Tulagi is twenty miles north of us.

Star shells glowed in the sky. The Japs were illuminating the Tulagi shore. One of our observation posts phoned in the report that there were three Jap ships, probably cruisers, and that they were firing salvos.

THURSDAY, *September 10*

This morning we heard that the Japs had shelled Tulagi harbor last night and again hit Capt. Theodore's ship, which was still beached.

I went to the CP of Maj. Nickerson (the Raider officer) and talked to some of the men who did outstanding work on the excursion to Tasimboko, day before yesterday. Among them, two young corpsmen, Pharmacist's Mate Alfred W. Cleveland (of South Dartmouth, Mass.) and Pharmacist's Mate, second class, Karl B. Coleman (of McAndrews, Ky.). They told me how they had used a penknife to amputate the ragged stump of one Raider's arm after it had been shattered by a 75 explosion; the wounded man had been the one whom I had seen, lying in a foxhole, just after he had been treated and bandaged. These two lads, Nick told me, had saved the wounded man's life by amputating the remnants of his arm; the medicos themselves had said that the man would have died if the two lads had not done such a good and quick job in the field.

Pvt. Andrew J. Klejnot (of Fort Wayne, Ind.) told me how he had picked off one of the crew of one of the Jap 75's.

"There were only two men on the gun," he said. "I picked off one, and the other went and hid behind some boxes in a little ammunition dump. I fired into the dump and set it afire."

I moved my worldly possessions from Col. Hunt's CP out to Gen. Vandegrift's headquarters today. The general has moved into the "boon-docks," as the marines call the jungles; and the new spot is too much of a trek from Col. Hunt's headquarters.

A tent has been put up for us correspondents, near the general's headquarters. The members of our "press club" now are Bob Miller, Till Durdin, Tom Yarbrough, and there is a new arrival, Carlton Kent.

The Japs air-raided us at about noontime; twenty-seven of the usual silver-colored, two-engine type, flying lower than usual today. But the sticks of bombs fell a long distance from our location at the time.

The general's new CP is located in the thick of the jungle. Sui, pet dog of the Commissioner, Martin Clemens, proved it tonight by dragging an iguana, a small dragon-like lizard, into plain view as we sat at dinner over the crude board table to-night. Sui had unearthed the iguana at the jungle edge, which stands up straight and dense as a wall only a few feet from our mess table.

The tent which has been put up for correspondents is one of a number located at the foot of a ridge, facing the jungle. The general's tent is atop the ridge. Tonight we were told to be on the alert, since the Japs had been reported infiltrating the jungle which we faced. We were told that if an attack came, we should retire up the ridge to the crest, where a stand would be made.

"I wish I had a pistol," said Yarbrough, as we correspondents lay in our bunks, after dark. And the rest of us were nervous, and not anxious to go to sleep. We kept up a clatter of conversation to help our spirits.

The situation was not without an element of humor. For, as we lay awake, the mackaws sat overhead in the trees and bombed our tent. The plopping of their missiles was loud and frequent. The birds seemed to have singled out our tent for the heaviest bombardment. Maj. Jim Murray, the general's adjutant, chided us about the fact. "Those birds have got the correspondents' number, all right," he said.

FRIDAY, *September 11*

The Japs who were supposed to be investing the jungle in front of our tent did not put in an appearance last night. There was not even any firing out in the "boon-docks."

In today's air raid—by twenty-six Jap two-engined bombers—I had my closest escape from a bomb explosion. When the air-raid alert came in, Miller, Durdin and I went to the top of the ridge and walked down it, looking for a good high spot from which we could watch the bombers.

We found three or four men at work building a shelter at a spot several hundred yards away, where the ridge was bare of any foliage except grass, and one had a wonderful view of the sky. The incipient shelter, now only a pit, was just what we wanted in the way of a box seat for the show. It was deep and wide. We could sit on the edge until the bombers were just overhead, then still have plenty of time to dive for cover.

We did just that. The planes came as usual in a wide line that was a very shallow V, stretching across the sky. As usual, the anti-aircraft guns put up bursts in the vicinity, and as usual the bombers plowed on steadily, holding their formation and course.

Then the bombs came. When we heard them rattling down, we piled into the pit, layer upon layer of humanity, and waited. The bombs made a slightly different sound this time, perhaps because they were closer than before. Their sound was louder and more of a whistle. And the explosions were deafening. You could hear fragments skittering through the air over the top of the pit, and in that second all of us must have known that if we had been lying on the bare ridge we would have been hit and hurt.

Till Durdin said, "Hot." I saw that he was touching the sole of his shoe. He pulled a piece of metal out of the leather and held it gingerly between two fingers. It was a bomb fragment, still warm from the explosion.

Miller and I were anxious to see how close the craters had

been this time. We spotted a small crater about forty yards from our pit. It was this missile, probably, that had thrown the fragments over our heads.

Beyond the small crater were other, larger holes. One of them must have been thirty feet across. That one lay about three hundred yards from our pit, fortunately beyond effective range. It was one of an irregularly spaced line of craters that led into the jungle beyond the grass.

Now, from the jungle, we heard excited shouting and cries for a corpsman. We knew that meant that there had been some people hurt down there. We saw several being brought out on stretchers.

Our fighter planes were already avenging the casualties. We heard the sounds of a dogfight in the sky, and later came word that they had knocked down six of the bombers and one Zero.

Later this afternoon, our dive-bombers came in from a trip to Gizo. This time they had found a small ship, a patrol-boat type of craft, lying off the base, and had sunk it. They had also bombed the buildings of the base again.

At air-operations headquarters I found a box which had been sent by plane, from my shipmates on a former task-force excursion. It included cans of beans, brown bread, salmon, peaches. Miller, Pvt. Frank Schultz, who drives our jeep, Jim Hurlbut (the Marine Corps correspondent) and I went down to the Lunga, taking the box along, and had a swim in the swift, clear water. Then we opened the cans and had a feast.

SATURDAY, *September 12*

This morning, as an urgent air alert was flashed, we of the Press Club decided to go down to Lunga Point to watch the show for today. So we piled into a jeep and our driver turned out one of the fastest cross-country records such a vehicle has ever achieved. He was not inclined to be caught on the road when the bombers arrived.

At the Point, Miller put on the headphones of the radio set and began calling out the interplane conversations of our fighters, who were by that time rising to search for the foe.

At 11:42 Maj. Smith called: "Control from Smith. They're coming in from the south—a big squadron of 'em." And then we saw them, the usual impressive span of two-motored silver bombers, Mitsubishi 96's, moving like a slender white line of cloud across the blue sky.

This time the planes were set against an almost cloudless sky, and had a long course of blue to traverse before they reached dropping point over the airport. That gave the anti-aircraft an unusually good opportunity to range on them.

At first, the puffs of ackack fire were too high and ahead of the Japs. We saw the silver bodied planes pass under the spotty cloud formed as the bursts spread out and merged. And then the AA began to come on the range. The flashes of the bursts came just in front of the silver-bodied planes; the one bomber in the left side of the formation was hit. We saw the orange flash of the explosion just under his wing, under the starboard motor nacelle, and then the motor began to trail a pennant of white smoke and the plane pulled off and downward, and left the formation.

Just as the plane pulled clear of the formation, another anti-aircraft shell burst directly under the belly of one of the planes at the center of the formation. A tongue of flame spread across the middle of the plane, then receded and was swallowed in a torrent of black smoke, and, in an instant, the plane was nosing straight down toward the ground. Now I saw one wing sheer off as if it were paper, and flutter after the more swiftly falling fuselage. Then the plane simply disintegrated, chunks fluttering away and falling, while the center part of the plane plunged at ever-accelerating speed toward the ground.

By this time the remainder of the Jap bomber formation had passed on out to sea. But one of the planes, possibly crippled by anti-aircraft fire, had become separated from the rest. One of our fighters was quick to pounce on him.

There was quite a group of us on the Point this day, watching the "show." Now they were cheering like a crowd at a football game. "Whoooo-ee," shouted someone, "look at that fighter. He's got him."

The tiny speck of the fighter, looking like a bumblebee in comparison to the bigger, clumsier bomber, was diving now. And we heard the rattlesnake sound of his guns. The bomber slewed, came up in a whipstall, and fell off in a steep dive toward the ocean.

The other bombers had disappeared somewhere in the blue, but we could hear our fighters going after them.

In the beautiful amphitheatre of the sky, the kill of the isolated bomber by the fighter was continuing. We saw the bomber diving straight toward the sea, vertically, but the fighter, like a malevolent mosquito, hovered about the larger object, watching for signs of life.

The bomber dived a few thousand feet, and then, suddenly, pulled out of the dive and climbed straight up into the sky, up and up, like an animal gasping for air in its death struggle.

Quickly, the fighter closed and its machine guns rattled again, for seconds on end, in a long burst. And then the bomber paused, fell off on one wing and with spinning wings fluttered vertically toward Tulagi Bay.

A few seconds later the spinning plane hit the water, and from the spot where it struck came a great backfire of ruddy flame and black smoke. And the watchers on the shore cheered madly, as if our side had made a touchdown.

Back at the airport, we found that the final score for the day was ten bombers and three Zeros; another goodly addition to a total that is mounting much too fast to please the Japs.

Capt. Smith came in to report that he had downed his fourteenth and fifteenth planes today; he did not say so, but it was told at the airport that he has been promoted to the rank of major, an award richly deserved.

We found that Lieut. Ken Frazier (Kenneth D. Frazier of Burlington, N.J.) was the pilot who had destroyed the crippled bomber so spectacularly while we watched from Lunga Point. He had shot down another plane as well.

"The first one went down in flames," he said. "The straggler was simple. I dived on him, saw the tracers falling a little short, pulled up a little, and then watched the chunks fly off the plane."

On one edge of the airfield, we found pieces of the Jap bomber which had disintegrated while we watched. There was quite a large section of the fuselage. The metal seemed much more fragile than the skin of the American bombers I have seen.

The cocoanut grove at one edge of the airfield had been

struck by a stick of large bombs. The craters were huge. But the bombs had hit nothing of value. A 100-pound bomb had smashed directly into a shack, killing one man, destroying some radio equipment. That was the only visible damage of the bombing.

When somebody came into our tent, at about 9:00 o'clock, and shouted, "Get up, fellas, we're moving up the ridge," we did not waste any time, but grabbed helmets and shoes and left. Only a few minutes later, from the ridge-top, we saw a pinpoint of bright green light appear in the sky to the north. The light spread into the glow of a flare, and then we heard the mosquito-like "double-hummer" tone of a Jap float plane. It was "Louie the Louse"—a generic name for any one of the Jap float planes which come to annoy us at night.

"Louie" flew leisurely, as he always does, over the island, dropping more flares, and then we saw the distinctive flashes of naval gunfire coming from the direction of Kukum.

Just as we heard the boom of the gun, the shell whizzed over our heads and crashed a few hundred yards around. There was a second's pause, and then more flashes followed, so continuously that the sky seemed to be flickering constantly, and shells whined overhead almost in column. They kept coming for minutes on end, fortunately hitting the jungle several hundred yards beyond us, skimming over the trees under which we were lying. We simply lay there clutching the side of the ridge and hoping the Japs would continue to fire too high.

The barrage kept up for about twenty minutes, then halted. And we waited in silence—the general and the rest of us lying on the ground, waiting to see if the firing would begin again.

We had just got to our feet when an outburst of rifle and machine-gun fire came from the south, apparently only a few hundred yards away. We wondered then if another big Jap effort to break through our lines had begun.

The firing continued, and the noise was augmented by mortar explosions. Then there came the flash of naval gunfire again, this time from the direction of Tenaru. We hit the deck pronto, but the shells were not coming in our direction. The sound of the explosions indicated they were falling along shore.

Our observation posts reported that four Jap warships—
cruisers and destroyers in the usual force—were swinging
along the beach, bombarding the shoreline at their leisure,
then turning back and making the run in the opposite direction to repeat their performance.

Then the shelling stopped, and gradually, the small arms
and mortar fire coming from the south dwindled in volume.
But we did not go back into the valley to sleep this night. I
slipped my poncho over my head, put on my mosquito headnet and my helmet, and lay down on the top of the hard ridge
to sleep.

SUNDAY, *September 13*

We heard this morning that a Jap patrol nipped off one end
of our outpost line, last night, a few hundred yards south of
the general's CP, on the ridge. That was the firing we heard.
The Raiders, who hold the line, are falling back to a better
position today, in case a big Jap push develops today or tonight. Last night's fighting was only a minor sort of engagement.

Miller and I went to Kukum this morning to watch the
daily air raid, which came in at about noon, on schedule. Interception was good. The bombers got frightened and jetti-
soned their loads. And Zeros and our Grummans had a
terrific dogfight. From Kukum, we could see them dodging in
and out of the towering cumulus clouds, occasionally diving
down over the water. We saw one Wildcat (Grumman) come
diving down like a comet from the clouds, with two Zeros on
his tail. He was moving faster than they, and as he pulled out
of his dive and streaked across the water, he left them behind.
They gave up the chase and pulled sharply back up into the
sky. We had a good view of their long, square-tipped wings,
and the round red ball of the rising sun insignia, as they
turned. They appeared, as the pilots had told me, to be very
maneuverable planes.

Many planes were dogfighting in and about the masses of
cumulus clouds. I watched two planes, one chasing the other,
pop out of the tower of cloud, describe a small, precise semicircle, and go back in again.

A few moments later they made another circle, like two

beads on the same wire. Other planes popped in and out of their levels in the cloud structure, and the whole area of the sky resounded with the rattling of machine guns. With so many guns firing at once, there was a cumulative effect as loud and magnificent as thunder.

Back at air headquarters, we waited for the tally of today's score. It was four bombers, four Zeros.

We went to bed in our tents tonight, but were shortly told to move out and up the ridge-top. This time I had enough foresight to take along a blanket, and my satchel full of notes.

We could hear rifle fire coming from our front lines a few hundred yards to the south. Then machine guns. Flares went up occasionally and shed a glow over the sky.

I spread out my poncho and blanket and tried to sleep. I was awakened by the blasting of our own artillery batteries, to the north of us. The shells were whirring just over our position in the ridge-top, skimming over the trees, then hitting and exploding a few hundred yards to the south, apparently in the area where the fighting was going on.

MONDAY, *September 14*

Shortly after midnight this morning the din of firing grew so tremendous that there was no longer any hope of sleeping. Our batteries were banging incessantly, the rifle and machine-gun fire from the direction of the Raider lines had swelled into a cascade of sound, Louie the Louse was flying about, and flares were dropping north, south, east and west.

We were drawing up a strong skirmish line on the ridge-top. Reinforcements were on their way up. We knew that the Raiders, Col. Edson's people, out on the ridge, had their hands full. We knew then that a major Japanese effort to break through our lines and seize the airport had begun.

Another storm of rifle, machine-gun and mortar fire came now from the direction of Tenaru. Was this another attempt to break through? For the present there was no way to find out.

Naval gunfire began to boom from the north. But it was not coming near us.

The general said to Col. Thomas: "Say, Jerry, ask air headquarters is it feasible to send a plane to see if there are any transports—just to see." The general was as calm and cheery as usual.

Some "shorts" from our own artillery fell in the valley where our tents are located. The flashes were as bright as day. One man standing near where I sprawled on the ground was knocked down by the concussion. We thought at first that the shells were Jap projectiles from their ships, ranging on the CP.

The sounds of firing had now become a din. A gray mist began to drift in among the trees on the ridge. It was thicker in the valley. Was it smoke from our artillery? It might be gas. (It was smoke, released by the Japs to create a gas scare.)

An artillery observer came into our communication dugout and reported to Col. Thomas, who was busy with phone calls, checking on the latest information from all outposts, giving orders. The observer said his telephone line, reaching farther toward the front, had been blown out. He had come back to relay firing instructions to our artillery batteries. He said the Japs were trying to advance down the ridge, but that our artillery fire, coupled with determined resistance from the Raiders on one of the knolls of the ridge, was holding up the enemy.

The observer found a line open from this point back to our batteries. "Drop it five zero and walk it back and forth across the ridge," he said. Then we heard the loud voice of the officer directing the battery: "Load . . . fire!" Then the bang of the cannon, the shells whizzing overhead.

The barrage continued. And after a few minutes, a runner came back from Col. Edson's lines. "Col. Edson says the range is perfect in there," he said, breathlessly. "It's right on. It's knocking the hell out of 'em."

Snipers were moving in on us. They had filtered along the flanks of the ridge, and taken up positions all around our CP. Now they began to fire. It was easy to distinguish the sounds of their rifles. There were light machine guns, too, of the same caliber. Ricocheting bullets skidded amongst the trees. We plastered ourselves flat on the ground.

I went to the communication dugout to see if there might be any room inside. But the shack was filled. I picked a spot amidst some sparse bushes at the foot of a tree. A bullet whirred over my head. I moved to another tree.

A stream of tracer bullets arched through the trees from behind us. We heard Jap .25's opening up from several new directions. It seemed now that they were all around.

The whispered word went round that the Japs were landing parachute troops (later proved false). More reinforcements came through our position on the ridge, while the Japs were firing. But we wondered if we could hold our place. If the Japs drove down the ridge in force, and broke through Col. Edson's lines, they would be able to take the CP. If they had already cut in behind our position, as we suspected they had, they would box us in, and perhaps capture the general and his staff.

But the general remained calm. He sat on the ground beside the operations tent. "Well," he said cheerfully, "it's only a few more hours till dawn. Then we'll see where we stand."

Occasionally, he passed along a short, cogent suggestion to Col. Thomas. He was amused at my efforts to take notes in the dark.

The telephone line to Col. Edson's front had been connected again. The colonel called Col. Thomas to say that the Raiders' ammunition was running low; he needed a certain number of rounds of belted machine-gun bullets—and some hand grenades. Col. Thomas located some of the desired items by phone after a quick canvass. They would be sent over soon, he told Col. Edson.

But at about 3:00 o'clock Col. Edson called again to say that he was "almost out." The ammunition had not arrived.

We were wondering if the Raider line was going to cave in when more Jap planes came over. There were probably two of them. They dropped more flares.

The sounds of heavy firing to our left rear had broken out again. Col. Thomas checked by phone. "It's in McKelvy's area," he said. "The Japs got into his wire."

Snipers were still popping at us from all sides. We had our hands full. But then Col. Edson called back to say that ammunition and grenades had arrived, and the news had a good effect on morale.

At about 4:00 o'clock the snipers were still shooting into our camp, but they had not attacked our skirmish lines on the ridge. Our artillery fire had slackened a little. And the sounds of firing in the Raider area were sporadic. I rolled myself in blanket and poncho (for the early mornings on Guadalcanal are always chill) and lay down in some underbrush on the slope of the ridge. I was able to sleep for about an hour.

As the first light of dawn came, the general was sitting on the side of the ridge, talking to some of his aides. A Jap machine gun opened up, and they high-tailed for the top of the ridge, with me right behind. We were heading for a tent, where we would at least have psychological shelter. Just as we reached the tent, a bullet clanged against a steel plate only two or three feet from us. It was amusing to see the rear ends of the dignified gentlemen disappearing under the edge of the tent. I made an equally undignified entrance.

It was not safe to walk about the camp this morning. Snipers had worked their way into camouflaged positions in trees through the area, and there were some machine gunners, with small, light .25 caliber guns. One had to watch one's cover everywhere he moved.

There were large groups of Japs on the left or east side of the ridge, in the jungles. There was a lot of firing in that area. We had a firing line of men extending south from the CP, out along the ridge, facing those groups of Japs. The men lay along the edge of a road that ran down the exposed top of the ridge, protected only by grass. The Japs were firing at them from the cover of the jungle.

Beyond that firing line, the ridge curved and dipped. It rose like the back of a hog into a knoll, beyond the dip. It was on this knoll that the Raiders had been doing their fiercest fighting.

I worked my way out along the ridge to the firing line, to get a look at the knoll where the Raiders had been fighting. I lay flat next to a machine gunner while the Japs fired at us with a .25 light gun. A man to our right, farther out on the ridge, was wounded. We saw him crawling back toward us, a pitiful sight, like a dog with only three serviceable legs. He had been shot in the thigh. Beyond the bend in the ridge, the machine gunner told me, there were several more wounded. A group of six or seven of our men had been hit by machine-gun fire. Two of them were dead.

In the jungle at the foot of the ridge we heard our own

guns firing as well as the Japs'. Some of our troops were pushing through there, mopping up the groups of Japs.

It was evident that the main Jap attempt, down the top of
the ridge, had failed. I moved out a little farther along the
ridge, nearly to the bend in the road where the wounded lay,
and I could see the knoll where the fighting had been going
on. It was peopled with marines, but they were not fighting
now.

We heard the characteristic whine of pursuit planes coming.
Then we saw them diving on the knoll, and heard their machine guns pop and rattle as they dived. "They've got a bunch
of Japs on the other side of the hill," said a haggard marine
next to me. "That's the best way to get at 'em."

I worked my way back to the CP and got some coffee. I
was cleaning my mess cup when I heard a loud blubbering
shout, like a turkey gobbler's cry, followed by a burst of
shooting. I hit the deck immediately, for the sound was close
by. When the excitement of the moment had stopped, and
there was no more shooting, I walked to the spot, at the entrance to the CP on top of the ridge, and found two bodies of
Japs there—and one dead marine. Gunner Banta told me
that three Japs had made a suicide charge with bayonets.
One of them had spitted the marine and had been shot. A
second had been tackled and shot, and the third had run
away. These three had been hiding in a bush at the edge of
the ridge road, evidently for some time. I had passed within
a few feet of that bush on my way out to the firing line and
back. The animal-like cry I had heard had been the Jap
"Banzai" shout.

Col. Edson and Col. Griffith, the guiding powers of the
Raiders, came in to our CP this morning to make a report to
Gen. Vandegrift and shape further plans. The mere fact that
they had come in was a good sign. It meant that the fighting
was at least slackening and perhaps ending, for they would
not have left their front lines if there had been any considerable activity.

Maj. Ken Bailey, one of the Raider officers and a hero of
the Tulagi campaign, also appeared, dirty and rumpled but
beaming like a kid on the night before Christmas. Bailey
loved a fight. He showed us his helmet, which had been

pierced front and back by a Jap bullet. The slug had grazed his scalp without injuring him.

The Raider officers' conversations with the general and Col. Thomas were held in the general's secret sanctum. But I talked to Col. Edson as he left the shack. He said that the large main body of Japs, who had been trying to drive down the ridge, had fallen back.

He said that a force of between 1,000 and 2,000 Japs had tried to storm the ridge, with lesser forces infiltrating along the base. His estimate of the Jap casualties, at that time, was between 600 and 700 in the ridge area alone. Our artillery fire, he said, had smacked into the midst of a large group of Japs and wiped out probably 200 of them. Our own casualties had been heavy, for the fighting was furious.

The colonel gave the impression that the big battle of the ridge had ended; that the only fighting in the area now was the mopping up of small, isolated Japanese groups by our patrols.

But snipers were scattered through the trees of the area. I had a brush with one of them during today's first air raid.

I was sitting on the side of the ridge that looks over the valley where our tents are located. A throng of Zeros were dogfighting with our Grummans in the clouds and I was trying to spot the planes.

Suddenly I saw the foliage move in a tree across the valley. I looked again and was astonished to see the figure of a man in the crotch of the tree. He seemed to be moving his arms and upper body. I was so amazed at seeing him so clearly that I might have sat there and reflected on the matter if my reflexes had not been functioning—which they fortunately were. I flopped flat on the ground just as I heard the sniper's gun go off and the bullet whirred over my head. I then knew that his movement had been the raising of his gun.

But there was no time to reflect on that fact either. I retreated behind a tent. And then anger caught up with me. Again the war had suddenly become a personal matter. I wanted to get a rifle and fire at the sniper. Correspondents, in theory at least, are non-combatants. Several of our men, however, fired into the crotch of the tree where the sniper was located.

Miller had come in from Kukum, where he spent last night. He and I went out on the ridge, later in the day, to have a look at the battleground. We climbed the steep knoll where our troops had made their stand and turned back the main Jap drive.

The hill was quiet now. Small fires smoldered in the grass. There were black, burned patches where Jap grenades had burst. Everywhere on the hill were strewn hand-grenade cartons, empty rifle shells, ammunition boxes with ragged, hasty rips in their metal tops.

The marines along the slope of the hill sat and watched us quietly as we passed. They looked dirty and worn. Along the flank of the hill, where a path led, we passed strewn bodies of marines and Japs, sometimes tangled as they had fallen in a death struggle. At the top of the knoll, the dead marines lay close together. Here they had been most exposed to Jap rifle and machine-gun fire, and grenades.

At the crest of the knoll we looked down the steep south slope where the ridge descended into a low saddle. On this steep slope there were about 200 Jap bodies, many of them torn and shattered by grenades or artillery bursts, some ripped, a marine told us, by the strafing planes which we had seen this morning. It was up this slope that the Japs had sent their heaviest assaults many times during the night, and each time they tried they had been repulsed.

Beyond the saddle of the ridge rose another knoll, and there we could see more bodies, and the pockmarks of shelling. The whole top of this knoll had been burned off and wisps of smoke still rose from the smoldering grass.

Miller and I still stood on the open crest of the knoll. "Better watch it," a marine said. "There's a sniper in the jungle over there."

We moved away from the hill crest and had walked about fifty feet when we heard a shout behind us. A man had been hit at the spot where we had been standing. He had a bad wound in the leg. Our luck was holding.

We went to Kukum to watch for further air raids. But no more planes appeared until late in the afternoon. In the meantime, we heard heavy artillery pounding into the jungle near Matanikau, and saw smoke rising in great clouds above the trees. We heard that a large body of Japs were trying to make a break-through in that area. The first reports had it that casualties were heavy, but later we found that the fighting here had been only a protracted skirmish and our casualties were few.

It was dusk when Jap seaplanes made a low-altitude attack. Three of them, monoplane float aircraft, passed back and forth over Kukum, drawing streams of anti-aircraft fire. Others swung over the beach farther to the east, and the island became alive with ackack; the sky was trellised with the bright lines of tracer.

Again the Japs dropped many flares, and once we saw an extremely bright white light flaming over the Tenaru, which we thought was a flare—and found out later that it was caused by two Jap planes burning simultaneously.

The Jap planes, we learned at air operations headquarters, had tried to make a bombing attack on the airport. A group of fifteen to twenty Jap seaplanes, slow, ancient biplanes, had sneaked over the mountains in southern Guadalcanal, and tried to make a low-altitude attack. But they had been caught by our Grummans, and nine of them shot down. Four Zero float planes had also been shot down. And in the earlier raid of the day, two Zeros and one bomber had been downed—and the bombers had been turned back long before they reached Guadalcanal. The Jap air attacks of the day, like their land effort of last night, had been a failure.

Tonight the general and his staff had moved from the old CP on the ridge to a slightly safer spot, and of course there had been no time during the day to erect tents, cots or the other elementary comforts of Guadalcanal living. So for the third successive night I slept on the bare ground. The senior surgeon of all Gen. Vandegrift's medical troops lay down near by; he, too, had only a poncho for a mattress, and took the discomfort without complaint. "I'm afraid I'm going to have my joints oiled up a bit if this keeps on," he said. And that was his only comment.

TUESDAY, *September 15*

Yarbrough and Kent have shoved off. They sailed aboard a small ship which came in today and made for a rendezvous with a larger craft. Durdin seems to be somewhat pessimistic about the general situation. Miller and I, being somewhat punch-drunk, are more inclined to view the future cheerfully.

This morning we corraled Col. Thomas and asked him to give us a quick outline of the big battle which has been going on for the last two days. He gave us a lucid summary.

The Japs had assembled three large units of troops, by a process of slow accumulation, said the colonel. Two of these large units, totaling 3,000 to 4,000 and possibly more (the figures were estimates based on the observations of our patrols) were massed to the east of the airport; the third, a smaller group, to the west.

"We couldn't get at them because of the terrain," said the colonel, "although we did raid the landing area of the two eastern detachments." (That was the raid which Col. Edson's troops had made on Tasimboko.)

The three groups made three separate attacks, said the colonel. The principal of these was a drive toward the airfield from the south along the top of Lunga Ridge. It was here that the Raiders had had their tough fight.

Two other, much lighter, attacks were made: one from the west, from the Matanikau area; and the second from the east, which was apparently intended to flank our positions along the Tenaru.

Our patrols discovered several days ago that the two eastern groups were moving in, one on our flank, one swinging around to make an attack from the south, our rear.

"On the night of the 12th and 13th," said the colonel, "the Japs came up from the rear (the south) and infiltrated our lines, but did no damage.

"Then, our outpost line being too long, it was withdrawn several hundred yards. One hour after dark on the night of the 13th-14th, groups of 50 to 100 men each broke through the line and attacked the ridge. Col. Edson moved his men 300 to 400 yards to the rear and took up a position on a rugged hill (the step knoll we had visited on the ridge). At about 11:00 o'clock in the evening, the Japs charged in large numbers. Edson had a few hundred men, the Japs about 2,000. Our artillery fire was laid down, causing many casualties.

From then on until 6 A.M. the Japs made many assaults on the hill, including bayonet charges. They lost 500 men."

On the same night the Japs attacked our eastern flank, but ran into barbed-wire entanglements and retired, leaving about thirty dead Japs in the wire, said the colonel. The attack from the west did not come until yesterday, and, thanks to our artillery and stubborn resistance by our troops, that attempt was also pushed back.

Miller, Durdin and I made another swift survey of the high knoll where Edson's men had fought, and decided that since it had no other name, it should be called "Edson Hill" in our stories.

Later in the day we went to Col. Edson's headquarters to get his story of the battle. He told us about the individual exploits of his men and their collective bravery, but did not mention the fact that he himself had spent the night on the very front line of the knoll, under the heaviest fire.

He did not mention it, but the fact was that two bullets had actually ripped through his blouse, without touching him. Another Raider officer whispered that information to me and I nodded absently, then was startled to see that the colonel was still wearing the garment. Bullet holes marred the collar and waist.

The Raiders told us some good stories of valor; about a sergeant named John R. Morrill (of Greenville, Tenn.), who with two buddies had been cut off from the rest of the marines by a Jap advance. And how Sgt. Morrill had walked with impunity through the Jap positions during the darkness.

Then there was a private, first class, named Ray Herndon (of Walterboro, S.C.), whose squad occupied a very exposed position on the south side of Edson Hill at the time the Japs made their heaviest attacks. The Jap firing hit right into the squad and left only four of them alive, three unwounded, and Ray, hit mortally through the stomach. And then Ray, knowing he was hit badly, had asked one of his buddies to give him a .45 automatic, and said: "You guys better move out. I'm done for anyhow. With that automatic, I can get three or four of the bastards before I kick off."

Then there was a young, round-faced lad from Greensburg, Pa., named Corp. Walter J. Burak, the colonel's runner, who had twice during the night traversed the exposed crest of the ridge the whole distance from the knoll to the general's CP, under the heaviest fire. He had made the first trip with a telephone wire, when the line had been blown out. And the second trip, toting a forty-pound case of hand grenades, when in the early hours of the morning, the shortage of that item became pressing.

But the outstanding story was Lewis E. Johnson's (of De Beque, Col.). Lewis was wounded three times in the leg by fragments of a grenade, and at daybreak placed in the rear of a truck with about a dozen other wounded, for evacuation. But as the truck moved down the ridge road, a Jap machine gunner opened up and wounded the driver severely. The truck stopped. Then Johnson painfully crawled from the rear of the vehicle, dragged himself to the cab, got into the driver's seat, and tried to start the motor. When it would not start, he put the car in gear, and, using the starter for traction, pulled the truck a distance of about 300 yards over the crest of the ridge. Then he got the engine going and drove to the hospital. By that time, he was feeling so refreshed, that he drove the truck back to the front and got another load of wounded.

To get the story of the attacks on the other two fronts, we went first to Col. Cates' headquarters, to cover the attack that had come from the east, and then to Col. Hunt's for news on the attack which had come from the west, the direction of Matanikau.

Col. Cates referred us to Lieut. McKelvy (William N. McKelvy of Washington, D.C.), the immediate commander of the troops who had held back the Japs attacking from the east.

"The entire attack was delivered against a road called the Overland Trial," he began.

"On the night of the 13th–14th, and about 10:15, I heard shooting. At 10:30 Capt. Putnam (Robert J. Putnam of Denver, Col.) called to say that one of his listening posts had been jumped. He said that a man came in to his CP, and as he arrived he said, 'They got 'em all,' and fainted.

"At about 11:00 o'clock, Capt. Putnam called and said the Japs had put out a few bands of fire—a few rifle shots, but that there was nothing serious yet.

"Then everything opened up. There was a terrific outburst

of firing, and Capt. Putnam said, 'They're inside the wire. They're being bayoneted.' We found twenty-seven bodies on the wire in the morning.

"We were putting down our big mortars and all the rest. All the activity was on that one flank. The Japs were trying hard to take the road."

The colonel stopped to get a large map and point out the road, a trail which led from the east into our lines, toward the airport.

"At 5:30 the attack stopped and the Japs withdrew. They didn't want to be caught in daylight.

"That morning—that was the 14th—we were given a reserve of six tanks. There was high grass across from our positions and we were afraid the Japs were lying doggo in there. While the tanks were in, one of our own lieutenants jumped on one of the tanks. He was a Lieut. Turzai (Joseph A. Turzai of Great Neck, L.I.), who had been wounded by shrapnel, and stayed surrounded by the Japs all night.

"Lieut. Turzai told us there were Jap machine guns in a shack in the high grass. Later in the day we sent the tanks after them. They accomplished their mission with some losses. (We lost three tanks when the Japs opened fire at point blank range with anti-tank guns.)

"At 11:00 o'clock last night, the Japs hit us again. It was a minor attack. They shelled us with light mortars.

"Just at daybreak this morning we spotted about 300 Japs in a group. We had our artillery batteries laid for a concentration in that area; the fire fell right on them. They undoubtedly lost a lot of people there."

At Col. Hunt's CP, Lieut. Wilson gave us an outline of the fighting in the Matanikau vicinity. That, too, had been of a minor character compared to the finish fight that had raged along the ridge.

"Yesterday morning, just at daybreak, there was mortar and machine-gun fire into our left flank positions," he said. "Col. Biebush (Lieut. Col. Fred C. Biebush of Detroit, Mich.) was commanding our troops.

"At about 8:30 A.M. there came a bayonet charge. But it was repelled with heavy losses for the Japs. The Japs tried it again at 10:30.

"The Japs tried a break-through between two groups of troops on our left flank. They were trying to see how far our wire extended. They were beaten back.

"At about noontime, a patrol went out to reconnoiter the enemy position. Maj. Hardy (former Capt. Bert W. Hardy), who led the patrol, sent back a message, saying, 'The woods are infested with snipers and automatic riflemen. I am pushing forward.'

"Information gathered by our reconnaissance enabled us to put down a heavy concentration of mortar and artillery fire which stopped the attack."

I slept in a shack at Kukum tonight, on the bare board floor. I came awake, once in the night, to hear people shouting. I asked a man next to me what was happening. He grunted. "Those silly sailors don't secure their boats," he said, "so when Oscar goes by, they all bust loose when his wake hits 'em." But he was wrong. It was not Oscar who had gone by, but a couple of Jap destroyer-type warships, apparently paying us a visit after landing troops at Cape Esperance, to the east.

WEDNESDAY, *September 16*

We had some copy to get to Gen. Vandegrift's headquarters for censorship this morning, and were about to start out for the CP, when an air alert came in. But there was no raid, and we reached our destination with our stories and got them off. Till Durdin feared they would be our last.

Today our dive-bombers and torpedo planes from Henderson Field went north on an attack mission. We checked at the airport later in the day and found that they had been after some Jap cruisers and destroyers located between Bougainville and Choiseul. It was believed they got one torpedo hit on a cruiser and got a bomb hit on a second.

THURSDAY, *September 17*

Till Durdin's worry that our story on the Jap attack might be our last, fortunately is not being substantiated. Things seem to be calming down on Guadalcanal. Our patrols on all our fronts contacted no Japs today, and to the east and south, it seems, they have withdrawn a goodly distance. Along Col.

McKelvy's front, we heard, our troops have found abandoned mortars and machine guns, some of them in brand-new condition, indicating the Japs fled in some haste.

Nor was there any air raid today, although our fighters, Pursuits and Grummans, went down to Cape Esperance on a strafing mission. Again they had found Jap landing boats on the shore there but no Japs visible. Evidently they had landed at night on the regular schedule and had time to take good cover.

The dust is getting thick on Guadalcanal. If you move on the roads now, you stir up a cloud of the dirty gray stuff. Planes and trucks moving across the airport trail huge triangular black clouds. You put on clean clothes at nine o'clock and walk down the road and at 9:30 you look like a chimney sweep. When you ride in a car the dust of passing vehicles chokes your lungs and blots out your vision. We now ride about with our helmets held over our faces in an attempt to keep them relatively clean. Schultz has dug up a pair of fancy polaroid goggles somewhere. Also, incidentally, a cowboy-effect belt set with large paste-stones, ruby and emerald-colored. Where he collects such items on Guadalcanal is a mystery. He has also adopted the glamorous sun-helmet which Yarbrough left behind. Schultz' ambition is to be a state cop in Illinois (he's from Chicago) or a border patrol trooper, after the war.

At air headquarters today we saw a complete tabulation of the number of planes shot down by our fighters to date. The total is 131; of these, our marine fighters (Grummans) have knocked down 109; the Army Pursuits, four; our Navy fighters (also Grummans), who have been here only a short time, seventeen; and one of our dive-bombers got a Zero. Our anti-aircraft batteries, in addition, credited with five.

Of the 131 enemy planes destroyed, about half were fighters or other single-engine planes, and about half the fast, two-motored Mitsubishi 97's.

Today I talked to a Coast Guard seaman named Thomas J. Canavan (of Chicago, Ill.), who had just got back after recuperating from a terrible adventure. That adventure happened about a month ago, when Canavan was out on anti-submarine patrol; there were three small boats in the patrol, and they were surprised by three Jap cruisers and sunk. Canavan was the only survivor. He saved his life by floating in the water, playing dead while one of the cruisers came close by and looked over his "body." Then he swam for seventeen hours, trying to get to Florida Island. He finally made the shore.

Canavan, who still looked and talked as if he could feel a ghost looking over his shoulder, said he had only a cocoanut for nourishment during two days on Florida. This he promptly upchucked. He saw fierce-looking natives with spines of bones stuck through their noses and ran from them, but he found later they had been cordially inclined. For when he woke up after falling asleep exhausted on the beach, he found someone had covered him with palm fronds to protect him from the rain and nightly cold. He tried twice to swim to Tulagi Island, and the first time was thwarted by tides. The second time he succeeded.

Our dive-bombers and torpedo planes laden with bombs went out today to target the buildings of the Cape Esperance area where the Japs have been landing. They reported they set the buildings afire.

There are two persistent reports on the "scuttlebutt" circuit today: one is that reinforcements are coming to Guadalcanal—and, on that count, estimates of numbers vary; and the other is that our aircraft carrier *Wasp* has been sunk.

FRIDAY, *September 18*

The rumor that reinforcements were en route to Guadalcanal was substantiated today, when they arrived. Early this morning, a certain colonel told me: "I can't say anything more about it, but I'd recommend that you go for a walk on the beach." I went to the beach and saw cargo and warships and transports steaming into sight.

Miller and I went to the landing point to watch the ships unload. All along the beach our weary veterans stood and watched the process, passively. We had been talking about reinforcements, and waiting for a long time.

They were marines, these new troops, thousands of them, boatload after boatload; they wore clean utility suits and new helmets, and talked tough and loud as they came ashore.

One of our veterans told me he had been talking to some of the new arrivals. "Chees," he said, "these guys want to tell *us* about the war." And we knew then that it would take some time with these men, as it had with us, to get rid of that loud surface toughness and develop the cool, quiet fortitude that comes with battle experience.

Two correspondents came in with the shiploads of re-inforcements. They are Jack Dowling and Frank McCarthy, who is relieving Miller. Miller was delighted and made much noise about the fact that when he hit the deck of the ship that would take him out of here, he was going to shave off his beard. We all cheered, for Miller's beard is one of the true horrors of Guadalcanal. It is almost as raggedy as my mustache.

A very reputable source told me today that the report of the *Wasp*'s having been sunk is true. He said she took two torpedoes in an isolated attack by a submarine (actually she took three), and was abandoned by her personnel.

Another persistent rumor these days is that our naval forces and the bulk of the Jap Navy in this area have fought a great battle somewhere to the north. But there is no confirmation from any official, or even informed direction. The truth seems to be that there has been no major naval action by surface forces since the battle of Savo Island.

Durdin and I sat on the beach most of the afternoon, waiting for the Jap air raid which we thought was inevitable. Our fleet of cargo and transport ships would make excellent targets. But the Japs, fortunately, did not come this afternoon.

They did come tonight, a force of ships estimated to range from two to six. They were too late, for our ships had gone. But Louie the Louse flew over for some time, dropping flares, looking for our ships, and the Jap ships, probably cruisers, lay well offshore and lobbed shells into our coastline.

SATURDAY, *September 19*

At the airport operations building this morning, we watched our dive-bombers taking off for some mission to the north. Probably bombing Gizo, or Rekata Bay, or one of the other Jap bases in the Solomons. Our people have been attacking some such objective frequently during the last few days, but have not had much luck in catching the Japanese ships, although they have damaged shore installations.

I checked over our records in an attempt to find out just how many ships our dive-bombers are credited with sinking since the first group of planes arrived here nearly a month ago. The total of ships sunk, I found, is three destroyers, one cruiser, and two transports. Probably a dozen other ships, mostly cruisers and destroyers, have been damaged by hits or near misses; altogether a good score, considering the fact that poor weather conditions and night operations generally make the location of the enemy difficult.

Still the enemy landings at Guadalcanal go on. Bit by bit, they are building up their forces—even now, so soon after their second big attack to break through our lines and take the airport has failed. Last night the group of ships which came in and shelled us probably also landed their daily load of troops.

This afternoon we talked with some of the Raiders about the Battle of the Ridge, and heard some interesting stories about the Japs, how, for instance, they often ask to be killed when they are captured, but seem relieved when we do not oblige. Then they feel they have complied with their part of the death-before-dishonor formula, and make no further attempt to deprive themselves of life.

Several of the Jap prisoners captured on the ridge it seems, said "Knife" when they were captured, and made hara-kiri motions in the region of the belly. But when no knife was forthcoming, they seemed relieved, and after that made no attempt to kill themselves.

Later this afternoon we heard that a large body of our troops is going out tomorrow to conduct a reconnaissance in force to the south of the airport, to try to find out how far the Japs have fallen back. Durdin, McCarthy, Dowling and I decided to go along.

Sunday, *September 20*

Our reconnaissance started at about 5:00 o'clock this morning and after that, for thirteen solid hours, we plowed through jungle and slipped and slid up and down the steepest ridges I have ever climbed. It was a lesson in the geography of Guadalcanal which I will not forget.

Much of the time we were hiking was spent in traversing the sides of ridges. The trails were muddy and slippery from rain which fell early this morning, and I found that a tripod posture, the three supports being formed by two legs and one arm, was the best way to stay on your feet.

We also spent considerable time in the thickest and most unpleasant jungles I have seen. We followed trails most of the time, but even these were covered with tangles of brambly vines, prickly leaves and tree branches protected by long spines.

But our group of troops, led by Col. Edson, at least did not run into any Japs. Other groups which joined in our reconnaissance found a few snipers. A group of our new reinforcements fired continuously, as we had done when we first came to Guadalcanal; they were as chary of shadows and as "trigger-happy" as we had been.

We found evidences that the Japs had moved away in a great hurry and in great disorganization. We found bivouac areas where they had left packs, shoes, flags behind. And I spotted a pile of canvas cases by the side of one trail and found they were filled with parts of a serviceable 75 mm. pack howitzer. And others found rifles and ammunition. We found the shattered remains of a few Japs who had been hit by our artillery and others who had evidently died of their wounds.

Today our dive-bombers and torpedo planes had gone out to bomb Rekata Bay, we found on getting back to camp. They had bombed and strafed the base, and uncovered a cruiser near by and got a hit which damaged, but did not sink it.

MONDAY, *September 21*

The ships which brought us reinforcements, also brought supplies, including clothes. I went to the quartermaster depot this morning, got some clothes that smelled delightfully like the dry-goods department in a store, and went up to the Lunga and had a good bath before putting on the new things. Then to Juan Morrera's mess, which the marines call the Book-Cadillac, and afterward felt like a new man.

We sat about at Col. Hunt's CP and talked about the reason for the slackening in the Jap air raids. The optimists said the Japs had taken such a drubbing from our fighters that they had no planes left. The pessimists said the foe were simply consolidating their forces for another and bigger effort; perhaps they would send over more planes less frequently, instead of twenty-five or twenty-seven every day.

TUESDAY, *September 22*

At Kukum this afternoon, I saw Dick Mangrum (now a lieutenant colonel) and Lieut. Turner Caldwell, who led, respectively, the original marine and naval dive-bomber groups which came to this island to work out of Henderson Field. Both Turner's and Dick's original squadrons have been largely supplanted by new fresh groups, but the two leaders continued to fly until recently.

They had both grown thin as scarecrows, since I last saw them, and their faces were haggard. They told me they were exhausted from the night-and-day stint of work they had been doing.

"When the medicos used to tell us about pilot fatigue," said Turner, "I used to think they were old fuds. But now I know what they meant. There's a point where you just get to be no good; you're shot to the devil—and there's nothing you can do about it."

I heard tonight that both Turner and Dick are going to be sent out of Guadal soon for a rest in some peaceful region.

WEDNESDAY, *September 23*

"Signs of civilization are coming to Guadalcanal," said Gen. Vandegrift this morning. He told me how an engineer had come into his quarters and asked where he wanted the light. The general said he was surprised to find that the engineer was actually towing an electric wire behind him. The Jap power house which we had captured was in working order, and they had extended a line to the general's camp.

The general said that he felt our situation on Guadalcanal was brightening a bit. The reinforcements had been a great help, he said, and he seemed assured that the naval protection of our shores would improve. I found out later in the day that

a group of motor torpedo boats are on their way to help protect our coastline from the continued Japanese landings.

There is much "scuttlebutt" about more reinforcements
coming into Guadalcanal. But the general feeling seems to be
that if Army troops are brought in, they will only reinforce,
not supplant, the marines, at least for the time being. The old
dream of being home for Christmas is fading.

Many of our officers, however, are being sent home, to
rest, and to train new groups of troops. That is another sign
that we have reached at least a "breather." And the Japs have
confirmed the impression by abstaining from air-raiding us for
another day, and failing even to send in the usual landing
force of troop-carrying warships this evening.

THURSDAY, *September 24*

We went to the Raiders' CP for breakfast this morning, and
had a good time yarning over pancakes. We talked about
some of the close escapes we have had during this campaign,
and Maj. Ken Bailey, one of the heroes of Tulagi and the
battle on the ridge, said something touching about taking
chances.

"You get to know these kids so well when you're working
with 'em," he said, "and they're such swell kids that when it
comes to a job that's pretty rugged, you'd rather go yourself
than send them."

(Maj. Bailey was killed three days later during a patrol
action.)

Guadalcanal Diary, 1943

Negroes Are Saying . . .

by Roi Ottley

*If I were a Negro I would live in constant fury and prob-
ably would batter myself to death against the bars inclos-
ing my condition.*—Westbrook Pegler

LISTEN to the way Negroes are talking these days!

Gone are the Negroes of the old banjo and singin' roun' the cabin doors. Old Man Mose is dead! Instead, black men have become noisy, aggressive, and sometimes defiant. Actually, this attitude is a reflection of a cold enthusiasm toward the war brought on by what the Pittsburgh *Courier* calls 'The War Against Negroes.' The fact is, there still is considerable doubt and apathy in the minds of the Negro civilian and military populations, which seriously hampers the war effort, particularly among those who are unable to lift their eyes to the hills. This is not the idle speculation of irresponsible observers, but an implacable fact that is revealed by the casual remarks dropped daily by the Negro man-in-the-street, and by his overt acts as well.

Recently a Harlem physician was summoned to court for driving about with a large sign tied to the rear of his automobile. It read:

IS THERE A DIFFERENCE?

JAPS BRUTALLY BEAT
AMERICAN REPORTER

GERMANS BRUTALLY BEAT
SEVERAL JEWS

AMERICAN CRACKERS
BRUTALLY BEAT
ROLAND HAYES & NEGRO SOLDIERS

JOIN THE AUTO CLUB PLACARD BRIGADE

A picture of this inflammatory display was reproduced on
the entire front page of Harlem's *People's Voice*, with a story
applauding the doctor's daring and denouncing his arrest by
the police. Such attitudes are by no means sectional. During a
quarrel with her white employer in Raleigh, North Carolina,
an unnamed Negro woman retorted, 'I hope Hitler does
come, because if he does he will get you first!' She was sent to
prison for three years. Charles Steptoe, a Negro, twenty-four
years of age, was sentenced to ten days in the workhouse because he refused to stand while 'The Star-Spangled Banner'
was played in a Harlem theater. When, in another instance, a
young Georgia-born Negro, Samuel Bayfield, came before
the federal court for sentencing on an admitted attempt to
evade the draft, he was asked where he was born. Bayfield
told the court, 'I was born in this country against my will!' A
Philadelphia Negro truck driver, Harry Carpenter, was held
on charges of treason. He was accused of having told a Negro
soldier: 'You're a crazy nigger wearing that uniform—you're
only out fighting for white trash. This is a white man's government and war and it's no damned good.'

A story is going the rounds in Washington's Negro circles
of an old Negro woman who boarded a streetcar and sat in
the only available seat—one next to a white sailor. He instantly jumped to his feet and angrily stalked off. The Negro
woman calmly spread into the vacancy, and, in mock humil-
ity, said, 'Thanks, son, for the whole seat.' Then she slowly
appraised the white-clad figure. 'Nice suit you're wearing that
Joe Louis bought!'

Sterling Brown, a Negro poet and gifted reporter of Southern life, heard a Negro bragging at a gas station: 'I done
regist. Expect to be called soon. That Hitler. Think he can
whup anybody. I'm gonna capture Hitler. I'm gonna
deliver him to President Roosevelt. At the front door of the
White House.' The white bystanders applauded—but froze

when he added, 'Then I'm gonna fight for some rights over here.'

A reporter for Harlem's *Amsterdam-Star News* interviewed James Miller, a Negro aged sixty-two, who had served thirty years in the Navy, concerning Negroes enlisting in the Navy—'a branch of our military service where they are apparently not wanted,' so one question ran. 'Unless they get the same opportunity as white men,' he said, 'I don't think it fair to mislead them.' A veteran of both the Spanish-American War and the first World War, he was bitter because he recalled how two of his uncles had served the Navy with distinction. It was not until 1922, he recalled, that the Navy set up a Jim Crow policy restricting Negroes to certain branches of the service. The Negro seaman added: 'We're the most loyal race in the world. We're supposed to be citizens of this country and our integrity as soldiers remains unquestioned, but they still don't want us.'

A fairly typical attitude is that of the Negro soldier who said, 'Sometimes I feel very proud of being a member of this big, huge army, until I pick up a paper and see where a Negro soldier was lynched and it makes me feel like, "What am I doin' here!"' Other soldiers are disappointed with their own treatment by the Army. One stationed at a camp deep in the South complained in a letter to a Harlem friend that the post restaurant—where he was stationed—was divided with one side marked 'Colored' and the other 'White.' According to his report, two Negro soldiers went into the 'Colored' section and, finding it crowded, went across into the 'White' one. A white officer was called and ordered them to leave, and when they refused, he had them arrested. 'This,' the letter concluded, 'is just one of the milder insults that we go through down here. It will not be long before the [Negro] boys here will resent these un-American practices. . . .'

This sort of attitude is heard in other quarters. A group of rural Negroes living outside Richmond, Virginia, were having a heated argument over what difference there was between the *old* and *new* Negro. 'Well, as I sees it,' drawled an octogenarian finally, 'when the old Negro was insulted he shed a tear; today, when these young ones is insulted they sheds blood.'

This extravagant talk is perhaps wishful thinking on the

old man's part. What is a fact, though, is that events since Pearl Harbor have stirred a sorely driven people. While Nazi spies and saboteurs went to trial one after another in an atmosphere of judicial fairness and public calm—six Negroes were lynched! One of these, Cleo Wright, was burned, his body mutilated and tied to an automobile, and dragged through the streets of Sikeston, Missouri. Right on the heels of this, a Negro sharecropper, Odell Waller, was executed in Pittsylvania County, Virginia, for the killing of his white landlord, though the liberal opinion of the country, acknowledging extenuating circumstances, clamored for clemency. Yet a week or so later a white man, Eugene Ekland, who vowed to exterminate the Negro race and in the process murdered five Negroes in the nation's capital, was sentenced only to fifteen years in prison! A sort of melancholy footnote was the discovery of two fourteen-year-old Negro boys hanging from a bridge in the town of Meridian, Mississippi. They had been taken from a jail, where they had been confined for reportedly confessing to an attempted rape.

When Southern gentlemen take the law in their own hands, Negro women too are victims. An Army nurse, Lieutenant Nora Green, stationed at the Tuskegee Army Air Corps School, received orders to prepare for overseas service. Before sailing, she went on a shopping tour in Montgomery, Alabama. On her return trip to Tuskegee she boarded a bus, and the white driver pummeled her into unconsciousness following a dispute over the denial of a seat she had reserved in advance. Afterward a Negro editor was heard to say, 'Something like that makes you wonder if Montgomery isn't still the capital of the Confederacy.'

Even before the United States entered the war, disturbing reports were tumbling out of the Army camps. There were race riots at Fort Oswego. Fighting between races at Camp Davis. Discrimination against Negroes at Fort Devens. Jim Crow conditions were prevalent at Camps Blanding and Lee. Stabbings occurred at Fort Huachuca, killings at Fort Bragg, and the edict 'not to shake a nigger's hand' at Camp Upton. Nearly every day reports were heard of Negroes going A.W.O.L. So moved was Harlem's *Amsterdam-Star News* that it described the situation with this headline:

TERROR REIGN SWEEPS
NATION'S ARMY CAMPS
NEGROES GO A.W.O.L.

One morning in the summer of 1941, the New York *Times* calmly reported that following friction with the white population near Little Rock, Arkansas, forty-three Negroes of the Ninety-Fourth Engineers (labor) battalion, stationed at Camp Custer, had departed from the maneuver area. Actually, they had run off to seek safety from violence of the white citizens and state police. 'As we were walking along the highway,' one of the soldiers said afterward, 'we saw a gang of white men with guns and sticks, and white state troopers were with them. They told us to get the hell off the road and walk in the mud at the side of the highway. One of our white lieutenants walked up to a state trooper and said something. I don't know what. Anyway, the trooper told him to get them blacks off the highway "before I leave 'em laying there." Then out of a clear blue sky the state trooper slapped the white lieutenant. . . . Some of our men began to talk about returning to Camp Custer for protection. That night they left by bus, train, and walking. Three of us hopped freight trains after walking forty-two miles to avoid white people, who we felt would attack us because of our uniforms.'

A Negro who has lived in the freer atmosphere of the North and has become aware of his rights will not relinquish them or put up with abuse because he happens to be in the South. That he wears the uniform of the United States Army increases his self-respect. To some Southerners such a man is a dangerous 'nigger' who must be made to 'know his place' — with violence and terror, if necessary. The prejudiced Southerner refuses to accord even the ordinary decencies to the Negro and is not impressed by the statements of the federal government about this being a war for democracy. In his view, democracy is not a way of life for all, but a luxury for better-class white people only.

'Make way for that *white* Lord God Jehovah!'

Senator John D. Bankhead of Alabama expressed the Southern viewpoint in a letter to General George C. Marshall, Army Chief of Staff. He suggested that Northern Negroes be quartered in Northern states only. 'Our people feel,' he said, 'that the government is doing a disservice to the war effort by locating Negro troops in the South in immediate contact with white troops at a time when race feeling among the Negroes has been aroused and when all the energies of both the whites and blacks should be devoted to the war effort.' If Negro soldiers must be trained in the South, he said finally, 'as a result of social and political pressure, can't you place Southern Negro soldiers there and place the Northern Negro soldiers in the North, where their presence is not likely to lead to race wars?'

The South proposes to be unbending in extending even the simple dignities to an Army uniform—if a Negro wears one. Negroes are equally insistent that, if they must die as equals, then they must be treated as equals. These sharply differing views met head-on in a flare-up at Fort Bragg, North Carolina, the result of an affray in which a Negro soldier and a white military policeman were killed. In this instance, however, the killing of the white man was the act of a Southern Negro whose resentments against injustice mounted to a desperate thrust for human dignity. The soldier, Ned Turman, had voiced objections to an attack on a fellow Negro soldier and, for his pains, was clubbed over the head by two white M.P.'s. In wrestling to protect himself, the Negro managed to snatch the gun of one of his assailants. Brandishing it, he stepped back and cried, 'I'm gonna break up you M.P.'s beating us colored soldiers!' And with that he fired the fatal shot. The other white M.P., standing near-by, shot the Negro to death. After the shooting, whole companies at Fort Bragg not involved in the affair—their Negro officers included—were forced to stand all night with their hands above their heads while armed military policemen patrolled the camp.

This affair occurred before the war. Today, with national unity desperately needed, racial tensions have increased rather than abated. The N.A.A.C.P. urged the War Department to include in its military instructions courses on the racial implications in the war, believing that such instructions were greatly needed to counteract racial bigotry. The suggestion was courteously but firmly turned down. Meanwhile, friction

between white and Negro troops reached a critical stage at
Fort Dix, in New Jersey, which certainly suggests that the
problem is not sectional. Three soldiers were killed and five
wounded in a fifteen-minute gun battle. According to the official Army version, the trouble started when a soldier stepped
out of a telephone booth in the Waldron Sports Palace, an
amusement center across a highway from a Negro barracks,
and two other soldiers in the waiting line outside the booth
made a simultaneous rush for it. A scuffle ensued, the military
police were called, and they attempted to separate the participants. A Negro lunged for the M.P.'s pistol, but only ripped
the holster and then ran out of the tavern.

The M.P. ran after him, commanding him to halt, and
fired a warning shot into the air. This was the signal for a
fusillade of rifle shots from the Negro barracks across the
road. One of the M.P.'s fell mortally wounded at almost the
first volley. White and Negro soldiers began pouring out of
the tavern and the barracks. The military police were called
out, and a battle began from opposite sides of the highway.
The M.P.'s were armed with pistols and the colored soldiers
with rifles. At the height of the battle, two white officers
came running up the highway, yelling the order to cease firing, and both sides obeyed. By then about fifty shots had
been fired. Fifteen Negroes were involved and fifty white
military policemen.

There was more to this affair than met the eye. Under-
scored by smoldering resentments, the gunplay had climaxed
a series of Negro-white clashes, caused mainly by an influx of
a detachment of Southern M.P.'s. Until that time relations
between Negro and white troops were on the whole good,
and were steadily getting better. A Negro officer told a *PM*
reporter that soon after the arrival of the M.P.'s, 'they immediately started kicking the Negro troops around. They'd flare
up at the drop of a hat. Things were especially bad on buses
to and from camp. If the bus was filled and Negro soldiers
had seats, those Southern M.P.'s would order them to stand
up and surrender their places to whites.' Fights became frequent. Race friction increased. Morale declined noticeably.
The Negro regiment, it should be mentioned, was the same

unit whose commanding officer, Colonel Riley E. McGarragh, posted a particularly offensive notice at temporary regimental headquarters at Marcus Hook, Pennsylvania:

> Any cases between white and colored males and females, whether voluntary or not, is considered rape and during time of war the penalty is death.

This order was later rescinded following protests from Negro organizations. 'I've been at Fort Bragg, where things were bad enough,' said the Negro officer. 'But this is worse. Hell may break loose unless something's done quick.' He felt the situation could be improved by removing the Southern M.P.'s because 'the colored man gets on well with Northern soldiers, and even with many Southerners who've learned that we've got to fight against a common enemy, not against each other.' Evidently the authorities paid him no mind. A few months later, Fort Dix was the scene of another fatal brawl in which a Negro soldier was killed.

'It is all right to be loyal if it is encouraged,' ran a letter to the editor of Harlem's *Amsterdam-Star News*. 'But I fail to see where America is doing anything to encourage the loyalty of black men. . . . Remember, that which you [Negroes] fail to get now you won't get after the war.' That comment appeared one week after Pearl Harbor. The issue of the paper that published this comment contained twenty articles by staff writers which dealt critically with the treatment of Negroes. Two weeks later, sixty prominent Negroes met in New York City in a conference called by the N.A.A.C.P. and the National Urban League to consider the Negro's part in the war effort. The group passed with only five dissenting votes a resolution introduced by Judge William H. Hastie, then civilian aide to the Secretary of War, that 'the colored people are not wholeheartedly and unreservedly all out in support of the present war effort.' Walter White, executive secretary of the N.A.A.C.P., attributed this country-wide apathy of Negroes to discrimination in the Army, Navy, and Air Corps, and especially in the war industries.

This situation has its roots in the very immediate past. In the first World War Negroes at once sought to participate as soldiers. With full consciousness of their duties as citizens and with the desire to act the rôles of men, they gladly bore their share of the war effort. W. E. B. Du Bois, then the acknowledged leader of the Negro community, articulated the race's view toward the conflict in his now famous 'Close Ranks' statement to the nation as well as to certain skeptical Negroes:

We of the colored race have no ordinary interest in the outcome. That which the German power represents spells death to the aspirations of Negroes and all dark races for equality, freedom, and democracy. Let us not hesitate. Let us, while this war lasts, forget our special grievances and close ranks shoulder to shoulder with our own white fellow-citizens and the allied nations who are fighting for democracy. We make no ordinary sacrifice, but we make it gladly and willingly with our eyes lifted to the hills.

This stirred Negroes in 1918. The conditions facing Negroes did not cause any lag when the call for volunteers was heard. Also, more than two million Negroes were registered under the Selective Service Law, and more than three hundred thousand were called. To the number drafted throughout the country were added 37,723, representing the Negro regulars and National Guard members. About two hundred thousand saw service in France, fifty thousand in actual combat. The fighting units constituted the 92d and 93d Divisions. To the 92d was attached the 367th United States Infantry, popularly known as the 'Buffaloes,' while the 15th Regiment (the New York National Guard) was part of the 93d. Two Negroes, Henry Johnson and Needham Roberts, were the first American privates to receive the *Croix de Guerre*, the French award for bravery.

Not until the war was over did the full measure of ill-treatment meted out to the Negro troops come to light and then only after Du Bois had visited Europe in 1919 to attend the Pan-African Congress. Documentary evidence of the discriminatory conditions faced by Negro troops was published by *The Crisis* magazine. One section alone will illustrate the attitude of the American high command, a memorandum called 'Secret Information Concerning Black American Troops.' It began with this statement:

It is important for French officers who have been called upon to exercise command over black American troops, or to live in close contact with them, to have an exact idea of the position occupied by Negroes in the United States. The information set forth in the following communication ought to be given to these officers and it is to their interest to have these matters known and widely disseminated. It will devolve likewise on the French Military Authorities, through the medium of Civil Authorities, to give information on this subject to the French population residing in the cantonments occupied by American colored troops.

Here are a few typical passages:

We must prevent the rise of any pronounced degree of intimacy between French officers and black officers. We may be courteous and amiable with these last, but we cannot deal with them on the same plane as with the white American officers without deeply wounding the latter. We must not eat with them, must not shake hands or seek to talk or meet with them outside of the requirements of military service. . . .

Make a point of keeping the native cantonment population from 'spoiling' the Negroes. [White] Americans become greatly incensed at any public expression of intimacy between white women and black men. . . .

The increasing number of Negroes in the United States (about 15,000,000) would create for the white race in the Republic a menace of degeneracy were it not that an impassable gulf has been made between them . . .

This indulgence and this familiarity are matters of grievous concern to the Americans. They consider them an affront to their national policy. They are afraid that contact with the French will inspire in black Americans aspirations which to them [the whites] appear intolerable. . . .

It developed that the Negro soldiers had themselves found a way of showing resentment. In a field near Metz on Thanksgiving evening in 1918, the regiment whose bravery in combat in the great offensive at Champagne had only a month before earned it the *Croix de Guerre* (their casualties were eleven hundred) was ordered to sing 'My Country, 'Tis of Thee.' The music boomed and the soldiers, the black warriors from America, some three thousand of them, stood silent with grim and sober faces. From all that great assemblage rose only the voices of the regiment's six white officers!

While these were the conditions abroad, the Negro civil population was the victim of some of the bloodiest race riots in American history. Even regiments in training in the United States were forced to undergo indignities and violence. One regiment was sent to Spartanburg, South Carolina, and at once the men were beset by Jim Crowism. The white population was no less considerate. The proprietor of a local hotel ordered a Negro officer named Noble Sissle, today a well-known band leader, to remove his hat when he entered the lobby—contrary to Army regulations—and kicked him into the street when he refused. A riot was averted only by the restraining influence of Lieutenant 'Jim' Europe, the regiment's popular band leader. On another occasion fifty Negroes marched on the city to 'avenge' two missing buddies and only the efforts of a sympathetic white colonel prevented bloodshed.

At the close of the war, administration leaders began a campaign to convince Negroes that no great change in their traditional position in America could be expected. With such a government policy, Negroes became the victims of new outrages throughout the country. Even the Ku Klux Klan was revived. In view of these events, Du Bois was forced to confess that he was less sure today than then of the soundness of his war attitude. 'I did not realize the full horror of war and its wide impotence as a method of social reform,' he wrote sadly. 'I doubt if the triumph of Germany in 1918 could have had worse results than the triumph of the Allies. Possibly passive resistance by my twelve millions to war activity might have saved the world for black and white. . . .'

Today, the prejudice shown by Army officials seems very little different from that of yesterday. Reports have trickled back from England—to illustrate—that the American high command is attempting to impose various forms of segregation and discrimination on the Negro troops. The British liberal *New Statesman and Nation* reports examples of discrimination and even assault against Negro soldiers. A British soldier wrote to complain that in a certain English port, Negroes were barred from a well-known restaurant. He said English soldiers were instructed not to eat and drink with Negroes, and restaurant employees were told to bar them. 'I have met [white] Southerners,' an English writer said, 'who seemed rational enough until the Negro problem was mentioned, and who would then show a terrified, lynching spirit, which was about the ugliest thing imaginable.' He also noticed that they 'took it for granted that it is their duty to interfere if they see black troops with white girls.' A most recent episode involves a Southern white soldier who was invited to an English home, and created a scene when he discovered that a fellow guest was an American Negro soldier. He attacked the Negro in the presence of the guests, ruining the evening for everybody.

The *New Statesman and Nation* made this significant comment:

> What is to be done? The American government must face the problem itself. It must use every device of persuasion and authority to let white Southern troops know that it is against discipline to treat Negro soldiers in the way to which their training and education has accustomed them. . . . If things are left to drift, unhappy incidents will occur . . . and the British will instinctively take the side of the Negroes against their white assailants.

One interesting fact about these reports is that they were passed by the British censor, which may suggest the emergence of a new British policy on race. Even the conservative elements in the House of Lords have been stirred. The Lord Chancellor, Viscount Simon, is quoted as attacking a proposal to accept the American segregation pattern with the indignant retort: 'I do not suppose Lord Shaftesbury is proposing that any distinction should be drawn between white and colored soldiers. That is the last thing the British Parliament would tolerate for a moment.'

From all reports, Negro troops are very popular with the English people, who have arranged many entertainments for them—much to the disgust and indignation of some white Americans. This very spirit in certain unrelaxing whites is what caused a bloody race riot in the United States, when two thousand whites engaged in pitched battle with five hundred Negroes to prevent them from occupying the Sojourner Truth Homes, a Detroit housing project built with public funds for Negro war workers. Immediately, this occurrence was seized upon by Axis agents to stir up racial strife and disrupt war production. Mob rule gripped one of the country's principal arteries of war industry, and demonstrated the federal government's weakness on the race issue.

A firm stand by the government on racial questions, would be translated into acts by the humblest white citizen in America—not to mention the white troops abroad. More important, though, is the fact that native Fascists, prodded by Axis agents, defied the government in Detroit. This riot was perhaps one of the most successful acts of sabotage during this war. At secret meetings, Ku Kluxers received orders to keep the Negro workers from entering their new homes. The F.B.I. investigation revealed surprising scope to Ku Klux Klan activities in Detroit, even to boring from within labor's ranks, and to links with Axis agents. The National Workers' League, a pro-Nazi group whose officials were later indicted, cooperated with the Klan in preparing and staging the subsequent riot in which scores of people were injured.

Today, however, the importance of millions of Negroes is being increasingly recognized in administration circles—to wage total war, a total population must be set in motion. The President wrote the N.A.A.C.P. convention in the summer of 1942: 'I note with satisfaction that the theme of your significant gathering read, "Victory Is Vital to Minorities." This theme might well be reversed and given to the nation as a slogan. For today, as never before, "Minorities Are Vital to Victory."' The status of the Negro in 1942 is considerably different from that of 1917. For one thing, his opportunities are definitely broadening, but only under public pressure. For example, an aviation unit was established at Tuskegee, though there is provision to train only a dozen Negro pilots a year. With few exceptions, the officer personnel is Negro. The ranking administrative officer is Lieutenant Colonel Benjamin O. Davis, Jr., a graduate of West Point in 1936, son of Brigadier General Benjamin O. Davis, first and only Negro general. This fact, incidentally, reminds me that in the last war, to prevent the promotion that was rightfully due him, the ranking Negro officer, Colonel Charles Young, was retired on the pretext that he suffered from high blood pressure. To prove

that he could withstand the rigors of a military campaign, he
rode horseback from Chillicothe, Ohio, to Washington, D.C.!

Decidedly on the credit side of the ledger has been the
partial removal of a long-standing discrimination in the Navy.
It recently agreed to enlist Negro 'reservists,' a step forward,
since it hitherto admitted Negroes only in the most menial
capacities. Unfortunately, this development was marred by official Jim Crow, Negroes having been placed in distinct units
separate from the whites. At the outbreak of the war abroad,
there were about fourteen thousand Negro soldiers in the
Regular Army, whereas only about four thousand of some
hundred and forty thousand enlisted men in the Navy were
Negroes. The draft brought many hundreds of thousands into
the Army. The War Department has announced that at full
strength there will be three hundred and seventy-five thousand Negro soldiers in the Army. However, the Army's more
liberal policy toward Negroes has not been duplicated by the
Navy— This is, however, somewhat like a choice between the
frying pan and the fire. The Army is training several thousand
Negro officers, but the Navy has made no provision for training officer material. A high degree of morale has been attained at the Army's Officer-Candidate Infantry School at
Fort Benning. Here—on Talmadge's Georgia soil—white
and Negro candidates attend the same classes, eat in the same
mess hall, sleep in the same barracks, and generally fraternize
together. There have been no racial incidents. Encouraging
too was the launching of the merchant ship *Booker T. Washington*, with a mixed crew of Chinese, Filipinos, Negroes, and
whites, and with a Negro captain, Hugh Mulzac, in full
charge of operations. Incidentally, a former British seaman, he
sailed his first ship in the United States under the colors of
Marcus Garvey's Black Star Line.

These things represent progress. Witness the acts of Negroes. During a drive in Austin, Texas, three Negro brothers—Arthur, Felix, and Osle Jackson—each bought twenty
thousand dollars' worth of war bonds. Eddie Anderson, the
Negro comedian known as 'Rochester,' invested his earnings
in a San Diego parachute factory—and significantly enough,
employs Negro, Mexican, and white workers. Two song writers, Andy Razaf and Eubie Blake, turned out a patriotic song

called 'We Are Americans Too,' which is currently popular in Negro communities. While pro-Axis agitators shout, the masses of Harlem seek to be included in the war program and confidently carry out the tasks assigned them. For instance, the Negro community has shown better discipline during the city-wide blackout tests than any other area, according to the city officials. Said Newbold Morris, President of the City Council, 'If you give Harlem a chance, the people will respond.'

Listen to the simple faith of a Negro youngster. Alice Godwin, a Harlem high-school student, wrote the following composition in her French class:

> I am a member of a race without a chance to do what it wants to do and without liberty in the whole world. I have been told that this war is a war for liberty for everybody. That is the reason this war is important to me. . . . It is with great fear that I consider my future under the heel of Hitler. He has said, hasn't he, that I am only half of a human creature? . . . I shall be glad to wear old shoes not in style. These things are very little compared with the suffering in a world under Hitler. Each little sacrifice I make, I make joyously. It is for a new world, tomorrow, isn't it?

Hope among Negroes rides high. But a minority of vocal whites are determined that the Negro shall not advance. When white liberals and the federal administration appease such elements, the Negro's thinking is confused and his morale lowered. The almost insurmountable prejudice of employers and backward labor unions is no abstraction—but a solid fact the Negro faces day after day. He well knows there are white men in America who would rather lose the war— even their own freedom—than see any change in the racial *status quo.* This attitude has received provocative encouragement from Axis sources.

One of the curious paradoxes of this war, despite its notorious ballyhoo of racism is the fact that Nazi agents have attempted to capitalize on the dissatisfaction of Negroes as well as whites. Adolf Hitler himself seems to have set the pattern. Back in the spring of 1932, he entertained a Georgia-born Negro, Milton S. J. Wright, in a dinner party at the Europäisch Hof, a fashionable hotel in Heidelberg. The Nazi leader had invited Wright, then a student at Heidelberg University, to

talk with him about life in the United States. 'As I recall,' says
Wright, today a professor at Wilberforce University, 'he mentioned the names of Booker T. Washington, Paul Robeson,
Jack Johnson, Florence Mills, W. C. Handy, Josephine Baker,
and the Scottsboro boys.' He spoke loudly, long, and with air
of authority on American affairs, but stung his Negro guest
with this:

'Negroes must be definitely third-class people,' Hitler said
slyly, 'to allow the whites to lynch them, beat them, segregate
them, without rising against their oppressors!'

A report of this incident was printed in the Negro press.
Obviously handicapped by loud pronouncements of 'Aryan'
racial superiority, the Nazi agents—Negro and white—have
made some amazing détours. Both in the French colonies and
the United States, they have tried to rouse the black man
against the Jew. Sometimes they have baldly tried to convince
Negroes that the Nazis are not anti-Negro. Mercer Cook, a
Negro professor at Atlanta University, tells the story of a German professor in a Negro college who invited Jesse Owens to
his class to counteract what he called 'the charges of the Jew-
financed American press.' He informed his students that the
Nazis had treated the colored athletes with every consideration during the 1936 Olympic Games, and that Hitler had
not refused to shake the hands of the 'black auxiliaries.'

The Berlin incident once came up in my conversations with
Jesse Owens. When he arrived in New York from abroad, I
was one of several hundred newspapermen—Nazi and Japanese correspondents included—who met the boat on his return. The American reporters showered him with questions as
to how the Nazis had treated the Negro athletes. He was
evasive—at least so I felt. After this mass interview, Owens
and I, along with two other Negro Olympic competitors,
rode up to Harlem in a taxi and I again put the question to
him point-blank. He told me candidly—as one Negro to another—that the Nazis bent backward in making things comfortable for them, even to inviting them to the smartest hotels
and restaurants. If the Nazis disapproved of the American Negro athletes' associations with the German girls, the athletes
said, nothing in what they said or did suggested it. But we
know now that that was a shrewd bit of propaganda by the

Nazi leaders, for the story was widely if naïvely told in Negro circles!

Negroes in America have even received reports that the Nazis have cleverly postponed the application of Hitler's anti-Negro dictums in France—perhaps because of the increasing importance of Africa in the war. Mercer Cook, a student of French life, received a report of a Negro soldier from Guadeloupe, demobilized in June, 1940, and about to return to his native land, who was convinced that he had nothing to fear from the Nazis and was persuaded to continue his work on the *agrégation* at the Sorbonne. Even Negroes married to 'Aryans' have been permitted to remain in business in the Paris area. The French Negro author, René Maran, whose *Batouala* won the Goncourt Prize in 1921 and was widely read by American Negroes, was forced to go into hiding in 1940. Yet, after a year of ominous silence, he was again published. Today he is believed to have returned to his apartment in the rue Bonaparte, and in the summer of 1942 received the Grand Prix Broquette-Gonin, awarded by the French Academy. Perhaps to offset the acts of the Negro Governor Félix Eboué, who brought French Equatorial Africa to the side of democracy and gave the Free French movement a territorial base, Hitler allowed Marshal Pétain to name a Martinique Negro, Senator Henry Lémery, as Minister of Colonies! Actually, though an admitted descendant of slaves, he espoused the Rightist cause and openly admired Léon Daudet. Last reports have dispelled this short-lived illusion. In a reshuffle of the Pétain cabinet, Lémery disappeared on Hitler's order.

Negroes today boldly look beyond the horizon of the Negro community, even beyond the borders of the United States, and are concerned with the condition and future of colored peoples elsewhere in the world. Harlem's *People's Voice*, in a long editorial, observed that 'The United Nations must immediately rethink the entire Colonial Problem,' and concluded with the remark, 'The Axis can only be beaten by a free world.' The recent outbreak of rioting at Nassau in the Bahamas, which assumed the proportions of a labor revolt, was not lost on American Negroes. Native despair and unrest in Jamaica, in the face of increasingly serious food shortages, which are being felt throughout the Caribbean, have brought

Negroes to voice their indignation to the British and American governments.

Negroes sometimes suspect that there is a tacit understanding among English and American leaders to limit democracy to white men only. Observations of this character are suggested by the demand of the British government that the United States send no American Negroes to work on the West Indian bases; and, what is more important, the fact that the American administration quietly acquiesced. Nor are such feelings dispelled by revelations of wage differentials. Congressman Vito Marcantonio called attention to conditions existing at Borinquen Field, Puerto Rico, where skilled white workers received a dollar and fifty cents per hour and native skilled workers only forty cents per hour.

Negroes are keenly conscious of the ironic fate which has thrown Africa into the vortex of struggling empires. The war's objectives of freedom and democracy are ardently desired by American Negroes for the Africans, who are playing no small part in the contribution of men and resources for the defense of democracy. Du Bois, in a recent lecture at Yale University, expressed the general attitude of American Negroes. He stressed the fact that the white world had millions of dollars invested in Africa, which obviously makes that continent an important part of the world economy. Yet in current plans and discussions, nothing is said about its future. If white America is little concerned, certainly such groups as the African Students' Association in the United States are keeping the issue alive among American Negroes.

These issues are of undoubted propaganda value to the Axis. The unyielding attitude of Britain in India, with the American government's tacit support of this policy, has been the subject of much discussion in Negro circles. To Negroes, these issues are tied to the ultimate objectives of the war! Said the *Courier* editorially, 'The rule of India, like that of other colonies, is based on military force, and when that force remains in the hands of alien rulers there can be no real independence nor successful defense against foreign invaders, as recently demonstrated in Malaya, Burma, and Java.' Pearl Buck, very much admired by Negroes, has expressed the view

that the progressive character of the war changed when Indian freedom was rejected.

What all this adds up to in the minds of Negroes is a pattern of continued white domination of colored peoples.
Therefore conflicts between the races are regarded as inevitable—that is, without cooperation and desire by whites to
see that freedom is the desire and right of all peoples. These,
and manufactured issues, are daily dinned into the ears of
black men by the Axis. From Berlin, of all places, a broadcast
was heard commenting upon the announcement of a new all-
Negro United States infantry division. Said the announcer:
'President Roosevelt stated recently that he was against race
discrimination. One might ask the President why he was segregating Negroes in a special troop.'

'New World A-Coming,' 1943

The Girls of Elkton, Maryland

by Mary Heaton Vorse

IT WAS pay day at the munitions plant. There seemed to be a run on the bank at Elkton. The queue extended a half block down the street. There were girls in slacks and coats, bright kerchiefs on their heads, girls in navy reefers, even a few girls in fur coats. They came out of the bank smiling. They felt rich. "I've got as much money as Carter's got Little Liver Pills," said one girl. A pay check of around sixty dollars every two weeks looks good. More girls were packing into the Greyhound bus to spend their money in Wilmington. "Looks like the Black Hole of Calcutta," a woman commented. "It's worse'n the subway rush."

The Elkton post office was almost as crowded as the bus, and a queue like a serpent wound around the lobby of the new gray-stone building. The girls were sending off packages. The little town was crammed to bursting with girls. Houses were full, restaurants were full, stores were full of war workers. The population of 3,800 has doubled. The conversion of a local factory to a munitions plant was followed by further expansions and additions until the plant now employs many thousands. Another munitions company nearby added nearly 2,000 more; 80 per cent of both are women. Girls between eighteen and twenty-five are what both companies prefer.

These girls are part of the vast migration that's going on all over the country. They are the pioneers in the mobilization of the great army of women workers. Many of them are on their first jobs.

Ask a group of girls why they came and you get answers like this: "I wanted to help." "My husband's in the Navy. I felt nearer to him, working like this." "My brother enlisted. I wanted to enlist too."

They have come for service but they have come for adventure also. Their one discipline is that of the munitions plant.

They are accountable to no one. They are the recruits of industry and like the boys in the armed forces they are eager for life, eager for fun. They want to dance. There is a massed vitality in these girls that is formidable, and their coming has changed the life, not only of Elkton, but of the whole county.

Before the war the most restful spot between Wilmington and Washington was lovely Cecil County, Maryland. Elkton is the county seat. Its citizens are conservative and have deep-seated convictions which came from the past. It is largely a dairy-farming community and its pleasant people were free from the problems of an industrial age. They were modestly prosperous, even during the depression.

Off the great highways flowing north and south, nothing disturbed the somnolence of Cecil County except the wedding shouts of Elkton's many marriages. Elkton is the great American Gretna Green. There are large blue signs with foot-high letters—MARRIAGES • MINISTER—on all the roads leading to town. The nuptial glee of its elopements (6,000 last year) resounds through the hotels until far into the night.

War shocked the contented community into a reluctant awakening. Not only Elkton, but the other nearby communities, had small munitions factories, each employing a few hundred workers. To the south there was a Naval Training Station, and ten thousand construction workers spilled over the countryside seeking rooms as they prepared the quarters for the naval trainees. The population of the county doubled even before the Naval Training Station added its thousands more.

The draft and the munitions plants between them took the workers from every other enterprise. People sold their dairy farms because there was no one left to milk the cows. By June, 1941, half the stores and all the restaurants displayed "Help Wanted" signs. Household help had practically vanished.

The local children felt the stir of change. Families were upset and family life disrupted because parents in war jobs worked on different schedules. Delicate as a seismograph, the Office of Child Welfare recorded the upset state of Cecil County. Little girls ran away in unprecedented numbers. Boys took to pilfering and "borrowing" cars. The load of juvenile delinquency bounced up. This occurred even in families where parents had not gone away. The less stable of the children felt the impact of war.

The very appearance of the Elkton streets changed. At night girl war workers who had no other place to go strolled up and down. Car prowlers from Wilmington swooped by, agog for a pickup. It got so that nice Elkton girls would not go uptown for a walk or to have a soda at Lyons' drug store. Sailors from the Naval Station jostled soldiers from Aberdeen, and it was necessary to clap on an eleven o'clock curfew. "Be whoopin' it up all night with the twelve o'clock shift, else," people said.

Married couples coming to work could not find a place to stay, and they doubled in with other people. Quickly there was overcrowding. Promising little slums sprang up here and there. Three families lived where one had been before. While there was neither the crowding nor the profiteering that there had been in some boom towns, there was not an empty room in Elkton.

One man even moved out of his home and rented the rooms to twenty-two girls at three dollars and fifty cents apiece. Four girls sleep in the living room, two in the kitchen. There is only one bathroom for the whole lot and the sun porch is the only place not occupied by beds. But there is never a vacancy in this crowded house. The girls say of the hostess: "She treats us like a mother. She comes to see us every day."

The presence of many Negro workers made another problem. Elkton has a Negro population of five hundred. Their houses are small, their families are large. There was no place to put the more than doubled colored population which flowed into town. Colored workers sat up all night in kitchens and sitting rooms, since their hosts had no beds for them; girls who came in jitneys and jalopies in the first rush sometimes worked by day and slept cramped in the cars.

Their pastor, The Reverend D. M. Collins, is the only one to look out for their interests, and he meets almost as many emergencies as there are days. Over Thanksgiving he housed fifteen

stranded people—men, women, and children, migratory
workers from Florida who had just finished digging potatoes
in New Jersey. They had heard Elkton described in glowing
terms by someone they believed was connected with the
plant; so there they were.

The company does not assume any responsibility for the
Negro girls that come looking for work, nor for finding them
places to live, as it does for the white girls. The theory is that
the Negroes employed shall all commute, and if they come to
Elkton they come at their own risk. There is one small Negro
restaurant, and unless the girls have kitchen privileges they eat
bakery stuff and sardines in their rooms. In the plant they
mostly work in separate departments from the white girls,
though there are some white foremen who direct the Negroes. Of course numerous local people expected "trouble,"
but there hasn't been any. The only ripple has been caused by
some Northern white girls who twit the Southern girls about
their attitude toward the Negroes.

In the end one problem piled on another created a situation too difficult for a small community to meet. There wasn't
enough of anything—rooms, food, or restaurants. There was
no place for sick people and not a single place of amusement,
except a couple of small movie houses, for the crowds of boys
and girls adrift on the streets. Even the water system was
overtaxed. Moreover the town sulked at what were euphemis-
tically referred to as "certain elements" in the plant, and certain elements in the plant feuded with the town. In the
newspaper office, courthouse, and stores people were saying,
"They can't cram those girls down our throats." Elkton practiced an almost Gandhi-like non-co-operation with anything
which altered its way of life.

Stores were slow to enlarge their stocks to cater to the girls'
needs, though seven thousand girls wanting shoes and clothes
streamed through the town daily with money to spend. Instead of new restaurants opening, the difficulties of getting
equipment, help, and even food were so great that restaurants
closed or opened under new management. Only one new
shop opened. The Housing Director of the company, Mrs.
Margaret Cronin, always looking as if she had stepped from

the pages of *Vogue*, sponsored the Victory Shop, which had a full assortment of what the well-dressed war-worker should wear.

Shock followed shock for Elkton's inhabitants. On October 12, 1942, people noticed that the Navy, complete with soup kitchen, was encamped down by the primary school. At first they thought this was only a maneuver. Consternation spread through the town when it was found that the Navy was taking over the plant, and that the Vice President and Manager of the plant was in the hands of the F.B.I. under charges of bribery.

From then until the end of December, 1942, Commander A. B. McCrary was the head of the plant.

Shock No. 2 was the letter in the newspaper which the Commander addressed to the town, in which he raked Elkton over the coals. If he did not call them a generation of vipers, he implied that they hadn't done right by our Nell, and that they were holding out on rooms for the girls employed in the plant. He asked for a recount of Elkton's housing facilities.

A delegation of indignant citizens waited upon him. They pointed to the fact they had a Housing Committee and a Nutrition Committee, and that dances for the girls had been given in the Armory, and that everyone had rented rooms to the girls. A recanvass of the town revealed less than a dozen empty rooms. Elkton was chock-a-block, and the people felt vindicated.

The Commander wrote another letter to the paper, to the people of Elkton, explaining that he had received his information from sources animated with too great zeal for the girls' welfare. The explosion cleared the air. Then the U.S.O. moved into Elkton. The organization proved to be the catalyst that precipitated the latent good will of the town.

What had ailed Elkton has ailed almost every new munitions town. There have been few such towns where the obvious needs—food, shelter, doctors, and recreation—have been handled efficiently. The old residents always feel put upon by the new arrivals. Food for workers is treated as an afterthought and recreation as a luxury, instead of being provided as a matter of course just as motor fuel and oil are provided for the machines.

For a lack of these things the plant was plagued with a fairly high turnover, absenteeism, and rejects, while Elkton was the target of so much criticism from various sources for conditions which it did not make, and which it felt it could not control, that it became as sensitive as an old-fashioned Singer sewing machine.

II

During the last six months of 1942 Cecil County, though set in its ways, began to adjust itself. Surprising things were happening in Elkton. Before that families had been shivering in unheated houses on the edge of the Chesapeake. A few lived in trailers, while for months three hundred and fifty government houses waited for some essential furnace parts and about twenty-five feet of pipe to connect them up with the town water. In Newark, Delaware, six miles away, eighty more houses awaited completion.

Now Grafton Brown of the War Manpower Commission, friendly as a next-door neighbor, handsome as Paul McNutt, sat in the U.S. Employment Service office, in the cellar of the courthouse. Unlike many of the other government officials who had streamed through Elkton, he stayed a while, whereas others "made a sourpuss at us and went away."

With him appeared an expediter from the Federal Public Housing Administration, and it began to look as if the houses might some day be finished. Mr. Brown, the wonder man, took up his telephone and spoke into it. Furnace parts appeared; pipes appeared; plumbers and carpenters appeared. Meantime he stirred around and got acquainted, listened to people's difficulties, and poured oil on troubled waters. Seeing him work was like watching a prestidigitator.

Even the *Whig* published Mr. Brown's release, which announced that the houses were now ready for occupancy. Mrs. Cronin got ready to hang Christmas wreaths on the houses over in Newark, though skeptics were heard to remark, "If those houses are ready to live in, then I'm a desert camel."

Now there are several more dormitories almost finished, and they are going to open progressively. There are to be eleven dormitories for white occupants, complete with a com-

munity house which will have a grill, a sandwich bar, and an
infirmary. Ground will soon be broken for the four much-
needed Negro dormitories, which are also to have a community house. A seventy-five-room addition to the hospital has
had its specifications signed, and Elkton is to have a new
sewer system.

Until these dormitories are completed the girls must find
lodging where they can. Mrs. Cronin's housing canvass included not only Elkton but other towns within a radius of
thirty-five miles. Many girls can get a room and two meals for
$9.00 a week. The Ross Transportation Co., which was orga-
nized to haul them to work, charges from $1.20 to $3.60 a
week for transportation.

Those of the girls who board in private homes like the
homes and the people with whom they live, though of course
there are instances where the twain do not meet successfully.

The Sandy Cove summer hotel is an example and the Kitty
Knight House is another. Sandy Cove was formerly a club for
professional women who paid $50.00 a week for accommoda-
tions. The ladies who run the place have turned the club over
to the girls—$9.00 a week for room and two meals—as a
war contribution. In the summer there are swimming, tennis,
and water sports; there are free indoor games and a fine dance
floor. But some girls hate the place. They must walk four
miles through woods to get to the State highway and they
can't stand being so far away. No strolling up and down Main
Street, no picking up drives from boys from Wilmington; call-
ers sternly discouraged.

As for the Kitty Knight House, this famous Colonial mansion, with thirty-two rooms and two cottages, can house over
a hundred girls. Mrs. Tomlinson, the owner, has opened her
place to them as a contribution to the war, but some of her
young charges upset and bewilder her. Even the excellent
meals and the Simmons beds don't make up for the fact that
it is miles from a movie. The girls don't care whether George
Washington slept here or not. Accustomed to evaporated milk
from a can, some don't appreciate the lumpy cream from
Kitty Knight's pure-bred cows.

Meantime the atmosphere in the office of James Flannery,
the head of the Federal Public Housing Administration, is

electric. The telephone rings all day. A young man arrives and
announces darkly, "Navy's got our dormitory sheets. They've
sent blankets like horse blankets that'll take the hides off them
gals instead of what we specified." It seems the Navy is always
getting everything which by rights belongs to Federal Housing. No. 4 Dormitory 'phones to find out where the janitor
is—the furnace is going out. A young lady of the office force
comes in and says with the quiet triumphant voice of one
announcing the crack of doom, "Eighteen NYA girls have
come from South Carolina and want to know where they go
from here."

III

Over in the new dormitories the new manager, Mrs. Edith
Alexander, is also leaping from crisis to crisis. The dormitories
are T-shaped, and the long tight corridors make one think of
the corridors on a ship with staterooms on each side. Here
the girls get a comfortable room and maid service for $3.50 a
week. There are both double and single rooms, shower and
baths and tubs and clean towels every day. The lounge is
larger than in the old dormitories and there is a room with
three ironing boards.

Although Mrs. Alexander is employed by the government
as manager of the eleven new dormitories, the girls have
adopted her as a new mother. Every problem a girl can have,
complicated by sickness and homesickness, is brought to her
door. They come to her for everything.

The new North Carolina girls are full of complaints. They
had been told that they could get room and board at the
dormitory for $12.00 a week, and one of them has quinsy sore
throat. Edith, one of the colored maids, comes in to announce with gloomy self-importance, "Mis' Alexander, some
of them new girls done stuff up th' toilet! Water's a runnin'
all ovah the washrooms just lak th' flood." Dora is sick and
wants her husband 'phoned for.

A group of girls chatter excitedly about the U.S.O., whose
opening on Christmas changed the whole outlook for hundreds of the girls.

For the first time the girls have a place of their own besides a beer parlor or juke joint where they can dance, play games, write a letter, or receive friends. The clubhouse is theirs. It was made over from a fine old three-storey house and has assembly rooms, game rooms, a writing room, and spare bedrooms for stranded girls.

The girls and the town have been brought together through the U.S.O. There was plenty of good will in Elkton but no channel through which it could flow. Now a gradual welding is going on between the war production workers and townspeople.

The second night the clubhouse was open the U.S.O. were hosts to the town after the community carol singing. It was sleeting, so the singers had to crowd inside the doors of the courthouse. But it was very gay and Christmaslike with the girls handing out the carol sheets to the community members. Afterward the various church choirs and community chorus groups were invited to the new clubhouse for cocoa and cookies. The girls were the hostesses of the evening, they greeted the townspeople at the door, they acted as guides round the house. They showed everyone the way to the coatroom and helped with serving, so that from the very beginning there was the feeling that the house belonged to the girls.

There was a continuous series of parties through the Christmas season. Open house was held on Christmas Day and there was a buffet supper. So many came that the people ate in three shifts. Word went round like wildfire that there was a grand new U.S.O. It spread among the soldiers at Aberdeen and the sailors at the Naval Training Station. On New Year's Eve alone there were five hundred boys and girls in and out, dancing, playing games, or just sitting about chatting. After the soldiers and sailors left at midnight—the curfew had been extended an hour for them—another party was held for the girls who had been working from four to twelve. They came there from work and stayed until half-past three in the morning. Every week-end the place fairly swarmed with soldiers and sailors, and more and more of the men war production workers filtered in.

Mrs. Rhoda Sutton and Miss Archambault are the U.S.O. workers, and Mrs. Sutton is responsible for every detail of the clubhouse. It seems like a dream come true to them when they listen to the comments of the boys and girls.

"This is just like home! This is the friendliest place we've been in since we have been in the Army! We never dreamed there was a place like this in Elkton! We'd rather come here than anywhere! This is the swellest thing that could have happened!"

The boys and girls are allowed to cook. They are encouraged to keep the place clean. Committees of soldiers and sailors and girls are appointed every night to keep track of things. They come to Mrs. Sutton and Miss Archambault and beg to wear a U.S.O. armband, which is the badge of the House Committee. The boys keep one another in line and the same is true of the girls. Every night except Sunday there is continuous dancing until eleven o'clock. The U.S.O. clubhouse with its open fires and its ready welcome has given heart to the lonely boys and girls.

Changes for the better are going on also at the plant. When the rest house for newcomers is under operation, the big turnover which occurs the first two weeks will shrink.

Almost every day busses, each holding forty girls, drive up to the personnel office. They have been on the road anywhere from twelve to eighteen hours. The girls have been recruited from the mining regions of West Virginia, the anthracite coal regions of Pennsylvania, and some of the steel areas, though now North Carolina, Tennessee, and Kentucky are being tapped.

The girls are interrogated, photographed, fingerprinted, blood-typed, and undergo a physical examination. You may see them any day slumped on the wooden benches outside the room marked "Investigation," or leaning against the wall or waiting in the busses, their heads in their hands.

There are young little mammas' girls with their hair curling in page-boy bobs over their shoulders. Fluttery high-school girls on the great adventure of their first jobs. The handsome, well-dressed girl was a doctor's assistant until two days ago.

"Two days ago I didn't know anything about this. I saw the advertisement in the paper and now I don't know what it's all about," one girl told me.

"We don't any of us know what it's all about. We're dead

on our feet. We've been traveling all night. We got here at seven this morning—and it's now after three."

By the time the ordeal is over many girls have made up their minds they are not going to stay. When the white farmhouse is made over into a place where the girls can wash and lie down and have something to eat things will be better.

There is no one thing that has caused more complaint among the girls than food—they complain it is poor, dear, and far off. Although there is now a cafeteria with good food near the dormitories, the girls complain that the food is dear—and it is more expensive than the Savarin or Childs'. Many girls go through the day on a cup of coffee and a piece of toast, or munch doughnuts on the way to work. They have a sandwich and a cup of coffee for lunch and only one good meal a day. The girls get so fat eating starches that their clothes burst the seams and they ultimately lose their pep and bounce, and absenteeism grows.

It's so hard to find a place open on Sunday that asking girls to Sunday dinner is becoming an Elkton custom. Most eating places close at nine o'clock at night, so the girls coming off the twelve o'clock shift who want something to eat are out of luck. Few places in Elkton board girls and such places as afford kitchen privileges are at a premium. Neither the plant nor private enterprise nor the government has as yet made plans for industrial feeding.

IV

It is in the dormitories that one gets to know the girls. A feeling of adventure streams through them. Take the case of Ellen Dearson. One Sunday morning she was a solitary girl standing near the bus station. There was never anyone as lonely and forsaken-looking as she. Her skirt flapped about her ankles, her hair fell lank about her ears. Everything about her spoke of some remote Southern hill town.

She had started on her journey from West Virginia in a company bus full of newly recruited girls, and had got separated from them and had been sent on by the regular bus, but her suitcase hadn't come with her. She didn't know what company she was working for. She didn't remember the name of the man who had hired her and she hadn't a penny in her pocket. She had had nothing to eat since the day before, but would accept only a cup of coffee. "I don't feel hungry—you mustn't spend all this money on me," she protested. She was frightened but she was self-contained and kept her fierce reticence. She was going to let no "foreigner" see her disturbance, but you could feel her all aquiver like a taut violin string.

Two months later she had on a wine-colored corduroy skirt, a pretty shirtwaist, and some costume jewelry, little red flowers that went with her dress. Her dark hair was swept back from her eyes, which had been so guarded and lackluster before, but now shone with pride as though to say, "You wouldn't know me." There was a discreet touch of rouge on her thin face. I'd see her running in and out of the dormitory, always with a group of girls, her face alight. She was rich. She made more money than she had ever thought possible. The dormitory was luxury. The clothes were something she had not even dreamed of. Here all at once was companionship, adventure, a different status.

There are girls from all over and women of all ages, but they all share in the spirit of adventure. The woman in the corner room, for instance, is over sixty. She had left a well-paying job in which she had worked for years because she wanted to be part of the war effort. She wore jodhpurs the first few days. The inspectors are supposed to wear skirts and this earned her the nickname of "Hi-yo Silver."

Next door is a bride. She's the daughter of a steel worker from Johnstown. A very little girl with tiny hands as pretty as a picture, she makes more than anyone else in the dormitory. Her soldier husband is in Aberdeen. The two girls next door are sisters—college girls. Clausine is line leader and makes $74.00 every two weeks. Like many college girls, she came to work during her vacation, and felt that the work being done there was more important than school, and stayed on.

There were two little girls, shy as wood creatures, from a tiny mining town in West Virginia. They had been here less than two weeks, and it seemed wonderful to them that they could live on the pay of one girl and send the whole of the other's pay home. Their father's a crippled miner and there are younger brothers and sisters. There are many women working here whose husbands and whose fathers have been hurt in the mines.

Life in the dormitory has a definite beat and rhythm. By listening you can tell what time it is by the noises in the corridor. Long before light there's a stir and shuffling. Doors bang. The girls are getting ready for the eight o'clock morning shift. In midwinter these girls walk a mile in darkness, up a road swarming with cars and busses. From then on to about ten—until the night shift girls have gone to bed—there's a stir around the place. Then there's a quiet interval until noon, when the girls of the 4 P.M. shift begin to get up. From then on girls wash clothes, visit about, go out to meals. Almost all the girls wear neat zippered housecoats and their hair is done carefully. The movies and the women's magazines don't live in vain. A girl with hair on end, untidy slippers, and a sleazy negligée stands out like a blackbird in snow. There is always a girl ironing clothes. The coming and going never stops until late at night when the girls through working at midnight come in, one by one.

This is a new dormitory and has not yet begun to have a life of its own. It's very largely a West Virginia crowd and they have the reticent ways of a mountain people. At night the girls go out in ones and twos, some of them as beautiful as movie stars. You can hardly recognize them as the same girls who went plowing through the snow in the dark, looking like a flock of refugees in long coats and slacks and kerchiefs over their heads.

Over in the old dormitory there is the feeling of an established community. Around six the lobby fills up. The girls iron and press their clothes. One of the girls, who was formerly in a beauty shop, is doing some handsome hairdressing. The girls are waiting in their coats for their beaus to pick them up.

Outside is a line of cars which beep softly and urgently from time to time like sea monsters calling to their mates. Until recently a large sign reading "ABSOLUTELY NO MEN ALLOWED ON THESE PREMISES" barred the way to the dormitory grounds. This sign has been taken down. Men are allowed to come in only if they have a pass from the main office and then just to call for a girl. So they beep their horns or flash the headlights on and off.

At each new beep Jinny, a little girl with electric red hair and a face like a Toulouse-Lautrec drawing, goes to the door and shouts "What do you want?" The boy shouts back and Jinny rushes off to tell Celia or Mamie that her date has come. Jinny is eighteen, but her mother, who works here too, won't let her go out, and she is getting a vicarious excitement being master of ceremonies. One after another the girls file out, perhaps to go dancing in Wilmington or maybe to the movies or to sit in a beer parlor.

Uncle Sam gives orders that strict morality is to be observed on his premises. But what the girls do after they leave government-owned territory is none of anyone's business. The girls come and go at their will. There are no hours to be kept. The doors of the dormitories are always open, and they must be to the three shifts.

One single soldier has come to get his date. He is an older fellow and sits stolidly while the girls chat. One girl, as pretty as a Christmas card, makes discreet eyes at him, and the others kid him. There's a sense of excitement and of adventure, something just a little forbidden in the beeping cars, but there's good nature and chaff, and above all there's youth. As I go out a sailor looms up. He says "Scuse me, ma'am, is Myrt there?"

"What does she look like?" I ask.

"Did you ever see a dream walking?" he counters.

Romance is on the rampage in Elkton. The streets are full of soldiers and sailors and there are always cars waiting for a pickup. As the girls walk down to go to the cafeteria at night cars follow them and open their doors invitingly. The girls stick their heads in the air or advise the drivers to go about their business.

"They must think we're nitwits to get into a strange car," they comment.

The very danger in which the girls work intensifies the tempo of life. They feel the importance of their jobs. When the lounge, with its green leather chairs, is full of girls having their morning cigarettes the talk crackles with danger.

"Did you hear how Rose got burned?"

"Oh, she wasn't burnt bad. She went right off to First Aid and she was right back to work again."

"I thought I'd die when that new girl come in our department. 'I can't work on this machine,' she says, 'it makes my stomach hop up and down like they do.' You know our machines hop up and down awful fast. You have to look out."

It's amazing how the girls stand up to the danger of their occupation. "Those who can take it stay, and those who can't take it clear out, and the sooner the better for the rest of us. If the boys can take what they do I guess we can," the girls say. The danger of the work identifies them with the men of their family who are overseas.

They never talk about the war and seem to have no curiosity about it. They seldom listen to news broadcasts and rarely look at a newspaper. In this they follow a pattern that is common throughout the munitions towns of the country. Though there are more miners' daughters than anything else, if they have a yearning for a union they never mention it. Nor has any attempt been made to organize them.

The girls like their jobs and complaints about working conditions in the plant are rare. There are a few inevitable clashes of personality between girls and foremen but they're not conspicuous.

There is a feeling among them that is electric and vital. They have shown such a pioneering and adventurous spirit in coming at all that one feels they are waiting for something, perhaps for a way to be found to fill their minds and to bring them closer to the great currents of thought sweeping through the world. They are so near to the war, and are playing so important a part, and their clever fingers are so necessary—yet there is lacking here, as elsewhere, a final urgency which war demands. These girls are waiting for some voice to speak a message which will release all their energy for total war.

Harper's Magazine, March 1943

The Foamy Fields

by A. J. Liebling

I

IF THERE is any way you can get colder than you do when you sleep in a bedding roll on the ground in a tent in southern Tunisia two hours before dawn, I don't know about it. The particular tent I remember was at an airfield in a Tunisian valley. The surface of the terrain was mostly limestone. If you put all the blankets on top of you and just slept on the canvas cover of the roll, you ached all over, and if you divided the blankets and put some of them under you, you froze on top. The tent was a large, circular one with a French stencil on the outside saying it had been rented from a firm in Marseilles and not to fold it wet, but it belonged to the United States Army now. It had been set up over a pit four feet deep, so men sleeping in it were safe from flying bomb fragments. The tall tent pole, even if severed, would probably straddle the pit and not hit anybody. It was too wide a hole to be good during a strafing, but then strafings come in the daytime and in the daytime nobody lived in it. I had thrown my roll into the tent because I thought it was vacant and it seemed as good a spot as any other when I arrived at the field as a war correspondent. I later discovered that I was sharing it with two enlisted men.

I never saw my tentmates clearly, because they were always in the tent by the time I turned in at night, when we were not allowed to have lights on, and they got up a few minutes before I did in the morning, when it was still dark. I used to hear them moving around, however, and sometimes talk to them. One was from Mississippi and the other from North Carolina, and both were airplane mechanics. The first night I stumbled through the darkness into the tent, they heard me and one of them said, "I hope you don't mind, but the tent

245

we were sleeping in got all tore to pieces with shrapnel last night, so we just moved our stuff in here." I had been hearing about the events of the previous evening from everybody I met on the field. "You can thank God you wasn't here last night," the other man said earnestly. The field is so skillfully hidden in the mountains that it is hard to find by night, and usually the Germans just wander around overhead, dropping their stuff on the wrong hillsides, but for once they had found the right place and some of the light anti-aircraft on the field had started shooting tracers. "It was these guns that gave away where we was," the first soldier said. "Only for that they would have gone away and never knowed the first bomb had hit the field. But after that they knew they was on the beam and they came back and the next bomb set some gasoline on fire and then they really did go to town. Ruined a P-38 that tore herself up in a belly landing a week ago and I had just got her about fixed up again, and now she's got shrapnel holes just about everywhere and she's hopeless. All that work wasted. Killed three fellows that was sleeping in a B-26 on the field and woke up and thought that was no safe place, so they started to run across the field to a slit trench and a bomb got them. Never got the B-26 at all. If they'd stayed there, they'd been alive today, but who the hell would have stayed there?"

"That shrapnel has a lot of force behind it," the other voice in the tent said. "There was a three-quarter-ton truck down on the field and a jaggedy piece of shrapnel went right through one of the tires and spang through the chassix. You could see the holes both sides where she went in and come out. We was in our tent when the shooting started, but not for long. We run up into the hills so far in fifteen minutes it took us four hours to walk back next morning. When we got back we found we didn't have no tent." There was a pause, and then the first soldier said, "Good night, sir," and I fell asleep.

When the cold woke me up, I put my flashlight under the blankets so I could look at my watch. It was five o'clock. Some Arab dogs, or perhaps jackals, were barking in the hills, and I lay uncomfortably dozing until I heard one of the soldiers blowing his nose. He blew a few times and said, "It's funny that as cold as it gets up here nobody seems to get a real cold. My nose runs like a spring branch, but it don't never develop."

When the night turned gray in the entrance to the tent, I woke again, looked at my watch, and saw that it was seven. I got up and found that the soldiers had already gone. Like everyone else at the field, I had been sleeping in my clothes. The only water obtainable was so cold that I did not bother to wash my face. I got my mess kit and walked toward the place, next to the kitchen, where they were starting fires under two great caldrons to heat dish water. One contained soapy water and the other rinsing water. The fires shot up from a deep hole underneath them, and a group of soldiers had gathered around and were holding the palms of their hands toward the flames, trying to get warm. The men belonged to a maintenance detachment of mechanics picked from a number of service squadrons that had been sent to new advanced airdromes, where planes have to be repaired practically without equipment for the job. That morning most of the men seemed pretty cheerful because nothing had happened during the night, but one fellow with a lot of beard on his face was critical. "This location was all right as long as we had all the planes on one side of us, so we was sort of off the runway," he said, "but now that they moved in those planes on the other side of us, we're just like a piece of meat between two slices of bread. A fine ham sandwich for Jerry. If he misses either side, he hits us. I guess that is how you get to be an officer, thinking up a location for a camp like this. I never washed out of Yale so I could be an officer, but I got more sense than that."

"Cheer up, pal," another soldier said. "All you got to do is dig. I got my dugout down so deep already it reminds me of the Borough Hall station. Some night I'll give myself a shave and climb on board a Woodlawn express." Most of the men in camp, I had already noticed, were taking up excavation as a hobby and some of them had worked up elaborate private trench systems. "You couldn't get any guy in camp to dig three days ago," the Brooklyn soldier said, "and now you can't lay down a shovel for a minute without somebody sucks it up."

Another soldier, who wore a white silk scarf loosely knotted around his extremely dirty neck, a style generally affected by fliers, said, "What kills me is my girl's brother is in the horse cavalry, probably deep in the heart of Texas, and he used to razz me because I wasn't a combat soldier."

The Brooklyn man said to him, "Ah, here's Mac with a parachute tied around his neck just like a dashing pilot. Mac, you look like a page out of *Esquire*."

When my hands began to feel warm, I joined the line which had formed in front of the mess tent. As we passed through, we got bacon, rice, apple butter, margarine, and hard biscuits in our mess tins and tea in our canteen cups. The outfit was on partly British rations, but it was a fairly good breakfast anyway, except for the tea, which came to the cooks with sugar and powdered milk already mixed in it. "I guess that's why they're rationing coffee at home, so we can have tea all the time," the soldier ahead of me said. I recognized the bacon as the fat kind the English get from America. By some miracle of lend-lease they had now succeeded in delivering it back to us; the background of bookkeeping staggered the imagination. After we had got our food, we collected a pile of empty gasoline cans to use for chairs and tables. The five-gallon can, known as a flimsy, is one of the two most protean articles in the Army. You can build houses out of it, use it as furniture, or, with slight structural alterations, make a stove or a locker out of it. Its only rival for versatility is the metal shell of the Army helmet, which can be used as an entrenching tool, a shaving bowl, a wash basin, or a cooking utensil, at the discretion of the owner. The flimsy may also serve on occasion as a bathtub. The bather fills it with water, stands in it, removes one article of clothing at a time, rubs the water hastily over the surface thus exposed, and replaces the garment before taking off another one.

There was no officers' mess. I had noticed Major George Lehmann, the commanding officer of the base, and First Lieutenant McCreedy, the chaplain, in the line not far behind me. Major Lehmann is a tall, fair, stolid man who told me that he had lived in Pittsfield, Massachusetts, where he had a job with the General Electric Company. When I had reported, on my arrival at the field, at his dugout the evening before, he had hospitably suggested that I stow my blanket roll wherever I could find a hole in the ground, eat at the general mess shack, and stay as long as I pleased. "There are fighter squadrons and some bombers and some engineers and anti-aircraft here, and you can wander around and talk to anybody that interests you," he had said.

Father McCreedy is a short, chubby priest who came from Bethlehem, Pennsylvania, and had been assigned to a parish in Philadelphia. He always referred to the pastor of this parish, a Father McGinley, as "my boss," and asked me several times if I knew George Jean Nathan, who he said was a friend of Father McGinley. Father McCreedy had been officiating at the interment of the fellows killed in the raid the evening before, and that was all he would talk about during breakfast. He had induced a mechanic to engrave the men's names on metal plates with an electric needle. These plates would serve as enduring grave markers. It is part of a chaplain's duty to see that the dead are buried and to dispose of their effects. Father McCreedy was also special-services officer of the camp, in charge of recreation and the issue of athletic equipment. "So what with one thing and another, they keep me busy here," he said. He told me he did not like New York. "Outside of Madison Square Garden and the Yankee Stadium, you can have it." He wore an outsize tin hat all the time. "I know a chaplain is not supposed to be a combatant," he said, "but if parachute troops came to my tent by night, they'd shoot at me because they wouldn't know I was a chaplain, and I want something solid on my head." He had had a deep hole dug in front of his tent and sometimes, toward dusk, when German planes were expected, he would stand in it waiting and smoking a cigar, with the glowing end of it just clearing the hole.

When I had finished breakfast and scrubbed up my mess kit, I strolled around the post to see what it was like. As the sun rose higher, the air grew warm and the great, reddish mountains looked friendly. Some of them had table tops, and the landscape reminded me of Western movies in Technicolor. I got talking to a soldier named Bill Phelps, who came from the town of Twenty-nine Palms, California. He was working on a bomber that had something the matter with its insides. He confirmed my notion that the country looked like the American West. "This is exactly the way it is around home," he said, "only we got no Ayrabs." A French writer has described the valley bottoms in southern Tunisia as foamy seas of white sand and green alfa grass. They are good, natural airfields, wide and level and fast-drying, but there is always plenty of dust in the air. I walked to a part of the field where there were a lot of P-38's, those double-bodied planes that look so very futuristic, and started to talk to a couple of sergeants who were working on one. "This is Lieutenant Hoelle's plane," one of them said, "and we just finished putting a new wing on it. That counts as just a little repair job out here. Holy God, at home, if a plane was hurt like that, they would send it back to the factory or take it apart for salvage. All we do here is drive a two-and-a-half-ton truck up under the damaged wing and lift it off, and then we put the new wing on the truck and run it alongside the plane again and fix up that eighty-thousand-dollar airplane like we was sticking together a radio set. We think nothing of it. It's a great ship, the 38. Rugged. You know how this one got hurt? Lieutenant Hoelle was strafing some trucks and he come in to attack so low he hit his right wing against a telephone pole. Any other plane, that wing would have come off right there. Hitting the pole that way flipped him over on his back, and he was flying upside down ten feet off the ground. He gripped that stick so hard the inside of his hand was black and blue for a week afterward, and she come right side up and he flew her home. Any one-engine plane would have slipped and crashed into the ground, but those two counter-rotating props eliminate torque." I tried to look as though I understood. "Lieutenant Hoelle is a real man," the sergeant said.

I asked him where Hoelle and the other P-38 pilots were, and he directed me to the P-38 squadron's operations room, a rectangular structure mostly below ground, with walls made out of the sides of gasoline cans and a canvas roof camouflaged with earth. A length of stovepipe stuck out through the roof, making it definitely the most ambitious structure on the field.

*　　*　　*

Hoelle was the nearest man to the door when I stepped down into the operations shack. He was a big, square-shouldered youngster with heavy eyebrows and a slightly aquiline nose. I explained who I was and asked him who was in charge, and he said, "I am. I'm the squadron C.O. My name's Hoelle." He pronounced it "Holly." There was a fire in a stove, and the shack was warm. Two tiny black puppies lay on a pilot's red scarf in a helmet in the middle of the dirt floor, and they seemed to be the centre of attention. Six or eight lieutenants, in flying togs that ranged from overalls to British Army battle dress, were sitting on gasoline cans or sprawled on a couple of cots. They were all looking at the puppies and talking either to them or their mother, a small Irish setter over in one corner, whom they addressed as Red. "One of the boys brought Red along with him from England," Hoelle said. "We think that the dog that got her in trouble is a big, long-legged black one at the airport we were quartered at there."

"These are going to be real beautiful dogs, just like Irish setters, only with black hair," one of the pilots said in a defensive tone. He was obviously Red's master.

"This is a correspondent," Hoelle said to the group, and one of the boys on a cot moved over and made room for me. I sat down, and the fellow who had moved over said his name was Larry Adler but he wasn't the harmonica player and when he was home he lived on Ocean Parkway in Brooklyn. "I wouldn't mind being there right now," he added.

There was not much in the shack except the cots, the tin cans, a packing case, the stove, a phonograph, a portable typewriter, a telephone, and a sort of bulletin board that showed which pilots were on mission, which were due to go on patrol, and which were on alert call, but it was a cheerful place. It reminded me of one of those secret-society shacks that small boys are always building out of pickup materials in vacant lots. Adler got up and said he would have to go on patrol. "It's pretty monotonous," he said, "like driving a fast car thirty miles an hour along a big, smooth road where there's no traffic. We just stooge around near the field and at this time of day nothing ever happens."

Another lieutenant came over and said he was the intelligence officer of the squadron. Intelligence and armament officers, who do not fly, take a more aggressive pride in their squadron's accomplishments than the pilots, who don't like to be suspected of bragging. "We've been out here for a month," the intelligence officer said, "and we have been do-ing everything—escorting bombers over places like Sfax and Sousse, shooting up vehicles and puncturing tanks, going on fighter sweeps to scare up a fight, and flying high looking for a target and then plunging straight down on it and shooting hell out of it. We've got twenty-nine German planes, includ-ing bombers and transports with troops in them and fighters, and the boys have flown an average of forty combat missions apiece. That's more than one a day. Maybe you'd like to see some of the boys' own reports on what they have been doing."

I said that this sounded fine, and he handed me a sheaf of the simple statements pilots write out when they put in a claim for shooting down a German plane. I copied part of a report by a pilot named Earnhart, who I thought showed a sense of literary style. He had had, according to the intelli-gence officer, about the same kind of experience as everybody else in the squadron. Earnhart had shot down a Junkers 52, which is a troop-carrier, in the episode he was describing, and then he had been attacked by several enemy fighters. "As I was climbing away from them," he wrote, "a 20-millimetre explosive shell hit the windshield and deflected through the top of the canopy and down on the instrument panel. Three pieces of shell hit me, in the left chest, left arm, and left knee. I dropped my belly tank and, having the ship under control, headed for my home base. On the way I applied a tourniquet to my leg, administered a hypodermic, and took sulfanilamide tablets. I landed the ship at my own base one hour after I had been hit by the shell. The plane was repaired. Claim, one Ju 52 destroyed." The intelligence officer introduced Earnhart to me. He was a calm, slender, dark-haired boy and he per-sisted in addressing me as sir. He said he came from Lebanon, Ohio, and had gone to Ohio State.

Still another lieutenant I met was named Gustke. He came from Detroit. Gustke had been shot down behind the Ger-man lines and had made his way back to the field. He was a tall, gangling type, with a long nose and a prominent Adam's apple. "I crash-landed the plane and stepped out of it wearing my parachute," he told me, "and the first thing I met was some Arabs who looked hostile to me, and as luck would have it I had forgotten to bring along my .45, so I tripped my parachute and threw it to them, and you know how crazy Arabs are about cloth or anything like that. They all got fighting among themselves for the parachute, and while they were doing that I ran like the dickens and got away from them. I got to a place where there were some Frenchmen, and they hid me overnight and the next day put me on a horse and gave me a guide, who brought me back over some mountains to inside the French lines. I had a pretty sore tail from riding the horse."

A pilot from Texas named Ribb, who stood nearby as Gustke and I talked, broke in to tell me that they had a fine bunch of fellows and that when they were in the air they took care of each other and did not leave anybody alone at the end of the formation to be picked off by the enemy. "In this gang we have no butt-end Charlies," he said feelingly.

I asked Lieutenant Hoelle what was in the cards for the afternoon, and he said that eight of the boys, including himself, were going out to strafe some German tanks that had been reported working up into French territory. "We carry a cannon, which the P-40's don't, so we can really puncture a tank the size they use around here," he said. "We expect to meet some P-40's over the target, and they will stay up high and give us cover against any German fighters while we do a job on the tanks. Maybe I had better call the boys together and talk it over."

A couple of pilots had begun a game of blackjack on the top of the packing case, and he told them to quit, so he could spread a map on it. At that moment an enlisted man came in with a lot of mail and some Christmas packages that had been deposited by a courier plane. It was long after Christmas, but that made the things even more welcome, and all the pilots made a rush for their packages and started tearing them open. Earnhart, one of the men who were going on the strafe job, got some National Biscuit crackers and some butterscotch candy and a couple of tubes of shaving cream that he said he couldn't use because he had an electric razor, and the operations officer, a lieutenant named Lusk, got some very rich home-made cookies that an aunt and uncle had sent him from Denver. We were all gobbling butterscotch and cookies as we gathered round the map Hoelle had spread. It was about as formal an affair as looking at a road map to find your way to Washington, Connecticut, from New Milford. "We used to make more fuss over briefings in England," the intelligence officer said, "but when you're flying two or three times a day, what the hell?" He pointed out the place on the map where the tanks were supposed to be, and all the fellows said they knew where it was, having been there before. Hoelle said they would take off at noon. After a while he and the seven other boys went out onto the field to get ready, and I went with them. On the way there was more talk about P-38's and how some Italian prisoners had told their captors that the Italian army could win the war easy if it wasn't for those fork-tailed airplanes coming over and shooting them up, a notion that seemed particularly to amuse the pilots. Then I went to the P-38 squadron mess with Adler, who had just returned from patrol duty and wasn't going out on the strafe job, and Gustke, who was also remaining behind. This mess was relatively luxurious. They had tables with plates and knives and forks on them, so they had no mess tins to wash after every meal. "We live well here," Adler said. "Everything high-class."

"The place the planes are going is not very far away," Gustke said, "so they ought to be back around half past two."

When we had finished lunch, I took another stroll around the post. I was walking toward the P-38 squadron's operations shack when I saw the planes begin to return from the mission. The first one that came in had only the nose wheel of its landing gear down. There was evidently something the matter with the two other wheels. The plane slid in on its belly and stopped in a cloud of dust. Another plane was hovering over the field. I noticed, just after I spotted this one, that a little ambulance was tearing out onto the field. Only one of the two propellers of this plane was turning, but it landed all right, and then I counted one, two, three others, which landed in good shape. Five out of eight. I broke into a jog toward the operations shack. Gustke was standing before the door looking across the field with binoculars. I asked him if he knew whose plane had belly-landed, and he said it was a Lieutenant Moffat's and that a big, rough Texas pilot whom the other fellows called Wolf had been in the plane that had come in with one engine out. "I see Earnhart and Keith and Carlton, too," he said, "but Hoelle and the other two are missing."

A jeep was coming from the field toward the operations shack, and when it got nearer we could see Wolf in it. He looked excited. He was holding his right forearm with his left hand, and when the jeep got up to the shack he jumped out, still holding his arm.

"Is it a bullet hole?" Gustke asked.

"You're a sonofabitch it's a bullet hole!" Wolf shouted. "The sonofabitching P-40's sonofabitching around! As we came in, we saw four fighters coming in the opposite direction and Moffat and I went up to look at them and they were P-40's, coming away. The other fellows was on the deck and we started to get down nearer them, to about five thousand, and these sonofabitching 190's came out of the sun and hit Moffat and me the first burst and then went down after the others. There was ground fire coming up at us, too, and the sonofabitches said we was going to be over friendly territory. I'm goddam lucky not to be killed."

"Did we get any of them?" Gustke asked.

"I know I didn't get any," Wolf said, "but I saw at least four planes burning on the ground. I don't know who the hell they were."

By that time another jeep had arrived with Earnhart, looking utterly calm, and one of the mechanics from the field. "My plane is all right," Earnhart told Gustke. "All gassed up and ready to go. They can use that for patrol."

The telephone inside the shack rang. It was the post first-aid station calling to say that Moffat was badly cut up by glass from his windshield but would be all right. The mechanic said that the cockpit of Moffat's plane was knee-deep in hydraulic fluid and oil and gas. "No wonder the hydraulic system wouldn't work when he tried to get the wheels down," the mechanic said. The phone rang again. This time it was group operations, calling for Earnhart, Keith, and Carlton, all three of them unwounded, to go over there and tell them what had happened. The three pilots went away, and a couple of the men got Wolf back into a jeep and took him off to the first-aid station. Hoelle and the two other pilots were still missing. That left only Gustke and me, and he said in a sad young voice, like a boy whose chum has moved to another city, "Now we have lost our buddies."

A couple of days later I learned that Hoelle had bailed out in disputed territory and made his way back to our lines, but the two other boys are either dead or prisoners.

II

Not many Mondays ago I was standing in a chow line with my mess tins at an airfield in southern Tunisia, waiting to get into a dugout where some mess attendants were ladling out a breakfast of stew and coffee. The field is enormous, a naturally flat airdrome of white sand and alfa grass that doesn't hold rainwater long enough to spoil the runways—terrain of the kind a French writer once said looked like foamy seas. All around the field there are bulky, reddish mountains. To the east, the sun was just coming up over one of them, and the air was very cold. The mess shack was covered on top and three sides by a mound of earth. It served officers and men of a squadron of P-40 fighters, and on that particular Monday morning I stood between a corporal named Jake Goldstein, who in civilian life had been a Broadway songwriter, and a private named John Smith, of New Hope, Pennsylvania, who used to help his father, a contractor, build houses. Goldstein told me about a lyric he had just written for a song to be called "Bombs." "The music that I think of when it goes through my head now," he said, "is kind of a little like the old tune called 'Smiles,' but maybe I can change it around later. The lyric goes:

> There are bombs that sound so snappy,
> There are bombs that leave folks sad,
> There are bombs that fell on dear old Dover,
> But those bombs are not so bad.

The idea is that the real bad bomb is when this girl quit me and blew up my heart."

"It sounds great," I told the Corporal.

"It will be even bigger than a number I wrote called 'What Do You Hear from Your Heart?'" Goldstein said. "Probably you remember it. Bing Crosby sang it once on the Kraft Cheese Hour. If you happen to give me a little writeup, remember that my name in the songwriting business is Jack Gould." Private Smith started to tell me that he had once installed some plumbing for a friend of mine, Sam Spewack, the writer, in New Hope. "His wife, Bella, couldn't make up her mind where she wanted one of the bathroom fixtures," Smith said, "so I said—"

I never heard any more about Bella Spewack's plumbing, because Major Robert Christman, the commanding officer of the squadron, came up to me and said, "Well, it's a nice, quiet morning." He had his back to the east. I didn't get a chance to answer him, because I started to run like hell to get to the west side of the mound. A number of soldiers who had been scattered about eating their breakfasts off the tops of empty gasoline cans had already started running and dropping their mess things. They always faced eastward while they ate in the morning so that they could see the Messerschmitts come over the mountains in the sunrise. This morning there were nine Messerschmitts. By the time I hit the ground on the lee side of the mound, slender airplanes were twisting above us in a sky crisscrossed by tracer bullets—a whole planetarium of angry worlds and meteors. Behind our shelter we watched and sweated it out. It is nearly impossible to tell Messerschmitts from P-40's when they are maneuvering in a fight, except when one plane breaks off action and leaves its opponent hopelessly behind. Then you know that the one which is distanced is a P-40. You can't help yelling encouragement as you watch a fight, even though no one can hear you and you cannot tell the combatants apart. The Messerschmitts, which were there to strafe us, flew right over the mess shack and began giving the runways and the planes on the field a going-over.

We had sent up four planes on patrol that morning and they tried to engage the strafing planes, but other Germans, flying high to protect the strafers, engaged the patrol. Some "alert" planes that we had in readiness on the perimeter of the field took off in the middle of the scrap, and that was a pretty thing to watch. I saw one of our patrol planes come in and belly-land on the field, smoking. Then I saw another plane twisting out of the sky in a spin that had the soldiers yelling. We all felt that the spinning plane was a Messerschmitt, and it looked like a sure thing to crash into one of the mountains north of us. When the plane pulled out and disappeared over the summit, the yell died like the howl at Ebbets Field when the ball looks as if it's going into the bleachers and then is snagged by a visiting outfielder. It was a Messerschmitt, all right. A couple of minutes later every one of the German planes had disappeared, with our ships after them like a squad of heavy-footed comedy cops chasing small boys.

The fellows who had ducked for cover hoisted themselves off the ground and looked around for the mess things they had dropped. They were excited and sheepish, as they always are after a strafe party. It is humiliating to have someone run you away, so you make a joke about it. One soldier yelled to another, "When you said 'Flop!' I was there already!" Another, who spoke with a Brooklyn accent, shouted, "Jeez, those tracers looked just like Luna Park!"

We formed the chow line again and one fellow yelled to a friend, "What would you recommend as a good, safe place to eat?"

"Lindy's, at Fifty-first Street," the other soldier answered.

"The way the guys ran, it was like a Christmas rush at Macy's," somebody else said.

Everybody tried hard to be casual. Our appetites were even better than they had been before, the excitement having joggled up our internal secretions. There were arguments about whether the plane that had escaped over the mountain would crash before reaching the German lines. I was scraping the last bits of stew from my mess tin with a sliver of hard biscuit when a soldier came up and told me that Major ——, whom I had never met, had been killed on the field, that five men had been wounded, and that one A-20 bomber had been ruined on the ground.

*   *   *

After I had washed up my tins, I walked over to the P-40 squadron operations shack, because I wanted to talk to a pilot familiarly known as Horse about a fight he had been in two days before. The day it had happened I had been visiting a P-38 squadron's headquarters on the field. I had seen eight P-38's go out to attack some German tanks and only five come back, two of them badly damaged. A lot of Focke-Wulf 190's had attacked the P-38's over the target, and Horse and three other P-40 pilots, who were protecting the 38's, had been up above the 190's. Horse was a big fellow with a square, tan face and a blond beard. He came from a town called Quanah, in Texas, and he was always showing his friends a tinted picture of his girl, who was in the Waves. Horse was twenty-five, which made him practically a patriarch in that squadron, and everybody knew that he was being groomed to command a squadron of his own when he got his captaincy. He was something of a wit. Once I heard one of the other boys say that now that the field had been in operation for six weeks, he thought it was time the men should build a shower bath. "The next thing we know," Horse said, "you'll be wanting to send home for your wife."

I found Horse and asked him about the fight. He said he was sorry that the 38's had had such a bad knock. "I guess maybe it was partly our fault," he said. "Four of our ships had been sent out to be high cover for the 38's. They didn't see any 38's or Jerries either, so when their gas was beginning to run low they started for home. Myself and three other fellows had started out to relieve them and we passed them as they came back. The 38's must have arrived over the tanks just then, and the 190's must have been hiding at the base of a cloud bank above the 38's but far below us. When we got directly over the area, we could see tracers flying way down on the deck. The 190's had dived from the cloud and bounced the 38's, who never had a chance, and the 38's were streaking for home. We started down toward the 190's, but it takes a P-40 a long time to get anywhere and we couldn't help. Then four more 190's dived from way up top and bounced us. I looped up behind one of them as he dived. My two wing men were right with me. I put a good burst into the sonofabitch and he started to burn, and I followed him down. I must have fired a hundred and twenty-five rounds from each gun. It was more fun than a county fair. Gray, my fourth man, put a lot of lead into another 190, and I doubt if it ever got home. The other two Jerries just kept on going."

The P-40 operations shack was set deep in the ground and had a double tier of bunks along three of its walls. Sand and grass were heaped over the top of the shack, and the pilots said that even when they flew right over it, it was hard to see, which cheered them considerably. The pilots were flying at least two missions a day and spent most of the rest of the time lying in the bunks in their flying clothes, under as many coats and blankets as they could find. The atmosphere in the shack was a thick porridge of dust diluted by thin trickles of cold air. Major Christman, the squadron leader, once said in a pleased tone, "This joint always reminds me of a scene in 'Journey's End.'" The pilots, most of whom were in their earliest twenties, took a certain perverse satisfaction in their surroundings. "Here we know we're at war," one of them said to me. "Not that I wouldn't change for a room and bath at a good hotel."

During most of my stay at the field I lived not in the Journey's End shack but in one known as the Hotel Léon because technically it belonged to a French lieutenant named Léon, a liaison officer between the French forces and our fliers. It was the newest and finest dugout on the field, with wooden walls and a wooden floor and a partition dividing it down the middle, and the floor was sunk about five feet below ground level. When I arrived at the field, there were plans to cover the part of the shack that projected above ground with sand, in which Léon intended to plant alfa. I was travelling with an Associated Press correspondent named Norgaard, and soon after our arrival Léon, a slender man with a thin, intelligent face and round, brown eyes, welcomed us to his palace. We put our stuff into the shack and emerged to find Léon throwing a modest shovelful of sand against one of the walls. Norgaard offered to help him. "There is only one shovel," Léon said with relief, pressing it into Norgaard's hands. "It is highly interesting for our comfort and safety that the house be covered entirely with sand. I am very occupied."

Then he walked rapidly away, and Norgaard and I took turns piling sand around the Hotel Léon for endless hours afterward. Léon always referred to a telephone switchboard as a switching board, oil paper as oily paper, a pup tent as a puppy tent, and a bedding roll as a rolling bed.

After my talk with Horse, I walked over to the Hotel Léon and found it crowded, as it usually was. Only Léon and Norgaard and I, together with Major Philip Cochran and Captain Robert Wylie, lived in the hotel, but during the day Cochran and Léon used it as an office, and that was why it was crowded. When I had first come to the field, it had been operating for six weeks practically as an outpost, for there was just a unit of American infantry, fifty miles to the southeast, between it and the region occupied by Rommel's army. Cochran, though only a major, had run the field for almost the entire period, but by the time I arrived he had reverted to the status of operations officer. The shack had telephone lines to detachments of French troops scattered thinly through the hills to our east, and they called up at all hours to tell Léon where German tanks were moving or to ask our people to do some air reconnaissance or drop bags of food to a platoon somewhere on a mountain. The French had no trucks to transport food. Sometimes Cochran flew with American transport planes to tell them where to drop parachute troops and sometimes he flew with bombers to tell them where to drop bombs. Because of Cochran's and Léon's range of activities, they always had a lot of visitors.

Attached to the partition in the shack were two field telephones, one of which answered you in French and the other in English. Two soldier clerks, who were usually pounding typewriters, sat on a bench in front of a shelf along one wall. One of them was Corporal Goldstein, the songwriter. The other was a private first class named Otto, who wore metal-rimmed spectacles with round lenses and belonged to the Pentecostal brethren, an evangelical sect which is against fighting and profanity. Otto owned some barber tools, and he cut officers' hair during office hours and enlisted men's at night. That morning he was cutting the hair of Kostia Rozanoff, the commandant of the Lafayette Escadrille, a French P-40 outfit that was stationed at the field. Rozanoff was a blond, round-headed Parisian whose great-grandfather was Russian. Otto, perhaps taking a cue from the shape of Rozanoff's skull, had clipped him until he looked like Erich Von Stroheim, but there was no mirror, so Rozanoff was happy anyway. Cochran, dressed in a dirty old leather flying jacket, had just come back from a mission in the course of which he thought he had destroyed a 190, and was trying to tell about that while nearly everybody else in the shack was trying to tell him about the morning's strafing. Also in the shack was Colonel Edson D. Raff, the well-known parachutist, who had once unexpectedly found himself in command of all the American ground forces in southern Tunisia and for weeks had successfully bluffed enemy forces many times larger. He had flown in from his post in Gafsa in a small plane which he used as his personal transport. He was crowded in behind Otto's barbering elbow and was trying to talk to Cochran over Rozanoff's head. Raff is short and always wears a short carbine slung over his left shoulder, even indoors. He invariably flies very low in his plane to minimize the risk of being potted by a Messerschmitt. "I have one foot trailing on the ground," he says.

Lieutenant Colonel William Momyer, the commanding officer of the field, was sitting between Rozanoff and Corporal Goldstein, telling about a mission he had been on himself that morning, escorting a lot of A-20's over Kebili, a town where the Italians had begun to repair a dynamited causeway across the Chott Djerid. "I bet the wops will never get any workmen to go back to that place," Momyer said. "We scared hell out of them." Momyer had shot down a Junkers 88 and Messerschmitt within a week. He was hot.

Among the others in the shack that morning were Norgaard, the Associated Press man, and a tall P-40 pilot named Harris, who kept asking Léon whether any French unit had telephoned to report finding the Messerschmitt he had been shooting at during the strafing episode, because he was sure it must have crashed. It was the Messerschmitt we had seen pull out of the spin over the mountain. The English-speaking telephone rang and Captain Wylie answered it. He has the kind of telephone voice that goes with a large, expensive office, which he probably had in civilian life. It was somebody up the line asking for Major ——, the officer who had just been machine-gunned in the strafing. "Major —— has been killed," Wylie said. "Is there anything I can do for you?"

There was a variety of stuff on the field when I was there. In addition to Christman's P-40 squadron and the Lafayette Escadrille, there was a second American P-40 squadron commanded by a Major Hubbard, which had a full set of pilots but only five ships. This was because the powers that be had taken away the other ships and given them to the Lafayettes in the interest of international good will. Hubbard's pilots were not sore at the Lafayettes, but they didn't think much of the powers that be. There was also a bomber squadron. The people on our field were not by any means sitting targets. They constantly annoyed the Germans, and that is why the Germans were so keen on "neutralizing" the field. But they didn't come back that day, and neither lunch nor dinner was disturbed.

The guests of the Hotel Léon often didn't go to the mess shack for dinner, because Léon would prepare dinner for them on the premises. He was a talented cook who needed the stimulation of a public, which was, that Monday evening, us. He also needed Wylie to keep the fire in the stove going, Cochran to wash dishes, and me and Norgaard to perform assorted chores. He got eggs from the Arabs and wine from a nearby French engineer unit, and he had gathered a choice assortment of canned goods from the quartermaster's stores. He also bought sheep and pigs from farmers. Léon's idea of a campaign supper was a *soufflé de poisson*, a *gigot*, and an *omelette brûlée à l'armagnac*. He made the *soufflé* out of canned salmon. The only trouble with dining at Léon's was that dinner was seldom ready before half past eight and it took until nearly midnight to clean up afterward.

During that Monday dinner we speculated on what the enemy would do next day. Norgaard said it was hell to have to get up early to catch the Germans' morning performance, but Cochran, the airfield's official prophet, and a successful one, said, "They'll want to make this one a big one tomorrow, so you can sleep late. They won't be over until two-thirty in the afternoon." Momyer, who was having dinner at the hotel that night, agreed that there would be something doing, but he didn't predict the time of day. Léon said, "I think also that there is something cooking in." Momyer decided to maintain a patrol of eight planes over the field all day. "Of course, maybe that's just what they want us to do, use our planes defensively, so we will fly less missions," he said, "but I think this time we ought to do it."

I had such faith in Cochran that it never occurred to me that the Germans would attack us before the hour he had named, and they didn't. The only enemy over the field the following morning was Photo Freddie, a German reconnaissance pilot who had become a local character. He came every morning at about forty thousand feet, flying a special Junkers 86 job so lightened that it could outclimb any fighter. The anti-aircraft guns would fire, putting a row of neat, white smoke puffs a couple of miles below the seat of Freddie's pants, the patrol planes would lift languidly in his direction, like the hand of a fat man waving away a fly, and Photo Freddie would scoot off toward Sicily, or wherever he came from, to develop his pictures, thus discovering where all the planes on the field were placed. The planes were always moved around after he left, and we used to wonder what the general of the Luftwaffe said to poor Freddie when the bombers failed to find the planes where he had photographed them. Now and then some pilot tried to catch Photo Freddie by getting an early start, climbing high above the field, and then stooging around until he appeared. Freddie, however, varied the hour of his matutinal visits, and since a P-40 cannot fly indefinitely, the pilot would get disgusted and come down. I do not think anybody really wanted to hurt Freddie anyway. He was part of the local fauna, like the pet hens that wandered about the field and popped into slit trenches when bombs began to fall.

At about twenty minutes past two that afternoon Norgaard and I returned to the Hotel Léon to do some writing. An Alsatian corporal in the French army was working in front of the shack, making a door for the entrance. The corporal had been assigned by the French command to build Léon's house, and he was a hard worker. He always kept his rifle by him while he was working. He had a long brown beard, which he said he was going to let grow until the Germans were driven out of Tunisia. Only Goldstein and Otto were inside the hut this time. I said to Goldstein, "Why don't you write a new number called 'One-Ninety, I Love You'?" Otto, who had been reading the *Pentecostal Herald*, said, "I do not think that would be a good title. It would not be popular." At that precise moment all of us heard the deep woomp of heavy ack-ack. It came from one of the British batteries in the mountains around the field. We grabbed our tin hats and started for the doorway. By the time we got there, the usual anti-aircraft show was on. In the din we could easily distinguish the sound of our Bofors guns, which were making their peculiar seasick noises—not so much a succession of reports as one continuous retch. The floor of the shack, as I have said, was five feet below ground level and the Alsatian had not yet got around to building steps down to the entrance, so we had a nice, rectangular hole just outside from which to watch developments. The Germans were bombing now, and every time a bomb exploded, some of the sand heaped against the wooden walls was driven into the shack through the knot-holes. The only trouble was that whenever a bomb went off we pulled in our heads and stopped observing. Then we looked out again until the next thump. After several of these thumps there was a straight row of columns of black smoke a couple of hundred yards to our right. I poked my head above ground level and discovered the Alsatian corporal kneeling and firing his rifle, presumably at an airplane which I could not see. The smoke began to clear and we hoisted ourselves out of the hole to try and find out what had happened. "I do not think I touched," the Alsatian said. A number of dog-fights were still going on over the mountains. Scattered about the field, men, dragging themselves out of slit trenches, were pointing to the side of a mountain to the north, where there was smoke above a downed plane.

Léon had a little and old Citroën car, which he said had become, through constant association with the United States Army, "one naturalized small jeeps." He had left it parked behind the shack, and as Norgaard and I stood gawping about, Léon came running and shouted that he was going out to the fallen plane. We climbed into the naturalized jeeps and

started across the field toward the mountainside. At one of
the runways, we met a group of P-40 pilots, including Horse,
and I yelled to them, "Was it theirs or ours?" "Ours, I think,"
Horse said. We kept on going. When we reached the other
side of the field, we cut across country, and Léon could not
make much speed. A couple of soldiers with rifles thumbed a
ride and jumped on the running boards. As we went out
across plowed fields and up the mountain toward the plane,
we passed dozens of soldiers hurrying in the same direction.

When we arrived where the plane had fallen, we found
three trucks and at least fifty men already there. The plane
had been a Messerschmitt 109 belonging to the bombers'
fighter escort. Flames were roaring above the portion deepest
in the earth, which I judged was the engine. Screws, bolts,
rings, and unidentifiable bits of metal were scattered over an
area at least seventy-five yards square. Intermingled with all
this were widely scattered red threads, like the bits left in a
butcher's grinder when he has finished preparing an order of
chopped steak. "He never even tried to pull out," a soldier
said. "He must have been shot through the brain. I seen the
whole thing. The plane fell five thousand feet like a hunk of
lead." There was a sour smell over everything—not intolerable, just sour. "Where is the pilot?" Norgaard asked. The
soldier waved his hand with a gesture that included the whole
area. Norgaard, apparently for the first time, noticed the red
threads. Most of the soldiers were rummaging amid the
wreckage, searching for souvenirs. Somebody said that the
pilot's automatic pistol, always the keepsake most eagerly
sought, had already been found and appropriated. Another
soldier had picked up some French and Italian money. How
these things had survived the pilot's disintegration I do not
know. While the soldiers walked about, turning over bits of
the plane with their feet, looking for some object which could
serve as a memento, an American plane came over and everybody began to run before someone recognized it for what it
was. Just as we came back, a soldier started kicking at something on the ground and screaming. He was one of the fellows who had ridden out on our running boards. He yelled,
"There's the sonofabitch's God-damn guts! He wanted my
guts! He nearly had my guts, God damn him!" Another

soldier went up to him and bellowed, "Shut up! It ain't nice to talk that way!" A lot of other men began to gather around. For a minute or so the soldier who had screamed stood there silently, his shoulders pumping up and down, and then he began to blubber.

Léon picked up a large swatch of the Messerschmitt's tail fabric as a trophy, and as the soldiers walked away from the wreck most of them carried either similar fragments or pieces of metal. After a while Norgaard and I climbed into Léon's car and the three of us started back toward the field. When we arrived, we learned that a lieutenant named Walter Scholl, who had never been in a fight before, had shot down the Messerschmitt. He was the fellow who, in the Cornell-Dartmouth football game of 1940, threw the famous fifth-down touchdown pass for Cornell, the one that was completed for what was considered a Cornell victory until movies of the game showed that it shouldn't have been Cornell's ball at all and the decision had to be reversed. Two other pilots had shot down two Junkers 88 bombers. One of our planes on the ground had been destroyed, and a slit trench had caved in on two fellows, nearly frightening them to death before they could be dug out.

III

Norgaard, the Associated Press correspondent who was with me during a small war that took place at an airfield in southern Tunisia a while ago, often said that the country reminded him of New Mexico, and with plenty of reason. Both are desert countries of mountains and mesas, and in both there are sunsets that owe their beauty to the dust in the air. The white, rectangular Arab houses, with their blue doors, are like the houses certain Indians build in New Mexico, and the Arabs' saddle blankets and pottery and even the women's silver bracelets are like Navajo things. The horses, which look like famished mustangs, have the same lope and are similarly bridle-wise; burros are all over the place, and so is cactus. These resemblances are something less than a coincidence, because the Moors carried their ways of house-building and their handicraft patterns and even their breed of horses and method of breaking them to Spain, and the Spaniards carried them to New Mexico eight hundred years later. All these things go to make up a culture that belongs to a high plateau country where there are sheep to furnish wool for blankets and where people have too little cash to buy dishes in a store, where the soil is so poor that people have no use for heavy plow horses but want a breed that they can ride for long distances and that will live on nearly nothing.

"This horse is young," an Arab once said to Norgaard and me as he showed us a runty bay colt tied in front of a combined general store and barbershop in a village about a mile from the airfield. "If I had had a little barley to feed him, he would be bigger, but what barley we had we have ourselves eaten. It is a poor country."

We used to go down to this village to get eggs when we were too lazy to make the chow line for breakfast or when we felt hungry at any time of day. We'd take them back to the shack a bunch of us were living in and cook them. Solitary Arabs squat along the roadsides all over North Africa, waiting for military vehicles. When one comes into sight, the Arab pulls an egg out from under his rags and holds it up between thumb and forefinger like a magician at a night club. The price of eggs—always high, of course—varies in inverse ratio to the distance from a military post. Near big towns that are a long way from any post the Arabs get only five francs (ten cents at the new rate of exchange) for an egg, but in villages close to garrisons eggs are sometimes hard to find at any price. Norgaard and I followed a standard protocol to get them. First we went into the general store and barbershop, which was just a couple of almost empty rooms that were part of a mud house, and shook hands with all the male members of the establishment. Naturally, we never saw any of the females. Then we presented a box of matches to the head of the house, an ex-soldier who spoke French, and he invited us to drink coffee. The Arabs have better coffee and more sugar than the Europeans in North Africa. While we drank the coffee, we sat with the patriarch of the family on a white iron bed of European manufacture. The patriarch had a white beard and was always knitting socks; he stopped only to scratch himself. Once, as we were drinking coffee, we watched our

French-speaking friend shave a customer's head. He simply started each stroke at the top of the cranium and scraped downward. He used no lather; the customer moistened his own poll with spittle after each stroke of the razor. Once, when the customer made a particularly awful face, all the other Arabs sitting around the room laughed. During the coffee-drinking stage of the negotiations we presented the Arabs with a can of fifty English cigarettes. After that they presented us with ten to fifteen eggs. Soldiers who were not such good friends of theirs usually got twenty eggs for fifty cigarettes, but it always costs something to maintain one's social life. One day I asked the barber why the old man scratched himself, and he said, laughing, "Because of the black spots. We all have them, and they itch." With much hilarity the Arabs showed us the hard, black spots, apparently under their skins, from which they were suffering. I judged the trouble to be a degenerate form of the Black Death, tamed during the centuries by the rugged constitutions of our hosts. Norgaard thought that the spots were just chiggers.

The Germans had come over our airfield on a Monday morning and strafed it and they had come back on Tuesday afternoon and bombed the place. They were going to start an offensive in southern Tunisia, we later learned, so they wanted to knock out this, the most advanced American field. On Wednesday morning the Germans made no attack. That afternoon Norgaard and I decided that we needed some eggs, so we walked down to the Arab village. I carried the eggs home in my field hat, a visored cap which has long flaps to cover your neck and ears when it is cold and which makes a good egg bag. We got back to our shack, which we preferred to call the Hotel Léon, between five and six o'clock. Major Philip Cochran, the airfield's operations officer, who lived in our shack and also used it as an office, was out flying, and Léon, the French liaison officer at the airfield and the titular proprietor of our premises, was out foraging. Jake and Otto, two soldier clerks who worked there during the day, had gone to chow. There was less than an hour of daylight left.

Cochran, who had a fine instinct for divining what the Germans were likely to do, had been sure that they would come over for the third day in succession, and Lieutenant Colonel William Momyer, the commanding officer of the field, had maintained a patrol of P-40's over the field all day. Cochran was among those taking their turns on patrol duty now. In forty minutes more all the planes would have to come down, because the field had no landing lights. And nothing had happened yet.

The walk had made Norgaard and me hungry and we decided to have our eggs immediately. We threw some kindling wood in the stove to stir the fire up and I put some olive oil in the mess tin in which I was going to scramble the eggs. The olive oil belonged to Léon, who went in for *haute cuisine* whenever he could assemble a quorum of majors and lieutenant colonels to act as scullions for him. I took the lid off the hole in the top of the stove, put the mess tin over the hole, and broke all the eggs into the oil. I think there were eleven of them. They floated around half submerged, and although I stirred them with a fork, they didn't scramble. We decided that I had used too much oil, so we added some cheese to act as a cement. Before the cheese had had time to take effect, we heard a loud explosion outside—plainly a bomb—and felt the shack rock. Norgaard grabbed his tin hat and ran out the door to look, and I was just going to follow him when I reflected that if I left this horrible brew on the stove hole a spark might ignite the oil and thus set fire to the shack. I carefully put the mess on a bench and replaced the lid on the stove. I put on my helmet and followed Norgaard out into a kind of foxhole outside our door. More bombs exploded and then all we could hear was the racket of the Bofors cannon and .50 calibre machine guns defending the field. I went back inside, removed the stove lid, and put the eggs on again. Just as some warmth began to return to the chill mess, another stick of bombs went off. In the course of the next minute or so, I repeated my entire routine. Before I finished cooking dinner, I had to repeat it three times more. Finally the eggs and the cheese stuck together after a fashion and I drained the oil off. Then, since no bombs had dropped for a couple of minutes, I poured half the concoction into Norgaard's canteen cup, I put what was left in my mess tin, and we ate.

After we had eaten, we left the shack and started toward

the large, round pit, some fifty yards away, which served as a control room for the field. Night had closed in. There had been no firing now for ten minutes, but as we approached the pit, our anti-aircraft opened up again, firing from all around the field simultaneously. The Bofors tracer shells, which look like roseate Roman candles, reminded me of the fireworks on the lagoon at the World's Fair in Flushing. The burst ended as abruptly as it had begun, except that one battery of .50's kept on for an extra second or two and then stopped in an embarrassed manner.

We saw a lot of our pilots clustered around the pit. A corporal named Dick usually stood in the pit talking to our planes in the air by radio telephone, but a major named Robert Christman, the C.O. of one of the post's fighter squadrons, was in Dick's place. I recognized Christman's voice as he spoke into the telephone, asking, "Did you see the gunfire? Did you see the gunfire?" You wouldn't ask a Jerry that if you were shooting at him, so I knew they were firing the anti-aircraft guns to light one or more of our planes home. Christman asked again, "Did you see the gunfire? Did you see the gunfire?" Then he said to somebody else in the pit, probably Dick, "Hold this a minute." He stuck his head up over the side of the pit and shouted in the direction of a nearby dugout, "They say they saw the fire! Cochran's going to lead in and land to show the other ship the way! Lord, how that Cochran swears when he's excited! Tell the ack-ack to hold everything!" The switchboard through which the control room communicated with all the ack-ack batteries was in the dugout. Nothing was convenient on that field. It sometimes seemed that one of the pilots had scratched the whole thing out of the ground with a broken propeller blade after a forced landing.

We could see a plane showing red and green lights slowly circling over the field, descending gradually in long, deliberate spirals, as if the pilot wanted somebody to follow him. Then there was a blast of machine-gun fire and a fountain of tracers sprayed up from a distant edge of the field. "God damn them!" Christman yelled. "Tell them to hold that fire! What do they want to do—shoot Phil down?" The plane coasted slowly, imperturbably lower. It was Cochran's firm belief, I knew, that the ack-ack on the field had never hit anything, so he probably wasn't worried. The plane skimmed over the surface of the field. There was one pitiful red light on the field for it to land by, like the lantern one hangs on the tail of a hobbled donkey to keep him from being hit by a pushcart. "He'll never make it that way," a pilot near me said. "What the hell is he doing? He'll overshoot. No, there he goes up again."

In a minute Christman, back at the phone once more, said, "Cochran went up because the other fellow couldn't see him. The other ship says he saw the gunfire, though. Now he wants a burst on the southern edge of the field only." Somebody in the switchboard dugout yelled, "Come on now! Battery C only, Battery C only! Everybody else *hold* it!" All the guns on the field immediately fired together. I could hear Momyer's voice yelling in the dugout, "God damn it, I'll have them all court-martialled!" Christman shouted, "He says he saw it and now he can see Cochran! He's coming in!" Cochran was again circling in the blackness above the field. The pilot next to me said, "This is sure sweating it out." I recognized him, partly by his voice and partly by the height of his shoulders, as a fellow the other boys called Horse, a big Texan who wore a square beard.

"Did we get any of theirs?" I asked Horse.

"Yes, sir," Horse said. "Bent got one for sure. He's in already. And a French post has telephoned that another one is down near there in flames and that pilot out there with Cochran had one smoking. He must have chased it so far he couldn't get back before dark. Must have forgot himself. I don't rightly know who he is."

The ack-ack batteries fired again. They apparently did what was wanted this time, because nobody cursed. Christman called up from the pit, "They want one more burst, all together, and then they're coming in!" The message was relayed and the ack-ack fired another salvo. Now there were two planes, both showing lights, moving in the sky above the field, one high and one low. "Cochran's coming in," Horse said. "Look at him. Just like it was day and he could see everything." The lower pair of lights drifted downward, straightened out and ran forward along the field, and stopped. The other lights slowly followed them down, seemed to hesitate a moment, then slanted toward the ground, and coasted into a horizontal. "Good landing," Horse said. "We sure sweated that one." The second pilot to land turned out to be a lieutenant named Thomas, who had become too absorbed in the pursuit of a Junkers 88 to turn back until he had shot it down. That made three Junkers for us, each carrying a crew of four men. I learned that the German bombs had spoiled, to use the airmen's term, two of our planes on the field. A couple of minutes later a jeep that had gone out to meet Cochran's plane brought him to where the rest of us were standing. He is a short, box-chested man, and the two or three flying jackets he was wearing made him look shorter and stockier than he really is. He was feeling good. "I'm sorry I cursed you out, Bob! I was excited!" he yelled down into the control pit to Christman. Momyer, who had come out of the dugout, made as if to grab Cochran and hug him, but stopped in astonishment when he heard Cochran being so polite. It seemed to remind him of something. Looking rather thoughtful, he went back into the dugout and called up the lieutenant colonel in command of the ack-ack, which he had been abusing. "Thank you very much, Colonel," I heard him say. "Your boys certainly saved the day."

That evening was a happy one. Léon's shack was crowded with pilots talking about the successful fight and scrambling eggs and eating them out of mess tins. Cochran felt so good that he decided to have his first haircut since he had left New York three months before, so he sent over to the enlisted men's quarters for Otto, who was a barber as well as a clerk, to do the job. Otto is a young man with reddish hair and white eyebrows and a long nose, and he had a habit of getting interested in a conversation between two senior officers and breaking into it. Once, hearing Colonel Edson D. Raff, the parachute-troop commander, telling Lieutenant Colonel Momyer that he could take Tunis with no more than four hundred and fifty men, Otto blurted out, "How can you be so sure?" Aside from this failing he is a good soldier and when he gives a haircut he really cuts off hair, so nobody can say he is looking for a return engagement in the near future.

It was well after dark when Léon came in from his foraging, which had been a success too. "I have bought three small peegs," he announced triumphantly, "and when they are theek enough we shall eat them." He had left them in the care of a *hôtelier* in a town a few miles away. They were subsequently taken, and presumably eaten, by the Germans. At the time, however, Léon thought it a safe *logement* for the pigs. "I have also talked with the aide of General Koeltz," Léon said to Cochran and Momyer, "and he says that in the case any pilot sees any trucks moving on the road of which we have spoken yesterday, he is allowed to shoot without permission." While Otto cut Cochran's hair, we added up the box score of the three-day German attack on the field. The home team felt that it had done pretty well. During the Monday strafing the Germans had spoiled one of our planes on the field and another in the air and had killed one officer, a major, with machine-gun bullets. We had merely damaged one of their fighters. On Tuesday, while they had spoiled two more of our planes on the ground with bombs, we had shot down a Messerschmitt 109 and two Junkers 88's. That meant that we had lost a total of three planes but only one life while they had lost three planes and nine lives. One of our missions had also destroyed a Focke-Wulf 190 on Monday morning and a Messerschmitt had been badly damaged in the dogfight that had accompanied the strafing of our field. Wednesday evening we had destroyed three more planes and twelve men, and the Germans had succeeded only in damaging two planes on the ground, which gave us an imposing lead. "They won't be over tomorrow morning," Cochran said. "Maybe not all day. They'll want to think things over and try something big to make up for their losses and get the lead back. They'll be like a guy doubling his bet in a crap game."

That field had been fought over many times before in the course of history and a corner of it had been the site of a Carthaginian city. Bent, a pilot who talked with a British accent and had once done some digging among old ruins in England, said that every time he flew over that corner he could plainly see the gridiron pattern of the ancient streets on the ground. Horse, the bearded pilot, was irreverent about Bent's claims. "Maybe a couple of thousand years from now,"

he said, "people will dig around this same field and find a lot
of C-ration cans that we've left and attribute them to arche-
ology. They'll say, 'Those Americans must surely have been a
pygmy race to wear such small helmets. It scarcely seems possible they had much brains. No wonder they rode around in
such funny airplanes as the P-40.'"

Another officer who turned up in Léon's shack that
evening was Major (afterward Lieutenant Colonel) Vincent
Sheean, who always points out these days that he was once a
correspondent himself. He said he had been driving in a jeep
on a road near the field when the bombing started, so he had
stopped and jumped into a ditch. Sheean had come down
from the second highest headquarters of the African Air
Forces to see that the French pilots of the Lafayette Escadrille, which had recently arrived at our field, received understanding and kind treatment from their American comrades.
A couple of the Lafayette pilots happened to be in the shack
when he arrived; they had received so much kind treatment
that they could hardly remember the words of "Auprès de Ma
Blonde," which they were trying to teach to Momyer on a
purely phonetic basis.

The next day, Thursday, was as quiet as Cochran had said it
would be. The Germans left us completely alone. In the
morning the Lafayette Escadrille fellows went on their first
mission, covering a French local offensive in a mountain pass,
and returned without meeting any enemy aircraft.

The exposed position of our mess shack had begun to
worry Major Christman's men after the strafing we had received the Monday before, and he had ordered the chow line
transferred to a place called the Ravine, a deep, winding gulch
on the other side of the high road along one end of the field.
Most of the men lived in the Ravine and felt safe there. They
had scooped out caves in its sides and used their shelter halves
to make doors. One stretch of the gully was marked by a sign
that said "Park Avenue." Sheean and I stood in the chow line
for lunch and then took an afternoon stroll along Park Avenue. Afterward I went back to Léon's shack to write a letter
and found it crowded, as usual. An engineer officer who had
been at the field a couple of days was asking Cochran how he

could be expected to get on with the construction job he had been sent there to do if new bomb holes appeared on the field every day and his detachment had to fill them up. "We've been filling up bomb holes ever since we been here, and it looks like we won't get a chance to do anything else," the engineer said. "My colonel sent me down here to build revetments for airplanes and he's going to expect me back soon." Another visitor, a captain in the Royal Engineers, asked him if there were any unexploded bombs on the runways. Men on the field always referred to this British captain as the booby-trap man, the planting of fiendish traps for the enemy being his specialty, and added with respect, "Even the parachute troops say he's crazy." He had made several jumps with Colonel Raff's parachutists to install his humorous devices in places where he thought German soldiers would later get involved with them. The American officer told him that there were several unexploded bombs on the runways and that he had marked off their positions with empty oil drums.

"But haven't you removed the fuses?" the booby-trap man asked with obvious astonishment.

"To hell with that!" his American colleague said with feeling. "They won't do any harm if they do go off. It's a big field."

"Oh, but they'll make quite a lot of noise," the booby-trap man said, still vaguely unhappy.

The American officer looked at the booby-trap man and Cochran as if they were both lunatics and went out of the hut without saying anything more. "How *extraordinary!*" the booby-trap man said. "He didn't even seem interested." He sounded hurt, like a young mother who has just learned that a visitor does not care for babies.

The booby-trap man looked like a conventional sort of Englishman, with a fair, boyish face and a shy smile. He spoke with the careful accent of the north countryman who has been to a university and he did not himself use the term "booby trap." He preferred to call his darlings, variously, trip mechanisms, push mechanisms, pull mechanisms, and antipersonnel switches. Trip mechanisms, for instance, are the ones soldiers inadvertently set off by stumbling over a concealed wire, and pull mechanisms are those they explode by picking up some innocent-seeming object like a corned-beef tin. The captain was an amateur botanist and seldom went out without a couple of pocketfuls of small devices to set about the countryside in likely spots as he ambled along collecting specimens of Tunisian grasses. I asked him that afternoon how he had started on what was to become his military career, and he said with his shy smile, "I expect it was at public school, when I used to put hedgehogs in the other boys' beds. After a while the hedgehogs began to pall and I invented a system for detuning the school piano, so that when the music master sat down to play 'God Save the King' it sounded god-awful."

"I sometimes try to imagine what your married life will be like, Captain," Cochran said. "Someday the baby will be in the crib and your wife will go to pick it up and the whole house will blow up because you've wired the baby to a booby trap."

"I trust I shall be able to restrain my professional instincts to fit the circumstances of domestic life," the booby-trap man said rather stiffly. He was a man who really took his branch of warfare seriously.

IV

Sleep in the Hotel Léon, which was the colloquial name of a shack on a Tunisian airfield in which I lived for a while not so long ago, was usually interrupted in the gray hour before dawn by the jangle of a field telephone that spoke French. Then Léon, the French liaison officer at our post, who had had the shack built according to his specifications and whom the rest of us residents called *Monsieur le patron*, would sit up and pull the telephone from the holster in which it hung at the foot of his bed. He slept wearing all the clothes he possessed, which included several sweaters, a long military overcoat, and a muffler. When he grabbed the phone, he would say, *"Allo! Oui?"* (The rest of us sometimes would sing "Sweet Allo, Oui" to the tune of "Sweet Eloise.") The French voice at the other end of the phone was almost always audible, and, so that the half-awake American officers in the shack would get the idea of what was going on, Léon would reply in a hybrid jargon. He would say, for example, "One *ennemi apparait* flying sousewest over point 106? *Merci, mon capitaine.*" Then he would hang up and fall back into bed, muttering, "*Imbécile,* why he don't fly west? He will be losted."

A partition divided Léon's shack into a bedroom, in which four of us slept side by side, and an office, in which only two slept. In the bedroom were Léon, Major Philip Cochran, an Associated Press correspondent named Norgaard, and myself. A captain named Robert Wylie and Major (later Lieutenant Colonel) Vincent Sheean slept in the office. We would try to ignore Léon's first morning call, but before long there would be another; Cochran, the operations officer at the field, would be asking what was going on, and we would hear the roar of the motors down on the field being warmed up for the dawn patrol and the morning missions. Then we would hear Wylie clattering around our stove in his G.I. shoes and there would be a glow in the shack when he put the match to the paper with which he started the fire. Wylie, who wasn't a flying officer, always tried to have the shack warm by the time Cochran got up, and he wanted the Major to stay in bed until the last minute. He was as solicitous as a trainer with a favorite colt, and the rest of us benefited from the care he took of Cochran, because we didn't get up early, either. Wylie is a wiry man with a high forehead and a pepper-and-salt mustache. He wears glasses and looks like an advertising artist's conception of an executive who is in good humor because he has had an excellent night's sleep owing to Sanka. He is a highly adaptable man. After Wylie had puttered around for a while, we would sit up one by one and stretch and complain about being disturbed or about the cold and then go outside to wash. Mornings on which the anti-aircraft opened up against early visitors, the tempo was accelerated. Cochran undressed at night by loosening the knot in his tie and drew it tight again in the morning as a sign that he was dressed. These were symbolic gestures he never omitted.

On the morning of the fifth and last day of a small private war during which the Germans had been trying hard to knock out our field, it was the anti-aircraft that brought us out of bed. We scrambled for the door, lugging our tin hats, our toothbrushes, and our canteens. The Germans were already almost over our field, but they were quite high, since our patrol planes had engaged them on the way in and they could not break off the fight to strafe us. The German planes were single-engined fighters, which sometimes carry wing or belly bombs, but this time they were not bombing. Some of the defending planes were marked with the tricolor *cocarde* of the French Army. It was, I suppose, a historic combat, because the pilots of the Lafayette Escadrille, which was stationed at the field, were making the first French air fight against the Germans since the armistice of 1940. The Escadrille, which had been equipped with a number of our Curtiss P-40's in Morocco, had been with us only a few days.

As we watched, a plane fell, apparently far on the other side of a ridge of mountains near the field, and we yelled happily, thinking it was a Messerschmitt. After the fight we were to learn that it had been a P-40 with a French sergeant pilot. Cochran kept up an expert running commentary on what all the pilots were trying to do, but he frequently didn't know which were French and which Germans. During the battle we simultaneously watched and brushed our teeth. A couple of the French planes landed on the field while the others were still fighting, so we knew that they must have been shot up. Finally, one group of planes above the field started away and the others chased them, but the first planes simply outclimbed their pursuers and left them behind; then there was no longer any doubt about which were Messerschmitts and which were Curtisses. One German plane remained over the field, at perhaps thirty thousand feet, even after the rest of the invaders had disappeared. "That's what kills me," Cochran said, pointing to the lone plane. "There's that sucker stooging around and casing the joint for a future job and he's so high nobody can bother him." Finally the stooge, evidently having found out all he wanted to know, took his leisurely departure.

A group of P-40's from one of the two American P-40 squadrons at the field rose to relieve the Lafayettes, and the French planes came buzzing in like bees settling on a sugared stick. In a few minutes Kostia Rozanoff, commandant of the Escadrille, and his pilots had gathered in Léon's shack to discuss the fight. All of them had had combat experience in 1939 and 1940, but the engagement this morning had been the *rentrée*, and they were as excited as if they had never seen a Messerschmitt before. Despite the fact that they were old hands, Cochran said, they had fought recklessly, climbing up to meet the Messerschmitts instead of waiting until the Germans dived. "If they don't dive," Cochran had frequently warned his own pilots, "you just don't fight." The French pilots' ardor had got them a beating, for besides the pilot whom we had seen fall and who, Rozanoff said, had not bailed out and was quite certainly killed, the two planes that had landed during the combat were riddled and would be of no use except for salvage, and one of their pilots had been wounded. The Germans apparently had suffered no damage at all. Rozanoff, a chunky, blond man who gets his name, as well as his coloring and his high cheekbones, from his Russian ancestry, is thirty-seven and has a deep voice, like Chaliapin's. He said that the pilot who had been killed was his wing man and he could not understand how he had failed to see the Messerschmitt that had attacked him from the rear. "I cry him turn," Rozanoff kept saying. "I turn. He turns not. Poor little one."

It was extremely sad that the first Escadrille combat had not been a victory; it would have been such a fine story to bolster French morale all over the world. I remembered the sergeant pilot, who had been a likable fellow. An officer of the district gendarmerie brought the sergeant's wedding ring back to the field later in the morning.

My friend Norgaard and I had chosen that Friday for our departure from the field. We were going in to the big city, where the censors and the cable offices were, to write some stuff and get it off. There was air transportation between our field and the more settled places to the west, where staff officers and diplomats lived, but the service did not run on a formal schedule. Big Douglas transports skimmed in over the mountains once and sometimes twice a day, carrying mail and supplies, and they usually had room for passengers going back. They came at a different hour each day to make it as hard as possible for the Germans to waylay them. When they came, they stayed merely as long as was necessary, and the only way to be sure of a ride was to have your bedding roll made up and to stay near the landing field waiting for the transports to appear. When they did, an officer would drive you and your luggage out to them in a jeep and you would get your stuff aboard. Norgaard and I hung around in front of our shack that morning, waiting. As the day wore on, a strong wind came up and blew great clouds of sand. At about eleven o'clock two transports arrived, escorted by some Spitfires. Cochran had planned to drive us down to the transports, but he was called to the telephone, and Major Robert Christman, the C.O. of one P-40 squadron, said that he would drive us instead.

When we arrived where the transports were standing on the runway, the transport captain, whose name, I noted from the leather strip on the breast of his flying jacket, was Lively, came over to the jeep and asked where his Spits could get gas. His ship was named the Scarlett O'Hara. He and Christman started discussing what was the quickest way to get the gas. Christman and Norgaard and I stayed in the jeep. Dust was blowing over the field a mile a minute. Suddenly Christman looked over his shoulder, called on God, and vanished. Within a moment Lively was also gone. I turned around to speak to Norgaard, and discovered that he too had evaporated. I hate to sit in an empty jeep when I don't know why the other passengers have jumped. I do not remember actually getting out myself, but I know that I was already running when I heard somebody yell, "Hit the dirt!" Under the circumstances, this sounded so sensible that I bellyflopped to the ground, and I landed so hard that I skinned my knees and elbows. No surface in the world offers less cover than a runway. I regretted that my body, which is thick, was not thinner. I could guess what had happened: German strafers had ridden in on the dust storm and nobody had seen them until they opened fire. I knew that the very nasty noises above me were being made by airplane cannon and that the even nastier ones close to me came from the detonation of the small explosive shells they fire. The strafers, I figured, were heading for the transports—large, expensive, unarmored jobs that you could punch holes in with a beer-can opener. I was therefore in line with the target and was very sorry to be where I was.

As soon as there was a lull in the noises overhead, I got up and ran toward the edge of the runway to get away from the transports, but more noises came before I made it, so I flopped again. After they had passed, I got up and ran off the runway. I saw a soldier in a fine, large hole nearly six feet deep. He shouted, "Come right in, sir!" You can have Oscar of the Waldorf any time; I will always remember that soldier as my favorite host. I jumped in and squeezed up against him. Almost immediately the noises came a third time and two transport pilots jumped down on my back. I was astonished that I had been able to outrun such relatively young men.

By this time all of our machine guns along the edges of the field were firing away, and there was a fourth pass, as the fliers say, and a loud crash, as if one of the Germans had dropped a bomb. A minute or two later the noise began to die down. Looking up from the bottom of the hole, we could see a man descending in a parachute. The big, white chute was swaying this way and that in the wind. The man had an awful time landing. We could see that even from a distance. The chute dragged him and bounced hell out of him after he landed. Afterward, word got around the field that he was an American. I didn't find out until a couple of days later, though, that the man with the chute had been a fellow called Horse, a big, square-bearded, twenty-five-year-old Texan pilot I had come to know well. In landing, he hit his head against the ground and suffered a concussion of the brain. They put him in an ambulance and started for the nearest hospital, which was forty miles by road, but he had bad luck. The Germans had been strafing that road, too, that morning, and when the ambulance got within five miles of the hospital, it was blocked by two burning ammunition trucks. The shells on the trucks were exploding. The squadron surgeon and the ambulance-driver put Horse on a stretcher and carried him around the trucks to a safe point on the other side, and an ambulance from the hospital came out to pick him up, but by the time it got there he was dead.

When the shooting at the field was over, the pilots and the soldier and I got out of the hole and walked back toward the transports, which were still there. Norgaard climbed out of another hole not far away. He said that when he had jumped out of the jeep he had crawled under it, and there he had found a transport lieutenant who had had the same idea. They had given up the jeep after the first pass and run for it, just as I had already done. We stared at the parallel furrows the Messerschmitt cannon had plowed down the runway, as if they had been the teeth of a rake, and ourselves the field mice between them. The transport boys borrowed our jeep to get gas for the Spits, which had been immobilized during the raid because their tanks were empty. When the boys came back, we climbed into one of the transports. The big planes took off almost immediately. "Leave them laughing," Norgaard said to me when he recovered sufficient breath to say anything.

We learned later that the strafing had been done by eight Messerschmitts flying in four loose pairs, and that was why there had been four passes. Another Messerschmitt, making a run by itself, had dropped one bomb, ineffectually. There had also been a high cover of Messerschmitts; one of them had accounted for Horse. We were told that Cochran had said, with a hint of admiration in his voice, "It is getting so that the Germans patrol our field for us." A lot of Air Forces generals who were on a tour of inspection visited the field shortly after we left, said that the situation was very grave, and left, too. This point in the war over the field may be compared to the one in a Western movie at which the villain has kicked hell out of the heroine and just about wrestled her to the brink of ruin in a locked room.

At about two-thirty that same afternoon the Lafayette Escadrille was patrolling the field, in the company of two pilots from the American P-40 squadron that was commanded by a Major Hubbard. This squadron had its full complement of pilots but only five planes. The pilots took turns flying the five ships, so they were not getting a great deal of practice. Nevertheless, Hubbard's squadron had already scored two victories that week. The two American pilots in the air were Hubbard and a man named Beggs. Two of their mates, Boone and Smith, were on the ground on alert call, sitting in their planes ready to reinforce the patrol if they were called.

This field didn't have one of those elaborate radio airplane-detectors that warn swank airdromes of the approach of enemy aircraft. It had to rely on its patrol system and on tips that watchers telephoned in. The tipsters were not infallible, as Norgaard and I had noticed that morning, and in the afternoon they slipped up again. Ten Junkers 88 bombers unexpectedly appeared, flying toward the field at three thousand feet. There was an escort of four fighters, unusually small for so many bombers, flying high above them and, as someone described it to me, acting oddly uninterested. The Frenchmen on patrol, also flying high, made one swipe at the escort and it disappeared, not to be seen again. Nine of the bombers were flying in three loose V's and one ship was trailing the third V. Hubbard took the bomber on the right of the first V and shot it down. Beggs got the middle one and a Frenchman knocked down the one on the left. The other Junkers had begun to drop their bombs. Boone and Smith came up off the field through the falling bombs to join the battle. Hubbard shot down another plane, and Boone, who had never fired a shot at a man or a plane before, came up behind one Junkers and blasted it out of the sky; it caromed against another Junkers on the way down, which gave Boone two planes with one burst of fire. He went on to destroy two more. Smith, opening fire at extreme range for fear that he would be shut out, blew the rudder off another Junkers, which also crashed. The tenth Junkers headed for home, but it never got there; the French picked off that one. It was the jack pot, ten out of ten. It was also the end of the five-day war over our airfield. No producer of Westerns ever wound up a film more satisfactorily. The Germans stayed away, in fact, for nineteen days and then came back only once, for a quick sneak raid.

Of the ten German bomber crews, only four men came out of the fight alive and two of these died in the hospital. The two others said that the ten bombers had been escorted by four Italian Macchi C. 202 fighters, which had deserted them. Why the Luftwaffe should have entrusted four Macchis with the protection of ten Junkers 88's is harder to explain than the result. The Germans, fortunately for our side, sometimes vary their extreme guile with extreme stupidity.

*   *   *

I didn't have a chance to return to the airfield for about ten days, and then I stopped in on my way down to Gafsa, where the Americans were supposed to be launching a ground offensive. Captain Wylie, who told me about the big day at the field, said that Boone had come into the operations shack looking rather incredulous himself. "Probably I'm crazy," he had said to Wylie, "but I think I just shot down four planes." The Frenchmen thought up a gag. They said it was a victory for three nations — "The Americans shot down seven planes, we shot down two, and the Italians shot down the tenth so the crew couldn't tell on them."

The Americans left the field undefeated, for the two P-40 squadrons were relieved not long afterward by other outfits and sent back from the fighting zone to rest. Christman's squadron had been fighting there steadily for two months. I met the fellows from Christman's bunch again while I was trying to get a ride into civilization from another airfield, a bit west of the one where they had been stationed. A lot of trucks drove up and deposited the officers and men of the squadron on the field, with their weapons, their barracks bags, and their bedding rolls. Christman was there, and Private Otto, the squadron barber, and Corporal Jake Goldstein, the reformed songwriter. I renewed my acquaintance with a pilot named Fackler, whom I remembered especially because he had once, finding himself flying formation with two Messerschmitts who thought he was another Messerschmitt, shot one of them down, and I again met Thomas, the Oklahoma boy who had been lost in the air one night and had been lighted home by the fire of the field's anti-aircraft guns, and a non-flying lieutenant named Lamb, who used to practice law in New York, and a dozen others. I felt as if I had known them all for a long time.

Eleven transports came in to take the squadron west, and I arranged to travel in one of them. I was in the lead ship of the flight, and the transport major who commanded it told me that his orders were to drop the squadron at a field only about an hour's flight away. Then the transports would go on to their base, taking me along with them. It was pleasant to see the faces of the P-40 boys aboard my transport when it took off. They didn't know anything about the field they were going to, but they knew that they were going for a rest, so they expected that there would at least be huts and showers there. They looked somewhat astonished when the transports settled down in a vast field of stubble without a sign of a building anywhere around it. There were a few B-25 bombers on the field and in the distance some tents. A transport sergeant came out of the pilot's compartment forward in our plane and worked his way toward the tail of our ship, climbing over the barracks bags heaped in the space between the seats. "I guess this is where you get out," he told the P-40 fellows.

A couple of soldiers jumped out and the rest began passing out bags and rifles to them. Pretty soon all the stuff was piled outside the plane and the soldiers were standing on the field, turning their backs to a sharp wind and audibly wondering where the hell the barracks were. A jeep with an officer in it drove out from among the tents and made its way among the transports until it arrived at our ship. The transport major talked to the officer in the jeep, and then they both drove over to the transport Christman was travelling in and picked him up, and the three of them drove back to the tents. Some soldiers who had been near the jeep had heard the field's officer say that nobody there had been notified that they were coming. The transport major had replied that all he knew was that he had orders to leave them there. The soldiers who had heard the conversation communicated the news to the others by Army telegraphy. "Situation normal!" one soldier called out, and everybody laughed. Soldiers are fatalistic about such situations.

Some time before a report had circulated among the men that the squadron was to go back to the United States. Now I heard one soldier say, "This don't look like no United States to me."

Another one said, "When we get back there, Freddie Bartholomew will be running for President." He didn't seem sore.

Somebody said, "I hear they're going to start us here and let us hack our way through to South Africa."

Somebody else began a descant on a favorite Army fantasy: what civilian life will be like after the war. "I bet if my wife gives me a piece of steak," he said, "I'll say to her, 'What the hell is this? Give me stew.'"

Another one said, "I bet she'll be surprised when you jump into bed with all your clothes on."

The delicacy of their speculations diminished from there on.

After a while the jeep came back. The transport major got out and said, "There seems to be some mistake. You'd better put your stuff back in the ship." We all got back into the planes, and the major told me that this obviously wasn't the place to leave the men but that he would have to wait until base operations could get headquarters on the telephone and find out their destination. We sat in the planes for an hour; then another officer came out in a jeep and said that nobody at headquarters knew anything about the squadron, so the major had better not take it any place else. The major told his sergeant to instruct the men to take their luggage off the planes. "We enjoy doing this. It's no trouble at all," one of the soldiers in my plane said. The transports took off and left them standing there. I learned later that they eventually got straightened out. After two or three days someone at headquarters remembered them; the pilots were sent to western Morocco and the ground echelon was moved to another field.

All this happened what seems now to be long ago, in the pioneer days of the American Army in Tunisia. The old field, from which I had watched the five-day war, was never knocked out from the air, but it was taken by German ground troops with tanks, and then the Americans took it back and went on. The Hotel Léon, if the Germans hadn't burned it, was certainly full of booby traps for the Americans when they got there. I shouldn't like to have slept in it. Léon is now in a large Algerian city, where he has been assigned to a calmer liaison job. Cochran has been promoted and decorated and posted to a new command. A lot of very fine fellows are dead, and I like to think that the best possible use was made of them.

The New Yorker, March 20, April 3, 10, 17, 1943

The War in Tunisia

---

by Ernie Pyle

"Only Slightly Above the Caveman Stage"

THE TUNISIAN FRONT — (by wireless) — It must be hard for you folks at home to conceive how our troops right at the front actually live. In fact it is hard to describe it to you even when I'm among them, living in somewhat the same way they are.

You can scarcely credit the fact that human beings — the same people you've known all your life — could adjust themselves so acceptingly to a type of living that is only slightly above the caveman stage.

*   *   *

Some of our troops came directly to the Tunisian front after the original occupation of North and West Africa, and have been here ever since. They have not slept in a bed for months. They've lived through this vicious winter sleeping outdoors on the ground. They haven't been paid in three months. They have been on British rations most of the time, and British rations, though good, get mighty tiresome.

They never take off their clothes at night, except their shoes. They don't get a bath oftener than once a month. One small detachment acquired lice and had to be fumigated, but all the rest have escaped so far. They move so frequently they don't attempt to put in many home touches, as the men do at the more permanent camps toward the rear. Very few of the front-line troops have ever had any leave. They never go to town for an evening's fun. They work all the time.

Nobody keeps track of the days or weeks. I'll wager that 90% of our frontline troops never know when Sunday comes.

Furthermore, the old traditional differences between day and night have almost ceased to exist. Nighttime no longer necessarily means rest, nor daytime work. Often it's just reversed. The bulk of our convoying of supplies and shifting of troops is done at night. The soldiers are accustomed to traveling all night, sometimes three or four nights in a row. Irregularity of sleep becomes normal. One soldier told me he once went three days and nights without sleep.

You see men sleeping anywhere, anytime. The other day I saw a soldier asleep in blankets under an olive tree at 2 in the afternoon. A few feet away a full colonel was sleeping soundly on the ground. In battle you just go until you drop.

It isn't always possible to get enough food up to the fighting soldiers. I have just been with one artillery outfit in the mountains who were getting only one cold meal a day.

Nurses tell me that when the more seriously wounded reach the hospital they are often so exhausted they fall asleep without drugs, despite their pain.

*   *   *

The war coarsens most people. You live rough and talk rough, and if you didn't toughen up inside you simply wouldn't be able to take it. An officer friend of mine, Lieut. Lennie Bessman of Milwaukee, was telling me two incidents of a recent battle that touched him deeply.

One evening he and another officer came up to a tiny farmhouse, which was apparently empty. To be on the safe side he called out "Who's there?" before going in. The answer came back:

"Captain Blank, and who the hell wants to know?"

They went in and found the captain, his clothes covered with blood, heating a can of rations over a gasoline flame. They asked if they could stay all night with him. He said he didn't give a damn. They started to throw their blankets down, and the captain said:

"Look out for that man over there."

There was a dead soldier lying in a corner.

The captain was cooking his supper and preparing to stay all night alone in that same room. The flood and fury of death about him that day had left him utterly indifferent both to the companionship of the living and the presence of the dead.

The other incident was just the opposite. Another captain happened to be standing beside Bessman. It was just at dusk and they were on the desert. The night chill was coming down. The captain looked to the far horizon and said, sort of to himself:

"You fight all day here in the desert and what's the end of it all? Night just closes down over you and chokes you."

A little later Bessman got out a partly filled bottle of gin he had with him and asked this same sensitive captain if he'd like a drink. The captain didn't even reach out his hand. He simply answered:

"Have you got enough for my men too?"

He wouldn't take a drink himself unless the enlisted men under him could have some.

All officers are not like that, but the battlefield does produce a brotherhood. The common bond of death draws humans toward each other over the artificial barrier of rank.

Scripps-Howard wire copy, February 19, 1943

"What a Tank Battle Looks Like"

THE TUNISIAN FRONT, March 1—(By wireless)—This and the next few columns will be an attempt to describe what a tank battle looks like.

Words will be poor instruments for it. Neither can isolated camera shots tell you the story. Probably only Hollywood with its machinery of many dimensions is capable of transferring to your senses a clear impression of a tank battle.

The fight in question was the American counter attack on the second day of the battle at Sidi Bou Zid which eventually resulted in our withdrawal.

It was the biggest tank battle fought so far in this part of the world. On that morning I had a talk with the commanding general some 10 miles behind the front lines before starting for the battle scene.

He took me into his tent and showed me just what the battle plan was for the day. He picked out a point close to the expected battle area and said that would be a good place for me to watch from.

The only danger, he said, would be one of being encircled and cut off if the battle should go against us.

"But it won't," he said, "for we are going to kick hell out of them today and we've got the stuff to do it with."

Unfortunately, we didn't kick hell out of them. In fact the boot was on the other foot.

I spent the forenoon in the newly picked, badly shattered forward command post. All morning I tried to get on up where the tanks were but there was no transportation left around the post and their communications were cut off at noontime.

We sat on the ground and ate some British crackers with jam and drank some hot tea. The day was bright and mellow. Shortly after lunch a young Lieutenant dug up a spare jeep and said he'd take me on up to the front.

We drove a couple of miles east along a highway to a crossroads which was the very heart center of our troops' bivouacs. German airmen had been after this crossroads all morning. They had hit it again just a few minutes before we got there. In the road was a large crater and a few yards away a tank was off to one side, burning.

The roads at that point were high and we could see a long way. In every direction was a huge semi-irrigated desert valley. It looked very much like the valley at Phoenix, Ariz.—no trees but patches of wild growth, shoulder-high cactus of the prickly pear variety. In other parts of the valley were spotted cultivated fields and tiny square stucco houses of Arab farmers. The whole vast scene was treeless, with slightly rolling big mountains in the distance.

As far as you could see out across the rolling desert in all four sections of the "pie" formed by the intersecting roads was American equipment—tanks, half tracks, artillery, infantry—hundreds, yes, thousands of vehicles extending miles and miles and everything standing still. We were in time; the battle had not yet started.

We put our jeep in super low gear and drove out across the sands among the tanks. Ten miles or so east and southeast were the Germans but there was no activity anywhere, no smoke on the horizon, no planes in the sky.

It all had the appearance of an after-lunch siesta but no one was asleep.

As we drove past tank after tank we found each one's crew

at its post inside—the driver at his control, the commander
standing with his head sticking out of the open turret door,
standing there silent and motionless, just looking ahead like
the Indian on the calendars.

We stopped and inquired of several what they were doing.
They said they didn't know what the plan was—they were
merely ready in place and waiting for orders. Somehow it
seemed like the cars lined up at Indianapolis just before the
race starts—their weeks of training over, everything mechanically perfect, just a few quiet minutes of immobility before the
great struggle for which they had waited so long.

Suddenly out of this siesta-like doze the order came. We
didn't hear it for it came to the tanks over their radios but we
knew it quickly for all over the desert tanks began roaring and
pouring out blue smoke from the cylinders. Then they started
off, kicking up dust and clanking in that peculiar "tank
sound" we have all come to know so well.

They poured around us, charging forward. They weren't
close together—probably a couple of hundred yards apart.
There weren't lines or any specific formation. They were just
everywhere. They covered the desert to the right and left,
ahead and behind as far as we could see, trailing their eager
dust tails behind. It was almost as though some official starter
had fired his blank pistol. The battle was on.

(Continued tomorrow)

Scripps-Howard wire copy, March 1, 1943

"The Fantastic Surge of Caterpillar Metal"

THE TUNISIAN FRONT, March 2.—(By Wireless)—We were
in the midst of the forward rushing tanks, but didn't know
what the score was. So I pulled the jeep to the side, gradually
easing a way out.

We decided to get to a high spot and take a look at what
was happening, before we got caught. So we bounced over
gullies and ditches, up the side of a rocky hill.

There—in a hidden gully—we found the commanding
colonel, standing beside a radio half-track. We stood close
enough to the radio to hear the voice of the battalion com-

mander, who was leading the tank attack. At the same time, through binoculars, we watched the fantastic surge of caterpillar metal move forward amidst its own dust.

Far across the desert, in front of us, lay the town of Sidi bou Zid. Through the glasses we could see it only as a great oasis whose green trees stood out against the bare brown of the desert. On beyond were high hills, where some of our troops were still trapped after the surprise attack of the day before.

Behind our tanks, leading the attack, other armored vehicles puffed blue smoke. New formations began to move forward swiftly. The artillery went first, followed by armored infantry in half-tracks and even in jeeps. Now the entire desert was surging in one gigantic movement.

Over the radio came the voice of the battalion commander:

"We're in the edge of Sidi bou Zid, and have struck no opposition yet." So our tanks were across the vast plain, which the Germans had abandoned during the night—after the chaos of the previous day.

This peaceful report from our tank charge brought no comment from any one around the command truck. Faces were grave: It wasn't right—this business of no opposition at all; there must be a trick in it somewhere . . .

Suddenly, brown geysers of earth and smoke began to spout. We watched through our glasses. Then, from far off, came the sound of explosions.

Again the voice from the radio:

"We're getting shelled, but can't make out where it's coming from." Then a long silence, while the geysers continued to burst . . .

"I'm not sure, but I think it's artillery along the road north of town . . . Now there is some from the south."

We looked, and could see through our glasses the enemy advancing. They were far away, perhaps 10 miles—narrow little streaks of dust, like plumes, speeding down the low sloping plain from the mountain base toward the oasis of Sidi bou Zid.

We could not see the German tanks, only dust plumes extending and pushing forward.

Just then I realized we were standing on the very hill the

general had picked out for me on his map that morning. It was not good enough. I said to the young lieutenant:

"Let's get on up there." He replied: "I'm ready."

So we got into the jeep, and went leaping and bounding up toward what was—but we didn't know it then—the most ghastly armored melee that has occurred so far in Tunisia.

(Continued tomorrow)

Scripps-Howard wire copy, March 2, 1943

"Into the Thick of Battle"

THE TUNISIAN FRONT, March 3—(By Wireless)—It was odd, the way we went up into the thick of the battle in our jeep. We didn't attach ourselves to anybody. We didn't ask anybody if we could go. We just started the motor and went.

Vehicles ahead of us had worn a sort of track across the desert and through irrigated fields. We followed that awhile, keeping our place in the forward-moving procession. We were just a jeep with two brown-clad figures in it, indistinguishable from anyone else.

The line was moving cautiously. Every now and then the procession would stop. A few times we stopped too. We shut off our motor to listen for planes. But, finally, we tired of the slow progress. We dashed out across the sand and the Arabs' plowed fields, skirting cactus fences and small farmyards.

As we did this, a sensation of anxiety—which had not touched me before—came over me. It was fear of mines in the freshly dug earth; the touch of the wheel—we could so easily be blown into little bits. I spoke of this to the lieutenant, but he said he didn't think they had had time to plant mines.

I thought to myself: "Hell, it doesn't take all night to plant a mine." We did not—it is obvious to report—hit any mines.

The battlefield was an incongruous thing. Always there is some ridiculous impingement of normalcy on a field of battle.

Here on this day were the Arabs. They were herding their camels, just as usual. Some of them continued to plow their fields. Children walked along, driving their little sack-ladden burros, as tanks and guns clanked past them. The sky was filled with planes and smoke bursts from screaming shells.

As we smashed along over a field of new grain, which pushed its small shoots just a few inches above earth, the asinine thought popped into my head: "I wonder if the Army got permission to use this land before starting the attack."

Both sides had crossed and recrossed these farms in the past 24 hours. The fields were riddled by deep ruts and by wide spooky tracks of the almost mythical Mark VI. tanks.

Evidence of the previous day's battle was still strewn across the desert. We passed charred half-tracks. We stopped to look into a burned-out tank, named Temes, from which a Lieut. Colonel friend of mine and his crew had demolished four German tanks before being put out of commission themselves.

We passed a trailer still full of American ammunition, which had been abandoned. The young lieutenant wanted to hook our own jeep to it as a tow when we returned, but I talked him out of it. I feared the Germans had booby-trapped it during the night.

We moved on closer to the actual tank battle ahead, but never went right into it—for in a jeep that would have been a fantastic form of suicide. We stopped, I should judge, about a mile behind the foremost tanks.

Behind us the desert was still alive with men and machines moving up. Later we learned that some German tanks had maneuvered in behind us, and were shooting up our half-tracks and jeeps. But, fortunately, we didn't know all this at the time.

Light American tanks came up from the rear and stopped near us. They were to be held there in reserve, in case they had to be called into the game in this league which was much too heavy and hot for them. Their crews jumped out the moment they stopped, and began digging foxholes against the inevitable arrival of the dive bombers.

Soon the dive bombers came. They set fires behind us. American and German tanks were burning ahead of us.

Our planes came over, too, strafing and bombing the enemy.

One of our half-tracks, full of ammunition, was livid red,

with flames leaping and swaying. Every few seconds one of its shells would go off, and the projectile would tear into the sky with a weird whang-zing sort of noise.

Field artillery had stopped just on our right. They began shelling the German artillery beyond our tanks. It didn't take long for the Germans to answer.

The scream of an approaching shell is an appalling thing. We could hear them coming—(You sort of duck inside yourself, without actually ducking at all).

Then we could see the dust kick up a couple of hundred yards away. The shells hit the ground and ricocheted like armor-piercing shells, which do not explode but skip along the ground until they finally lose momentum or hit something.

War has its own peculiar sounds. They are not really very much different from sounds in the world of peace. But they clothe themselves in an unforgettable fierceness, just because born in danger and death.

The clank of a starting tank, the scream of a shell through the air, the ever-rising whine of fiendishness as a bomber dives—these sounds have their counterparts in normal life, and you would be hard put to distinguish them in a blindfold test. But, once heard in war, they remain with you forever.

Their nervous memories come back to you in a thousand ways—in the grind of a truck starting in low gear, in high wind around the eaves, in somebody merely whistling a tune. Even the sound of a shoe, dropped to the floor in a hotel room above you, becomes indistinguishable from the faint boom of a big gun far away. A mere rustling curtain can paralyze a man with memories.

Scripps-Howard wire copy, March 3, 1943

"Brave Men. Brave Men!"

NORTHERN TUNISIA—(by wireless)—I was away from the front lines for a while this spring, living with other troops, and considerable fighting took place while I was gone. When I got ready to return to my old friends at the front I wondered if I would sense any change in them.

I did, and definitely.

The most vivid change is the casual and workshop manner in which they now talk about killing. They have made the psychological transition from the normal belief that taking human life is sinful, over to a new professional outlook where killing is a craft. To them now there is nothing morally wrong about killing. In fact it is an admirable thing.

I think I am so impressed by this new attitude because it hasn't been necessary for me to make this change along with them. As a noncombatant, my own life is in danger only by occasional chance or circumstance. Consequently I need not think of killing in personal terms, and killing to me is still murder.

Even after a winter of living with wholesale death and vile destruction, it is only spasmodically that I seem capable of realizing how real and how awful this war is. My emotions seem dead and crusty when presented with the tangibles of war. I find I can look on rows of fresh graves without a lump in my throat. Somehow I can look on mutilated bodies without flinching or feeling deeply.

It is only when I sit alone away from it all, or lie at night in my bedroll re-creating with closed eyes what I have seen, thinking and thinking and thinking, that at last the enormity of all these newly dead strikes like a living nightmare. And there are times when I feel that I can't stand it and will have to leave.

*   *   *

But to the fighting soldier that phase of the war is behind. It was left behind after his first battle. His blood is up. He is fighting for his life, and killing now for him is as much a profession as writing is for me.

He wants to kill individually or in vast numbers. He wants to see the Germans overrun, mangled, butchered in the Tunisian trap. He speaks excitedly of seeing great heaps of dead, of our bombers sinking whole shiploads of fleeing men, of Germans by the thousands dying miserably in a final Tunisian holocaust of his own creation.

In this one respect the front-line soldier differs from all the rest of us. All the rest of us—you and me and even the thousands of soldiers behind the lines in Africa—we want terribly yet only academically for the war to get over. The front-line soldier wants it to be got over by the physical process of his destroying enough Germans to end it. He is truly at war. The rest of us, no matter how hard we work, are not.

*   *   *

Say what you will, nothing can make a complete soldier except battle experience.

In the semifinals of this campaign—the cleaning out of Central Tunisia—we had large units in battle for the first time. Frankly, they didn't all excel. Their own commanders admit it, and admirably they don't try to alibi. The British had to help us out a few times, but neither American nor British commanders are worried about that, for there was no lack of bravery. There was only lack of experience. They all know we will do better next time.

The First Infantry Division is an example of what our American units can be after they have gone through the mill of experience. Those boys did themselves proud in the semifinals. Everybody speaks about it. Our casualties included few taken prisoners. All the other casualties were wounded or died fighting.

"They never gave an inch," a general says. "They died right in their foxholes."

I heard of a high British officer who went over this battlefield just after the action was over. American boys were still lying dead in their foxholes, their rifles still grasped in firing position in their dead hands. And the veteran English soldier remarked time and again, in a sort of hushed eulogy spoken only to himself:

"Brave men. Brave men!"

Scripps-Howard wire copy, April 22, 1943

"Little Boys Again, Lost in the Dark"

NORTHERN TUNISIA—(By wireless)—We moved one afternoon to a new position just a few miles behind the invisible line of armor that separates us from the Germans in Northern Tunisia. Nothing happened that first night that was spectacular, yet somehow the whole night became obsessed with a spookiness that leaves it standing like a landmark in my memory.

We had been at the new camp about an hour and were still setting up our tents when German planes appeared overhead. We stopped work to watch them. It was the usual display of darting planes, with the conglomerate sounds of ack-ack on the ground and in the sky.

Suddenly we realized that one plane was diving straight at us, and we made a mad scramble for foxholes. Two officer friends of mine had dug a three-foot hole and set their tent over it. So they made for their tent, and I was tramping on their heels. The tent flap wouldn't come open, and we wound up in a silly heap. Finally it did open, and we all dived through the narrow opening all at once.

We lay there in the hole, face down, as the plane came smack overhead with a terrible roar. We were all drawn up inside, waiting for the blow. Explosions around us were shatteringly loud, and yet when it was all over we couldn't find any bomb holes or anybody hurt.

But you could find a lot of nervous people.

*   *   *

Dusk came on, and with dusk began the steady boom of big guns in the mountains ahead of us. They weren't near enough for the sound to be crashing. Rather it was like the lonely roll of an approaching thunderstorm—a sound which since childhood has always made me sad with a kind of portent of inevitable doom.

We went to bed in our tents. A nearby farmyard was full of dogs and they began a howling that lasted all night. The roll of artillery was constant. It never stopped once in 24 hours. Once in a while there were nearer shots which might have been German patrols or might not.

We lay uneasily in our cots. Sleep wouldn't come. We turned and turned. I snapped on a flashlight.

"What time is it?" asked Chris Cunningham from the next cot.

"Quarter to one," I answered. "Haven't you been asleep?"
He hadn't.

A plane droned faintly in the distance and came nearer and nearer until it was overhead.

"Is that a Jerry or a Beaufighter," Chris asked out of the darkness.

"It hasn't got that throb-throb to it," I said, "so it must be a Beaufighter. But hell, I never can tell really. Don't know what it is."

The plane passed on, out of hearing. The artillery rolled and rolled. A nearer shot went off uncannily somewhere in the darkness. Some guinea hens set up a terrific cackling.

I remembered that just before dusk a soldier had shot at a snake in our new camp, and they thought it was a cobra. We'd just heard our first stories of scorpions, too. I began to feel creepy and wondered if our tent flaps were tight.

Another plane throbbed in the sky, and we lay listening with an awful anticipation. One of the dogs suddenly broke into a frenzied barking and went tearing through our little camp as though chasing a demon.

My mind seemed to lose all sense of proportion, and I was jumpy and mad at myself.

Concussion ghosts, traveling in waves, touched our tent walls and made them quiver. Ghosts were shaking the ground ever so lightly. Ghosts were stirring the dogs to hysteria. Ghosts were wandering in the sky peering for us in our cringing hideout. Ghosts were everywhere, and their hordes were multiplying as every hour added its production of new battlefield dead.

You lie and think of the graveyards and the dirty men and the shocking blast of the big guns, and you can't sleep.

"What time is it?" comes out of darkness from the next cot. I snap on the flashlight.

"Half past 4, and for God's sake go to sleep!"

Finally just before dawn you do sleep, in spite of everything.

*   *   *

Next morning we spoke around among ourselves and found one by one that all us had tossed away all night. It was an unexplainable thing. For all of us had been through dangers greater than this. On another night the roll of the guns would have lulled us to sleep.

It's just that on some nights the air becomes sick and there is an unspoken contagion of spiritual dread, and you are little boys again, lost in the dark.

Scripps-Howard wire copy, April 27, 1943

"The Greatest Damage Is Psychological"

AT THE FRONT LINES IN TUNISIA—(by wireless)—When our infantry goes into a big push in northern Tunisia each man is issued three bars of D-ration chocolate, enough to last one day. He takes no other food.

He carries two canteens of water instead of the usual one. He carries no blankets. He leaves behind all extra clothes except his raincoat. In his pockets he may have a few toilet articles. Some men carry their money. Others give it to friends to keep.

In the days that follow they live in a way that is inconceivable to us at home. They walk and fight all night without sleep. Next day they lie flat in foxholes, or hide in fields of freshly green, kneehigh wheat.

If they're in the fields they dare not even move enough to dig foxholes, for that would bring the German artillery. They can't rise even for nature's calls. The German feels for them continually with his artillery.

*   *   *

The slow drag of these motionless daylight hours is nearly unendurable. Lieut. Mickey Miller of Morgantown, Ind., says this lifeless waiting in a wheatfield is almost the worst part of the whole battle.

The second evening after the attack begins, C-rations and five-gallon cans of water are brought up across country in jeeps, after dark. You eat in the dark, and you can't see the can you are eating from. You just eat by feel. You make cold coffee from cold water.

One night a German shell landed close and fragments punctured 15 cans of water.

Each night enough canned rations for three meals are

brought up, but when the men move on after supper most of them either lose or leave behind the next day's rations, because they're too heavy to carry. But, as they say, when you're in battle and excited you sort of go on your nerve. You don't think much about being hungry.

The men fight at night and lie low by day, when the artillery takes over its blasting job. Weariness gradually creeps over them. What sleeping they do is in daytime. But, as they say, at night it's too cold and in daytime it's too hot. Also the fury of the artillery makes daytime sleeping next to impossible. So does the heat of the sun. Some men have passed out from heat prostration. Many of them get upset stomachs from the heat.

But as the third and fourth days roll on weariness overcomes all obstacles to sleep. Men who sit down for a moment's rest fall asleep in the grass. There are even men who say they can march while asleep.

Lieut. Col. Charlie Stone, of New Brunswick, N.J., actually went to sleep while standing up talking on a field telephone—not while listening, but in the middle of a spoken sentence.

When sometimes they do lie down at night the men have only their raincoats to lie on. It is cold, and the dew makes the grass as wet as rain. They don't dare start a fire to heat their food, even in daytime, for the smoke would attract enemy fire. At night they can't even light cigarets in the open, so after digging their foxholes they get down and make hoods over their heads with their raincoats, and light up under the coats.

They have plenty of cigarets. Those who run out during battle are supplied by others. Every night new supplies of water and C-rations are brought up in jeeps.

*   *   *

You can't conceive how hard it is to move and fight at night. The country is rugged, the ground rough. Everything is new and strange. The nights are pitch black. You grope with your feet. You step into holes, and fall sprawling in little gullies and creeks. You trudge over plowed ground and push through waist-high shrubs. You go as a man blindfolded, feeling unsure and off balance, but you keep on going.

Through it all there is the fear of mines. The Germans have mined the country behind them beyond anything ever known before. We simply can't take time to go over each inch of ground with mine detectors, so we have to discover the mine fields by stumbling into them or driving over them. Naturally there are casualties, but they are smaller than you might think—just a few men each day.

The greatest damage is psychological—the intense watchfulness our troops must maintain.

The Germans have been utterly profligate with their mines. We dug out 400 from one field. We've found so many fields and so many isolated mines that we have run out of white tape to mark them with. But still we go on.

Scripps-Howard wire copy, May 1, 1943

"The God-Damned Infantry"

IN THE FRONT LINES BEFORE MATEUR—(by wireless)— We're now with an infantry outfit that has battled ceaselessly for four days and nights.

This northern warfare has been in the mountains. You don't ride much any more. It is walking and climbing and crawling country. The mountains aren't big, but they are constant. They are largely treeless. They are easy to defend and bitter to take. But we are taking them.

The Germans lie on the back slope of every ridge, deeply dug into foxholes. In front of them the fields and pastures are hideous with thousands of hidden mines. The forward slopes are left open, untenanted, and if the Americans tried to scale these slopes they would be murdered wholesale in an inferno of machine-gun crossfire plus mortars and grenades.

Consequently we don't do it that way. We have fallen back to the old warfare of first pulverizing the enemy with artillery, then sweeping around the ends of the hill with infantry and taking them from the sides and behind.

*   *   *

I've written before how the big guns crack and roar almost constantly throughout the day and night. They lay a screen ahead of our troops. By magnificent shooting they drop shells on the back slopes. By means of shells timed to burst in the air a few feet from the ground, they get the Germans even in their foxholes. Our troops have found that the Germans dig foxholes down and then under, trying to get cover from the shell bursts that shower death from above.

Our artillery has really been sensational. For once we have enough of something and at the right time. Officers tell me they actually have more guns than they know what to do with.

All the guns in any one sector can be centered to shoot at one spot. And when we lay the whole business on a German hill the whole slope seems to erupt. It becomes an unbelievable cauldron of fire and smoke and dirt. Veteran German soldiers say they have never been through anything like it.

*   *   *

Now to the infantry—the God-damned infantry, as they like to call themselves.

I love the infantry because they are the underdogs. They are the mud-rain-frost-and-wind boys. They have no comforts, and they even learn to live without the necessities. And in the end they are they guys that wars can't be won without.

I wish you could see just one of the ineradicable pictures I have in my mind today. In this particular picture I am sitting among clumps of sword-grass on a steep and rocky hillside that we have just taken. We are looking out over a vast rolling country to the rear.

A narrow path comes like a ribbon over a hill miles away, down a long slope, across a creek, up a slope and over another hill.

All along the length of this ribbon there is now a thin line of men. For four days and nights they have fought hard, eaten little, washed none, and slept hardly at all. Their nights have been violent with attack, fright, butchery, and their days sleepless and miserable with the crash of artillery.

The men are walking. They are fifty feet apart, for dispersal. Their walk is slow, for they are dead weary, as you can tell even when looking at them from behind. Every line and sag of their bodies speaks their inhuman exhaustion.

On their shoulders and backs they carry heavy steel tripods, machine-gun barrels, leaden boxes of ammunition. Their feet seem to sink into the ground from the overload they are bearing.

They don't slouch. It is the terrible deliberation of each step that spells out their appalling tiredness. Their faces are black and unshaven. They are young men, but the grime and whiskers and exhaustion make them look middle-aged.

In their eyes as they pass is not hatred, not excitement, not despair, not the tonic of their victory—there is just the simple expression of being here as though they had been here doing this forever, and nothing else.

The line moves on, but it never ends. All afternoon men keep coming round the hill and vanishing eventually over the horizon. It is one long tired line of antlike men.

*   *   *

There is an agony in your heart and you almost feel ashamed to look at them. They are just guys from Broadway and Main Street, but you wouldn't remember them. They are too far away now. They are too tired. Their world can never be known to you, but if you could see them just once, just for an instant, you would know that no matter how hard people work back home they are not keeping pace with these infantrymen in Tunisia.

Scripps-Howard wire copy, May 2, 1943

I Saw Regensburg Destroyed

by Beirne Lay, Jr.

IN the briefing room, the intelligence officer of the bombardment group pulled a cloth screen away from a huge wall map.
Each of the 240 sleepy-eyed combat-crew members in the
crowded room leaned forward. There were low whistles. I felt
a sting of anticipation as I stared at the red string on the map
that stretched from our base in England to a pin point deep
in Southern Germany, then south across the Alps, through
the Brenner Pass to the coast of Italy, then past Corsica and
Sardinia and south over the Mediterranean to a desert airdrome in North Africa. You could have heard an oxygen mask
drop.

"Your primary," said the intelligence officer, "is Regensburg. Your aiming point is the center of the Messerschmitt
One Hundred and Nine G aircraft-and-engine-assembly
shops. This is the most vital target we've ever gone after. If
you destroy it, you destroy thirty per cent of the Luftwaffe's
single-engine-fighter production. You fellows know what that
means to you personally."

There were a few hollow laughs.

After the briefing, I climbed aboard a jeep bound for the
operations office to check up on my Fortress assignment. The
stars were dimly visible through the chilly mist that covered
our blacked-out bomber station, but the weather forecast for
a deep penetration over the Continent was good. In the office, I looked at the crew sheet, where the line-up of the lead,
low and high squadrons of the group is plotted for each mission. I was listed for a copilot's seat. While I stood there, and
on the chance suggestion of one of the squadron commanders who was looking over the list, the operations officer erased
my name and shifted me to the high squadron as copilot in
the crew of a steady Irishman named Lieutenant Murphy,
with whom I had flown before. Neither of us knew it, but

that operations officer saved my life right there with a piece of rubber on the end of a pencil.

At 5:30 A.M., fifteen minutes before taxi time, a jeep drove around the five-mile perimeter track in the semi-darkness, pausing at each dispersal point long enough to notify the waiting crews that poor local visibility would postpone the take-off for an hour and a half. I was sitting with Murphy and the rest of our crew near the Piccadilly Lily. She looked sinister and complacent, squatting on her fat tires with scarcely a hole in her skin to show for the twelve raids behind her. The postponement tightened, rather than relaxed, the tension. Once more I checked over my life vest, oxygen mask and parachute, not perfunctorily, but the way you check something you're going to have to use. I made sure my escape kit was pinned securely in the knee pocket of my flying suit, where it couldn't fall out in a scramble to abandon ship. I slid a hunting knife between my shoe and my flying boot as I looked again through my extra equipment for this mission: water canteen, mess kit, blankets and English pounds for use in the Algerian desert, where we would sleep on the ground and might be on our own from a forced landing.

Murphy restlessly gave the Piccadilly Lily another once-over, inspecting ammunition belts, bomb bay, tires and oxygen pressure at each crew station. Especially the oxygen. It's human fuel, as important as gasoline, up where we operate. Gunners field-stripped their .50-calibers again and oiled the bolts. Our top-turret gunner lay in the grass with his head on his parachute, feigning sleep, sweating out his thirteenth start.

We shared a common knowledge which grimly enhanced the normal excitement before a mission. Of the approximately 150 Fortresses who were hitting Regensburg, our group was the last and lowest, at a base altitude of 17,000 feet. That's well within the range of accuracy for heavy flak. Our course would take us over plenty of it. It was a cinch also that our group would be the softest touch for the enemy fighters, being last man through the gantlet. Furthermore, the Piccadilly Lily was leading the last three ships of the high squadron — the tip of the tail end of the whole shebang. We didn't relish it much. Who wants a Purple Heart?

The minute hand of my wrist watch dragged. I caught myself thinking about the day, exactly one year ago, on August 17, 1942, when I watched a pitifully small force of twelve B-17's take off on the first raid of the 8th Air Force to make a shallow penetration against Rouen, France. On that day it was our maximum effort. Today, on our first anniversary, we were putting thirty times that number of heavies into the air—half the force on Regensburg and half the force on Schweinfurt, both situated inside the interior of the German Reich. For a year and a half, as a staff officer, I had watched the 8th Air Force grow under Maj. Gen. Ira C. Eaker. That's a long time to watch from behind a desk. Only ten days ago I had asked for and received orders to combat duty. Those ten days had been full of the swift action of participating in four combat missions and checking out for the first time as a four-engine pilot.

Now I knew that it can be easier to be shot at than telephoned at. That staff officers at an Air Force headquarters are the unstrung heroes of this war. And yet I found myself reminiscing just a little affectionately about that desk, wondering if there wasn't a touch of suicide in store for our group. One thing was sure: Headquarters had dreamed up the biggest air operation to date to celebrate its birthday in the biggest league of aerial warfare.

At 7:30 we broke out of the cloud tops into the glare of the rising sun. Beneath our B-17 lay English fields, still blanketed in the thick mist from which we had just emerged. We continued to climb slowly, our broad wings shouldering a heavy load of incendiary bombs in the belly and a burden of fuel in the main and wing-tip Tokyo tanks that would keep the Fortress afloat in the thin upper altitudes eleven hours.

From my copilot's seat on the right-hand side, I watched the white surface of the overcast, where B-17's in clusters of six to the squadron were puncturing the cloud deck all about us, rising clear of the mist with their glass noses slanted upward for the long climb to base altitude. We tacked on to one of these clutches of six. Now the sky over England was heavy with the weight of thousands of tons of bombs, fuel and men being lifted four miles straight up on a giant aerial hoist to the western terminus of a 20,000-foot elevated highway that led east to Regensburg. At intervals I saw the arc of a sputtering red, green or yellow flare being fired from the cabin roof of a group leader's airplane to identify the lead squadron to the high and low squadrons of each group. Assembly takes longer when you come up through an overcast.

For nearly an hour, still over Southern England, we climbed, nursing the straining Cyclone engines in a 300-foot-per-minute ascent, forming three squadrons gradually into compact group stagger formations—low squadron down to the left and high squadron up to the right of the lead squadron—groups assembling into looser combat wings of two to three groups each along the combat-wing assembly line, homing over predetermined points with radio compass, and finally cruising along the air-division assembly line to allow the combat wings to fall into place in trail behind Col. Curtis E. Le May in the lead group of the air division.

Formed at last, each flanking group in position 1000 feet above or below its lead group, our fifteen-mile parade moved east toward Lowestoft, point of departure from the friendly coast, unwieldy, but dangerous to fool with. From my perch in the high squadron in the last element of the whole procession, the air division looked like huge anvil-shaped swarms of locusts—not on dress parade, like the bombers of the Luftwaffe that died like flies over Britain in 1940, but deployed to uncover every gun and permit maneuverability. Our formation was basically that worked out for the Air Corps by Brig. Gen. Hugh Knerr twenty years ago with eighty-five-mile-an-hour bombers, plus refinements devised by Colonel Le May from experience in the European theater.

The English Channel and the North Sea glittered bright in the clear visibility as we left the bulge of East Anglia behind us. Up ahead we knew that we were already registering on the German RDF screen, and that the sector controllers of the Luftwaffe's fighter belt in Western Europe were busy alerting their *Staffeln* of Focke-Wulfs and Messerschmitts. I stole a last look back at cloud-covered England, where I could see a dozen spare B-17's, who had accompanied us to fill in for any abortives from mechanical failure in the hard climb, gliding disappointedly home to base.

I fastened my oxygen mask a little tighter and looked at the little ball in a glass tube on the instrument panel that indicates proper oxygen flow. It was moving up and down, like a visual heartbeat, as I breathed, registering normal.

Already the gunners were searching. Occasionally the ship shivered as guns were tested with short bursts. I could see puffs of blue smoke from the group close ahead and 1000 feet above us, as each gunner satisfied himself that he had lead poisoning at his trigger tips. The coast of Holland appeared in sharp black outline. I drew in a deep breath of oxygen.

A few miles in front of us were German boys in single-seaters who were probably going to react to us in the same way our boys would react, emotionally, if German bombers were heading for the Pratt & Whitney engine factory at Hartford or the Liberator plant at Willow Run. In the making was a death struggle between the unstoppable object and the immovable defense, every possible defense at the disposal of the Reich, for this was a deadly penetration to a hitherto inaccessible and critically important arsenal of the *Vaterland*.

At 10:08 we crossed the coast of Holland, south of The Hague, with our group of Fortresses tucked in tightly and within handy supporting distance of the group above us, at 18,000 feet. But our long, loose-linked column looked too long, and the gaps between combat wings too wide. As I squinted into the sun, gauging the distance to the barely visible specks of the lead group, I had a recurrence of that sinking feeling before the take-off—the lonesome foreboding that might come to the last man about to run a gantlet lined with spiked clubs. The premonition was well founded.

At 10:17, near Woensdrecht, I saw the first flak blossom out in our vicinity, light and inaccurate. A few minutes later, at approximately 10:25, a gunner called, "Fighters at two o'clock low." I saw them, climbing above the horizon ahead of us to the right—a pair of them. For a moment I hoped they were P-47 Thunderbolts from the fighter escort that was supposed to be in our vicinity, but I didn't hope long. The two FW-190's turned and whizzed through the formation ahead of us in a frontal attack, nicking two B-17's in the wings and breaking away in half rolls right over our group. By craning my neck up and back, I glimpsed one of them through the roof glass in the cabin, flashing past at a 600-mile-an-hour rate of closure, his yellow nose smoking and small pieces flying off near the wing root. The guns of our group were in action. The pungent smell of burnt cordite filled the cockpit and the B-17 trembled to the recoil of nose and ball-turret guns. Smoke immediately trailed from the hit B-17's, but they held their stations.

Here was early fighter reaction. The members of the crew sensed trouble. There was something desperate about the way those two fighters came in fast right out of their climb, without any preliminaries. Apparently, our own fighters were busy somewhere farther up the procession. The interphone was active for a few seconds with brief admonitions: "Lead 'em more." . . . "Short bursts." . . . "Don't throw rounds away." . . . "Bombardier to left waist gunner, don't yell. Talk slow."

Three minutes later the gunners reported fighters climbing up from all around the clock, singly and in pairs, both FW-190's and Me-109-G's. The fighters I could see on my side looked like too many for sound health. No friendly Thunderbolts were visible. From now on we were in mortal danger. My mouth dried up and my buttocks pulled together. A co-ordinated attack began, with the head-on fighters coming in from slightly above, the nine and three o'clock attackers approaching from about level and the rear attackers from slightly below. The guns from every B-17 in our group and the group ahead were firing simultaneously, lashing the sky with ropes of orange tracers to match the chain-puff bursts squirting from the 20-mm. cannon muzzles in the wings of the jerry single-seaters.

I noted with alarm that a lot of our fire was falling astern of the target—particularly from our hand-held nose and waist guns. Nevertheless, both sides got hurt in this clash, with the entire second element of three B-17's from our low squadron and one B-17 from the group ahead falling out of formation on fire, with crews bailing out, and several fighters heading for the deck in flames or with their pilots lingering behind under the dirty yellow canopies that distinguished some of their parachutes from ours. Our twenty-four-year-old group leader, flying only his third combat mission, pulled us up even closer to the preceding group for mutual support.

As we swung slightly outside with our squadron, in mild

evasive action, I got a good look at that gap in the low squadron where three B-17's had been. Suddenly I bit my lip hard.
The lead ship of that element had pulled out on fire and exploded before anyone bailed out. It was the ship to which I
had been originally assigned.

I glanced over at Murphy. It was cold in the cockpit, but
sweat was running from his forehead and over his oxygen
mask from the exertion of holding his element in tight formation and the strain of the warnings that hummed over the
interphone and what he could see out of the corners of his
eyes. He caught my glance and turned the controls over to
me for a while. It was an enormous relief to concentrate on
flying instead of sitting there watching fighters aiming between your eyes. Somehow, the attacks from the rear, although I could see them through my ears via the interphone,
didn't bother me. I guess it was because there was a slab
of armor plate behind my back and I couldn't watch them,
anyway.

I knew that we were in a lively fight. Every alarm bell in my
brain and heart was ringing a high-pitched warning. But my
nerves were steady and my brain working. The fear was unpleasant, but it was bearable. I knew that I was going to die,
and so were a lot of others. What I didn't know was that the
real fight, the *Anschluss* of Luftwaffe 20-mm. cannon shells,
hadn't really begun. The largest and most savage fighter resistance of any war in history was rising to stop us at any cost,
and our group was the most vulnerable target.

A few minutes later we absorbed the first wave of a hail-
storm of individual fighter attacks that were to engulf us clear
to the target in such a blizzard of bullets and shells that a
chronological account is difficult. It was at 10:41, over Eupen,
that I looked out the window after a minute's lull, and saw
two whole squadrons, twelve Me-109's and eleven FW-190's
climbing parallel to us as though they were on a steep escala-
tor. The first squadron had reached our level and was pulling
ahead to turn into us. The second was not far behind. Several
thousand feet below us were many more fighters, their noses
cocked up in a maximum climb. Over the interphone came
reports of an equal number of enemy aircraft deploying on
the other side of the formation.

For the first time I noticed an Me-110 sitting out of range on our level out to the right. He was to stay with us all the way to the target, apparently radioing our position and weak spots to fresh *Staffeln* waiting farther down the road.

At the sight of all these fighters, I had the distinct feeling of being trapped—that the Hun had been tipped off or at least had guessed our destination and was set for us. We were already through the German fighter belt. Obviously, they had moved a lot of squadrons back in a fluid defense in depth, and they must have been saving up some outfits for the inner defense that we didn't know about. The life expectancy of our group seemed definitely limited, since it had already appeared that the fighters, instead of wasting fuel trying to overhaul the preceding groups, were glad to take a cut at us.

Swinging their yellow noses around in a wide U turn, the twelve-ship squadron of Me-109's came in from twelve to two o'clock in pairs. The main event was on. I fought an impulse to close my eyes, and overcame it.

A shining silver rectangle of metal sailed past over our right wing. I recognized it as a main-exit door. Seconds later, a black lump came hurtling through the formation, barely missing several propellers. It was a man, clasping his knees to his head, revolving like a diver in a triple somersault, shooting by us so close that I saw a piece of paper blow out of his leather jacket. He was evidently making a delayed jump, for I didn't see his parachute open.

A B-17 turned gradually out of the formation to the right, maintaining altitude. In a split second it completely vanished in a brilliant explosion, from which the only remains were four balls of fire, the fuel tanks, which were quickly consumed as they fell earthward.

I saw blue, red, yellow and aluminum-colored fighters. Their tactics were running fairly true to form, with frontal attacks hitting the low squadron and rear attackers going for the lead and high squadrons. Some of the jerries shot at us with rockets, and an attempt at air-to-air bombing was made with little black time-fuse sticks, dropped from above, which exploded in small gray puffs off to one side of the formation. Several of the FW's did some nice deflection shooting on side attacks from 500 yards at the high group, then raked the low group on the breakaway at closer range with their noses cocked in a side slip, to keep the formation in their sights longer in the turn. External fuel tanks were visible under the bellies or wings of at least two squadrons, shedding uncomfortable light on the mystery of their ability to tail us so far from their bases.

The manner of the assaults indicated that the pilots knew where we were going and were inspired with a fanatical determination to stop us before we got there. Many pressed attacks home to 250 yards or less, or bolted right through the formation wide out, firing long twenty-second bursts, often presenting point-blank targets on the breakaway. Some committed the fatal error of pulling up instead of going down and out. More experienced pilots came in on frontal attacks with a noticeably slower rate of closure, apparently throttled back, obtaining greater accuracy. But no tactics could halt the close-knit juggernauts of our Fortresses, nor save the single-seaters from paying a terrible price.

Our airplane was endangered by various debris. Emergency hatches, exit doors, prematurely opened parachutes, bodies and assorted fragments of B-17's and Hun fighters breezed past us in the slip stream.

I watched two fighters explode not far beneath, disappear in sheets of orange flame; B-17's dropping out in every stage of distress, from engines on fire to controls shot away; friendly and enemy parachutes floating down, and, on the green carpet far below us, funeral pyres of smoke from fallen fighters, marking our trail.

On we flew through the cluttered wake of a desperate air battle, where disintegrating aircraft were commonplace and the white dots of sixty parachutes in the air at one time were hardly worth a second look. The spectacle registering on my eyes became so fantastic that my brain turned numb to the actuality of the death and destruction all around us. Had it not been for the squeezing in my stomach, which was trying to purge, I might easily have been watching an animated cartoon in a movie theater.

The minutes dragged on into an hour. And still the fighters came. Our gunners called coolly and briefly to one another, dividing up their targets, fighting for their lives with every round of ammunition—and our lives, and the formation. The tail gunner called that he was out of ammunition. We sent another belt back to him. Here was a new hazard. We might run out of .50-caliber slugs before we reached the target.

I looked to both sides of us. Our two wing men were gone. So was the element in front of us—all three ships. We moved up into position behind the lead element of the high squadron. I looked out again on my side and saw a cripple, with one prop feathered, struggle up behind our right wing with his bad engine funneling smoke into the slip stream. He dropped back. Now our tail gunner had a clear view. There were no more B-17's behind us. We were last man.

I took the controls for a while. The first thing I saw when Murphy resumed flying was a B-17 turning slowly out to the right, its cockpit a mass of flames. The copilot crawled out of his window, held on with one hand, reached back for his parachute, buckled it on, let go and was whisked back into the horizontal stabilizer of the tail. I believe the impact killed him. His parachute didn't open.

I looked forward and almost ducked as I watched the tail gunner of a B-17 ahead of us take a bead right on our windshield and cut loose with a stream of tracers that missed us by a few feet as he fired on a fighter attacking us from six o'clock low. I almost ducked again when our own top-turret gunner's twin muzzles pounded away a foot above my head in the full forward position, giving a realistic imitation of cannon shells exploding in the cockpit, while I gave an even better imitation of a man jumping six inches out of his seat.

Still no letup. The fighters queued up like a bread line and let us have it. Each second of time had a cannon shell in it. The strain of being a clay duck in the wrong end of that aerial shooting gallery became almost intolerable. Our Piccadilly Lily shook steadily with the fire of its .50's, and the air inside was wispy with smoke. I checked the engine instruments for the thousandth time. Normal. No injured crew members yet. Maybe we'd get to that target, even with our reduced fire power. Seven Fortresses from our group had already gone down and many of the rest of us were badly shot up and short-handed because of wounded crew members.

Almost disinterestedly I observed a B-17 pull out from the

group preceding us and drop back to a position about 200 feet from our right wing tip. His right Tokyo tanks were on fire, and had been for a half hour. Now the smoke was thicker. Flames were licking through the blackened skin of the wing. While the pilot held her steady, I saw four crew members drop out the bomb bay and execute delayed jumps. Another bailed from the nose, opened his parachute prematurely and nearly fouled the tail. Another went out the left-waist-gun opening, delaying his opening for a safe interval. The tail gunner dropped out of his hatch, apparently pulling the ripcord before he was clear of the ship. His parachute opened instantaneously, barely missing the tail, and jerked him so hard that both his shoes came off. He hung limp in the harness, whereas the others had shown immediate signs of life, shifting around in their harness. The Fortress then dropped back in a medium spiral and I did not see the pilots leave. I saw the ship, though, just before it trailed from view, belly to the sky, its wing a solid sheet of yellow flame.

Now that we had been under constant attack for more than an hour, it appeared certain that our group was faced with extinction. The sky was still mottled with rising fighters. Target time was thirty-five minutes away. I doubt if a man in the group visualized the possibility of our getting much farther without 100 per cent loss. Gunners were becoming exhausted and nerve-tortured from the nagging strain—the strain that sends gunners and pilots to the rest home. We had been aiming point for what looked like most of the Luftwaffe. It looked as though we might find the rest of it primed for us at the target.

At this hopeless point, a young squadron commander down in the low squadron was living through his finest hour. His squadron had lost its second element of three ships early in the fight, south of Antwerp, yet he had consistently maintained his vulnerable and exposed position in the formation rigidly in order to keep the guns of his three remaining ships well uncovered to protect the belly of the formation. Now, nearing the target, battle damage was catching up with him fast. A 20-mm. cannon shell penetrated the right side of his airplane and exploded beneath him, damaging the electrical system and cutting the top-turret gunner in the leg. A second

20-mm. entered the radio compartment, killing the radio operator, who bled to death with his legs severed above the knees. A third 20-mm. shell entered the left side of the nose, tearing out a section about two feet square, tore away the right-hand-nose-gun installations and injured the bombardier in the head and shoulder. A fourth 20-mm. shell penetrated the right wing into the fuselage and shattered the hydraulic system, releasing fluid all over the cockpit. A fifth 20-mm. shell punctured the cabin roof and severed the rudder cables to one side of the rudder. A sixth 20-mm. shell exploded in the No. 3 engine, destroying all controls to the engine. The engine caught fire and lost its power, but eventually I saw the fire go out.

Confronted with structural damage, partial loss of control, fire in the air and serious injuries to personnel, and faced with fresh waves of fighters still rising to the attack, this commander was justified in abandoning ship. His crew, some of them comparatively inexperienced youngsters, were preparing to bail out. The copilot pleaded repeatedly with him to bail out. His reply at this critical juncture was blunt. His words were heard over the interphone and had a magical effect on the crew. They stuck to their guns. The B-17 kept on.

Near the initial point, at 11:50, one hour and a half after the first of at least 200 individual fighter attacks, the pressure eased off, although hostiles were still in the vicinity. A curious sensation came over me. I was still alive. It was possible to think of the target. Of North Africa. Of returning to England. Almost idly, I watched a crippled B-17 pull over to the curb and drop its wheels and open its bomb bay, jettisoning its bombs. Three Me-109's circled it closely, but held their fire while the crew bailed out. I remembered now that a little while back I had seen other Hun fighters hold their fire, even when being shot at by a B-17 from which the crew were bailing. But I doubt if sportsmanship had anything to do with it. They hoped to get a B-17 down fairly intact.

And then our weary, battered column, short twenty-four bombers, but still holding the close formation that had brought the remainder through by sheer air discipline and gunnery, turned in to the target. I knew that our bombardiers were grim as death while they synchronized their sights on the great Me-109 shops lying below us in a curve of the winding blue Danube, close to the outskirts of Regensburg. Our B-17 gave a slight lift and a red light went out on the instrument panel. Our bombs were away. We turned from the target toward the snow-capped Alps. I looked back and saw a beautiful sight—a rectangular pillar of smoke rising from the Me-109 plant. Only one burst was over and into the town. Even from this great height I could see that we had smeared the objective. The price? Cheap. 200 airmen.

A few more fighters pecked at us on the way to the Alps and a couple of smoking B-17's glided down toward the safety of Switzerland, about forty miles distant. A town in the Brenner Pass tossed up a lone burst of futile flak. Flak? There had been lots of flak in the past two hours, but only now did I recall having seen it, a sort of side issue to the fighters. Colonel Le May, who had taken excellent care of us all the way, circled the air division over a large lake to give the cripples, some flying on three engines and many trailing smoke, a chance to rejoin the family. We approached the Mediterranean in a gradual descent, conserving fuel. Out over the water we flew at low altitude, unmolested by fighters from Sardinia or Corsica, waiting through the long hot afternoon hours for the first sight of the North African coast line. The prospect of ditching, out of gasoline and the sight of other B-17's falling into the drink seemed trivial matters after the vicious nightmare of the long trial across Southern Germany. We had walked through a high valley of the shadow of death, not expecting to see another sunset, and now I could fear no evil.

With red lights showing on all our fuel tanks, we landed at our designated base in the desert, after eleven hours in the air. I slept on the ground near the wing and, waking occasionally, stared up at the stars. My radio headset was back in the ship. And yet I could hear the deep chords of great music.

The Saturday Evening Post, November 6, 1943

Fear of Death as Green
Troops Sail to Invasion

by John Steinbeck

SOMEWHERE IN THE MEDITERRANEAN THEATER—On the iron floors of the L. C. I.'s, which stands for Landing Craft Infantry, the men sit about and for a time they talk and laugh and make jokes to cover the great occasion. They try to reduce this great occasion to something normal, something ordinary, something they are used to. They rag one another, accuse one another of being scared, they repeat experiences of recent days, and then gradually silence creeps over them and they sit silently because the hugeness of the experience has taken them over.

These are green troops. They have been trained to a fine point, hardened and instructed, and they lack only one thing to make them soldiers, enemy fire, and they will never be soldiers until they have it. No one, least of all themselves, knows what they will do when the terrible thing happens. No man there knows whether he can take it, knows whether he will run away or stick, or lose his nerve and go to pieces, or will be a good soldier. There is no way of knowing and probably that one thing bothers you more than anything else.

And that is the difference between green troops and soldiers. Tomorrow at this time these men, those who are living, will be different. They will know then what they can't know tonight. They will know how they face fire. Actually there is little danger. They are going to be good soldiers for they do not know that this is the night before the assault. There is no way for any man to know it.

In the moonlight on the iron deck they look at each other strangely. Men they have known well and soldiered with are strange and every man is cut off from every other one and in their minds they search the faces of their friends for the dead.

Who will be alive tomorrow night? I will, for one. No one ever gets killed in the war. Couldn't possibly. There would be no war if any one got killed. But each man, in this last night in the moonlight, looks strangely at the others and sees death there. This is the most terrible time of all. This night before the assault by the new green troops. They will never be like this again.

Every man builds in his mind what it will be like, but it is never what he thought it would be. When he designs the assault in his mind he is alone and cut off from every one. He is alone in the moonlight and the crowded men about him are strangers in this time. It will not be like this. The fire and the movement and the exertion will make him a part of these strangers sitting about him, and they will be a part of him, but he does not know that now. This is a bad time, never to be repeated.

Not one of these men is to be killed. That is impossible, and it is no contradiction that every one of them is to be killed. Every one is in a way dead already. And nearly every man has written his letter and left it somewhere to be posted if he is killed. The letters, some misspelled, some illiterate, some polished and full of attitudes, and some meager and tight, all say the same thing. They all say: "I wish I had told you, and I never did, I never could. Some obscure and impish thing kept me from ever telling you, and only now when it is too late, can I tell you. I've thought these things," the letters say, "but when I started to speak something cut me off. Now I can say it, but don't let it be a burden on you. I just know that it was always so, only I didn't say it." In every letter that is the message. The piled up reticences go down in the last letters. The letters to wives, and mothers, and sisters, and fathers, and such is the hunger to have been a part of some one, letters sometimes to comparative strangers.

The great ships move through the night though they are covered with silence. Radios are dead now, and the engines make no noise. Orders are given in soft voices and the conversation is quiet. Somewhere up ahead the enemy is waiting and he is silent too. Does he know we are coming, and does he know when and in what number? Is he lying low with his machine guns ready and his mortars set on the beaches, and

his artillery in the hills? What is he thinking now? Is he afraid
or confident?

The officers know H-hour now. The moon is going down.
H-hour is 3:30, just after the moon has set and the shore is
black. The convoy is to moonward of the shore. Perhaps with
glasses the enemy can see the convoy against the setting
moon, but ahead where we are going there is only a musty
pearl-like grayness. The moon goes down into the ocean and
ships that have been beside you and all around you disappear
into the blackness and only the tiny shielded position-lights
show where they are.

The men sitting on the deck disappear into the blackness
and the silence, and one man begins to whistle softly just to
be sure he is there.

New York *Herald Tribune*, October 3, 1943

"Then I Got It"

by Richard Tregaskis

November 22

This morning we could see how close the shells had landed. One fresh crater, no more than fifty feet away from the house, had come closest. Three others had landed within a radius of 100 feet.

Col. Yarborough, Capt. Tomasik and I started out in a jeep for Ranger headquarters, to check on the latest developments on Mount Corno. Maj. Saam said that the fighting had quieted down after last night's outburst, but that the Germans still held the cave on the far side of Mount Corno near the top.

"It's something to see," he said. "You can watch 'em sticking out their heads and throwing grenades. Our plan for today is to carry up bangalore torpedoes. The boys on Corno will try to lower 'em close to the cave and blow out the Krauts. We've already flopped with dynamite and grenades. This has got to work. There's only a squad of Germans in the cave itself, but on the far slope, two fresh battalions of enemy troops are moving up. If the squad in the cave can hold on long enough, the rest of the Krauts will creep up and grab the ridge."

Tomasik, Yarborough and I started up the steep, craggy slope of Mount Corno in our jeep.

"We might as well go as far as we can by jeep," said Yarborough. "It'll take us long enough to walk up the darn mountain after that."

So we chugged through a stony orchard, bouncing over the outcrops of rock, and came to a virtually insurmountable slope. We left the jeep and began to clamber up the rocks on foot.

Col. Yarborough said, "I know a place where you can

watch the fireworks, if you want to. You'd better leave that mackinaw behind." He indicated the heavy coat I was wearing. "We'll work up enough of a sweat if we go in shirt-sleeves. It's only a couple of miles, but it'll take a couple of hours."

We were certainly perspiring as we passed beyond the fringe of scrub trees which covers the lower slopes of the mountain. Progress was slow up the stony mule track leading toward the bare summit.

There was no firing now. I kept my eyes on the rocks underfoot—and soon realized that we were following a literal trail of blood! Some of the stones were spattered with dark-red spots. This trail was the only negotiable route up the precipitous slope. Consequently, the wounded were bound to leave marks on the white rocks as they staggered or were carried down the winding path.

The track had a macabre fascination for me. I watched the variations in the trail of red spots; occasionally, the drops covered more rocks in one area, indicating, possibly, that a man had been wounded at that spot, or had stopped for a rest as he struggled to the aid station.

We walked in single file, at wide intervals, so that we would not all be killed or wounded by a single shell. This territory might be under heavy enemy fire at any moment, without warning. We halted several times and sat down in the trail, streaming sweat, but even when we rested, we remained scattered.

After another hour of climbing, we heard the sound of tumbling rocks from somewhere above us. Tomasik whipped out his .45; we halted and listened. "It might be an enemy patrol," Tomasik whispered. The sounds continued: falling stones, large objects brushing through the tall grass on the flank of the hill above.

We waited, frozen, and then saw an American helmet, then another, in the underbrush—one of our own patrols. We breathed more freely.

Farther up the trail, we spotted a single figure of a man, wearing an American uniform. When he came closer, we recognized Col. Darby. The Ranger leader was grimy and disheveled. A great rent had been torn in his trousers, exposing his long woolen underwear. Despite his ragged appearance, he spoke with his usual energy. "Rough up here last night," he said. "The damn Krauts were giving us hell." He pointed out a great knout of rock clinging to the flank of the ridge. At the top of the rock mass, we could see a sharp cleft through which the trail passed. "The sons of bitches were laying 'em right on there. Had to hang on so we wouldn't get blown off."

Yarborough, Tomasik and I stopped at the cleft in the rock, where twenty or thirty bedraggled and dirty Rangers sprawled. They had been up on the white rock at the top of Mount Corno, battling with the Germans who were trying to seize the peak. Other forces had relieved them.

They looked utterly exhausted, all the more unhappy because they reclined amidst a litter of ration cans, pasteboard boxes and empty shell cartons.

Gradually we progressed along the flank of the ridge running between the peaks of Mount Corno and Mount Croce. Near the top of this great massif, I realized, as always in mountainous terrain, the vastness of the hills in which we are fighting, and how puny our destructive efforts have been. We could wipe a town off the map with concentrated shelling, but we could not do more than scratch the hide of the earth. Up here, we were like fleas picking our way across the ribs of a mammoth animal.

We turned off the mule trail and started up the steepest part of the ridge. "You can get a good look at the fighting on Mount Corno from the top of this ridge," Yarborough offered.

He and Tomasik moved along toward Mount Croce, to inspect other positions. I stayed behind. At the top of the ridge, a few hundred yards from the crest of Mount Corno, I found an American observation post. The view of the peak and the large white rock on the German side was magnificent. With binoculars, I could make out occasional helmeted heads of Americans, barely distinguishable round spots, marking positions where Rangers were dug in on the summit of Mount Corno. While I watched, a squirt of black smoke dabbed the skyline. Then another, and another. They were German hand grenades, probably tossed from the base of the great white boulder. Somewhere at the foot of that boulder, I knew, the Germans were hiding in their cave. Presumably, the American helmets moving across the peak were the squad which had the job of lowering bangalore torpedoes over the rock and down into positions where they might blast the German strong point.

To the west of the peak of Mount Corno, the mountain mass, speckled with small trees, sloped steeply downward. Somewhere on that slope, the Germans were dug in. From the stubble of vegetation, a far-spreading cloud of smoke was rising. Large, rapidly springing bursts leaped from the woods as shells were striking. Our big 4.2-inch mortars were trying to keep back the tide of Germans inching up the grade.

From the ridge top where I was lying, there spread below me to the west the vast panorama of Italy. The brown scattering of roofless buildings in the next valley was the village of Concasale, where the cancerous pittings of shell craters disfigured the green face of the ground. Two ridges beyond, the town of Cassino sprawled up the mountainside. And beyond that, gray in the mist of distance, the mountain ridges were piled up, one on top of the other as far as we could see, like giant stony steps ascending gradually to Rome. Where, I wondered, was the "level, straight route" which is supposed to be ours once we conquer Cassino?

Near me, in a shallow, rocky foxhole, sat Maj. Bill Hutchinson, shouting corrections by phone to his 4.2 mortar batteries near Venafro. He cautioned me sharply against exposing myself in my movements across the ridge.

"We're within machine-gun range of Mount Corno," he said.

One of the group of men scattered over the ridge top was Capt. Shunstrom, the same wild man who had operated the mobile artillery so effectively with the Rangers back at Chiunzi Pass. Now he was fiddling with a 60-mm. mortar tube, preparing to add a few shells to the torrent of explosives falling on the German positions atop Mount Corno. "Here's the way to shoot one of these things," he announced. He braced the base-end of the tube against the ground and gave a demonstration, firing the powerful field weapon as if it were a pistol or rifle.

Usually, the 60-mm. mortar tube, which throws a projectile about two and a half inches in diameter and nearly a foot long, is attached to a heavy base plate when it is set up for firing, with a bipod supporting the tube at the proper angle. A mortar man drops the projectile down the mouth of the barrel and steps back to keep clear of the shell as it speeds from the muzzle. But Shunstrom had his own system. He wrapped the bare tube, without stand or bipod, in an old glove—which would insulate the heat of the barrel—seized the tube with his left hand, aimed it approximately, and dropped the mortar shell down the mouth with his right hand.

His marksmanship was surprisingly accurate. The first burst sprang up less than fifty feet from the top of the white rock at the peak of Mount Corno, and the second blew up on the rock itself. Shunstrom fired ten or eleven shells, three of them landing on the stone, and one close to the cave where the Germans must have been dug in. Shunstrom gave a grunt of satisfaction.

I watched the fireworks: the firing of the heavy mortars which were giving the Germans hell on the far slope of Corno, and had set fire to some of the trees there; Shunstrom's wildcat marksmanship with his mortar; the slender plume of smoke raised by a German hand grenade near the top of Corno. Finally, I saw a great explosion blossoming from the white rock itself—perhaps the detonation of the bangalore torpedoes, or a charge of dynamite. Maj. Hutchinson said, "Great fun, as long as we're dishing it out and not taking it."

Yarborough and Tomasik came back from their inspection tour, and we started down the tedious trail toward home. I felt a healthy fatigue. For the first time in several weeks, I had a bang-up eyewitness story of an action at a crucial sector of the front. But there was an even better story ahead of me.

We reached the cleft rock, the local C.P., and I stopped for a few minutes to talk to some of the Rangers, while Tomasik and Yarborough went on. I would catch up with them later. I got the notes I wanted and hurried after them. Past the curve in the trail where we had listened, tautly, to the approach of a patrol on our way up, I was making my way along the relatively straight stretch where the German mortar shells had been falling on the previous day. Then I got it.

I heard the scream of something coming, and I must have dived to the rocks instinctively. Months of conditioning on many battlefields resolved themselves in that instantaneous, life-saving reflex. Then a smothering explosion descended around me. It seemed to flood over me from above. In a fraction of a second of consciousness, I sensed that I had been hit. A curtain of fire rose, hesitated, hovered for an infinite second. In that measureless interval, an orange mist came up quickly over my horizon, like a tropical sunrise, and set again, leaving me in the dark. Then the curtain descended, gently.

I must have been unconscious for a few seconds. When a rudimentary awareness came back, I knew everything was all wrong. I realized I had been badly hit. I was still stretched on the rocks. A couple of feet from me lay my helmet which had been gashed in at least two places, one hole at the front and another ripping through the side.

Catastrophe had struck me down. My shocked perceptions groped for an understanding of what had happened. It was no use.

There was no pain. Everything seemed finished, quiet, as if time had stopped. I sat up and looked back at the path. Now I saw the motion of figures of men running up the trail at a half crouch, as a man would zigzag through shellfire. There must be danger. I was aware of that at least. I tried to shout at them, but only incoherent sounds tumbled from my mouth, and my voice rattled, as if it were coming from some place far off and beyond my control. It was like a broken, muted phonograph.

My mind formulated frantic questions. What's wrong? Why can't I talk? What am I going to do? And then I felt a slight easing of tension, a slight relaxation. I knew, then, that even though I could not utter the words, I could still think. I had lost my power of speech, not my power to understand or generate thought. It was clear to me what I wanted to say, but I couldn't say it.

By this time the men had gone, and it was evident that they were too concerned with something else to come back and pay attention to me.

A shell was coming. I knew that because I heard the sound of the approaching projectile. But the sound was just a tinny little echo of something which had once been terrifying and all-powerful. And the explosion, while it seemed to rattle my skull, was certainly not terrifying. I couldn't understand the fear written on the face of a soldier who had skidded into the ground near me as he sought to take cover from the bursting of the shell.

I tried, with my distant and almost uncontrollable voice, to talk intelligibly to the frightened soldier during the few seconds he was there. I was trying to say, "Can you help me?" And after a number of unconnected, stumbling syllables, I finally managed two words, "Can help?"

I heard the tinny sound of a little shell, and saw the soldier's face, hollowed by terror. He was saying, "I can't help you, I'm too scared." And then he was gone, running, up the trail.

I have no recollection how soon the first-aid man dropped to the ground beside me and bandaged my head. But it was done, in those few minutes, and I saw the needle of the hypo as he gave me a shot of morphine. I did not feel the prick of the needle. The first-aid man was gone. I was alone on the mountainside.

I knew, then, that if I wanted to get back to the field dressing station, I would have to go under my own power. I would have to get up and walk down the trail in the hope that I might still catch up with Col. Yarborough. Somehow, shock seemed to have allayed any pain I might otherwise have experienced. The quick administration of morphine within a few minutes of the time of injury dulled my concern about my wound.

My glasses were lying on the rocks a few inches away. Miraculously, they had been blown off without being broken. I tried to move my right hand to pick up the spectacles, and realized that the whole arm was as inert as a board. I grabbed the glasses with my left hand and put them on. They were not very secure because my head was bandaged, and they were askew on my nose. I picked up my helmet. It would be a fine souvenir, I thought illogically. That too sat precariously on my bandaged head. I grasped my right arm in my left hand.

Touching it was like touching a foreign body, and when I dropped it, it fell limply, beyond control, at my side.

I stood up and started down the trail. My helmet bobbed on the bulky bandages around my head, and finally it slid off and bounced on the ground. Determined to save it at all costs, I picked it up and put it back on my head.

Then a shell came. I heard the same ragged, distant whistling, and the rattling explosion, as I automatically fell to the rocks for protection. I waited for the rest of the group of shells to arrive, and they were close. I looked up and saw tall spouts of smoke and high explosive jumping up all around me—but it was all unreal, like a movie with a feeble sound track. Probably the concussion of the shell burst which had hit me had also deafened me. I was amazed, but not frightened, as one huge shell burst suddenly sprang into being, towered over me like a genie. It was so close that I could have reached out and touched it. Yet none of the flying fragments had brushed me.

When the burst of firing was over, I scrambled to my feet again. Dropping my helmet, I stubbornly picked it up and put it back on my head. My glasses slipped down on my nose again and again. A red drapery of blood ran down over the glasses and blurred my vision. Staggering down the trail, I dropped my helmet again, several times, and doggedly retrieved it. My right arm and hand dangled loosely. I muttered to myself, trying to talk straight, practicing—and still able to mouth only a sort of ape-chatter. If anyone had been there to see me, I would have been a grotesque apparition.

Shells were coming again. This time I headed for a shallow cave carved in the rock at the side of the trail, and took refuge in it. A feeling of simple contentment came over me because the shells were landing harmlessly outside, while I was secure in my hideaway. Here, in a shelter originally dug by a German, I smiled, sat and waited for the spell of firing to cease. I remembered that I must go on as soon as the firing stopped. My mind fixed on the idea that the only way to get out of this was by catching up with Yarborough and Tomasik. If I had to stay up on the mountain overnight, and wait for someone to find me, before I could be carried down, I might not be alive in the morning.

When the firing stopped, I staggered onto the path. I went as fast as I could, dropping my helmet occasionally and picking it up; I was determined to preserve it. I heard the rustle of the shells again, and automatically sprawled on the rocks. The muffled explosions seemed quite a distance away now. I got up. If only I could catch up with Yarborough. Nothing else seemed too important. After all, I had realized the odds and often speculated upon them. Already I had more than used up my chances. If I could get through this thing alive, I thought, I could start on a fresh bunch of chances.

I came around a bend of the trail, and felt a surge of pleasure as I saw Col. Yarborough and Capt. Tomasik, bending over a wounded man. Fortunately for me, they had stayed behind to care for him. Yarborough started to wave to me, then noticed the bandaged head, the bloody glasses and red-stained shirt.

More shells squeaked and rattled into the side of the ridge, and we ducked. When it was over, Bill Yarborough and I started together down the trail. My one usable arm was draped over his shoulder. He provided support for my staggering feet.

Once, we had to stop to shoo from the trail three wild-eyed pack mules, frightened by the shelling and deserted by their keeper. Once, we had to take shelter when the shells came again. Twice or three times, I lost my dubious balance and fell. Yarborough helped me to my feet. The trail seemed endlessly long—actually it was about a mile that we had to travel—and it would have seemed nightmarish had it not been for the shot of morphine, and the great shock of the wound. Still, there was not the faintest trace of pain.

And so we reached a command post, in a peasant house at the fringe of the woods. Two aid men sat me down, looked at my head and expertly slit the sleeve of my shirt to inspect my useless arm. There were no marks on the arm. Then I knew it had been paralyzed in some way. Yarborough gave me five or six sulfa tablets. The dashing parachutist doctor, Capt. Alden, looked at my head, said nothing. I tried to talk. The words were still unintelligible. I lay on the dirt floor and looked up at the line of soldiers staring at me, the Badly Wounded Man.

I must have stared just that way at many a wounded man whom I had seen. Now I was on the other side of the picture, for a change.

I had another shot of morphine, and dozed. I remember being sick. Then I was stretched out in the rear of a jeep. I asked again and again whether my notes, and especially my helmet, were aboard. They were. The air felt cool as we began to move down the steep mountain side. A faint light hovered in the sky. It was late afternoon. The time must have been about four-thirty, about two hours after I was hit.

Once we had begun to move, I lost consciousness. We must have stopped somewhere, for I remember being in a tent, and hearing voices that said something about "tetanus shot." I did not see or feel the needle.

Then I became aware that it was dark and cold, and that I was being carried on a stretcher. They put me down inside a tent, where a bright electric light glared. I heard gruff voices. The stretcher bearers picked me up again. We passed into the night, the stretcher bumping with the steps of the aid men. They carried me into another tent, less garishly lighted than the first. It was cold. I lay and shivered.

I was brought to still another tent, which seemed warmer. A voice asked me about my right arm, and, in general, how I felt. I tried to explain these matters, but my words would not come out right. They were as badly tangled as before. Instead of saying something like "The arm's been like that since I got hit up on the mountain," I said, "The sam—I mean farm—I mean tam—farm, sam—like that since I got bit—rot—rat—hut, on the rountain, I mean fountain—bounty—fountain."

I was feeling warmer. The stretcher bearers came in again and picked me up and carried me to still another tent, which, even in my present drugged condition, I recognized as an X-ray room. I knew that I had been set down on the floor, still on my stretcher, while loud voices could be heard talking. I was sensitive, as I suppose patients in general must be, to the tone of the voices. These were rough and grumbling.

Very different was the next voice I heard talking to me as I was carried back to the tent which I had just left. It was cheerful, very considerate. The man said that he was sorry but that he was going to have to shave my head. He did not want it to hurt.

Another man came in, looked down at me and informed me, "We're going to have to operate on you." This voice was very brusque. I wanted to ask him something. It was the question, "Am I going to die?" After several attempts, I conveyed the intended meaning, but the man, evidently the doctor, wouldn't commit himself.

Then there was another, pleasant man, sitting by my side. I realized that he must be a minister. His voice was very calm and soothing. He was saying a prayer. I thanked him; the mere sound of the words was comforting. Then I had another shot of morphine.

Invasion Diary, 1944

from *Tarawa: The Story of a Battle*

by Robert Sherrod

"I Didn't Know Whether We Had the Heart to Fight a War"

I spent a lot of time studying the Marines. They looked like any group of ordinary, healthy young Americans. The range of their background was as broad as America: farmers, truck drivers, college students, runaway kids, rich men's sons, orphans, lawyers, ex-soldiers. One day Lieutenant William B. Sommerville, the battalion supply officer, himself a Baltimore lawyer, was showing me around the ship. On deck we passed a Marine corporal with a bandaged thumb. Sommerville stopped and asked what happened.

"I let my air hose get away from me," grinned the corporal. We walked on. "That guy," said Sommerville, "was a county judge in Texas when he enlisted."

All these Marines were volunteers. Only now, several months after voluntary enlistments had been stopped—to the unconcealed disgust of old-line Marine sergeants who had from time immemorial been able to fall back on the final, scathing word, "Nobody asked you to be a Marine, bub"—were the first Marine draftees being sent overseas as replacements.

The Marines ate the same emergency rations that soldiers ate in battle. They used the same weapons. They came from the same places.* They went to the same schools. What, then, had gained the Marines a reputation as fighting men far ex-

---

*With some differences. A glance at the roster of men aboard the *Blue Fox* showed a preponderance of Midwesterners, Southerners, and Californians, and almost no New Englanders. Thus, of 1,618 Marines and attached naval units aboard, 115, or seven percent, were from Texas, whereas Texas holds just under five percent of the U.S. population. But I had seen no units overseas in this war, outside some National Guard outfits, to which Texas had not contributed more than her pro-rata share. Texans were sometimes immodest on this point, but their boast was well-founded.

celling any attributed to the average young U.S. citizen in a soldier's uniform?

I had been curious about this question for at least a year before the United States went to war. I recalled a White House press conference in June, 1940, when President Roosevelt said angrily that a year of military training would be good for the mollycoddled youth of the United States—at least, it would teach them to live with their fellow men. The weeks I spent on maneuvers with the Army in the swamps of Louisiana and in the Carolina hills did not serve to ease my fears that perhaps we had grown too soft to fight a war; at that time some low-moraled outfits were threatening to desert, rather than stay in the Army. Almost none of them deserted, but the threat was an unhealthy sign, and it could not be blamed entirely on poor leadership.

When I came back to the United States after half a year in Australia, in August, 1942, I went around Cassandra-fashion, crying, "We are losing the war—you don't realize it, but we are losing the war!" I talked to several men at the top of the Army and Navy. I went to the White House and sang my mournful tune to the President. To bear bad tidings is a very rocky road to popularity, but I felt that somebody had to do it.

What worried me was not our productive ability, although it was barely in evidence at the time. I knew we could make the machines of war. But I didn't know whether we had the heart to fight a war. Our men who had to do the fighting didn't want to fight. Their generation had been told in the all-important first ten years, in its teens, and at the voting age that it was not necessary to fight. Sometimes it almost seemed that they had been taught that peace was more important than honor. Our men just wanted to go home.

I could not forget my conversation one chilly August day in a room in Lennon's Hotel in Brisbane. My companion was an Army general, a friend of many years. I asked his opinion of the American soldier. He became very depressed. He said, "I'm afraid, Bob. I'm afraid the Americans of this generation are not the same kind of Americans who fought the last war."

In the spring of 1943 I went to the Aleutians. The Battle of Attu in its early stages was not well handled. Our equipment was poor. Nearly fifteen hundred men became casualties from exposure because of their poor equipment, and because their leaders allowed them to be pinned down for days in icy water on the floor of Massacre Valley. But the Battle of Attu did not make me feel any worse. In this primitive, man-against-man fighting enough of our men rose up to win. I thought I learned a lesson on Attu which probably applied to all armies: not all soldiers are heroes—far from it; the army that wins, other things being fairly equal, is the army which has enough men to rise above duty, thus inspiring others to do their duty. There were many such Americans on Attu—men received the fairly commonplace Silver Star for deeds that would have earned a Congressional Medal of Honor earlier in the war. I thought I learned another lesson on Attu: no man who dies in battle dies in vain. There is no time for mourning during a battle, but the after-effect a soldier's battlefield grave has on his comrades is sometimes overpowering. Five weeks after the Battle of Attu ended, a memorial service was held for the six hundred Americans who died there. No man of the 17th, 32nd, or 4th Regiments who attended this service is likely ever to forget that hundreds of men scaled Attu's summer-clad brown peaks to pick wild mountain flowers, with which they made wreaths for the graves of their brothers-in-arms. Could the living fail to gain from their own dead an inspiration which would sustain them in future battles? Can one American watch another die in his cause, by his side, without realizing that that cause must be worth while, and, therefore, must be pursued to a victorious end, whatever the cost?

This was the hard way of gaining an education, but, since we in America had made such an abominable job of educating a generation, we had no other method during the first two years of war. Therefore, our soldiers showed up poorly in their first battles. The number of "war neuroses" or "shell-shock" cases among them simply reflected the fact, in my opinion, that they were not mentally prepared to bridge the vast gap between the comforts of peace and the horrors of war. In other words, they had been brought up to believe that it was only necessary to wish for peace to have peace, and the best way to avoid war was to turn our heads the other way when war was mentioned. I had no words to describe the effect the first bombs and bullets had on many of the men educated in such fashion. Fortunately, most of them recovered their equilibrium after the initial shock. Fortunately, there were signs after two years of war that the oncoming generation of soldiers—those who had been conscious for two years of the nearness of war to them—would go into battle better prepared, better educated.

I thought Attu could be told in the story of the sergeant. On top of one of those snowy, marrow-chilling peaks in May, 1943, the platoon leader, a second lieutenant, ordered the sergeant to take a squad and go over there and knock out that Jap machine-gun nest. The sergeant just stared. His mouth was open. He was horrified. He had been in the Army two years; now, all of a sudden, he was told to go out and risk his life. He, like most Americans, had never thought of the war in terms of getting killed. In disgust, the second lieutenant said, "All right, sergeant, you just sit here. If any of you bastards," turning to the rest of his men, "have got the guts, follow me. We've got to get that machine gun. A lot of our men are getting killed by that machine gun."

Well, about ten men followed the second lieutenant. They killed the Japs and the machine gun didn't kill any more Americans.

That afternoon the sergeant went to the second lieutenant and said, "Sir, I am ashamed of myself. Give me another chance." By then there was another machine gun to be knocked out. So, the second lieutenant ordered the sergeant to take a squad and knock it out. The sergeant did just that. In fact, he knocked it out personally. The necessity of risking his life had finally been demonstrated to him.

Why didn't the sergeant on Attu do as he was told? Why did he volunteer to do the same thing the second time? I think men fight for two reasons: (1) ideals, (2) *esprit de corps*. The sergeant's education had not included any firm impression of the things that are worth fighting for, so he didn't see why he should risk his life the first time. But the second time he was willing to risk his life for his fellows, for the lieutenant and the ten men who had risked *their* lives, possibly for him, in the morning. The bonds of their common peril of the moment had gripped him as nothing in the past could.

In talking to the Marines aboard the *Blue Fox* I became convinced that they didn't know what to believe in, either—except the Marine Corps. The Marines fought almost solely on *esprit de corps*, I was certain. It was inconceivable to most Marines that they should let another Marine down, or that they could be responsible for dimming the bright reputation of their corps. The Marines simply assumed that they were the world's best fighting men. "Are you afraid?" Bill Hipple asked one of them. "Hell, no, mister," he answered, "I'm a Marine."

View of the Carnage

Betio had been declared "secured" at 1312 on the fourth day, seventy-five hours and forty-two minutes after the first Marines hit the beach. Occasional snipers would fire from holes and rubble-and-corpse-packed pillboxes for days afterward. Until the battle ended I had covered only a small part of the island—perhaps a total of four hundred yards along the beach, and no more than one hundred yards inland. To understand what had happened in each sector, it was necessary to walk over the island yard by yard. This I did for a day and a half before I flew out of the lagoon on a PB2Y on the afternoon of the sixth day.

What I saw on Betio was, I am certain, one of the greatest works of devastation wrought by man. Words are inadequate to describe what I saw on this island of less than a square mile. So are pictures—you can't smell pictures.

So that the reader may be able to place the scenes I describe in their approximate positions, I have inserted three drawings of the three trips I made over Betio. (See pp. 338, 348, 353.)

Here on the south beach the coconut-log and sand and concrete pillboxes are larger and more powerfully constructed than on the beach we invaded. Undoubtedly, the Japs, who had themselves landed on the north beach, expected us to land there, and not through the lagoon. In the water there are rows of land mines and double fences of barbed wire. There are fifteen dead Japs in and around the first pillbox next to the tank trap, all dressed in green uniforms, wrap-around leggings, and hobnailed shoes except one who wore a Navy flyer's blue uniform. Two of the fifteen have blown their guts out with hand grenades, as evidenced by their missing stomachs and right hands. Most of the bodies are already turning a sickly green, though they have been corpses only two days—as against five for most of the five thousand putrefying bodies on Betio.

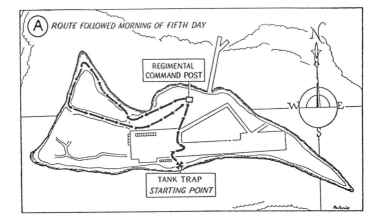

Down the beach, it is possible to see these mighty fortresses, one after another, as far as the eye can reach. There are twelve Japs inside the second pillbox—more than the smaller machine-gun boxes on the north shore could contain—and there are thirteen outside. Some of these wear only shorts, some only the G-string shorts which do not cover the flanks.

After a brief alert, caused by friendly planes, which we spend in a foxhole on the beach, Dick Johnston and I start across the airstrip toward the regimental command post near the northern shore. On the edge of the airstrip we find that the huge, fifteen-foot-high, box-like structures made of coconut logs are not blockhouses, but revetments to contain two planes. All the bombing and shelling have blown a few logs off these three-sided pens (the open side faces toward the runway), but generally they are surprisingly intact. There are perhaps a dozen Jap planes—Zeros and twin-engined bombers—along the runway, but only two inside the revetments which are fairly well riddled by shrapnel and bullets. The first light, maneuverable Zero we examine is in fairly good condition, however. The red ball of the Japanese is painted on both sides of the fuselage just back of the cockpit and on the top and bottom near each end of the wings.

A bullet-riddled, brown truck is on the edge of the runway. Inside the next big coconut-log revetment there are three identical trucks. Though they are Japanese-made, the dashboards of the trucks have their instruments labeled in English. Here is an example of the Japanese tendency to imitate: the "water" thermometer dial is in the centigrade of the French, as is the "kilos" of the speedometer; "oil" and "amperes" dials might have been taken from either the Americans or the British, but the fuel indicator is labeled "gasoline" instead of the British "petrol." The tires on this truck are four different brands: Dunlop, Bridgestone, Yokohama, and Firestone. An uncamouflaged black sedan nearby, also of Japanese make, had been hit and burned until there is less than half of it left. It has a license plate with the Navy anchor insignia on it, and the number 7/233. The blackout oilcloth over the headlights has no ordinary little hole through which a small beam of light might show; it has a Navy anchor, which gives the headlights the appearance of a Hallowe'en pumpkin.

Beside one of the revetments four naked Marines take a bath in a well of brackish water. The well, many years old, had been there before the Japs came. It had gone through the Battle of Betio unharmed.

At headquarters Captain J. L. Schwabe, one of the regimental staff officers, says we will find at the northwest tip of the island (the bird's beak) spots where our flamethrowers killed thirty and forty Japs at a time. He estimates that 250 Marines were killed in the water along the north beach between headquarters and the beak. Estimates of casualties in the Second Regiment are sickening: First Battalion 63 killed, 192 wounded, 41 missing; Second Battalion has 309 left out of 750 who landed; Third Battalion has 413 left, about the same as Major Crowe's Second Battalion of the Eighth. These figures were found later to be somewhat exaggerated, but they indicate how forcefully the first casualty compilations struck us. Five cemeteries have been started thus far—by 0800 of the fifth day—and less than one-fourth of our dead have been buried. The largest cemetery, next to the regimental command post, has 134 graves; the others 80, 53, 20, and 41 respectively.

A bandy-legged little Korean who wears white cotton pants and golf stockings is trying to talk to the M.P.'s who are taking him to an interpreter. He is trying to tell the M.P.'s how many were on the island. He says "Nippon" and draws "6000" in the sand; then he says "Korean" and draws "1000."

Going westward up the beach, beyond the farthest point I had yet reached, we see on the beach the bodies of Marines who have not yet been reached by the burial parties. The first is a husky boy who must have been three inches over six feet tall. He was killed ten feet in front of the seawall pillbox which was his objective. He is still hunched forward, his rifle in his right hand. That is the picture of the Marine Corps I shall always carry: charging forward. A bit further up the beach there are four dead Marines only a few feet apart; ten feet along, another; fifteen feet further another; then there are six bunched together. These men, we are told, are from I and K companies of the Third Battalion, Second Regiment.

Fifty feet further up the beach, ten Marines were killed on the barbed wire on the coral flats. One of them was evidently shot as he placed his foot on the top rung of the wire—his trouser leg was caught on the barbs and the leg still hangs in the air. There are eighty more dead Marines scattered in a twenty-foot square of the beach just beyond. Six more . . . two more . . . four more. Here four got to the very mouth of the coconut-log pillbox, but none of them made it, because there are no dead Japs inside. But in the next pillbox there are two Japs sprawled over their machine gun, and in the next, five yards further along the seawall, there are three. All appear to have been killed by hand grenades.

We detour inland a few yards. Here, perhaps thirty feet back of the seawall, four Marines lie dead outside a larger pillbox. There are six dead Japs inside. Still thirty feet further inland three dead Japs lie inside another pillbox, and there are three Marines lying around the pillbox. It is not difficult to see that the Marines were determined to keep on killing Japs while the breath of life remained in them, whether that last breath was drawn in the water, at the barricade, or at some undetermined point inland. What words can justify such bravery in the face of almost certain death? They died, but they came on. Those machine guns were killing other Marines out in the water, and who ever heard of one Marine letting another down?

Here Amphtrack Number 15—name: "Worried Mind"—is jammed against the seawall. Inside it are six dead Marines; next to it are three more. Two more lie impaled on the barbed wire next to the twenty-eight-seater Jap privy over the water. Their clothing ties them to the wire. They float at anchor. A half dozen Marines, members of the engineer regiment, are walking around the beach, examining the bodies. "Here's Larson," says one. "Here's Montague," says another. The bodies, as they are identified, are tenderly gathered up and taken fifteen or twenty yards inland, where other Marines are digging graves for them.

This is unusual, because most of the Marines are being gathered up by burial parties, which have not progressed this far. But these men are looking for the dead from their own particular company. Since they are leaving by transport in a few hours, I suppose they think: "Here is the last thing we can do for these boys we have known so long. We'll do it with our own hands."

When I passed that way again several hours later, the Eighteenth Marines had gone, had sailed away. But I noticed the fifteen graves this particular company had dug. A rude cross had been erected over each grave—undoubtedly replaced later by a neat white cross—and on the cross had been written the name of the Marine who lay underneath it, the designation that he was a Marine, and the date of his death, thus:

A. R. Mitlick
U.S.M.C.
20-11-43

In front of the fifteen graves, so that all would know which outfit they came from, and that they all came from D Company of the Eighteenth, the Marines had proudly erected a larger cross:

3−2−18

The names of these fifteen, right to left, were: R. C. Mc-Kinney, G. G. Seng,* R. C. Kountzman, R. L. Jarrett, Max J. Lynnton, C. Montague,* S. R. Parsons, M. W. Waltz, H. H. Watkins, H. B. Lanning, J. S. Castle, A. B. Roads, A. R. Mitlick, W. A. Larson, and R. W. Vincent, First Lieutenant.

Just behind the coconut-log wall where the men of D Company had died there is a pit containing a 77-mm. gun, whose ammunition supply had been half exhausted. A few yards further along the wall there is a 13-mm. machine gun. Inside the gun pit is a half-pint bottle of the only brand of whisky I have ever seen in Japanese possession. The label, like the labels of many Japanese commercial products, is in English:

Rare Old Island Whisky
SUNTORY
First Born in Nippon
Choicest Products
Kotobukiya Ltd.
Bottled at our own Yamazaki Distillery

A Marine near the gun pit had evidently been hit squarely by a 77-mm. shell (77 mm. is about three inches). There is a hole through his midsection, and he is badly burned—so badly that he could hardly be identified as a Marine but for the laced leggings under his trouser legs. A Marine who is standing nearby, Pfc. Glenn Gill of Oklahoma, explains that the remnants of the first and second waves of 3/2 rushed over the barricade, where they were pinned down as the third wave got all the machine-gun attention.

A hundred yards inland we find an air-raid sound detector, which is sandbagged all around, and a power plant, which was protected only by a tin roof that was smashed to a thousand pieces. There are wooden-compartmented boxes full of

---

*Gene Seng and Charlie Montague, aged twenty-one, had been childhood friends. They had gone to school together in Texas. On February 3, 1942, they had volunteered for the Marines together. On November 20, 1943, on Tarawa, they died together.

carpenter's tools and some more delicate instruments. Next to the power plant there is a thirty-six-inch searchlight, and in the middle of a group of buildings and pillboxes a hole ten feet deep, twenty feet in diameter. The sixteen-inch shell or one-thousand-pound bomb which made that hole could not have fallen anywhere else within a hundred yards without destroying something. Near the shellhole there are two Japs blown completely in two. Only the lower extremities of either are anywhere in sight—one was cut in two at the waist, the other at the hips. In a smaller shellhole there are six dead Japs around a 77-mm. gun—this had once been a Jap gun pit. On the rim of the gun pit lies a dead Marine, who looks as if he might have been killed while diving in. Another 77-mm. gun—they are very thick along this northwest beach—has been knocked out by shellfire. The barrel is splintered and twisted. In a bomb crater there are fourteen Japs, evidently tossed in there by Marines cleaning out pillboxes before inhabiting them. Another 77-mm. gun has not been touched by shellfire, but the eight Japs in the pit were killed by rifle fire.

Amphtrack Number 48 is jammed against the seawall barricade. Three waterlogged Marines lie beneath it. Four others are scattered nearby, and there is one hanging on the two-foot-high strand of barbed wire who does not touch the coral flat at all. Back of the 77-mm. guns there are many hundreds of rounds of 77-mm. ammunition.

At the tip of the Betio bird's beak, there is the first big Jap gun I have seen: 5.5 inches. It is set in a concrete cup, and the degrees of the compass are painted on the rim of the cup. Shells for the gun, which are about twenty inches long, are contained in six little compartments, six shells to a compartment, inside the walls of the cup. Outside the cup there are hundreds more shells. The gun turret has been hit by about fifty fifty-caliber strafing bullets which probably also killed the gun crew, who have been removed, but otherwise the gun is untouched.

Turning southward up the Betio bird's forehead, we find another 5.5-inch gun thirty yards away. Shells or bombs have nicked the inside of its cup at 170 degrees, 220 degrees, and 30 degrees. The four Japs inside the pit have been charred to sticks of carbon.

Outside the gun emplacement a dog, suffering from severe shell shock, wanders drunkenly. When some Marines whistle and call him he trembles and tries to run, but falls. Not far away there is a placid cat with a dirty red ribbon around his neck. A sergeant of an engineer platoon calls the roll of his outfit, which arrived late and had only one man wounded. But its flamethrowers killed dozens of the reeling Japs.

The pillboxes here along the west beach, spaced only ten feet apart, are connected by trenches. Near another 77-mm. gun there is another 36-inch searchlight. Like all seven searchlights on Betio, this one was a favorite target of strafing planes, and all were destroyed. Between this 77-mm. gun and another similar gun thirty yards up the beach the Japs have pointed a coconut log out to sea. To a pilot five hundred feet in the air it could very well be mistaken for a six-inch gun.

About halfway up the west beach we turn inland and start back through the center of the island, past the body of a bloated Jap officer lying next to more dull-brown trucks. A bit further toward the center, the Marines have thrown a few shovelfuls of sand over the ghastly, mangled bodies of a dozen Japs. Dead Japs are strewn liberally along the road that leads through the center, eight here, two there, thirty over there where they were caught by a flamethrower. Two lie beside a Jap light tank, which is camouflaged in the navy fashion of World War I. On the other side of the tank lies a Marine, whose body's site is marked for burial parties by the age-old method; his bayoneted rifle jabbed upright into the ground.

Here was a Jap warehouse, which burned to the ground at least three days ago. It was filled apparently with foodstuffs, mostly canned: salmon, shrimp, rice. Whoever dreams of starving out Japs should know that they always have enough food to last many months, not counting fish that they can catch, birds that they can kill, and coconuts they can pick. Near the warehouse there are the mangled remains of a dozen bicycles, of which the Japs must have had a thousand on Betio, in addition to perhaps a hundred cars and trucks, and great quantities of miniature rail equipment. Further on there are bales of sacks labeled in English: "Stores Government— Stores Department." Great stacks of cases of rifle ammunition have not been touched by the terrific bombardment. A Seabee walks out of a pillbox with a fencing costume that looks like a baseball catcher's equipment: a steel face mask and a "belly protector" made of laced bamboo and heavy blue cloth. Scattered along the road are several one-man sniper pits: gasoline drums sunk into the ground, with a lid for cover.

Between the road and the north beach, spaced some fifty yards apart, there are three big coconut-log bomb shelters, about twenty by fifty feet inside. Outside they are covered on the top and on the sides by three to ten feet of sand. None was touched either by aerial or naval bombardment. The occupants, cowering in their corners, had been killed by TNT and flamethrowers. A Marine intelligence officer tells his sergeant to tell his men to search the bodies for documents. "Sir, don't ask them to," pleads the sergeant. "They are puking already."

A tank trap has been constructed diagonally across the section of the island north of the runway that forms part of the air-strip triangles. It is a long, deep ditch whose sides are braced by upright coconut logs. Nearby there is another twenty-by-fifty bomb shelter, which is reinforced concrete inside, tiers of coconut logs in the middle and sand on the outside covered by palm fronds. I wonder: would the heaviest bomb ever made tear up this unbelievable fortification? Or if the bomb hit on the rounded sides of the blockhouse, would it not glance off and explode harmlessly alongside the blockhouse? Several bomb holes around the sides of the blockhouse indicate that "near misses" do no good.

Another burned warehouse contains hundreds of bottles of sake, most of them broken. Also stacks of uniforms, hundreds of pots and pans, several gross of little blue enamelware cereal bowls and cups with the Navy anchor stenciled on them, about eighty bicycles, and a number of pressure cookers. Like other navies, the Japanese Navy apparently is far more luxuriously equipped than the Army.

By 1030 the Seabees are working like a thousand beavers on the airfield, which must be prepared quickly in order that the Americans on Betio will have fighter protection. Actually, there is not a great deal for them to do before planes can land. The main runway, along the longitudinal center of the island, is concrete and it is in almost perfect condition. The shorter runways, of gravel, are almost as well preserved. The planes and ships had orders to lay off the runways. If their accuracy was such that they could lay off specified areas, then why could they not hit the targets assigned to them? The Seabees, many of them skilled workmen old enough to be the fathers of most of the Marines, are having a great time. Little, rubber-tired Jap carts provide much amusement for Seabees who wheel supplies up and down the runways with them. One Seabee boasts that his outfit has already killed two Jap snipers this morning.

More evidence of the care the Japs had used in building up Betio: an unharmed gasoline truck sunk into an underground revetment, a twelve-by-thirty concrete water storage tank, still three-quarters filled with water, another big warehouse—the battleships and bombers really tore up the unprotected warehouses, two black automobiles, three more destroyed buildings.

Two hundred yards west of the regimental command post there is an American graveyard which by now contains seventy Marines, and seven more bodies lie on the ground awaiting burial. The first grave is marked, on a crude piece of packing-case lumber, "Unidentified." Other names I note at random: Lieutenant Colonel David K. Claude,* J. F. Svoboda, Duffy, Jenkins, P. L. Olano, W. R. Jay, W. A. Carpenter, M. D. Dinnis, C. E. McGhee, W. C. Culp, F. R. Erislip, W. H. Soeters, "Unknown," L. N. Carney, Hicks, R. E. Bemis, E. R. Pero, C. J. Kubarski, H. Schempf.

Before I returned to regimental (now division) headquarters, the corps commander of the Gilbert Islands assaults (i.e., both Makin and Tarawa) had arrived: Major General Holland McTyeire Smith, one of the most colorful figures in the Marine Corps. Alabama-born Holland Smith is the father of amphibious training of U.S. armed forces. Many years ago he foresaw that one day it would be necessary for American soldiers and Marines to land on enemy beaches in the face of hostile fire. In awarding him the Distinguished Service Medal,

---

*Later that day someone remarked, "I wonder where Colonel Claude is. I haven't seen him in two days." Colonel Claude was an observer from another division, unattached to any particular outfit. He was killed up front with the Scout and Sniper Platoon.

Navy Secretary Frank Knox had said of him: "He laid the groundwork for amphibious training of practically all American units, including at various times the First and Third Marine Divisions, the First, Seventh, and Ninth Infantry Divisions of the Army and numerous other Marine Corps and Army personnel. His proficient leadership and tireless energy in the development of high combat efficiency among the forces under his supervision were in keeping with the highest traditions of the United States Naval Service."

Nonetheless, Holland Smith, beloved by the Marine Corps, had assumed the aspects of a barnacle, so far as much of the regular Navy was concerned. He spoke his mind whenever he saw something wrong, even if that something were a brain child of his own. And in the regular Navy the first rule is to speak softly, particularly if the speech contains something that might not reflect credit on everybody else. Holland Smith at sixty-one was a military liberal, which few men in the U.S. Navy dare to be after fifty.

I had known General Smith a long time, in San Diego where he was training amphibious forces, on Attu, on Kiska, aboard a transport, a battleship, and a couple of airplanes. Because he was an unusual major general, he was delightful, and I was glad to see him. Although his route over the western end of the island duplicated some of the territory I had covered in the morning, I looked forward to listening to his comments on an inspection during the afternoon, along with his Tarawa division commander, Julian Smith, his aide Major Clifton A. Woodrum, Jr., and two newsmen who had accompanied him by plane from Makin, Bernard McQuaid of the Chicago *Daily News* and Robert Trumbull of the New York *Times*. Said one of the newsmen—I forget which—"I guess we had a pretty tame show on Makin, compared to what the Marines had here." On Makin the 165th New York Infantry— the onetime "Fighting Sixty-Ninth"—had found about 250 Japs, plus some Korean laborers. In exterminating them, the 165th had had 65 killed, 121 wounded. "A lot of our casualties were caused by the wild firing of our men"—but that was not news; it always happens when green troops go into battle. The 165th had had the misfortune to lose its colonel, Gardiner Conroy, who was killed by a Jap sniper.

Before the tour started there was, at Julian Smith's suggestion, a double flag-raising near headquarters; U.S. and British
flags went up on twin flagpoles. There had been a devil of a
time finding a British flag. Finally, Major Frank Lewis George
Holland, who had been schoolmaster of the Gilberts before
he was forced to flee when the Japs came, produced a British
flag about half the size of the Stars and Stripes. In the words
of Henry Keys, the Australian correspondent representing the
London *Daily Express*, "Major Holland looked in his bag. It
contained one pair of drawers and the Union Jack."

The generals' tour of the island started from headquarters
southward, then west on the south shore, down the western
end, then eastward along the northern shore:

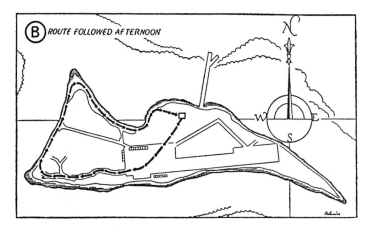

The first three dead men the generals see are Marines; one
near a disabled Jap tank on the edge of the runway, two more
in a shellhole not far away. Fifty yards before they reach the
south shore, after crossing the runway, they find the hastily
scooped graves of three more Marines. I note the casualty tag
on one grave: "W. F. Blevins, Killed in Action, 11-22-43."
Nearby there is the lone grave of "Pvt. J. M. Redman, Killed
in Action, 11-23-43." His helmet hangs on the cross, a bullet
hole through the center of it. A Marine near the south beach
reports that some of his buddies killed Japs in a machine-gun
nest over there only three hours ago. And there are still snipers scattered throughout the island that the Marines just can't

find. "Uh-huh," uh-huhs Holland Smith, who carries a carbine slung from his shoulder.

"There was one thing that won this battle, Holland," says
Julian Smith, "and that was the supreme courage of the Marines. The prisoners tell us that what broke their morale was
not the bombing, not the naval gunfire, but the sight of Marines who kept coming ashore in spite of their machine-gun
fire. The Jap machine-gun fire killed many Marines in the water and on the beach. But other Marines came behind those
who died. They landed on the beaches, they climbed the seawall, and they went into those enemy defenses. The Japs
never thought we would get to those defenses. They never
thought they would lose this island. They told their men a
million of us couldn't take it." Julian Smith tells Holland
Smith about Lieutenant Hawkins, that he is going to name
the airfield for Hawkins. "His will be my first recommenda-
tion for the Medal of Honor," says Julian Smith.

On the beach there is a twin-mount 5.5-inch seacoast gun,
which obviously had been demounted from a ship for shore
duty. Three dead Japs are inside the cup surrounding the gun,
and there are two more in a cut-back which has been hit directly. In the area of this twin-mount naval gunfire has obviously been very effective. On a sand hill thirty yards behind
the guns the Japs had mounted a fire director and range
finder.

A hundred yards or so west of the first guns there is another twin-mount 5.5-inch set of guns. This is a grisly sight.
There are two Japs under the gun barrels who have committed suicide with hand grenades. Four more are in a ditch leading from a nearby dugout. Only one of these is a suicide, but
another's heart bulges out of his chest, which apparently has
been rent open by a shell, and a third is only a stick of char.

The generals marvel at the strength of the machine-gun
emplacements on this south shore—almost a solid wall of apparently impregnable defenses all the way up to the southwest
tip of the island. They concede that one-six must have done a
thoroughgoing job.

At the southwest tip of the island they see two of the four
eight-inch guns which the Japs had on Betio. Both guns are
pointed toward the direction from which our transports

approached, but it is obvious that they were put out of action by some of the first salvos fired by our battleships. Hardly a round of eight-inch shells has been fired. It is easy to see what did the trick: a direct hit on the concrete powder chamber next to the guns. A gaping hole through the powder chamber indicates that a sixteen-inch shell perforated there. Inside the chamber there are about twenty-five charred Japs. Others are hanging on the jagged edge of the hole and for fifty yards beyond the hole Japs are spewed out over the sandy terrain. That must have been the terrific explosion we saw on the third battleship shot.

Next to the exploded powder chamber is the biggest hole on the pockmarked island of Betio—some sixty feet in diameter and much deeper than the sub-surface water level of the island. Scattered about the rim of the great hole are about two hundred rounds of eight-inch ammunition, evidence that the ammunition dump as well as the powder house blew up.

These two guns were served by a small mechanical trolley whose tracks circle the inside of the gun emplacements. The guns are labeled V. S. and M. (Vickers), indicating that they were captured from the British, or purchased from the British when Japan was an ally. Both eight-inch guns have been hit directly many times. The smaller guns, notably 77-mm. and machine guns, might escape hits from the terrific bombing and shelling which preceded our attack, but the larger ones were comparatively easy targets.

The generals and their inspecting party turn north and head back from the Betio bird's tufted head toward its beak. They see what had been a Japanese radar screen, mounted on a concrete pedestal. In front of a sign—"Danger: Mines"—battle-weary Marines are swimming nude, attempting to wash the crust, the scum, and the odors of Betio from their tanned bodies. There are no dead bodies on the western end of the island to impede the swimming. The generals note the lone grave of Captain Thomas Royster of the Second Amphibious Tractor Battalion. As they pass two of the deadly 77-mm. guns which are still in working condition, Julian Smith remarks, "These are the guns that kill our people; we can knock out the big guns."

Three pigs lie in a pen. One of them is dead from shrapnel hits. The other two act dazed, merely grunt.

The Generals Smith examine a 13-mm. machine gun at the northwest tip of Betio. Hundreds of empty shells show that it was fired many times before the nearby Jap had the top of his head blown off. "That gun killed a lot of Marines," says Julian Smith.

When we reach the northern shore—the bird's throat—we notice an amazing phenomenon: the full tide is now washing against the seawall to a depth of three feet, and the Marines who were lying on the beach this morning are now floating against the seawall. In other words, the tide during those first two critical days was exceptionally low, perhaps due to a wind from the south, or the Marines would have had no beachhead at all! This was truly an Act of Providence.

The Marines floating in the water are now pitiful figures. Many of them have had the hair washed off their heads by this time. Julian Smith orders an additional burial party formed to speed up the interment of the Americans. The eyes of the two veteran major generals are misty when they view the bodies of gallant Marines who were killed just before they reached the seawall. Says Holland Smith, "You must have three or four hundred here, Julian." But the most stirring sight is the Marine who is leaning in death against the seawall, one arm still supported upright by the weight of his body. On top of the seawall, just beyond his upraised hand, lies a blue and white flag, a beach marker to tell succeeding waves where to land. Says Holland Smith, "How can men like that ever be defeated? This Marine's duty was to plant that flag on top of the seawall. He did his duty, though it cost him his life. *Semper fidelis* meant more to him than just a catch phrase." We pass on down the seawall rather quickly, because it is impossible to look at such a sight, and realize its implications, without tears.

Three dead Japs lie in a pillbox behind the seawall. Near one of them there is a green-covered bound volume of the *National Geographic* for September–December, 1931, with markings in Japanese on the ends. The first article in the volume is about New Hampshire. Says New Hampshire–born

Barney McQuaid, sticking the volume under his arm, "I am not ordinarily a souvenir-hunter, but, gentlemen, this is my souvenir."

The generals are awestruck when they inspect the pillboxes the assault troops had to knock out. "By God," says Holland Smith, "those Marines just kept coming. Many of them were killed, but more came on. It looks beyond the realm of a human being that this place could have been taken. These Japanese were masters of defensive construction. I never saw anything like these defenses in the last war. The Germans never built anything like this in France. No wonder these bastards were sitting back here laughing at us! They never dreamed the Marines could take this island, and they were laughing at what would happen to us when we tried it."

Back at headquarters there is the first complete report on what happened on the other twenty-four islands of the Tarawa Atoll. The Second Battalion of the Sixth Infantry had landed on the next island, Bairiki, where a few Japs offered light resistance. But most of them fled to Abaokora, northernmost island of the atoll, with the Marines pursuing hotly. From there the Japs could go no further. The Marines killed the 150 to 200 Japs who fought to the last. Three officers and twenty-six men of the battalion were killed, and about six officers and sixty men were wounded. On Abemama, the other Gilbert atoll where there were Japs, about thirty Marine scouts had landed and hemmed in the Japs. One Marine was killed; the twenty-five Japs committed suicide.

By now the LST's have nosed up to the edge of the shelf that surrounds Betio. At low tide they discharge trucks by the dozen which carry supplies ashore over the coral flats, through the hole that has been cut into the seawall. Within a very few days Betio will be a strong American base—stronger offensively than the Japs had made it defensively.

Not until next day did we learn that three Marines had been killed on the western end of the island by Jap snipers, shortly after the generals had passed that point.

On the sixth day I walked over the eastern half of Betio—the half which got almost as much attention prior to the landing as the western half, plus an additional four days' pounding by every gun in the U.S. Navy, every gun up to 75 mm. in the

U.S. Marine Corps, and many hundreds of Navy bombers and fighters. If the western half was a shambles, the tail end was the acme of destruction and desolation. Shellholes and bomb craters, uprooted coconut trees, exploded ammunition dumps, some pulverized pillboxes, big guns broken and bent, and many hundreds of rotting Japanese bodies. This is the route I took in viewing the carnage on the tail end of Betio:

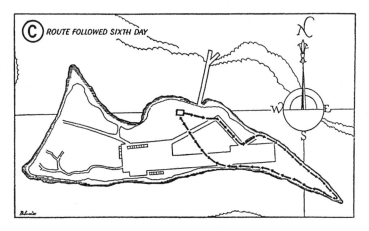

At the pillbox near Major Crowe's headquarters where I had seen the first Jap fried by a flamethrower, I note the details of the fortification, now that it has been stripped down by repeated charges of TNT. The three feet of sand that covered its rounded top has been blasted away. The top actually was a cone-shaped piece of armor, two layers of quarter-inch steel. Beneath that steel turret there were two layers of eight-inch coconut logs—the turret armor was used apparently to give the top a rounded shape which would deflect bombs. This pillbox was five-sided, each side about ten feet, with a buffer tier at the entrance for protection against shrapnel. Each side consisted of a double tier of coconut logs, hooked together by steel spikes with sand between the tiers. Over the whole, including the sides, there was a deep layer of sand, which gave the pillbox the appearance of a tropical igloo. There were two entrances to the pillbox—one to seaward and one to the east.

The machine-gun emplacements on the north side of the

island's tail are much the same as those on the west end. Beside them and back of them there are trenches, some containing twenty-five Jap dead. Inland thirty yards there is a fifteen-foot-high cement-and-coconut-log, sand-covered ammunition dump. There are gashes in the coconut logs where the sand has been blasted away, but no penetration by hundreds of rounds of high explosives.

A mess kitchen, with two-by-four walls and a tin roof, has been blasted to bits. It measures about twenty-five by one-hundred feet and there are many ten-gallon pots laid on the fire holes in the cement stoves. A hen sets calmly inside the debris. At the east end of the kitchen there are thousands upon thousands of cans of food and broken bottles. Nearby there are a dozen half-Japs whose life had been flicked away by a flamethrower. One of them is only a charred spinal cord and a lump of burnt flesh where his head had been. A little further on, there are fifty more dead Japs—they seem to be thicker on this end of the island. Scattered around a big blockhouse and what apparently had been a power plant there are at least 150 more who had been hit by a variety of weapons: some are charred, others have their heads blown off, others are only chests or trunks. Only one of them appears to be a suicide. In the midst of them there is a lone Marine, lying under two sprawling Japs. What had been this man's fate— this man whose pack containing two cans of C ration had been ripped by shrapnel? Had he been killed by a Jap bullet, or hit by some of our own high explosives? Or had he single-handed tried to attack 150 Japs? No reporter is ever likely to answer that question.

The march up the tail of the island is strewn with carnage. Now, on the sixth day, the smell of the dead is unbelievable. The ruptured and twisted bodies which expose their rotting inner organs are inexpressibly repelling. Betio would be more habitable if the Marines could leave for a few days and send a million buzzards in. The fire from a burning pile of rubble has reached six nearby Jap bodies, which sizzle and pop as the flame consumes flesh and gases. Fifteen more are scattered around a food dump, and two others are blown to a hundred pieces—a hand here, a head there, a hobnailed foot farther away.

There is a warehouse near the end of the Burns Philp pier, whose contents have been scattered over many hundreds of square feet. A small trolley leads from the end of the pier to the warehouse. Unlike the Jap Army on Attu, the Navy troops on Tarawa were well supplied with mechanized tools and vehicles. Next to the pier there is another armored turret that served atop a pillbox. This one is smashed in on two sides, and perforated a hundred times by strafing bullets. Two Japs are in a shellhole that was a coconut-log pillbox—here the additional four days of shelling proves that some of these pillboxes can be smashed by heavy gunfire. Under the Burns Philp pier lie a dozen Japs who machine-gunned the Americans as they waded ashore (a destroyer finally smashed the pier). Under a privy platform which is also smashed lie fourteen more Japs. At the end of this pier lies a pig, his hams shot off. Three wrecked barges are on the beach. Two of them have double-fuselaged bows, look something like P-38's.

Inland there is one of the biggest concrete blockhouses on the island—about sixty by forty, and twenty-five feet high. Four direct hits, probably from battleships, smashed through its walls, and a Marine souvenir-hunter says there are 300 charred Jap bodies inside. Steps lead to the roof of the blockhouse, where there are two 13-mm. machine guns. In one gun nest there are four dead Japs, in the other, two. Four others are scattered around the rooftop and two more are in a pen covered by sandbags. All apparently were killed by strafing planes, although some naval gun shrapnel nicked the extension of the walls which protect the roof-bound machine gunners. These nicks show that the entire thick concrete structure was laced with half-inch reinforcing steel. A Marine sits down on the roof, opens a can of C ration, and eats heartily.

Outside there are two burned Jap tanks, carrying license plates number 102 and 113 and the Navy anchor insignia. A black automobile in a nearby wooden garage has hardly been touched. None of the glass windows has been broken and there are only a few strafing bullets through the top of the car. An indifferent Marine gets in the car, steps on the starter. The engine runs like a sewing machine. Near the garage there is what was once a motor pool—the concrete blockhouse was undoubtedly a headquarters. A dozen motorcycles with side-cars are burned to steel skeletons, but one little motorcycle truck is in fairly good condition.

Another warehouse a hundred yards beyond is torn to pieces, but only one of the five coconut-log pillboxes surrounding it is not intact. Another warehouse was also the site of another motor pool. None of its trucks or motorcycles will run again!

Back on the north beach opposite the inland warehouses, there are three fifty-foot-long pillboxes and eight or ten smaller ones. One of the larger fortifications has its top blown completely off. The rest are untouched, but the mounted gun inside—37 mm. or 40 mm.—is twisted and broken, its wheels demolished. Further down the beach there are contiguous shellholes, and shellholes within shellholes, as far as the eye can see. A strong, small pillbox is smashed in, pinning a Jap machine gunner to the bottom of the dugout. The next pillbox also had an armored turret for a top, but it, too, is only a smashed steel cone.

Within a few hundred yards of the end of the island the Japs had used great bulbous roots of coconut trees for fortifications, back of layers of barbed wire and rows of mines on the beach. Back of the beach, where eight Japs lie in a blasted pillbox, there is a long tank trap fenced in on either side by barbed wire. A little Jap pack howitzer, about 75 mm., but having wheels only thirty inches in diameter, is the first of its kind I have seen on Betio. A 36-inch searchlight on the beach has been shattered. The coconut logs supporting it have been smashed to the ground and the machinery which operated the searchlight is good only for scrap iron.

Thirty yards inland from the searchlight there is another concrete blockhouse which was an ammunition dump serving the two nearby shattered twin-mount 5.5-inch guns. A direct hit on the ammunition dump had set off the shells inside, which blew the roof heaven knows where. There are hundreds of rounds of ammunition inside. The concrete walls are fairly well intact, however. These walls measure, by a twelve-inch shoe, just eight feet thick, which is a lot of concrete. There is evidence of only one Jap nearby: a leg and arms which probably matched. On the airfield to the west the first F6F lands on Betio.

Beside an unexploded five-hundred-pound bomb there is a hole caused by a bomb that was not a dud. Six Japs are in the hole, which is filled to a depth of two feet by seeping water. Inland there is another mess kitchen with a capacity for ten ten-gallon pots. Near it there had been a barracks building of which now only the floor remains. Scattered around the remains of the building are blankets, shoes, buttons, underwear, "writing pads"—so labeled in English, pans and cups carrying the Navy insignia, sake bottles. Much of the clothing is civilian—evidently there were quite a few Japanese civilians on Betio, or the Navy takes its civilian clothes with it. My souvenir of Betio is a fine, red-figured Japanese silk necktie.

Near the tail end of the island I cross the 150 yards to the southern shore. In the middle of the tail end of the island there are hundreds of tons of unrusted steel rail and at least a thousand wheels to fit those rails. Unmistakably, the Japs had big plans for Betio.

On the south shore, near the tail end, are the remains of two more eight-inch Vickers guns. One of the gun barrels is broken off about four feet from where it sticks out of the turret. The other gun is badly burned and strafing bullets had nicked the inside of the barrel so badly that it probably could not have been fired again. There are three searchlights within 300 yards, and numerous 13-mm. and 77-mm. anti-aircraft guns protect the big guns. Not far away there are twenty dead Japs in a shellhole. Perhaps they had worked at the mixer which had been pouring dozens of pyramidal concrete blocks for the defense of Betio against the expected American invasion.

By running most of the mile and a half back to the pier, past Seabees and trucks and graders and rollers working on the airfield, past several hundred more dead Japs and one well-hidden live Jap who pestered the Seabees, past hundreds of shellholes and bomb craters of varying depths, I made the plane for Funafuti. I was not sorry to leave the appalling wreckage of Betio and its 5,000 dead. I was thankful that I had lived through the toughest job ever assigned to the toughest outfit the U.S. has produced: the magnificent U.S. Marines.

That night as I gratefully soaped myself in an outdoor shower on Funafuti, Co-pilot Hugh Wilkinson said, "I hated to tell you this when you boarded the plane at Tarawa, but all of you smelled like dead Japs." Lieutenant Wilkinson gave me some of his clothing, for I had none except the dirty Marine dungarees I had worn for six days. "Can't I give you these in exchange?" I said. "Perhaps a native woman would wash them."

Said Wilkinson, "Thanks just the same, but I think we'll bury the dungarees. Let's go get a bottle of beer."

"The Hard Facts of War"

Just eight days after the first Marines hit the beach at Betio, I was again in Honolulu. Already there were rumblings about Tarawa. People on the U.S. mainland had gasped when they heard the dread phrase, "heavy casualties." They gasped again when it was announced that 1,026 Marines had been killed, 2,600 wounded.* "This must not happen again," thundered an editorial. "Our intelligence must have been faulty," guessed a member of Congress.

This attitude, following the finest victory U.S. troops had won in this war, was amazing. It was the clearest indication that the peacetime United States (i.e., the United States as of December, 1943) simply found it impossible to bridge the great chasm that separates the pleasures of peace from the horrors of war. Like the generation they educated, the people had not thought of war in terms of men being killed—war seemed so far away.

Tarawa, it seemed to me, marked the beginning of offensive thrusts in the Pacific. Tarawa appeared to be the opening key to offensive operations throughout the whole Pacific—as important in its way as Guadalcanal was important to the defense of the U.S.-Australian supply line. Tarawa required four

---

*This first estimate actually was somewhat higher than revised casualty figures: 685 killed, 77 died of wounds, 169 missing, about 2100 wounded.

days; Guadalcanal, six months. Total casualties among Marines alone, not even including malaria cases, were about twenty percent higher on Guadalcanal.

Tarawa was not perfectly planned or perfectly executed. Few military operations are, particularly when the enemy is alert. Said Julian Smith: "We made mistakes, but you can't know it all the first time. We learned a lot which will benefit us in the future. And we made fewer mistakes than the Japs did." Tarawa was the first frontal assault on a heavily defended atoll. By all the rules concerning amphibious assaults, the Marines should have suffered far heavier casualties than the defenders. Yet, for every Marine who was killed more than four Japs died—four of the best troops the Emperor had. Looking at the defenses of Betio, it was no wonder our colonels could say: "With two battalions of Marines I could have held this island until hell froze over."

Tarawa must have given the Japanese General Staff something to think about.

The lessons of Tarawa were many. It is a shame that some very fine Americans had to pay for those lessons with their lives, but they gave their lives that others on other enemy beaches might live. On Tarawa we learned what our best weapons were, what weapons needed improving, what tactics could best be applied to other operations. We learned a great deal about the most effective methods of applying Naval gunfire and bombs to atolls. Our capacity to learn, after two years of war, had improved beyond measure. The same blind refusal to learn, which had characterized many of our operations early in the war, had almost disappeared. We were learning, and learning how to learn faster.

The facts were cruel, but inescapable: Probably no amount of shelling and bombing could obviate the necessity of sending in foot soldiers to finish the job. The corollary was this: there is no easy way to win the war; there is no panacea which will prevent men from getting killed. To me it seemed that to deprecate the Tarawa victory was almost to defame the memory of the gallant men who lost their lives achieving it.

Why, then, did so many Americans throw up their hands at the heavy losses on Tarawa? Why did they not realize that there would be many other bigger and bloodier Tarawas in the three or four years of Japanese war following the first Tarawa? After two years of observing the Japanese I had become convinced that they had only one strategy: to burrow into the ground as far and as securely as possible, waiting for the Americans to dig them out; then to hope that the Americans would grow sick of their own losses before completing the job. Result: a Japanese victory through negotiated peace. It seemed to me that those Americans who were horrified by Tarawa were playing into Japanese hands. It also seemed that there was no way to defeat the Japanese except by extermination.

Then I reasoned that many Americans had never been led to expect anything but an easy war. Through their own wishful thinking, bolstered by comfort-inspiring yarns from the war theatres, they had really believed that this place or that place could be "bombed out of the war." It seemed to many that machines alone would win the war for us, perhaps with the loss of only a few pilots, and close combat would not be necessary. As a matter of fact, by the end of 1943 our airplanes, after a poor start, had far outdistanced anything the Japanese could put in the air. We really did not worry particularly about Japanese airpower. If we could get close enough, we could gain air supremacy wherever we chose. But did that mean we could win the war by getting only a few pilots killed? It did not. Certainly, air supremacy was necessary. But airpower could not win the war alone. Despite airplanes and the best machines we could produce, the road to Tokyo would be lined with the grave of many a foot soldier. This came as a surprise to many people.

Our information services had failed to impress the people with the hard facts of war. Early in the war our communiqués gave the impression that we were bowling over the enemy every time our handful of bombers dropped a few pitiful tons from 30,000 feet. The stories accompanying the communiqués gave the impression that any American could lick any twenty Japs. Later, the communiqués became more matter-of-fact. But the communiqués, which made fairly dry reading, were rewritten by press association reporters who waited for them back at rear headquarters. The stories almost invariably came out liberally sprinkled with "smash" and "pound" and other "vivid" verbs. These "vivid" verbs impressed the headline writers back in the home office. They impressed the reading public which saw them in tall type. But they sometimes did not impress the miserable, bloody soldiers in the front lines where the action had taken place. Gloomily observed a sergeant: "The war that is being written in the newspapers must be a different war from the one we see." Sometimes I thought I could see a whole generation losing its faith in the press. One night a censor showed me four different letters saying, in effect: "I wish we could give you the story of this battle without the sugar-coating you see in the newspapers."

Whose fault was this? Surely, there must have been some reason for tens of millions of people getting false impressions about the war. Mostly, it was not the correspondents' fault. The stories which gave false impressions were not usually the front-line stories. But the front-line stories had to be sent back from the front. They were printed somewhat later, usually on an inside page. The stories which the soldiers thought deceived their people back home were the "flashes" of rewritten communiqués, sent by reporters who were nowhere near the battle. These communiqué stories carrying "vivid" verbs were the stories that got the big headlines. And the press association system willy-nilly prevented these reporters from making any evaluation of the news, from saying: "Does this actually mean anything, and if it does, what does it mean in relation to the whole picture?" The speed with which the competing press associations had to send their dispatches did not contribute to the coolness of evaluation. By the time the radio announcers had read an additional lilt into the press association dispatches—it was no wonder that our soldiers spat in disgust.

Said a bomber pilot, after returning from the Pacific: "When I told my mother what the war was really like, and how long it was going to take, she sat down and cried. She didn't know we were just beginning to fight the Japs."

My third trip back to the United States since the war began was a let-down. I had imagined that everybody, after two years, would realize the seriousness of the war and the necessity of working as hard as possible toward ending it. But I found a nation wallowing in unprecedented prosperity. There was a steel strike going on, and a railroad strike was threatened. Men lobbying for special privilege swarmed around a Congress which appeared afraid to tax the people's new-found, inflationary wealth. Justice Byrnes cautioned a group of newsmen that we might expect a half million casualties within a few months—and got an editorial spanking for it. A "high military spokesman" generally identified as General Marshall said bitterly that labor strikes played into the hands of enemy propagandists. Labor leaders got furious at that. The truth was that many Americans were not prepared psychologically to accept the cruel facts of war.

The men on Tarawa would have known what the general and the justice meant. On Tarawa, late in 1943, there was a more realistic approach to the war than there was in the United States.

Tarawa: The Story of a Battle, 1944

"The Target Was To Be the Big City"

By Edward R. Murrow

YESTERDAY AFTERNOON, the waiting was over. The weather was right; the target was to be the big city. The crew captains walked into the briefing room, looked at the maps and charts and sat down with their big celluloid pads on their knees. The atmosphere was that of a school and a church. The weatherman gave us the weather. The pilots were reminded that Berlin is Germany's greatest center of war production. The intelligence officer told us how many heavy and light ack-ack guns, how many searchlights we might expect to encounter. Then Jock, the wing commander, explained the system of markings, the kind of flare that would be used by the Pathfinders. He said that concentration was the secret of success in these raids, that as long as the aircraft stayed well bunched, they would protect each other. The captains of aircraft walked out.

I noticed that the big Canadian with the slow, easy grin had printed "Berlin" at the top of his pad and then embellished it with a scroll. The red-headed English boy with the two weeks' old moustache was the last to leave the room. Late in the afternoon we went to the locker room to draw parachutes, Mae Wests and all the rest. As we dressed, a couple of the Australians were whistling. Walking out to the bus that was to take us to the aircraft, I heard the station loud-speakers announcing that that evening all personnel would be able to see a film, *Star Spangled Rhythm*, free.

We went out and stood around a big, black, four-motored Lancaster *D for Dog*. A small station wagon delivered a thermos bottle of coffee, chewing gum, an orange and a bit of chocolate for each man. Up in that part of England the air hums and throbs with the sound of the aircraft motors all day. But for half an hour before take-off, the skies are dead, silent and expectant. A lone hawk hovered over the airfield, absolutely still as he faced into the wind. Jack, the tail gunner, said, "It would be nice if *we* could fly like that."

D for Dog eased around the perimeter track to the end of the runway. We sat there for a moment. The green light flashed and we were rolling—ten seconds ahead of schedule! The take-off was smooth as silk. The wheels came up, and *D-Dog* started the long climb. As we came up through the clouds, I looked right and left and counted fourteen black Lancasters climbing for the place where men must burn oxygen to live. The sun was going down, and its red glow made rivers and lakes of fire on tops of the clouds. Down to the southward, the clouds piled up to form castles, battlements and whole cities, all tinged with red.

Soon we were out over the North Sea. Dave, the navigator, asked Jock if he couldn't make a little more speed. We were nearly two minutes late. By this time we were all using oxygen. The talk on the intercom was brief and crisp. Everyone sounded relaxed. For a while the eight of us in our little world in exile moved over the sea. There was a quarter moon on the starboard beam. Jock's quiet voice came through the intercom, "That'll be flak ahead." We were approaching the enemy coast. The flak looked like a cigarette lighter in a dark room—one that won't light. Sparks but no flame. The sparks crackling just above the level of the cloud tops. We flew steady and straight, and soon the flak was directly below us.

D-Dog rocked a little from right to left, but that wasn't caused by the flak. We were in the slip stream of other Lancasters ahead, and we were over the enemy coast. And then a strange thing happened. The aircraft seemed to grow smaller. Jack in the rear turret, Wally, the mid-upper gunner; Titch, the wireless operator—all seemed somehow to draw closer to Jock in the cockpit. It was as though each man's shoulder was against the other's. The understanding was complete. The intercom came to life, and Jock said, "Two aircraft on the port beam." Jack in the tail said, "Okay, sir, they're Lancs." The whole crew was a unit and wasn't wasting words.

The cloud below was ten tenths. The blue-green jet of the exhausts licked back along the leading edge, and there were other aircraft all around us. The whole great aerial armada was hurtling towards Berlin. We flew so for twenty minutes, when Jock looked up at a vapor trail curling across above us, remarking in a conversational tone that from the look of it he thought there was a fighter up there. Occasionally the angry red of ack-ack burst through the clouds, but it was far away, and we took only an academic interest. We were flying in the third wave. Jock asked Wally in the mid-upper turret and Jack in the rear turret if they were cold. They said they were all right, and thanked him for asking. Even asked how I was, and I said, "All right so far." The cloud was beginning to thin out. Up to the north we could see light, and the flak began to liven up ahead of it.

Boz, the bomb aimer, crackled through on the intercom, "There's a battle going on on the starboard beam." We couldn't see the aircraft, but we could see the jets of red tracer being exchanged. Suddenly there was a burst of yellow flame, and Jock remarked, "That's a fighter going down. Note the position." The whole thing was interesting, but remote. Dave, the navigator, who was sitting back with his maps, charts and compasses, said, "The attack ought to begin in exactly two minutes." We were still over the clouds. But suddenly those dirty gray clouds turned white. We were over the outer searchlight defenses. The clouds below us were white, and we were black. *D-Dog* seemed like a black bug on a white sheet. The flak began coming up, but none of it close. We were still a long way from Berlin. I didn't realize just how far.

Jock observed, "There's a kite on fire dead ahead." It was a great golden, slow-moving meteor slanting toward the earth. By this time we were about thirty miles from our target area in Berlin. That thirty miles was the longest flight I have ever made. Dead on time, Boz, the bomb aimer, reported, "Target indicators going down." The same moment the sky ahead was lit up by bright yellow flares. Off to starboard, another kite went down in flames. The flares were sprouting all over the sky—reds and greens and yellows—and we were flying straight for the center of the fireworks. *D-Dog* seemed to be standing still, the four propellers thrashing the air. But we didn't seem to be closing in. The clouds had cleared, and off to the starboard a Lanc was caught by at least fourteen searchlight beams. We could see him twist and turn and finally break out. But still the whole thing had a quality of unreality about it. No one seemed to be shooting at us, but it was getting lighter all the time. Suddenly a tremendous big blob of yellow light appeared dead ahead, another to the right and another to the left. We were flying straight for them.

Jock pointed out to me the dummy fires and flares to right and left. But we kept going in. Dead ahead there was a whole chain of red flares looking like stop lights. Another Lanc was coned on our starboard beam. The lights seemed to be supporting it. Again we could see those little bubbles of colored lead driving at it from two sides. The German fighters were at him. And then, with no warning at all, *D-Dog* was filled with an unhealthy white light. I was standing just behind Jock and could see all the seams on the wings. His quiet Scots voice beat into my ears, "Steady, lads, we've been coned." His slender body lifted half out of his seat as he jammed the control column forward and to the left. We were going down.

Jock was wearing woolen gloves with the fingers cut off. I could see his fingernails turn white as he gripped the wheel. And then I was on my knees, flat on the deck, for he had whipped the *Dog* back into a climbing turn. The knees should have been strong enough to support me, but they weren't, and the stomach seemed in some danger of letting me down, too. I picked myself up and looked out again. It seemed that one big searchlight, instead of being twenty thousand feet below, was mounted right on our wing tip. *D-Dog* was corkscrewing. As we rolled down on the other side, I began to see what was happening to Berlin.

The clouds were gone, and the sticks of incendiaries from the preceding waves made the place look like a badly laid out city with the street lights on. The small incendiaries were going down like a fistful of white rice thrown on a piece of black velvet. As Jock hauled the *Dog* up again, I was thrown to the other side of the cockpit, and there below were more incendiaries, glowing white and then turning red. The cookies— the four-thousand-pound high explosives—were bursting below like great sunflowers gone mad. And then, as we started down again, still held in the lights, I remembered that the *Dog* still had one of those cookies and a whole basket of incendiaries in his belly, and the lights still held us. And I was very frightened.

While Jock was flinging him about in the air, he suddenly flung over the intercom, "Two aircraft on the port beam." I looked astern and saw Wally, the mid-upper, whip his turret around to port and then look up to see a single-engined fighter slide just above us. The other aircraft was one of ours. Finally, we were out of the cone, flying level. I looked down, and the white fires had turned red. They were beginning to merge and spread, just like butter does on a hot plate. Jock and Boz, the bomb aimer, began to discuss the target. The smoke was getting thick down below. Boz said he liked the two green flares on the ground almost dead ahead. He began calling his directions. And just then a new bunch of big flares went down on the far side of the sea of flame and flare that seemed to be directly below us. He thought that would be a better aiming point. Jock agreed, and we flew on. The bomb doors were open. Boz called his directions, "Five left, five left." And then there was a gentle, confident, upward thrust under my feet, and Boz said, "Cookie gone." A few seconds later, the incendiaries went, and *D-Dog* seemed lighter and easier to handle.

I thought I could make out the outline of streets below. But the bomb aimer didn't agree, and he ought to know. By this time all those patches of white on black had turned yellow and started to flow together. Another searchlight caught us but didn't hold us. Then through the intercom came the word, "One can of incendiaries didn't clear. We're still carrying it." And Jock replied, "Is it a big one or a little one?" The word came back, "Little one, I think, but I'm not sure. I'll check." More of those yellow flares came down and hung about us. I haven't seen so much light since the war began. Finally the intercom announced that it was only a small container of incendiaries left, and Jock remarked, "Well, it's hardly worth going back and doing another run-up for that." If there had been a good fat bundle left, he would have gone back through that stuff and done it all over again.

I began to breathe and to reflect again — that all men would be brave if only they could leave their stomachs at home. Then there was a tremendous whoomp, an unintelligible shout from the tail gunner, and *D-Dog* shivered and lost altitude. I looked at the port side, and there was a Lancaster that seemed close enough to touch. He had whipped straight under us, missed us by twenty-five, fifty feet, no one knew how much. The navigator sang out the new course, and we were heading for home. Jock was doing what I had heard him tell his pilots to do so often—flying dead on course. He flew straight into a huge green searchlight and, as he rammed the throttles home, remarked, "We'll have a little trouble getting away from this one." And again *D-Dog* dove, climbed and twisted and was finally free. We flew level then. I looked on the port beam at the target area. There was a sullen, obscene glare. The fires seemed to have found each other—and we were heading home.

For a little while it was smooth sailing. We saw more battles. Then another plane in flames, but no one could tell whether it was ours or theirs. We were still near the target. Dave, the navigator, said, "Hold her steady, skipper. I want to get an astral site." And Jock held her steady. And the flak began coming up at us. It seemed to be very close. It was winking off both wings. But the *Dog* was steady. Finally Dave said, "Okay, skipper, thank you very much." And a great orange blob of flak smacked up straight in front of us. And Jock said, "I think they're shooting at us." I'd thought so for some time.

And he began to throw *D for Dog* up, around and about again. And when we were clear of the barrage, I asked him how close the bursts were and he said, "Not very close. When they're really near, you can smell 'em." That proved nothing, for I'd been holding my breath. Jack sang out from the rear turret, said his oxygen was getting low, thought maybe the lead had frozen. Titch, the wireless operator, went scrambling back with a new mask and a bottle of oxygen. Dave, the navigator, said, "We're crossing the coast." My mind went back to the time I had crossed that coast in 1938, in a plane that had taken off from Prague. Just ahead of me sat two refugees from Vienna—an old man and his wife. The co-pilot came back and told them that we were outside German territory. The old man reached out and grasped his wife's hand. The work that was done last night was a massive blow of retribution for all those who have fled from the sound of shots and blows on the stricken Continent.

We began to lose height over the North Sea. We were over England's shore. The land was dark beneath us. Somewhere down there below American boys were probably bombing-up Fortresses and Liberators, getting ready for the day's work. We were over the home field. We called the control tower, and the calm, clear voice of an English girl replied, "Greetings, *D-Dog*. You are diverted to Mule Bag." We swung around, contacted Mule Bag, came in on the flare path, touched down very gently, ran along to the end of the runway and turned left. And Jock, the finest pilot in Bomber Command, said to the control tower, "*D-Dog* clear of runway."

When we went in for interrogation, I looked on the board and saw that the big, slow-smiling Canadian and the red-headed English boy with the two weeks' old moustache hadn't made it. They were missing. There were four reporters on this operation—two of them didn't come back. Two friends of mine—Norman Stockton, of Australian Associated Newspapers, and Lowell Bennett, an American representing International News Service. There is something of a tradition amongst reporters that those who are prevented by circumstances from filing their stories will be covered by their colleagues. This has been my effort to do so.

In the aircraft in which I flew, the men who flew and fought it poured into my ears their comments on fighters, flak and flares in the same tones they would have used in reporting a host of daffodils. I have no doubt that Bennett and Stockton would have given you a better report of last night's activities.

Berlin was a kind of orchestrated hell, a terrible symphony of light and flame. It isn't a pleasant kind of warfare—the men doing it speak of it as a job. Yesterday afternoon, when the tapes were stretched out on the big map all the way to Berlin and back again, a young pilot with old eyes said to me, "I see we're working again tonight." That's the frame of mind in which the job is being done. The job isn't pleasant; it's terribly tiring. Men die in the sky while others are roasted alive in their cellars. Berlin last night wasn't a pretty sight. In about thirty-five minutes it was hit with about three times the amount of stuff that ever came down on London in a night-long blitz. This is a calculated, remorseless campaign of destruction. Right now the mechanics are probably working on *D-Dog*, getting him ready to fly again.

CBS Radio Broadcast, December 3, 1943

San Pietro a Village of the Dead;
Victory Cost Americans Dearly

by Homer Bigart

WITH THE 5TH ARMY, Dec. 18 (Via London) (Delayed).
—We crossed the valley to San Pietro through fields littered
with dead. The village, rising in terraces on the southern
hump of Monte Samucro, loomed out of the blue haze of
battle smoke like an ancient ruined castle, and even from the
creek bed we could see that not one house in that tight little
cluster of buildings had escaped ruin.

The Germans had cleared out—that much had been established late yesterday when patrols penetrated the outskirts
without drawing fire. But we heard that enemy snipers were
still clinging to their bunkers in the ravine north of the village
and, since San Pietro was likely to receive further pastings
from German artillery, no infantrymen ventured into the
death trap. Instead, a force led by Lieutenant James Epper-
man, of Hot Springs, Tex., skirted the town and took up positions on the high ground just beyond.

We followed a unit of medical-aid men into San Pietro. In
the wrecked buildings, sprawling on blood-drenched rubble,
were American as well as German wounded. Three times during Wednesday's initial attack American assault parties had
penetrated San Pietro. Each time they had been driven off
with severe casualties.

Early today litter bearers had cleared the lower buildings of
wounded. In darkness they groped through narrow alleys
choked with rubble, shouting into open doorways and listening intently for some response.

From the wine cellar of a house, sheered off nearly to the
ground by weeks of shelling, came a faint cry for help. On the
straw-covered earthen floor lay three wounded Americans
who had been there two days and nights, too weak to get

371

back to friendly lines. One had been wounded three times on successive days. In Wednesday's assault he received shell fragments in the right hip, and lay helpless in a dugout just outside the village. Next day the Germans renewed their shelling, and his right hip was subject to a near miss. Yesterday, while crawling toward a wine cellar, another fragment pierced his right hip.

He had used all his sulfa tablets. A comrade, less seriously hurt, gave him more. Without sulfa he would have died of shock. His condition is good, and he will receive the Purple Heart with Oak Leaf Cluster.

With him were two other privates mangled by shell fragments. One had sulfa and, despite grave injuries, will live. The third youth found the stuff too nauseous. He will lose a leg.

At noon, when we cleared the eastern base at Monte Rotunda and struck out across the valley, the battlefield was strangely still. A thick haze lay stagnant above the pass and a wan sun bathed the scene in sickly light. There was not a sound except our own cautious footsteps as we crossed the pasture, still uncleared of mines.

Near the forward aid station we met Captain Ralph Phelan, of Waurika, Okla, who had done such a heroic job evacuating wounded from within the range of snipers. Phelan warned us not to enter San Pietro. The town, he said, was full of booby traps and subject to intermittent shelling.

He showed us a path up the steep bank of the creek, where three days previously Major Milton Landry's men formed for their bloody, futile assault on San Pietro. We merged on the field, so thickly pocked with shell holes that there must have been a hundred bursts within an acre of bare rocky ground.

The assault waves had met an intense and deadly hail of artillery at the very line of departure. On the far side of the field sprawled some dead. One boy lay crumpled in a shallow slit trench beneath a rock. Another, still grasping his rifle, peered from behind a tree, staring with sightless eyes toward the Liri plain. A third lay prone where he had fallen. He had heard the warning scream of a German shell. He had dropped flat on his stomach but on level ground affording no cover. Evidently some fragment had killed him instantly, for there had been no struggle. Generally, there is no mistaking the dead—their strange contorted posture leaves no room for doubt. But this soldier, his steel helmet tilted over his face, seemed merely resting in the field. We did not know until we came within a few steps and saw a gray hand hanging limply from a sleeve.

Somehow we became separated from the medical aid patrol. We crossed another field scattered with abandoned rifles, cartridge belts, blood-stained bandages and other debris of battle, and reached a pass curving along the walled terrace. It was along this wall that American remnants which had survived a dash across the fields crept in a desperate effort to gain the village.

We heard a sudden rushing noise that made us stop, involuntarily. It was only a brook that tumbled down a wall and crossed our path beneath strands of enemy barbed wire. The brook was kind to us. It had carried away the dirt which covered a German Teller mine.

The mine lay just to the left of the path. A thin strand of trip wire ran from it directly across our trail. Don Whitehead, Associated Press reporter, was scrambling over the barbed wire. One of us saw that the trip wire was draped over the bottom strand. We were very careful getting across that barrier.

[Mr. Whitehead in his dispatch credited Mr. Bigart with noticing the trip wire and shouting a warning.]

Now the path widened and became a cobbled alley. We passed the first house. A rifle was in position near the door step. Looking within we saw an American man lying beneath a heap of straw.

There were three other dead in the shallow gully house. Every approach to San Pietro, every ravine and sunken path offering shelter from machine-gun fire had been covered by German snipers.

The cobbled lane wound steeply up the slope into the heart of San Pietro. The village was a ghastly sight. Pounded for three weeks by American guns and bombed many times from the air, this village of 500 peasants was reduced to one great pile of shattered stone. Whole blocks were obliterated. The street pattern was almost unrecognizable, for the narrow lanes were buried under five feet of rubble. A high wall, towering above the lesser buildings, showed where the Church of St.

Michael and Archangel had stood. The choir loft hung crazily above an altar almost buried under masonry.

In alcoves against the wall stood the statues of St. Michael, and beneath the statue of St. Peter was the inscription: "By the devotion of Americans from San Pietro." A young woman who had followed us into the church explained that natives had emigrated to America and that her uncle Pietro Rossai had a farm near Syracuse.

She showed us a large iron crucifix which, she said, had "passed many miracles." In September the natives had prayed for peace and a few days later the armistice had come. The crucifix had survived the great earthquake of 1915, but the bombardment was 100 times worse than the earthquake. Now the figure of Christ was headless, the Madonna of the Waters had lost an arm.

The Germans had evacuated San Pietro last Thursday afternoon. The steep slopes on both sides of the village were honeycombed with bunkers strongly walled with sandbags and roofed with stone. With flanking heights the Germans could have held out for weeks. They had taken a terrific toll from units attacking frontally and down the valley from the east. But now the Italians held Monte Lungo, to the west, and repeated German counter-attacks had failed to budge the Americans from the crest of Monte Samucro above the town.

So the 15th Panzer Grenadiers became panicky and left six German wounded in the town. A medical-aid sergeant stayed with them. They begged for food and water when the Americans arrived.

The German wounded were evacuated early this morning. As a precaution against a counter-attack, Corporal John Ahrens, of Middle Village, Queens, set up a machine gun at the head of the main street, while medical-aid men went to work. Corporal Peter Vaglia, of 1740 Melville Street, the Bronx, said that one German with a shattered shoulder cursed his comrades for deserting him.

Since the dawn the German guns have been silent and now San Pietro's survivors have emerged from caves and gathered around the Americans. There were about a score of middle-aged men, a few women and children, all very dirty and unkempt, but showing no signs of hysteria. One old man ran behind the medical patrol, pointing toward a collapsed building and mumbling, "Many dead, many dead." But the patrol was concerned with the living.

Near a ruined cathedral two German trucks lay buried beneath a collapsed wall, and across the street were piles of enemy ammunition in cans. Great vats of water had been stored in one building and in an adjoining house we made a curious discovery. The floor was strewn with letters addressed to an American soldier and on a table was a baseball glove. Evidently the Germans had taken letters from an American prisoner. But the baseball glove was unexplained.

Above the village of Piazza the street narrowed and became nothing more than a steep lane between ghostly shells of houses. Occasionally we found a home with some of the lower rooms well intact. In one, Medical Aid Private Benjamin Selleck, of 10 Sunset Road, Bay Shore, L.I., and Private Albert Schempp, of Pittsburgh, were dressing some wounded Italians. One of the natives had retrieved a case of wine from the ruins and toasts were offered to the American victory.

In another house, strongly built and with the lower floor undamaged, we found what apparently had been the enemy's command post. A copy of the "Voelkischer Beobachter" dated Dec. 6 lay on the table. It was the edition published in Posen, indicating that one of the officers recently passed through eastern Germany, probably en route from the Russian front.

Dead mules and pigs lay amid the debris in the eastern section of the village. Rounding a curve on the edge of the town we found two charred hulks of the only American tanks to reach San Pietro during Wednesday's abortive tank attack. They had been knocked out by German anti-tank guns before they could support the infantry advancing across the valley from the south. Farther up the road were other tanks, disabled by mines.

We went back across the fields, reaching the safety of Monte Rotunda, just as the German 88's began shelling San Pietro. At the command post Lieutenant Colonel Aaron Wyatt, of Tarrytown, N.Y., said the battle had been the grimmest since the Volturno crossing.

The assault was led by Major Landry, of San Antonio, Tex.,

who told us how two sergeants, Nolan Peele, of Robstown, Tex., and Frauston, of El Paso, rounded up remnants of the company's cruelly mauled men in the initial attack and attached them to other companies preparing a new thrust.

"It is awfully hard to try to attack more than once in one night," Landry explained. "The men were desperately tired, and they suffered losses grim enough to demoralize any one.

"All officers were dead or wounded. The German outpost laid low until the Americans were well within the trap, then opened with automatic fire. In the company all officers were killed or wounded. Sergeant Frauston, assuming command, gathered thirty-two survivors and led them back.

"They could have melted into darkness, lying low until dark and then come straggling back to the regiment with the story of how they were cut off without officer leadership in no-man's-land. No one would have blamed them. They had been in the line twenty-seven days.

"Many had 'fox hole feet'—their arches were cracked and swollen from wearing wet shoes for days without a change. Yet such was their morale that they reported to the nearest officer and were ready when the attack was resumed a few hours later."

Wednesday's casualties were so heavy that Captain William Farley, of St. Louis, the regimental surgeon, ran out of litter squads. A call for volunteers brought twenty-five replacements from anti-aircraft and coast artillery units. They included several who had never been to the front.

That night they made two trips into no-man's-land, bringing back wounded, despite snipers and shell fire. Among the volunteers were Private Robert Guertin Manville, of Rhode Island, who had fought the Japanese in Java and the Vichy French in New Caledonia. "I figured some day I'd need the medics, so I joined," he said.

In attempting to cover their withdrawal from San Pietro the Germans threw a final vicious counter-attack against the Americans attacking on the east. Just after dark Thursday night enemy troops swarmed from pillboxes on Monte Samucro's southern slope and struck hard at the right flank of a battalion led by Lieutenant Colonel Howard K. Dodge, of Temple, Tex.

Back at the American command post the regimental commander heard the sudden clatter of small arms fire. Through the telephone he could hear the confused shouting of riflemen trying to stem the assault. He heard one infantryman groan: "My God, when are we going to get artillery support?"

"At first we thought it was merely the usual enemy patrol probing our position and we didn't dare to fire for fear of endangering our men," the colonel said. "But when the firing increased in intensity we ordered a barrage. It came within a few minutes and fell smack where we wanted it. It must have caught a lot of Germans, for we could hear them hollering and moaning in a draw just beyond our lines."

The attack lasted four hours. Three times the Germans tried to crack the American lines. Their last attempt nearly succeeded. Company I, commanded by Lieutenant David R. Fields, was badly chewed up by mortar and machine-gun fire and a break-through was prevented in the nick of time by the arrival of Company E, led by Lieutenant Eben C. Bergman, who quickly organized a stonewall defense. Not one inch of ground was abandoned.

Company K, which shared the brunt of the attack, fought valiantly under the cool leadership of Lieutenant Henry C. Bragaw, of Wilmington, N.C., whose name has been put up for battlefield promotion. Bragaw, a mild-mannered horticulturist with a strawberry-colored handlebar mustache, steadied his men when the weight of the attack shifted from the right to the center and fell furiously against his line.

On his right Bergman's men saw the German wave fall back in disorder. They were too tired to cheer. On the previous afternoon they had supported the abortive tank attack on San Pietro, and their casualties were sore. No sooner did the survivors of the tank attack return than they were pressed back into action to save Company I.

Dawn saw a noticeable lessening of enemy artillery fire. The Americans who had tried to attack San Pietro across an open valley from the south were able to recover their dead and wounded, cut down by machine guns and snipers' bullets Thursday.

A force atop Monte Samucro, commanded by Major David Frazior, of Houston, Tex., advanced and seized the extreme northwestern rim of the crest. Frazior's battalion had beaten off a dozen desperate counter-attacks in five days, leaving the slopes littered with at least 500 dead and wounded Germans. His battalion took forty prisoners.

Outstanding among Frazior's men was Lieutenant Rufus J. Cleghorn, of Waco, Tex., a barrel-chested football player from Baylor University. Exulting in battle, Cleghorn clambered to the highest rock of Samurco's pinnacle and howled insults at the Germans, pausing now and then to toss grenades. For variety, Cleghorn occasionally put his weight against a huge bowlder and sent it rolling down the slope. He roared with laughter as Germans attempted to dodge the hurtling bowlders.

The supply problem was terrific. Every available rifleman was needed in the line, so cooks and clerks donned pack-boards and carried food, clothing and ammunition up the mountain. Each man carried a forty-two-pound can of water, plus two bandoliers of ammunition, mail and Sterno cans. They filled their pockets with hand grenades. Ahead of them was a grueling three-hour climb of an 1,000-foot slope, so steep that the men had to crawl hand over hand up the guide ropes.

Captain William R. Lynch, of Huntsville, Tex., estimated that Frazior's battalion had thrown 2,000 hand grenades—more than a division would expend in a normal combat. They used more than three times the normal amount of mortar shells.

It is very cold these December nights on Samurco's peak, and the uniforms and overcoats issued to the men were none too warm. Yesterday Army cooks carried war combat suits to the troops and a can of Sterno to each man.

New York Herald Tribune, December 20, 1943

Over the Lines

by Margaret Bourke-White

"THIS STRIP is really a nerve jerker," Lieutenant Mike Strok called to me over his shoulder.

We were circling above the tiniest airfield I had ever seen. The landing strip was so pocked with shell craters that I did not see how my Grasshopper pilot was going to slip in among them. It was nothing more than the beaten edge of a plowed field, but for the Air OP's, the "Eyes of the Artillery" as they are called in heavy-gun circles, this strip was their most forward operating base.

Lieutenant Strok had to divide his attention between the shell pits below and the sky above. This was because we were landing in the region airmen called Messerschmitt Alley. If an unarmed, unarmored observation plane such as our Cub is attacked, the pilot's means of escape is to outmaneuver the enemy.

"Good idea to make sure there's no Jerry fighter hanging about," said Lieutenant Strok. "If you can see him first, then he doesn't get the chance to blast the daylights out of you."

A final inspection confirmed that the sky was clear, and he brought our tiny Cub to a standstill on a piece of earth as big as a back yard in Brooklyn.

The commanding officer of the field and his ground crew of one ran up to greet us.

The ground crew spoke first. "If that ain't an American girl, then I'm seeing things!" he exclaimed.

The young officer laughed. "Sorry we're out of red carpet," he said. "We live like gypsies up here."

The CO of the Grasshoppers was twenty-six-year-old Captain Jack Marinelli of Ottumwa, Iowa. He was chief pilot and supervisor for a group of artillery liaison pilots who hedge-hopped along the front lines in their Cubs, acting as flying

Margaret Bourke-White, Life Magazine, © Time Warner Inc.

Below us lay the Volturno and ahead stood the mountain barrier, heavy with the menace of German guns. The Cub's job was to hunt them out, and direct with accuracy the fire of our artillery.

observation posts to spot enemy targets and adjust fire for Fifth Army artillery. I had seldom seen a flier who bore less resemblance to Hollywood's idea of a pilot than Captain Marinelli. He looked more like the tractor and hay-machine demonstrator which I learned he had been back in Iowa before the war. He was plump, pleasant, and easygoing. This last characteristic, I was to find, faded as soon as the enemy was in sight. He had the reputation of being the coolest and most resourceful artillery pilot on the Fifth Army front.

Mike Strok explained that I wanted to take airplane pictures of the front, and Captain Marinelli said, "Well, I've just had a call to go out on a mission. There's a *Nebelwerfer* holding up an infantry division and they asked me to go out and try to spot it. She can come along if she wants to."

"Jees, you don't want to take a girl on a mission," said the ground crew of one.

"She'll go if you'll take her," stated Lieutenant Strok.

"What's a *Nebelwerfer*?" I inquired.

"You've heard of a screaming meemie, haven't you? Wicked weapon! It's a multiple mortar: eight-barreled rocket gun."

By the time the screaming meemie was explained to me, I had been strapped into the observer's seat, and the ground crew was adjusting a parachute to my back and shoulders.

Knowing that one of the functions of observer is to watch all quadrants of the sky for enemy planes, I said to the Captain, "I'm not going to make a very good observer for you. Most of the time I'll have my face buried in my camera, and even when I haven't, I'm not sure I'll know the difference between an enemy fighter and one of ours."

"Don't worry about that," Captain Marinelli said. "If you see anything that looks like an airplane, you tell me and I'll decide whether it's a bandit or an angel."

I placed my airplane camera on my knees and arranged additional equipment and a couple of spare cameras, telephoto lenses, and some aerial filters on the low shelf behind my shoulders. The space was so cramped, and any extra movement so pinched, with the parachute crowded on my back, that I wanted to be sure I had everything near at hand where I could reach it in a hurry. There was no room in the Cub to

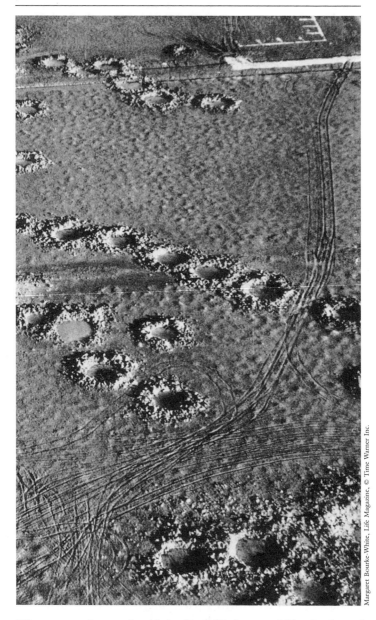

Wherever we flew we found the face of Italy scarred like the face of the moon. This airfield shows the pattern.

wear helmets, as our heads touched the roof. Someone had
lent me one of the fur caps used by our Alaska troops, and I
tucked my hair back under it and tied it firmly around my
chin. When you lean out into the slipstream with an airplane
camera, any escaping strand of hair will lash into your eyes
and sometimes blind you during just that vital second when
you are trying to catch a picture. The Captain lowered the
whole right side of the airplane, folding it completely out of
the way so I would have an unobstructed area in which to
lean out and work. Then he spoke into his microphone.
"Mike-Uncle-Charlie! This is Mike-Uncle-Charlie five-zero.
I'm taking off on a mission. Stand by!"

"Who is Mike-Uncle-Charlie?" I asked.

"That's our brigade HQ's code word for today," replied
the Captain. "Just our phonetic alphabet for MUC—today's
call letters. When I find something that radio guy will be sitting up there with his ear phones on, listening."

The ground crew spun the props. "We'll be back in time
for lunch," shouted Captain Marinelli to Lieutenant Strok as
we started to taxi between the shell craters. I glanced at my
watch, which registered quarter after eleven, and couldn't
help wondering if we really would be back for lunch. I was
trying hard not to wonder whether we would be back at all.

As we headed toward the front I was impressed with how
regular the pattern of war, seemingly so chaotic from the
ground, appears from the air. The tracks of pattern bombing
on an airfield were as regular as though drawn with a ruler
and compass. In some olive groves the traffic patterns made
by trucks and jeeps which had parked there looked as if a
school child had drawn circles in a penmanship exercise, his
pen filled not with ink but with a silvery mud-and-water mixture which held the light of the sun. Each bridge had been
demolished with a Teutonic precision. The delicate arches of
the small bridges were broken through the crest; larger
bridges were buckled like giant accordions. Paralleling these
were bypasses and emergency bridges which our engineers
had thrown up. Most regular of all was German railroad
demolition. Between the rails an endless succession of V's
marched into the distance, an effect produced by the giant
plow which the retreating Germans had dragged from their

Below us, always, the tracks of war. Moving in mud, tanks, heavy trucks, artillery could not conceal their footprints.

last railroad train, cracking each tie in two so neatly that it seemed as if someone had unrolled a narrow length of English tweed, flinging this herringbone strip over the hills and valleys of Italy.

The irregularities were furnished by the smashed towns, so wrecked that seldom did two walls stand together, and never was a roof intact. Flying low, sometimes we could see Italian civilians picking through the sickening rubble that once had been their homes.

As we flew over the ghastly wreckage of Mignano and headed toward the still more thoroughly wrecked town of San Pietro, suddenly our plane was jarred so violently that it bounced over on its side, and we heard what sounded like a thunderclap just below.

"That's a shell leaving one of our big hows," Marinelli said as he righted the plane.

"Sounded close," I said.

"I'd hate to tell you how close," Captain Marinelli replied.

"How are you going to know when you get to the front?" I asked.

"Oh, that's easy," he explained. "When you stop seeing stars on things you know you've left your own side behind."

I looked down and saw our jeeps, trucks, and half-trucks crawling along Highway Six below us, each plainly marked with its white star.

"But the best way to tell is by the bridges," he continued. "As long as you see trestle bridges below you know we're over friendly territory, because those are bridges our engineers have built. When you begin spotting blown-out bridges you know we're approaching no man's land. The last thing the Germans do when they pull out is to blow up their bridges, and if they haven't been repaired it's because it's been too hot for our men to get in and mend them.

"When you see a stretch of road with no traffic at all, that's no man's land. And when you see the first bridge intact on the other side, you know you're crossing into Jerry territory."

We were flying over the crest of hills which surrounded Cassino valley like the rim of a cup. Highway Six wound between bald, rocky mountains here, and we almost scraped their razorback edges as we flew over. I could look down and see entrenchments and gun emplacements set in layers of rock. Then the land dropped away sharply, and all at once we were high over Cassino corridor.

As I looked down, the earth seemed to be covered with glistening polka dots—almost as though someone had taken a bolt of gray coin-spotted satin and unrolled it over the landscape. I knew these were shell holes, thousands of them, and made by the guns of both sides, first when we shelled the Germans here, and now by their guns shelling us. As we rose higher I could look down and see hundreds of thousands of these holes filled with rain and glistening in the sun.

"It's been so rough down there," said Captain Marinelli, "that the boys are calling it Purple Heart Valley."

I could hardly believe that so many shells could have fallen in a single valley. It was cruelly contradictory that with all this evidence of bloodshed and destruction, the valley seemed to clothe itself in a sequin-dotted gown.

As we flew on, we glanced back toward our own territory and could see the muzzle flashes from our guns winking on and off as though people were lighting matches over the hillsides. Each gun flash left a smoke trail until our Allied-held hills appeared to be covered with the smoke of countless campfires.

"The worst of that smoke is from our howitzers," Marinelli said.

And then he added, "Usually we don't fly across the lines unless the mission absolutely requires it. But it looks to me as though we're going to have to today, to find that *Nebelwerfer*. O.K. with you?"

"I'm right with you, Captain."

We circled lower over a loop of Highway Six where wrecked tanks were tumbled around the curve of road. "First day they've brought tanks out into the open," said Marinelli. "I want to radio back a report." The tanks seemed to have been picked off one by one as they tried to round the bend, but I could see one tank charging bravely ahead. Then as we bobbed over it, I could see a giant retriever coming in with a derrick to evacuate one of the blasted tanks.

Just beyond we began seeing demolished bridges, and we circled above these also, because the Captain's secondary mission was to report on any bridges that had been blown up. He was just phoning back his observations, and I was taking pictures, when suddenly our plane was rocked sharply back and forth and we heard a sound like freight trains rumbling under us.

"Jerry shells," said Marinelli. "High explosives! You know, they've been missing that road junction by a hundred yards every day this week."

We were tossing around violently now, and dark whorls and spirals of greasy smoke were blanketing the ground beneath.

"We've got infantry troops down there," the Captain said. The realization was almost more than I could bear—that our own boys were trying to slog through that fatal square of earth being chewed up by high-explosive shells.

An instant later we were flying over a desolate stretch of road with no traffic at all. This, then, was no man's land. At the farther end we saw a beautifully arched ancient bridge, its masonry quite intact.

"Jerry territory," said the Captain, and took the plane sharply upward.

Over our own side the Cubs make a practice of flying low, because this makes an attack by enemy fighters more difficult, as they cannot come in under; but when the observation planes cross the lines, they must increase altitude, for without armor they are very vulnerable to small-arms fire.

In search of the German rocket gun, we flew four miles over enemy territory and Captain Marinelli began hunting for the *Nebelwerfer* in the region of San Angelo.

"That's the 'Gargling River,'" he pointed out. "GI for Garigliano. And there's the Rapido." The road to Rome stretched forward into the distance, with a railroad running parallel some distance to the left. A hairpin turn branched upward toward the Benedictine monastery, at that time still intact. The ruins of Cassino lay in white smudges at the foot of snowcapped Mt. Cairo.

Cassino corridor presented an extraordinary appearance, with white plumes rising up at intervals from the valley floor. These were phosphorus shells from our own Long Toms, falling on the enemy. Whenever one landed close below us we

Italian villages which died in Purple Heart Valley.

could see it opening out into a pointed splash of fire, which quickly became transformed into a rising chunk of smoke.

Suddenly I spotted a tiny silhouette in the sky, behind us. "There's a plane," I yelled.

"Just another Cub out on a mission," said Marinelli. "But you did the right thing. Tell me anything you see."

Just then he picked up the flash of the German *Nebelwerfer*—too quick for my untrained eye—and caught sight of the shrubbery blowing back on the ground from the gun blast.

"Mike-Uncle-Charlie," he spoke into his microphone. "This is Mike-Uncle-Charlie five-zero. Enemy gun battery located at co-ordinate 86-16-2. I can observe. Over."

Then to me, over his shoulder, "It's going to take them a little time now, because they've got to compute their data and consult their fire-direction chart to see which guns can reach the target. They'll let me know when they've assigned a battery. We'll be hanging right around here, so speak up if you want to be put into position for anything special."

There were many things that I wanted to be put into position for. Below us it looked as though someone were shaking an enormous popcorn shaker with white grains of popcorn bursting all over the valley floor. These were thickest in front of Cassino. The Captain maneuvered the plane so that I was practically lying on my side over the valley, and—strapped in safely—I could get an unobstructed view of the battleground below.

In a few minutes a message came through that Xray-King-Item would fire. While I took pictures of the popcorn-sprinkled valley, Marinelli carried on his radio conversation with Xray-King-Item, the battery assigned to knock out the *Nebelwerfer*.

I was overwhelmed to learn that it would be my pilot, up in our little Cub, who would actually give the command to fire. The next message he received was, "Mike-Uncle-Charlie five-zero, this is Xray-King-Item. Will fire on your command. Over."

"Fire," said Marinelli, and the reply came back, "Seventy-two seconds. On the way."

It seemed amazing that the shell traveling from the Long

Tom battery several miles back of us would take almost a minute and a quarter to reach the enemy gun target below. The Captain was checking with his watch. "Don't want to sense the wrong round," he explained.

He had to make this precise time check because with other guns peppering the valley it was easy to make an error, and it would have caused great confusion had he started correcting the aim of some other gun.

On the seventy-second second, a white geyser began rising toward us from below, and we knew that this was Xray-King-Item's smoke shell. Marinelli spoke into his microphone: "Xray-King-Item; this is Mike-Uncle-Charlie five-zero; five hundred yards right, one hundred yards short. Over."

Then he explained, "We've got to give them a little time again to make their correction. They're laying number-one gun on it now. When they get it adjusted they'll tie in the whole battery."

Soon another message came from Xray-King-Item: seventy-two seconds on the way. Again at the end of seventy-two seconds a feather of smoke rose from below. The aim was closer now: "Five-zero right; seven-zero short," Captain Marinelli radioed.

I realized that the Captain was handling a great many tasks at once. Not only was he checking his watch during each seventy-two-second interval, radioing his sensings in terms of deflection and elevation data, but he was keeping an eye on the sky for enemy planes. And taking care of me, too! Every time I saw a fresh shell burst I would yell to be put in position, and he would maneuver the Cub so that I could photograph while he observed.

Suddenly he exclaimed, "We're being shot at." We could hear faint sounds as though twigs were snapping against the plane—a little like hot grease spitting in a frying pan just beyond us. "It's a Spandau," said Marinelli, and he knew exactly what to do. Since the Spandau, a German machine gun, has an effective range up to 2400 feet, he simply circled up to 3200 feet, where he went on making his observations and I went on taking photographs.

"Hands cold?" he called.

They were almost numb. At our higher altitude the air was

colder and I had been leaning out into the windstream with the camera. The Captain, more protected by the nose of the Cub, stripped off his gloves and gave them to me.

The whole process of adjusting fire had gone on for about fourteen minutes when Captain Marinelli finally radioed, "Deflection correct, range correct. Fire for effect."

"They're bringing in several batteries this time," said the Captain. "And this time it will be HE shells."

At the end of seventy-two seconds we could see that whole area being blanketed, not with white smoke bursts as before, but with the deadlier high-explosive shells. Curls and twists of black smoke spurted over the ground and billowed upward, and we knew that the *Nebelwerfer* was being chewed to bits.

"This is Mike-Uncle-Charlie five-zero," called Captain Marinelli. "Target area completely covered. Fire effective. Enemy battery neutralized."

Less than a minute later he exclaimed, "I see a fighter." Then, "I see two fighters."

Coming around Mt. Cevaro I could see them too: a black speck growing larger and behind it another smaller speck. In less time than it takes to tell, they had taken on the size and shape of airplanes.

We were in such a steep dive by that time that I was practically standing on my head, when I heard Marinelli say, "I see four fighters."

Sure enough, there were four shapes coming toward us, looking unmistakably like Focke-Wulf 190's.

This was the steepest dive I had ever been in in my life. I tried to take a picture, a plan I very quickly had to abandon because, with the whole side of the plane completely open, and the shelf behind me full of cameras and lenses, it was all I could do to hold back my equipment with my elbows and shoulders, to keep it from sailing into space.

I was bracing myself with the back of my neck when Captain Marinelli exclaimed, "I've lost my mike. Can you find my mike for me?" I knew he needed his microphone so he could report the fighters as a warning to all the other Cubs in the air. Groping with my left hand, and holding back my cameras with my right elbow, I retrieved his mike and handed it to him. We were still gliding down at a terrific angle when he reported, "Four enemy fighters sighted."

We were within fifteen feet of the ground when he pulled out of that dive. I have never seen such flying. He ducked into a gully and began snaking along a stream bed. Soon we were behind a small hill and over our own territory, where the fighters could not follow us in so low. In another instant we were behind a mountain and blocked from sight of the enemy planes.

We flew back to our field in time for mess, and when we rolled into the tiny landing strip, the ground crew came running up, bursting with news. To Captain Marinelli this news was much more exciting than being chased by four Focke-Wulfs: there was steak for lunch.

They Call It "Purple Heart Valley," 1944

THE DEATH OF AN INFANTRY OFFICER
ITALY: JANUARY 1944

"This One Is Captain Waskow"

by Ernie Pyle

AT THE FRONT LINES IN ITALY, Jan. 10—(by wireless)—In this war I have known a lot of officers who were loved and respected by the soldiers under them. But never have I crossed the trail of any man as beloved as Capt. Henry T. Waskow, of Belton, Tex.

Captain Waskow was a company commander in the 36th Division. He had been in this company since long before he left the States. He was very young, only in his middle 20s, but he carried in him a sincerity and gentleness that made people want to be guided by him.

"After my own father, he comes next," a sergeant told me.

"He always looked after us," a soldier said. "He'd go to bat for us every time."

"I've never known him to do anything unkind," another one said.

*   *   *

I was at the foot of the mule trail the night they brought Captain Waskow down. The moon was nearly full, and you could see far up the trail, and even part way across the valley. Soldiers made shadows as they walked.

Dead men had been coming down the mountain all evening, lashed onto the backs of mules. They came lying belly down across the wooden packsaddle, their heads hanging down on the left side of the mule, their stiffened legs sticking awkwardly from the other side, bobbing up and down as the mule walked.

The Italian mule skinners were afraid to walk beside dead men, so Americans had to lead the mules down that night. Even the Americans were reluctant to unlash and lift off the bodies, when they got to the bottom, so an officer had to do it himself and ask others to help.

The first one came early in the morning. They slid him down

394

from the mule, and stood him on his feet for a moment. In the half light he might have been merely a sick man standing there leaning on the other. Then they laid him on the ground in the shadow of the stone wall alongside the road.

I don't know who that first one was. You feel small in the presence of dead men, and you don't ask silly questions.

We left him there beside the road, that first one, and we all went back into the cowshed and sat on watercans or lay on the straw, waiting for the next batch of mules.

Somebody said the dead soldier had been dead for four days, and then nobody said anything more about him. We talked for an hour or more; the dead man lay all alone, outside in the shadow of the wall.

*   *   *

Then a soldier came into the cowshed and said there were some more bodies outside. We went out into the road. Four mules stood there in the moonlight, in the road where the trail came down off the mountain. The soldiers who led them stood there waiting.

"This one is Captain Waskow," one of them said quickly.

Two men unlashed his body from the mule and lifted it off and laid it in the shadow beside the stone wall. Other men took the other bodies off. Finally, there were five lying end to end in a long row. You don't cover up dead men in the combat zones. They just lie there in the shadows until somebody else comes after them.

The uncertain mules moved off to their olive groves. The men in the road seemed reluctant to leave. They stood around, and gradually I could sense them moving, one by one, close to Captain Waskow's body. Not so much to look, I think, as to say something in finality to him and to themselves. I stood close by and I could hear.

One soldier came and looked down, and he said out loud: "God damn it!"

That's all he said, and then he walked away.

Another one came, and he said, "God damn it to hell anyway!" He looked down for a few last moments and then turned and left.

Another man came. I think he was an officer. It was hard to tell officers from men in the dim light, for everybody was grimy and dirty. The man looked down into the dead captain's face and then spoke directly to him, as though he were alive:

"I'm sorry, old man."

Then a soldier came and stood beside the officer and bent over, and he too spoke to his dead captain, not in a whisper but awfully tenderly, and he said:

"I sure am sorry, sir."

Then the first man squatted down, and he reached down and took the captain's hand, and he sat there for a full five minutes holding the dead hand in his own and looking intently into the dead face. And he never uttered a sound all the time he sat there.

Finally he put the hand down. He reached up and gently straightened the points of the captain's shirt collar, and then he sort of rearranged the tattered edges of his uniform around the wound, and then he got up and walked away down the road in the moonlight, all alone.

The rest of us went back into the cowshed, leaving the five dead men lying in a line end to end in the shadow of the low stone wall. We lay down on the straw in the cowshed, and pretty soon we were all asleep.

Scripps-Howard wire copy, January 10, 1944

"Wide Awake on an Island Beachhead"

by Vincent Tubbs

No Picturesque Battle Scenes in SWP War

WITH MARINES AT CAPE GLOUCESTER — (Via Air Mail) — You can't see much of the battle because this war isn't being fought like battles of old such as Washington crossing the Delaware, the Crossing of the Marne or the charge up San Juan Hill.

There will be no painting of the general standing in the bow of the boat, long line of advancing and defending troops or fiery steeds charging up a hill to come out of this war — not unless the artist has a terrific imagination or is a whale of a liar.

Most of the news about a battle comes from the injured returning from the front, from a soldier being relieved or from an officer who is in on the planning and execution.

You can't see much of a battle even if it's just up the road from you and you go to it yourself. I know because I've just returned from Hill 660, the final objective of marines who established the beachhead in this sector.

Hill 660 is ours. We took it last night after some of the meanest fighting the marines have ever experienced — including the struggle for Guadalcanal. Jap casualties exceeded 3,000; ours were not meagre.

I started to the war, in company with Enoc Waters of the Defender, aboard a GI truck. We walked a while, grabbed another truck, walked some more — traveling thusly over disgustingly bumpy and muddy roads, to the regimental command post of the unit that assaulted the Hill. Here I saw my first Jap — a live one.

We had started away when my brain registered "that's a Jap

you're about to pass." I jerked back to look at him; stopped almost in front of him. He smiled wryly, knowing my thoughts.

We stumbled on toward the war—over tree stumps, mud bogs and debris of every description. A terrific barrage had been laid on this area by our heavy field guns.

"Hello there," a voice to our left called. "Where y'all going?" a marine drawled from beneath a shelter half under which was built an uncovered pallet of small tree limbs.

"Up the hill to the war, if we can make it. What's cooking around here?"

"Oh, nothing much now. We hear they took the hill last night. The fighting was right here yesterday, y'know."

"Yep, looks like it. What sort of outfit is this?"

"We're a mortar platoon—did a little work yesterday. Laid down a barrage up yonder," one of the muddy men said. "There were lots of Japs in here then. Y'all been over by Hill 150?"

"Naw, where's that?"

"Right there," he said, pointing to a small hump behind us. "There's a lot of Jap bodies over there. Seen any?"

"Yeah, we saw one back there at headquarters alive. Next one we see we want him to be dead."

"Well, come on over here; we'll show you some."

What they exhibited defies description, but there was, among other revolting sights, remnants of a Jap machine gunner who had knocked off nearly 20 marines before they got him and they didn't leave much.

On the verge of vomiting, we debated whether we should go further. The marines pointed out a trail, said there was a wire to guide us, conjected the journey little short of 660 yards; so we pushed on.

Before we left, a tiny marine returning from sick bay where he was treated for combat fatigue said there was scuttlebutt about 30 Japs who escaped during last night's action and who were reported headed toward the tank trail which we must ultimately cross.

Nevertheless, we went along bravely, with warnings about snipers ringing in our ears.

One hundred steps along the muddy, mosquito-infested

trail we got a scare. The top of a tree split by shell from one of our 105-mm. guns teetered in the sultry breeze; then toppled to earth with a resounding crash.

We, like veteran bush fighters, dropped to the ground, submerged ourselves in mud a foot deep; then abused everything that grows out of the ground when we discovered we weren't being attacked by the 30 stray Japs.

Plowing along, holding to the wire for both guidance and support, we reached the tank trail, forded a small stream and came upon two marines sitting on boxes beneath a shelter half. Before them was a switchboard. Here we waited for a tank to take us to the Advanced CP. The communications post is as interesting a spot as can be found in a battle area. All information is transmitted through the switchboard; so this correspondent just sat there and listened to operations going on at the crest of the hill a few hundred yards away.

Here sat two fellows, the operator and his troubleshooter, who listened last night, just as you listened to your radio, to the battle up the hill. They told the story:

The Japs were dug into the side of the hill in pillboxes and machine gun nests that stair-stepped up the incline. Our first assault was an attempt to storm these positions, but the Japs sat in their little caves and mowed down our men.

The attack was repulsed so we drew back to lick our wounds and work out new strategy.

It turned out that 105-mm. guns, 75-mm. howitzers and 50-cal. machine guns joined mortar platoons in blasting into the hillside.

In the meantime, the weapons company of the marine division circled the foot of the hill, set up gun positions on the Japs' north flank and began to blast away with the same type of artillery.

Detachments from two companies stole around the opposite side of the hill to attack from the south and east. Other elements of these companies, along with another company, attacked up the hill's west side.

The Japs were almost completely encircled and, like in other such instances, found it impossible to get out of the pocket so dug in to fight it out.

General Sherman tanks joined the assault, some rumbling

as far as 300 yards up the steep hillside. When a stubborn pillbox was encountered, the tank rolled up, stuck the muzzle of its 75-mm. gun into the bunker and blasted away. There was silence.

In other instances the Sherman would run atop such a pill-box and wriggle itself there until the bunker caved in, bringing both bunker and tank crashing down on the occupants. There was silence.

Troops leaving the regimental command post were brought up aboard other tanks which themselves could advance only about half way up the hill.

Men climbing the hill from this point crawled along like babies—on all fours, their muddy hands grasping vines and digging into the earth where the heel of the preceding man had left a dent.

All the time the enemy fought back from caves, nests and pillboxes that had survived the barrage. The marines fought for almost every inch of ground.

"I don't see how we ever did it," the operator said. "It was hell just to have to climb up—to say nothing about fighting while you climbed."

A crack of bush broke the conversation and brought our heads about with a start. Out walked two heavily armed soldiers and one big, strong-looking man who carried no arms.

He looked at me, asked: "What are you doing up here?"

When I showed my insignia which was being worn on the underside of my collar because shining metal makes a good target, he said something about correspondents getting into the thick of things like saps and, after a few other questions, signed my identification card.

"Go on up the hill," he added as he went off, his protectors before and after him. My card now bore the signature of a colonel in the U.S.M.C.

Back at the switchboard calls were now coming through rapidly. One conversation was that a Jap carrying one of our 30-cal. carbines had just been killed.

During a lull, the fellows pulled out a Jap's belt of a thousand stitches (supposed to protect the wearer from harm), gave me bills of Jap Government Philippine and Australian invasion money.

Then—the rains came.

Our 105's opened up on Jap positions along Borgen Bay, just beyond the hill's crest. The concussions sent gusts of wind around us that rocked the broken treetops above our heads. We watched them closely.

Then came the grinding sound of an approaching tank. Soon it was in the ravine there below us. Thumbs went up and the driver yelled out we'd have to wait until he reached a spot with better traction before we could board.

We pulled along beside the tank to a spot some twenty yards distant and climbed aboard. We were frightful sights of mud and muck.

When the tank ended its run we were at what is called Advance Command Post. The mud came above our knees.

Things were surprisingly casual here. One marine yelled:

"Souvenir hunters right up the hill there. You can find all you want. Chow will be served right here." And he began to take the warm food containers off the tank.

The marine with me said they had been living in the mud for twenty-one days—no change of clothing, no water for washing, the food C Ration until the day before, but there had been hot coffee last night . . . right in the midst of the battle, when someone made a fire and a brew.

We moved off to climb to the top of the hill. We had to crawl hand over foot. Half the time we were prone in the mud, scrambling for a firm footing.

From the hilltop we could look down into Borgen Bay, across its expanse and into what we were told was the Jap bivouac area into which the 105's were firing.

Things were so quiet, so disinteresting (we couldn't even see the Japs that were being knocked off) that we turned and slid back down the hill to the CP.

Our tank was about to take off so we climbed aboard, found there was standing room only.

A few hundred feet down the track we came upon a group of men trudging along in the muck. The tank stopped. A marine behind me nudged and said, "That's General Rupertus." The general climbed aboard. Back at the regimental command post the tank stopped to let the general off. We then climbed on trucks that took us to the site of our original landing on this island. We walked an additional two miles to our campsite.

The little actual shooting we saw is called "mopping up." We couldn't see much of that.

Baltimore Afro-American, February 12, 1944

Homesick Joe in Pacific

CAPE GLOUCESTER (Via Air Mail)—"It's gone and started raining. I'm lonesome as a man can be-e-e. It's gone and started raining . . ."

The rain was beating a tattoo on the tent top. We were tired, wet, miserable, heart sick. We didn't know where the singing was coming from and we didn't care but we did know that it sounded good and the guy was singing right out of the depths of his heart.

"If you read my letter, baby . . . you sho musta read my mind. . . ."

We just lay there in the mid-afternoon heat and listened to the rain and the singing. The rain and the heat are perpetually with us here. The singing—especially this kind—isn't. It comes very rarely—only when a man gets full . . . very full.

"Y'know, I love my wife," a soldier said. "I really love my wife and I've never known how much I love her until right this minute."

Nobody answered the soldier. It wasn't necessary. We all knew what was going on inside of that man. We all knew what he was thinking; we were all thinking the same thing, so we just sat there and thought.

Then the soldier got up and walked out of the tent into the rain. As he moved away we could hear his voice rising in song:

"Take me back, baby. Try me one more time-e. Take me back, baby. Try me one more ti-ime."

Those of us left in the tent looked at each other; then went back to our individual thoughts. The rain kept beating on the tent top.

Baltimore Afro-American, February 26, 1944

Men Can't Sleep; They Talk, Dream of Home

CAPE GLOUCESTER—(Via Air Mail—Censored)—Nobody sleeps at night in the camp area of the quartermaster truck unit with which this correspondent is making home on this beachhead.

When dusk comes the men saunter into their tents and bed down. There's an awful lot of time between dusk and daybreak, a fact that you can appreciate, in case you never knew it before, if you will just try lying on a canvas cot those 12 hours, while the rain beats down outside, and any side you may lie on jabs into the hard canvas and gets sore after a spell.

Anyhow, we all bed down at dusk . . . but some don't sleep . . . for several reasons. First, we sort of "sweat out" an air raid; secondly, we don't want to be asleep if a Jap decides to run up into our camp, starts throwing grenades and generally raises hell.

Sometimes we talk but not much. However, what we talk about—when we do talk—should warm up some hearts and writing pens back there in the States.

This correspondent can find no better way to put these conversation pieces down than in the form in which they appear in my notebook. These are the voices of the men who are keeping war from American shores and the talk might go like this:

"Wonder how things are going back there? Wonder whether the folks are in this thing with us—up to the hilt? Do you think we'll find things better when we get back?" begins Voice No. 1.

"They had damned well better be. I suspect if I hailed a cab and the driver tried to hand me some stuff, I'd pull him out by the collar and peel his head like it was a banana," will go a second voice.

"What do I want?" is the third voice. "Oh, I don't know exactly, but I guess it's something like a good job—no charity—just the privilege of a free man's place in a free man's world and the opportunity to build the kind of life I want to live."

Here there might come a lull in the conversation while ears

prick up at the sound of movement outside the tent. A long interval of silence; then a voice from a dark corner:

"Gee, I'm going to be glad to see my sister. This guy she married is supposed to be the perfect man. I want to see the bloke—sort of size him up."

"And man, am I gonna have a time raiding the ice box. I can see it all now—those glistening hardwood floors, the clean walls, that knee-deep bed with clean sheets and my slippers beside it."

"I can see mine, too," another voice whose owner is also hidden by the night, will put in.

"It ain't nothing like that, but it's mine—a sort of tumble-down shack, you might say. Holes in the roof and a bucket always handy to catch the rain.

"Some pasteboard boxes I'm saving in a corner so I could use them for inner soles when my shoes got thin . . . that old, creaking rocking chair, a couple of missing boards in the porch and the rickety steps I planned to fix. Still it's mine."

"Hacienda or hovel, it's home just the same," sympathizes Voice No. 1.

Silence again—another long interval of it. Then the sound of soft snoring in one corner and movement in another as a soldier sits up under his mosquito net, beginning to talk again.

"That guy had better be nice to my sister. I'll twist his neck if he don't."

"I wonder how my old man is getting along," another reminiscent voice will sing out, almost as if the owner had been jabbed with a hat-pin.

"He's getting kinda old now. They don't go into detail in the letters; just say he's okay. Guess he's still going squirrel hunting, though. Boy, he sure can shoot not to be able to see any better than he can. Can't read a paper without his glasses but he's hell on a squirrel."

"I hope my dog ain't dead. He was getting a little weak in the hind legs and couldn't hear very well," the voice with the married sister interrupts.

"Whatahell you mean bringing up your dog when I'm talking about my old man?"

"Cut it," an impatient sergeant's voice will say. "Let me see whether I can think out what home means to me.

". . . That cafe next to the show with the fried fish in the window smelling up the whole neighborhood . . . that drug store where they never had enough ice-cream to last until after 9 o'clock . . . that scale outside the door where I used to stand and watch the female chassis go by.

"That church down the street where Mom used to go every Sunday and where I always cropped up when there was a Sunday school picnic . . . that straw hat and those white trousers I used to sport on Easter Sunday.

"That sharp black Alpaca overcoat I got just before I was drafted . . . that number I've got scratched on the wall beside the telephone and the girl who answers when I call it.

"Man, that's home to me—and I'm going to sleep tonight and dream about it. Hell, if they get us, we're just got—then we won't have to worry about ANYTHING anymore."

"Break it off, Jack, break it off," an irritated voice from another tent will howl out—and the howl will bring a hundred more requests for silence, some of which will be annotated with plain and fancy swearing; others with threats of untold physical violence.

These are the dreams of men wide awake on an island beachhead. They are dreams that tantalize—even torture, but they come nocturnally with the surety and quickness of Pacific nightfall, repeating themselves and adding embellishments as the weeks wear on.

Nostalgia is perpetually with us over here, expressing itself in hundreds of ways, but never more vividly to this correspondent than from the lips of the young marine returning from the battle for Hill 660.

When climbing onto the muddy, bumping truck, he banged his knee against the steel bed, then sprawled around the feet of a dozen tired men to find himself staring in the face of a dead buddy lying on a litter square.

He picked himself up and threw a hurt glance in the direction of a jovial marine who said: "Didn't your mother warn you there'd be days like this?"

The little fellow looked over the truck's side at the feet of a dead Jap jutting out of the mud in which rain had almost buried him and said to the jungle toward which he lifted his eyes:

"Gee, I'll be glad when I get back home."

Baltimore Afro-American, March 18, 1944

Search for a Battle

by Walter Bernstein

THE ATTACK was to jump off at nine in the morning. The objective of my infantry regiment was a long, steep ridge that stood like a door at the head of the valley we occupied. The pattern of attack was familiar and orthodox: first an hour of dive-bombing to soften the objective, then a half hour of artillery, and finally the infantry to do the dirty work. It was a pattern that had been followed ever since we had landed in Italy. Everyone was getting tired of it. Our regiment had fought through Sicily and all the way up from Salerno, and the men were particularly tired of walking. They were not tired of fighting, if fighting meant that they would get home sooner, but they were very weary of long night marches and then hours of fancy mountain climbing in the face of enemy fire. This struck them as a hell of a way to fight a war that was supposed to be so mechanized and motorized, and they frequently said so. My job in this operation was going to be with the headquarters of one of the attacking battalions. I was now on duty at regimental headquarters, which was in a one-room farmhouse by the side of a dirt road, and the plan was for me to join the battalion as it marched past the regimental command post during the night on its way to the jump-off point. The battalion was scheduled to come by at two in the morning, and someone was supposed to wake me. No one did. When the guard was changed at midnight, the old guard forgot to tell the new guard. At four-thirty the regimental C.P. moved out, leaving me behind. I was asleep in a haystack and they could have moved the whole Fifth Army without my hearing them. A horse nibbling at the hay was what finally woke me. It was six o'clock.

There was no one around the place when I slid out of the hay, and the road was deserted. It was just getting light. Fog lay like chalk over the valley, twisting at the bottom as it be-

gan to rise. The air was cold and damp. The only living thing
in sight seemed to be the horse, and he was no bargain. I
dressed, put on my helmet and pistol belt, then went up to
the farmhouse and looked in. There was nothing inside but
guttered candles, torn and empty K-ration boxes, and piles of
straw on which the officers had slept. I returned to the haystack and made up my bedding roll. Most of the line troops
carried only a raincoat and half a blanket. At night they
wrapped the half blanket around their head and shoulders,
put the raincoat over that, and lay on the ground. I had a
whole blanket and a shelter half, a combination which, by
comparison, was equal to an inner-spring mattress. After making up the roll, I ate a bar of K-ration chocolate. As the fog
lifted, it revealed the mountains along the valley. At the end
of the valley was the ridge we were going to take, looming
black and forbidding through the mist. I finished the chocolate, slung the bedding roll over one shoulder, and started
along the road toward the front.

There was no activity at all on the road, which seemed
strange, considering that an attack was coming off. The valley
was completely quiet. There were not even the ordinary
morning-in-the-country noises. I walked for about a mile
without seeing anyone and then passed an artillery battery
dug in beside the road. The guns were camouflaged with
nets. The men sat beside them, eating out of C-ration cans.
No one looked up as I passed. Ahead of me, growing larger,
was the high ridge. Before it were a few small hills. Between
these hills and the ridge was another, smaller valley, running
at right angles to the one I was following. Our men would
have to cross it under fire. It was seven o'clock now, and
there was still no sound of gunfire.

I had gone half a mile past the artillery when I heard a car
behind me. A jeep was coming up the road. It stopped when
I thumbed it. A colonel was sitting next to the driver, and he
said, "Hop in." I climbed into the back and sat on my bedding
roll. "We're going to the regimental C.P.," the colonel said.
That suited me; I could find out there where my battalion was.
The colonel must have been important, because the driver,
a staff sergeant, drove very carefully, as if he were driving

a sedan instead of a jeep. The road was full of holes, and he actually went into second for some of them, which is a rare thing to do with a jeep. I kept my eye out for planes. The ceiling was still very low, but you never could tell. The road curved to the right, when we came to the first of the little hills, and then headed straight for the ridge. The colonel told the driver to slow down. We caught up to a young lieutenant walking along the road, and the colonel leaned out and asked him where the regimental C.P. was. "Damned if I know," the lieutenant said. He needed a shave and looked tired. "Well, what outfit are you?" the colonel asked. "Support battalion," the lieutenant said. He turned off the road and started across a field toward some vehicles parked under a tree. The colonel looked as though he were going to call him back, but finally he ordered the driver to go ahead. A hundred yards beyond, we came to a crossroads, and there was an M.P. here. The colonel shouted his question about the regimental C.P. at him and the M.P. waved us to the left. We took the road he had indicated, but it soon turned into a cow path and finally petered out altogether in front of an old farmhouse. Another M.P. was standing there, scratching his head. We stopped beside him and the colonel asked directions again. The M.P. kept scratching his head, but he pointed across a field to a wooded hill. The driver started off again. The M.P. called, "Hey!" We stopped, and the M.P. said mildly, "You better be careful crossing that field. It's supposed to be mined." None of us said anything for a moment; then the colonel sighed and told the driver to go ahead.

The driver went slowly across the field, following what he probably hoped were wheel tracks. I shifted around so that I was sitting on the side of the jeep with my feet on the back seat. I wondered briefly whether I shouldn't sit on my helmet, but decided that it wasn't really necessary. We didn't hit any mines, but we thought about them and it seemed like a long time before we got across that field. There was a dirt road on the other side and we followed it as we ascended the hill. Halfway up the hill we reached the C.P., which was in a grove of trees. I saw the regimental commander and his executive officer standing in a large excavation; the C.O. was talking over a telephone. The drivers and other headquarters-company men were digging foxholes and putting up a black-out tent. We parked under a tree. I thanked the colonel for the lift and went off to see if I could find someone I knew. I finally found the sergeant in charge of the intelligence platoon, a New Yorker named Vrana, whom I had been with in Sicily. He was sitting in a ditch by the side of the road, fooling around with a hand radio. I asked him where the battle was and he said it hadn't started yet. "We got observation on top of this hill," he said. "I was just talking to them. They said they couldn't see a damned thing." Vrana thought that the best way to find the battalion was to go up to the observation post and try to spot it from there. I could climb to the crest of the hill and walk along it until I found the post. He thought it was safe. He said that there had been only a little shelling, and that the enemy had settled down to throwing one shell into the C.P. every twenty minutes. "But on the nose," Vrana said. "You can set your watch by those bastards."

I said goodbye and started up the hill. It was easy climbing and I got to the top without much trouble. I came across a telephone wire there and followed it along the crest. The hill dipped into a saddle. I went down into it and was halfway up the other side when I heard the sound of men descending above me. They turned out to be two infantrymen, looking very dirty and completely bushed. One carried a rifle and the other had the base plate of a mortar. The rifleman said wearily, "How do you get out of this damned place?" I told them to follow the wire.

"You know where C Company is?" the mortar man asked me.

I asked him what outfit.

"Second battalion," he said.

"We just got relieved," the rifleman said. "Only nobody knows where we're supposed to go."

"I ain't even sure we been relieved," the mortar man said.

"I'm sure," the rifleman said. "The lieutenant come by and said we were relieved. That's good enough for me."

"The lieutenant got killed," the other man said.

"So what?" the rifleman said. "He relieved us before he got killed."

I said that I didn't know where C Company was but that they could probably find out at the C.P., and then it developed that they weren't even from our regiment. Their outfit had been in the line for eight days, and had held the hill we were on against four counterattacks; they had been spread all over the place and when our regiment had moved through, the night before, they had got mixed up. Now all they wanted was some hot chow and a place to sleep for a few days. Finally they decided to go down to the C.P., and moved off, cursing with the mechanical passion that everyone picks up in the Army.

I continued to follow the wire. It led up the slope to the top of the hill, which I suddenly realized was now flat and grassy. I felt very conspicuous. I ducked low and was creeping along beside the wire when a voice called my name. In a hollow between some rocks were three members of our regiment's intelligence platoon. The man who had called me was a private named Caruso, a small, dark man whom I had also known in Sicily. I crawled down to them. They said that they were the observation post. The two others were a lieutenant named Bixby and a private named Rich. You couldn't see anything from the hollow, but they said it was more comfortable there. "It's also healthier," Caruso explained. At that moment we heard the whine of a shell, growing steadily louder, and then a great swish, as though someone were cutting the tops of the trees with a giant scythe.

"See what I mean?" Caruso said.

"They throw one like that every twenty minutes," Lieutenant Bixby said. "You can set a clock by it."

I said I had heard about that before; the shells were landing below, in the C.P.

Caruso laughed. "I bet they're sweating down there," he said.

The fact that the shells were aimed at the C.P. and not at them seemed to make them happy. Caruso reached behind a rock and drew out a cardboard box full of rations. "How about something to eat?" he said.

"You just finished breakfast," Rich said.

"I got something better to do?" Caruso asked. He rummaged around in the box and came up with a can of meat balls and spaghetti. He opened it with a trench knife and ate the whole can, using the knife as a spoon.

While Caruso was eating, the lieutenant kept looking at his watch. Finally he said, "Listen." Very far away there was the faint cough of a gun, and then a rising whine and a sudden heavy rush of air as another shell passed over our heads. "See?" the lieutenant said, looking very pleased with himself. "Twenty minutes on the nose."

When Caruso had finished his meal, we climbed out of the hollow and up to the crest of the hill, where we lay on our stomachs, looking across the smaller valley toward the ridge. The lieutenant had a pair of field glasses. He looked through them and said, "There's fighting on the side of the ridge." He handed me the glasses. Through them I could see faint puffs of smoke halfway up the ridge and movement among the trees and rocks. "That's for me," I said. I was greatly tempted just to stay at the observation post. Sitting in the hollow was safe and secret, and no shell in the world would find me there. The air was getting warmer and the grass was soft and only a little wet. I could sleep. But I had to find the battalion, so I stood up, shouldered my roll, said goodbye, and started off again.

Lieutenant Bixby had said to follow the wire, which he thought led to the ridge. There was not even a suggestion of a path, and if you didn't know regimental wire teams you wouldn't think the wire could possibly lead anywhere. Finally, halfway down the hill, the wire brought me onto a muddy path that ran diagonally down the hill. The path was screened by trees and seemed insulated from the rest of the world. The air was cold down there. The only sound was the squish of my shoes in the mud, and even that was a cold, clammy sound. It was easy going, but there was nothing pleasant about it. It was like walking in a cold jungle. But I soon lost myself in the rhythm of walking. It wasn't until I was almost at the foot of the hill that I discovered that I had also lost the wire. I walked back a few yards, then decided that it wasn't worth going all the way back up the hill. I had no idea where the path led, but if the fighting was halfway up the ridge the valley was probably safe. If it wasn't safe, I was just out of luck. I started to descend again, only slower. It was very quiet. The path straightened out near the bottom of the hill and the trees became sparser. Then it dipped suddenly and I began to walk fast.

The path turned abruptly. Ahead of me was a group of men. I went for the ground, but it was unnecessary—they were Americans. There were four of them, carrying a blanket stretched out between them. Lying on the blanket was another soldier. His feet were drawn up and his face was buried in his arms. He lay very still. The men came slowly toward me, carrying the blanket with great care. They all had rifles slung over their shoulders; their faces were drawn and their eyes were deep in their sockets. They stopped when they reached me and one of the two front men said, "You know where the medics are?" His voice was too tired to have any expression; it seemed to come from a great distance. I said I didn't know. "We got to find the medics," the soldier said. "We got a man hurt bad." I said they would have to climb the hill and then maybe they could send down from the observation post for one of the first-aid men at the C.P. The soldier was silent for a while, then he said again, "We got to find the medics." The three other men stood silent, looking at the one who was talking. The blanket was stiff with caked blood. The wounded man was scarcely breathing. Once in a while his fingers twitched and tapped weakly on the blanket. I said that they would pick up a wire further along and that it would take them to the observation post. "Thank you," the man who had spoken to me said. He shifted his feet, moving very gently so as not to disturb the wounded man. "All right," he said to the others. "Left foot." They began to walk again, synchronizing their steps so that they wouldn't shake the blanket. As they passed, I stepped aside, but not quickly enough to avoid brushing against one of the rear men. He said, "Excuse me." They moved up the path slowly, like sleepwalkers, and I watched until they turned the corner and were out of sight. Then I went on along the path, following the tiny trail of blood they had left.

The path broadened at the foot of the hill and before I knew it I was in the valley. It was wider than I had thought, looking at it from above; the ridge seemed a couple of miles away. The path ended at a dirt road running through the valley, but I decided to cut straight across and head for the ridge. The ground was soft and grassy; it felt good to be walking on the level again. There was a lovely tranquillity in the valley, and the ridge was quiet again. I had walked about two hundred yards from the foot of the hill when there was a rush of air and a clap of thunder, and I fell flat on my face. When the ground had settled down, I lifted my head and looked around. A thin cloud of smoke and dust hung peacefully in the air a hundred feet to my left. There was nothing else to be seen. I lay there until I began to feel a little foolish, then stood up and began walking toward the ridge again. This time I got about twenty yards before there was the flat wham of something going very fast and another thunder clap. This time the smoke was closer. Then, while I was still lying on the ground, another shell hit only thirty feet away, throwing dirt all over the place. I stood up, bent low, and ran like hell. Another shell landed somewhere behind me, but I didn't stop until I got back to the foot of the hill. The first thing I saw was a ditch, and I hopped into that. It was full of water, but it was deep. It could have been full of hydrochloric acid as long as it was deep.

I lay in the ditch perhaps twenty minutes. There was no more shelling. The echoes still rang in my ears, but the valley was quiet again. Finally I climbed out of the ditch and started along the base of the hill, keeping under cover as much as I could. The road through the valley curved toward me, and I found myself walking on it. I went slowly, trying to look all around me at once. My clothes were wet and I began to shiver. The valley was deathly quiet. I couldn't stop shivering, and then I felt afraid. I wasn't afraid of snipers, or even of mines, which can irritate you so much that eventually you say the hell with them, just to be able to walk freely and with dignity again. But there is something about heavy artillery that is inhuman and terribly frightening. You never know whether you are running away from it or into it. It is like the finger of God. I felt cowardly and small at the base of this tremendous hill, walking alone on the floor of this enormous valley. I felt like a fly about to be swatted. It was a lousy feeling. I was very angry until I realized that there was nothing I could do about it. Then I began to wish I were somewhere else.

The road hugged the base of the hill and then swung out into the valley again. I stayed on it, partly from inertia and partly to assert myself. All of a sudden I heard an automobile horn. I looked up and down the road, but nothing was in sight. The horn blew again. It was a nice, raucous city horn; I thought I was imagining things. The horn blew again and a voice called out, "You dumb son of a bitch, where do you think *you're* going?" The voice came from the hill. I looked over and saw a soldier standing above me near some bushes, waving. "Come back here!" he yelled. "You want your goddam head blown off?" I started toward him. I had almost reached him when he yelled "Run!" and jumped in among the bushes. I started to run, and then there was the whistle of a shell and a loud crack and a piece of the hill flew into the air. I hit the ground, digging with my nose, and the soldier stuck his head out of the bushes and yelled, "Here! In here!" I got up and ran toward him and he pulled me through the bushes. There was a shallow cleft in the hill, hidden by foliage, and parked in the cleft was a jeep. In the jeep was another soldier and on the back was a reel of telephone wire. "I hope you got insurance," the soldier in the jeep said, "because the way you travel around this country you're sure going to need it." As soon as I got my breath, I asked him what he meant, and the first soldier took me by the arm and pulled me back to the bushes. He held them apart and asked me what I saw. I couldn't see anything. "Over there by the foot of the ridge," he said. I looked again. "You see it?" he said. I saw it. A German tank was sitting in a field below the ridge. It was far away, but you could see that it was a heavy tank and you could see the black cross on the side. "Get a load of that kraut bastard," the soldier said. "He nearly blew us off the road."

We went back to the jeep and he explained that they and another man had come around the other side of the hill along a wide trail, stringing wire for the battalion, and the tank had opened fire, forcing them to take cover in the cleft. The tank was apparently afraid to come down into the valley, since we had covering fire on it, but it would fire on anything that moved. The one who had yelled to me was short and red-faced; his name was Jenkins. The other was tall, with a long, sad face and huge hands, and Jenkins called him Tex. "He really comes from Oklahoma," Jenkins said, "but he served two years at Fort Sam Houston, so everyone calls him Tex." I asked if they had done anything about the tank. Jenkins said they had sent the third man up to the artillery observation post to put some fire on it. He said we had men working their way up the ridge; he didn't think they were meeting much opposition, since all the firing he had heard had been light and sporadic. There seemed to be nothing to do but wait, so I sat down in the jeep and relaxed. The two other men went into what was apparently a running argument about the relative attractions of French women in Algiers and Italian women in Italy. Jenkins was upholding the French.

"They got more class," he kept saying to Tex.

"Maybe so," Tex said, unimpressed, "but what good is it if you can't get anywhere?"

"That's just what I mean," Jenkins said triumphantly. "That's *class*."

Just then there was the crackle of a shell overhead. "That's it!" Jenkins said. He rushed to the bushes and held them apart so that he could look across the valley. Tex and I followed him. "It's our goddam artillery," Tex said. "They finally realized there's a war on." The shell had hit a hundred yards or so from the tank. The tank began to move, obviously trying to retreat, but something must have been wrong, because it turned only part way around. Another shell landed closer, and Jenkins whispered, "You kraut bastard, stay there, stay there!" The tank looked like a huge bug, twitching as it strained to get away. Another shell came over, but this one was farther off, and then two more, closer.

"How can you hit a tank from that distance?" Tex asked. "It'd be a miracle."

"Shut your face!" Jenkins said, without looking at him. He was whispering to the artillery, "Hit the bastard, hit him, *hit* him!"

But the next shell was off the target and the two after that were even farther off, and then the tank spun around, wobbled for a second, and lumbered out of sight. Two more shells went over, but it was too late. The tank was hidden now.

"God *damn!*" Jenkins said, turning back to us. He looked as if he were going to cry.

"Listen," Tex said. "Them guns have been firing since Salerno. I bet right now they got bores as smooth as a baby's bottom. You're lucky they get as close as two hundred yards to what they're aiming at."

Jenkins got into the driver's seat of the jeep and started the motor. "That tank ain't going to stick his nose out no more," he said. "We might as well get this wire laid." Tex went around behind the jeep, so that he could follow it and see that the wire didn't get tangled as it was reeled out, and I got into the front seat. We drove out through the bushes and headed across the valley toward the ridge but bearing away from the part of the ridge where the tank had disappeared. "He ain't going to bother us," Jenkins said, "but there ain't no sense giving him the chance." We drove across the valley in second, Tex walking behind, paying out the wire. Once we heard the crackle of a shell going over. Jenkins slammed on the brakes and we both spilled out, but the shell kept going and we heard it hit on the other side of the ridge. When we got to the base of the ridge, Jenkins parked the car and said he'd be damned if he was going to lug that wire up a mountain; he was going to wait for the man they had sent to the artillery observation post. I offered to help them, but he said they'd better wait for him. I said I thought I'd be on my way then. I got my bedding roll and thanked them for saving my life. "Hell," Tex said. "He might have missed you." Jenkins warned me to watch out for trip wires on the way up; while they had been pinned down by the tank, they had heard some explosions on the ridge that sounded like mines, and trip wires were the favorite German method of mining a mountain. I thanked them again and started off.

There was no path up the ridge here, so I went straight up. It wasn't hard going at first; the ground was soft and I had to fight my way through bushes, but they weren't too thick. Then the soft ground ended and rocks began. They were big rocks, with thickets growing between them, and I had to hop from one to another. Even this wasn't too bad, but then the rocks ended and there was nothing but thickets, which I had to claw my way through. They were full of thistles, and after a few minutes my hands and face were bleeding. Finally I stopped and looked back. The valley was just the same, calm and green and peaceful. In the distance I could see dust on the road, which meant that trucks were moving up. Then I heard the sharp sounds of small-arms fire above me and to the right, so I headed that way. The sounds grew louder and distinguishable: the crack of a rifle and the riveting-machine burst of a German machine pistol, and then the slower, measured answer of our machine guns. I stopped to get my breath, and when I started again my legs felt very heavy. My pistol dragged at my side and the bedding roll felt as heavy as a sack of flour. But as I approached the firing, I began to feel life-size. The valley fear and sense of insignificance disappeared and I felt human, and very important. I didn't know how close I was to the top of the ridge, but that didn't matter now.

The ridge grew steeper; the rocks appeared again, and then the bushes. I ripped my way through. My uniform was soaked with sweat and my helmet bounced up and down on my head and slid over my eyes. At last I got on a trail which went uphill. The firing was very near now, but it had slackened. Alongside the path, I saw, ahead of me, three soldiers with red crosses on their arms, standing over another soldier on the ground. They paid no attention to me. When I got closer, I saw that two of them were working on the man on the ground, cutting away his uniform around a lumpy brown stain on his side. The third man was standing a little apart. He was a medical captain. I asked him where the battalion C.P. was and he pointed up the trail without speaking. I kept on the trail and began to encounter signs that there had been a fight. There was a German machine-gun emplacement dug in between two trees, the gun still pointing down the mountain, and two dead Germans lying beside the gun. Farther up, cases of German ammunition were scattered around. The trail widened. It mounted a little further and then ran for a while along the side of the ridge, hidden from the top by an overhanging cliff. I came upon the mouth of a cave in the cliff.

Two officers were sitting before it, looking at a map. One was the battalion commander, a young, tough colonel with a mustache. The other was the regimental intelligence officer, a child lieutenant who looked about eighteen when he was shaved. He was one of the people I was supposed to have gone with. When he saw me, all he said was, "You're a little late, aren't you?" I told him what had happened. "You missed all the fun," he said. "We've already chased the krauts off the hill." I asked what the shooting was, and he said it was just some isolated snipers the boys were cleaning up. "You can go on up to the top of the hill if you want," he said. "Just keep your head down."

I said I'd take a quick look and continued up the trail. There were infantrymen scattered along it, opening packages of K ration or sleeping or just sitting and smoking. None of them were talking. There were also several men lying on the ground with blankets over their faces. The path grew steeper and then dribbled out among some rocks. I started to climb up over the rocks and a voice said, "Keep your head down." A soldier was sitting behind a large rock at the top. I kept low and climbed up to him. "This is the end of the line," he said. "Unless you want your head handed to you." I dropped my bedding roll, climbed the rock, and looked over. Everything was exactly the same. There was the other side of the ridge dropping off beneath me and at the bottom was a green little valley, and then another ridge. Beyond that were more ridges, rising and falling in the same pattern. There seemed to be no end; it was like being in an airplane over a sea of clouds that stretched forever into space. It was very quiet on top of the ridge. There was no more firing and the air was warm and motionless. Then there was the sound of planes and two of our dive-bombers appeared, flying very high and fast, heading for the next ridge. When they were over it, they gunned their motors and then heeled over and went down with terrible directness in a long, plummeting dive, the motor sound lost in the screaming of the wings; and when it seemed that they would never pull out, they pulled out, and from the bottom of the planes, like droppings from a bird, the bombs fell beautifully down and hit and exploded. Then the planes flattened out and climbed and sped swiftly back toward their field.

I lay there for a while longer and then climbed down to the soldier behind the rock. "How does it look?" he asked.

"It looks familiar," I said.

The New Yorker, September 23, 1944

Issei, Nisei, Kibei

by The Editors of *Fortune*
drawings by Miné Okubo

WHEN the facts about Japanese brutality to the soldier prisoners from Bataan were made known, Americans were more outraged than they had been since December 7, 1941. Instinctively they contrasted that frightfulness with our treatment of Japanese held in this country; and, without being told, Americans knew that prisoners in the U.S. were fed three meals a day and had not been clubbed or kicked or otherwise brutalized. Too few, however, realize what persistent and effective use Japan has been able to make, throughout the entire Far East, of U.S. imprisonment of persons of Japanese descent. This propaganda concerns itself less with *how* the U.S. treats the people imprisoned than *who* was imprisoned. By pointing out, again and again, that the U.S. put behind fences well over 100,000 people of Japanese blood, the majority of them citizens of the U.S., Japan describes to her Far Eastern radio audiences one more instance of American racial discrimination. To convince all Orientals that the war in the Pacific is a crusade against the white man's racial oppression, the enemy shrewdly notes every occurrence in the U.S. that suggests injustice to racial minorities, from the Negroes to the Mexicans and Japanese.

The enemy, of course, deliberately refrains from making distinctions among the various kinds of detention we have worked out for those of Japanese blood in this country. Unfortunately, Americans themselves are almost as confused as the Japanese radio about what has happened to the Japanese minority in this country—one-tenth of 1 per cent of the nation's total population. There are three different types of barbed-wire enclosures for persons of Japanese ancestry. First there are the Department of Justice camps, which hold 3,000 Japanese aliens considered by the F.B.I. potentially dangerous to the U.S. These and these alone are true internment camps.

Second, there are ten other barbed-wire enclosed centers in the U.S., into which, in 1942, the government put 110,000 persons of Japanese descent (out of a total population in continental U.S. of 127,000). Two-thirds of them were citizens, born in the U.S.; one-third aliens, forbidden by law to be citizens. No charges were brought against them. When the war broke out, all these 110,000 were resident in the Pacific Coast states—the majority in California. They were put behind fences when the Army decided that for "military necessity" all people of Japanese ancestry, citizen or alien, must be removed from the West Coast military zone.

Within the last year the 110,000 people evicted from the West Coast have been subdivided into two separate groups. Those who have professed loyalty to Japan or an unwillingness to defend the U.S. have been placed, with their children, in one of the ten camps called a "segregation center" (the third type of imprisonment). Of the remainder in the nine "loyal camps," 17,000 have moved to eastern states to take jobs. The rest wait behind the fence, an awkward problem for the U.S. if for no other reason than that the Constitution and the Bill of Rights were severely stretched if not breached when U.S. citizens were put in prison.

Back in December, 1941, there was understandable nervousness over the tight little Japanese communities scattered along the West Coast. The long coast line seemed naked and undefended. There were colonies of Japanese fishermen in the port areas, farmlands operated by Japanese close to war plants, and little Tokyos in the heart of the big coastal cities. There were suspected spies among the Japanese concentrations and there was fear of sabotage. Californians were urged to keep calm and let the authorities take care of the problem. In the first two weeks the Department of Justice scooped up about 1,500 suspects. A few weeks later all enemy aliens and citizens alike were removed from certain strategic areas such as Terminal Island in Los Angeles harbor, and spots near war plants, power stations, and bridges. But Californians did not completely trust the authorities. While the F.B.I. was picking up its suspects, civilian authorities were besieged with tele-

Citizens and Aliens, all people of Japanese blood on the West Coast were carted off to custody.

The Tanforan Race Track, near San Francisco, was one of fifteen Army assembly centers.

phone calls from citizens reporting suspicious behavior of their Oriental neighbors. Although California's Attorney General Warren (now governor) stated on February 21, 1942, that "we have had no sabotage and no fifth-column activity since the beginning of the war," hysteria by then had begun to spread all along the coast. Every rumor of Japanese air and naval operations offshore, and every tale of fifth-column activity in Hawaii, helped to raise to panic proportions California's ancient and deep antagonism toward the Japanese-Americans.

For decades the Hearst press had campaigned against the Yellow Peril within the state (1 per cent of the population) as well as the Yellow Peril across the seas that would one day make war. When that war prophecy came true, the newspapers'

Horse Stalls had to be cleaned, for human use, but the smell of manure persisted for months.

For their food handout, the *évacués* waited in long queues at the central mess hall.

campaign of hate and fear broke all bounds. And, when Hearst called for the removal of all people of Japanese ancestry, he had as allies many pressure groups who had for years resented the presence of Japanese in this country.

The American Legion, since its founding in 1919, has never once failed to pass an annual resolution against the Japanese-Americans. The Associated Farmers in California had competitive reasons for wanting to get rid of the Japanese-Americans who grew vegetables at low cost on $70 million worth of California land. California's land laws could not prevent the citizen-son of the Japanese alien from buying or renting the land. In the cities, as the little Tokyos grew, a sizable commercial business came into Japanese-American hands—vegetable commission houses, retail and wholesale enterprises of all kinds. It did not require a war to make the farmers, the Legion, the Native Sons and Daughters of the Golden West, and the politicians resent and hate the Japanese-Americans. The records of legislation and press for many years indicate that the antagonism was there and growing. War turned the antagonism into fear, and made possible what California had clearly wanted for decades—to get rid of its minority.

By early February both the Hearst press and the pressure groups were loudly demanding the eviction of all people of Japanese blood—to protect the state from the enemy, and to protect the minority from violence at the hands of Filipinos and other neighbors. A few cases of violence had, indeed, occurred, and spy talk ran up and down the coast. On February 13, a group of Pacific Coast Congressmen urged President Roosevelt to permit an evacuation; a week later the President gave that authority to the Army. On February 23, a Japanese submarine shelled the coast near Santa Barbara. Lieutenant General John L. DeWitt, on March 2, issued the order that all persons of Japanese descent, aliens and citizens, old and young, women and children, be removed from most of California, western Oregon and Washington, and southern Arizona. The greatest forced migration in U.S. history resulted.

At first the movement inland of the 110,000 people living within the prohibited zone was to be voluntary. The

Regimentation for men, women, and children made these little Tokyos more ingrown than ever.

Privacy was gained only by hanging curtains between crowded beds. There was too much idle time.

Japanese-Americans were merely told to get out. Within three weeks 8,000 people had packed up, hastily closed out their business affairs, sold their possessions or left them with neighbors, and set forth obediently toward the east. But Arizona remembered all too well how California had turned back the Okies in the past, and many Japanese-Americans were intercepted at this border. Kansas patrolmen stopped them. Nevada and Wyoming protested that they did not want to receive people found too dangerous for California. About 4,000 got as far as Colorado and Utah. It became apparent that the random migration of so many unwanted people could result only in spreading chaos. By March 29 voluntary evacuation was forbidden, and the Army made its own plans to control the movement.

They packed up again, after six months, and were all herded out of the Army centers.

Jammed into trains, they were sent farther inland into new soldier-guarded camps.

The *évacués* reported to local control stations where they registered and were given a number and instructions on what they could take (hand luggage only) and when they should proceed to the first camps, called assembly centers. Although they were offered government help in straightening out their property problems, many thousands, in their haste and confusion, and in their understandable distrust of government, quickly did what they could for themselves. They sold, leased, stored, or lent their homes, lands, personal belongings, tractors, and cars. Their financial losses are incalculable.

The Army, in twenty-eight days, rigged up primitive barracks in fifteen assembly centers to provide temporary quarters for 110,000. Each *évacué* made his own mattress of straw, took his place in the crowded barracks, and tried to adjust to his new life. By August 10 everyone of Japanese descent (except those confined to insane asylums and other safe institutions) was behind a fence, in "protective custody." They were held here (still within the forbidden military zone) until a newly created civilian agency, the War Relocation Authority, could establish other refuges farther inland. WRA's job was to hold the people until they could be resettled in orderly fashion.

WRA appealed to the governors of ten nearby western states. With one exception, Colorado's Governor Carr, they protested that they did not want the Japanese-Americans to settle in their domain, nor did they want any relocation center erected within their borders unless it was well guarded by the Army. Finally nine remote inland sites were found, all of them on federally owned land. (One assembly center in eastern California became a relocation camp.) Most of them were located, for lack of better acreage, on desolate but irrigable desert tracts. More tar-papered barracks were thrown up, more wire fences built, and once more the people moved. By November, 1942, all the *évacués* had packed up their miserably few possessions, had been herded onto trains, and deposited behind WRA's soldier-guarded fences, in crowded barracks villages of between 7,000 and 18,000 people.

They felt bitterness and anger over their loss of land and home and money and freedom. They knew that German and

Deposited in a desert camp, whipped by sandstorms, they were put in new barracks.

Crowded into a single room, this family managed to improvise a Christmas celebration.

Italian aliens—and indeed, Japanese aliens in other parts of the U.S.—had been interned only when the F.B.I. had reason to suspect them. Second-generation citizens of German and Italian origin were not evacuated from California; nor were the second-generation citizens of Japanese descent elsewhere in the U.S. put behind fences.

Although the *évacués'* resentment at regimentation within WRA's little Tokyos is deep, it is seldom expressed violently. Considering the emotional strains, the uprooting, and the crowding, no one can deny that the record of restraint has been remarkable. Only twice have the soldiers been asked to come within a WRA fence to restore order.

But WRA and its director, Dillon Myer, have been under almost continual attack by congressional committees in Wash-

Victory gardens are planted even though minimum food is given to everyone.

Public showers and latrines are provided but the Japanese tradition of tub bathing persists.

ington, and by a whole long list of badgering groups and individuals on the West Coast. The Dies Committee goes after WRA* and the Japanese minority at frequent intervals. Even Hedda Hopper, the movie gossip, prattles innuendoes. Not wishing to "imply anything," she noted last December that "we've had more than our share of explosions, train wrecks, fires, and serious accidents" since WRA has released so many of the *évacués*. Actually, not one of the 17,000 has been convicted of anti-American activity.

WRA has usually been criticized for the wrong reasons. It has been accused of turning loose, for resettlement, "dangerous Japs." The implication usually is that no Japanese-American should be released, although from the very beginning WRA's prescribed purpose was to help the *évacués* to find some place to live outside the prohibited zone. Again and again, the pressure groups and California Congressmen have urged that WRA's ten centers be turned over to the Army. (In February the President, instead, dropped WRA intact, with its Director Dillon Myer, into the Department of Interior.) Most frequently Mr. Myer has been charged with pampering the Japanese-Americans. Almost every day the Hearst papers fling the word "coddling," with the clear implication that all persons of Japanese descent, citizen or no, women and infants, should be treated strictly as prisoners of war, which of course they are not.

No one who has visited a relocation center and seen the living space, eaten the food, or merely kept his eyes open could honestly apply the word "coddling" to WRA's administration of the camps. The people are jammed together in frame barracks. A family of six or seven is customarily allotted an "apartment" measuring about twenty by twenty-five feet. It is a bare room, without partitions. The only privacy possible is achieved by hanging flimsy cotton curtains between the crowded beds.

Furniture is improvised from bits of scrap lumber: a box for a table, three short ends of board made into a backless chair.

*Herman P. Eberharter, a member of the Dies Committee, has said of its September, 1943, findings, ". . . the report . . . is prejudiced, and most of its statements are not proven." The committee wound up by suggesting three policies, all of which the WRA had already adopted.

The rabble rouser spreads disaffection among the *évacués*, distrusted and discarded by society.

At Americanization classes the old people learn the three R's and some history of the U.S.

The family's clothing and few personal possessions are somehow stuffed neatly away—on shelves if scrap lumber, a priceless commodity in all camps, is available. Otherwise, they are stuffed away under the beds. The quarters are usually neat. There are no cooking facilities and no running water in the barracks, unless the *évacué* has brought his own electric plate or had a friend "on the outside" send one in. As in Army camps, each block of twelve or fourteen barracks (250 to 300 people) has its central mess hall, laundry building, public latrines, and showers.

With faithful regularity, irresponsible yarns are circulated that the *évacués* are getting more and better food than other Americans. Actually, the food cost per day is held below 45

The loyal *évacué*, who has courage to face race prejudice "outside," can go east for a job.

cents per person. For 15 cents a meal the food is possibly adequate, but close to the edge of decent nutrition. In most camps, located far from dairy districts, milk is provided only for small children, nursing and expectant mothers, and special dietary cases. There are two meatless days a week and a heavy emphasis on starches. Nearly a third of the food requirements are grown on the irrigated fields of the camp itself. This reduces the actual cash outlay for food to 31 cents per person.

Practically everyone who wants a job can work, and most of the able bodied do. They plant and till the camp's vegetable acreage, prepare the food in the mess halls, do stenographic work for the Caucasian staff, work in the cooperative store.* In some centers they make furniture for the administration building or cotton mattresses to take the place of the hard straw pallets. Some are barbers and cobblers for the community, doctors in the hospital, scrubwomen in the latrines, garbage collectors. The maximum wage (a doctor, for instance) is $19 a month; the minimum, $12; the average, $16. In addition, those who work get a clothing allowance for themselves and their dependents—at the most, $3.75 a month for an adult in the northernmost center.

Individual enterprise is forbidden. To set up one's own dressmaking service within the community, or to sell shell jewelry or anything else to the outside is prohibited. In order to keep the center wage uniform, all economic activities must be conducted through the community cooperative, which pays its barbers and other workers the standard stipend. With their small monthly wage, and by dipping into their prewar savings, most *évacués* buy extras to eat, but they can get only nonrationed food, since they possess no ration books. They send to the mail-order houses for some of their clothes, buy shoes, yard goods, and clothing at the cooperative store. Their children go to school in the barracks village, and when they are sick, to the center hospital.

Thus the pampering and thus the humiliation. A doctor distinguished in his profession, who lived with grace and

*WRA has a lexicon of its own: Caucasian is the term for appointed administrative personnel, to distinguish them from the *"évacués,"* sometimes called "colonists"; beyond the gate is "the outside."

charm in a decently comfortable home before the war, is to day huddled in a small room with all his family. He practices his profession for $19 a month at the center hospital, serving under a Caucasian of lesser accomplishments, hired for considerably more money. A man who spent twenty years building up his own florist business or commission house, or who operated a large vegetable farm in one of California's valleys, is merely "stoop labor" on the center's acreage.

The record of Japanese-Americans during the depression indicated that they did not take to public relief. They were too proud. They stuck together, helped each other, and almost never appeared on WPA or home-relief lists. To virtually all of them it is now galling to be distrusted wards of the nation, their meager lodging and food a scanty handout, the payment for their labor somewhat the same.

They have always been an isolated, discarded, and therefore ingrown people. Today this is more true than ever. The barracks village as a rule is literally isolated. At Manzanar, California, for example, the center is but a tiny square in a vast and lonely desert valley, between two great mountain ranges. Spiritually the people are just as isolated as that. Thrown together in a compact racial island of their own frustrated people, they grow in upon themselves and each other; they become almost completely detached from American life, the war, the world. Their small children speak more Japanese than they would if they competed daily with other American school children. The teen-age boys and girls are ostentatiously American in clothes, slang, and behavior. It is as if they were trying too hard to convince themselves that they *are* Americans. They know that they must and will go out the gate soon.

The adults think about themselves, and about the past they left. With time and distance, California's farm valleys, towns, and cities become more golden-hued than ever to the *évacués*. They brood vaguely and fearfully on the future; the war, sometimes, seems like a vague abstraction, the cause of their troubles. And they think about rumors—which they often trust more than they do printed, official announcements. It may be a rumor that the Army will take over. Or that the

évacués in this center will all be transported to another. This is
the most nightmarish rumor of all to people who have moved
so much in the past two years.

They think, too, about the endless details of their camp life.
Each group of 250 or so *évacués* has a block manager who gets
$16 a month for listening to their complaints and, if possible,
straightening out innumerable daily problems. The food in
the mess hall is badly prepared; there is no toilet paper in the
ladies' latrine; the neighbors play the radio too late and too
loud; the roof of No. 29 barracks has a small leak.

Finally, there are gossip and politics. The Japanese-
Americans back in California went their way without much
participation in politics as most American citizens know it. In
the barracks village of WRA there is little real self-
government. Most of the centers have a Council made up of
block representatives or managers. But there is only a slight
area within which such a congress can make community decisions. Usually at the meeting of the Council the members do
little more than listen to new rules, new plans of WRA,
handed down from Washington or the local director. The
block representatives are expected to pass on this information
to all the people.

Originally WRA ruled that citizens alone could hold office in
the centers, but this proved to be unwise. Two-thirds of the
évacués are citizens, but most of these American-born Nisei
are from eighteen to twenty-eight years of age—too young
to take on such responsible jobs as the block manager's. Besides, among the Japanese-Americans born here are hundreds
of Kibei—young men who were sent to Japan for part of
their education. Not all—but a large percentage of them—
are pro-Japan, particularly those who gained the latter part of
their education in Japan. Disliked by the Nisei majority, outnumbered and maladjusted, the Kibei often have become a
nuisance, creating little areas of disaffection in the center.

Thus it turned out that the Issei—the aliens, parents of the
Nisei and Kibei—could best provide the authority, stability,
and seasoned wisdom needed in a block manager. They possessed a tradition of family and community leadership, and
had commanded respect in the past. Above all they usually

have an earnest desire to make the block of 250 or more people in which they live function in an orderly and quiet fashion. They are aliens primarily because U.S. law forbade them to become citizens. Many of them have a real loyalty to the U.S., not because the U.S. has invited their loyalty but because they look to their children's American future for their own security.

Politics in the centers has nothing to do with office or votes or *apparent* power. But it *is* power—the power of demagoguery, of spreading the infection of bitterness, exaggerating an instance or affront into an issue that may even get to the point of a small strike against WRA. The leaders have not invariably been pro-Japan. Some, both aliens and citizens, who had been good Americans became indignant at their loss of freedom and their right to participate in the life of the nation.

It may be that the administration was not willing to permit a big funeral for a man accidentally killed when a work truck overturned; it may be that three or four of the Caucasian staff displayed signs of race discrimination; it may be a rumor more plausible than fact. The "politicians" take any one of these, or a series, and worry it into a big camp issue. How great an issue it becomes depends most of all on the degree of confidence the center as a whole has in its director and the coolness and fairness with which he customarily handles his people. Too often the administration is out of touch with the main issues and grievances within the camp. WRA suffers, like every other agency, from the manpower shortage. Competent center directors and minor personnel are scarce. Often enough the director finds his Caucasian staff more of a problem than the *évacués*.

The two so-called "riots," which brought the Army over the fence, arose from the accumulation of small grievances, whipped up to a crisis by groups struggling for power and eager to put the administration on the spot. There was, in each instance, a strike. Actually a strike in a relocation center is self-defeating since almost all labor in the community works to provide goods and services for the *évacués* themselves; no more than a handful work in the staff mess and office building.

Only when violence occurred, and the director thought he needed help in maintaining order, was the Army invited in.

But trouble rarely reaches either the strike stage or violence. The people in the Pacific Coast's little Tokyos rarely appeared on police blotters in the past, and now the crime record of WRA centers compares favorably with that of any small cities of their size, or, indeed, with any Army camp. Most of the policing is done by the *évacués* themselves, appointed to the "internal security" staff of each center.

Policing should be simpler than ever from now on. The ideological air has been cleared; the pro-Japan people have been moved out. The process of sifting the communities, separating the loyal and the disloyal, is virtually complete. The "disloyal" have been sent to a segregation center in northeastern California, leaving the other nine centers populated only by the loyal.

To all the *évacués* the two words, registration and segregation, are almost as charged with emotion as that disturbing term, evacuation. Quite simply the two nouns mean that a questionnaire was submitted to all adults in the centers to determine their loyalty or disloyalty. On the basis of this, plus F.B.I. records and in some instances special hearings, WRA granted or denied the *évacués* "leave clearance," the right to go East and find a job. The same information was used as a basis for segregating the "disloyal" in a separate center. About 18,000 (the "disloyal" and all their dependents) will sit out the war at Tule Lake, within a high, manproof, barbed-wire enclosure, unless Japan shows more enthusiasm than she has to date for their repatriation. (These 18,000 must not be confused with the few thousand interned by the Department of Justice.)

But separating the loyal and the disloyal is not so simple a job as it might seem. Loyalty is difficult to measure accurately on any scales, and the sifting of the *évacués* was clumsily handled. The process began in February, 1943, when the Army decided to recruit a combat unit of Japanese-Americans. A registration form was printed containing twenty-eight questions to determine loyalty and willingness to fight.

It was to be filled out by all men of military age. Someone realized that it would be well to have just such records on all adults in the centers. Plans were suddenly changed and everyone from seventeen years of age up was given the twenty-eight questions.

Nothing is more disastrous in a rumor-ridden, distrustful, neurotic community like a relocation center than to make one explanation of purpose today and a quite different one tomorrow. The people, newly arrived in the WRA centers, were still stunned by their evacuation, loss of property and freedom, and were acutely conscious of their stigma as "enemy." There was misunderstanding about the purpose of registration at most of the centers. The questionnaire was so carelessly framed its wording had to be changed during the process of registration. A few thousand refused to fill out the form at all. Others, remembering that they had lost business, home, and their civil rights, wrote angry ("disloyal") answers. They had no enthusiasm for defending a democratic America that had imprisoned them for no crime and without trial.

WRA, in an effort to be fair, has granted hearings in recent months for those who wished to explain the answers they made in anger or confusion. Pride made a few people stick to what they first wrote. There is little question that the majority of adults sent to Tule Lake feel loyalty to Japan, but there are also behind Tule's fences a few thousand who are not disloyal.

Most of the Issei who chose Tule Lake are there because of firm ties of loyalty to Japan, or strong ties of family relationships. Some Issei were afraid of bringing reprisals upon their relatives in Japan by affirming loyalty to the U.S. The parents who chose Tule Lake usually have taken all their children with them. Only a few sons and daughters over seventeen, who had the right to choose for themselves, could resist strong family pressure. It is ironic and revealing that at the high school at Tule Lake, civics and American history are popular elected courses.

Japan, however, makes no legal claims of protective interest in the Nisei or Kibei. When the Spanish consul visits Tule to report conditions to Japan, he is legally concerned only with the welfare of the Issei, the nationals of Japan. And, under U.S. law, the Nisei and Kibei cannot abrogate their American citizenship during wartime, even if they want to. Their expatriation, and even the repatriation of most of the Issei to Japan, during the war, is unlikely. Negotiations for the exchange of civilian war prisoners have been slow, and the delay is due to Japan, not to the U.S. State Department.

To a minority living at Tule Lake, Japan's unwillingness to arrange frequent exchange of prisoners is not disheartening. This minority does not want to set sail for Japan; it wants to stay in the U.S. People are at Tule Lake for many complicated reasons besides "disloyalty" and family relationships. There is evidence, for example, that some chose this kind of imprisonment for reasons of security and weariness. This is indicated

by the percentages of people in the various centers who said they wanted to be segregated. When the decision was made last fall to turn the Tule Lake camp into a segregation center, nearly 6,000 out of 13,000 residents of that center decided to stay put. This high percentage of "disloyal," the highest in any center, is explained in part by unwillingness to be uprooted and moved again. In the Minidoka relocation center, in Idaho, only 225 people out of 7,000 chose to go to Tule.

There are a few tired and discouraged people from other WRA centers who went to Tule Lake because they knew that the barbed-wire fences in that camp would stand permanently throughout the war. They reasoned that they would have certain refuge for the duration, while the other centers, according to *évacué* rumor, might be abruptly closed, and everyone turned loose without resources.

Some chose Tule Lake imprisonment as a gesture against what they consider the broken promises of democracy. For example, there is a young Nisei who enlisted in California early in 1941 because he felt strongly about fascism. He was abruptly thrown out of his country's army after Japan attacked the U.S. and put behind the fences along with all the other *évacués*. In February, 1943, when he was handed a questionnaire on loyalty and his willingness to defend the U.S., he was too angry to prove his "loyalty" that way; he had already amply demonstrated it. He is at Tule Lake, not because of his love for Japan, but as a protest to the government he honestly wanted to serve back in 1941.

There is the Japanese-American who fought in the last war in the U.S. Army, and is a member of the American Legion. When the Japanese struck Pearl Harbor, he offered his services to the Army and to industry in California. He was turned down. Sent to a relocation center he became a "troublemaker," with the slogan, "If you think you are an American, try walking out the gate." He was packed off to an "isolation center," and finally wound up at Tule Lake. Last year the U.S. Treasury received a check from him, mailed from behind Tule's barbed wire. It was a sum in excess of $100 and represented his income tax for the calendar year, 1942, when he had received belated payment for his 1941 services as navigator on a Portuguese ship. He insisted on paying his tax, as usual. He has, of course, no wish to go to Japan. He too sits out the war at Tule Lake in protest against the failure of democracy.

The minority who are in Tule for reasons of weariness or protest are not important numerically. But they show what can happen to people who are confused, discouraged, or justifiably angry. They reveal some ugly scars inflicted by our society. It is too early to speculate about what will happen to these 18,000 prisoners. A few thousand, at the most, may get aboard the *Gripsholm*. Will all the rest be shipped finally to a defeated Japan? Or will they be a postwar U.S. problem?

Where the Tule Lake prisoners will end their days is less important to consider than what is to become of those "loyal" *évacués* who are still in the nine other centers. Everyone deemed loyal, by the sifting process of registration and hearings, has been granted "leave clearance." Fortified with a handful of official papers, a numbered identification card bearing his picture and fingerprints, an *évacué* can set forth to the East. He gets his railroad fare, $3 a day travel money, and if he has no savings, $25 in cash.

During the last twelve months, 17,000 *évacués* have had the courage to go "outside." They are, with rare exceptions, young and single, or married but childless. A Nisei has to muster considerable courage to go out into the society that rejected him two years ago. From behind the fence "the outside" has become vague, enormous, and fearful. The huddling together, which is resented, is nonetheless a cohesive, protective force, hard to overcome. As he leaves the soldier-guarded gate, the young Nisei is about as lonely as any human being could be; he faces even more prejudice than his father did as immigrant contract labor.

The most powerful magnets to draw him out are letters from friends who have already gone east. Those who have made the plunge usually report back to their friends enthusiastically. The people who have started a new life—most of them from eighteen to thirty years old—are the pioneers. In the factories and in the restaurants and hotels, in the offices and in the kitchens where they work, they are building a future not merely for themselves, but for those who may follow. When they write back, "We can eat in *any* restaurant in New York," they spread a little hope. Or, "I attracted very little attention on the train." Or, "In Chicago, nobody seems to care that I have a Japanese face." They tell of the church groups who are almost alone in providing some kind of organized social protection for those who relocate in cities like Chicago.

They are being sent "outside" wherever a not-too-prejudiced community provides opportunity. Seven WRA regional officers have staffs scouting for job prospects, talking to employers of farm and industrial labor, sounding out public opinion, and, in general, smoothing the way. Illinois has taken more relocated American Japanese than any other state—4,000. Most of these have found jobs in and around Chicago. Winnetka housewives compete for Nisei servants, and even the Chicago *Tribune* has been calm. Only Hearst howls.

Ohio's industrial cities have taken about 1,500 from the relocation centers. Although special clearances have been needed for the eastern defense area, a few hundred have already gone to New York City, and the stream to the northeastern states will increase steadily. Scattered throughout midwestern states like Wisconsin, Montana, and Iowa are hundreds more.

There are, of course, areas of resistance. Antagonism to WRA's *évacués* is apt to increase not diminish when the European war ends and the casualty lists come only from the Pacific. Utah has taken about 2,000 *évacués*—mostly in Ogden and Salt Lake City where at first they were quietly absorbed. But last month the state A.F. of L. petitioned Salt Lake City authorities to deny business licenses to people of Japanese ancestry. Two thousand have gone to Colorado, but recent campaigns like Hearst's in the Denver *Post* and proposed new discriminatory legislation keep the state aroused. Wayne W. Hill, a state representative in Colorado, wearing the uniform of a sergeant in the U.S. Army, got emergency leave from his camp last month to beg the Colorado Legislature not to pass a bill barring Japanese aliens from owning land. About to be discharged from the Army, he said, "I am just as willing to die a political death as I am to die in battle to preserve American freedom." He was warmly applauded, but the House passed the bill; the Senate turned it down fifteen to twelve.

Arizona has had such a spree of race hating in the last year that WRA does not try to place people of Japanese ancestry there. A year ago the governor signed a bill making it impossible to sell anything—even a pack of cigarettes—to a person of Japanese descent without first publishing in the newspaper, days in advance, one's intention to do so, and filing documents with the governor. The law was declared unconstitutional after a few months' operation. It was not aimed merely at the new WRA settlers who number fifty-seven. It was intended to strangle Arizona's prewar Japanese-American population (632), many of whom make a good living in the highly competitive business of vegetable farming.

With only 17,000 young, unencumbered, and fairly bold Nisei out on their own, the biggest and hardest job of re-settlement remains. The supply of young people without dependents is not unlimited. Early this year the Army, which had previously accepted only volunteers,* decided to draft the Nisei, like Negroes, for segregated units. This new turn of events will draw off a few thousand *évacués*. But the most difficult problems are obviously the large families and the older people. Depending heavily on the well-known tightness of the family unit of its *évacués*, WRA believes that many of the young men and women already relocated will soon bring their parents and small sisters and brothers out. Perhaps these Nisei who are so aggressively American themselves will not want their families held behind the fences.

However, in WRA centers there are hundreds of families with several young children, none old enough to leave alone. He is a courageous father who dares to start a new life with these responsibilities when, at the center, food, shelter, edu-cation, medical care, $16 a month, and clothing are provided. Farm families are often afraid to go to the Midwest to try a totally new kind of agriculture. And many feel that they are too old to start again as day laborers. There are the men who had retail, export, import, wholesale, commission businesses. The concentrated little Tokyos in California made possible a whole commercial structure in which the Japanese provided goods and services for each other. Presumably there will be no more little Tokyos to serve.

Even if the *évacués* were allowed back on the Pacific Coast tomorrow, they could not readily establish themselves in the old pattern. Quite apart from race prejudice, the gap they left has closed in two years. Except for the few who own land, they would have to build in California as patiently as they

---

*No less than 1,200 Nisei have already volunteered from behind the wire fences of the centers. Including Hawaiian Nisei, the total in the armed forces in January was close to 10,000. Some are doing intelligence work in the South Pacific. An all-Japanese-American battalion did distinguished service in Italy, with heavy losses.

now do in the East. They have been more thoroughly dislocated than they realize as they think nostalgically about California.

No one can gauge how soon the prewar unwillingness to accept charity or government relief deteriorates into a not-unpleasant habit of security. It is too much to expect of any people that their pride be unbreakable. Some of the old farm women who were "stoop labor" all their lives, even after their Nisei sons' landholdings or leased acres became sizable, have had the first rest in their history. Most of the old bachelors who had always been day laborers frankly enjoy the security of the centers.

If the war lasts two more years, and if WRA has succeeded in finding places for 25,000 more Japanese-Americans in the next twenty-four months (and WRA hopes to better that figure), it will be a job well done. That would leave some 45,000 in the relocation centers, as continuing public wards, not to mention over 20,000 at Tule Lake and the Department of Justice internment camps. Whatever the final residue, 25,000 or 45,000, it is certain that the "protective custody" of 1942 and 1943 cannot end otherwise than in a kind of Indian reservation, to plague the conscience of Americans for many years to come.

Meanwhile in the coming months, and perhaps years, a series of cases testing the constitutionality of evacuation and detention, even suits for recovery of property will come before the higher courts. Verdicts of "unconstitutional," or even eventual settlement of property claims cannot undo the record. It is written not only in military orders, in American Legion resolutions, Hearst headlines, and Supreme Court archives. It is written into the lives of thousands of human beings, most of them citizens of the U.S.

When future historians review the record, they may have difficulty reconciling the Army's policy in California with that pursued in Hawaii. People of Japanese blood make up more than one-third of the Hawaiian Islands' population, yet no large-scale evacuation was ordered after Pearl Harbor and Hickam Field became a shambles. Martial law was declared; certain important constitutional rights of *everyone* were suspended. The Department of Justice and the military authorities went about their business, rounded up a few thousand suspects. In Hawaii, unlike California, there was no strong political or economic pressure demanding evacuation of the Japanese-Americans. Indeed, had they been removed, the very foundation of peacetime Hawaiian life, sugar and pineapple growing, would have been wrecked. General Delos C. Emmons, who commanded the Hawaiian district in 1942, has said of the Japanese-Americans there: "They added materially to the strength of the area."

For two full years the West Coast "military necessity" order of March, 1942, has remained in force—an unprecedented *quasi*-martial law, suspending a small minority's constitutional rights of personal liberty and freedom of action. Those loyal *évacués* who can take jobs in war plants in the East have reason to ask why they are forbidden to return to California to plant cabbages. Mr. Stimson and Mr. Knox have assured the nation that the Japanese enemy is *not* coming to our shores. The Pacific Coast is now a "defense command," no longer "a theatre of operations," in the Army's own terminology. Each month the March, 1942, order seems more unreasonable.

Perhaps the Army forbids the *évacués* to return home less for military reasons than because of strong California pressures and threats. The Hearst papers on the Pacific Coast promise pogroms if any Japanese citizen or alien is permitted to come home. New groups like the Home Front Commandos of Sacramento have risen to cry: "They must stay out—or else." The Associated Farmers and the California Grange, the American Legion and the Sons and Daughters of the Golden West reiterate the theme of *or else*. Politicians listen and publicly urge that the despised minority be kept out of California for the duration.

There are Californians who care about civil liberties and human justice and see the grave danger of continued *quasi*-martial law but they have difficulty getting their side heard. The California C.I.O., the League of Women Voters, and segments of the church are all putting up a fight against continued "protective security." They work side by side with the Committee on American Principles and Fair Play, a group that includes such distinguished Californians as President Robert G. Sproul of the University of California, Ray Lyman Wilbur, and Maurice E. Harrison.

Lieutenant General John L. DeWitt, who ordered the evacuation in 1942, encouraged California's racist pressure groups when he said, "I don't care what they do with the Japs as long as they don't send them back here. A Jap is a Jap." General Delos C. Emmons, who succeeded DeWitt on the West Coast last September, says very little. He is the same General Emmons who decided *not* to order wholesale evacuation of the Japanese from Hawaii.

The longer the Army permits California and the rest of the

Pacific Coast to be closed to everyone of Japanese descent the more time is given the Hearst papers and their allies to convince Californians that they will indeed yield to lawlessness if the unwanted minority is permitted to return. By continuing to keep American citizens in "protective custody," the U.S. is holding to a policy as ominous as it is new. The American custom in the past has been to lock up the citizen who commits violence, not the victim of his threats and blows. The doctrine of "protective custody" could prove altogether too convenient a weapon in many other situations. In California, a state with a long history of race hatred and vigilanteism, antagonism is already building against the Negroes who have come in for war jobs. What is to prevent their removal to jails, to "protect them" from riots? Or Negroes in Detroit, Jews in Boston, Mexicans in Texas? The possibilities of "protective custody" are endless, as the Nazis have amply proved.

Fortune, April 1944

Working at the Navy Yard

by Susan B. Anthony II

MY FIRST NIGHT on the midnight shift at the Washington Navy Yard, I met Esther, a fellow ordnance worker, who ran the machine next to mine. Dreading the changeover from swing shift to "graveyard," I asked Esther's advice on the best hours for eating and sleeping after 8 a.m.

"When do you go to bed?" I asked.

"Bed!" exclaimed Esther, a swarthy woman of about 35. "I haven't slept in a bed for five months."

Esther, the mother of five children, then told me the seemingly unbelievable schedule she has followed for the five months she has been working on ordnance to pad her husband's daily wage of $4.83, made as a trucker on the railroad.

"I have to run out of here to catch my bus at 8:10 in the morning so I can get home right after he leaves for work," said Esther. "I see that the three older kids are dressed OK for school and have had something to eat. Then I feed the little ones. Tommy is four and Mary is almost three. I feed myself and wash the dishes, straighten up the house, wash if I have to and take the kids out with me to buy groceries. Then I give the little ones lunch and make some sandwiches for the kids that go to school.

"After lunch I try to get some sleep—not in bed though—I just sit in a big chair in the living room and prop my feet up. Have you ever tried getting to sleep and staying asleep while watching two little kids tear the house apart?"

I could only look at Esther's tired face and wonder how many more months she could continue on such a regime. Next month, Tommy will go to half-day kindergarten. There are no nursery schools in the neighborhood for Mary, however, and the only one near the navy yard has a waiting list of 40 children.

Two nights after my talk with Esther, I came in at midnight and found her the center of a buzzing, indignant group of women workers.

"Esther's house almost caught fire this morning," explained Louise excitedly. "The new ruling that we have to take our coats all the way down to the ladies' room at the far end of the shop instead of hanging them in here, made Esther lose her bus. When she got home the kids were fooling with the gas stove and a towel had already caught fire."

The master mechanic, head of the shop, had decreed that we must take a ten-minute round-trip walk to hang up our coats. This meant that women workers had to get to work ten minutes earlier and were delayed ten minutes afterwards.

"Why can't we have lockers right up here near the elevator, like most of the men?" protested one of women.

This led to a petition asking for conveniently located lockers which we planned to get all the women in the shop to sign and then present to the master mechanic. Only four of us had a chance to sign it, however, before a personnel man on his daily check-up rounds, picked it up and turned it over to the master mechanic. We four were called on the carpet.

"Your request for lockers is ridiculous and will never be granted," he said. "Don't ever let me hear another word of this."

Two of the women who had signed were immediately transferred from our room. I was threatened with disciplinary action and was asked to explain my conduct in writing. I did explain. I protested the women's lack of representation on any grievance body. For our locker gripe was the least of our grievances. Working at the navy yard is like working in a completely open shop, since women are not members of the main union at the plant—the International Association of Machinists, AFL. We therefore had no shop steward, no grievance committee, no representation on union bodies and, least of all, no benefits of equal pay, promotion policies or other standards that a union contract would ensure.

Take our wages, for example. Though research for my book* had shown stories of high pay for women workers to

---

*Out of the Kitchen—Into the War (New York: Stephen Daye, Inc.).

be an utter myth, I had no idea, until I became a war worker myself, how *low* wages actually were. When my skimpy little paycheck of $23 a week came to me, I wondered how on earth I could ever live on that in wartime Washington if I were forced to pay my own room, board, transportation, doctors' bills and other necessities out of it. Then I would look around the shop and wonder how the married women and mothers—the majority there—could support their children and parents as well as themselves on these wages.

Navy-yard women start at $4.65 a day, which, with time and one-half for the sixth day, is $29.64 a week. Deduct the 20-percent withholding tax, and you find that we luxuriate on $23 a week. The highest-paid woman on production in our shop receives $6.95 a day, a peak she has attained after two years at the yard. Men get as high as $22 a day. The same low wages for beginning women workers prevail at most of the other eight navy yards in the country. Welders, however, and others who get preëmployment training are better paid. Welders at one yard receive $1.14 an hour. The wages of mechanics-learners, which is the classification we came under at the Washington yard and in which many women start at other yards, begin at 57 or 58 cents an hour.

Not only do the women start at a low wage—they stay at it. At the Washington yard and at the other navy yards in the East and West, there are no automatic raises. Miriam, who had been in the yard for eighteen months, said to me:

"At this place, it ain't what you know—it's who you know."

Raises were accorded on some indeterminate basis. Promotions to supervisory jobs seem to be unknown not only at Washington but elsewhere in navy yards. I could discover no women foremen, no women job instructors, or "snappers"— the lowest rank in the supervisory hierarchy. Up to last fall, I had heard of only three women "snappers" working at all navy yards. Others may have been promoted since then, but the going is slow.

Equal pay and promotions for women are one of the government standards of employment supported in writing by the Navy Department and seven other federal agencies. The navy yards themselves seem to be unaware of the fact; nor do they observe other standards adhered to on paper by the Department.

A few minutes before my first lunch on the day shift, I saw a woman, crouching almost double, come over to a bucket of dirty water used for cooling tools. She glanced furtively through the glass partitions separating our room from the rest of the shop and then stooped quickly and washed her hands in the filthy water.

"We aren't allowed to go out to the ladies' room and wash our hands before lunch—so this is the only water in the room and at least I can get some of the grease off my hands before I eat. If one of the bosses catches you washing you get docked and suspended," she explained, while keeping an eye out for the bosses.

Following most of the women workers, I quickly adapted myself to eating sandwiches held between grimy hands. I also had to learn to gulp down lunch in 15 minutes. The yard gave us 20 minutes for lunch, but at least five minutes were gone by the time you had raced and waited at the understaffed canteen for cold, watery chocolate milk or cola drinks (no coffee except on the midnight shift). The government standard of 30-minute lunch periods, hot lunches and a decent place to eat them is ignored by the Washington yard, which is nearer being the rule than the exception. Four out of seven yards in the nation give workers lunch periods of less than 30 minutes—15 in one yard, 20 in two and 25 in a fourth. In the other three yards, the lunch period, which is on the workers' own time, is 30, 40 and 45 minutes, respectively. Some of these other yards have hot lunches served from mobile or stationary canteens. We had to choose between cold sandwiches bought from the yard and cold sandwiches which we brought with us.

Another standard neglected by yard officials was the 15-minute rest period, morning and afternoon, advocated for women workers. I don't think many of us at the Washington yard missed these breathing spells, however. The fact was that although the work in our room was physically hard and required standing almost eight hours at a stretch in some cases (such as mine), there was such a slowdown, stemming from the top, that no one hurried. When I first caught on to my particular job, I began working at my normal speed, which is fast. The woman next to me said to me in a blasé tone:

"Don't break your neck working so fast—no one else does and the bosses won't like you any better for it."

Later a boss actually warned me:

"Take it easy; there's no rush. If you finish that there won't be anything else for you to do for a while."

On day shift we were kept fairly busy. The swing shift, from four to midnight, was the slowest. Workers stood around obviously idle for want of work, and would look alert only when a naval officer came by. The workers accepted the slowdown along with the bosses. When I asked one man the cause of it, he replied:

"Oh, it's red tape. The stuff we need in this shop is laying around in another shop and the orders to send it over here are tied up somewhere else."

I do not know whether workers at the other navy yards need rest periods more than those at Washington. Only two out of seven yards reporting have said that their women get formal rest periods, and in one of these, rests were given in the machine shop alone. In the other, women in the sail loft were given a rest period of 10 minutes every two hours. Rest periods for women, just like convenient lunch facilities for all workers, seem to be considered luxuries by yard officials.

At the Washington yard the lack of formal rest periods could not be attributed to the rush of work. Nor could one attribute it to a shortage of workers or overvaluation of the workers' time. I had mistakenly thought before going to work at the yard that minutes were precious in production. Once on the job, personnel officers and posters proclaimed the need for punctuality and perfect attendance. I was naturally surprised to learn after one day's work that the main method of disciplining these "precious" workers was to lay them off for as much as a week at a time.

Bertha, who took two or three days without permission to be with her sailor husband who was shipping out for a long time, was laid off for an entire week as a penalty. If you were one minute late in the morning, you were made to stand idle for one hour and be docked accordingly. If you forgot to tag in upon arrival at work or at lunch time, after three offenses you were laid off for a day.

There were other penalties besides being laid off, I learned when I was on the midnight shift. I saw Miriam, who had held the day shift for months, standing at a machine one night and asked her why she had changed from day work.

"You can bet your life I didn't change because I wanted to. The boss told me today at the end of my shift that I had to come in tonight."

Miriam had just married a soldier. She had accumulated one week's annual leave so she could take her honeymoon when her husband got his furlough. Before her vacation began, however, she took a day's sick leave. When she put in a slip for her vacation, the personnel officer, who had previously promised her the week off, told her:

"You don't get that week's leave now. Taking that day off when you were sick means that you can't take the week."

Miriam decided she would go ahead and take her honeymoon as planned. The result was that her first day back on the job she was forced to work 16 hours, 8 on the day shift and 8 on midnight. She was being punished by assignment to midnight for two weeks.

"Why do you stand for it?" I asked.

"I need the money, that's why," she replied simply.

That was the attitude of most of the women whom I met at the yard. They would stand for practically anything—five months without sleeping in a bed, a solid year on the graveyard shift so as to be home with the kids during the day, the double job, indigestible lunches, long hours and no promise of a future after the war—all for miserably low wages. The longer I worked side by side with them, the more I admired their endurance—but the more I seethed to see them organized in a union that would help solve their problems. And the more I saw the necessity for really planned production, planned community service, labor-utilization inspectors, labor-management committees that function and are recognized, and a program to educate the workers about the issues of the war abroad and at home. I admired the patience of the women who stuck by their jobs, day after day, though it was obvious that their usefulness to the war effort was cut in half by the very working conditions which they endured.

The New Republic, May 1, 1944

Omaha Beach After D-Day

by Ernie Pyle

"And Yet We Got On"

NORMANDY BEACHHEAD—(by wireless)—Due to a last-minute alteration in the arrangements, I didn't arrive on the beachhead until the morning after D-day, after our first wave of assault troops had hit the shore.

By the time we got here the beaches had been taken and the fighting had moved a couple of miles inland. All that remained on the beach was some sniping and artillery fire, and the occasional startling blast of a mine geysering brown sand into the air. That plus a gigantic and pitiful litter of wreckage along miles of shoreline.

Submerged tanks and overturned boats and burned trucks and shell-shattered jeeps and sad little personal belongings were strewn all over these bitter sands. That plus the bodies of soldiers lying in rows covered with blankets, the toes of their shoes sticking up in a line as though on drill. And other bodies, uncollected, still sprawling grotesquely in the sand or half hidden by the high grass beyond the beach.

That plus an intense, grim determination of work-weary men to get this chaotic beach organized and get all the vital supplies and the reinforcements moving more rapidly over it from the stacked-up ships standing in droves out to sea.

* * *

Now that it is over it seems to me a pure miracle that we ever took the beach at all. For some of our units it was easy, but in this special sector where I am now our troops faced such odds that our getting ashore was like my whipping Joe Louis down to a pulp.

In this column I want to tell you what the opening of the second front in this one sector entailed, so that you can know and appreciate and forever be humbly grateful to those both dead and alive who did it for you.

Ashore, facing us, were more enemy troops than we had in our assault waves. The advantages were all theirs, the disadvantages all ours. The Germans were dug into positions that they had been working on for months, although these were not yet all complete. A 100-foot bluff a couple of hundred yards back from the beach had great concrete gun emplacements built right into the hilltop. These opened to the sides instead of to the front, thus making it very hard for naval fire from the sea to reach them. They could shoot parallel with the beach and cover every foot of it for miles with artillery fire.

Then they had hidden machine-gun nests on the forward slopes, with crossfire taking in every inch of the beach. These nests were connected by networks of trenches, so that the German gunners could move about without exposing themselves.

Throughout the length of the beach, running zigzag a couple of hundred yards back from the shoreline, was an immense V-shaped ditch 15 feet deep. Nothing could cross it, not even men on foot, until fills had been made. And in other places at the far end of the beach, where the ground is flatter, they had great concrete walls. These were blasted by our naval gunfire or by explosives set by hand after we got ashore.

Our only exits from the beach were several swales or valleys, each about 100 yards wide. The Germans made the most of these funnel-like traps, sowing them with buried mines. They contained, also, barbed-wire entanglements with mines attached, hidden ditches, and machine guns firing from the slopes.

This is what was on the shore. But our men had to go through a maze nearly as deadly as this before they even got ashore. Underwater obstacles were terrific. The Germans had whole fields of evil devices under the water to catch our boats. Even now, several days after the landing, we have cleared only channels through them and cannot yet approach the whole length of the beach with our ships. Even now some ship or boat hits one of these mines every day and is knocked out of commission.

The Germans had masses of those great six-pronged spiders, made of railroad iron and standing shoulder-high, just beneath the surface of the water for our landing craft to run into. They also had huge logs buried in the sand, pointing upward and outward, their tops just below the water. Attached to these logs were mines.

In addition to these obstacles they had floating mines offshore, land mines buried in the sand of the beach, and more mines in checkerboard rows in the tall grass beyond the sand. And the enemy had four men on shore for every three men we had approaching the shore.

And yet we got on.

*   *   *

Beach landings are planned to a schedule that is set far ahead of time. They all have to be timed, in order for everything to mesh and for the following waves of troops to be standing off the beach and ready to land at the right moment.

As the landings are planned, some elements of the assault force are to break through quickly, push on inland, and attack the most obvious enemy strong points. It is usually the plan for units to be inland, attacking gun positions from behind, within a matter of minutes after the first men hit the beach.

I have always been amazed at the speed called for in these plans. You'll have schedules calling for engineers to land at H-hour plus two minutes, and service troops at H-hour plus 30 minutes, and even for press censors to land at H-hour plus 75 minutes. But in the attack on this special portion of the beach where I am—the worst we had, incidentally—the schedule didn't hold.

Our men simply could not get past the beach. They were pinned down right on the water's edge by an inhuman wall of fire from the bluff. Our first waves were on that beach for hours, instead of a few minutes, before they could begin working inland.

You can still see the foxholes they dug at the very edge of the water, in the sand and the small, jumbled rocks that form parts of the beach.

Medical corpsmen attended the wounded as best they could. Men were killed as they stepped out of landing craft. An officer whom I knew got a bullet through the head just as the door of his landing craft was let down. Some men were drowned.

The first crack in the beach defenses was finally accomplished by terrific and wonderful naval gunfire, which knocked out the big emplacements. They tell epic stories of destroyers that ran right up into shallow water and had it out point-blank with the big guns in those concrete emplacements ashore.

When the heavy fire stopped, our men were organized by their officers and pushed on inland, circling machine-gun nests and taking them from the rear.

As one officer said, the only way to take a beach is to face it and keep going. It is costly at first, but it's the only way. If the men are pinned down on the beach, dug in and out of action, they might as well not be there at all. They hold up the waves behind them, and nothing is being gained.

Our men were pinned down for a while, but finally they stood up and went through, and so we took that beach and accomplished our landing. We did it with every advantage on the enemy's side and every disadvantage on ours. In the light of a couple of days of retrospection, we sit and talk and call it a miracle that our men ever got on at all or were able to stay on.

Before long it will be permitted to name the units that did it. Then you will know to whom this glory should go. They suffered casualties. And yet if you take the entire beachhead assault, including other units that had a much easier time, our total casualties in driving this wedge into the continent of Europe were remarkably low—only a fraction, in fact, of what our commanders had been prepared to accept.

And these units that were so battered and went through such hell are still, right at this moment, pushing on inland without rest, their spirits high, their egotism in victory almost reaching the smart-alecky stage.

Their tails are up. "We've done it again," they say. They figure that the rest of the army isn't needed at all. Which proves that, while their judgment in this regard is bad, they certainly have the spirit that wins battles and eventually wars.

Scripps-Howard wire copy, June 12, 1944

"The Wreckage Was Vast and Startling"

NORMANDY BEACHHEAD, D Day Plus Two—(by wireless, delayed)—I took a walk along the historic coast of Normandy in the country of France.

It was a lovely day for strolling along the seashore. Men were sleeping on the sand, some of them sleeping forever. Men were floating in the water, but they didn't know they were in the water, for they were dead.

The water was full of squishy little jellyfish about the size of your hand. Millions of them. In the center each of them had a green design exactly like a four-leaf clover. The good-luck emblem. Sure. Hell yes.

I walked for a mile and a half along the water's edge of our many-miled invasion beach. You wanted to walk slowly, for the detail on that beach was infinite.

The wreckage was vast and startling. The awful waste and destruction of war, even aside from the loss of human life, has always been one of its outstanding features to those who are in it. Anything and everything is expendable. And we did expend on our beachhead in Normandy during those first few hours.

*   *   *

For a mile out from the beach there were scores of tanks and trucks and boats that you could no longer see, for they were at the bottom of the water—swamped by overloading, or hit by shells, or sunk by mines. Most of their crews were lost.

You could see trucks tipped half over and swamped. You could see partly sunken barges, and the angled-up corners of jeeps, and small landing craft half submerged. And at low tide you could still see those vicious six-pronged iron snares that helped snag and wreck them.

On the beach itself, high and dry, were all kinds of wrecked vehicles. There were tanks that had only just made the beach before being knocked out. There were jeeps that had burned to a dull gray. There were big derricks on caterpillar treads that didn't quite make it. There were half-tracks carrying office equipment that had been made into a shambles by a single shell hit, their interiors still holding their useless equipage of smashed typewriters, telephones, office files.

There were LCT's turned completely upside down, and lying on their backs, and how they got that way I don't know.

There were boats stacked on top of each other, their sides caved in, their suspension doors knocked off.

In this shoreline museum of carnage there were abandoned rolls of barbed wire and smashed bulldozers and big stacks of thrown-away lifebelts and piles of shells still waiting to be moved.

In the water floated empty life rafts and soldiers' packs and ration boxes, and mysterious oranges.

On the beach lay snarled rolls of telephone wire and big rolls of steel matting and stacks of broken, rusting rifles.

On the beach lay, expended, sufficient men and mechanism for a small war. They were gone forever now. And yet we could afford it.

We could afford it because we were on, we had our toe-hold, and behind us there were such enormous replacements for this wreckage on the beach that you could hardly conceive of their sum total. Men and equipment were flowing from England in such a gigantic stream that it made the waste on the beachhead seem like nothing at all, really nothing at all.

*   *   *

A few hundred yards back on the beach is a high bluff. Up there we had a tent hospital, and a barbed-wire enclosure for prisoners of war. From up there you could see far up and down the beach, in a spectacular crow's-nest view, and far out to sea.

And standing out there on the water beyond all this wreckage was the greatest armada man has ever seen. You simply could not believe the gigantic collection of ships that lay out there waiting to unload.

Looking from the bluff, it lay thick and clear to the far horizon of the sea and on beyond, and it spread out to the sides and was miles wide. Its utter enormity would move the hardest man.

As I stood up there I noticed a group of freshly taken German prisoners standing nearby. They had not yet been put in the prison cage. They were just standing there, a couple of doughboys leisurely guarding them with Tommy guns.

The prisoners too were looking out to sea—the same bit of sea that for months and years had been so safely empty before their gaze. Now they stood staring almost as if in a trance.

They didn't say a word to each other. They didn't need to. The expression on their faces was something forever unforgettable. In it was the final horrified acceptance of their doom.

If only all Germany could have had the rich experience of standing on the bluff and looking out across the water and seeing what their compatriots saw.

Scripps-Howard wire copy, June 16, 1944

"This Long Thin Line of Personal Anguish"

NORMANDY BEACHHEAD—(by wireless)—In the preceding column we told about the D-Day wreckage among our machines of war that were expended in taking one of the Normandy beaches.

But there is another and more human litter. It extends in a thin little line, just like a high-water mark, for miles along the beach. This is the strewn personal gear, gear that will never be needed again, of those who fought and died to give us our entrance into Europe.

Here in a jumbled row for mile on mile are soldiers' packs. Here are socks and shoe polish, sewing kits, diaries, Bibles and hand grenades. Here are the latest letters from home, with the address on each one neatly razored out—one of the security precautions enforced before the boys embarked.

Here are toothbrushes and razors, and snapshots of families back home staring up at you from the sand. Here are pocketbooks, metal mirrors, extra trousers, and bloody, abandoned shoes. Here are broken-handled shovels, and portable radios smashed almost beyond recognition, and mine detectors twisted and ruined.

Here are torn pistol belts and canvas water buckets, first-aid kits and jumbled heaps of lifebelts. I picked up a pocket Bible with a soldier's name in it, and put it in my jacket. I carried it half a mile or so and then put it back down on the beach. I don't know why I picked it up, or why I put it back down.

Soldiers carry strange things ashore with them. In every invasion you'll find at least one soldier hitting the beach at H-Hour with a banjo slung over his shoulder. The most ironic piece of equipment marking our beach—this beach of first despair, then victory—is a tennis racket that some soldier had brought along. It lies lonesomely on the sand, clamped in its rack, not a string broken.

Two of the most dominant items in the beach refuse are cigarets and writing paper. Each soldier was issued a carton of cigarets just before he started. Today these cartons by the thousand, watersoaked and spilled out, mark the line of our first savage blow.

Writing paper and air-mail envelopes come second. The boys had intended to do a lot of writing in France. Letters that would have filled those blank, abandoned pages.

Always there are dogs in every invasion. There is a dog still on the beach today, still pitifully looking for his masters.

He stays at the water's edge, near a boat that lies twisted and half sunk at the waterline. He barks appealingly to every soldier who approaches, trots eagerly along with him for a few feet, and then, sensing himself unwanted in all this haste, runs back to wait in vain for his own people at his own empty boat.

*   *   *

Over and around this long thin line of personal anguish, fresh men today are rushing vast supplies to keep our armies pushing on into France. Other squads of men pick amidst the wreckage to salvage ammunition and equipment that are still usable.

Men worked and slept on the beach for days before the last D-Day victim was taken away for burial.

I stepped over the form of one youngster whom I thought dead. But when I looked down I saw he was only sleeping. He was very young, and very tired. He lay on one elbow, his hand suspended in the air about six inches from the ground. And in the palm of his hand he held a large, smooth rock.

I stood and looked at him a long time. He seemed in his sleep to hold that rock lovingly, as though it were his last link with a vanishing world. I have no idea at all why he went to sleep with the rock in his hand, or what kept him from dropping it once he was asleep. It was just one of those little things without explanation, that a person remembers for a long time.

*   *   *

The strong, swirling tides of the Normandy coastline shift the contours of the sandy beach as they move in and out. They carry soldiers' bodies out to sea, and later they return them. They cover the corpses of heroes with sand, and then in their whims they uncover them.

As I plowed out over the wet sand of the beach on that first day ashore, I walked around what seemed to be a couple of pieces of driftwood sticking out of the sand. But they weren't driftwood.

They were a soldier's two feet. He was completely covered by the shifting sands except for his feet. The toes of his G.I. shoes pointed toward the land he had come so far to see, and which he saw so briefly.

Scripps-Howard wire copy, June 17, 1944

Battle and Breakout in Normandy

by Ernie Pyle

"A Ghastly Relentlessness"

IN NORMANDY—(by wireless)—Our frontlines were marked by long strips of colored cloth laid on the ground, and with colored smoke to guide our airmen during the mass bombing that preceded our break-out from the German ring that held us to the Normandy beachhead.

Dive bombers hit it just right. We stood in the barnyard of a French farm and watched them barrel nearly straight down out of the sky. They were bombing about half a mile ahead of where we stood.

They came in groups, diving from every direction, perfectly timed, one right after another. Everywhere you looked separate groups of planes were on the way down, or on the way back up, or slanting over for a dive, or circling, circling, circling over our heads, waiting for their turn.

The air was full of sharp and distinct sounds of cracking bombs and the heavy rips of the planes' machine guns and the splitting screams of diving wings. It was all fast and furious, but yet distinct, as in a musical show in which you could distinguish throaty tunes and words.

*   *   *

And then a new sound gradually droned into our ears, a sound deep and all encompassing with no notes in it—just a gigantic faraway surge of doom-like sound. It was the heavies. They came from directly behind us. At first they were the merest dots in the sky. You could see clots of them against the far heavens, too tiny to count individually. They came on with a terrible slowness.

They came in flights of 12, three flights to a group and in

461

groups stretched out across the sky. They came in "families" of about 70 planes each.

Maybe these gigantic waves were two miles apart, maybe they were 10 miles, I don't know. But I do know they came in a constant procession and I thought it would never end. What the Germans must have thought is beyond comprehension.

Their march across the sky was slow and studied. I've never known a storm, or a machine, or any resolve of man that had about it the aura of such a ghastly relentlessness. You had the feeling that even had God appeared beseechingly before them in the sky with palms outward to persuade them back they would not have had within them the power to turn from their irresistible course.

I stood with a little group of men, ranging from colonels to privates, back of the stone farmhouse. Slit trenches were all around the edges of the farmyard and a dugout with a tin roof was nearby. But we were so fascinated by the spectacle overhead that it never occurred to us that we might need the foxholes.

The first huge flight passed directly over our farmyard and others followed. We spread our feet and leaned far back trying to look straight up, until our steel helmets fell off. We'd cup our fingers around our eyes like field glasses for a clearer view.

And then the bombs came. They began ahead of us as the crackle of popcorn and almost instantly swelled into a monstrous fury of noise that seemed surely to destroy all the world ahead of us.

From then on for an hour and a half that had in it the agonies of centuries, the bombs came down. A wall of smoke and dust erected by them grew high in the sky. It filtered along the ground back through our own orchards. It sifted around us and into our noses. The bright day grew slowly dark from it.

By now everything was an indescribable cauldron of sounds. Individual noises did not exist. The thundering of the motors in the sky and the roar of bombs ahead filled all the space for noise on earth. Our own heavy artillery was crashing all around us, yet we could hardly hear it.

*   *   *

The Germans began to shoot heavy, high ack-ack. Great black puffs of it by the score speckled the sky until it was hard to distinguish smoke puffs from planes.

And then someone shouted that one of the planes was smoking. Yes, we could all see it. A long faint line of black smoke stretched straight for a mile behind one of them.

And as we watched there was a gigantic sweep of flame over the plane. From nose to tail it disappeared in flame, and it slanted slowly down and banked around the sky in great wide curves, this way and that way, as rhythmically and gracefully as in a slow motion waltz.

Then suddenly it seemed to change its mind and it swept upward, steeper and steeper and ever slower until finally it seemed poised motionless on its own black pillar of smoke. And then just as slowly it turned over and dived for the earth—a golden spearhead on the straight black shaft of its own creation—and it disappeared behind the treetops.

But before it was done there were more cries of, "There's another one smoking and there's a third one now."

Chutes came out of some of the planes. Out of some came no chutes at all. One of white silk caught on the tail of a plane. Men with binoculars could see him fighting to get loose until flames swept over him, and then a tiny black dot fell through space, all alone.

And all that time the great flat ceiling of the sky was roofed by all the others that didn't go down, plowing their way forward as if there were no turmoil in the world.

Nothing deviated them by the slightest. They stalked on, slowly and with a dreadful pall of sound, as though they were seeing only something at a great distance and nothing existed in between. God, how you admired those men up there and sickened for the ones who fell.

Scripps-Howard wire copy, August 8, 1944

"The Universe Became Filled with a Gigantic Rattling"

IN NORMANDY—(by wireless)—It is possible to become so enthralled by some of the spectacles of war that you are momentarily captivated away from your own danger.

That's what happened to our little group of soldiers as we stood in a French farmyard, watching the mighty bombing of the German lines just before our break-through.

But that benign state didn't last long. As we watched, there crept into our consciousness a realization that windrows of exploding bombs were easing back toward us, flight by flight, instead of gradually forward, as the plan called for.

Then we were horrified by the suspicion that those machines, high in the sky and completely detached from us, were aiming their bombs at the smokeline on the ground—and a gentle breeze was drifting the smokeline back over us!

An indescribable kind of panic comes over you at such times. We stood tensed in muscle and frozen in intellect, watching each flight approach and pass over us, feeling trapped and completely helpless.

And then all of an instant the universe became filled with a gigantic rattling as of huge, dry seeds in a mammoth dry gourd. I doubt that any of us had ever heard that sound before, but instinct told us what it was. It was bombs by the hundred, hurtling down through the air above us.

Many times I've heard bombs whistle or swish or rustle, but never before had I heard bombs rattle. I still don't know the explanation of it. But it is an awful sound.

We dived. Some got in a dugout. Others made foxholes and ditches and some got behind a garden wall—although which side would be "behind" was anybody's guess.

*   *   *

I was too late for the dugout. The nearest place was a wagon-shed which formed one end of the stone house. The rattle was right down upon us. I remember hitting the ground flat, all spread out like the cartoons of people flattened by steam rollers, and then squirming like an eel to get under one of the heavy wagons in the shed.

An officer whom I didn't know was wriggling beside me. We stopped at the same time, simultaneously feeling it was hopeless to move farther. The bombs were already crashing around us.

We lay with our heads slightly up—like two snakes—staring at each other. I know it was in both our minds and in our eyes, asking each other what to do. Neither of us knew.

We said nothing. We just lay sprawled, gaping at each other in a futile appeal, our faces about a foot apart, until it was over.

There is no description of the sound and fury of those bombs except to say it was chaos, and a waiting for darkness. The feeling of the blast was sensational. The air struck you in hundreds of continuing flutters. Your ears drummed and rang. You could feel quick little waves of concussions on your chest and in your eyes.

At last the sound died down and we looked at each other in disbelief. Gradually we left the foxholes and sprawling places, and came out to see what the sky had in store for us. As far as we could see other waves were approaching from behind.

When a wave would pass a little to the side of us we were garrulously grateful, for most of them flew directly overhead. Time and again the rattle came down over us. Bombs struck in the orchard to our left. They struck in orchards ahead of us. They struck as far as half a mile behind us. Everything about us was shaken, but our group came through unhurt.

*   *   *

I can't record what any of us actually felt or thought during those horrible climaxes. I believe a person's feelings at such times are kaleidoscopic and uncatalogable. You just wait, that's all. You do remember an inhuman tenseness of muscle and nerves.

An hour or so later I began to get sore all over, and by mid-afternoon my back and shoulders ached as though I'd been beaten with a club. It was simply the result of muscles tensing themselves too tight for too long against anticipated shock. And I remember worrying about War Correspondent Ken Crawford, a friend from back in the old Washington days, who I knew was several hundred yards ahead of me.

As far as I knew, he and I were the only two correspondents with the Fourth Division. I didn't know who might be with the divisions on either side—which also were being hit, as we could see.

Three days later, back at camp, I learned that AP Photographer Bede Irvin had been killed in the bombing and that Ken was safe.

We came out of our ignominious sprawling and stood up

again to watch. We could sense that by now the error had been caught and checked. The bombs again were falling where they were intended, a mile or so ahead.

Even at a mile away a thousand bombs hitting within a few seconds can shake the earth and shatter the air where you are standing. There was still a dread in our hearts, but it gradually eased as the tumult and destruction moved slowly forward.

Scripps-Howard wire copy, August 9, 1944

"Anybody Makes Mistakes"

IN NORMANDY—(by wireless)—With our own personal danger past, our historic air bombardment of the German lines holding us in the Normandy beachhead again became a captivating spectacle to watch.

By now it was definite that the great waves of four-motored planes were dropping their deadly loads exactly in the right place.

And by now two Mustang fighters, flying like a pair of doves, patrolled back and forth, back and forth, just in front of each oncoming wave of bombers, as if to shout to them by their mere presence that here was not the place to drop— wait a few seconds, wait a few more seconds.

And then we could see a flare come out of the belly of one plane in each flight, just after they had passed over our heads.

The flare shot forward, leaving smoke behind it in a vivid line, and then began a graceful, downward curve that was one of the most beautiful things I've ever seen.

It was like an invisible crayon drawing a rapid line across the canvas of the sky, saying in a gesture for all to see: "Here! Here is where to drop. Follow me."

And each succeeding flight of oncoming bombers obeyed, and in turn dropped its own hurtling marker across the illimitable heaven to guide those behind.

Long before now the German ack-ack guns had gone out of existence. We had counted three of our big planes down in spectacular flames, and I believe that was all. The German ack-ack gunners either took to their holes or were annihilated.

How many waves of heavy bombers we put over I have no

idea. I had counted well beyond 400 planes when my personal distraction obliterated any capacity or desire to count.

I only know that 400 was just the beginning. There
were supposed to be 1800 planes that day, and I believe it
was announced later that there were more than 3000.

It seemed incredible to me that any German could come
out of that bombardment with his sanity. When it was over
even I was grateful in a chastened way I had never experienced before, for just being alive.

*　　*　　*

I thought an attack by our troops was impossible now, for
it is an unnerving thing to be bombed by your own planes.

During the bad part a colonel I had known a long time was
walking up and down behind the farmhouse, snapping his fingers and saying over and over to himself, "goddamit, goddamit!"

As he passed me once he stopped and stared and said,
"goddamit!"

And I said, "There can't be any attack now, can there?"
And he said "No," and began walking again, snapping his
fingers and tossing his arm as though he was throwing rocks
at the ground.

The leading company of our battalion was to spearhead the
attack 40 minutes after our heavy bombing ceased. The company had been hit directly by our bombs. Their casualties,
including casualties in shock, were heavy. Men went to pieces
and had to be sent back. The company was shattered and
shaken.

And yet Company B attacked—and on time, to the
minute! They attacked, and within an hour they sent word
back that they had advanced 800 yards through German territory and were still going. Around our farmyard men with
stars on their shoulders almost wept when the word came
over the portable radio. The American soldier can be majestic
when he needs to be.

*　　*　　*

There is one more thing I want to say before we follow the
ground troops on deeper into France in the great push you've
been reading about now for days.

I'm sure that back in England that night other men—

bomber crews—almost wept, and maybe they did really, in the awful knowledge that they had killed our own American troops. But I want to say this to them. The chaos and the bitterness there in the orchards and between the hedgerows that afternoon have passed. After the bitterness came the sober remembrance that the Air Corps is the strong right arm in front of us. Not only at the beginning, but ceaselessly and everlastingly, every moment of the faintest daylight, the Air Corps is up there banging away ahead of us.

Anybody makes mistakes. The enemy makes them just the same as we do. The smoke and confusion of battle bewilder us all on the ground as well as in the air. And in this case the percentage of error was really very small compared with the colossal storm of bombs that fell upon the enemy.

The Air Corps has been wonderful throughout this invasion, and the men on the ground appreciate it.

Scripps-Howard wire copy, August 10, 1944

"This Weird Hedgerow Fighting"

ON THE WESTERN FRONT—(by wireless)—I know that all of us correspondents have tried time and again to describe to you what this weird hedgerow fighting in northwestern France has been like.

But I'm going to go over it once more, for we've been in it two months and some of us feel that this is the two months that broke the German Army in the west.

This type of fighting is always in small groups, so let's take as an example one company of men. Let's say they are working forward on both sides of a country lane, and this company is responsible for clearing the two fields on either side of the road as it advances.

That means you have only about one platoon to a field. And with the company's understrength from casualties, you might have no more than 25 or 30 men in a field.

Over here the fields are usually not more than 50 yards across and a couple of hundred yards long. They may have grain in them, or apple trees, but mostly they are just pastures of green grass, full of beautiful cows.

The fields are surrounded on all sides by immense hedgerows which consist of an ancient earthen bank, waist high, all matted with roots, and out of which grow weeds, bushes, and trees up to 20 feet high.

The Germans have used these barriers well. They put snipers in the trees. They dig deep trenches behind the hedgerows and cover them with timber, so that it is almost impossible for artillery to get at them.

Sometimes they will prop up machine guns with strings attached, so they can fire over the hedge without getting out of their holes. They even cut out a section of the hedgerow and hide a big gun or a tank in it, covering it with brush.

Also they tunnel under the hedgerows from the back and make the opening on the forward side just large enough to stick a machine gun through.

But mostly the hedgerow pattern is this: a heavy machine gun hidden at each end of the field and infantrymen hidden all along the hedgerow with rifles and machine pistols.

*   *   *

Now it's up to us to dig them out of there. It's a slow and cautious business, and there is nothing very dashing about it. Our men don't go across the open fields in dramatic charges such as you see in the movies. They did at first, but they learned better.

They go in tiny groups, a squad or less, moving yards apart and sticking close to the hedgerows on either end of the field. They creep a few yards, squat, wait, then creep again.

If you could be right up there between the Germans and the Americans you wouldn't see very many men at any one time—just a few here and there, always trying to keep hidden. But you would hear an awful lot of noise.

Our men were taught in training not to fire until they saw something to fire at. But that hasn't worked in this country, because you see so little. So the alternative is to keep shooting constantly at the hedgerows. That pins the Germans in their holes while we sneak up on them.

The attacking squads sneak up the sides of the hedgerows while the rest of the platoon stay back in their own hedgerow and keep the forward hedge saturated with bullets. They shoot rifle grenades too, and a mortar squad a little farther back keeps lobbing mortar shells over onto the Germans.

The little advance groups get up to the far ends of the hedgerows at the corners of the field. They first try to knock out the machine guns at each corner. They do this with hand grenades, rifle grenades and machine guns.

*　　*　　*

Usually, when the pressure gets on, the German defenders of the hedgerow start pulling back. They'll take their heavier guns and most of the men back a couple of fields and start digging in for a new line.

They leave about two machine guns and a few riflemen scattered through the hedge, to do a lot of shooting and hold up the Americans as long as they can.

Our men now sneak along the front side of the hedgerow, throwing grenades over onto the other side and spraying the hedges with their guns. The fighting is very close—only a few yards apart—but it is seldom actual hand-to-hand stuff.

Sometimes the remaining Germans come out of their holes with their hands up. Sometimes they try to run for it and are mowed down. Sometimes they won't come out at all, and a hand grenade, thrown into their hole, finishes them off.

And so we've taken another hedgerow and are ready to start on the one beyond.

This hedgerow business is a series of little skirmishes like that clear across the front, thousands and thousands of little skirmishes. No single one of them is very big. But add them all up over the days and weeks and you've got a man-sized war, with thousands on both sides being killed.

Scripps-Howard wire copy, August 11, 1944

The Siege of St. Malo

by Lee Miller

I THUMBED a ride on an L.S.T. to the Siege of St. Malo. I had brought my bed, I begged my board, and I was given a grandstand view of fortress warfare reminiscent of Crusader times. I arrived the 13th of August, and there were still armed marauders being dug out of cellars and cleared out of backyards in the mainland towns . . . snipers who lay in wait for the Brass or the unwitnessed or unwary . . . hoping to rejoin a fighting unit some place else, and not knowing how far behind the real line they were.

So the war wasn't over in this section, and the soldiers who were fighting assault battles, the artillery who were in their turn spotted and shelled by Hun counter-battery, the combat M.P.s who scraped the town for hidden enemies, the Civil Affairs team who aided bewildered civilians and kept them out of the hair of the Army, in fact, all of the Division wondered what they'd tell their grandchildren they'd done in the great war, since it was "all over" where they were still fighting on for weeks . . . bloody, heroic, tricky battles. . . . [*Censors just released that it was the 83rd Division, 329th Regiment at St. Malo.*]

The Germans called a truce from the Château in Old St. Malo, and asked that they be allowed to send out all the French people who were sheltering in the burning town. They chose the hour before darkness, typically, and the Civil Affairs sent scouts around quickly to organize hospitalization and food, to find local patriots who would recognize any conspirators or phonies in the lot . . . the *gendarmerie* to control the line. The military sent their counter-intelligence men, and ambulances were provided. From past experience with the Huns, we didn't dare risk sending trucks down to the causeway to meet the refugees, as it might have been a bait to get

471

all our transport concentrated. The shooting suddenly stopped again, and a long stream of people came out into view and passed down the causeway . . . the injured and ill first . . . then old women, with bundles and dazed eyes, little hand-holding groups of girls, stumbling along . . . couples with babies, prams piled with all they had saved of their possessions . . . boys, men shambling from shock . . . prim women, and nuns in immaculate white, and whores. A few were hoisted out of line by the police for their crimes, and a few trustworthy others kept at the bridgehead to help identify any possibly escaping Germans.

There were farewell scenes as the injured were separated and taken off in ambulances . . . and the mass moved on. There were twice the 600 the Germans had announced were on the way. There was no way to control them if they dropped off and went to their own houses, or scattered or got lost, but nearly all wanted the food stocks being given out at the school, and hoped for transport further behind the battle. There was some frigid division among the people, but no haircutting . . . all these people had shared the hardship of battle and were friends again. For the moment.

A couple of counter-intelligence characters came to the Civil Affairs villa, to pick up the prison warden who was there. They wanted to interview a woman they had (on the advice of the *Résistance* people) put in jail the night before. The counter-intelligence deals only with those who are dangerous to the military situation. All other collaborators and such are turned over to the civilian authorities. The jail had a big hole through it, but wasn't blasted at all. The woman and her three children were brought in to the warden's office and her own portfolio of papers put on the desk. Two of the little girls were dressed in blue velvet coats with white bunny collars, and the third was a toddler. The papers contained receipts for salary from the German labour "Todt" organization where she had had a secretarial position. Identity cards and ration books in order . . . and letters signed Heil Hitler, all swastika-ed. There were also some pornographic photographs, which for some strange reason she clung to. When any difficult question came along, she bent over the small child in her lap in madonna-like poses. The CIC man spoke to her in much more halting French than I knew he knew, and with a Bing Crosby voice. It was like snake and bird hypnosis. She claimed that she had never turned in military information to the enemy, and that if her husband or nephew, the authors of the Nazi-minded letters had, she didn't know it, and anyway they had gone away she knew not where.

We parked her back in her cell. She made a pretty pose with her children when I wanted to photograph her. The kids ate some coloured Life-Savers without tasting them, their big, sullen eyes glued to me. They were neither timid nor tough, but gloomy, and I felt like vomiting.

We dodged up to Parame, and found the house where she had lived. It was an ugly cobblestone and brick villa, with a detached shed-garage. We forced the shutters and climbed into a disorderly, slovenly room. Everything in it was sluttish . . . children's clothes and Nazi propaganda were strewn around together . . . unwashed dishes . . . laundry . . . sewing and pornography . . . empty booze bottles and suitcases. In the bathroom, the tub was full of water like all the houses in town, as the water plant had been turned off for a long time. The cupboard was full of men's clothes with the maker's address, "Kiel" inside.

Some young, attractive girls from down the street came in and levelled more accusations at the woman; said that a few nights before, two German officers had come in with suitcases and left in civilian clothes. Also that they had heard that the woman's husband, a Frenchman who organized labour for the Germans, was supposed to be in Rennes and was coming back to fetch her that night. In the garage were the Germans' clothes, also heaps of propaganda material, et cetera. That really clinched the job. It was only a question of picking up the husband. The two girls, by the way, had had a tough time. They were charming and intelligent, if venomous toward their neighbour. Both were students preparing for college, and one has spent 16 months in a concentration camp, accused, rightly, of sheltering and aiding de Gaullists. The other, who was younger, had just done four months for wearing the Cross of Lorraine under her lapel.

*   *   *

Photo by Lee Miller/© Lee Miller Archives

Interrogation of a Frenchwoman who has had her hair shaved for consorting with Germans. Note her earrings.

In the meantime, old St. Malo was busy organizing a surrender. I wasn't allowed to go, as the quai was still under close machine-gun fire, so I called in at the command post of the regiment to see what was cooking there. They seemed to have plenty on their minds, and Major Speedie, the battalion commander, took me on a tour of observation posts which he was setting up for an assault next day on the "Fort de la Cité," the famous Citadel, located on a promontory off St. Servan, and guarding the mouth of the Rance and the Port of St. Malo.

Since 1940 the Germans had been arming the Fort with pillboxes and secret weapons, digging galleries fifty feet into solid granite, building ventilation systems, food stores and 'phone connections to the other fortresses of Cap Frehel, Cézambre, and Grand Bey. When the land fighting of the mainland had driven the Germans to the water's edge, and to surrender, the "Mad Colonel," von Aulock, left his celebrated mistress behind, and decided to make a name for himself by holding out the impregnable "Cité." He had been military governor of the whole area and our people had a wholesome respect for him in a soldier's way. His mistress, a German beauty known for her past with certain Russian royalty, was registered as his secretary interpreter, and was well known by the people of St. Malo and St. Servan, who admire some of the things she did for them on the side, with humanity and discretion . . . for whatever reason she may have had.

The Colonel had now announced that he was going to hold out to the last man. Thus he put the seal of doom on the towns of St. Malo and St. Servan.

Some combat MPs told me of the exploits of various officers of the regiment whom I'd met that day. Captain David Gray, of Topeka, Kansas, had manoeuvred several risky exchanges of prisoner-wounded with Herr Doktor Weller, the interpreter medico of the Fortress. They were always putting up white flags, once to ask for medical supplies in exchange for our wounded prisoners from an unsuccessful night assault on the Fortress. Some of them were recognized truces by both sides, others were risky deals. Walking across the *digue* to meet Weller halfway, with machine-gun fire going on from both sides . . . bargaining for our wounded, shrewdly and fairly . . . taking out Germans and Americans, also two women who had served various purposes in the Fortress.

One of his walks "into the jaws" was to insist on getting a wounded American who had been refused a time before, as too ill to travel. Weller showed the medical chart of his leg amputation, and the Hun marine doctor asked for the return of a captive surgeon we had. It was arranged that a report on the situation should be made under white flag next day at two o'clock, if we recognized their signal. However, Colonel Craibill decided that there should be "no more white flags except for surrender," and enough of this nonsense. Dr. Weller came down, however, on his own, without protection, and was met by Gray and Colonel Craibill who explained that he would not call off the planned aerial bombardment scheduled for one hour from then for just one man, but only for the whole garrison.

There was heavy fire again as the white flag was hauled down on the Fort, Colonel von Aulock having refused the terms. Dr. Gray walked up to the pillbox again to ask for his patient. The Colonel sent word to him that all negotiations were over and "thanks for the fair fighting." There were stories about Captain Boyd, who stamped up to a pillbox with a white flag unrecognized, to see if they'd changed their minds . . . and was waved back by a hand reaching out of the gunhole.

Major Speedie, Gray, and a volunteer named Rifferetti made a reconnaissance with their flag once to see if anyone was left . . . there was. It was confusing enough to catch up with the different exploits without being told that the MP who had been telling me was also guilty of having gone up bare-handed to meet a German white flag, to which we had refused recognition, on the excuse that a combat MP's duties include taking charge of prisoners, and there might have been some. He was an enormous and extraordinary character, and I'm glad he liked me. I take back everything that's been said about MPs . . . they are wonderful.

The next morning I hung around hoping to get into St. Malo proper, and ate breakfast with the MPs who managed everything, including hot water which they boiled in the basement. Fires, like lights and outdoor cigarettes, were strictly forbidden as attracting snipers and enemy OPs, although casual French civilians lit everything, and since the refugees had come back there had been a lot of trouble with shooting at lights, and even some signalling to enemy posts, as well as a few cases of arson. Houses had been fired with German incendiary gadgets within two hours after the refugee truce. Undoubtedly the Huns had sent out saboteurs and soldiers in disguise along with the French, and had confused us also in our inspection by sending more than a thousand people instead of the announced 600.

A company of soldiers was filing out of St. Malo, ready to go into action, grenades hanging on their lapels like Cartier clips, menacing bunches of death. Everybody was leaving as if from the proverbial doomed ship, without even cleaning up the bodies which lay along the streets. War was their business, and they went on in a sloping march across the town of St. Servan, to a small square before the Mairie . . . a nice little square if it had been Bastille Day, but hell now, with its dugout shelters and hand-grenades. I went on to the command post in the boys' school . . . the telephone exchange and the wireless reception were on the courtyard balcony just outside the major's office.

The blackboards were still chalked with German-French lessons and German tourist posters decorated the walls. In the next room it was French or German-English and the silly 1900 pictures of the "Famille Durand" with their cats, canaries, and crowded rooms were on the walls, with a long pointer for reaching to the sideburned gent *"ce monsieur est un soldat."*

In Major Speedie's office, soldiers of all ranks came in and looked at maps and front elevations. There were sketches from prisoners' information . . . and drawings of mined areas given by deserters. At the end of the balcony a Captain was briefing his group.

There were flashes from delayed action bombs buried in the earthworks. The next wave was light incendiaries . . . a lot fell in the water to the right. Many hit the sloping earth towards us, and more into the fort. Our artillery started its

Major Speedie (later made Lt. Col.), who received St. Malo's surrender from Col. Von Aulock, in German ex-headquarters.

barrage . . . the soldiers had started moving down the streets with the last air bombs, assembling between the burning buildings at the approach to the fort. The dry, fast cough of our machine guns echoed ghost-like. The enemy's 20mm., 200-a-minute cannons made savage probes . . . our mortars and smokescreen . . . pounded and drifted—our heavy guns battered into the moat . . . on to the fortress and around the pillboxes . . . our soldiers were leaving the houses. I could see them next to the orange-tiled one creeping down to the rocks and moving single-file up the steep approach to the fort, while another platoon crept from the houses to the rocks, crouching, waiting their turn. It was a heavy climb . . . and they were earth-coloured like the burnt soil they were traversing.

I projected myself into their struggle, my arms and legs aching and cramped . . . the first man scrambled over the sharp edge, went along a bit, and turned back to give a hand in hauling up the others . . . on and on the men went up . . . veering off to the right . . . it was awesome and marrow-freezing.

The building we were in and all the others which faced the Fort were being spat at now . . . ping, bang . . . hitting above our window . . . into the next . . . breaking on the balcony below . . . fast, rapid, queer noise . . . impact before the gun noise itself . . . following the same sound pattern . . . hundreds of rounds . . . crossing and recrossing where we were.

Machine-gun fire belched from the end pillbox . . . the men fell flat . . . stumbling and crawling into the shelter of shell-holes . . . some crept on, others sweeping back to the left of the guns' angle, one man reaching the top. He was enormous. A square-shouldered silhouette, black against the sky between the pillbox and the fort. He raised his arm. The gesture of a cavalry officer with sabre waving the others on . . . he was waving to death, and he fell with his hand against the Fort.

The men were flowing away from the path he had followed . . . moving toward the left . . . it was retreat. Singly and together they picked themselves up and threw themselves down into another hole, stooping, hunched . . . scrambling, helping each other. There was silence—poised—desperate. I could hear yells from the slopes . . . orders . . . directions . . . with nightmare faintness. There was a great black explosion where the most forward men had been a minute before. Cézembre was firing on her sister fortress . . . shells which would not penetrate or injure the occupants but which could blast our men, who were oozing down the escarpment . . . and sliding down the path which they had so painfully climbed. Other bursts from Cézembre swept the sides of the Fort. They were directed by telephone, probably from the Cité . . . they followed with hideous knowledge. One burst hiding and shattering the men at the bottom . . . our mortar fire was peppering the pillboxes to keep them silent . . . smoke screens and artillery pummelled the fortress just above our men to keep the krauts from slaughtering them in retreat.

They got back among the houses . . . our machine guns keeping a steady tattoo . . . Cézembre bursts hunting angrily in the rocks, slopes and buildings, hungry for more of the withdrawing soldiers. The Cité guns could not reach them there and turned more attention to us . . . we separated to different rooms . . . everyone was sullen . . . silent . . . and aching, like a terrible hangover. The men came back into the square . . . the ambulance men had the wounded, the dead had been left.

Stricken lonely cats prowled. A swollen horse had not provided adequate shelter for the dead American behind it . . . flower-pots stood in roomless windows. Flies and wasps made tours in and out of underground vaults which stank with death and sour misery. Gunfire brought more stone blocks down into the street . . . I sheltered in a kraut dugout, squatting under the ramparts. My heel ground into a dead detached hand . . . and I cursed the Germans for the sordid ugly destruction they had conjured up in this once beautiful town. I wondered where my friends were . . . that I'd known here before the war . . . how many had been forced into disloyalty and degradation . . . how many had been shot, starved or what. I picked up the hand and hurled it across the street and ran back the way I'd come, bruising my feet and crashing in the unsteady piles of stone and slipping in blood. Christ, it was awful.

Everybody was busy making plans for a new assault on the
Citadel in the afternoon. A low level attack—all oil bombs
and incendiaries—barrage . . . men . . . that Cézembre
should be attacked during the infantry assault to keep its guns
silent . . . that St. Malo should be evacuated . . . that the
civilians would, for heaven's sake, keep back of the bombline
. . . that the fat man in the white helmet refused to leave the
bank and had to be taken from St. Malo by the force of civilian police, crying. Streams of refugees haunted the Civil Affairs, tracing families, begging to go into the town of St.
Malo.

In the Hotel Victoria the telephone was on the bed, and
Major Speedie kept going out too far on the balcony. His
sergeant pulled him in by the belt. The attack was scheduled
for three. It was nearly that now. There was no fire from the
Fort. We weren't bothering either. Somebody thought they
saw white flags way down on the left. If they were, they
weren't in the agreed position. The wind was the wrong way
and it certainly was white and it hadn't been there before. But
it looked more like two white sticks, not very straight. Frantic
phoning went on. The switchboards tried to break down.
Other O.P.'s were contacted. Had they a better view? Could
the air attack be called off? Was it a real surrender? A trick?
The phones traced air command . . . a General. It couldn't
be stopped. They were here . . . on their bomb run.

We could see Capt. Boyd now, running up to the left part
of the Fort with his flag-bearer and interpreter. There were
other people there. Germans. Somebody else. It was MacFar-
lane, racing up through the buildings toward them for warning. The planes were nearer. Boyd and his group backed up
toward the buildings a few yards. Waving flags, spreading
scarlet boundary markers to signal the P-38 pilots that the
place was ours. The Major said, "Goddamit, those are my
boys!" as a pair of bombs hurled from the first plane over
their heads and into the opened belly of the Fort.

There was a burst of flame and billowing smoke, and the
second plane veered off without bombing . . . and the third.
They circled through the smoke at crazy angles, deprived of
their prey, standing by to watch for trickery. We raced down

through the streets, up through the causeway buildings. The terrain was soft with shelling, and hard with broken stones, weapons, twisted track rails, scattered ties, unexploded German grenades, and mines to be stepped over. A large metal barrow blocked the narrow street which was still burning.

As we came out into the open we could see Boyd and Mac-Farlane and the others turning over the markers into some other signal pattern. They went down the back of the Fort to the tunnel entrance. Major Speedie made me stay at the markers, and they disappeared at the turn. A messenger went up, the walkie-talkie. A platoon disarmed themselves at the boundary, and carefully spaced out up the hill. It wasn't too late for the Cézembre guns to give us a swipe, and orders were passed back to keep well spread. An armed platoon went up . . . that must mean that the surrender was real and complete.

Captain Boyd had gone to the hole—shouted for a German, and disappeared inside, but I couldn't disobey the Major and had to stay. I caught sight of him escorting a tall figure, certainly not G.I., and preceded by a police dog. It was Colonel von Aulock. He wore a flapping camouflage coat, a battered peaked hat. I took a picture and stepped out in front. Seeing the camera he held a grey-gloved hand up in front of his face. He was pale, monocled. An iron cross and ribbon at his neck. He kept on walking, and obviously, recognized that I was a woman. He said "something Frau" in a loud voice and flushed little red spots in each cheek like rouge. I kept scrambling on in front, turning around to take another shot of him, stumbling, running. He wasted as much energy as I did, and ruined his dignified departure in hiding his face. He seemed awfully thin under his clothes, as he stood in the jeep and said farewell to the men who had carried his bags down. He shook them by the hand, waved the dog away, and was whisked up to headquarters.

I went back to the Citadel, and stood around with Major Speedie and Captain White, while droves of prisoners came down carrying suitcases and bundles. Some straggled, some lingered and had to be ordered to move faster. Some recognized me as a girl and set up conversation, which was forbidden. The German Captain Waller stood nearby. He told our

Col. Von Aulock (the Mad Colonel) waits for jeep after surrender. On left, Maj. Speedie; on right, Capt. White.

Captain, Dr. Gray, "You understand, that to me this scene is
very unhappy." He gave assurances that the tunnels were not
mined, that there were no booby traps in return for what they
thought was our clean fighting. He picked out six German
N. C. O.'s to return with our men into the Fort to act as
guides and to keep the ventilation and lights going. Major
General Macon raced up the hill like a gazelle and congratulated Major Speedie on having effected the surrender: the
last of the hordes of Germans had passed, and the wounded
came out.

It was difficult to get the litters out of the crumbled entrance to the tunnel. The bearers had to stoop and crawl,
gently, because the first boy was the American prisoner who
had been refused evacuation. There were other Americans,
too. One, unwounded, who knew the works of the Fort by
now, said the aerial bombardment hadn't upset anyone at
all. . . . They just went into a deeper tunnel and waited . . .
but that many of the gun turrets had been knocked out and
could only be used by hand-fire, although that was effective
too, and could have made our assault a costly affair. A Polish
boy came out very ill. Our Polish-speaking soldiers sat next to
him while he got used to the air. The Germans were surprised
at the surrender. They had been asked to put all their small
arms into a big bonfire of the commander's papers. There had
been plenty of food, water, ammunition.

I went into the tunnel. A short, rough-hewn passage
turned at an angle into a long higher tunnel. There were rails
for a metal barrow, and electric lights at 50 foot intervals.
Rooms opened off each side, lofty, rough, curved to the ceiling . . . double-decker bunks in disorder . . . bottles,
clothes, photographs, letters, loot from French towns. There
were store-rooms, offices, telephones, power plants, dumps of
ammunition and cellars of wine, rum and bottled water. Our
boys found plenty of souvenirs. The wounded were lying in
litters up and down the main passage outside the hospital
corridors.

The Hun Marine medical officer refused to be photographed and quoted the Geneva Convention at me through
the interpreter. There was only one surgery. It was only "adequate" in equipment. Nothing like what I had seen in our

travelling advance field hospitals. They still had medical supplies of their own in spite of having begged ours in exchange
for wounded.

I went back out into the light. There were crowds of
people now. Reporters had gathered like vultures for the kill,
all the way from Rennes. French people were already trying to
move back into the houses. I didn't walk around the pillbox
to see the man who had waved . . . and I put off going to
the top and walking down where I had seen the little men
crawl up. I never did go. Dr. Gray's American flag was waving
on the top, and that was enough. The war left St. Malo and
me—behind.

Daily News Writer Sees Man Slain at Her Side in Hail of Lead

by Helen Kirkpatrick

PARIS, Saturday, Aug. 26.—Paris' celebration of its liberation was very nearly converted into a massacre by the Fascist militia's attempt to eliminate French leaders and to start riots during the afternoon's ceremonies.

All Paris streamed into the center of the town—to the Arc de Triomphe, the Place de la Concorde, along the Champs Elysees, at the Hotel de Ville and to Notre Dame Cathedral.

Gens. De Gaulle, Koenig, Leclerc and Juin led the procession from the Etoile to Notre Dame amid scenes of tremendous enthusiasm.

Lt. John Reinhart, U.S.N., and I could not get near enough to the Arc de Triomphe to see the parade, so we turned back to Notre Dame where a Te Deum service was to be held. We stood in the door of the cathedral awaiting the arrival of the French generals at 4 o'clock this afternoon and were about to fight our way through the crowd to leave when they began arriving.

French tanks were drawn up around the square in front of the cathedral. Crowds pushed desperately to get nearer the church, which was already filled with the families of French Forces of the Interior men who had fallen during the Battle of Paris. We stood beside the police who formed a lane into the cathedral.

The generals' car arrived on the dot of 4:15. As they stepped from the car, we stood at salute and at that very moment a revolver shot rang out. It seemed to come from behind one of Notre Dame's gargoyles. Within a split second a machine gun opened from a nearby room—one behind the Hotel de Ville. It sprayed the pavement at my feet. The generals entered the church with 40-odd people pressing from behind to find shelter.

I found myself inside in the main aisle, a few feet behind the generals. People were cowering behind pillars. Someone tried to pull me down.

The generals marched slowly down the main aisle, their hats in their hands. People in the main body were pressed back near the pillars. I was pushed forward down the aisle.

Suddenly an automatic opened up from behind us—it came from behind the pipes of Notre Dame's organ. From the clerestory above other shots rang out and I saw a man ducking behind a pillar above. Beside me F.F.I. men and the police were shooting.

For one flashing instant it seemed that a great massacre was bound to take place as the cathedral reverberated with the sound of guns. Outside, machine guns were rattling. There was a sudden blaze and a machine gun sprayed the center aisle, flecking the tiles and chipping the pillars to my left.

Time seemed to have no meaning. Spontaneously a crowd of widows and bereaved burst forth into the Te Deum as the generals stood bareheaded before the altar.

It seemed hours but it was only a few minutes, perhaps 10, when the procession came back down the aisle. I think the shooting was still going on but, like those around me, I could only stand amazed at the coolness, imperturbability and apparent unconcern of French generals and civilians alike who walked as though nothing had happened. Gen. Koenig, smiling, leaned across and shook my hand.

I fell in behind them and watched them walk deliberately out and into their cars. A machine gun was still blazing from a nearby roof.

Once outside, one could hear shooting all along the Seine. From F.F.I. friends and from Americans I learned later that shooting at the Hotel de Ville, the Tuilleries, the Arc de Triomphe and along the Elysees had started at exactly the same moment.

It was a clearly planned attempt probably designed to kill as many of the French authorities as possible, to create panic and to start riots after which probably the mad brains of the militia, instigated by the Germans, hoped to retake Paris.

It failed for two reasons: First, the militia were such incredibly bad shots that they hit only onlookers in the crowd. Second, the French people did not panic, although all the elements to create a panic were there.

They say today that between 15 and 25 persons were wounded or killed in Notre Dame. I doubt it. I saw one man killed. He stood beside me in the main aisle. A woman behind me fainted, but otherwise the only other person I saw killed was the militiaman who was trapped by the police in the clerestory, and then shot by F.F.I. men from below.

Outside Notre Dame, when only Gen. Leclerc and his staff remained, I saw the police bringing three militiamen, dressed in gray flannels and sleeveless sweaters, from the cathedral.

I was told later that they had caught four there. As we drove past the Crillon, at the Place de la Concorde, they were bringing out a solitary German who apparently had begun shooting at 4:15 with the militia.

Political conflict there may and probably will be in France. But the moment when blood might have been shed on a very large scale was over by 4:30 this afternoon. The prestige of those French generals and the civilians with them is enormous—deservedly so.

Paris was never more beautiful than during the last hours of its fight for freedom Friday afternoon. Friday night it is a madhouse of celebration.

We came through the Porte d'Orleans with French tanks at 2 o'clock in the afternoon, through streets lined with wildly cheering people, heedless of the snipers who were lying low on rooftops and in cellars. We got as far as Boulevard Raspail when we had to turn back because of the fighting ahead.

The police took us in tow to the prefecture of the 6th district, where the honorary mayor of Paris, 70-year-old Henri Boussard, received us with formal dignity and tears.

He presented us to the police commissioner who organized the Paris police for the fight against the Germans. From the windows of the prefecture, St. Sulpice rose majestically in the afternoon sun.

Paris that night was still noisy but behind closed doors. Every few minutes a truck loaded with F.F.I. dashed down the boulevard blowing its horn continuously, and then snipers down at the corner of Raspail opened up. The Palais des Bourbon was burning and the flames made a lurid light.

Germans were still holding out, but Paris was free. Its freedom is heady and intoxicating.

The Chicago Daily News, August 26, 1944

from *Up Front*

by Bill Mauldin

"Let 'im in. I wanna see a critter I kin feel sorry fer."

Dig a hole in your back yard while it is raining. Sit in the hole until the water climbs up around your ankles. Pour cold mud down your shirt collar. Sit there for forty-eight hours, and, so there is no danger of your dozing off, imagine that a

"Maybe Joe needs a rest. He's talkin' in his sleep."

guy is sneaking around waiting for a chance to club you on the head or set your house on fire.

Get out of the hole, fill a suitcase full of rocks, pick it up, put a shotgun in your other hand, and walk on the muddiest road you can find. Fall flat on your face every few minutes as you imagine big meteors streaking down to sock you.

After ten or twelve miles (remember—you are still carrying the shotgun and suitcase) start sneaking through the wet brush. Imagine that somebody has booby-trapped your route with rattlesnakes which will bite you if you step on them. Give some friend a rifle and have him blast in your direction once in a while.

Snoop around until you find a bull. Try to figure out a way to sneak around him without letting him see you. When he does see you, run like hell all the way back to your hole in the back yard, drop the suitcase and shotgun, and get in.

If you repeat this performance every three days for several months you may begin to understand why an infantryman sometimes gets out of breath. But you still won't understand how he feels when things get tough.

"A experienced field sojer will figure out a way to sleep warm an' dry. Lemme know when ya do."

One thing is pretty certain if you are in the infantry—you aren't going to be very warm and dry while you sleep. If you haven't thrown away your blankets and shelter half during a march, maybe you can find another guy who has kept his shelter half and the two of you can pitch a pup tent. But pup tents aren't very common around the front. Neither is sleep, for that matter. You do most of your sleeping while you

*"Ya wouldn't git so tired if ya didn't carry extra stuff.
Throw th' joker outta yer decka cards."*

march. It's not a very healthy sleep; you might call it a sort of
coma. You can't hear anybody telling you to move faster but
you can hear a whispering whoosh when the enemy up ahead
stops long enough to throw a shell at you.

You don't feel very good when you wake up, because there
is a thick fuzz in your head and a horrible taste in your mouth
and you wish you had taken your toothbrush out before you
threw your pack away.

It's a little better when you can lie down, even in the mud.
Rocks are better than mud because you can curl yourself
around the big rocks, even if you wake up with sore bruises
where the little rocks dug into you. When you wake up in the
mud your cigarettes are all wet and you have an ache in your
joints and a rattle in your chest.

"This damn tree leaks."

You get back on your feet and bum a cigarette from some-body who has sense enough to keep a pack dry inside the webbing of his helmet liner. The smoke makes the roof of your mouth taste worse but it also makes you forget the big blister on your right heel. Your mind is still foggy as you fin-ger the stubble on your face and wonder why there are no "Burma Shave" signs along the road so you could have fun reading the limericks and maybe even imagine you're walking home after a day's work.

Then you pick up your rifle and your pack and the en-trenching tool and the canteen and the bayonet and the first-aid kit and the grenade pouches. You hang the bandoleer around your neck and you take the grenades out of the pouches and hang them on your belt by the handles.

You look everything over and try to find something else you can throw away to make the load on the blister a little lighter. You chuckle as you remember the ad you saw in the tattered magazine showing the infantryman going into battle with a gas mask and full field pack.

Then you discover something and you wonder why the hell you didn't think of it long ago—the M-1 clip pouches on your cartridge belt are just the right size for a package of cigarettes. That will keep the rain off the smokes.

You start walking again but you are getting close now so you keep five yards between yourself and the next guy and you begin to feel your heart pounding a little faster. It isn't so bad when you get there—you don't have time to get scared. But it's bad going there and coming back. Going there you think of what might happen and coming back you remember what did happen and neither is pleasant to think about.

Of course, nothing's really going to get you. You've got too much to live for. But you might get hurt and that would be bad. You don't want to come back all banged up. Why the hell doesn't somebody come up and replace you before you get hurt? You've been lucky so far but it can't last forever.

You feel tighter inside. You're getting closer. Somebody said that fear is nature's protection for you and that when you get scared your glands make you more alert. The hell with nature. You'd rather be calm the way everybody else seems to be. But you know they're just as jumpy as you are.

Now they're pulling off the road. Maybe you don't have to go up there tonight. You don't. You start to dig a slit trench because the enemy might come to you if you don't go to him. But there's a big root halfway down. Mud and roots seem to follow you wherever you go. You dig around the root and then you try the hole for size. You look at the sky and it looks like rain.

A weapons carrier slithers up the trail and the driver tosses out the packs you all threw away a couple of miles back. Maybe the army is getting sensible. Hell, you got the wrong pack and somebody else got yours. The blankets are damp but they would have been soaked anyway even if you had carried them.

"Me future is settled, Willie. I'm gonna be a expert on types of European soil."

You throw some brush in the bottom of the trench. You squeeze in. You don't like it. You get out and sleep beside the hole. You wake up two hours later and you're glad you didn't get in the hole because it's raining and the hole is half full of water. Your head still feels fuzzy and your heart is still pounding but it's better because you have been lying down. A pool of water has collected right in the center of the shelter half you threw over yourself and the water is dribbling right through to your skin. You brush the water out and pull the canvas tight around you. The rain continues, the weather is getting colder, and you try to go to sleep quick so you won't feel it.

*

"Now that ya mention it, Joe, it does sound like th' patter of rain on a tin roof."

Sometimes when the doggies are on the march they find a gutted house with part of the roof still hanging out from the top of the wall. This makes very fine shelter indeed and it's a happy time when they go into bivouac near such a house. But when the guys are really lucky they find a barn, and every doggie knows that barns are far better than houses. He knows that vermin are awful things to have and, since he never gets a chance to take a bath, he avoids houses and questionable mattresses if he can find a luxurious barn full of hay. A farmer who has reason to be suspicious of soldiers prefers to have the guys sleep in his barns because even if the doggies swipe some hay they can't carry off his favorite rocking chair and daughter.

*"Aim between th' eyes, Joe. Sometimes they charge when
they're wounded."*

When you are in a barn you don't have to bother about
being nice to the hostess because she is probably a cow. You
can put one blanket under you and one over you and lots of
hay on top of that and you will be very, very warm.

The only bad thing about a barn is that you find a lot of
rats there. You don't mind it so much when they just scurry
over you if they leave your face alone and don't get curious
about your anatomy. A barn rat likes nothing better than to
bed down with his guest and carry on a conversation in Braille
all night.

The best nights I've spent in the field have been in barns.
And the best night I ever spent in a barn was when I woke up
and found a cow standing over me. She had a calf but I shoul-

Breakfast in bed.

dered the little creature aside and milked the mother in my
best New Mexico style. The farmer came in when I was almost finished and I pointed to a small lump on the cow's
udder. That showed he hadn't stripped her well and I showed
him how to do a nice job of stripping with thumb and forefinger. He was well content when I left and so was I because
that was the first fresh milk I had drunk since I left the States.

The dogfaces love to find haystacks and an infantry company will tear down a stack in five minutes. They line their
holes with the stuff and, if they've got bedsacks, they'll fill
them too. If they don't have bedsacks they find some stack
that hasn't been torn down and dozens of guys will crawl into
this one stack and disappear. It's wonderfully soft and wonderfully warm but if it's old hay a lot of people who suffer

"We gotta probe fer Willie."

from hay fever have to pass it up. But even if you don't have hay fever there's another bad thing about haystacks: the enemy has used them and he figures you are going to use them too, so he often mines them and, if he is within shooting range, every now and then throws a shell into them. Bombers and artillerymen blow up haystacks and barns just on general principle sometimes.

Caves are nice and you find them sometimes in the mountains. Nice thing about a cave is that you can throw up a little dirt around the entrance and you're safe from almost anything. Air bursts and butterfly bombs make open holes uncomfortable sometimes.

Barns are still about the best, though.

*

*'Sure they's a revolution in Germany. Git down so they
won't hit ya wit' a wild shot."*

¹ nights, and it got below freezing at night and he
ᵗʰad any cover. He didn't have a sleeping bag, and
ʰn't have used one anyway, because you can't get
ᵇe quickly if Jerry sneaks up on you with a grenade
ᵂt.

pneumonia, and while he was waiting for the am-
ᵃˢcome up to the aid station, I talked to him. He
ᵐerseas three months, and he didn't look any dif-
ˡoᵗ the men who had been over three years. He
thᵉₐ different, though, because he griped about
ₐthree-year men accept with deadened senses.
ₐ griping, he had stayed on that muddy em-
his eyes open for German patrols until his
the ᶜbad his buddies were afraid he would die or

tip off the Germans to his position, and so they made him come up to the aid station.

Sometimes the doctor kidded the two sick men and sometimes he was gruff with them, but they knew what kind of guy he was by the way he acted. When the ambulance came up, both men were evacuated to the hospital.

No men came out of the misery and death and mud below us unless they were awfully sick. They didn't want to stay down there, but they knew they were needed. They were full of bitches and gripes and cynicism about the whole war, but they stayed, and so they had a right to say anything they pleased.

"I wish to hell I could send every man in every hole back to hot food and a hospital bed with sheets," said the captain, and then he realized he had said something serious, so he made a silly crack to neutralize it.

The little field phone rang. One of the guys in the aid station answered it. It was Charley company with a casualty. The medic took his blankets off the litter he had intended to sleep on, and he carried it out to the medical jeep, which sat in a revetment of sandbags at the side of the building. He asked me if I wanted to go with him. I didn't, but I got up and put on my helmet.

"Now what in hell do you want to go for?" asked one of the Anzio guys I had beaten at hearts. "Haven't you ever seen a foxhole at night before?"

I was grateful to him, because I really didn't want to go. I didn't care if I never saw another foxhole again. But you have to play the game, and so while the two guys were getting ready to go I said:

"Well, you are using barbed wire here, and I guess I ought to see it."

"Haven't you ever seen barbed wire before?" my benefactor asked. Still playing the game, I said yes, I had seen barbed wire before, but well, hell, and I fingered my helmet.

"Besides, there's only room for two in the car with the stretcher in back," he said.

"Well, hell," I said again. "If there isn't any room, there isn't any room. Besides, it's an awfully steep hill." I sat down and took off my helmet. The game was over.

"We'll be here quite a while, boys. Ya kin take yer shoes
off tonight."

They were back in five minutes, because it was only a thousand yards, and they used the jeep because the hill was steep and the machine was faster than men on foot with a litter. The Germans would have killed the medics just as quickly on foot as with the jeep, if they had felt like killing medics that night. I was glad they got back okay.

The boy screamed as the litter bumped the door coming in.

"Goddam it, be careful," said one of the medics to the other.

They laid the litter on two old sawhorses in the middle of the room, and the bantering, good-natured doctor grabbed the kerosene lantern and went to work. He was strangely different now. His warm, sympathetic eyes got cool and quick and his fingers gently unrolled the bandages, now dark red, which the company aid man had wrapped hastily but efficiently around the wounded man's face. The boys who had kidded and bulled about Anzio and Florida maneuvers and Old Sport were very serious now. One took a pair of surgical scissors and slit through layers of muddy, bloody clothing until the boy was stark-naked in the warm room. His face was a pulp, and one arm and a leg were shattered and riddled.

"God, I'm hurt," he said. "God, they hurt me." He couldn't believe it. His unhurt hand reached for his face and one of the medics grabbed his arm and held it—not roughly, but the way a woman would have done.

"Easy, boy," he said.

"God, I'm hurtin'. Give me a shot," the boy screamed.

"We gave you a shot, Jack," said one of the medics who had read his dogtags and was filling out a slip. "Just a minute, and you'll feel better."

While the doctor and the others worked on the bandages and the splint for the shattered arm, the medic with the pencil said:

"What got you, Jack?"

"God, I don't know. It was a tank. Where's the chaplain?"

"You don't need the chaplain, Jack," said the medic. "You're going to be okay. What got you? There weren't any tanks around a while ago."

"It was a grenade," said Jack, his hand still reaching for his face. "Where's the chaplain? God, why do you let me hurt like this?"

"How old are you, Jack?" asked the medic persistently. He had already marked "grenade," because the wounds showed that. It had been a German potato-masher grenade, because the holes in his body looked like bullet wounds, but didn't go clear through him, and they weren't as jagged as shell or mortar fragment wounds. Evidently the German had sneaked up while the boy was down in his hole.

Jack said he was twenty years old, he was a staff sergeant, and he was from Texas.

The questioning seemed heartless at this time, but there is a reason for it. If the patient is able to answer, it distracts him

"Do retreatin' blisters hurt as much as advancin' blisters?"

from his pain; and if the information isn't gained here, they have to get it back at the hospital.

Jack had guts. Of course he was scared. He knew he was hurt bad, and it's a shock to anybody to get hit. But when they told him he shouldn't reach for his face, he said okay a little sleepily, because the morphine was taking effect.

"Hold a flashlight," the doctor said to me. "The lantern isn't strong enough."

I grabbed a flashlight and held it on the boy while they worked on him. I thought, "Christ, twenty years old!" I felt like an old man at twenty-three. I looked at the holes which had riddled his right arm and practically severed his little finger, and I looked at the swollen bloody gashes on his leg. I looked at his horribly wounded face and head, and I thought of how twenty minutes ago he was sitting quietly in his hole wondering how soon he could get home.

I handed the flashlight to the medic who had finished filling out the slip, and I went over to the litter and sat on it with my head between my knees and tried to keep from being sick on the floor.

The medic took the flashlight without even a glance, and nobody looked at me. They went right on working. Pretty soon Jack's face was fixed and it didn't look so bad with a neat bandage and the blood washed off. His arm was fixed in a splint and it looked very neat indeed. He was wrapped up in blankets, and the ambulance came up and took him away. He was full of morphine and probably dreaming of home.

Up Front, 1945

Democracy?

by Rupert Trimmingham and others

Dear YANK:

Here is a question that each Negro soldier is asking. What is the Negro soldier fighting for? On whose team are we playing? Myself and eight other soldiers were on our way from Camp Claiborne, La., to the hospital here at Fort Huachuca. We had to lay over until the next day for our train. On the next day we could not purchase a cup of coffee at any of the lunchrooms around there. As you know, Old Man Jim Crow rules. The only place where we could be served was at the lunchroom at the railroad station but, of course, we had to go into the kitchen. But that's not all; 11:30 A.M. about two dozen German prisoners of war, with two American guards, came to the station. They entered the lunchroom, sat at the tables, had their meals served, talked, smoked, in fact had quite a swell time. I stood on the outside looking on, and I could not help but ask myself these questions: Are these men sworn enemies of this country? Are they not taught to hate and destroy . . . all democratic governments? Are we not American soldiers, sworn to fight for and die if need be for this our country? Then why are they treated better than we are? Why are we pushed around like cattle? If we are fighting for the same thing, if we are to die for our country, then why does the Government allow such things to go on? Some of the boys are saying that you will not print this letter. I'm saying that you will. . . .

Fort Huachuca, Ariz.   —Cpl. RUPERT TRIMMINGHAM

Yank, April 28, 1944

Dear YANK:

I am writing to you in regard to the incident told in a letter to you by Cpl. Trimmingham (Negro) describing the way he was forced to eat in the kitchen of a station restaurant while a group of German prisoners were fed with the rest of the white civilians in the restaurant. Gentlemen, I am a Southern rebel, but this incident makes me none the more proud of my Southern heritage! Frankly, I think that this incident is a disgrace to a democratic nation such as ours is supposed to be. Are we fighting for such a thing as this? Certainly not. If this incident is democracy, I don't want any part of it! . . . I wonder what the "Aryan supermen" think when they get a first-hand glimpse of our racial discrimination. Are we not waging a war, in part, for this fundamental of democracy? In closing, let me say that a lot of us, especially in the South, should cast the beam out of our own eyes before we try to do so in others, across the seas.

—Cpl. HENRY S. WOOTTON JR.*
Fairfield-Suisun AAF, Calif.

* Also signed by S/Sgt. A. S. Tepper and Pfc. Jose Rosenzweig.

Dear YANK:

You are to be complimented on having the courage to print Cpl. Trimmingham's letter in an April issue of YANK. It simply proves that your policy is maturing editorially. He probes an old wound when he exposes the problem of our colored soldiers throughout the South. It seems incredible that German prisoners of war should be afforded the amenities while our own men—in uniform and changing stations—are denied similar attention because of color and the vicious attitude of certain portions of our country. What sort of a deal is this? It is, I think, high time that this festering sore was cut out by intelligent social surgeons once and for all. I can well understand and sympathize with the corporal's implied but unwritten question: why, then, are we in uniform. Has it occurred to anyone that those Boche prisoners of war must be still laughing at us?

Bermuda   —S/Sgt. ARTHUR J. KAPLAN

Dear YANK:

. . . I'm not a Negro, but I've been around and know what the score is. I want to thank the YANK . . . and congratulate Cpl. Rupert Trimmingham.

Port of Embarkation —Pvt. GUSTAVE SANTIAGO

Yank, June 9, 1944

Dear YANK:

Just read Cpl. Rupert Trimmingham's letter titled "Democracy?" in a May edition of YANK. We are white soldiers in the Burma jungles, and there are many Negro outfits working with us. They are doing more than their part to win this war. We are proud of the colored men here. When we are away from camp working in the jungles, we can go to any colored camp and be treated like one of their own. I think it is a disgrace that, while we are away from home doing our part to help win the war, some people back home are knocking down everything that we are fighting for.

We are among many Allied Nations' soldiers that are fighting here, and they marvel at how the American Army, which is composed of so many nationalities and different races, gets along so well. We are ashamed to read that the German soldier, who is the sworn enemy of our country, is treated better than the soldier of our country, because of race.

Cpl. Trimmingham asked: What is a Negro fighting for? If this sort of thing continues, we the white soldiers will begin to wonder: What are *we* fighting for?

Burma —Pvt. JOSEPH POSCUCCI (Italian)*

*Also signed by Cpl. Edward A. Kreutler (French), Pfc. Maurice E. Wenson (Swedish) and Pvt. James F. Malloy (Irish).

Dear YANK:

Allow me to thank you for publishing my letter. Although there was some doubt about its being published, yet somehow I felt that YANK was too great a paper not to. . . . Each day brings three, four or five letters to me in answer to my letter. I just returned from my furlough and found 25 letters awaiting me. To date I've received 287 letters, and, strange as it may seem, 183 are from white men and women in the armed service. Another strange feature about these letters is that the most of these people are from the Deep South. They are all proud of the fact that they are of the South but ashamed to learn that there are so many of their own people who by their actions and manner toward the Negro are playing Hitler's game. Nevertheless, it gives me new hope to realize that there are doubtless thousands of whites who are willing to fight this Frankenstein that so many white people are keeping alive. All that the Negro is asking for is to be given half a chance and he will soon demonstrate his worth to his country. Should these white people who realize that the Negro is a man who is loyal—one who would gladly give his life for this our wonderful country—would stand up, join with us and help us to prove to their white friends that we are worthy, I'm sure that we would bury race hate and unfair treatment. Thanks again. *Fort Huachuca, Ariz.*   —Cpl. RUPERT TRIMMINGHAM

Since YANK printed Cpl. Trimmingham's letter we have received a great number of comments from GIs, almost all of whom were outraged by the treatment given the corporal. His letter has been taken from YANK and widely quoted. The incident has been dramatized on the air and was the basis for a moving short story published recently in the *New Yorker* magazine.

Yank, July 28, 1944

Young Man Behind Plexiglass

by Brendan Gill

JOSEPH THEODORE HALLOCK, who has light-blue eyes and an engaging smile and is usually called Ted, is a first lieutenant in the United States Army Air Forces. Two years ago he was an undergraduate at the University of Oregon; today he is a veteran bombardier who has completed thirty missions in a B-17 over Germany and Occupied Europe. Eighteen months ago he fainted when an Army doctor examining him pricked his finger to get a sample of blood; today he wears the Purple Heart for wounds received in a raid on Augsburg, the Air Medal with three oak-leaf clusters, and the Distinguished Flying Cross. Before he got into the Air Forces, he had been rejected by the Navy and Marines because of insufficient chest expansion; he still weighs less than a hundred and thirty pounds, and this gives him an air of tempered, high-strung fragility. When he relaxes, which is not often, he looks younger than his twenty-two years, but he doesn't think of himself as being young. "Sometimes I feel as if I'd never had a chance to live at all," he says flatly, "but most of the time I feel as if I'd lived forever."

Hallock and his wife, Muriel, recently spent a three-week leave in New York, and I met him through friends. I took him aside one morning and talked with him for an hour or two about his part in the war. I was naturally curious to know what it felt like to complete thirty missions in a Flying Fortress, but I also saw, or thought I saw, that he was eager to speak to someone of his experiences. Apparently he considers himself typical of thousands of young men in the armed forces, and he rejects any suggestion that he has done more than was specifically demanded of him. "Whatever I tell you," he said, "boils down to this: I'm a cog in one hell of a big machine. The more I think about it, and I've thought about it a lot lately, the more it looks as if I've been a cog in one thing after another since the day I was born. Whenever I get set to do what I want to do, something a whole lot bigger than me comes along and shoves me back into place. It's not especially pleasant, but there it is.

"As a matter of fact, my father had about the same deal. He'd graduated from Oregon State and was just starting in business when we got mixed up in the first World War. He joined the Navy, and from what he says I guess he disliked the war but liked his job. He'd been trained as a radio engineer, and that was the sort of work they gave him to do, so he got to be a C.P.O. and kept on working for the Navy for quite a while after the war was over. He and Mother moved around from Mare Island to Portland, down to Los Angeles and San Diego, and so on, and they seem to have had a good enough time. Like Muriel and me, they probably didn't try to figure what was going to happen to them next. I was their only child, and I was born on October twenty-fifth, 1921." Hallock shrugged. "In a way, it's funny my being born then. I was arguing about the war with a fellow the other night, and he kept telling me what Wilson should have done and what Wilson shouldn't have done. I got sore finally. Why, hell's bells, I hadn't even been born when Wilson was president! I don't give a hoot about Wilson, I told this guy, Wilson's been dead for years; it's 1944 I'm worrying about.

"Things must have been pretty unsettled when I was a baby, just as they've been ever since I grew up. Whatever that boom was I've heard about, I doubt if it meant anything ritzy for the Hallocks. My father helped found a company that manufactured radios—he was in on the ground floor in radio, from crystal pickup sets to those big old-fashioned jobs with all the knobs and dials—but he figured the fad wouldn't last. That was what he used to say—'Radio won't last.' Those early sets cost too much for the average guy, Dad thought, and it didn't occur to him that the prices were bound to come down someday. So he drifted into one job or another, some good and some bad, up to the time of the crash.

"Naturally, I don't remember anything about Harding and Coolidge. One of my earliest memories is of betting marbles with the kids at school about who was going to win the election, Hoover or Roosevelt. I bet on Roosevelt. I suppose my mother and father had been talking about him at home — about how bad things were and about how the country needed a change. While I don't remember good times, I'd hear Mother and Dad talking about what they'd had once and didn't have any more — nothing like yachts or fur coats, just something like security, whatever that is. It's the same thing Muriel and I talk about sometimes, wondering what the hell it looks and tastes like. Most of the other guys in the Army who grew up when I did feel the same way. We keep trying to figure out what it was our parents had before we grew up, or what our grandparents had. There must have been something back there someplace, or we wouldn't miss it so much.

"Moving around the country during those bad times, I had plenty of trouble with schools, and I guess it's a wonder I managed to learn anything at all. In California, for instance, I'd have to take French but not Latin, and in Maryland I'd have to take Latin but not French. I finally graduated from a Portland, Oregon, high school in 1939. I wasn't very popular at school, partly because I never was in a place long enough to know anybody well, but mostly because I spent my time reading books and listening to good jazz, which can be a lonely thing to do. I was a pretty serious character in those days, and I boned up a lot on the first World War. I listened to my father talk and I read about the munitions kings and I felt sure I'd never be willing to fight in any war about anything. I delivered the commencement address when I graduated from high school, and I called it 'Cannon Fodder?' You can bet I made that question mark a big one.

"Then I began to grow confused. I was disgusted when the League of Nations gave in to Mussolini on the Ethiopian grab, and even before that, when the Spanish War broke out, I saw that that was a war the Loyalists had to fight, and I also saw that it was a war the Loyalists had to win. I was only fifteen or sixteen at the time, but I wanted them to win more than anything else in the world. Besides, there was the Jap attack on China. Naturally, I sided with the Chinese right from the start. What it came down to was that I believed in other people's wars but I didn't believe in any American war.

I guess I was as bad as a lot of people in that respect, like the other kids who were brought up on Senator Nye and the Veterans of Future Wars.

"I wanted to go to Reed College, in Portland, so after I got out of high school I spent a year working as busboy, dishwasher, and things like that to make some money. I also got a job at a radio station, where I had charge of the record library and helped out the announcers on the night shift, and I played drums in a local band. Being on the air when the flash announcing the second World War came through, I remember the time exactly: it was 2:17 A.M., on September third, 1939. As soon as I got home that morning, I asked my father if he thought we'd ever get into the war, and he said, 'No, of course not.' But I suspected we might, and I hated the thought of it. My father had already taken the Civil Service exams for a job with the Federal Communications Commission and passed them, and at about that time he was sent to an F.C.C. job in Texas. I found out that I couldn't afford to go to Reed College unless I was able to live board-free at home, so I had to plan on going to the University of Oregon instead. My family and I got separated back there in 1940, and I've been away from them pretty steadily ever since. There were only the three of us, and we miss each other." Hallock smiled without embarrassment and said, "Damn it, we miss each other a lot."

Hallock and I talked about his family for a while, then got back to the war. "All the time up to Pearl Harbor, I kept trying to pretend that the war wasn't really happening," he said. "I kept telling myself that this was a different kind of war from the Chinese and Spanish wars. When my roommate at college woke me up on Sunday morning, December seventh, 1941, and told me that the Japs had attacked Pearl Harbor, I didn't believe it. It sounded like Warner Brothers stuff to me, so I went back to sleep. Later on I was listening to the André Kostelanetz program when the announcer cut in with some news flashes, and this time I believed it. I guess it's typical of me that as far as I was concerned the war started in the middle of the Coca-Cola program, 'the pause that refreshes on the air.'

"Nearly everybody at college got drunk and burned his books. My roommate and I killed a bottle of kümmel between us and I painted our windows with black enamel as an air-raid precaution. I spent the next two weeks scraping off the enamel with a razor. Undergraduate guards were posted on the library roof, and when the rumor got around that San Francisco had been bombed, 22-calibre rifles started showing up around the campus. Everybody else seemed to be doing something, so I wired my father that I wanted to enlist in the Signal Corps. My father wired back for me to sit tight until the Army told me what to do. In spite of him, I tried enlisting as a cadet in the Navy and Marines, but they said I had insufficient chest expansion and too few college credits. I didn't mind terribly when they turned me down. I had no real convictions about the war in Europe, and I was more or less willing to wait my turn at taking a crack at the Japs. I'd started an orchestra at college called Ted Hallock's Band, which played at sorority and fraternity dances, and during the year I'd had an article on jazz published in *Downbeat*. I'd even made a quick trip to New York and haunted all the night clubs that had good bands. I'd had to hock my Speed Graphic camera to do it, but it was worth it. I felt I was really on my way.

"Besides all that, and a lot more important than all that, I had Muriel, back in Portland. That is, I'd fallen in love with her and I wanted to marry her, but she didn't give me much encouragement. She just wouldn't say anything when I'd ask her to marry me, and I figured that if I got into the Army I might never have a chance to see her again. I wanted time to see her. I wanted time to do a lot of things I hadn't been able to do, and every day outside the Army was worth weeks and months in terms of Muriel and jazz and reading and ordinary living. Finally, in June, 1942, thinking I was bound to be drafted soon, I enlisted as an aviation cadet in the Army Air Forces. I was underweight the first time I took my physical, but I ate fifteen bananas, drank three quarts of milk, passed a second physical, and was sick as a pup for a couple of days afterward.

"The Air Forces told me they'd notify me when to report for training. I didn't feel like going back to college, and I was sore at Muriel because she wouldn't say she'd marry me, so I went down to Galveston to visit my mother and father. I got a job there as a pipe-fitter's apprentice—a fine fate for someone who thought of himself as a rising young authority on jazz and other fine arts. When I couldn't stand not hearing from Muriel, I returned to Portland and got a job in a record shop in a department store. Later, I set up a pitch as a disc jockey at the radio station, playing jazz records and ad-libbing from midnight to eight A.M. I managed to pick up sixty-five or seventy dollars a week, and Muriel and I had some fine times. It seemed as if for once I wasn't just a cog in something bigger than me; I was doing what I wanted to do, but of course that feeling was too good to last. I was ordered to report for duty on February second, 1943, at the A.A.F. base at Santa Ana, California, where I received my pre-flight training.

"That training was really rugged. We had two and a half months of calisthenics led by Fred Perry and Joe DiMaggio, obstacle races, drill, and studies. The saying there was that the discipline was so tough you'd be gigged if they found air under your bed. We took enough mathematics in six weeks to go from two plus two makes four to trig and calculus. I suspected that I might be washed out as pilot material, so to keep from getting a broken heart like a lot of other fellows, I applied to be sent to bombardier school. That was just good strategy on my part, but apparently the officers liked it. We—the bombardier candidates—were sent on to Deming, New Mexico. We arrived there and lined up in one hell of a sandstorm, in terrible heat, feeling a million miles from anywhere. I can still remember the C.O. yelling, as the sand blew down his throat and blinded his eyes, 'Welcome to Deming, men!'

"There were a thousand men at the base and two bars in the town, and things were about as unpleasant as that sounds. We had three months of training with the Norden bomb sight at Deming. The men who had been trained before us had not even been allowed to take notes on what they learned. We could take notes, but we had to burn them as soon as we finished memorizing them. We used to take our notes out to the latrines at night after lights out and study them there. We had to learn how to strip and assemble a bomb sight, a job that became sort of a religious ritual with me. The more I found out about the bomb sight, the more ingenious and inhuman it seemed. It was something bigger, I kept thinking, than any one man was intended to comprehend. I ended up with a conviction, which I still have, that a bombardier can't help feeling inferior to his bomb sight—at least, this bombardier can't. It's not a good feeling to have; it doesn't help you very much when you're over Germany and going into your run to realize that everything depends on your control of something you'll never fully understand, but the feeling is there.

"In July, 1943, I finished the course at Deming and got my wings as a second lieutenant. Muriel had stopped corresponding with me for the umptieth time by then, and I had got so sore that I had written her that I would never see her again. At the last minute, though, I hopped on a train and stood up all the way back to Portland. As soon as I saw Muriel, I told her, 'You know you're going to marry me, don't you?' She said, 'Well, maybe,' which was the greatest encouragement she'd ever given me. I wasted a lot of time—three whole days—making up her mind for her, which left us only three days of my leave in which to get married and have a honeymoon. We spent our honeymoon in a hotel in Portland. Then we took a train to Ephrata, Washington, the training center for B-17s to which I'd been ordered to report.

"Muriel stayed at a hotel in Wenatchee, several miles away. That meant that I was A.W.O.L. a good deal of the time. But I guess I learned something. I didn't like the first pilot to whom I was assigned, so the C.O. assigned me to another pilot, a fellow just my age, with whom I got along fine. It's literally a matter of life and death for everybody in the crew of a Fort to get on well; the ship just won't fly otherwise. There are ten men in a Fort crew—the pilot, co-pilot, navigator, bombardier, and six gunners, and there's more than enough responsibility to go around. The bombardier, for example, is also gunnery officer and in charge of fire control, first aid, and oxygen. Most of those jobs are theoretical in practice flights, but they can all need you at once in a hot raid.

"After a couple of months at Ephrata, where we got the hang of flying a Fort, we were sent on to Rapid City, South

Dakota, for some bomb practice on the target ranges there.
Muriel and I felt really married for the first time in Rapid
City, because we rented a bungalow and Muriel, who'd never
cooked before, practiced her cooking on me. As it turned out,
we lived on spaghetti most of the time. Muriel and I had a lot
of scraps at Rapid City. I'd come down from a flight looking
for trouble, looking for someone to pick on, and Muriel was
always the easiest to hurt. That kind of irritability seems to be
a characteristic of high flying. I blame it mostly on using oxygen, but, oxygen or no oxygen, there's no doubt the sky does
something to you. There it is around you, and it's so damn
big, and yet you have a false feeling of having mastered it.
And when you come down out of it you feel like elbowing all
the civilians you see into the streets that from above looked
like little trickles of nothing. The difficulty is, you have to try
to live in two different scales of worlds, the one up there and
the one down here, and it's not a natural thing to do.

"Muriel must have understood what was going on inside
me, because in spite of the way I behaved we had a good time
in that cheap little bungalow. As soon as I finished the course
at Rapid City, we went to Washington, so I could say good-
bye to my parents. My father had been made chief of the
Facility Security Division of the F.C.C. when the war broke
out, and he and Mother had had to move to Washington.
Later, we came up here to New York for a day or two before I
went across. We spent most of our time at Nick's, in the Village, getting a last fill of good music. In November, 1943, I
shipped out to England, and Muriel went back to Portland
and got a job at an advertising agency there."

I asked Hallock a few questions about Muriel, and then
he took up his story again. "Right from the start, I liked
England. That helped me to stand my separation from Muriel
and the fact that I was fighting in a war I'd never particularly believed in fighting. England was so much older physically and spiritually than I had expected that I felt shocked. I
understood for the first time that there were people in the
world who looked the same as us but thought differently
from us, and I began to wonder if the Germans were maybe
as much different from the English and us as a lot of writers

and politicians claimed. After a day or two in an indoctrination pool, our crew was assigned to an old and well-established operational base south of London and given our Fort, which our pilot christened Ginger. None of us ever found out why he named the ship Ginger, but it's the pilot's privilege to choose any name he likes; probably ginger was the color of his girl's hair or the name of his dog—something like that. We never painted the name on our Fort, because the Forts with names seemed to get shot up more than the ones without.

"My first raid was on December thirty-first, over Ludwigshaven. Naturally, not knowing what it was going to be like, I didn't feel scared. A little sick, maybe, but not scared. That comes later, when you begin to understand what your chances of survival are. Once we'd crossed into Germany, we spotted some flak, but it was a good long distance below us and looked pretty and not dangerous: different-colored puffs making a soft, cushiony-looking pattern under our plane. A bombardier sits right in the plexiglass nose of a Fort, so he sees everything neatly laid out in front of him, like a living-room rug. It seemed to me at first that I'd simply moved in on a wonderful show. I got over feeling sick, there was so much to watch. We made our run over the target, got our bombs away, and apparently did a good job. Maybe it was the auto-pilot and bomb sight that saw to that, but I'm sure I was cool enough on that first raid to do my job without thinking too much about it. Then, on the way home, some Focke-Wulfs showed up, armed with rockets, and I saw three B-17s in the different groups around us suddenly blow up and drop through the sky. Just simply blow up and drop through the sky. Nowadays, if you come across something awful happening, you always think, 'My God, it's just like a movie,' and that's what I thought. I had a feeling that the planes weren't really falling and burning, the men inside them weren't really dying, and everything would turn out happily in the end. Then, very quietly through the interphone, our tail gunner said, 'I'm sorry, sir, I've been hit.'

"I crawled back to him and found that he'd been wounded in the side of the head—not deeply but enough so he was bleeding pretty bad. Also, he'd got a lot of the plexiglass dust from his shattered turret in his eyes, so he was, at least for the time being, blind. The blood that would have bothered me back in California a few months before didn't bother me at all then. The Army had trained me in a given job and I went ahead and did what I was trained to do, bandaging the gunner well enough to last him back to our base. Though he was blind, he was still able to use his hands, and I ordered him to fire his guns whenever he heard from me. I figured that a few bursts every so often from his fifties would keep the Germans off our tail, and I also figured that it would give the kid something to think about besides the fact that he'd been hit. When I got back to the nose, the pilot told me that our No. 4 engine had been shot out. Gradually we lost our place in the formation and flew nearly alone over France. That's about the most dangerous thing that can happen to a lame Fort, but the German fighters had luckily given up and we skimmed over the top of the flak all the way to the Channel.

"Our second raid was on Lille, and it was an easy one. Our third was on Frankfort. France was the milk run, Germany the bad news. On the day of a raid we'd get up in the morning, eat breakfast, be briefed, check our equipment, crawl into the plane, maybe catch some more sleep. Then the raid, easy or tough, and we'd come back bushed, everybody sore and excited, everybody talking, hashing over the raid. Then we'd take lighted candles and write the date and place of the raid in smoke on our barracks ceiling. Maybe we wouldn't go out again for a week or ten days. Then we'd go out for four or five days in a row, taking chances, waiting for the Germans to come up and give us hell. They have a saying that nobody's afraid on his first five raids, and he's only moderately afraid on his next ten raids, but that he really sweats out all the rest of them, and that's the way it worked with me and the men I knew.

"When we started our missions, we were told that after twenty-five we would probably be sent home for a rest, so that was how we kept figuring things—so many missions accomplished, so many missions still to go. We worked it all out on a mathematical basis, or on what we pretended was a mathematical basis—how many months it would take us to finish our stint, how many missions we'd have to make over Germany proper, what our chances of getting shot down were. Then, at about the halfway mark, the number of missions we would have to make was raised from twenty-five to thirty. That was one hell of a heartbreaker. Supposedly, they changed the rules of the game because flying had got that much safer, but you couldn't make us think in terms of being safer. Those five extra raids might as well have been fifty.

"The pressure kept building up from raid to raid more than ever after that. The nearer we got to the end of the thirty missions, the narrower we made our odds on surviving. Those odds acted on different guys in different ways. One fellow I knew never once mentioned any member of his family, never wore a trinket, never showed us any pictures, and when he got a letter from home he read it through once and tore it up. He said he didn't trust himself to do anything else, but still it took guts. Most of the rest of us would lug a letter around and read it over and over, and show our family pictures to each other until they got cracked and dirty. There was also a difference in the way we faked our feelings. Some of the guys would say, 'Well, if I managed to get through that raid, it stands to reason they'll never get me,' but they didn't mean it. They were knocking on wood. Some of the other guys would say, 'I'm getting it this time. I'll be meeting you in Stalag Luft tonight,' but they were knocking on wood, too. We were all about equally scared all the time.

"My best friend over there was an ardent Catholic. He used to pray and go to confession and Mass whenever he could. I kept telling him, 'What's the use? The whole business is written down in a book someplace. Praying won't make any difference.' But whenever I got caught in a tight spot over Germany, I'd find myself whispering, 'God, you gotta. You gotta get me back. God, listen, you gotta.' Some of the guys prayed harder than that. They promised God a lot of stuff, like swearing off liquor and women, if He'd pull them through. I never tried to promise Him anything, because I figured that if God was really God he'd be bound to understand how men feel about liquor and women. I was lucky, anyhow, because I had something to fall back on, and that was music. I went up to London several times between missions and visited some of those Rhythm Clubs that are scattered all over the country. I listened to some good hot records and a few times I even delivered lectures on jazz. The nearest town to our base had its own Rhythm Club, and I spoke there to about a hundred and fifty people on Duke Ellington and Louis Armstrong. Now and then I got a chance to play drums in a band. That helped a lot and made it seem less like a million years ago that I'd been leading Ted Hallock's Band out at Oregon."

Hallock got onto the subject of jazz, then abruptly switched back to his story again. "The missions went on and on," he said, "and the pressure kept on building. Guys I knew and liked would disappear. Somebody I'd be playing ping-pong with one day would be dead the next. It began to look as if I didn't have a chance of getting through, but I tried to take it easy. The worst raid we were ever on was one over Augsburg. That was our twenty-sixth, the one after what we expected to be our last mission. When we were briefed that morning and warned that we might be heading for trouble, I couldn't help thinking, 'By God, I'm getting rooked, I ought to be heading home to Muriel and New York and Nick's this very minute.'

"There was never any predicting which targets the Germans would come up to fight for. I was over Berlin five times, over Frankfort four times, over Saarbrücken, Hamm, Münster, Leipzig, Wilhelmshaven, and I had it both ways, easy and hard. We had a feeling, though, that this Augsburg show was bound to be tough, and it was. We made our runs and got off our bombs in the midst of one hell of a dogfight. Our group leader was shot down and about a hundred and fifty or two hundred German fighters swarmed over us as we headed for home. Then, screaming in from someplace, a twenty-millimetre cannon shell exploded in the nose of our Fort. It shattered the plexiglass, broke my interphone and oxygen connections, and a fragment of it cut through my heated suit and flak suit. I could feel it burning into my right shoulder and arm. My first reaction was to disconnect my heated suit. I had some idea that I might get electrocuted if I didn't.

"I crawled back in the plane, wondering if anyone else needed first aid. I couldn't communicate with them, you see, with my phone dead. I found that two shells had hit in the waist of the plane, exploding the cartridge belts stored there, and that one waist gunner had been hit in the forehead and the other in the jugular vein. I thought, 'I'm wounded, but I'm the only man on the ship who can do this job right.' I placed my finger against the gunner's jugular vein, applied pressure bandages, and injected morphine into him. Then I sprinkled the other man's wound with sulfa powder. We had no plasma aboard, so there wasn't much of anything else I could do. When I told the pilot that my head set had been blown off, the tail gunner thought he'd heard someone say that my head had been blown off, and he yelled that he wanted to jump. The pilot assured him that I was only wounded. Then I crawled back to the nose of the ship to handle my gun, fussing with my wounds when I could and making use of an emergency bottle of oxygen.

"The German fighters chased us for about forty-five minutes. They came so close that I could see the pilots' faces, and I fired so fast that my gun jammed. I went back to the left nose gun and fired that gun till *it* jammed. By that time we'd fallen behind the rest of the group, but the Germans were beginning to slack off. It was turning into a question of whether we could sneak home without having to bail out. The plane was pretty well shot up and the whole oxygen system had been cut to pieces. The pilot told us we had the choice of trying to get back to England, which would be next to impossible, or of flying to Switzerland and being interned, which would be fairly easy. He asked us what we wanted to do. I would have voted for Switzerland, but I was so busy handing out bottles of oxygen that before I had a chance to say anything the other men said, 'What the hell, let's try for England.' After a while, with the emergency oxygen running out, we had to come down to ten thousand feet, which is dangerously low. We saw four fighters dead ahead of us, somewhere over France, and we thought we were licked. After a minute or two, we discovered that they were P-47s, more beautiful than any woman who ever lived. I said, 'I think now's the time for a short prayer, men. Thanks, God, for what you've done for us.'

"When we got back to our base, I found a batch of nineteen letters waiting for me, but I couldn't read a single one of them. I just walked up and down babbling and shaking and listening to the other guys babble. I had my wounds looked at, but they weren't serious. The scars are already beginning to fade a little, and the wounds didn't hurt me much at the time. Still, I never wanted to go up again. I felt sure I couldn't go up again. On the day after the raid I didn't feel any better, and on the second day after the raid I went to my squadron commander and told him that I had better be sent up at once or I'd never be of any use to him again. So he sent me up in another plane on what he must have known would be a fairly easy raid over France, the milk run, and that helped.

"That was my twenty-seventh mission. The twenty-eighth was on Berlin, and I was scared damn near to death. It was getting close to the end and my luck was bound to be running out faster and faster. The raid wasn't too bad, though, and we got back safe. The twenty-ninth mission was to Thionville, in France, and all I thought about on that run was 'One more, one more, one more.' My last mission was to Saarbrücken. One of the waist gunners was new, a young kid like the kid I'd been six months before. He wasn't a bit scared— just cocky and excited. Over Saarbrücken he was wounded in the foot by a shell, and I had to give him first aid. He acted more surprised than hurt. He had a look on his face like a child who's been cheated by grownups.

"That was only the beginning for him, but it was the end for me. I couldn't believe it when I got back to the base. I kept thinking, 'Maybe they'll change the rules again, maybe I won't be going home, maybe I'll be going up with that kid again, maybe I'll have another five missions, another ten, another twenty.' I kept thinking those things, but I wasn't especially bitter about them. I knew then, even when I was most scared, that fliers have to be expendable, that that's what Eaker and Doolittle had us trained for. That's what war is. The hell with pampering us. We're supposed to be used up. If the Army worried one way or another about our feelings, it'd never get any of us out of Santa Ana or Deming."

I asked Hallock how long he had to wait before he was ordered back to the States. "In just a few days," he said, "the word came through that I could go home for a three-week leave. I cabled Muriel and she met me here in New York. I must have looked a lot different to her, and acted different, but she looked and acted the same to me. She brought along whatever money she'd managed to save out of what I'd sent her, so we could shoot it all on a good time. I'd been made a first lieutenant, and I get good pay, but saving any of it is something else again. Muriel and I both figure we'd better spend it while we're here to spend it. After a couple of days in Washington with my mother and father, we settled ourselves here in New York. We've just been eating and sleeping and listening to jazz and wandering around the town in a nice daze. I don't care if things are booming, if the civilians are all pulling down big dough, if no one seems to know there's a war on. For the moment, I don't care about any other damn thing in the world except that I'm here in New York with Muriel.

"We haven't made any plans. Hell's bells, I've *never* been able to make any plans. As soon as my leave's up, I have to report to a rehabilitation centre in Miami, and I suppose I'll be sent on from there to another post. Frankly, I'd like to land a job somewhere on the ground. I don't care where. Even Deming sounds beautiful to me. I don't particularly want to fly again. Pilots and navigators seem to feel different about the flying end of it; they don't seem to get that feeling of never wanting to go up again. Maybe that's because they're really flying the ship. When you're only one of the hired hands, who's being carried along to do the dirty work, to drop the bombs and do the killing, you don't feel so good about it.

"As for after the war, we don't dare to think too much about that. We're not ready to settle down and have kids and all that stuff. We feel as if we'd been cheated out of a good big chunk of our lives, and we want to make it up. I want to go back to college. Damn it, I want to play drums in a band again, in Ted Hallock's Band. I want to feel that maybe I can look two days ahead without getting scared. I want to feel *good* about things. You know what I mean. It seems to me that sooner or later I'm going to be entitled to say to myself, 'O.K., kid, relax. Take it easy. You and Muriel got a lifetime in front of you. Do what you damn please with it.' I want to be able to tell myself, 'Listen, Hallock, all that cannon-fodder stuff never happened. You're safe. You're fine. Things are going to be different for Muriel and you. Things are going to be great. You're not a damn little cog any more. You're on your way.' "

The New Yorker, August 12, 1944

Peleliu Landing

by Tom Lea

This is not a page from a history book, not an account of a battle. It is the simple narrative of an experience in battle; like combat itself such a narrative is bound to be personal, confused, benumbed and in its deepest sense lonely. D-morning, 15 September, 1944, I landed on Peleliu Island, about fifteen minutes after the first troops hit the beach, with marines under command of Captain Frank Farrell, Headquarters Company, Seventh Regiment. I remained with Farrell and his men under fire for the first thirty-two hours of the assault. As a LIFE War Artist my purpose in going ashore was to record the United States Marines in combat. On the beach I found it impossible to do any sketching or writing; my work there consisted of trying to keep from getting killed and trying to memorize what I saw and felt under fire. On the evening of D-plus-one I returned to a naval vessel offshore where I could record in my sketch book the burden of this memory. Before my hand steadied I put down the words and pictures that compose this book. The narrative is printed here as I first wrote it except for minor chronological rearrangement. The sketches are untouched.

MY WATCH said *0340* when I woke up on the blacked-out weatherdeck below the bridge. Barefooted and in my skivvies, I got off my cot and stood by the rail rubbing grit from my eyes. Dead ahead, framed between the forward kingposts, there was flickering light on the black horizon. Sick yellow balls of fire flashed low in the clouds like heat lightning, but continuous. It was the Navy shelling Peleliu with the final punch before we landed. The black silhouette of a seaman on watch by the rail turned to me and said, "Them Japs are catching hell for breakfast."

Dawn came dim with low overcast. In the first gray light I saw the sea filled with an awe-inspiring company of strangers to our troop ships. Out to the horizon in every direction were lean men-of-war, fat transports, stubby landing craft, gathered around us like magic in the growing light. It was D-day.

We ate our last meal together, dressed in baggy green dungarees, on the plank benches of the troop officers' mess. We washed the food down our dry throats with big mugs of coffee, and put all the oranges in our pockets. Getting up to go, Captain Farrell repeated his instructions for Martin and me, the two correspondents, "Be at Number Three Net, starboard side, at *0600*."

Growing dawn had brought the ship violently to life. Power winches rumbled, hoisting our landing craft over the side. The marines, after long captivity in their crowded holds, moved at last to their stations by the rail, battle gear buckled, the last oil in the gun, the last whet to the knife. I felt some almost palpable spirit walking the emptying holds and passageways and along the crowded decks, with a word for every man.

In the corner where I kept my gear I checked it carefully and finally. There was the belt with the two filled canteens, first-aid kit and long black-bladed knife; and the pack with the poncho and shovel, the gloves, headnet and K-ration, the waterproofed cigarettes and matches and candy bar—and my sketch book and pencils and camera and films wrapped in the target balloon. All set. I checked my pockets for my watch and identification wrapped in rubbers—and my grizzly coin for luck.

Martin and I buckled our belts, slung our packs and put on our helmets. Inching along through the marines, we found Farrell and his men standing shoulder to shoulder with all their gear on the jampacked maindeck near the rail over Number Three Net. The maindeck looked queer without the landing craft that had loomed overhead on the long convoy days, making shade for marine card games. Now these boats were down in the water ready for the loads.

"Free Boat Two," bellowed the squawkbox on the bridge and Farrell said, "That's us. Let's go."

We gave a hitch to our packs, hoisted our legs over the rail and went down the rope net, down the scaly side of our sea-bitten ship by swinging handgrips and tricky footholds between the swaying knots, down to where the bobbing net met the pitching deck of our little iron tub. When we were loaded the coxswain gunned our engine in a blue stink of smoke and we cast off.

Our ship seemed to fall away from us and grow small as we moved out; there was a kind of finality about leaving it. Yet final or not, there was relief in action, and release from morbid imagination. For a moment we even partook of the gaiety of our bobbing tub on the foam-tracked sea. Emotions of an hour ago seemed suddenly unimportant as we looked back at the transport and remembered the parting words we posted on the bulletin board in the Ship's Officers' Wardroom:

A MESSAGE OF THANKS

From: Marines aboard *U.S.S. Repulsive*
To: Officers and Men aboard *U.S.S. Repulsive*

1. It gives us great pleasure at this time to extend our sincere thanks to all members of the crew for their kind and considerate treatment of Marines during this cruise.

2. We non-combatants realize that the brave and stalwart members of the crew are winning the war in the Pacific. You Navy people even go within ten miles of a Japanese island, thereby risking your precious lives. Oh how courageous you are! Oh how our piles bleed for you.

3. Because of your actions during this voyage it is our heartfelt wish that:

    a. The *U.S.S. Repulsive* receives a Jap torpedo immediately after debarkation of all troops.

    b. The crew of the *U.S.S. Repulsive* is stranded on Beach Orange Three where Marine units which sailed aboard the ship may repay in some measure the good fellowship extended by the crew and officers during the trip.

4. In conclusion we Marines wish to say to all you dear, dear boys in the Navy: "Bugger you, you bloody bastards!"

Sixteen thousand yards off the beach the LCVPs circled at the sides of their transports, awaiting H-hour. From the air the big vessels must have seemed like a flock of fat ducks with broods of iron ducklings playing ring-around-the-rosy at their mothers' sides.

We circled until *0714* when our signal came to straighten out and head for the transfer line just outside the reef. The circles of iron ducklings suddenly unwound into parallel files of LCVPs gray with the seriousness of war, heading full speed for the flame.

For an hour we plowed toward the beach, the sun above us coming down through the overcast like a silver burning ball. Peleliu was veiled with the smoke of our shelling. New hits against that veil made brown and gray pillars like graceful ghost-trees by Claude Lorrain. As we drew abreast of our battleships and cruisers 1000 yards outside the reef, the sound of their firing changed from dooming booms to the slamming of huge doors.

At *0747* the carrier planes, hundreds of them, noiseless in the roar of gunfire, started pouring death. I counted 96 over my head at once. I saw one flash and fall in a long slow arc of flame.

Over the gunwale of a craft abreast of us I saw a marine, his face painted for the jungle, his eyes set for the beach, his mouth set for murder, his big hands quiet now in the last moments before the tough tendons drew up to kill.

At *0759* I noticed the amphibious tanks and tractors, the LVTAs and LVTs that would carry us over the reef, being spewed from the maws of LSTs. Sending twin plumes of foam from their tracks aft, they made their way to the transfer line.

At *0800* the rockets from LCI gunboats flashed pink and soared in flaming curves, by salvoes, into the wall of smoke on the beach.

At *0830* we wallowed aft the control boat on the transfer line, the reef a hundred yards ahead, and beyond the edge of the reef 700 yards of green shallow water thick with black niggerheads of coral. The first Jap mortar burst hit just inside the reef as our coxswain worked us up alongside an LVT for transfer. While the two craft bobbed and smashed at each other, we numbly piled ourselves and our gear into the LVT.

Going In—First Wave

The coxswain of the LCVP waved, backed his craft clear, and headed seaward.

The iron bulkheads of the LVT came above our heads—we could see only the sky. Farrell climbed on a pile of gear to see out, preparatory to giving our new coxswain the signal for heading in over the reef. Standing on a field radio case forward, I managed to poke my head up so I could see the first wave of LVTs go in. As I watched, the silence came into my consciousness; our shelling had ceased. Only our tank treads churning the water marred the quietness.

Then on the lip of the beach we saw many pink flashes— the Japs, coming out from under our shelling, were opening up with mortar and artillery fire on the first wave. Dead ahead there was a brighter flash. Looking through his binoculars, Farrell told us, "They hit an LVT."

As our coxswain watched the amphitracks toiling through the black obstructions on the reef, I heard him say to Farrell he doubted if it were possible to get us to our precise point on the far right of Beach Orange Three, and Farrell answered, "Well, take us as close as you can."

Mortar bursts began to plume up all over the reef and walk along the edge of the beach. Farrell, who could have waited another hour to take our Free Boat (not belonging to a specific assault wave) into the beach, abruptly put down his glasses, cupped his hands at the gunner by the coxswain, and bawled, "Let's quit this farting around. Tell him to take us in!"

The clatter of our treads rose to the pitch of a rock crusher and our hell ride began. In that clanking hearse it was impossible to stand without holding on to something, impossible to sit on the deck without the risk of fracturing our tailbones. So we grabbed and lurched and swore. Suddenly there was a cracking rattle of shrapnel on the bulkhead and dousing water on our necks.

"Get down! Squat!" yelled Farrell, and we bent down on our hunkers, grasping at each other's shoulders, at the bulkheads, at anything. That was the first mortar that came close. There were two more, and then the ping and whine of small arms in the air over us.

"Keep down!" yelled Farrell, with his head up over the bulkhead peering at the beach, "Still 300 yards to go."

We ground to a stop, after a thousand years, on the coarse coral. The ramp aft, seaward, cranked down fast and we tightened our holds on our gear. The air cracked and roared, filled our ears and guts with its sound while Farrell bellowed, "OK! Pile out! Scatter! But follow me to the right! The right, goddammit, remember!" And we ran down the ramp and came around the end of the LVT, splashing ankle-deep up the surf to the white beach.

Suddenly I was completely alone. Each man drew into himself when he ran down that ramp, into that flame. Those marines flattened in the sand on that beach were dark and huddled like wet rats in death as I threw my body down among them. There was a rattle and roar under my helmet while I undid the chin strap and smelled the flaming oil and popping ammunition from the burning LVTs around us. Men of the first wave had penetrated about 25 yards inland as I looked up the sandy slope.

Then I ran—to the right—slanting up the beach for cover, half bent over. Off balance, I fell flat on my face just as I heard the *whishhh* of a mortar I knew was too close. A red flash stabbed at my eyeballs. About fifteen yards away, on the upper edge of the beach, it smashed down four men from our boat. One figure seemed to fly to pieces. With terrible clarity I saw the head and one leg sail into the air. Captain Farrell, near the burst, never dodged nor hesitated but kept running, screaming at his men to follow him to their objective down the beach.

I got up to follow him, ran a few steps, and fell into a small shell hole as another mortar burst threw dirt on me. Lying there in terror looking longingly up the slope to better cover, I saw a wounded man near me, staggering in the direction of LVTs. His face was half bloody pulp and the mangled shreds of what was left of an arm hung down like a stick, as he bent over in his stumbling, shock-crazy walk. The half of his face that was still human had the most terrifying look of abject patience I have ever seen. He fell behind me, in a red puddle on the white sand.

I ran farther to the right, angling up the slope. Suddenly I recognized Martin's big back (he was unarmed like myself) under a three-foot ledge on the upper rim of the beach where

The Beach

My first view as I came around from the ramp of our LVT.

vegetation started. I made a final dash to throw myself under the ledge at Martin's side. The exertion was so great I fell down almost unconscious. When I opened my eyes again my throat burned, yet I was cold with sweat. We were lying with our heads to the ledge, not four feet from the aperture of a Jap "spider trap," a small machine-gun nest built into the face of the ledge with coco logs. Loose sand shovelled away from the aperture in two widening banks at either side made the trough in which we lay and gave additional cover. I wondered how well I could use my knife if a live Jap suddenly should poke an ugly face out at me from the opening formed by the logs.

Mortar shells whished and whapped through the air over our heads. They hit without apparent pattern on the beach and in the reef at our backs. Turning my head seaward I saw a direct center hit on an LVT. Pieces of iron and men seemed to sail slow-motion into the air. As bursts began to creep steadily from the reef in toward the beach, the shells from one mortar rustled through the air directly over our heads at intervals of a few seconds, bursting closer, closer. Then a flat cracking flash nearly buried me with sand. Wriggling out, and trying to wipe the sharp grains from my sweating eyelids, I saw in the clinging gray smoke that a burst had hit about six feet from my left foot, beyond the bank of loose sand at my side. In almost burying me, this sand had also saved me from shrapnel, except for one small spent piece that burned my left shin—which I did not know until later. I yelled to Martin, but he lay with face down, and did not answer. I could see no blood but I thought he was hit. A moment later he raised his head—I shouted, but he could not hear me. The blast had deafened him. Burst followed burst, creeping out to the reef and then back into the beach again. We hugged the earth and hung on.

Abruptly from close by, from over the ledge at our heads came a shuddering explosion, then a wild popping of .50-calibre shells. Later when we got up, we discovered an LVT on fire in the brush above us. It had run over a mine.

A different kind of shellburst began to come at us from a new direction. We judged it was 75-mm. artillery from a Jap battery down the beach on a peninsula to our right. We saw

The Price

hits on five or six LVTs as they came jolting in over the reef. As I looked over my shoulder a burst smashed into a file of marines wading toward our beach from a smoking LVT. Jap machine guns lashed the reef with white lines and marines fell with bloody splashes into the green water. The survivors seemed so slow and small and patient coming in, out there.

Our carrier planes were swarming the sky again. Fighters roared in low over our heads almost continuously, strafing beyond our perimeter inland. Dive bombers peeled off by sections, dropping their 1000-pounders, and TBFs made their roaring rocket runs, finishing off with bellies full of 100-pounders for the Japs. We had it all our way in the sky over Peleliu; there was not a Jap plane in the air. Airmen gave marines on Peleliu great support. Martin and I realized their efficiency and close contact with the ground command when we saw dive bombers making runs over the peninsula to our right. The Jap 75's were silenced.

For some reason mortar and sniper fire slackened too, and left us on our lonely beach in comparative quiet. We knew our lines were well toward the airstrip now.

Martin and I lay there weak, grateful and still, in the lull. Suddenly we were conscious of someone crawling up behind us from the beach, and we turned our heads. It was a corpsman. As we moved around to see him, he grinned and rasped, "Christ, I thought you were a couple of corpses!" We agreed.

The delicious lack of bursts in our immediate vicinity was like a life-renewing elixir. Tension broke for a few moments, and we lit cigarettes, the three of us. For myself, I was sampling the sheer joy of being alive.

The sector of the beach we could see from our trough in the sand was empty of living creatures. Two dead bodies and five wrecked LVTs were our closest company. I stared at the sand bank above my head and saw against the smoking sky the tangled, broken wrecks of coco palms and tropical trees with their big leaves hanging burned and dead. Two birds with long bills and short bodies lighted on a smashed palm frond and cried. Then the mortars started again.

Hugging the ground and turning our heads seaward, we watched the next wave of LVTs come in. They had good luck. I saw no hits. The amphitracks crawled in, pushed their snouts against the sand, and the men came up from the surf. Most of them streamed off to our right along the rim of the beach at the edge of the broken trees. Mortar fire shifted far to our left, and there was only the occasional zing of a sniper's bullet. Four men carrying posts and orange beach markers walked by, and another wave of LVTs discharged men along the whole length of the beach. We got up and started walking to our right. I remember the strange quietness, the dead marines in the white sand, the men with heavy loads trudging along in the smoke of the LVTs. Two rows of land mines, sown about six feet apart, lined our beach. The Japs had not tended them well; they were easy to see. We stepped carefully around their rusty bellies and forked horns.

Behind us came a burly man walking fast, as if on eggs. He bawled at the men he passed, "Where's the Seventh's CP?" and always got the reply, "Up that way, Colonel." We recognized him as the CO of our regiment, and fell in behind him, to find Farrell's bunch. When snipers' bullets and occasional mortar shells went over our heads on their way out to the reef, I instinctively pulled in my neck—though I could judge by now when they would be really close. It was interesting to watch the colonel ahead. He never bobbled nor missed a pace, but there was plenty in his stiff stride—almost an expression on the back of his neck—to describe the trouble in his mind.

We followed him inland from the beach, plunging into the burned and twisted jungle trees. We stumbled through debris into an open space where four LVTAs were parked, and thirty paces further into the trees we found our CP being set up in a trench dug by the Japs. It was six feet deep and about twenty yards long. Under our naval shelling the Japs had given it up just before we landed. Farrell had found it, cleared it of Jap machine-gun fire, and had it functioning as a command post when his superiors arrived. It was full of marines now, taking cover from sniper fire and mortars. A burst hit close at our backs just as Martin and I slid down into the trench. There was a yell for corpsmen—somebody was hit.

We sat in the trench, getting our breath. My legs trembled from exertion, but I felt very relieved, very secure. Out some

200 yards ahead, our front line inched forward and our perimeter grew more solid. Firing on our area slackened gradually.

By this time it was *1300*. Some of us climbed out of the trench and walked back in the smashed trees to stretch our cramped legs. Disposal squads were working through the area, digging out dud rockets, bombs and shells. When a projectile could not be disarmed with tools, disposal men would explode it. They would clear the necessary area, pass the word loudly to get down, and let 'er go— *blump!* All through the broken trees we found crude booby traps. Details were busy marking them and the land mines with red tape. Telephone linemen were unrolling their heavy spools of wire. Scout observation planes from warships wheeled high above our heads, directing naval gunfire. Occasionally they would go into a shallow dive and have awkward fun strafing.

Before noon the sun had bitten through the overcast of early morning and burned away all but a few white puffy clouds. Our planes were working against a background of bright, sharp blue. And as the sun, seven degrees above the equator, struck down upon us, it turned Peleliu into a bitter furnace.

Three of us had each carried a can of beer ashore in his pack. Giving each other the high-sign, we gathered behind a broken palm log, punched holes with our knives in the three cans, and drank a toast, *To the Marines on Peleliu.* The beer was hot, foamy and wonderful. When it was gone, we were still dry-mouthed. And not a bit hungry.

About thirty paces back of the Jap trench a sick bay had been established in a big shell crater made by one of our battleship guns. Lying around it were pieces of shrapnel over a foot long. In the center of the crater at the bottom a doctor was working on the worst of the stretcher cases. Corpsmen, four to a stretcher, came in continually with their bloody loads. The doctor had attached plasma bottles to the top of a broken tree stump and was giving transfusions as fast as he could after rough surgery. Corpsmen plied tourniquets, sulpha, morphine, and handled the walking wounded and lighter cases with first aid.

The padre stood by with two canteens and a Bible, helping.

Sick-Bay in a Shellhole:
The Padre read, "I am the Resurrection and the Light."

He was deeply and visibly moved by the patient suffering and death. He looked very lonely, very close to God, as he bent over the shattered men so far from home. Corpsmen put a poncho, a shirt, a rag, anything handy, over the grey faces of the dead and carried them to a line on the beach, under a tarpaulin, to await the digging of graves.

It is hard to remember how the minutes ticked away, while the sun climbed down from the top of the blazing sky. The battle pounded on ahead of us. During flurries of fire I slid down into the trench; during the lulls I tried to find shade from the sun. I was without emotion of any kind. I saw everything around me in sharp focus, yet it no longer crashed into my consciousness. My mind blanked itself for my body's sake.

Our front advanced slowly, if at all; the radio in our trench picked up few reports, and the inactivity began to pall on Martin and me as we grew more and more curious about the battle's progress in other sectors. We had no access to the messages runners brought in to the colonel.

Farrell was sending two men to establish contact with the Division command post which was supposed to be far down the beach to our left. Martin asked if we could go along and get news from the Division command. We buckled our canteen belts and joined the two marines.

It is hard to walk through a jungle that has been subjected to saturation bombing and bombardment for a week. Jagged holes in the scattered stone and dirty sand, splintered trees and tangled vines made a churned, burned wilderness. Strewn through this chaos were not only the remnants and remainders of the marines' advance, but also the new men and new gear that had poured ashore to back up the front line. These men were digging in, making holes for themselves for the long night ahead when the Japs would surely counterattack. We jumped over foxholes, climbed over and around smashed trees, sidestepped tapes denoting mines and booby traps, walked gingerly around those yet unmarked. Telephone wires in crazy criss-cross mazes were stretched along the broken ground. Scattered everywhere were discarded packs, helmets, rifles, boxes, clothes, rubber life belts—the rubbish of battle. Lying on the seared leaves and hot sand were dead bodies yet ungathered by corpsmen, the flesh bluish gray as the pitiless sun began to bring the peculiar and intolerable stench of human dead.

Planes came in strafing over our heads; the whump and chatter of firing to our right made a constant churning of sound. Sweat ran in streams from under our helmets which, without cloth covers, were burning to the touch. Our dungarees, wet with sweat, stuck to our legs and backs. The sand under our clothes scratched like sandpaper.

When we had snaked our way along for about 300 yards, the two marines with us began to ask the men we met where the Division command post was. Nobody knew. We hunted for an hour, and never did find it. Intolerably hot and thirsty, Martin and I left the marines to their search. We turned left and walked down to the edge of the beach, planning to make our way back to our own CP by walking along the beach, the way we had first gotten there. The water's edge was crowded with men bringing equipment ashore.

We had walked fifty paces along the sand, dodging around LVTs, when we heard a mortar shell whirr over us and saw it send up its column of grey water about sixty yards out on the reef. That was the first of several salvoes. They began to get hot.

We were passing by a big hole dug in the sand with a sign above it reading "Shore Party CP" when a burst hit about 25 yards down the beach at the water's edge, where we had been, and set an LVT on fire. We flopped into the very crowded Shore Party CP. The mortar fire lasted for about ten minutes, with most of the hits on that part of the beach we had just traversed. Later that evening we learned from the two marine messengers that in their further search for the Division CP they had been directly under this fire and had four men killed in the same hole with them. They came back shaken and no longer eager.

Meanwhile we lay packed in the hole with the shore party. The supply officer in charge was stretched flat on his belly and holding a telephone in his hand. He wanted to make a call, but he would not get up to crank the box to get the operator. So I cranked it for him, as I was right by it. By the time he got an answer, and I had cranked and cranked, the mortar bursts were hitting further down the beach away from us.

Some guy buried deep in the sand hole stuck his head up and began to gripe, "Goddammit, what are all you bastards in this hole for? Them bursts are a mile off. Scatter, you punks!" Just then a shell came whapping over and hit very close, and the guy buried his head again and said no more. Somebody grunted, "You're a brave son of a bitch walking around out there ain't you?"

In a few minutes Martin and I got up and continued our way down the beach through the welter of men, vehicles and ammunition cases. In some places things were so jammed up that we had to wade out into the surf to get around. The Jap mortars were far from silent, and direct hits on this kind of concentration really played hell. Yet regardless of fire, the marines were pouring everything they could get on the beach before nightfall and the expected counterattack. We watched sweating crews lift light artillery out of the amphitracks and haul them ashore. Martin muttered, "The more of those damn guns they put on here tonight the better I'll feel."

Turning in from the beach toward our CP we found the area thicker than ever with marines digging in for the night. There were foxholes every three or four feet, most of them barricaded with coral stones and logs moved around to help deepen and strengthen the cover. The men worked at their places for the night earnestly, without much conversation except short declarations of fact: "It's the ferking night time I don't like, when them little ferkers come sneakin' into your lap." They dug in the dirt and cleaned their guns.

I saw a big redheaded sergeant I knew, lying in a hole with his eyes closed. It was his first action, and the day's events had bitten too deeply into his mind. At noon, I had seen him sink down on the ground with his hands over his face and cry.

We found our CP. The trench was twice as wide at the bottom as it had been, and cleared of broken tree limbs and big rocks. As we came up a bomb disposal officer was carrying out a dud rocket he had dug from the side of the trench. Improvements were going on. Marines were filling new gunnysacks, making sandbags to pile around the radio set and around the section of the trench where the colonel would spend the night. Men were hacking roots from the sides of the trench and smoothing out bumps, making places to rest their backs. Others were cutting poles from broken trees, laying them crosswise over their part of the trench, and tying their ponchos across the poles. It was getting cosy around the CP.

We asked Farrell if we could spend the night in the trench and he told us he had a place for us down at the extreme left end where he would be.

Very heavy firing suddenly started on our left. The radio operator got busy. When he finished writing out the message he showed it to us before he passed it down the trench to the colonel. It said our center was under heavy counterattack, the enemy using tanks. We knew we had three Shermans ashore, and sat there listening and hoping they would be enough. Gradually the firing died down. The attack stalled after the Shermans had knocked out eleven Jap tanks. A lull settled over us, as both sides prepared for the night.

About sundown we settled into our places at the end of the trench. The low sun cast a sulphurous yellow light through the smoke, then faded. Somewhat to the left and behind us two batteries of 75-mm. were placed. They fired a few rounds over our heads and the crack and blast made me jump. Then there was almost silence in the growing dusk. Our planes left the sky, heading out for their carriers. I got the orange and candy bar out of my pack, ate the candy, split the orange three ways to share with Martin and Farrell. Warm water from my nearly empty canteen was dessert. Word was passed that the "smoking lamp" would be out all night, that if anybody wanted a cigarette this was the last chance before morning. So we sat smoking in the dusk.

Martin and I spread a poncho under us and I hung my knife on a tree root over my head where I could reach it easily. We settled down to sleep, as close into Mother Earth as we could get. Mosquitoes began to swarm and bite. Like everyone else, I finally rummaged in my pack, found my headnet and gloves, and put them on.

We had expected that it might cool off after sundown, but we were wrong. With our headnets over our helmets and tied at the bottom around our necks, and with our gritty gloves on, we sat and steamed in puddles of sweat. Gun flashes occasionally silhouetted the top of the trench against the sky of misty stars. So began the long night in which the waking and the dozing nightmare merged.

A deep and numb kind of weariness both of body and of mind made the trench and the battle, the anxiety and uncertainty unreal, without the power of fact. I did not give a damn. I accepted each moment as it came, as if watching the paying out of a coiled cable, not being able to see when the end would suddenly come, time's end, world's end. Meanwhile the cable unwound. I was neither contented nor disturbed.

Little balls of fire danced under my eyelids when I closed my eyes. Flurries of gunfire rattled and thumped, and I seemed to be drifting off remotely into the sea of sound out there amongst the waves of a death I neither desired nor despised. Somewhere in those great waves was a peace that would lose me everything. Drifting out into the darkness farther, I struggled with those waves like a man on a life raft alone.

The blurred ring of the telephone about five feet from where I lay was like a tug at my sleeve, pulling me back to my fellows, back to my life, back from those huge waves of sound where I struggled alone. The quiet voice of the man on watch was crisp as he relayed information to the officers whose voices answered in the darkness down the trench. I could not help hearing what they said about weakness in our perimeter, about over-extension of Baker Company, about lack of reserves, about failure to contact the Fifth, about our poor position for Jap counterattack. Hunched over in my hole, I had the dreamlike certainty that I was two people—one in a black pit who was too tired to live or die, the other standing by with a disembodied rather benign regret that living and dying were so similar and so confused.

Events were the only measurement of time as the night dragged on. I do not know what time it was when the counterattack came. There was a sudden flurry of rifle fire and blatting machine-guns, a sudden pause, then a crashing answering fire from somewhere out in the blackness ahead of our trench. The phone rang. A battalion CO reported the Japs' infiltration and the beginning of the counterattack. He asked what reserves were available and was told there were none. Small arms fire ahead of us became a continuous rattle. Abruptly three star shells burst in the sky. As soon as they died floating down, others flared to take their place. Then the howitzers just behind us opened up, hurling their charges over our heads, shaking the ground with their blasts. Jap mortars spotted them, and bursts came our way. Some hit very close but I do not know what casualties they caused. The howitzer batteries answered every few seconds. The black air above our trench was gradually filled with the whistle and whine of small arms fire coming our way and crackling in the tattered brush over the banks of our trench. Our machine-guns cracked in short deliberate bursts and were answered by the faster, higher chattering of the Japs' *Nambus.*

Then I heard, in pauses between bursts of fire, the high-pitched, screaming yells of the Japs as they charged, some-where out ahead. The firing would grow to crescendo, drowning out the yells, then the sound would fall dying like the recession of a wave. Four times I heard the screaming Japs; in the firing I could not judge how near they came, though the second wave of yammering seemed closest. From down our trench in the lulls I heard our colonel giving orders to his operations officer who sat by another phone calling out to battalion commanders. Suddenly the colonel stood up and called for one of his junior officers at our end of the trench. I heard him give orders to get forward every available machine-gunner and rifleman from the rear of our position. A runner crawled out to pass the word. Small arms fire over our heads increased. A few moments later three riflemen on their bellies wriggled up behind the coco log that lay broken at the end of our trench about ten feet from where I sat, and started firing over the log. Looking up, I saw the earth, the splintered trees, the men on their bellies all edged against the sky by the light of the star shells like moonlight from a moon dying of jaundice.

I do not know how long it took the marines to beat the Japs back. Perhaps it was an hour, perhaps longer. If my weariness detached me from a sense of bodily peril, it also detached me from a sense of the passage of time. I floated calmly at the bottom of the black eternal well, strangely unconcerned with the fire and the sound that troubled its dark waters. There

Counter attack.
The black well in the shaking earth
the BANZAI, the starshells

was no sudden cessation of battle; it slackened slowly. The words over the telephones were less frequent, the snapping whine of small arms became less steady, the artillery gradually ceased firing. Only the star shells kept going—like bursts of fever in the sky.

The borderline between sleeping and waking melted somewhere within this recession of battle. I dozed, feeling at the same time that I was awake, conscious of the hard stones against my back, the wet gritty sand against my skin, the aches in my bones, the dryness in my mouth. Yet I slept, I'm sure. Martin told me next morning that a fox-like creature with a bushy tail jumped into our hole, ran across my shoulder and up the sliding dirt at my back. I do not remember it. Yet I was awake later when Martin broke his snoring with a violent jerk and curse, and threw a land crab as big as his fist violently down the trench. It had pinched him on the backside and while he rubbed his behind and swore it seemed unbearably funny. I dozed again before daylight, for suddenly I opened my eyes and the sky was gray and the earth was silent. Quickly in the growing light the dark shapes of our trench acquired color, the three riflemen by the coco log grew sharp and clear.

The bottomless black well of night was a lie; the light of heaven had not forgotten us. The world lived again and so did we. Men stood up and grinned and perhaps were ashamed to speak their joy. Then from out of the silence there came a distant hum, growing steadily, becoming a roar. It was our planes: they had not forgotten either. As we climbed out of our trench men popped up out of foxholes everywhere like a magic army conjured from the debris of war.

The staccato rattle of strafing planes, the first rumbling blumps of the dive bombers began the second day of battle after the silence of dawn.

We wiped the slime off our front teeth and lighted cigarettes. Three of us shared our last orange, and I had a stick of chewing gum and the last water in my canteens for breakfast. Ground fire on our perimeter broke out again, and men buckled themselves for battle.

We learned more about what the Japs had done in the night. The nearest dead ones had been found about thirty yards in front of our position. They had infiltrated behind our perimeter, even stolen our aircraft markers and planted them far in our rear. There had been several charges—that explained the *Banzai* screams—but the marines had held them off in spite of thin spots in our lines. Japs wearing helmets of dead marines had sneaked into foxholes behind our front and cut throats. They had been slashed or shot by marines in hand to hand fighting in the darkness and there were bodies on the ground now in the morning light.

By *0800* our troops were beginning their day's push, with heavy air and artillery support. We knew the LVTs were pouring in over the reef again. The 105-mm. guns were at last being brought ashore and set up. The Jap mortars started again too, the bastards: corpsmen came in bearing the dead and the shattered.

Farrell turned to Martin and me. "I'm taking a patrol to see how things are going at the front. Would you like to go along?" We said we would, and a few minutes later we strung out in single file, with Farrell and eight of his marines, through the shattered jungle. We walked about 400 yards, skirting the airfield at its southern end.

This airfield was of course the prime reason for the Peleliu operation. It had big well-graded runways surfaced with finely crushed gravel. It danced now in the heat waves, wide and empty under the blistering sun. Although marines held two sides of the field, the Japs still commanded the 400-foot height along the left side and could, like the marines, register fire anywhere on the open space. It was no-man's-land that morning. Down at our end of the runway there was only one smashed Zero; up at the other end we could see big piles of wrecked Jap aircraft (117 by count later in the day).

At the southern end on our side of the field opposite the hill our artillerymen had dug holes and carried 75-mm. field howitzers to the sites. As we came down to them these batteries were firing continuously, throwing shells into the Jap hangars and buildings at the foot of the hill, and at caves in the hill where Jap mortar and artillery and machine-gun fire was dealing out misery to marines. The targets were almost completely obscured by the smoke and dust of the shelling. A naval scout observation plane spotted fire for our batteries

Field Howitzer at edge of airfield.
Punching at 'Bloody Nose'

and carrier aircraft strafed and dive bombed into the murk. Our patrol joined one of the 75-mm. gun crews for awhile, watching them fire. Farrell sent two of his scouts off into the mangrove swamps to locate a battalion commander whose outfit had taken the brunt of the Jap counterattack the night before. Farrell wanted his report for the regimental command. When the scouts returned and reported they had found him, we threaded our way into the tangled mangroves.

We found the battalion commander sitting on a smashed wet log in the mud, marking positions on his map. By him sat his radioman, trying to make contact with company commands on the portable set propped up in the mud. There was an infinitely tired and plaintive patience in the radioman's voice as he called code names, repeating time and again, "This is Sad Sack calling Charlie Blue. This is Sad Sack calling Charlie Blue—"

The whiskery, red-eyed, dirty marines sprawled around us were certainly sad sacks too. They had spent the night fighting in foxholes filled with stinking swamp water; they were slimy, wet and mean now.

The major was trying to establish the exact positions of his companies before moving out of the miserable swamp closer to his day's objective. His people were taking some high ground to our right and had the job of smashing several big blockhouses and pillboxes overlooking the two peninsulas at the southeastern tip of Peleliu. Tanks and flamethrowers were spearheading the advance. We were in the swamp an hour before word came that the high ground had been taken.

As the battalion headquarters group prepared to move forward a supply detail came in carrying cans of water for the outfit. We each filled one of our canteens with the warm brackish stuff that sloshed from the square tins, and had a drink. Just as we were forming up to proceed toward the ridge the Japs laid their mortars and artillery on us. The nearest burst hit about twenty yards from where I ducked down, but the thick trees stopped the shrapnel and none of us was hurt.

There were about sixty of us, including Farrell's patrol. We started eastward in single file, three or four yards between

"This is Sad Sack calling Charlie Blue"

each man, winding tortuously around muddy sink holes and uprooted trees and through the clinging network of vines and broken branches and seared leaves. Gradually we came to higher ground where bare stone sloped up in little ridges and defiles, and vegetation was not so thick. Sniper fire cracked in the trees above our heads, but we were not shelled.

As the sun climbed in the clear sky the heat grew. There was no breeze. Stinging sweat poured from our bodies and kept us wet in our muddy dungarees. That morning marines learned the full force of the sun on Peleliu, where coral rock bakes in the oven of the sky. The heat cut into our very marrow as we trudged up the ridge. The dead Japs we passed were also affected by the heat; they had started to stink before they were stiff.

We could hear the heavy slugging of the tanks and mortars and howitzers, our crackling gunfire and the answering fire of the Japs just ahead as we came into an open pocket near the top of the gentle slope we were climbing. The clearing was a Jap barracks area surrounded by small pillboxes and anti-aircraft positions. It was a smoking heap of rubble as we came into it. Everything in it was smashed, twisted, blasted. There were dead Japs on the ground where they had been hit and in two of the pillboxes I saw some of the bodies were nothing more than red raw meat and blood mixed with the gravelly dust of concrete and splintered logs. I felt no emotion except a kind of gladness that these bodies were dead. An occasional sniper bullet over my head gave some point to my gladness.

Over in some dry grass by a tree I stood a moment looking down at the face of a dead marine. He seemed so quiet and empty and past all the small things a man could love or hate. I suddenly knew I no longer had to defend my beating heart against the stillness of death. There was no defense. The burning hope of remaining restless, unwise and alive, forges frail armor for the beating heart.

The Japs had cleared a trail from their barracks to the top of a ridge where their strong points were. We walked carefully up the side of this trail littered with Jap pushcarts, smashed ammunition boxes, rusty wire, old clothes and tattered gear. Booby traps kept us from handling any of it. Looking up at the head of the trail I could see the big Jap blockhouse that commanded the height. The thing was now a great jagged lump of concrete, smoking. I saw our lead man meet a front line detail posted by the blockhouse while the other troops advanced down the hill with the three tanks and the flame-throwers. Isolated Jap snipers were at work on our slope; small groups of marines fanned out on both sides of the trail to clean them out, while we climbed toward the block-house.

To the left of the trail, about fifty paces from the summit, we came to an open-sided hut with a tattered palm-thatch roof, apparently the mess kitchen for nearby Jap installations. It was filthy and forlorn. Over the open fire pit hung three big blackened cooking pots, with nothing in them but a little charred stuff. On a dusty table were still strewn bright blue enamelware mess bowls with the Jap Navy anchor printed on their sides. A big gunnysack of rice was broken and spilled in the dirt. I looked around for tinned crabmeat or *saki* but

The Blockhouse and the Dead

found nothing worth taking. The Japs had provided fine sanitary arrangements for their kitchen: under the same roof was a chicken roost and pig sty. The poultry was gone, but lying in the sty was a dead hog where a million flies were feasting. A marine came in from the trail and stopped at my side. Looking down at the pig in the puddle of blood, he shook his head and remarked, "Ain't it the goddamdest thing how a dead Jap looks exactly like a stuck hog?"

Just as we walked into the clearing around the blockhouse, a Jap sniper gave us a short machine-gun burst that splattered on the concrete over our heads. We all hit the dirt, most of us bunched up under the blockhouse walls. After a moment somebody got up and yelled, "All right you bastards—break it up and spread out." We did. The Jap did not risk another burst for awhile.

Heavy fighting was in progress just over the brow of the hill beyond the blockhouse clearing. Marine riflemen were still in position along the crest fifty paces ahead of us. Jap mortars from below occasionally overshot our front and burst on the hilltop. The area all around the blockhouse was still subject to sporadic fire and we did not loiter in the open places.

Among the scattered marines on the edge of the clearing I came face to face with a young lieutenant who had been a messmate of mine on the troopship coming to Peleliu. We had seen each other at dawn only the day before, yet we grinned, grimy and proud, as if we had not seen each other for years, shook hands and went our ways. Later I realized we had said a good deal with the handshake.

The battalion headquarters group turned right and went down the slope for better cover, to set up a command post in the trees. Soon Farrell and his men were the only marines left in the immediate area of the blockhouse.

In addition to its primary strongpoint, the hilltop clearing held two concrete pits about thirty feet in diameter constructed as mounts for heavy guns. Their circular walls slanted outward like saucers and around them were neatly painted 360-degree marks. Their decks were about eight feet below ground level and in the circular walls were cut entrances to caves which served as shelters for the gun crews. The pits had been tightly roofed over with brush camouflage now entirely burned off. We found not a trace of the big guns for which the pits had been constructed. Either bombing and bombardment had obliterated them or, more likely, they had never been installed.

Farrell and his patrol had numerous duties in the area, and we sat in one of the gun pits for an hour, taking cover from Jap snipers and mortar fire while members of the patrol completed their work. Three of the six openings in the circular wall around us were blocked up with coral boulders. Peering in the caves behind the other three we found one was empty, another held two dead Japs. The last one, larger than the rest, was full of bloody bodies. They were piled up so tight it was hard to count them, but there were more than twenty. The marines were finding souvenirs, putting bloody Jap flags on the deck to dry in the sun, and examining the firearms and enemy gear scattered around us.

One marine found a beautiful and clean silk "belt of a thousand stitches." It was brilliant yellow with a purple rectangle at the middle top holding the embroidered name of the owner. Below the rectangle were ten lines of one hundred red stitches—little round red dots, embroidered. A thousand ladies had each sewn a stitch of well-wishing for the owner, but this feminine backing had done him damned little good. He was dead now and starting to stink there on the coral rock a long way from home.

The whole gun pit stunk, and the sun cut like a knife. I was glad when Farrell's patrol had covered the blockhouse area, and he decided to go forward, find a place on a ledge overlooking one of the peninsulas to the south, and observe the fighting. The marines were scheduled to take the peninsula that afternoon, but the Japs were putting up a bitter fight as they backed down the slope.

We made our way to the left side of the clearing where we cut into the woods. Then finding a narrow trace in the tangle of trees, we followed it out to the eastern rim of the ridge. At one point a dead Jap lay on his back in the trace. Farrell bent over the body and saw a wire tight around the top of the right shoulder. He tried to peer around under the arm to see if a booby trap grenade was rigged in the armpit, but he couldn't tell. So he said to one of his marines, "We're going on. But go get one of the disposal men, and a line. Secure the line on this arm, get back plenty, and yank—to see if this son of a bitch is rigged. I think he is." I wanted to see that, but I went on with the patrol.

There were mines and booby traps all along the trace, but they were crude and easy to see. Farrell tore narrow strips off his white handkerchief and tied them on the stakes by the trip wires, to mark them for the troops that would come later.

The ledge where we came out, overlooking the beach and the peninsula to the south, had been strongly barricaded by a rough wall of coral boulders. Apparently the Japs had planned some additional work with reinforced concrete, for all along the inland side of the wall we found bundles of steel rods. At first we were careful about lifting our heads above the top of the wall, for now we were the extreme left flank of the marine front that bulged in the center down the hill to our right. After some experimenting, and drawing no fire, we poked our heads up and looked around at will. It was a ringside seat for the battle going on below us, for 400 yards, out to the peninsula's end.

We had been in our position for only a short while when the hot and heavy firing below us eased off into a lull. Farrell explained that the marines were drawing back to positions clear of the area where our aircraft and naval guns were scheduled to soften the Japs on the peninsula for the final ground assault.

While we waited for the fireworks, the sun started down its afternoon journey to the west. It beat upon us unmercifully. The shade from the scraggly brush over our position was thin; the glittering heat simmered us in our own sweat under our iron helmets.

Suddenly 8-inch shells from heavy cruisers started hitting from 250 to 400 yards ahead of us. They burst in tall sprays of flame and grey smoke. The very earth would tremble, and then we would hear the triple booming reports of the salvoes. These giant fountains of flame spouted along the length and breadth of the peninsula again and again—then ceased as suddenly as they had begun.

Immediately from out of the sun dive bombers plummeted with the sound of some huge ripping fabric, as if they were tearing holes in the sky itself. We watched the black eggs leave the plane bellies, and as the divers pulled out and soared, the 1000-pounders would *blump* into the jungle. Over the peninsula there grew again high lazy trees of grey and mustard smoke, where seeds of fire had taken root.

Then torpedo bombers ran down the sky in steep slants, releasing their multiple rockets with a terrifying *whoosh*, and at the end of their runs dropping whole nests full of small black eggs that rattled in the air and roared as they tore into the earth. The torpedo planes did not soar out of their runs, but banked in tight turns and circled over us quite low. We could see their crews distinctly as they banked and peered down at us behind our wall. Two of the pilots waved.

Finally the fighters came, whole squadrons diving in by sections, strafing. We watched the flaming orange paths of their tracers while the air was filled to bursting with the stuttering din of their guns.

The planes were hardly out of sight before the marines below us opened fire to advance. Down the slope the broken trees and the smoke obscured the actual movement of the troops. We could locate the fighting only by the new smoke puffs that rolled up out of the trees. Minute after minute the artillery and small arms slugged and pounded, and the firing positions did not change.

Suddenly Farrell cracked, "All right—you have targets— commence firing!"

We saw a Jap running along an inner ring of the reef, from the stony eastern point of the peninsula below us. Our patrol cut down on him and shot very badly, for he did not fall until he had run a hundred yards along the coral. A moment later, another Jap popped out running—and the marines had sharpened their sights. The Jap ran less than twenty steps when a volley cut him in two, and his disjointed body splattered seaward into the surf.

Our patrol was immensely cheerful when Farrell trained his binoculars and found the caves the Japs had run from. Other Japs were poking their heads out to fire, and for several minutes Farrell and his men peppered the cave mouths with M-1 and carbine bullets. The range was over 350 yards. I strained my eyes until they watered, trying to judge the effect of the firing. The marines claimed at least two more hits, but I did not see them myself.

While we kept our eyes peeled for more Japs Farrell sent one of his men back to the battalion CP to find out how the marine advance was going. About half an hour later he came back with salt sweat rolling over his cracked lips and reported that Jap resistance was very stiff, that our men were catching hell from pillboxes and gaining very little ground in spite of high casualties.

Farrell suggested that we might see more of the fighting under the ridge if we crawled over our wall and made our way down to the beach. Two marines, Farrell, Martin and I decided to go, leaving the rest of the patrol above to cover us.

We crawled over the tearing coral boulders and down the steep slope in the biting sun, heading for a rotten tree about ten feet from the water's edge. Farrell, Martin and I finally squeezed ourselves against the crooked trunk, both for cover and for shade. The two marines squatted by big stones nearby. I suppose we had been there between five and ten minutes, craning our necks at the fighting along the slope to our right—and not getting a very satisfactory view—when suddenly CRACK, a mortar burst hit on the beach to our left, and snipers' bullets splattered on the rocks at our backs. The fire came unexpectedly from the headland up north, toward which Japs from the caves had run. The mortar hadn't ranged us yet, and the riflemen were rotten shots, but we were in a very unhealthy place. We scrambled up the slope and threw ourselves down between big rocks for cover. The heat between the stones out in the fiery sun was intolerable. As I lay there I grew dizzy and began to feel numb. I knew I had to move or I would faint. Without drawing another shot, I slid and crawled and wiggled back up the slope and over the wall. The other four men followed.

I flopped ten feet back of the barricade in a small patch of shade under some limp leaves. Our canteens had been empty since noon; I was very thirsty and infinitely tired. I lay there breathing fiery air over my dry teeth, wishing I had taken some training for this damned beachhead business.

War is Fighting and Fighting is Killing

Every few minutes a mortar would slam into the woods around us; stray rifle and machine-gun bullets sang and ricocheted in the brush over our heads. Down the slope to our right a couple of hundred yards I could hear our tanks trading wallops with Jap pillboxes. Fighter planes came in strafing with a razzle dazzle racket. I took it all for granted, more interested in my aches than in a battle. We waited for the front to advance so we could go down and have a look, but the front stalled, and the afternoon wore on.

About *1600* we heard marines talking as they came up the trace at our backs, then their voices were lost in the grinding and clanking of an LVT mashing a road up the trail we had travelled in the morning. Marines began to slouch by, loaded down with their packs and guns. Some of them went on over the ridge as reinforcements to the front; others filed down the ragged path back of our wall, and trampled through the brush up the slope at our backs. Farrell gave one man hell for stumbling by the strip of handkerchief tied as warning by a land mine about ten feet from where we were sitting. Marines were occupying our position in force to hold it during the night.

When I heard one of the new men say that the LVT had brought up some cans of water, I came to life immediately. I unbuttoned my canteens from my belt and without even putting on my helmet went off at a trot looking for the water cans. I spotted where the LVT had left them in a clearing at the top of the ridge and made for them. About fifteen paces from the water I nearly stepped in a big puddle of fresh blood. Looking up, I saw three marines carrying a man shot in the chest. They were taking him out of the clearing, and there was only one man standing at the water cans. I thought of nothing but getting some of that water and poured it into my canteens without saying a word to the other marine. A moment after I rejoined Farrell and Martin and we were drinking, a marine from our patrol came up puffing with his full canteen and said, "Goddammed snipers got two guys by me while I was pouring this. They got another guy just before that."

I drank several more hot swallows, feeling peculiar.

It appeared that the fighting was mostly finished for the day. Our perimeter for the night was being established; the troops around us were digging in. Farrell decided to go back to his regimental command and report.

Back in the blockhouse clearing we found two LVTs. One of them had brought up the water cans, the other had come up loaded with corpsmen, stretchers and first aid equipment. The coxswain of the one that had brought the water told us he was going to the beach and would take us. So we got in and grabbed hard to the bulkhead as we lurched away. The LVT slammed down the slope batting down trees, rocking over boulders, leaving a swathe of churned hillside and dust. We came out of the brush near the southeastern corner of the airfield, rolled out into the open and headed for the end of the long runway on the southwest edge of the field. As we clanked and roared at our full speed of maybe twelve knots, I stood on an ammunition box to see out over the side and get a look at the scores of Jap aircraft smashed and burned on the ground.

Across the field to the northwest grey skeletons of hangars and barracks and the ruins of a little town lay dead at the foot of the highest hill on Peleliu. Incessant bombardment and bombing had chewed the western end off the ridge, burned from it the living jungle green, shattered its stone into ruinous sawtooth pinnacles and jumbled defiles. Grey against the smoky light of the slanting sun, it stood like the broken wilderness of a dead world. Yet within its crust were living Japs and chattering guns and the blood of dead marines was caked upon the hot and ghostly stone. The gunner of the LVT nudged me and pointed at the hill. "Bloody Nose," he said.

The chartmakers had marked it Umorbrogol Hill; marines had marked it now another way—and found its right name.

Past the howitzer batteries we had visited in the morning we turned into the jungle and found bulldozers scraping roads and carving clearings. The Ducks were thick as ants, carrying supplies to dumps in the trees. Down on the beach where our LVT stopped at the water's edge, we got out to walk to our command post along the way Martin and I had first struggled on D-morning. Now it was totally unfamiliar, covered with vehicles and supplies and teeming with men. I felt lost in the maze of traffic, as if my memory lied about the

Down from BLOODY NOSE
Too Late
He's Finished - Washed up-Gone

lonely place under the terrible fire so long ago yesterday. Then a mortar burst hit close to the water's edge a hundred yards ahead, and made everything true again.

We got our packs at the CP and thanked Farrell and said good-bye. Marines chewing at K-rations looked up from the trench and did not hide their envy: "Hey, when you get back to that mudscow out there, will you go to the scuttlebutt and drink me about a gallon of that cold water?"

As we passed sick bay, still in the shell hole, it was crowded with wounded, and somehow hushed in the evening light. I noticed a tattered marine standing quietly by a corpsman, staring stiffly at nothing. His mind had crumbled in battle, his jaw hung, and his eyes were like two black empty holes in his head. Down by the beach again, we walked silently as we passed the long line of dead marines under the tarpaulins.

A Duck picked us up and took us out to an LCVP. The sun was going down as we headed seaward. A mortar burst cracked on the reef like a last baleful word from Peleliu.

Peleliu Landing, 1945

Now the Germans Are the Refugees

by William Walton

Aachen, Germany

SOMETIMES war is very personal when you see it all around you. It was that way when we went down from the surrounding hills into Aachen. The shelling and bombing had ceased because our infantrymen were creeping from house to house, rooting out every German with rifles, machine guns and grenades. Gunfire sounded, now loud, now whispering as we entered the streets of Aachen.

Every building was damaged or destroyed. Not a window remained. Dense smoke swirled over rows of houses that looked like the brownstone fronts of New York's East 80s, but in ruins. The air was full of tiny cinders that were grit in your eyes and bitter on your tongue.

We stopped at an intersection to watch spurts of rock thrown up by mortar shells farther down a side street. Then commenced one of the most remarkable sights I have ever seen. Slowly from a huge basement shelter down that street the people of Aachen began streaming out into the smoky sunshine. Heavy with weariness, with fear, and with the bulging bundles of their last possessions, they plodded in double files toward us. One block behind them guns poked from windows and ruined doorways and were blasting at one another, shattering chipped masonry, raising clouds of dust and smoke. The people walked on, casting only occasional frightened looks over their shoulders. For almost 10 days they had lived in that basement; some had been there for months. They blinked in the sunlight.

Three-fourths of them were women, many of them old. The old move very slowly even when the war is breathing hot behind them. They panted under loads of paper, suitcases, packages of clothing, shopping bags stuffed with small possessions. They panted and plodded on. One old crone in wooden-soled shoes pushed a baby carriage full of household goods. She seemed to see and hear nothing. Another passed, muttering gutturally, the wind ruffling her straggling white hair. Middle-aged ones looked more harassed and some were black with anger. In twos and threes they trudged, a long, winding line up the street.

The younger ones herded frightened children. One pushed a baby carriage in which a blank-faced one-year-old sat wedged among sacks of food. Another young woman, her face working with emotion, clutched the hand of her 8-year-old son, who looked wild with terror.

Two girls of 20 came abreast. They gave us a fierce burning look and then turned their faces to the wall as they walked by, not a casual gesture but a slow, studied movement of hate and revulsion.

The only smiles were from an elderly man who walked alone and waved as he passed, and from two blue-eyed women, who looked as though they might be charwomen and seemed to think their struggle with a two-handled basket was uproarious.

The men were old, some shepherding wives. Some pushing carts, some so elderly they barely shuffled, some moved 10 yards, set down mountainous bundles and took a breather before wearily plodding on. Only one old man walked without a single parcel or bag. In his arms was cradled a great gray cat.

Behind a cumbersome steel cart three people struggled up the hill while a fourth guided the cart from the front. One pusher was a fortyish woman in a neat, black, pin-stripe suit with a simple black hat. Twice she faltered on the hill but each time kept grimly on. The muscles in her slim legs bulged with the strain. She gave one more heave and then stumbled to a halt. The cart kept on going. Tears were streaming down her face. She shook convulsively and groped in her pocket for a handkerchief. A poorly dressed woman with a huge bundle strapped to her back walked up beside her and put a comforting arm around the woman in the black suit. She shook her head, then tentatively put one foot forward, then the other, and with infinite weariness continued on up the hill.

One flighty woman stopped to ask if she could wait for her

crippled sister-in-law. In German she said, "We are very glad you have come. Anything to end this terrible war." They were all obedient, turning into another street just as the doughboys directed. When they neared a cross street, some tried to turn off. "These are our homes," they said. "Can't we stay here?"

No. All civilians must leave the city until it is cleaned up entirely. Infantrymen could not risk having Germans, even old ones, at their backs.

Leaning against the wall beside me, Sgt. Eldridge Benefield said in his Texas drawl, "I hope I never live to see anything like this happen in America. These ruins. These people." He shook his head. "But sometimes I wish people over there could at least see it. Sometimes I think they don't quite understand what it's like."

As we watched the people of Aachen straggle down the street we saw them pass two first-aid men carrying a stretcher out of a half-ruined building. On the stretcher was the inert, blood-stained body of an American soldier. Machine guns still echoed behind that building.

More than an hour went by before the last weary refugee plodded out of sight. The sergeant and I had witnessed an historic turning point in World War II. For the first time the people of Germany were joining the long lines of Europe's refugees along the road over which they had forced so many other peoples before them. Now the German people would know how it had been for the Poles, Russians, Greeks, Norwegians and French. Now they would know where their politicians and generals and strutting Nazi youths had led them. Perhaps this was the only way they could learn the fruits of cruelty and oppression which their country had spread over all Europe and far beyond. None of the politicians and generals and strutting youths were in that procession. It was only the very old, the very young and helpless, moving past their ruined homes through the blasted streets of Aachen in poverty and in fear.

Life, November 6, 1944

U.S. Board Bares Atrocity Details
Told by Witnesses at Polish Camps

by John H. Crider

WASHINGTON, Nov. 25—In the first detailed report by a United States Government Agency offering eyewitness proof of mass murder by the Germans, the War Refugee Board made public today accounts by three persons of organized atrocities at Birkenau and Oswiecim [Auschwitz] in southwestern Poland that transcend the horrors of Lublin. The accounts were vouched for by the WRB.

While at Lublin 1,500,000 persons were said to have been killed in three years, 1,500,000 to 1,765,000 persons were murdered in the torture chambers of Birkenau from April, 1942, to April, 1944, according to these Government-verified reports. Many thousands of other deaths by phenol injection, brutal beatings, starvation, shooting, etc., also are recounted.

"It is a fact beyond denial that the Germans have deliberately and systematically murdered millions of innocent civilians—Jews and Christians alike—all over Europe," the WRB declared.

"This campaign of terror and brutality, which is unprecedented in all history and which even now continues unabated, is part of the German plan to subjugate the free peoples of the world," it added.

"So revolting and diabolical are the German atrocities that the minds of civilized people find it difficult to believe that they have actually taken place," the board stated. "But the Governments of the United States and of other countries have evidence which clearly substantiates the facts."

After describing the nature of the reports now made public, the WRB added:

"The board has every reason to believe that these reports present a true picture of the frightful happenings in these camps. It is making the reports public in the firm conviction that they should be read and understood by all Americans."

Simultaneously with Government publication of the narrative from two young Slovak Jews, who escaped last April 7 —the only Jews to have escaped from Birkenau—and a non-Jewish Polish major—the only survivor of sixty Poles moved to Birkenau from Lublin—Peter H. Bergson, chairman of the Hebrew Committee for National Liberation, announced at a news conference that the United Nations War Crimes Commission had "refused to take into consideration any acts committed against persons other than nationals of the United Nations."

German atrocities against Jews and others of nationalities included in the German sphere of influence have not been recognized by the commission, Mr. Bergson said.

He added that his committee was recommending the following action to the United Nations concerned:

"1. That they issue a joint declaration proclaiming that crimes committed against Hebrews in Europe, irrespective of the territory on which the crime was committed or the citizenship or lack of citizenship of the victim at the time of death, be considered as a war crime and punished as such.

"2. That the Governments of the United Nations concerned instruct their representatives on the War Crimes Commission to see to it that the above-mentioned declaration is put into effect.

"3. That representatives of the Hebrew people be given membership on the War Crimes Commission and that temporarily, until such time as a Hebrew national sovereignty be re-established, the Hebrew Committee of National Liberation be authorized to constitute the Hebrew representation on the War Crimes Commission."

The two Slovak youths cited in the WRB reports estimated the number of Jews gassed and burned at Birkenau in the two-year period at 1,765,000 in the following table, but the Polish officer estimated that about 1,500,000 Jews were killed in Oswiecim in that fashion. Here is the recapitulation by the two escaped Jews:

Poland (transported by truck)	300,000
Poland (transported by train)	600,000
Holland	100,000
Greece	45,000
France	150,000
Belgium	50,000
Germany	60,000
Yugoslavia, Italy and Norway	50,000
Lithuania	50,000
Bohemia, Moravia & Austria	30,000
Slovakia	30,000
Camps for foreign Jews in Poland	300,000
Total	1,765,000

In the report the Jewish youths described the gassing and burning technique as follows:

"At present there are four crematoria in operation at Birkenau, two large ones, I and II, and two smaller ones, III and IV. Those of Type I and II consist of three parts, i.e., (a) the furnace room, (b) the large hall, and (c) the gas chamber. A huge chimney rises from the furnace room, around which are grouped nine furnaces, each having four openings. Each opening can take three normal corpses at once, and after an hour and a half the bodies are completely burned. This corresponds to a daily capacity of about 2,000 bodies.

"Next to this is a large 'reception hall,' which is arranged so as to give the impression of the antechamber of a bathing establishment. It holds 2,000 people, and apparently there is a similar waiting room on the floor below. From there a door and a few steps lead down into the very long and narrow gas chamber. The walls of this chamber are also camouflaged with simulated entries to shower rooms in order to mislead the victims. The roof is fitted with three traps which can be hermetically closed from the outside. A track leads from the gas chamber toward the furnace room.

"The gassing takes place as follows: The unfortunate victims are brought into the hall (b), where they are told to undress. To complete the fiction that they are going to bathe, each person receives a towel and a small piece of soap issued by two men clad in white coats. Then they are crowded into the gas chamber (c) in such numbers that there is, of course, only standing room.

"To compress this crowd into the narrow space, shots are often fired to induce those already at the far end to huddle still closer together. When everybody is inside, the heavy doors are closed. Then there is a short pause, presumably to allow the room temperature to rise to a certain level, after which SS men with gas masks climb the roof, open the traps, and shake down a preparation in powder form out of tin cans labeled 'Cyklon,' for use against vermin, which is manufactured by a Hamburg concern.

"It is presumed that this is a 'cyanide' mixture of some sort which turns into gas at a certain temperature. After three minutes everyone in the chamber is dead. No one is known to have survived this ordeal, although it was not uncommon to discover signs of life after the primitive measures employed in the birch wood.

"The chamber is then opened, aired, and the 'special squad' carts the bodies on flat trucks to the furnace rooms, where the burning takes place. Crematoria III and IV work on nearly the same principle, but their capacity is only half as large. Thus the total capacity of the four cremating and gassing plants at Birkenau amounts to about 6,000 daily."

In his independent report the Polish officer described the mass extermination thus:

"The first large convoys arrived from France and Slovakia. Physically able men and women—those without children or the mothers of grown-up children—were sent to the camp of Birkenau. The remainder, i. e., old or weak men, women with small children and all those unfit for labor, were taken to the Birch Wood (Brzezinki) and killed by means of hydrocyanic gas. For this purpose special gassing barracks had been built there.

"These consisted of large halls, airtight, and provided with ventilators which could be opened or closed according to the need. Inside they were equipped so as to create the impression of bathing establishments. This was done to deceive the victims and make them more manageable. The executions took place as follows: Each death convoy consisted of some eight to ten trucks packed with the 'selectees'; the convoy was unguarded, as the whole frightful drama took place on camp territory."

Then the victims were taken to the gas chambers, according to the report, which continued:

"Everything was hermetically closed, and specially trained SS units threw hydrocyanic bombs through the ventilation openings. After about ten minutes the doors were opened and a special squad composed exclusively of Jews had to clear away the bodies and prepare for a new group of 'selectees.'

"The crematoria had not yet been constructed, although there was a small one at Auschwitz which, however, was not employed for burning these bodies. Mass graves were dug at that time into which the corpses were simply thrown.

"This continued into the autumn of 1942. By this time extermination by gas was being intensified and there was no more time even for such summary burial. Row upon row of bodies of murdered Jews, covered only by a thin layer of earth, were widely dispersed in the surrounding fields, causing the soil to become almost marshy through the putrification of the bodies.

"The smell emanating from these fields became intolerable. In the autumn of 1942 all that remained of the bodies had to be exhumed and the bones collected and burned in the crematoria (by that time four had been completed). An alternative was to gather the remains of the unfortunate victims into heaps, pour gasoline over them, and leave it to the flames to finish the tragedy. The immense quantity of human ashes thus collected was carted away in every direction to be scattered over the fields where these martyrs had found their last rest."

In addition to mass asphyxiations, the Germans resorted to executions, phenol injections and brutality to dispose of victims. Here is one eyewitness account of brutality recorded by the Polish major:

"One day a working comrade discovered a few pieces of turnip, which he carefully hid. He continued his work but, from time to time, took surreptitious bites off his treasure. Another prisoner having 'squealed' on him, the capo arrived a few minutes later.

"It must be remembered that the capo is absolute master of

his commando and that everybody tries to get into his good graces. Unfortunately, this favor often had to be attained to the detriment of the well-being or sometimes even of the lives of other prisoners.

"The capo proceeded to search our comrade and, finding the pieces of turnip, knocked the weakened man to the ground, hitting him brutally about the head and face and in the stomach. He then ordered him to sit up, hands outstretched in front of him on the ground with a weight of bricks on each hand; the pieces of turnip were stuck in his mouth.

"All the men were then assembled and informed that the unfortunate man was to stay in this position for a whole hour. We were warned that this punishment would befall any member of the commando who committed a similar 'offense.' The condemned man underwent this ordeal guarded by one of the foremen, very eager to fulfill his task to the satisfaction of the capo, so that he hit our friend every time he tried to shift his position slightly.

"After fifteen to twenty minutes the man became unconscious, but a bucket of water was poured over him and he was again forced into his original position. After he had slumped over, senseless, for a second time, his body was thrown aside and nobody was allowed to pay further attention to him. After roll call that evening he was taken to the 'infirmary,' where he died two days later."

The use of the hypodermic needle for murder was described by the Polish major as follows:

"The sick were classified into two groups, 'Aryans' and Jews. These groups were again subdivided into further groups, of which the first included the sick, who were to remain in hospital, being considered 'curable.' The second consisted of extremely rundown patients, chronic cases, and the half-starving or mutilated whose recovery could only be effected by a long stay in the hospital.

"This group was practically condemned to death by phenol injections in the heart region. Racial considerations played an important role. An 'Aryan' really had to be seriously ill to be condemned to death by injection, whereas 80 to 90 per cent of the Jews 'hospitalized' there were 'eliminated' in this manner. Many of them knew about this method and applied for admission as so-called 'suicide candidates,' not having the courage to throw themselves on the high tension wires."

The accounts of the Slovaks and the Polish major mentioned a special "hygiene institute" at Oswiecim, which was adjacent to Birkenau, and where mysterious "experiments" were conducted on Jewish prisoners, mostly on females. The Polish major's account, which provided the only clue of what went on in the "institute," said:

"Here sterilizing by X-ray treatment, artificial insemination of women, as well as experiments on blood transfusions, were carried on."

The reports mentioned several well-known individuals, such as Witold Zacharewicz, Polish actor, and a brother of Léon Blum, former French Premier, as having been executed.

"Prominent guests from Berlin were present at the inauguration of the first crematorium in March, 1943," the reports said.

The New York Times, November 26, 1944

"A SOLID MASS OF DARK, IMPENETRABLE GREEN": THE HUERTGEN FOREST, NOVEMBER 1944

War in the Huertgen Forest

---

by Mack Morriss

THE FIRS are thick, and there are 50 square miles of them standing dismal and dripping at the approaches to the Cologne plain. The bodies of the firs begin close to the ground, so that each fir interlocks its body with another. At the height of a man standing, there is a solid mass of dark, impenetrable green. But at the height of a man crawling, there is room, and it is like a green cave, low-roofed and forbidding. And through this cave moved the infantry, to emerge cold and exhausted when the forest of Huertgen came to a sudden end before Grosshau.

The infantry, free from the claustrophobia of the forest, went on, but behind them they left their dead, and the forest will stink with deadness long after the last body is removed. The forest will bear the scars of our advance long after our scars have healed, and the infantry has scars that will never heal.

For Huertgen was agony, and there was no glory in it except the glory of courageous men—the MP whose testicles were hit by shrapnel and who said, "Okay, doc, I can take it"; the man who walked forward, firing tommy guns with both hands until an arm was blown off and then kept on firing the other tommy gun until he disappeared in a mortar burst.

Men of the 25th, 43d, and 37th Divisions would know Huertgen—it was like New Georgia. The mud was as deep, but it was yellow instead of black. Trees were as thick, but the branches were stemmed by brittle needles instead of broad jungle leaves. Hills were as steep and numerous, but there were mines—S mines, wooden-shoe mines, teller mines, box mines.

Foxholes were as miserable, but they were covered, because

577

tree bursts are deadly, and every barrage was a deluge of fragmentation from the tops of the neat little firs. Carrying parties were burdened with supplies on the narrow trails. Rain was as constant, but in Huertgen it was cold, and on the line there was constant attack and a stubborn enemy.

For 21 days, the division beat its slow way forward, and there were two mornings out of those 21 when the order was to reform and consolidate. Every other morning saw a jump-off advance, and the moment it stopped, the infantry dug in and buttoned up, because the artillery and mortars searched for men without cover and maimed them.

There was counterattack, too, but in time the infantry welcomed it, because then and only then the German came out of his hole and was a visible target, and the maddened infantry killed with grim satisfaction. But the infantry advanced with its battle packs, and it dug in and buttoned up, and then the artillery raked the line so that there were many times when the infantry's rolls could not be brought up to them.

Rolls were brought to a certain point, but the infantry could not go back for them because to leave the shelter was insane. So the infantry slept as it fought—if it slept at all—without blankets, and the nights were long and wet and cold.

But the artillery was going two ways. The division support fire thundered into the forest, and it was greater than the enemy fire coming in. A tired battalion commander spoke of our artillery. "It's the biggest consolation we have," he said. "No matter how much we're getting, we know the kraut is getting more." So the infantry was not alone.

Tanks did the best they could, when they could. In the beginning, they shot up defended bunkers and dueled with machine guns in the narrow firebreaks, and they waddled down into the open spaces so that the infantry could walk in their tracks and feel the comfort of safety from mines. At the clearing before Grosshau, they lunged forward, and some of them still dragged the foliage of the forest on their hulls when they were knocked out.

One crew abandoned its tank, leaving behind all their equipment in the urgency of the escape. But they took with them the mascot rooster they had picked up at St. Lo.

The advance through Huertgen was "like wading through the ocean," said S-3 at the regiment. "You walk in it all right, but water is all around you."

There were thickets in the forest where two battalion CPs had been in operation for three days, and physical contact between them had been routine. Thirteen Germans and two antitank guns were discovered between them. The CPs were 800 yards apart. "Four thousand yards from the German lines," said S-3, who had been one of the battalion command-ers, "and we had to shoot krauts in our own front yard. Our prisoner-of-war interrogation team got its own captives to question. The engineers bridged the creek, and before they could finish their work they had 12 Germans sitting on a hill 200 yards away, directing artillery fire on them by radio." These things were part of Huertgen, a green monument to the *Wehrmacht*'s defense and the First Army's power.

At that, the monument is a bitter thing, a shattered thing. The Germans had four lines of defense in the forest, and one by one those lines were beaten down and the advance contin-ued. This was for the Fourth Division alone. There were other divisions and other lines. And these MLRs were pre-pared magnificently.

Huertgen had its roads and firebreaks. The firebreaks were only wide enough to allow two jeeps to pass, and they were mined and interdicted by machine-gun fire. In one break there was a teller mine every eight paces for three miles. In another there were more than 500 mines in the narrow break. One stretch of road held 300 teller mines, each one with a pull device in addition to the regular detonator. There were 400 antitank mines in a three-mile area.

Huertgen had its roads, and they were blocked. The Ger-man did well by his abatis, his roadblocks made from trees. Sometimes he felled 200 trees across the road, cutting them down so they interlocked as they fell. Then he mined and booby-trapped them. Finally he registered his artillery on them, and his mortars, and at the sound of men clearing them, he opened fire.

The first two German MLRs were screened by barbed wire in concertina strands. The MLRs themselves were log-and-earth bunkers six feet underground, and they were constructed carefully, and inside them were neat bunks built of forest wood, and the walls of the bunkers were paneled with wood. These sheltered the defenders. Outside the bunkers were the fighting positions.

The infantry went through Huertgen's mud and its splintered forest growth and its mines and its high explosives, mile after mile, slowly and at great cost. But it went through, with an average of perhaps 600 yards gained each day.

The men threw ropes around the logs of the roadblocks and yanked the ropes to explode the mines and booby traps in the roadblock, and then they shoved the trees aside to clear the way. The engineers on their hands and knees probed the earth with number-eight wire to find and uncover nonmetallic shoe mines and box mines that the Germans had planted by the thousands. A wire or bayonet was shoved into the ground at an angle in the hope that it would touch the mines on their sides rather than on the tops, for they detonated at two or three pounds' pressure. Scattered on that ground there were little round mines no larger than an ointment box, but still large enough to blow off a man's foot.

At times, when there was a clearing, the engineers used another method to open a path. They looped primacord onto a rifle grenade and then fired the grenade. As it lobbed forward, it carried with it a length of primacord, which was then touched off and exploded along the ground with enough force to set off or uncover any shoe mines or S mines hidden underground along its path. In other cases, when the area was known to be mined, it was subjected to an artillery concentration that blew up the mines by the force of the concussion. There could be no certainty that every mine was blown. The advance was costly; but the enemy suffered.

One regiment of the Fourth Division claimed the destruction of five German regiments in meeting 19 days of constant attack. The German had been told the value of Huertgen and had been ordered to fight to the last as perhaps never before. He did, and it was hell on him. How the German met our assault was recorded in the brief diary of a medic who later was taken prisoner, and because it is always good for the infantry to know what its enemy is thinking, the diary was published by the Fourth Division. The medic refers to the infantry as "Ami," colloquial for American. These are some excerpts:

It's Sunday. My God, today is Sunday. With dawn the edge of our forest received a barrage. The earth trembles. The concussion takes our breath. Two wounded are brought to my hole, one with both hands shot off. I am considering whether to cut off the rest of the arm. I'll leave it on. How brave these two are. I hope to God that all this is not in vain. To our left, machine guns begin to clatter—and there comes Ami.

In broad waves you can see him across the field. Tanks all around him are firing wildly. Now the American artillery ceases and the tank guns are firing like mad. I can't stick my head out of the hole— finally here are three German assault guns. With a few shots we can see several tanks burning once again. Long smoke columns are rising toward heaven. The infantry takes cover, and the attack slows down—it's stopped. It's unbelievable that with this handful of men we hold out against such attacks.

And now we go forward to counterattack. The captain is leading it himself. We can't go far, though. Our people are dropping like tired flies. We have got to go back and leave the whole number of our dead and wounded. Slowly the artillery begins its monotonous song again—drumming, drumming, drumming without letup. If we only had the munitions and heavy weapons that the American has, he would have gone to the devil a long time ago, but, as it is, there is only a silent holding out to the last man.

Our people are overtired. When Ami really attacks again, he has got to break through. I can't believe this land can be held any longer. Many of our boys just run away and we can't find them and we have to hold out with a small group, but we are going to fight.

Then, two days later, came the final entry:

Last night was pretty bad. We hardly got any sleep, and in the morning the artillery is worse than ever. I can hardly stand it, and the planes are here again. Once more the quiet before the storm. Then, suddenly, tanks and then hordes of Amis are breaking out of the forest. Murderous fire meets him, but he doesn't even take cover anymore. We shoot until the barrels sizzle, and finally he is stopped again.

We are glad to think that the worst is past, when suddenly he breaks through on our left. Hand grenades are bursting, but we cannot hold them any longer. There are only five of us. We have got to go back. Already we can see brown figures through the trees. As they get to within 70 paces, I turn around and walk away very calmly with my hands in my pockets. They are not even shooting at me, perhaps on account of the red cross on my back.

On the road to Grosshau, we take up a new position. We can hear tanks come closer, but Ami won't follow through his gains anyway. He's too cowardly for that.

Perhaps this German who called the infantry cowardly and then surrendered to it will never hear the story of one Fourth Division soldier in Huertgen. He stepped on a mine and it blew off his foot. It was one of those wounds in which the arteries and veins are forced upward so they are in a manner sealed, and bleeding is not so profuse as it otherwise would be.

The man lay there, but he wasn't able to bandage his own wounds. The medics tried to reach him but were fired upon. One was hit, and the trees around the man were white with scars of the machine-gun bullets that kept the medics away. Finally—after 70 hours—they managed to reach him.

He was still conscious, and for the medics it was a blessing that he was conscious; and for the man himself it was a blessing. For during the darkness the Germans had moved up to the wounded man. They took his field jacket from him, and his cigarettes. They booby-trapped him by setting a charge under his back, so that whoever lifted him would die. So the wounded man, knowing this, lay quietly on the charge and told the men who came to help him what the Germans had done. They cut the wires of the booby trap and carried him away.

The green monument of Huertgen is a bitter thing.

Yank, January 5, 1945

The Battle of the Bulge

by Martha Gellhorn

THEY all said it was wonderful Kraut-killing country. What it looked like was scenery for a Christmas card: smooth white snow hills and bands of dark forest and villages that actually nestled. The snow made everything serene, from a distance. At sunrise and sunset the snow was pink and the forests grew smoky and soft. During the day the sky was covered with ski tracks, the vapor trails of planes, and the roads were dangerous iced strips, crowded with all the usual vehicles of war, and the artillery made a great deal of noise, as did the bombs from the Thunderbolts. The nestling villages, upon closer view, were mainly rubble and there were indeed plenty of dead Krauts. This was during the German counteroffensive which drove through Luxembourg and Belgium and is now driven back. At this time the Germans were being "contained," as the communiqué said. The situation was "fluid"—again the communiqué. For the sake of the record, here is a little of what containing a fluid situation in Kraut-killing country looks like.

The road to Bastogne had been worked over by the Ninth Air Force Thunderbolts before the Third Army tanks finally cleared the way. A narrow alley was free now, and two or three secondary roads leading from Bastogne back to our lines. "Lines" is a most inaccurate word and one should really say "leading back through where the Germans weren't to where the Americans were scattered about the snowscape." The Germans remained on both sides of this alley and from time to time attempted to push inward and again cut off Bastogne.

A colleague and I drove up to Bastogne on a secondary road through breath-taking scenery. The Thunderbolts had created this scenery. You can say the words "death and destruction" and they don't mean anything. But they are awful words when you are looking at what they mean. There were some German staff cars along the side of the road: they had not merely been hit by machine-gun bullets, they had been mashed into the ground. There were half-tracks and tanks literally wrenched apart, and a gun position directly hit by bombs. All around these lacerated or flattened objects of steel there was the usual riffraff: papers, tin cans, cartridge belts, helmets, an odd shoe, clothing. There were also, ignored and completely inhuman, the hard-frozen corpses of Germans. Then there was a clump of houses, burned and gutted, with only a few walls standing, and around them the enormous bloated bodies of cattle.

The road passed through a curtain of pine forest and came out on a flat, rolling snow field. In this field the sprawled or bunched bodies of Germans lay thick, like some dark shapeless vegetable.

We had watched the Thunderbolts working for several days. They flew in small packs and streaked in to the attack in single file. They passed quickly through the sky and when they dived you held your breath and waited; it seemed impossible that the plane would be able to pull itself up to safety. They were diving to within sixty feet of the ground. The snub-nosed Thunderbolt is more feared by the German troops than any other plane.

You have seen Bastogne and a thousand other Bastognes in the newsreels. These dead towns are villages spread over Europe and one forgets the human misery and fear and despair that the cracked and caved-in buildings represent. Bastogne was a German job of death and destruction and it was beautifully thorough. The 101st Airborne Division, which held Bastogne, was still there, though the day before the wounded had been taken out as soon as the first road was open. The survivors of the 101st Airborne Division, after being entirely surrounded, uninterruptedly shelled and bombed, after having fought off four times their strength in Germans, look—for some unknown reason—cheerful and lively. A young lieutenant remarked, "The tactical situation was always good." He was very surprised when we shouted with laughter. The front, north of Bastogne, was just up the road and the peril was far from past.

At Warnach, on the other side of the main Bastogne road, some soldiers who had taken, lost and retaken this miserable village were now sightseeing the battlefield. They were also inspecting the blown-out equipment of two German tanks and a German self-propelled gun which had been destroyed here. Warnach smelled of the dead; in subzero weather the smell of death has an acrid burning odor. The soldiers poked through the German equipment to see if there was anything useful or desirable. They unearthed a pair of good bedroom slippers alongside the tank, but as no one in the infantry has any chance to wear bedroom slippers these were left. There was a German Bible but no one could read German. Someone had found a German machine pistol in working order and rapidly salted it away; they hoped to find other equally valuable loot.

The American dead had been moved inside the smashed houses and covered over; the dead horses and cows lay where they were, as did a few dead Germans. An old civilian was hopelessly shoveling grain from some burned and burst sacks into a wheelbarrow; and farther down the ruined street a woman was talking French in a high angry voice to the chaplain, who was trying to pacify her. We moved down this way to watch the goings-on. Her house was in fairly good shape; that is to say, it had no windows or door and there was a shell hole through the second-floor wall, but it was standing and the roof looked rainproof. Outside her parlor window were some German mines, marked with a white tape. She stood in her front hall and said bitterly that it was a terrible thing, she had left her house for a few moments that morning, and upon returning she found her sheets had been stolen.

"What's she saying?" asked an enormous soldier with red-rimmed blue eyes and a stubble of red beard. Everyone seems about the same age, as if weariness and strain and the unceasing cold leveled all life. I translated the woman's complaint.

Another soldier said, "What does a sheet look like?"

The huge red-bearded man drawled out, "My goodness," a delicious expression coming from that face in that street. "If she'd of been here when the fighting was going on, she'd act different."

Farther down the street a command car dragged a trailer; the bodies of Germans were piled on the trailer like so much ghastly firewood.

We had come up this main road two days before. First there had been a quick tempestuous scene in a battalion headquarters when two planes strafed us, roaring in to attack three times and putting machine-gun bullets neatly through the second-story windows of the house. The official attitude has always been that no Germans were flying reclaimed Thunderbolts, so that is that. No one was wounded or killed during this brief muck-up. One of the battalion machine-gunners, who had been firing at the Thunderbolts, said, "For God's sake, which side are those guys fighting on?" We jumped into our jeep and drove up nearer the front, feeling that the front was probably safer.

A solitary tank was parked close to a bombed house near the main road. The crew sat on top of the tank, watching a village just over the hill which was being shelled, as well as bombed by the Thunderbolts. The village was burning and the smoke made a close package of fog around it, but the flames shot up and reddened the snow in the foreground. The armed forces on this piece of front consisted, at the moment, of this tank, and out ahead a few more tanks, and somewhere invisibly to the left a squadron of tanks. We did not know where our infantry was. (This is what a fluid situation means.) The attacked village would soon be entered by the tanks, including the solitary watchdog now guarding this road.

We inquired of the tank crew how everything went. "The war's over," said one of the soldiers, sitting on the turret. "Don't you know that? I heard it on the radio, a week ago. The Germans haven't any gasoline. They haven't any planes. Their tanks are no good. They haven't any shells for their guns. Hell, it's all over. I ask myself what I'm doing here," the tankist went on. "I say to myself, boy, you're crazy, sitting out here in the snow. Those ain't Germans, I say to myself, didn't they tell you on the radio the Germans are finished?"

As for the situation, someone else on the tank said that they would gratefully appreciate it if we could tell them what was going on.

"That wood's full of dead Krauts," said another, pointing across the road. "We came up here and sprayed it just in case there was any around and seems the place was full of them, so it's a good thing we sprayed it all right. But where they are right now, I wouldn't know."

"How's your hen?" asked the Captain, who had come from Battalion HQ to show us the way. "He's got a hen," the Captain explained. "He's been sweating that hen out for three days, running around after it with his helmet."

"My hen's worthless," said a soldier. "Finished, no good, got no fight in her."

"Just like the Germans," said the one who listened to the radio.

Now two days later the road was open much farther and there was even a rumor that it was open all the way to Bastogne. That would mean avoiding the secondary roads, a quicker journey, but it seemed a good idea to inquire at a blasted German gun position. At this spot there were ten Americans, two sergeants and eight enlisted men; also two smashed German bodies, two dead cows and a gutted house.

"I wouldn't go up that road if I was you," one of the sergeants said. "It's cut with small-arms fire about a quarter of a mile farther on. We took about seventeen Heinies out of there just a while back, but some others must of got in."

That seemed to settle the road.

"Anyhow," the sergeant went on. "They're making a counterattack. They got about thirty tanks, we heard, coming this way."

The situation was getting very fluid again.

"What are you going to do?" I said.

"Stay here," said one of the soldiers.

"We got a gun," said another.

War is lonely and individual work; it is hard to realize how small it can get. Finally it can boil down to ten unshaven gaunt-looking young men, from anywhere in America, stationed on a vital road with German tanks coming in.

"You better take that side road if you're going to Bastogne," the second sergeant said.

It seemed shameful to leave them. "Good luck," I said, not knowing what to say.

"Sure, sure," they said soothingly. And later on they got a tank and the road was never cut and now if they are still alive they are somewhere in Germany doing the same work, as undramatically and casually—just any ten young men from anywhere in America.

About a mile from this place, and therefore about a mile and a half from the oncoming German tanks, the General in command of this tank outfit had his headquarters in a farmhouse. You could not easily enter his office through the front door, because a dead horse with spattered entrails blocked the way. A shell had landed in the farmyard a few minutes before and killed one cow and wounded a second, which was making sad sounds in a passageway between the house and the barn.

The air-ground-support officer was here with his van, checking up on the Thunderbolts who were attacking the oncoming German tanks. "Argue Leader," he said, calling on the radiophone to the flight leader. "Beagle here. Did you do any good on that one?"

"Can't say yet," answered the voice from the air.

Then over the loud-speaker a new voice came from the air, talking clearly and loudly and calmly. "Three Tigers down there with people around them."

Also from the air the voice of Argue Leader replied rather peevishly, "Go in and get them. Don't stand there talking about it." They were both moving at an approximate speed of three hundred miles an hour.

From the radio in another van came the voice of the Colonel commanding the forward tank unit, which was stopping this counterattack on the ground. "We got ten and two more coming," said the Colonel's voice. "Just wanted to keep you posted on the German tanks burning up here. It's a beautiful sight, a beautiful sight, over."

"What a lovely headquarters," said a soldier who was making himself a toasted cheese sandwich over a small fire that served everyone for warmth and cookstove. He had opened the cheese can in his K ration and was doing an excellent job, using a German bayonet as a kitchen utensil.

"Furthermore," said a lieutenant, "they're attacking on the other side. They got about thirty tanks coming in from the west too."

"See if I care," remarked the soldier, turning his bread carefully so as to toast it both ways. A shell landed, but it was farther up the road. There had been a vaguely sketched general ducking, a quick reflex action, but no one of course remarked it.

Then Argue Leader's voice came exultantly from the air. "Got those three. Going home now. Over."

"Good boys," said the ground officer. "Best there is. My squadron."

"Listen to him," said an artillery officer who had come over to report. "You'd think the Thunderbolts did everything. Well, I got to get back to work."

The cow went on moaning softly in the passageway. Our driver, who had made no previous comment during the day, said bitterly, "What I hate to see is a bunch of livestock all beat up this way. Goddammit, what they got to do with it? It's not their fault."

Christmas had passed almost unnoticed. All those who could, and that would mean no farther forward than Battalion Headquarters, had shaved and eaten turkey. The others did not shave and ate cold K rations. That was Christmas. There was little celebration on New Year's Eve, because everyone was occupied, and there was nothing to drink. Now on New Year's Day we were going up to visit the front, east of Luxembourg City. The front was quiet in the early afternoon, except for artillery, and a beautiful fat-flaked snowstorm had started. We decided, like millions of other people, that we were most heartily sick of war; what we really wanted to do was borrow a sled and go coasting. We borrowed a homemade wooden sled from an obliging little boy and found a steep slick hill near an abandoned stone quarry. It was evidently a well-known hill, because a dozen Luxembourg children were already there, with unsteerable sleds like ours. The sky had cleared and the ever present Thunderbolts returned and were working over the front less than four kilometers away. They made a lot of noise, and the artillery was pounding away too. The children paid no attention to this; they did not watch the Thunderbolts, or listen to the artillery. Screaming with joy, fear, and good spirits, they continued to slide down the hill.

Our soldier driver stood with me at the top of the hill and watched the children. "Children aren't so dumb," he said. I said nothing. "Children are pretty smart," he said. I said nothing again. "What I mean is, children got the right idea. What people ought to do is go coasting."

When he dropped us that night he said, "I sure got to thank you folks. I haven't had so much fun since I left home."

On the night of New Year's Day, I thought of a wonderful New Year's resolution for the men who run the world: get to know the people who only live in it.

There were many dead and many wounded, but the survivors contained the fluid situation and slowly turned it into a retreat, and finally, as the communiqué said, the bulge was ironed out. This was not done fast or easily; and it was not done by those anonymous things, armies, divisions, regiments. It was done by men, one by one—your men.

The Face of War, 1959

The First Three Days

by Robert Sherrod

By wireless from Iwo Jima

THE JAPS had expected for a long time that we would land on Iwo Jima and they prepared accordingly. Into their defense they poured all the ingenuity they could command, all the lessons they learned from Tarawa, Kwajalein, Saipan, Guam and Peleliu. For our attack on Iwo Jima, the island they could not afford to lose, they had saved their newest and best weapons.

Besides their meticulously built pillboxes and their concentrated hillside caves, the Japs had dozens of big guns, a new rocket projectile, hundreds of smaller guns and machine guns and the most fantastic array of mortars man ever assembled in defense of one island. Their soldiers—perhaps 20,000 of them—lived underground because our planes could destroy topside barracks. It is no wonder that Vice Admiral Richmond Kelly Turner, veteran of the toughest Pacific amphibious operations, said, "Iwo Jima is as well defended as any fixed position that exists in the world today."

Yet it is possible to say after three days that the Japs will lose Iwo Jima and we will have airfields within 675 miles of Tokyo. One reason is sheer power, including naval and air supremacy which made available some 800 ships and a total of perhaps 1,200 planes. But the ultimate factor in the fall of Iwo Jima will be the character and courage of the U.S. Marines.

Iwo Jima is shaped roughly like South America. The northern half of Iwo Jima's five-mile length is a high plateau rising over 300 feet and having steep cliffs around the perimeter as well as in between the various levels of the plateau. The southern tip of Iwo Jima is Mt. Suribachi, a volcano shaped like a scoop of ice cream which rises 554 feet. The only beaches on the island are between the plateau and the volcano at the southern tip. Our landings were made on the east beaches.

The island had been bombed for 74 straight days before D-Day. In January it had been thoroughly shelled by cruisers and battleships. For three days prior to D-Day many cruisers, battleships and destroyers poured more than 8,000 tons of high explosives on the eight square miles of Iwo Jima. To a British observer aboard our transport it seemed "that nothing could possibly be alive." The naval gunfire stripped away many tons of earth from the east side of Mt. Suribachi and from the cliffs at the underside of the bulge on the right flank. Thus the concrete-framed caves of the molelike Japs were revealed—rectangular frames leading to holes which extended far into the cliffs. Some of these concrete frames were wrecked. But from many others, though they had been laid bare, the Japs kept firing.

Several hundred carrier planes dropped their last bombs and completed their final strafing runs as the first wave of assault boats reached the shore of Iwo Jima's east beaches. It was 9 o'clock when regimental combat teams from the 4th Marine Division of Major General Clifton Cates and the new 5th Marine Division under Major General Keller Rockney landed abreast on the black sand.

The first objective was Motoyama Airfield No. 4 which lies midway between the east and west beaches of Iwo Jima. The airfield itself is on a plateau that looks deceptively low. But from the beach the airfield looks as high as a mountain. Furthermore the sand on Iwo Jima beaches is a coarse, loose, black sand which can be negotiated only by tracked vehicles—and not always by them. Many of our indispensable tanks stalled in the sand soon after they hit the beaches. There they became easy marks for heavy gunfire.

The first two hours were not easy. Mortars from Mt. Suribachi and the northern plateau rained on the beaches. The 4th Division was sprinkled by machine-gun fire from the cliffs. By 11 o'clock one division had advanced 300 yards to the steep embankment below the airfield, had almost crossed the island at its narrow neck just above Suribachi. But the first two hours were a picnic compared to what followed.

We had a toehold and it looked like a good one. Then,

before noon, all hell broke loose. From the north and from the south the hidden Japs poured artillery and six-inch mortars into the marines on the beachhead. Nearly all our tanks were clustered near the beaches like black beetles struggling to move on tar paper. A few others waddled up the steep, sandy incline toward the airfield, spouting flames now and then into the pillboxes.

Viewing the scene later, I could only marvel that any men got past those pillboxes. Their openings were mostly to the north and south. Naval gunfire might have destroyed them had their vents been exposed to the sea. But somehow these incredible marines had swept past the pillboxes, tossing grenades into them or shooting flame into them as they inched uphill toward the airfield.

It was sickening to watch the Jap mortars crash into the men as they climbed. These huge explosive charges—"floating ash cans" we called them—would crash among the thin lines of marines or among the boats bringing reinforcements to the beach, throwing sand, water and even pieces of human flesh a hundred feet into the air. Supporting naval gunfire and planes with bombs managed to knock out some of the mortars but the Japs continued throwing their deadly missiles all afternoon. By noon the assault battalions reported 20% to 25% fatalities.

Some units crossed the island in midafternoon and overran the southern extremity of the airfield but others were knocked back every time they struggled over the eastern embankments. Five tanks actually got on the airfield but three of them were quickly knocked out and the other two had to return. Our trouble was that the Japs had us covered from both ends of the island, from any point on the island. The marines could only advance and die, paving with their bodies a way for the men who came behind them.

By late afternoon we held perhaps 10% of the island, the most dangerous 10%. It was about 5 o'clock when orders came for Colonel Walter Irvine Jordan to take his 24th Regiment of the 4th Division to the beach. I had been assigned a spot in the boat of Jordan's executive officer, Lieut. Colonel Austin R. Brenelli.

The Higgins boat crunched on the shore. We ran up the

steep beach and started digging in for the night. Fashioning a foxhole out of that loose sand was, in the words of a marine from the Deep South, "like trying to dig a hole in a barrel of wheat." But we all finally managed to spade holes deep enough to protect our bodies against the shelling that was to come.

All night the Japs rained heavy mortars and rockets and artillery on the entire area between the beach and the airfield. Twice they hit casualty stations on the beach. Many men who had been only wounded were killed. The command post of one of the assault battalions received a direct hit which killed several officers. An artillery battalion based near the beach had 12 men killed and one of its guns knocked out. A six-inch mortar killed the captain of one assault company with two of his officers and five of his men. When the night had ended one group of medical corpsmen had been reduced from 28 to 11. The corpsmen were taking it as usual.

Many times during the night we blessed our naval gunfire and the few pieces of land-based artillery. They plastered the Jap nine tenths of the island so thoroughly that the enemy could never gather for a counterattack against our thinly held lines. Once a hundred Nips managed to rush against the 5th Division lines. Those who were not killed fled.

During the entire second day I saw only 12 dead Japs, though many others had undoubtedly been burned in their pillboxes by flamethrowers. The Jap plan of defense was plain. Only a few men would defend the beaches. The mortars and machine guns from the hillside caves, long ago registered on the beaches, would stop the landing. The Jap plan of defense failed because we had so much power we could stun them if we could not kill them, because the Navy's guns and planes could keep them down during our attacks. And it failed because the marines kept advancing despite their losses.

About the dead, whether Jap or American, there was one thing in common. They died with the greatest possible violence. Nowhere in the Pacific war have I seen such badly mangled bodies. Many were cut squarely in half. Legs and arms lay 50 feet away from any body. In one spot on the sand, far from the nearest cluster of dead men, I saw a string of guts 15 feet long. There are 250 wounded aboard the transport where this story is being written. One of the doctors tells me that 90% of them require major surgery. Off Normandy last summer, he says, only 5% who were brought aboard this transport needed such surgery. On the beach this morning I saw at least 50 men still fighting despite their wounds. Only the incapacitated request evacuation.

On the second day the 4th and 5th Divisions completed occupation of the airfield and pushed northward toward Motoyama Airfield No. 2, about 400 yards north of No. 1. The second night ashore was bitter cold but Jap firepower had decreased. After three days we hold about one quarter of Iwo Jima and we have finally gained some high ground. It seems certain that we will take Iwo Jima at a smaller cost in casualties than Saipan's 16,000. Probably no large percentage of the Jap defenders have yet been killed, but henceforth the Japs will kill fewer marines and the marines will kill more Japs.

Life, March 5, 1945

Jump-Off

by Howard Brodie

WITH THE NINTH ARMY—I joined K Company, 406th Regiment, 102d Division, the night before the shove-off, as an artist, not an infantryman.

We were part of a reserve regiment several miles behind the line and would not be committed until after the Roer had been crossed by forward elements.

I felt everyone of us sweated it out as we went to sleep that night. At 0245 our barrage awoke us, but we stayed in our sacks until 0400. After hot chow we saddled our packs and headed for an assembly area in a wrecked town about five miles away. It was a silent company of men spaced on either side of the road—the traditional soldier picture of silhouettes against the crimson flashes of shells bursting on the enemy lines in the distance.

In the assembly town, we waited in the shattered rooms of a crumbling building. It was not pleasant waiting, because a dead cow stank in an adjoining room. We shoved off at daylight and came to gutted Rurdorf. I remember passing crucifixes and a porcelain pee pot on the rubble-laden road and pussy willows as we came to the river. A pool of blood splotched the side of the road. We crossed the Roer on a pontoon bridge and moved on. The forward elements were still ahead of us a few miles.

We passed a still doughboy on the side of the road with no hands; his misshapen, ooze-filled mittens lay a few feet from him. Knots of prisoners walked by us with their hands behind their heads. One group contained medics. In their knee-length white sacks, emblazoned with red crosses, they resembled crusaders. In another group were a couple of German females, one of them in uniform. Mines like cabbages lay on either side of the road.

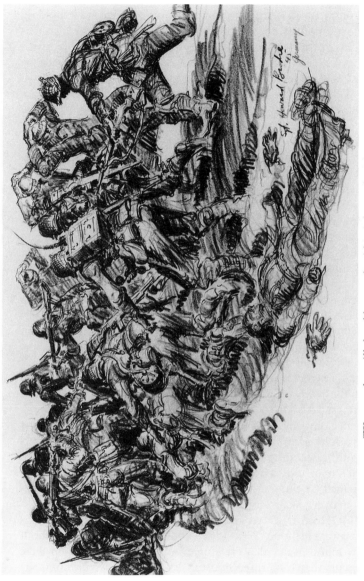

"We passed a still doughboy on the side of the road with no hands, his misshapen, ooze-filled mittens a few feet from him."

We entered the town of Tetz and set up the CP in a cellar. Two platoons went forward a few hundred yards to high ground overlooking the town and dug in. We were holding the right flank of the offensive finger. Several enemy shells burst in the town. Some tracers shot across the road between the CP and the dug-in platoons. The tracers seemed to be below knee level. Night fell.

The CP picked up reports like a magnet: "The Jerries are counterattacking up the road with 40 Tiger tanks . . . The Jerries are attacking with four medium tanks." Stragglers reported in from forward companies. One stark-faced squad leader had lost most of his squad. The wounded were outside, the dead to the left of our platoon holes. It was raining. I went to sleep.

The next day I went to our forward platoons. I saw a dough bailing his hole out with his canteen cup . . . saw our planes dive-bomb Jerry in the distance . . . saw our time-fire burst on Jerry, and white phosphorus and magenta smoke bombs. I saw platoon leader Lt. Joe Lane playing football with a cabbage. I saw a dead GI in his hole slumped in his last living position—the hole was too deep and too narrow to allow his body to settle. A partially smoked cigarette lay inches from his mouth, and a dollar-sized circle of blood on the earth offered the only evidence of violent death.

Night fell and I stayed in the platoon CP hole. We didn't stay long because word came through that we would move up to the town of Hottorf, the forward position of the offensive finger, preparatory to jumping off at 0910.

K Company lined up in the starlit night—the CO, the first platoon, MGs, third platoon, heavy weapons, headquarters and the second platoon in the rear—about 10 paces between each man and 50 between the platoons. The sky overhead was pierced by thousands of tracers and AA bursts as Jerry planes flew over. Again it was a silent company.

At Hottorf we separated into various crumbling buildings to await H-hour. We had five objectives, the farthest about 2¼ miles away. All were single houses but two, which were towns of two or three houses. We were the assault company of the Third Battalion.

H-hour was approaching. A shell burst outside the win-

"I saw a GI in his hole, slumped in his last living position."

dow, stinging a couple of men and ringing our ears. We huddled on the floor.

It was time to move now. The first platoon went out on the street followed by the MGs and the third platoon and the rest of us. We passed through doughs in houses on either side of the street. They wisecracked and cheered us on. We came to the edge of town and onto a broad rolling field. The third and first platoons fanned out in front of us. Headquarters group stayed in the center.

I followed in the footsteps of Pfc. Joe Esz, the platoon runner. He had an aluminum light case upon which I could easily focus the corner of my eye to keep my position and still be free to observe. Also, I felt if I followed in his footsteps I would not have to look down at the ground for mines. He turned to me and commented on how beautifully the company was moving, properly fanned and well-spaced.

Several hundred yards away I noticed Jerries running out of a gun position waving a white flag. A black puff of smoke a few hundred yards to my right caught my attention, then another closer. I saw some men fall on the right flank. The black puffs crept in. There were whistles and cracks in the air and a barrage of 88s burst around us, spaced like the black squares of a checkerboard surrounding the reds. I heard the zing of shrapnel as I hugged the earth. We slithered into the enemy 88 position from which I had seen the prisoners run. Somebody threw a grenade into the dugout.

We moved on. Some prisoners and a couple of old women ran out onto the field from a house, Objective One. There was the zoom and crack of 88s again. A rabbit raced wildly away to the left. We went down. I saw a burst land on the running Jerries. One old woman went down on her knees in death, in an attitude as though she were picking flowers.

A dud landed three feet in front of T/Sgt. Jim McCauley, the platoon sergeant, spraying him with dirt. Another dud ricocheted over Pfc. Wes Maulden, the 300 radio operator. I looked to the right flank and saw a man floating in the air amidst the black smoke of an exploding mine. He just disappeared in front of the squad leader, S/Sgt. Elwin Miller. A piece of flesh sloshed by Sgt. Fred Wilson's face. Some men didn't get up. We went on. A couple of men vomited. A piece of shrapnel cut a dough's throat as neatly as Jack the Ripper might have done it.

The right flank was getting some small-arms fire. I was so tired from running and going down that it seemed as though my sartorius muscles would not function. The 300 radio wouldn't work and we couldn't get fire on those 88s. Pfc. George Linton went back through that barrage to get another one from Hottorf. Medic Oliver Poythress was working on wounded in that barrage.

Objective Two loomed ahead—a large building enclosing

"A dud landed . . ."

a courtyard. Cow shed, stables, tool shed, hay loft, living quarters opened on the inner court. I saw an 88 explode over the arched entrance.

We filtered into the courtyard and into the surrounding rooms. The executive officer started to reorganize the company. The platoons came in. 1st Sgt. Dick Wardlow tried to make a casualty list. Many didn't make it. A plan of defense was decided on for the building. A large work horse broke out from his stable and lumbered crazily around the courtyard. T-4 Melvin Fredell, the FO radio operator, lay in the courtyard relaying artillery orders. An 88 crashed into the roof. The cows in their shed pulled on their ropes. One kicked a sheep walking around in a state of confusion.

A dying GI lay in the tool room; his face was a leathery yellow. A wounded GI lay with him. Another wounded dough lay on his belly in the cow shed, in the stench of dung and decaying beets. Another GI quietly said he could take no more. A couple of doughs started frying eggs in the kitchen. I went into the tool shed to the dying dough. "He's cold, he's dead," said Sgt. Charles Turpen, the MG squad leader. I took off my glove and felt his head, but my hand was so cold he felt warm. A medic came and said he was dead.

Lt. Bob Clark organized his company and set up defense. FO Phillip Dick climbed the rafters of the hay loft to report our artillery bursts. The wounded dough in the cow shed sobbed for more morphine. Four of us helped carry him to a bed in another room. He was belly down and pleaded for someone to hold him by the groin as we carried him: "I can't stand it. Press them up, it'll give me support." A pool of blood lay under him.

"One dough was hit as he ran."

I went to the cowshed to take a nervous leak. A shell hit, shaking the roof. I ducked down and found I was seeking shelter with two calves. I crossed the courtyard to the grain shed where about 60 doughs were huddled.

Tank fire came in now. I looked up and saw MG tracers rip through the brick walls. A tank shell hit the wall and the roof. A brick landed on the head of the boy next to me. We couldn't see for the cloud of choking dust. Two doughs had their arms around each other; one was sobbing. More MG tracers ripped through the wall, and another shell. I squeezed between several bags of grain. Doughs completely disappeared in a hay pile.

We got out of there and our tanks joined us. I followed a tank, stepping in its treads. The next two objectives were taken by platoons on my right, and I don't remember whether any 88s came in for this next quarter mile or not. One dough was too exhausted to make it.

We were moving up to our final objective now—a very large building, also enclosing a courtyard, in a small town. Jerry planes were overhead but for some reason did not strafe. Our tanks spewed the town with fire and led the way. Black bursts from Jerry time-fire exploded over our heads this time. We passed Jerry trenches and a barbed-wire barrier. Lt. Lane raced to a trench. A Jerry pulled a cord, setting off a circle of mines around him, but he was only sprayed with mud. S/Sgt. Eugene Flanagan shot at the Jerry, who jumped up and surrendered with two others.

Jerries streamed out of the large house. Women came out too. An 88 and mortars came in. I watched Pfc. Bob de Valk and Pfc. Ted Sanchez bring out prisoners from the basement, with Pfc. Ernie Gonzalez helping. An 88 crashed into the roof and a platoon leader's face dripped blood but it was a surface wound. Jerries pulled out their wounded on an old bed spring and chair.

We made a CP in the cellar. The wounded were brought down. Stray Jerries were rounded up and brought to the rear. Jittery doughs relaxed for a moment on the beds in the basement. Pfc. Frank Pasek forgot he had a round in his BAR and frayed our nerves by letting one go into the ceiling. A pretty Jerry girl with no shoes on came through the

"Two doughs had their arms around each other; one was sobbing."

basement. Doughs were settling down now. The CO started to prepare a defense for a counterattack. Platoons went out to dig in. L and M Companies came up to sustain part of our gains.

Most of us were too tired to do much. The battalion CO sent word he was relieving us. All of us sweated out going back over the field, although this time we would go back a sheltered way. We were relieved and uneventfully returned to a small town. The doughs went out into the rain on the outskirts and dug in. A few 88s came into the town and some time-fire near the holes. Early the next morning, K Company returned to its former position in the big house with the courtyard as the final objective. Just when I left, Jerry started counterattacking with four tanks and a company of men.

Yank, March 11, 1945 (Continental Edition)

"These Terrible Records of War"

by James Agee

THE PARAMOUNT newsreel issue about Iwo Jima subjects the tremendous material recorded by Navy and Marine Corps and Coast Guard camera men to an unusually intelligent job of editing, writing, and soundtracking. I noticed with particular respect a couple of good uses of flat silence; the use of a bit of dialogue on "intercoms," recorded on the spot, in a tank; and the use, at the end, of a still photograph down whose wall the camera moved slowly. Still photographs of motionless objects have a very different quality from motion-picture photographs of motionless objects; as Jean Cocteau observed, time still moves in the latter. The still used here was of dead men, for whom time no longer moved. The device is not a new one; Griffith (or William Bitzer) used it for the same purpose at the end of a battle in "The Birth of a Nation," and René Clair used stop-shots for a somewhat related purpose in "The Crazy Ray." But it is a device too basic to poetic resource on the screen to discard as plagiarized, and I am glad to see it put back into use so unpretentiously and well.

The Fox version of the same battle—the only other version I could find—drew on the same stock, and is interesting to compare with the Paramount. In one way it is to its credit that it is much less noisy and much less calculated to excite; it is in other words less rhetorical, and the temptations to rhetoric must be strong in handling such material, and usually result in falseness. But in this Paramount issue it seems to me that rhetoric was used well, to construct as well as might be in ten hours' work and in ten minutes on the screen an image of one of the most terrible battles in history. And that is not to mention plain sense: the coherent shape of violence in the Paramount version, which moves from air to sea to land; its intact, climactic use of the footage exposed through a tank-slit, which in the Fox version is chopped along through the picture; and its use of the recorded dialogue, which Fox didn't even touch. The Fox version does on the other hand have two shots—a magically sinister slashing of quicksilvery water along the sand, and a heartrending picture of a wounded Marine, crawling toward help with the scuttling motions of a damaged insect—which I am amazed to see omitted from a piece of work so astute as Paramount's.

Very uneasily, I am beginning to believe that, for all that may be said in favor of our seeing these terrible records of war, we have no business seeing this sort of experience except through our presence and participation. I have neither space nor mind, yet, to try to explain why I believe this is so; but since I am reviewing and in ways recommending that others see one of the best and most terrible of war films, I cannot avoid mentioning my perplexity. Perhaps I can briefly suggest what I mean by this rough parallel: whatever other effects it may or may not have, pornography is invariably degrading to anyone who looks at or reads it. If at an incurable distance from participation, hopelessly incapable of reactions adequate to the event, we watch men killing each other, we may be quite as profoundly degrading ourselves and, in the process, betraying and separating ourselves the farther from those we are trying to identify ourselves with; none the less because we tell ourselves sincerely that we sit in comfort and watch carnage in order to nurture our patriotism, our conscience, our understanding, and our sympathies.

The Nation, March 24, 1945

Letter from Cologne

by Janet Flanner (Genêt)

MARCH 19 (BY WIRELESS)
COLOGNE-ON-THE-RHINE is now a model of destruction. The nearby city of Aachen died in a different way: its handsome, melancholy skeleton is left upright; behind its elegant, carved façades, it was burned out. Cologne and its heavy, medieval pomp were blown up. By its river bank, Cologne lies recumbent, without beauty, shapeless in the rubble and loneliness of complete physical defeat. Through its clogged side streets trickles what is left of its life, a dwindled population in black and with bundles—the silent German people appropriate to the silent city.

Most of the people in Cologne have little to say. Dazed by a week of defeat, three years of bombings, and twelve years of propaganda, the old men and the women and children who now inhabit the city sound as if they had lost all ability to think rationally or to tell the truth. Nor did the last orders from their departing Nazi government encourage accurate conversation. One brand-new, fragile-looking item that is seen again and again along the sodden Cologne streets, battered by weather and war, is a propaganda poster pasted on the remaining walls. In Gothic letters, and with exclamation point, the poster advises *"Schweigen siegen!"*—"To keep silent is to win." This poster was put up just before the American First Army's triumphant entrance into the city. Having lost the war of arms, defeated Germany is apparently counting again on the psychological victory she won in the last peace— the victory of silence, lies, whining, energy, devotion, and guile. Even the children seem to have been given their orders to tell the same old patriotic little Nazi fibs. Some small boys I saw who were patently wearing their Hitlerjugend caps, from which the insignia had been removed, told me, with no timidity whatever, that these were ordinary winter caps. Then, overcome by the farcical ease of their first trick on the decadent democratic foreigner, they fled, giggling, to hide behind a ruined doorway. Theirs was the only laughter I have heard in Cologne. The other day, from the nearby city of Bonn, which our troops were then entering, news came to Cologne of an extraordinary proposition. Being a university town, Bonn felt competent to offer, for our American Army's help, the city's own selected corps of interpreters, all speaking perfect Oxford English and high German, who could thus replace, in our relations with the Bonn civilians, our own Army interpreters, many of whom are German Jews.

The only Cologne German I have talked to who has made sense began with the customary subservient lies but ended, at least, with his version of Teutonic truth. He lives near the gate of the Klingelpütz Gestapo prison and for forty years was a paper bundler for the *Kölnische Zeitung*, which was the town's leading conservative Catholic newspaper. He opened our conversation by mumbling mendaciously that no Germans had ever believed Germany could win the war, then admitted that the shocking idea of losing it had come to him and everyone else only when their Army failed to capture Stalingrad. I asked him if the Germans had not been discouraged when Japan pulled the powerful, productive United States into the conflict. He said that they had, on the contrary, rejoiced and had at once intelligently declared war on us themselves. By doing that, he explained, they forced upon us that war on two fronts which had long been the German high command's formula for military defeat. He actually seemed able to accept philosophically the idea of Germany's fast-approaching defeat—on two fronts—since it proved that the German high command had been, for Germany anyhow, absolutely right. He furthermore felt that somehow England had failed to keep a date with history by not falling by 1941.

He and his patient, nervous wife, whom I also talked with, had been bombed out three times, but she had been buried alive with him only twice, since in the terrible daylight bombing of September 17, 1944, she had been away from home in a food queue and had popped into one of the available *Bunker*, as the Germans call their air-raid shelters. It had never occurred to them to leave Cologne, where food was fairly easy to get. Anyway, every other place was being bombed, too, and refugees were resented. The couple showed me their cellar room, where they had been sleeping, cooking, and hoping for the past fourteen months. It looked and smelled orthodox in the circumstances—damp, dark, crowded with a mixture of bedding and skillets, family photographs, and mudstained clothes. The mud of Cologne is part wallpaper from the city's bombed homes, part window panes, part books, part slate roofs fallen from fine old buildings, and surely part blood from the two hundred thousand dead, the fourth of Cologne's population now in peace. The paper bundler and his wife were planning to sleep upstairs now that the Americans had come. *"Gott sei Dank,"* the woman said bleakly. "Anyhow, they bring an end to the war."

The power of survival of the poor apartment house in which this couple live was shared by few of the city's grand mansions. The bombs had left the paper bundler's ground-floor bedroom intact. From its single window was visible, in the rubble-strewn areaway outside, a discarded Nazi flag. It could have been tossed only from that room. Like all the Nazi flags that had been dumped, like scarlet garbage, into the corners of alleys, its arrival there was dated. It had surely lain there from precisely four-thirty of the Tuesday afternoon on which the American Army officially took over the city and began its appreciative collection of such German souvenirs as Nazi flags. Cologne was so thoroughly destroyed by bombings that the German Army did not bother to boobytrap its ruins, presumably figuring, incorrectly, that they contained nothing attractive to the American soldier.

The hundred thousand inhabitants of Cologne who lived like troglodytes in their caves during all our blitzes are now coming up from underground to present themselves, with pale servility, to the U.S. Army's Military Government, which has already got a census under way. Three hours after our Army had fought its last bleeding step in, this military government started to operate. Much of the impression we make on captive Germany and it makes on us will be formalized in our first civilian relations with Cologne, our first big conquered city. The dangerous, comfortable moment in Germany may come when the American administrators, quite naturally, find the obedient, obsequious, efficient enemy Germans easier to deal with than the scatter-brained, individualistic French have been, or the captious Belgians, or the obstinate Dutch.

Fraternization carries a heavy penalty in Cologne. What was called in Aachen, where we began our first relations with the Germans en masse, the sixty-five-dollar question—the amount of the fine, as ordered by General Eisenhower, a soldier had to pay for talking to a German *Mädchen*—has been raised in Cologne to a ten-year prison sentence. I saw a soldier take longer than necessary to discuss with a Cologne *Fräulein* the problem of getting his laundry done, in itself a permitted brief platonic dialogue. An M.P. picked him up, theoretically for ten years. Another soldier nipped by an M.P. proved to be a Pennsylvania Dutch reconnaissance man who was lost and asking his way, in bad German, along the ruined streets. Our Army captured some splendid colored *Stadtpläne*, or city maps, of Cologne, but unfortunately the streets they indicate are often no longer there. Even the city parks are plowed under. To the Germans, with their worshipful sense of iconography, it must be shocking to sit for a moment's rest in a park beneath a blasted tree and a headless statue of the beautiful old Kaiserin Louise.

Cologne contains two important chambers of horrors. It was good that a half dozen of us American journalists viewed them together, so that our eyewitness reports would be unanimous and would be believed. Sometimes it appears that Americans in general and the good-and-bad-Germans school in particular do not wish to hear about Nazi atrocities. One of the great differences between some officers and their men here is that the officers are inclined to believe, even at this late date, that German sadism is a lot of hysterical bunk, whereas their men usually know that it is an unpleasant truth. Certainly the wrecked human beings whom I saw tumbling to liberty through the grilled doorway of the Klingelpütz Gestapo prison on the cold Saturday after our Army had entered Cologne were scarred, starved, in-the-flesh proofs of the existence of very bad Germans indeed. During their first half hour's delirium of freedom and fresh air, these men and women who had been imprisoned for the adultness of their political faith acted like lunatics—sobbing, falling down on the cobblestones of the courtyard, wagging their heads, and holding their temples, where they had most often been beaten. From the nose of one French boy the blood spurted in a pale-pink, excited, pulsing jet. A tall, once strong Dutch workingman kept shouting, in German, "We must never forget! Swear it!" A thin young Belgian, in what had once been good tweeds, stood praying over a mound of earth in the prison courtyard. His father and four other prisoners had been buried there the night before our soldiers came in. The son had made a cross by binding two bits of wood together with a frayed strap he had been using as a belt for his trousers. Then he had prayed. He apologized to me in English for not being shaved. At first he refused a cigarette—"for fear of depriving you." He and his dead father had been resistance men. The most startling member of the group was the still exquisitely pretty Brussels girl in a saintly blue rain cape who had spent nineteen months of her nineteen years in Gestapo prisons for having helped R.A.F. fliers to escape. Another surprise was a seventy-year-old Dutch grandmother, complete with dignity, four languages, gold-rimmed glasses, and a decent black fur coat. She had listened to the London B.B.C. broadcasts. There were also several blond, tubercular Russian girls, some terrified-looking, speechless Poles, and three completely crazed Germans. One liberated Frenchman was a Montmartre café waiter who had refused to go to Germany to work and had therefore been sent there and put in a concentration camp, the first of a series of nine camps. He had escaped nine times and been caught nine times. His eyes, teeth, hands, head, and feet had all been injured by the beatings the Germans had given him. In one camp, on the Vistula River, he had labored one summer, along with some starving Poles, dredging sand to make a bathing beach for the *Herrenvolk* officers.

The second horror chamber was the Gestapo office in the Apellhof Platz, across from the court of appeals it had ignored. Near the curiously undamaged office, on a mattress in the middle of a wrecked street, lay three young non-German corpses. These were the bodies of men who were being dragged by two Gestapo men to the questioning room when an American shell fell and, perhaps fortunately, killed all five men. High above them lay a sixth victim of the same shell: a well-to-do, stay-at-home old German, still wearing a nice blue suit and his wedding ring, his prosperous person caught, but still intact, underneath the staircase on the second-floor landing of his big house, half of which had been sheared away just an inch from where he lay. Below the Gestapo office was a small sub-basement cell where, the Klingelpütz prisoners said, the Gestapo had hung other prisoners six at a time by crowding them into a row, standing them on stools, dropping nooses around their necks from an overhead bar, and then kicking the stools out from beneath their feet. One Italian became a legend by kicking his stool loose himself and shouting, as his final strangled words, *"Viva l'Italia! Viva la libertà!"*

The Gestapo sub-basement smelled of a rotting haunch of horsemeat from which a hoof still dangled. Supplies, apparently, had run low as the Americans approached the city. In the office were files containing some copies of an S.S. French-language leaflet destined for French slave-labor gangs in Germany. The leaflet said, "French comrades, conscious of the future of thy country, thou canst not remain neutral in this conflict, thou shouldst take up arms to fight at thy European brothers' sides. Thy country sinks beneath Jewish-Anglo-American bombs. Thy parents lie amid the ruins. Come avenge them. Come with us to chase these assassins from France, give thyself the honor of not leaving this task to Germans alone. Come combat with us the true enemies of thy land, those who turn it into a vast cemetery, the Jews. France will relive, thanks to thee, and thou wilt participate with us in its arising again in the new National Socialist regime which we will set up after our victory. Offer thy services to the French Armed Elite Guard or to the French National Socialist movement, 7 Freytagstrasse, in Düsseldorf."

The buildings of architectural interest in Cologne have been seventy-five-per-cent destroyed, the Fine Arts and Monuments section of our Army reports. The Wallraf-Richartz Museum, which contained good paintings of the South German and Cologne schools of 1300–1550, including various Altdorfers, Cranachs, and Dürers, and Stephan Lochner's famous "Madonna in an Arbor of Roses," was demolished, a loss in itself because of its fine cloisters, but the paintings had been evacuated. Our art experts figure only a ten-percent damage to Cologne Cathedral, which typical Hohenzollern egotism put over as one of the sublimest in the world, although its pleasant Gothic nave was finished in exactly 1880 (a priest was still on hand with a throwaway historical booklet to give our tourist soldiers) and is only slightly better than Fifth Avenue's St. Patrick's. The really great loss to Cologne and the world are its eleventh-century Romanesque churches, such as the decagonal St. Gereon, which has been cut in two, and, above all, the Apostles' Church, with its twelfth-century side aisles, superb mosaics, and magnificent domed crossing. I stumbled and crawled up a nobly proportioned aisle into which the mosaic dome had crumbled in colored ruin. Overhead, four of the dome's ribs and its lantern, miraculously intact, were outlined as naked, resistant, architectural principles—nearly a thousand years old in wisdom and balance—against the dull modern sky. Across that sky flew a gaggle of nine planes. The mortar shells of the Nazis still fighting on the other side of the Rhine began dropping, a long way off, into what had once been their fine city. The air shook and from the church's injured choir great drops of red mosaics bled down onto the altar.

It is reasonable to think that Cologne's panorama of ruin will be typical of what our rapidly advancing Army will see in city after city. Because Germany is populous, more cities have been destroyed there than in any other country in Europe. Defeat in the last war did not cost Germany a stone. This time the destroyer of others is herself destroyed. This physical destruction of Germany is the one positive reason for thinking that this time the Allies may win the peace. However they decide to divide Germany, her cities, if they are like Cologne, are already divided into morsels of stone no bigger than your hand.

The New Yorker, March 31, 1945

Das Deutsches Volk

by Martha Gellhorn

NO ONE is a Nazi. No one ever was. There may have been some Nazis in the next village, and, as a matter of fact, in that town about twenty kilometers away it was a veritable hotbed of Nazidom. To tell you the truth confidentially, there were a lot of Communists here. Oh, the Jews? Well, there weren't really many Jews in this neighborhood. I hid a Jew for six weeks. I hid a Jew for eight weeks. All God's chillun hid Jews.

We have been waiting for the Americans. You came to befriend us. The Nazis are *Schweinhunde*. The Wehrmacht wants to give up but they do not know how. No, I have no relatives in the army. I worked on the land. I worked in a factory. That boy wasn't in the army, either; he was sick. Ach! How we have suffered! The bombs. We lived in the cellars for weeks. We have done nothing wrong. We were never Nazis! . . .

It would sound better if it were set to music. Then the Germans could sing this refrain. They all talk like this. One asks oneself how the Nazi government to which no one paid allegiance managed to carry on this war for five and a half years. Obviously not a man, woman or child in Germany ever approved of the war.

On the other hand, we are not having any of this story and we stand around looking blank and contemptuous, and we listen without friendliness and certainly without respect. To see a whole nation passing the buck is not an enlightening spectacle. At night the Germans take pot shots at Americans or string wires across roads, apt to be fatal to men driving jeeps. They burn the houses of Germans who accept posts in our Military Government or they booby-trap ammunition dumps or motorcycles or anything that is likely to be touched. But that is at night. In the daytime we are the answer to the German prayer.

At the moment we are sitting on the west bank of the Rhine facing the Ruhr pocket. The Germans here are peeved and wish us to push the pocket back ten miles so they will no longer be troubled by their own artillery, which fires into their villages whenever it can spare some shells. The 504th Regiment of the 82d Airborne Division sent a company across the Rhine in landing craft one night and took and held a town for thirty-six hours. On the other side was the Wehrmacht, which was not giving up by any manner of means.

The company of paratroopers drew onto themselves a great deal of armed attention—two German divisions, it was estimated. This relieved pressure at another part of the front but the company lost heavily. When they got back, two officers and four sergeants were decorated with the Silver Star. This ceremony took place in a nondescript street amidst brick rubble and fallen telephone wires outside the regimental command post. The six who received medals were not dressed for the occasion. They had come directly from their work. Their faces were like gray stone from weariness, and their eyes were not like eyes you will see every day around you, and no one was talking about what he'd seen across the river.

The German civilians looked with wonder at this row of dirty, silent men standing in the street. It makes little or no difference to anyone around here whether the Germans are Nazis or not; they can talk their heads off, sing The Star-Spangled Banner. They are still Germans and they are not liked. No one has forgotten yet that our dead stretch back all the way to Africa.

The villages along the Rhine here are in pretty good shape. In the middle, of course, is Cologne, one of the great morgues of the world, but, by and large, these adjacent villages have nothing to complain of. There is food and clothing, coal, bedding, all household equipment and livestock. The Germans are nice and fat, too; clean, orderly and industrious. They carry on their normal lives within seven hundred yards of their army which is now their enemy.

The burgomasters whom we appoint rule the people by decrees which we publish and slap up on the walls. The Germans seem to love decrees and they stand in line busily to read anything new that appears. We went to call on one burgomaster of a front-line village; he was, he said, a Communist and a half-Jew and he may be, for all I know, but it is amazing how many Communists and half-Jews there are in Germany. He was a workingman before and he says there are plenty of people in the village who are furious about him being burgomaster; he has got above himself, they think, just because of the Americans.

If the Americans fired him he would be killed, he said. He stated this in a perfectly matter-of-fact way.

We said, "Then that means the people here are Nazis."

"No, no," he said. "It is that they think I have too good a position."

He spoke with some despair about the future of Germany and finished by saying that America must help Germany to recover. We listened to this remark with surprise and asked him why. He admitted that perhaps we had a reason to hate Germany, but the Germans were relying on our well-known humanitarianism.

"Nuts," said a sergeant who spoke German.

"Translate nuts," said a lieutenant.

The burgomaster went on to say that if the Americans did not occupy Germany for fifty years, there would be war again.

"Some man," he said, "with a bigger mouth than Hitler will come along and promise them everything, and they will follow, and there will be war again."

"I believe him," said the lieutenant.

"I'd just as soon leave him a little present when we go," the sergeant said. "I'd just as soon slip him in his pocket a hand grenade with the pin pulled—him and all the others."

After the tidy villages, Cologne is hard to believe. We are not shocked by it, which only goes to prove that if you see enough of anything, you stop noticing it. In Germany when you see absolute devastation you do not grieve. We have grieved for many places in many countries, but this is not one of the countries. Our soldiers say, "They asked for it."

Between two mountains of broken brick and backed by a single jagged wall, a German had set up a pushcart and was selling tulips, narcissuses and daffodils. The flowers looked a little mad in this *décor*, and considering there are no houses to put flowers in, the whole setup seemed odd. Two young men on bicycles rode up, and one of them bought a bunch of tulips. We asked him what he wanted tulips for, and he said he was Dutch. So of course he needed the tulips. He had been in forced labor in this city for three years. He and his friend came from Rotterdam. Anything that happened to Cologne was all right with them.

The flower vendor then came over to talk. He made very little money, but before we came, he sold his flowers to the hospitals as well as to some old customers. He was alone in the world now. His family, forty-two of them including his grandparents and parents, his wife and children, his sisters and their children and husbands, had all been buried in one cellar during one air raid. He brought pictures out of his wallet.

The two soldiers and I sat in the jeep and wondered why he talked to us; if forty-two members of our families had been killed by German bombs we would not talk pleasantly to Germans.

A crowd gathered around us; since no one speaks to Germans except on official business, you can collect a crowd anywhere simply by saying *"Guten Tag."* This desire to be chummy baffles us as much as anything. The crowd was varied and everyone talked at once. I asked them when things had started to go bad in Germany. I had a private bet with myself on the answer and I won. Things have been bad in Germany since 1933, they all said loudly.

I said, "No, I am talking about since the war. Since 1941 it has been bad. Why?"

"Because of the bombs."

"Danke schön," said I. Then I asked what form of government they hoped for after the war.

"Democracy," they cried.

But one day in another village it came out much better than that and much more truly; the women said that if they had enough to eat and could live quietly they did not care *who* ruled them. The men said they had not talked politics for eleven years and no longer knew anything about government. However, democracy is a fine word and in frequent use in Germany.

Then I asked them whether they had traveled during the war. Had anyone made a side trip to Paris? No one had traveled anywhere at all: they were assigned their work and they stayed to do it, twelve hours a day. After that, the talk degenerated into the usual condemnation of the Nazis.

We went down to the river front to call on some airborne pals. The company command post was in a candy factory and we were taken to see the vast stocks of sugar, chocolate, cocoa, butter, almonds and finished candies that remained. Then we were led to a huge wine cellar, only one of three they had located. Next we visited a flour warehouse which had more flour in it than any of us had seen at one time. After this (and by now we were all in a temper thinking how well off the Germans had been) we went through a jumble of factory buildings used as a general food depot and we looked with anger on rooms full of Dutch and French cheese, Portuguese sardines, Norwegian canned fish, all kinds of jams and canned vegetables, barrels of sirup and so on.

The Germans had not given up butter for guns but had done very nicely producing or stealing both.

There was a line of German women sitting outside the white tape which marked off the military zone. They were watching their houses. No roof or window remains, and often there is not a wall left, either, and almost everything in those houses has been blown about. But there they sat and kept mournful guard on their possessions. When asked why they did this, they started to weep. We have all seen such beastly and fantastic suffering accepted in silence that we do not react very well to weeping. And we certainly do not react well to people weeping over furniture.

I remembered Oradour, in France, where the Germans locked every man, woman and child of the village into the church and set the church afire, and after the people were burned, the village was burned. This is an extremely drastic way to destroy property. The Germans have taught all the people of Europe not to waste time weeping over anything easy like furniture. Farther down the river, the Military Government was registering German civilians in the villages.

During all the war this village had lost ten civilians dead; during the last week German shells had killed seven more. We talked with some German women about the horrors of war.

"The bombs," they said. "O God, the bombs! Two thousand eight hundred bombs fell on this village alone," they said.

"Don't be crazy," we told them. "There would be no sign of a village if that were true."

"Ah, the bombs!" they said, firmly convinced that their village was flat and they were all dead.

Just across the river the German ack-ack continues to operate. Yesterday it operated effectively and a B-26 was shot down and a column of black smoke rose straight and mountain-high. It looked like a funeral pyre to all of us. The tanks of the Thirteenth Armored Division were moving up across the river behind the burning plane, but the crew were there in a belt of Krauts and no one could reach them. From a 505th observation post, some paratroopers had seen four men get out of the plane. That was at about one o'clock on a soft clear day.

At six o'clock, across the river on the green bank, someone started waving a white flag. This was ignored because it does not necessarily mean anything. Then a procession came down to a landing pier. They carried a Red Cross flag; through binoculars we could see a priest, a medic, and two German soldiers carrying a stretcher. A landing craft put out from our bank, well covered by our machine guns in case this was all a sinister joke. Presently on both banks of the Rhine there was an audience. Normally you would never have moved in this area in daylight. Now we stood cheerfully in the sun and gaped.

Slowly three more stretchers were carried down to our boat. We could see civilians over there, children, German soldiers; everyone was out staring at everyone else. We could not quite believe it and were still prepared to dive for cover. Then the little boat was launched into the current. It landed, and our medic who had gone over to get these four wounded men—the survivors of the B-26 crew—shouted to clear the banks, because the Krauts said they'd give the ambulance time to load and then they would open up.

The war had stopped for approximately an hour on a hundred-yard front.

"I never saw the Krauts act so nice," one soldier said.

"They know our tanks are coming up," another soldier said. "Krauts don't act nice for nothing."

The DPs (Displaced Persons, if you have forgotten) tell us that Krauts never act nice. There are tens of thousands of Russians and Poles and Czechs and French and Yugoslav and Belgian slave laborers around here, and they pour in every day in truckloads to the camps which the 82d Airborne now runs.

There is apparently an inexhaustible supply of human beings who have been torn from their families and have lived in misery with no medical care and on starvation rations while working twelve hours a day for their German masters. They do not feel very kindly toward the Germans, as you can imagine. The only time I have seen a Russian cry was when a Russian nurse, a girl of twenty-five, wept with rage telling of the way her people were treated. They had all seen their dead thrown into huge lime-filled pits which were the communal graves.

"Everywhere the graves became as high as a mountain," she said. The anger of these people is so great that you feel it must work like fire in the earth.

British prisoners of war are starting to come through now, still joking, still talking in understatement but with bitterness behind the jokes and the quiet words. The ones we saw had walked for fifty-two days from the Polish frontier to Hannover, where their tank columns freed them, and on that fearful march those who fell out from hunger and exhaustion died. Their Red Cross parcels kept them alive during five years, but since last November no parcels had arrived. In one small group, nine men had died of starvation after the long march, and their bodies lay for six days in their crowded barracks because for some unknown reason the Germans did not feel like burying them or allowing them to be buried.

"They're not human is all," a New Zealander said.

"I wish they'd let us take charge of the German prisoners," a boy from Wales said.

A man who was lying on the grass near him now spoke up thoughtfully. "You can't really learn to like those people," he said, "unless they're dead."

Meantime, the Germans, untroubled by regret (because after all they did nothing wrong; they only did what they were told to do), keep on saying with energy, "We are not Nazis." It is their idea of the password to forgiveness, probably to be followed by a sizable loan. "We were never Nazis! We are friends."

There are hundreds of thousands of people in khaki around here—and equal numbers of foreigners in rags—who simply cannot see it that way.

Collier's, May 26, 1945

"A Soldier Died Today"

by James Agee

In Chungking the spring dawn was milky when an MP on the graveyard shift picked up the ringing phone in U.S. Army Headquarters. At first he heard no voice on the other end; then a San Francisco broadcast coming over the phone line made clear to him why his informant could find no words. A colonel came in. The MP just stared at him. The colonel stared back. After a moment the MP blurted two words. The colonel's jaw dropped; he hesitated; then without a word he walked away.

It was fresh daylight on Okinawa. Officers and men of the amphibious fleet were at breakfast when the broadcast told them. By noon the news was known to the men at the front, at the far sharp edge of the world's struggle. With no time for grief, they went on with their work; but there, while they worked, many a soldier wept.

At home, the news came to people in the hot soft light of the afternoon, in taxicabs, along the streets, in offices and bars and factories. In a Cleveland barbershop, 60-year-old Sam Katz was giving a customer a shave when the radio stabbed out the news. Sam Katz walked over to the water cooler, took a long, slow drink, sat down and stared into space for nearly ten minutes. Finally he got up and painted a sign on his window: "Roosevelt Is Dead." Then he finished the shave. In an Omaha poolhall, men racked up their cues without finishing their games, walked out. In a Manhattan taxicab, a fare told the driver, who pulled over to the curb, sat with his head bowed, and after two minutes resumed his driving.

Everywhere, to almost everyone, the news came with the force of a personal shock. The realization was expressed in the messages of the eminent; it was expressed in the stammering and wordlessness of the humble. A woman in Detroit said: "It doesn't seem possible. It seems to me that he will be back on the radio tomorrow, reassuring us all that it was just a mistake."

It was the same through that evening, and the next day, and the next: the darkened restaurants, the shuttered night-clubs, the hand-lettered signs in the windows of stores: "Closed out of Reverence for F.D.R."; the unbroken, 85-hour dirge of the nation's radio; the typical tributes of typical Americans in the death-notice columns of their newspapers (said one, signed by Samuel and Al Gordon: "A Soldier Died Today").

It was the same on the cotton fields and in the stunned cities between Warm Springs and Washington, while the train, at funeral pace, bore the coffin up April's glowing South in re-enactment of Whitman's great threnody.

It was the same in Washington, in the thousands on thousands of grief-wrung faces which walled the caisson's grim progression with prayers and with tears. It was the same on Sunday morning in the gentle landscape at Hyde Park, when the burial service of the Episcopal Church spoke its old, strong, quiet words of farewell; and it was the same at that later moment when all save the gravemen were withdrawn and reporters, in awe-felt hiding, saw how a brave woman, a widow, returned, and watched over the grave alone, until the grave was filled.

Time, April 23, 1945

"For Most of It I Have No Words"

---

by Edward R. Murrow

APRIL 15, 1945

During the last week, I have driven more than a few hundred miles through Germany, most of it in the Third Army sector—Wiesbaden, Frankfurt, Weimar, Jena and beyond. It is impossible to keep up with this war. The traffic flows down the superhighways, trucks with German helmets tied to the radiators and belts of machine-gun ammunition draped from fender to fender. The tanks on the concrete roads sound like a huge sausage machine, grinding up sheets of corrugated iron. And when there is a gap between convoys, when the noise dies away, there is another small noise, that of wooden-soled shoes and of small iron tires grating on the concrete. The power moves forward, while the people, the slaves, walk back, pulling their small belongings on anything that has wheels.

There are cities in Germany that make Coventry and Plymouth appear to be merely damage done by a petulant child, but bombed houses have a way of looking alike, wherever you see them.

But this is no time to talk of the surface of Germany. Permit me to tell you what you would have seen, and heard, had you been with me on Thursday. It will not be pleasant listening. If you are at lunch, or if you have no appetite to hear what Germans have done, now is a good time to switch off the radio, for I propose to tell you of Buchenwald. It is on a small hill about four miles outside Weimar, and it was one of the largest concentration camps in Germany, and it was built to last. As we approached it, we saw about a hundred men in civilian clothes with rifles advancing in open order across the fields. There were a few shops; we stopped to inquire. We were told that some of the prisoners had a couple of SS men

625

cornered in there. We drove on, reached the main gate. The prisoners crowded up behind the wire. We entered.

And now, let me tell this in the first person, for I was the least important person there, as you shall hear. There surged around me an evil-smelling horde. Men and boys reached out to touch me; they were in rags and the remnants of uniform. Death had already marked many of them, but they were smiling with their eyes. I looked out over that mass of men to the green fields beyond where well-fed Germans were ploughing.

A German, Fritz Kersheimer, came up and said, "May I show you round the camp? I've been here ten years." An Englishman stood to attention, saying, "May I introduce myself, delighted to see you, and can you tell me when some of our blokes will be along?" I told him soon and asked to see one of the barracks. It happened to be occupied by Czechoslovakians. When I entered, men crowded around, tried to lift me to their shoulders. They were too weak. Many of them could not get out of bed. I was told that this building had once stabled eighty horses. There were twelve hundred men in it, five to a bunk. The stink was beyond all description.

When I reached the center of the barracks, a man came up and said, "You remember me. I'm Peter Zenkl, one-time mayor of Prague." I remembered him, but did not recognize him. He asked about Benes and Jan Masaryk. I asked how many men had died in that building during the last month. They called the doctor; we inspected his records. There were only names in the little black book, nothing more—nothing of who these men were, what they had done, or hoped. Behind the names of those who had died there was a cross. I counted them. They totalled 242. Two hundred and forty-two out of twelve hundred in one month.

As I walked down to the end of the barracks, there was applause from the men too weak to get out of bed. It sounded like the hand clapping of babies; they were so weak. The doctor's name was Paul Heller. He had been there since 1938.

As we walked out into the courtyard, a man fell dead. Two others—they must have been over sixty—were crawling toward the latrine. I saw it but will not describe it.

In another part of the camp they showed me the children,

hundreds of them. Some were only six. One rolled up his sleeve, showed me his number. It was tattooed on his arm. D-6030, it was. The others showed me their numbers; they will carry them till they die.

An elderly man standing beside me said, "The children, enemies of the state." I could see their ribs through their thin shirts. The old man said, "I am Professor Charles Richer of the Sorbonne." The children clung to my hands and stared. We crossed to the courtyard. Men kept coming up to speak to me and to touch me, professors from Poland, doctors from Vienna, men from all Europe. Men from the countries that made America.

We went to the hospital; it was full. The doctor told me that two hundred had died the day before. I asked the cause of death; he shrugged and said, "Tuberculosis, starvation, fatigue, and there are many who have no desire to live. It is very difficult." Dr. Heller pulled back the blankets from a man's feet to show me how swollen they were. The man was dead. Most of the patients could not move.

As we left the hospital I drew out a leather billfold, hoping that I had some money which would help those who lived to get home. Professor Richer from the Sorbonne said, "I should be careful of my wallet if I were you. You know there are criminals in this camp, too." A small man tottered up, saying, "May I feel the leather, please? You see, I used to make good things of leather in Vienna." Another man said, "My name is Walter Roeder. For many years I lived in Joliet. Came back to Germany for a visit and Hitler grabbed me."

I asked to see the kitchen; it was clean. The German in charge had been a Communist, had been at Buchenwald for nine years, had a picture of his daughter in Hamburg. He hadn't seen her for almost twelve years, and if I got to Hamburg, would I look her up? He showed me the daily ration— one piece of brown bread about as thick as your thumb, on top of it a piece of margarine as big as three sticks of chewing gum. That, and a little stew, was what they received every twenty-four hours. He had a chart on the wall; very complicated it was. There were little red tabs scattered through it. He said that was to indicate each ten men who died. He had to account for the rations, and he added, "We're very efficient here."

We went again into the courtyard, and as we walked we talked. The two doctors, the Frenchman and the Czech, agreed that about six thousand had died during March. Kersheimer, the German, added that back in the winter of 1939, when the Poles began to arrive without winter clothing, they died at the rate of approximately nine hundred a day. Five different men asserted that Buchenwald was the best concentration camp in Germany; they had had some experience of the others.

Dr. Heller, the Czech, asked if I would care to see the crematorium. He said it wouldn't be very interesting because the Germans had run out of coke some days ago and had taken to dumping the bodies into a great hole nearby. Professor Richer said perhaps I would care to see the small courtyard. I said yes. He turned and told the children to stay behind. As we walked across the square I noticed that the professor had a hole in his left shoe and a toe sticking out of the right one. He followed my eyes and said, "I regret that I am so little presentable, but what can one do?" At that point another Frenchman came up to announce that three of his fellow countrymen outside had killed three S.S. men and taken one prisoner. We proceeded to the small courtyard. The wall was about eight feet high; it adjoined what had been a stable or garage. We entered. It was floored with concrete. There were two rows of bodies stacked up like cordwood. They were thin and very white. Some of the bodies were terribly bruised, though there seemed to be little flesh to bruise. Some had been shot through the head, but they bled but little. All except two were naked. I tried to count them as best I could and arrived at the conclusion that all that was mortal of more than five hundred men and boys lay there in two neat piles.

There was a German trailer which must have contained another fifty, but it wasn't possible to count them. The clothing was piled in a heap against the wall. It appeared that most of the men and boys had died of starvation; they had not been executed. But the manner of death seemed unimportant. Murder had been done at Buchenwald. God alone knows how many men and boys have died there during the last twelve years. Thursday I was told that there were more than twenty thousand in the camp. There had been as many as sixty thousand. Where are they now?

As I left that camp, a Frenchman who used to work for Havas in Paris came up to me and said, "You will write something about this, perhaps?" And he added, "To write about this you must have been here at least two years, and after that—you don't want to write any more."

I pray you to believe what I have said about Buchenwald. I have reported what I saw and heard, but only part of it. For most of it I have no words. Dead men are plentiful in war, but the living dead, more than twenty thousand of them in one camp. And the country round about was pleasing to the eye, and the Germans were well fed and well dressed. American trucks were rolling toward the rear filled with prisoners. Soon they would be eating American rations, as much for a meal as the men at Buchenwald received in four days.

If I've offended you by this rather mild account of Buchenwald, I'm not in the least sorry. I was there on Thursday, and many men in many tongues blessed the name of Roosevelt. For long years his name had meant the full measure of their hope. These men who had kept close company with death for many years did not know that Mr. Roosevelt would, within hours, join their comrades who had laid their lives on the scales of freedom.

Back in 1941, Mr. Churchill said to me with tears in his eyes, "One day the world and history will recognize and acknowledge what it owes to your President." I saw and heard the first installment of that at Buchenwald on Thursday. It came from men from all over Europe. Their faces, with more flesh on them, might have been found anywhere at home. To them the name "Roosevelt" was a symbol, the code word for a lot of guys named "Joe" who are somewhere out in the blue with the armor heading east. At Buchenwald they spoke of the President just before he died. If there be a better epitaph, history does not record it.

CBS Radio Broadcast, April 15, 1945

Ernie Pyle

by Evan Wylie

OKINAWA—Ernie Pyle covered Okinawa on D-Day with the Marines. Many of them did not recognize him at first and stared curiously at the small oldish-looking man with the stubby white whiskers and frayed woolen cap. When they did recognize him they said: "Hi, Ernie. What do you think of the war here in the Pacific?" And Pyle smiled and said a little wearily: "Oh, it's the same old stuff all over again. I am awful tired of it." The men watched him climb from the boat, his thin body bent under the weight of his field pack and draped in fatigue clothes that seemed too big for him and they said: "That guy is getting too old for this kind of stuff. He ought to go home."

Ie Shima, where Pyle died, is a small, obscure island off the western coast of Okinawa. The operation was on such a small scale that many correspondents didn't bother to go along. Pyle had been in the ship's sick bay for a week with one of his famous colds. The weather was perfect, with balmy air and bright sunshine. Pyle was ashore on D-plus-one. He stretched out on the sunny slope with Milton Chase, WLW radio correspondent, soaking up the sun and gazing at the picturesque landscape and gently rolling fields dotted with sagebrushlike bushes and clumps of low pine trees. The country, he said, was the way Italy must be in summertime. That was only a guess, he added, because he was in Italy in the middle of winter. Most of all, it reminded him of Albuquerque. "Lots of people don't like the country around Albuquerque," he said, "but it suits me fine. As soon as I finish this damned assignment I'm going back there and settle down for a long time."

A young officer came up to report that the Japs were blowing themselves up with grenades. "That's a sight worth seeing," he said. Chase asked Pyle what his reaction to the Jap dead was. Pyle said dead men were all alike to him, and it made him feel sick to look at one. A wounded soldier with a bloody bandage on his arm came up the slope and asked Pyle for his autograph. "Don't usually collect these things," he told Pyle sheepishly, "but I wanted yours. Thanks a lot."

The operation was going so well that most of the correspondents left that night. There had been hardly any casualties and only a very few of these were killed. Pyle was in the midst of preparing a story on a tank-destroyer team, so he stayed on. He was wearing green fatigues and a cap with a Marine emblem. He was with a few troops when he died, standing near Lt. Col. Joseph B. Coolidge of Helena, Mont. The Jap machine gun that got him took the group by surprise.

Pyle had proceeded to the front in a jeep with Col. Coolidge. As they reached a crossroads, still some distance from the front lines, the Jap machine gun, hidden in a patch of woods, suddenly opened up on them. The gun was a sleeper. Our troops had been moving up and down the road all morning and most of the day before. This was the first time it had revealed itself.

Pyle and the others jumped from the jeep and took cover in a ditch beside the road. The machine gun fired another long burst, and Pyle was dead. The rest withdrew. Several groups attempted to recover the body, once with the support of tanks, but each time they were driven back.

At 1500, Chaplain N. B. Saucier of Coffeeville, Miss., received permission to attempt to recover the body with litter-bearers. T-5 Paul Shapiro of Passaic, N.J., Sgt. Minter Moore of Elkins, W. Va., Cpl. Robert Toaz of Huntington, N.Y., and Sgt. Arthur Austin of Tekamah, Neb., volunteered to go with him. The crossroads lay in open country that offered no cover. The men crawled up the ditch, dragging the litter behind them. Army Signal Corps photographer Cpl. Alexander Roberts of New York City preceded them and was the first man to reach the body.

Pyle lay on his back in a normal resting position. His unmarked face had the look of a man sleeping peacefully. He had died instantly from a bullet that penetrated the left side of his helmet and entered the left temple. His hands folded across his chest still clutched his battered cap, said to be the same one he carried through his previous campaigns. The litter-bearers placed the body on the stretcher and worked their way slowly back along the ditch under sniper fire. The battle for Ie Shima still remained to be won.

The island probably will be remembered only as the place where America's most famous war correspondent met the death he had been expecting for so long.

Yank, May 18, 1945

"A Giant Whirlpool of Destruction"

by Virginia Irwin

BERLIN, Germany, April 27.—I am one of the first three Americans to enter Berlin. After a fantastic journey northward, after we crossed the Elbe River where the Russians and Americans made contact this afternoon, I arrived at Berlin at dark tonight with Andrew Tully, reporter for the Boston Traveler, and jeep driver Sgt. John Wilson of Roxbury, Mass.

The air is heavy with smoke. Everywhere around us is the clatter of small arms fire. Russian artillery is pouring an almost constant barrage into the heart of the city.

But in this Russian command post, where we are guests of Guards Major Nikolai Kovaleski, there is a terrific celebration going on. The arrival of three Americans in Berlin was the signal for the Russians to break out their best vodka and toss a terrific banquet in our honor.

I have just finished eating all sorts of strange Russian concoctions and being toasted by every officer in this command post. I have danced with at least a dozen Russians of various rank and degrees of terpsichorean ability. I have even been initiated into that great knee-bend brand of acrobatics which the Guards-Major says is "Russian Kosachec."

We arrived in Berlin a few minutes before 8 o'clock after the strangest journey I have ever undertaken. It was a nerve-shattering experience. We "ran off" the map and had to navigate by guess.

None of us understood Russian. German road signs had been removed and replaced with their Russian equivalent. We got to Berlin on the strength of a crude hand-made American flag flying from our jeep, several hundred handshakes and repeated assurances to fierce Russians who repeatedly stopped us that we were "Amerikanski."

And everywhere, as soon as we had convinced the Russians of our identity, we were mobbed. Russian infantry piled out of their horse-drawn wagons and crowded round. Refugees of all nationalities closed in around us and time after time the road had to be cleared almost by force before we could proceed.

Shortly after noon today at Torgau, east of the Elbe, we dined with Maj. Gen. Emil Reinhardt, commander of the Sixty-ninth American Division; Maj. Gen. Clarence R. Huebner, commander of the American Fifth Corps; Maj. Gen. Gleb Zlabimirovitzch Baklanoff, commander of the Thirty-fourth Russian Corps, and Gen. Vladimir Rusakov, commander of the Fifty-eighth Guards Infantry Division. The dinner was the official celebration of the meeting of the American and Russian troops at the Elbe River.

From Torgau we started north, behind the Russian lines, traveling sometimes over deserted roads, through dark forests. At other times, we hit highways clogged with the great body of the Russian Army, beating along in its motley array of horse-drawn vehicles of all sorts.

There were Russian troops riding in American 2½-ton trucks. There were Russian troops riding in two-wheeled carts, phaetons, in old-fashioned pony carts, in gypsy wagons, and surreys with fringed tops. They rode in everything that could be pulled.

The wagons were filled with hay and the soldiers lay on top of the hay like an army taking a holiday and going on a great mass hayride. It was the most fantastic sight I have ever seen. The fierce fighting men of the Red Army in their tunics and great boots, shabby and ragged after their long war, riding toward Berlin in their strange assortment of vehicles, singing their fighting songs, drinking vodka, were like so many holiday-makers going on a great picnic.

Before 8, we were well into Berlin with the forward elements of the Russian troops in the German capital.

German dead lay on the sidewalks, in the front yards of the bomb-shattered homes of the Berlin suburbs.

All streets were clogged with Russian tanks, guns, infantry in their shaggy fur hats, and everywhere the horses of the Russian Army ran loose about the streets.

But the Russians were happy—with almost indescribable wild joy. They were in Berlin. In this German capital lies their true revenge for Leningrad and Stalingrad, for Sevastopol and Moscow.

And the Russians are having their revenge. All along the road into Berlin, the fields along the roadways are littered with the carts and belongings of the Germans who tried to escape from the German capital. For the Russians are not so polite as the Americans are to Germans who clog the roads in the paths of American traffic. Americans wait for the Germans to pull off the road to let traffic pass, but the Russians drive over the German carts, push them off the road and upset them.

In the territory over which I traveled to reach Berlin, I saw very few Germans. They fear the Russians as no nation has ever feared a conquering army. The Russian Red Army is a mad, wonderful lot of fierce fighting men. They are also wonderful hosts.

American prisoners of war liberated from the great prison camps I passed on the way to Berlin told me that the Russians insisted on sharing their last morsel of food and their last drop of drink with every American they encounter. And to-night, here in Berlin, I am sampling Russian hospitality at its best.

This command post is in what is left of a German home in the battered city of Berlin, almost leveled by American bombers. There are no electric lights, no running water, but the Guards-Major is a kind of host who can rise above such difficulties. The minute I arrived he had his Cossack orderly, a fierce Mongolian with a great scar on his left cheek, ready with a dishpan of water. After I had washed my face the Guards-Major produced some German face powder, a quarter-full bottle of German perfume, and a cracked mirror.

I made myself as presentable as possible and sat down to a candlelit, flower-bedecked dinner table. The candelabra was upturned milk bottles and the flower vase was an old pickle jar, but the dinner was served with all the formality of a State function in Washington. At each toast the Russian officers stood up, clicked their heels, bowed deeply and drained tumblers of vodka. Besides vodka, there was cognac and a drink of dynamite strength the Major described simply as "spirits."

The food was served by a German woman and a Russian

laundress attached to artillery headquarters. The "appetizer" was huge platefuls of something that tasted like spiced salmon. Then came in huge platefuls of a strange dish that tasted like mutton cooked over charcoal, huge masses of mashed potatoes with meat oil poured all over them, a huge Russian cheese, and for dessert, platefuls of Russian-made pastries.

After each course there were toasts to "The late and great President Roosevelt," to Stalin, to President Truman, to Churchill, to "Capt. Andre Tooley," to "Capt. Veergeenee Erween," to the "Red Army," to "the American Army," to "Sarjaunt Wilson," and "to the American jeep."

As we drank our toasts the battle of Berlin raged only a few blocks away. As the artillery roared, the house shook and the candles fluttered. The candles are still fluttering as I write this story, this story of the most exciting thing that could ever happen to a newspaper reporter. It is all unreal.

Russian officers in their worn but military tunics bedecked with the medals of Leningrad, Stalingrad, and all the other great Russian battles, are unreal. The whole battle is somehow unreal.

And the thought keeps coming into my mind that here is the greatest city-dump in the world, with the remains of bombed buildings all dumped in the same place with the dead.

I asked the Guards-Major if Berlin was his greatest battle.

He smiled and said sadly, "No. To us there were greater battles. In those we lost our wives and children."

And then the Guards-Major told the story of the strange staff he has gathered around him. Every officer on that staff had lost his entire family to the Germans.

In that Major's story, I thought, lay the answer to the success of the fierce battle the Russians are waging for a Berlin that is almost all now in Russian hands.

———

BERLIN, April 28. — I almost had a jeep ride down the Unter den Linden today. After repeated attempts to reach the center of the city, I finally stopped at a Russian infantry command

post about 200 yards north of the intersection of the Tempel-
hofstrasse and Eberstrasse.

To have gone farther than this command post on the northern boundary of the Schoeneberg section of the city would
have been suicide. Russian artillery was laying down a merciless barrage on the heart of Berlin. Snipers were everywhere
on rooftops, in sewers, and behind road blocks that had been
thrown up at all main intersections.

The last 16 blocks that stand between me and the Unter
den Linden are too hot to navigate.

With me here in Berlin are Andy Tully, reporter for the
Boston Traveler, and jeep driver Johnny Wilson. We are the
only three Americans here, and even the Russians think we
are slightly mad to have dared the trip from Torgau on the
Elbe through the Russian lines.

It is now about 3 o'clock in the afternoon. We have spent
the day probing the main highways that lead into the heart of
the city. On our first three tries we were turned back after
running into pitched battles.

On the fourth try, we penetrated to within 10 blocks of the
Wilhelmstrasse. To get there we drove north, up the Berlinerstrasse, turned left on a Ringbahn near the Templehof and
then took a sharp right turn down the Sachsendamm to the
Innsbrueckerplatz. There we took another right turn and
edged our way about 200 yards down the Eberstrasse to the
Russian command post.

The Russians are fighting madly and doggedly beyond this
point.

As each block is cleared of organized resistance, there still
remains the job of fine-combing the buildings for snipers.
The crack of small-arms fire is everywhere. German dead still
lie in the streets.

This section of Berlin is not so badly damaged as I had
expected it to be. There are still plenty of houses and buildings that remain intact to provide good hiding places and
snipers. The few German civilians that have remained are in a
state of abject and shivering terror. They know that for them
the least suspicion of sniping means death.

The sight of our crude Russian-made American flag from
our jeep brings all German civilians running.

"When will the Americans be here?" is their one question.

Several Germans who spoke English have begged for the answer and it has given me considerable pleasure to reply: "The Americans will not be here. Berlin belongs to the Russians."

At this command post today we were told that somewhere in this section were two American flyers who had escaped from a prison camp and were fighting with the Russians. We spent about an hour trying to find them, but it was no use— hunting anybody in Berlin is like trying to find a dime on the bottom of the Atlantic.

At one point we thought we were within reach of them. We found a German woman who spoke English, but she was too frightened to be coherent and when we tried to follow her directions we were hopelessly lost.

This German woman tried to tell us how the Russians were treating the civilians in Berlin, but we paused only long enough to get the information about the American flyers. For us to be seen talking to a German behind the Russian lines might easily have meant death for us.

One look at this German woman told more than she could have said in words. There were circles under her eyes so deep and dark that they might have been etched there with lamp black. She shivered like some one with the ague.

The Russians have shown no mercy. They have played the perfect game of tit-for-tat. They have done to Berlin what the German Army did to Leningrad and Stalingrad.

Last night in the artillery command post where we three Yanks were guests of the Russian Guards-Maj. Nikolai Kovaleski, I heard from Russian officers the staggering numbers of Russian civilians killed in the battles of Smolensk, Sevastopol, Leningrad and Stalingrad; and as they talked the Russian artillery boomed the revenge of these cities.

Last night was a fantastic night. The artillery barrage went almost all night long. Between rounds there were unearthly sounds—the cracking of machine-gun fire tearing the night, the rumbling sounds of great buildings collapsing under the battering of the artillery barrage.

But in the guard-major's command post there was a great celebration. By the time the great feast was over, we had established beyond doubt in the guard-major's mind that we were not spies, but only three foolhardy Yanks who had taken our lives in our hands to get to Berlin. Once all suspicion was gone from the minds of the officers in the party, there was an air of camaraderie that is hard to describe.

They practically gave us the keys to Berlin. The guard-major insisted that "our brave and courageous Sergeant" Johnny Wilson have a seat of honor near the head of the table. Johnny was without appetite in the excitement, but the guard-major slapped his gun, pointed to Johnny's plate and roared good-naturedly "Mange, mange." Johnny understands a little French and knew that the Major was commanding him to eat. So, wide-eyed and almost choking with emotion over being the first American GI to enter Berlin, Johnny ate.

After the dinner, there was dancing to a beaten-up victrola. One young Captain was the Russian equivalent of the American jitterbug and danced, not only with me, but with Johnny. I am still puffing from the exertion.

At about 1 o'clock in the morning we three exhausted Yanks begged off from more dancing and vodka drinking and the Major showed us to our rooms. Still the perfect host, he gave up his bed to our Sergeant. While Johnny slept in style, the Major disposed himself on a divan in the living room.

Everywhere today the sight of three Yanks in Berlin was the sign for great mobs of Russian soldiers to gather around us. I have shaken hands until my right wrist is paralyzed. I have smiled and laughed until my ears ache.

BERLIN, April 28.—The Red Army in action is terrific. On the move it looks like a mixture of a scene from a De Mille movie of the Crusades and newsreel shots of American motorized supply columns.

American Studebaker trucks rub axles with antiquated farm carts loaded down with Russian infantry. Great herds of sheep and cows are mixed in with armored cars and half-tracks with household belongings lashed to their sides. Super tanks tangle with a fantastic mess of horse-drawn buggies, phaetons, surreys, pony carts and farm wagons, all loaded down with ammunition, food, women, wounded and animals.

To an American observer used to the ordered precision of the American Army on the move, the scene is unbelievable, but behind this seeming confusion there is an order, or purpose, that has already carried the Russians into the heart of Berlin.

As I write, the Russian artillery is pounding the heart of the city with a barrage I have never heard equaled in an American battle. The earth shakes. The air stinks of cordite and the dead. All Berlin seems confusion.

The fierce Russian infantry are pushing into the heart of the city. Wild horses turned loose after pulling supply carts roam the streets. German dead lie everywhere. Here and there, a horse, caught by some sniper's bullet, lies sprawled amidst the wreckage of the buildings.

We three Yanks, Andy Tully of the Boston Traveler, a jeep driver, Johnny Wilson of the Twenty-sixth U.S. Division, and I are the first Americans to see the Russian fighting army in action. They have practically given us the keys to the city and we have spent the day trying to keep the Russian infantry from sweeping us before them on their way down the Unter den Linden.

The ruthlessness and the determination of the Russian fighting men is hard to describe. Nobody seems to have any set duty. They all just pitch in and fight like hell wherever there is fighting to be done.

Today we managed to make ourselves understood to a Russian infantryman who acted as a sort of guide around the city. This fierce-looking youngster in a great fur shako took off without bothering to ask a superior officer's permission. He perched on the hood of our jeep and motioned directions with his riot gun. Finally, when we had had all we could take, we made him understand that we were going back toward the rear, where things were a little quieter, but, instead of going back with us to his command post where we had picked him up about a mile back, he shook hands with us and set off on foot to join some Russian infantrymen who were going into the heavy fighting right in the heart of Berlin.

The Russian Army does a fantastic job of mixing work and play. They fight like mad and play with a sort of barbaric abandon.

This morning after eating a heavy breakfast of charred veal and potatoes swimming in fat—all washed down with alternate drinks of hot milk and vodka—we three Yanks set off alone to try to see something of Berlin.

We made a wrong turn some place off the Berlinerstrasse and at a road block that had not been cleared got scared out of our field boots by a terrific burst of machine-gun fire off to our right.

Retracing our way, we went back to the command post of our friend, the Guards Maj. Nikolai Kovalesky.

When we returned, there was a mid-morning dance in full swing. Russian officers, their medals clanking on their chests, were dancing with a young Russian WAC Lieutenant; and there, practically in the middle of Berlin and in the middle of one of the bloodiest battles in history, I danced for an hour before we could pry ourselves away from the festivities.

I waltzed to the tune of "Kannst Du Mir Gut Sein," which I think was a German record of "Sonny Boy." I danced to "Magnolia" and "Love and Kisses" by Paul Whiteman and his orchestra. In fact, they swung me around until the scratchy old Victrola hopped on the table and I was a dripping mess of mud composed of three parts perspiration and one part German bomb rubble dust.

In between times, Russian noncoms would come in, click their heels smartly, salute and receive their orders for the fighting at hand.

At about 10:30 our Russian host insisted we eat another breakfast, well basted again with cognac and vodka. My Russian orderly, a fierce-looking Mongolian named Rachmann, turned up with a fresh bouquet of flowers and escorted me out into the hall for a shoeshine. He put enough black polish on my brown Army shoes to last a lifetime. He also blacked my stockings halfway to the knee.

The whole day was like being transported to another and strange world. I felt as though I had been caught in a giant whirlpool of destruction. There was such an air of unreality about the whole of the battle for Berlin that I thought at times I had lost my reason and was only imagining these strange and unearthly sights.

It was too much for my reason to accept the Russian women—in the uniforms of secretaries, laundresses and traffic cops—riding in the hay-filled ricks with the infantry.

It was too much to get out of our jeep to shake hands with a furiously milling mob of Russian soldiers—one of whom was serenading me on an accordion—and find that I was standing practically in the middle of a yard full of German dead.

All of these two days I have spent with the Russian Army is like a dream. I have only to close my eyes to see again the fantastic scene of the Russian Army on the move. The horse-drawn carts are, many of them, driven by infantrymen with their heads swathed in bandages. In the Russian Army, evidently, you have to be pretty seriously wounded to be relieved of duty and taken to a hospital.

I have only to close my eyes to see again the horses and cattle, American trucks and almost medieval carts, and anti-tank guns and tanks and the phaetons and buggies and gaily painted gypsy wagons are rolling down a road into Berlin.

The U.S. Army allows the German civilian to keep his cattle and chickens and sheep, so the Army won't have to feed him. The Russian Army sweeps the countryside and drives before it all the livestock in its path.

This was the most nerve-racking day of my life. We were continually caught in traffic jams. When I wasn't worried about being killed by a bursting shell or a German sniper, I was panic-stricken lest a horse chew my arm off.

Whenever a column would halt, there would be an unearthly din of truck horns mixed with the neighing of horses, the bleating of sheep and the cackling of chickens loaded in coops, with the infantry riding in farm carts. Over all could usually be heard the strains of some Russian tune being "rendered" on an accordion or a violin. Always there was the shouting in, to me, unintelligible Russian.

And over all this there has been the almost hysterical shouting of our American Sergeant, Jeep Driver Johnny Wilson of Roxbury, Mass., yelling "Amerikanski" and acting like the Grover Whalen of World War II. Johnny is the greatest ambassador of good will a nation ever had. He looks like a sad sack, but he is the personality kid with the Russians. He shows me off like Evelyn MacLean sporting the Hope diamond. If the Russians don't notice me at every hand, Johnny yells, "American woman," and brings to their attention that an American female is in Berlin, and he is right now telling a bunch of Russian officers that Andy Tully should be a battalion commander in the Red Army.

It has been a mad day, but a wonderful one.

If the pay was in something besides rubles, I'd join the Russian Army and try to help take Berlin.

St. Louis Post-Dispatch, May 9–11, 1945

The War in Europe Is Ended!
Surrender Is Unconditional;
V-E Will Be Proclaimed Today

by Edward Kennedy

REIMS, France, May 7—Germany surrendered unconditionally to the Western Allies and the Soviet Union at 2:41 A.M. French time today. [This was at 8:41 P.M. Eastern Wartime Sunday.]

The surrender took place at a little red schoolhouse that is the headquarters of Gen. Dwight D. Eisenhower.

The surrender, which brought the war in Europe to a formal end after five years, eight months and six days of bloodshed and destruction, was signed for Germany by Col. Gen. Gustav Jodl. General Jodl is the new Chief of Staff of the German Army.

The surrender was signed for the Supreme Allied Command by Lieut. Gen. Walter Bedell Smith, Chief of Staff for General Eisenhower.

It was also signed by Gen. Ivan Susloparoff for the Soviet Union and by Gen. Francois Sevez for France.

[The official Allied announcement will be made at 9 o'clock Tuesday morning when President Truman will broadcast a statement and Prime Minister Churchill will issue a V-E Day proclamation. Gen. Charles de Gaulle also will address the French at the same time.]

General Eisenhower was not present at the signing, but immediately afterward General Jodl and his fellow delegate, Gen. Admiral Hans Georg Friedeburg, were received by the Supreme Commander.

They were asked sternly if they understood the surrender terms imposed upon Germany and if they would be carried out by Germany.

They answered Yes.

Germany, which began the war with a ruthless attack upon Poland, followed by successive aggressions and brutality in internment camps, surrendered with an appeal to the victors for mercy toward the German people and armed forces.

After having signed the full surrender, General Jodl said he wanted to speak and received leave to do so.

"With this signature," he said in soft-spoken German, "the German people and armed forces are for better or worse delivered into the victors' hands.

"In this war, which has lasted more than five years, both have achieved and suffered more than perhaps any other people in the world."

The New York Times, May 8, 1945

The A.P. Surrender

by A. J. Liebling

THE GREAT ROW over Edward Kennedy's Associated Press story of the signing of the German surrender at Reims served to point up the truth that if you are smart enough you can kick yourself in the seat of the pants, grab yourself by the back of the collar, and throw yourself out on the sidewalk. This is an axiom that I hope will be taught to future students of journalism as Liebling's Law. The important aspect of the row, I am sure, is not that Kennedy got his dispatch out of Europe before the SHAEF Public Relations bosses wanted him to but that only three representatives of the American press were admitted to one of the memorable scenes in the history of man, and they only on condition that they promise not to tell about it until the brigadier general in charge of public relations gave them permission. *No* correspondent of a newspaper published in the United States was invited to the signing; besides Kennedy, Boyd Lewis of the United Press, and James Kilgallen of Hearst's International News Service, the official list included four radio men, an enlisted correspondent for *Stars & Stripes*, and a collection of French, Russian, Australian, and Canadian correspondents. Whether a promise extorted as this one was, in an airplane several thousand feet up, has any moral force is a question for theologians. The only parallel I can think of offhand is the case of Harold the Saxon, who was shipwrecked in the territories of William of Normandy at a time when Edward the Confessor was getting on in years. William, taking Harold into protective custody, made him swear not to claim the English throne after Edward died, but when Harold got home he cocked a snoot at William. Anglo-Saxon historians have since expressed a good deal of sympathy for Harold's point of view, but the Church held with William. I suppose that Kennedy should have refused to promise anything and thus made sure of

646

missing an event that no newspaperman in the world would want to miss, but I can't imagine any correspondent's doing it.

I do not think Kennedy imperilled the lives of any Allied soldiers by sending the story, as some of his critics have charged. He probably saved a few, because by withholding the announcement of an armistice you prolong the shooting, and, conversely, by announcing it promptly you make the shooting stop. Moreover, the Germans had broadcast the news of the armistice several hours before Kennedy's story appeared on the streets of New York, and Absie, the O.W.I.'s American Broadcasting Station in Europe, broadcast it in twenty-four languages, including English, within an hour after. The thing that has caused the most hard feeling is that Kennedy broke a "combination," which means that he sent out a story after all the correspondents on the assignment had agreed not to. But the old-fashioned "combination" was an agreement freely reached among reporters and not a pledge imposed upon the whole group by somebody outside it. Incidentally, the *Times* used to make its reporters at Police Headquarters stay out of combinations. The willingness of the large American news organizations in the European Theatre of Operations to be herded into the new-style combination, in return for favors that independent journalists didn't get, had led directly to the kind of official contempt for the press that the Reims arrangements indicated, with the accompanying view that opportunity to report history was what SHAEF calls a "SHAEF privilege," like a Shubert pass. The Associated Press was a leader in establishing this form of organized subservience, and the jam it now finds itself in is therefore a good illustration of the workings of Liebling's Law.

For many years before this war, the editorial end of the American newspaper business had been turning from news gathering to shopping for a packaged, mass-produced wordage sold by the press associations and syndicates. A few newspapers, such as the *Times* and *Herald Tribune* here and the *Tribune* and *Daily News* in Chicago, went into wholesaling in a modest way themselves by setting up their own syndicates, principally to peddle European news. The war, coupled with the excess-profits tax (which made many businessmen decide that they might as well pay their extra money to employees as to the tax collector), put an end, in a number of cases, to the newspapers' depending entirely on this sort of ready-made, or store, news, and scores of writers for magazines and newspapers began to arrive in the European Theatre of Operations. The large news organizations then faced the problem of proving that boughten coverage was not only cheaper but better than "original" reporting—say, Ernest Hemingway's. To accomplish this, they either suggested or accepted enthusiastically—it is not quite clear which—the Army's present principle of "limited facilities" for the coverage of news events. This meant that they concurred in the rear-area military maxim that there were never enough accommodations for the number of correspondents who wanted to see anything. The military, in return, conceded that the correspondents of the organizations which had large London bureaus should have first call on whatever accommodations there were. These bureaus established their importance with a SHAEF Public Relations personnel that seldom got out of London. The clearing house for the allotment of "facilities," which from then on assumed the character not of rights but of favors, was the Association of American Correspondents, whose headquarters were in London and which was dominated by the representatives of the large press organizations, and any facilities that were left over were distributed among the independent correspondents whom the members found most "reasonable." The key members of the Association further impressed the Public Relations soldiers with statistics about the number of readers each of their organizations served. The Associated Press claims to "fill the news needs of eight hundred million people," I.N.S. two hundred and twenty-five million, United Press (unaccountably modest) fifty-five million "in the United States alone," the Chicago *Tribune* syndicate a hundred and ten million, the *Herald Tribune* syndicate ten million, the *Times* syndicate six million, and Time-Life, Inc., which managed to wedge its way into the Association at an early date, twenty-two million. Together with the major radio chains, which reach a good billion people each, these press associations and syndicates served about twice the population of the world. This total does not even include the readers of the Chicago *Daily News* syndicate, figures for which are not on hand at this writing. Having once accepted the principle of limitation (i.e., to members of the Correspondents' Association) and having made a habit, for thirty months, of shouting publicly, "Headquarters is always right!," the dozen or so ruling members were hardly in a position to object when the Army decided on a further limitation of newspaper facilities — this time to zero.

The story that amused me most during armistice week was the one that appeared in the *Times* of Wednesday, May 9th, under the headline "Fiasco by SHAEF at Reims Is Bared: Reporters Barred from Seeing Historic Signing of the German Surrender." It was signed by Raymond Daniell, a sententious little man who, as chief of the *Times'* London bureau, had been the chief promoter of the limitations scheme, back in 1942. "The correspondents never liked the Army's plan, but they accepted it with reservations," Daniell wrote. "What made them especially angry, however, was the fact that when the time came for the surrender, it was the Army's plan for coverage in Berlin that was adopted, instead of an order of precedence drawn up at Dieppe by the newspaper representatives and followed ever since until last Sunday night by the Army where space was limited." Daniell, as president of the Correspondents' Association, had practically imposed the "order of precedence" on the Army press-relations chief in London after the Dieppe what-was-it. His reason was that it turned out after the raid that Quentin Reynolds of *Collier's* had been along without the sanction of the Association. It was never hinted that Reynolds' presence had anything to do with the sanguinary unsuccess at Dieppe, but Daniell and his opposite numbers in the other large news organizations nevertheless felt that magazine men should be discouraged. The bureau chiefs of the syndicates, conspicuously including Robert Bunnelle of the A.P., who is now involved in the Kennedy trouble, simply transferred to Europe the tendency of American district reporters to play ball with the police lieutenant on the desk. It is that which makes the rather spluttery rage of Brigadier General Frank Allen, the Supreme Headquarters Press Relations chief, so comprehensible. The Brigadier feels like a keeper at the Zoo who has been butted in the behind by his favorite gazelle. What made Daniell especially angry, apparently, was that the military found room at the surrender ceremony for twenty women friends of officers but left him standing outside. He seemed to feel that this was rubbing it in.

The Kennedy explosion has, I imagine, done no harm, except possibly to Kennedy—one of my favorite reporters, I might add. The Russians have not declined to end the war because of it. Maybe, in the absence of opposition, the Russians would have had to stop anyway, although this does not seem to have occurred to Supreme Headquarters spokesmen. The Russians had their own surrender show in Berlin, and probably had a better publicity break on it than they would have had if the two surrenders had been announced simultaneously. (They could do with a public-relations counsel, anyway.) One unconditional surrender of the Reich a day is about as much as the public can absorb. Moreover, the row can do a lot of good if it brings into the clear the whole disturbing question of military censorship imposed for political, personal, or merely capricious reasons and reveals the history of the prodigious amount of pure poodle-faking that has gone on under the name of Army Public Relations. I remember the period in North Africa when, for reasons of "military security," no correspondent was allowed to say anything against Admiral Darlan even after he was dead, and when a dispatch of my own was censored because I said that anti-Fascist Frenchmen thought our indulgence of the Fascists silly (information which obviously would have been of great interest to the German General Staff). In France, last summer, another of my stories was held up a week because I wrote about the torture and execution of an American parachutist by Vichy militiamen. It was evidently important to military security that the American public shouldn't think hard of our enemies. "Horror stuff," by which the censors meant any mention of ugly wounds or indecorous deaths, was for a long time forbidden, but recently it has been found compatible with security. Somebody must have told whoever makes the rules that the Germans know about it. But the worst form of censorship was the preventive kind exercised by Public Relations, which, in any echelon higher than an army in the field, acted on the principle that an inactive correspondent was potentially a source of less bother than a correspondent who was going somewhere. While the correspondent was in the United States, the object was to keep him from crossing to England, and once he got to England the game was to stop him from reaching Africa, Italy, France, or any other place he might find subject matter. If he arrived in any of those countries, there was one more line of defense — P.R.O. would try to hold him in Algiers, Naples, or Paris, as the case might be. Actually, he was safe only when he got to a front. He had nothing to worry him there but shells, for the higher echelons of Public Relations left him alone. To give Army Public Relations the only credit due it, some of the younger officers in the field were helpful, hard-working, and at times even intelligent.

The Public Relations situation reached a high point in *opera-buffa* absurdity in London in the spring of a year ago, before the invasion of France. There were at one time nine separate echelons of Public Relations in London at once: P.R.O. SHAEF; P.R.O. Twenty-first Army Group (Montgomery's command); P.R.O. FUSAG (First Army Group, which later became Twelfth Army Group); P.R.O. First Army; P.R.O. ETOUSA (European Theatre of Operations, U.S. Army), which handled the correspondents' mail, gave out ration cards, did publicity for Services of Supply, and tried to horn in on everything else; P.R.O. Eighth Air Force; P.R.O. Ninth Air Force; the P.R.O. for General Spaatz's highest echelon of the Air Forces command; and the Navy P.R.O. The Air Forces publicity people were unpretentious but aggressive; the Navy was helpful; the five other echelons spent most of their time getting in each other's way.

The P.R.O.s, mostly colonels and lieutenant colonels (a major, in this branch of service, was considered a shameful object, to be exiled to an outer office), had for the most part been Hollywood press agents or Chicago rewrite men in civilian life. They looked as authentic in their uniforms as dress extras in a B picture, but they had learned to say "Army" with an unction that Stonewall Jackson could never have achieved. One rewrite lieutenant colonel used to predict casualties as high as eighty per cent in the first assault wave on D Day. He had never heard a shot fired in anger. Others would seriously tell correspondents, that they, the correspondents, couldn't go along on D Day because there wouldn't be space enough on the landing craft to hold another man. The P.R.O.s were perhaps under the impression that you load ships for an invasion the way you would ferry boats, without regard to the organization of combat units. There was room for ninety more men on the Coast Guard LCI on which I finally crossed. The one point on which all the London officers were united was their detestation of the field army. One division commander who requested that a certain correspondent be allowed to accompany his outfit into action stirred such resentment in the London army that he was reprimanded by the Chief of Staff of SHAEF. The London P.R.O.s felt that the division commander, being a mere major general rich in battle experience, was guilty of insubordination when he disagreed with non-combatant lieutenant colonels. Daniell, Bunnelle, and the rest of the news-agency men adapted themselves to this squalid milieu and flourished in it. They agreed with everything the dress extras said, especially with the thesis that on fifty miles of Norman coast there would be room for only about twenty correspondents, who would of course represent the larger news organizations. The habit of saying yes to people you don't respect is hard to break, which is one reason I think well of Edward Kennedy for breaking it. Also, I think that if any severe punishment is inflicted on the first journalist to disobey an unreasonable order, an era of conformity will set in that will end even the pretense of freedom of the press in any area where there is a brigadier general to agree with.

Having finished with what I consider the deeper implications of the Kennedy case, I would like to say that it has produced some delightful examples of journalism right here in this country. On the afternoon of Tuesday, May 8th, after most of the papers had played up Kennedy's story real big and the Army had then denounced it as "unauthorized," Roy W. Howard, president of the Scripps-Howard newspapers and overlord of the United Press, the A.P.'s chief rival, broke into print with a plea for the Associated Press. Howard said that he himself had been pilloried like Kennedy in November, 1918, when he had reported the armistice four days before it had happened. The two cases were an exact parallel except that Kennedy's report was right and Howard's was wrong.

The *Times*, on that same Tuesday morning, carried Kennedy's story in two columns on the right-hand side of the front page, in twelve-point type, under two cross-lines and two banks dropping from its four-line streamer headline. On Thursday it published an editorial saying Kennedy had done a "grave disservice to the newspaper profession." A *Times* man I met in a saloon that afternoon said they had run the story because it looked authentic but they had run the editorial because they didn't like the way the story had been sent out. On Tuesday they also carried a boxed dispatch from Drew Middleton, one of their own men in Paris, saying that all the correspondents except Kennedy had been caught in "the most colossal 'snafu' in the history of the war."

Wednesday morning brought Daniell's remarkable *Times* story, cited above (which read exactly the way a *Nebelwerfer* sounds) and a perfectly deadpan account of the Reims function by Drew Middleton, who presumably had not been there, since he wasn't on the list of correspondents invited by SHAEF. Middleton's story appeared twenty-four hours after the *Times* had carried the Kennedy story and was practically a duplicate of it. The *Herald Tribune* had an equally deadpan account by John O'Reilly, who presumably wasn't there either, and an editorial, better-tempered than the *Times*', chiding Kennedy. It also had on its front page an excellent eyewitness story about Berlin in the final days of the Russian attack upon it, written by its own correspondent Seymour Freidin, who was still under suspension by SHAEF for having gone to Berlin without Brigadier General Allen's permission. The story had been held up six days. The *Times* had a similar story by the equally excommunicated John Groth, but it wasn't so good. *PM*, that same P.M., had a long, involved "Letter from the Editor," by the Editor, toward the end of which it came out that the Editor was in favor of the decision Kennedy had made.

After that, the excitement seemed to be dying away, but Friday morning, Robert McLean, publisher of the Philadelphia

Bulletin and president of the Associated Press, issued a statement censuring Kennedy. Friday afternoon brought an editorial in *Editor & Publisher*, the trade journal of the newspaper business, a publication that usually reflects high-echelon newspaper sentiment. *Editor & Publisher* made a magnificent grab for the best of both worlds simultaneously, just as if it were a newspaper. It said, "We agree with Kennedy that no military security was involved and that it was political censorship. . . . The Paris correspondents also declare they have no degree of confidence in the Public Relations Division of SHAEF, and we don't blame them. [Actually, when a motion of no confidence was proposed at a correspondents' meeting in Paris after the surrender incident, the correspondents tabled it, preferring to gang up on their colleague Kennedy.] We hope this will serve as a lesson to the military and political leaders of the Allied nations that a story of that magnitude cannot be kept secret." But the editorial also said, "Kennedy apparently violated one of the cardinal principles of good journalism—that of respecting a confidence. No amount of explanation . . . is justification." Of course, the Allied leaders would not have learned the lesson if Kennedy had not repudiated the confidence. Neither McLean nor *Editor & Publisher* challenged SHAEF's right to impose such a condition. The top side of the newspaper business obviously believes that freedom of the press goes no farther than the right to complain about corporation taxes.

To wind up, and illustrate, my morality tale, the *Times*, on Saturday morning, carried a story that SHAEF was going to retain control over correspondents in Europe even though fighting has ceased and that censors have been empowered to suppress anything they consider "unauthorized, inaccurate, or false reports, misleading statements and rumors, or reports likely to injure the morale of the Allied forces (or nations)." This means that correspondents may send no news, even though it is verified and vital to American understanding of what is happening, unless it is "authorized" by some Army political adviser like Robert Murphy, who in 1942 gave a sample of his stuff by stopping all stories unfavorable to the State Department filed in North Africa. It also means that the censors—or rather, in the last analysis, the censors' Army superiors—will decide what is true and accurate or false and misleading, and what is calculated to injure the morale of Allied forces. For example, a correspondent might say there was a strong republican movement in Italy, but the censor might decide that such knowledge would diminish the Royal Italian Army's enthusiasm for the Royal House the Allies insist on propping up. So he would stop the correspondent from sending the story to America. And so it might go—and will, if the press continues to truckle to the dress extras.

The New Yorker, May 19, 1945

Attack on Carrier Bunker Hill

by Phelps Adams

ABOARD A FAST CARRIER IN THE FORWARD PACIFIC AREA, May 11 (Delayed).—Two Japanese suicide planes carrying 1,100 pounds of bombs plunged into the flight deck of Admiral Marc A. Mitscher's own flagship early today, killing several hundred officers and men, and transforming one of our biggest and finest flattops into a floating torch, with flames soaring nearly a thousand feet into the sky.

For eight seemingly interminable hours that followed, the ship and her crew fought as tense and terrifying a battle for survival as has ever been witnessed in the Pacific, but when dusk closed in the U.S.S. Bunker Hill—horribly crippled and still filmed by thin wisps of smoke and steam from her smoldering embers, was valiantly plowing along under her own power on the distant horizon—safe! Tomorrow she will spend nearly eight equally interminable hours burying at sea the men who died to save her.

Only once before during the entire war against Japan has any American carrier suffered such wounds, fought such fires, and lived—and that was when the battered, gutted hulk of the Franklin managed miraculously to steam away from these waters under her own power.

Like the Franklin, the Bunker Hill took everything the Japs could give her, under the most unfavorable circumstances, and survived it. And tonight, as she licks at her wounds and nurses her wounded, she stands as a living monument to the fact that no major unit of the American fleet has ever been sunk by a suicide plane or by any combination of them. She constitutes one more link in the chain of evidence which must, by now, have convinced the Japs that all the maniacal, suicidal fury that they can unleash against us cannot save them.

From the deck of the neighboring carrier a few hundred yards distant I watched the Bunker Hill burn, and I do not yet see how she lived through it. It is hard to believe that men could survive those flames, or that metal could withstand such heat.

I still find it incredible, too, that death could strike so swiftly and so wholly unexpectedly into the very heart of our great Pacific fleet. At one minute our task force was cruising in lazy circles about sixty miles off Okinawa without a care in the world and apparently without a suggestion of the presence of an enemy plane in any direction. In the next minute the Bunker Hill was a pillar of flame. It was as quick as that—like summer lightning without any warning rumble of thunder.

The Oriental equivalent of Lady Luck was certainly riding with Japan's suicide corps today. Everything broke for them with unbelievable good fortune.

A series of fleecy-white, low-hanging clouds that studded a bright sky concealed the intruders from the vigilant eyes of all the lookouts manning all the stations on all of the ships that go to make up this great armada called Task Force 58. Not until they began their final screaming plunge from the cover of these clouds did the Jap kamikazes become visible.

And it was sheer luck, of course, that they happened to strike on the particular day and at the exact hour when their target was most vulnerable. Because there was no sign of the enemy and because the Bunker Hill and the men aboard her were weary after fifty-eight consecutive days in the battle zones off Iwo Jima, Tokyo, the Inland Sea and Okinawa her crew was not at General Quarters when she was hit. For the first time in a week our own ship had secured from General Quarters an hour or two before. Some of the watertight doors that imprisoned men in small, stifling compartments were thrown open. The ventilators were unsealed and turned on, and those men not standing the regular watch were permitted to relax from the deadly sixteen-hour vigil that they had put in at their battle stations every day since we had entered the danger zone.

So it was on the Bunker Hill. Exhausted men not on watch were catching a catnap. Aft on the flight deck thirty-four planes were waiting to take off. Their tanks were filled to the last drop of capacity with highly volatile aviation gasoline.

Their guns were loaded to the last possible round of ammunition. Earnest young pilots, mentally reviewing the briefing they had just received, were in the cockpits warming up the motors. On the hangar deck below more planes—also crammed with gasoline and ammunition—were all set to be spotted on the flight deck, and in the pilots' ready rooms other young aviators were kidding around while waiting their turn aloft.

Just appearing over the horizon were the planes returning from the early mission. They jockeyed into the landing circle and waited until the Bunker Hill should launch her readied craft and clear the deck for landing.

And it was at this precise moment that a keen-eyed man aboard our ship caught the first glimpse of three enemy planes and cried a warning. But before General Quarters could be sounded on this ship, and before half a dozen shots could be fired by the Bunker Hill, the first kamikaze had dropped his 550-pound bomb and plunged squarely into the midst of the thirty-four waiting planes in a shower of burning gasoline.

The bomb, fitted with a delayed action fuse, pierced the flight deck at a sharp angle, passed out through the side of the hull and exploded in mid-air before striking the water. The plane—a single-engined Jap fighter—knocked the parked aircraft about like ten-pins, sent a huge column of flame and smoke belching upwards and then skidded crazily over the side.

Some of the pilots were blown overboard, and many managed to scramble to safety; but before a move could be made to fight the flames another kamikaze came whining out of the clouds, straight into the deadly anti-aircraft guns of the ship. This plane was a Jap dive bomber—a judy. A five-inch shell that should have blown him out of the sky, set him afire and riddled his plane with metal, but still he came. Passing over the stern of the ship, he dropped his bomb with excellent aim right in the middle of the blazing planes. Then he flipped over and torched through the flight deck at the base of the island. The superstructure, which contains many of the delicate nerve centers from which the vessel is controlled, was instantly enveloped in flames and smoke which were caught in turn by the maws of the ventilating system and sucked down into the inner compartments of the ship, where the watertight doors and hatches had just been swung shut and battened down. Scores of men were suffocated in these below deck chambers.

Minutes later a third Jap suicider zoomed down to finish the job. Ignoring the flames and the smoke that swept around them, the men in the Bunker Hill's gun galleries stuck courageously to their posts, pumping ammunition into their weapons and filling the sky with a curtain of protective lead. It was a neighboring destroyer, however, which finally scored a direct hit on the Jap and sent him splashing harmlessly into the sea.

That was the end of the attack and beginning of an heroic and brilliant fight for survival. The entire rear end of the ship was burning with uncontrollable fury. It looked very much like the newsreel shots of a blazing oil well, only worse—for this fire was feeding on highly refined gasoline and live ammunition. Greasy black smoke rose in a huge column from the ship's stern, shot through with angry tongues of cherry-red flame. Blinding white flashes appeared continuously as ready ammunition in the burning planes or in the gun galleries was touched off. Every few minutes the whole column of smoke would be swallowed in a great burst of flame as another belly tank exploded or as the blaze reached another pool of gasoline flowing from the broken aviation fuel lines on the hangar deck below.

For more than an hour there was no visible abatement in the fury of the flames. They would seem to be dying down slightly as hundreds of thousands of gallons of water and chemicals were poured on them, only to burst forth more hungrily than ever as some new explosion occurred within the stricken ship.

The carrier itself had begun to develop a pronounced list, and as each new stream of water was poured into her the angle increased more dangerously. Crippled as she was, however, she ploughed ahead at top speed and the wind that swept her decks blew the flame and smoke astern over the fantail and prevented the blaze from spreading forward on the flight deck and through the island structure. Trapped on the fantail, men faced the flames and fought grimly on, with only the ocean behind them, and with no way of knowing how much of the ship remained on the other side of that fiery wall.

Then, somehow, other men managed to break out the huge openings in the side of the hangar deck, and I got my first glimpse of the interior of the ship. That, I think, was the most horrible sight of all. The entire hangar deck was a raging blast furnace, white-hot throughout its length. Even from where I stood the glow of molten metal was unmistakable.

By this time the explosions had ceased and a cruiser and three destroyers were able to venture alongside with hoses fixed in their rigging. Like fireboats in New York Harbor, they pumped great streams of water into the ship and the smoke at last began to take on that greyish tinge which showed that somewhere a flame was dying.

Up on the bridge, Capt. George A. Seitz, the skipper, was growing increasingly concerned about the dangerous list his ship had developed, and resolved to take a gambling chance. Throwing the Bunker Hill into a 70-degree turn, he heeled her cautiously over onto the opposite beam so that tons of water which had accumulated on one side were suddenly swept across the decks and overboard on the other. By great good fortune this wall of water carried the heart of the hangar deck fire with it.

That was the turning point in this modern battle of the Bunker Hill. After nearly three hours of almost hopeless fighting, she had brought her fires under control, and, though it was many more hours before they were completely extinguished, the battle was won and the ship was saved.

A thick book could not record all the acts of heroism that were performed aboard that valiant ship today. There was the executive officer, Commander H. J. Dyson, who was standing within fifty feet of the second bomb when it exploded and who was badly injured; yet he refused medical aid and continued to fight the blaze until it was safely under control.

Then there was a squad of Marines who braved the white heat of the hangar deck and threw every bomb and rocket out of a nearby storage room.

But the most fruitful work of all, perhaps, was performed

by the pilots of the almost fuelless planes that had been circling overhead for a landing when the ship was struck. In the hours that followed, nearly three hundred men went overboard, and the fact that 269 of these were picked up by other ships in the fleet later was due, in no small measure, to the work of these sharp-eyed airmen.

Although our own flight deck had been cleared for their use and they had been instructed to land on it, these pilots kept combing every inch of the surface of the sea, tearing packets of dye marker from their own life jackets and dropping them to guide destroyers and other rescue vessels to the little clusters of men they saw clinging to bits of wreckage below them. Calculating their fuel supply to a hairbreadth nicety, some of them came aboard us with such a close margin that a single wave-off would have sent them and their planes into the sea before they could make another swing of the landing circle and return.

In all, I am told, 170 men will be recommended for awards as a result of this day's work.

Late today Admiral Mitscher and 60 or more members of his staff came aboard us to make this carrier his new flagship. He was unhurt—not even singed by the flames that swept the Bunker Hill, but he had lost three officers and six men of his own staff and a number of close friends in the ship's company. It was the first time in his long years of service that he had personally undergone such an experience.

As he was hauled aboard in a breeches buoy across the churning water that separated us from the speedy destroyer that had brought him alongside, he looked tired and old and just plain mad. His deeply lined face was more than weather beaten—it looked like an example of erosion in the dustbowl country—but his eyes flashed fire and vengeance. He was a man who had a score to settle with the Japs and who would waste no time going about it. He had plans that the Japs will not like.

But as a matter of fact, the enemy is already on the losing end of the Bunker Hill box score. Since she arrived in the Pacific in the fall of 1943 the Bunker Hill has participated in every major strike that has occurred. She was initiated at Rabaul, she took part in the invasions of the Gilberts and the

Marshalls, pounding at Kwajalein and Eniwetok. With Task Force 58, she has struck twice at Tokyo and also at Truk, the China Coast, the Ryukyus, Formosa, the Bonins, Iwo Jima and Okinawa.

During this period the pilots of her air groups have sunk, probably sunk and damaged, nearly a million tons of Jap shipping. They have shot 475 enemy planes out of the air, 169 of them during the past two months. In two days here off Okinawa they splashed sixty-seven Nipponese aircraft, and the ship herself has brought down fourteen more by anti-aircraft fire.

On a raid last March at Kure Harbor when the Japanese fleet was hiding out in the Inland Sea, Bunker Hill planes scored direct bomb hits on three carriers and one heavy cruiser, and then sent nine torpedoes flashing into the side of the enemy's beautiful new battleship, the Yamato, sinking her.

That is our side of the box score.

In the Jap column stands the fact that at the cost of three pilots and three planes today the enemy killed a probable total of 392 of our men, wounded 264 others, destroyed about 70 planes and wrecked a fine and famous ship. The flight deck of that ship tonight looks like the crater of a volcano. One of the great fifty-ton elevators has been melted almost in half. Gun galleries have been destroyed and the pilots' ready rooms demolished. Virtually the entire island structure with its catwalks and platforms is a twisted mass of steel, and below decks tonight hospital corpsmen are preparing 352 bodies for burial at sea, starting at noon tomorrow.

But the ship has not been sunk. Had it been it would have taken years to build another. As it is the Bunker Hill will steam back to Bremerton Navy Yard under her own power and there will be repaired. While she remains there one American carrier with a hundred or so planes and a crew of 3,000 men will be out of action, but within a few weeks she will be back again, sinking more ships, downing more planes, and bombing out more Japanese airfields.

Perhaps her next task will be to cover the Invasion of Tokyo itself. Who knows?

The New York Sun, June 28, 1945

"A GIANT PILLAR OF PURPLE FIRE":
NAGASAKI, AUGUST 9, 1945

Atomic Bombing of Nagasaki Told by Flight Member

by William L. Laurence

WITH THE ATOMIC BOMB MISSION TO JAPAN, Aug. 9 (Delayed)—We are on our way to bomb the mainland of Japan. Our flying contingent consists of three specially designed B-29 "Superforts," and two of these carry no bombs. But our lead plane is on its way with another atomic bomb, the second in three days, concentrating in its active substance an explosive energy equivalent to 20,000 and, under favorable conditions, 40,000 tons of TNT.

We have several chosen targets. One of these is the great industrial and shipping center of Nagasaki, on the western shore of Kyushu, one of the main islands of the Japanese homeland.

I watched the assembly of this man-made meteor during the past two days, and was among the small group of scientists and Army and Navy representatives privileged to be present at the ritual of its loading in the "Superfort" last night, against a background of threatening black skies torn open at intervals by great lightning flashes.

It is a thing of beauty to behold, this "gadget." In its design went millions of man-hours of what is without doubt the most concentrated intellectual effort in history. Never before had so much brain-power been focused on a single problem.

This atomic bomb is different from the bomb used three days ago with such devastating results on Hiroshima.

I saw the atomic substance before it was placed inside the bomb. By itself it is not at all dangerous to handle. It is only under certain conditions, produced in the bomb assembly, that it can be made to yield up its energy, and even then it gives only a small fraction of its total contents—a fraction,

663

however, large enough to produce the greatest explosion on earth.

The briefing at midnight revealed the extreme care and the tremendous amount of preparation that had been made to take care of every detail of the mission, to make certain that the atomic bomb fully served the purpose for which it was intended. Each target in turn was shown in detailed maps and in aerial photographs. Every detail of the course was rehearsed—navigation, altitude, weather, where to land in emergencies. It came out that the Navy had submarines and rescue craft, known as Dumbos and Superdumbos, stationed at various strategic points in the vicinity of the targets, ready to rescue the fliers in case they were forced to bail out.

The briefing period ended with a moving prayer by the chaplain. We then proceeded to the mess hall for the traditional early morning breakfast before departure on a bombing mission.

A convoy of trucks took us to the supply building for the special equipment carried on combat missions. This included the "Mae West," a parachute, a lifeboat, an oxygen mask, a flak suit and a survival vest. We still had a few hours before take-off time, but we all went to the flying field and stood around in little groups or sat in jeeps talking rather casually about our mission to the Empire, as the Japanese home islands are known hereabouts.

In command of our mission is Maj. Charles W. Sweeney, 25, of 124 Hamilton Avenue, North Quincy, Mass. His flagship, carrying the atomic bomb, is named The Great Artiste, but the name does not appear on the body of the great silver ship, with its unusually long, four-bladed, orange-tipped propellers. Instead it carried the number 77, and someone remarks that it was "Red" Grange's winning number on the gridiron.

Major Sweeney's co-pilot is First Lieut. Charles D. Albury, 24, of 252 Northwest Fourth Street, Miami, Fla. The bombardier, upon whose shoulders rests the responsibility of depositing the atomic bomb square on its target, is Capt. Kermit K. Beahan of 1004 Telephone Road, Houston, Tex., who is celebrating his twenty-seventh birthday today.

Captain Beahan has the awards of the Distinguished Flying Cross, the Air Medal and one Silver Oak Leaf Cluster, the

Purple Heart, the Western Hemisphere Ribbon, the European Theatre Ribbon and two battle stars. He participated in the first Eighth Air Force heavy bombardment mission against the Germans from England on Aug. 17, 1942, and was on the plane that transported Gen. Dwight D. Eisenhower from Gibraltar to Oran at the beginning of the North African invasion. He has had a number of hair-raising escapes in combat.

The navigator on The Great Artiste is Capt. James F. Van Pelt Jr., 27, of Oak Hill, W. Va. The flight engineer is M/Sgt. John D. Kuharek, 32, of 1054 Twenty-second Avenue, Columbus, Neb.; S/Sgt. Albert T. De Hart of Plainview, Tex., who celebrated his thirtieth birthday yesterday, is the tail gunner; the radar operator is S/Sgt. Edward K. Buckley, 32, of 529 East Washington Street, Lisbon, Ohio. The radio operator is Sgt. Abe M. Spitzer, 33, of 655 Pelham Parkway, North Bronx, N.Y.; Sgt. Raymond Gallagher, 23, of 572 South Mozart Street, Chicago, is assistant flight engineer.

The lead ship is also carrying a group of scientific personnel, headed by Comdr. Frederick L. Ashworth, USN, one of the leaders in the development of the bomb. The group includes Lieut. Jacob Beser, 24, of Baltimore, Md., an expert on airborne radar.

The other two Superfortresses in our formation are instrument planes, carrying special apparatus to measure the power of the bomb at the time of explosion, high speed cameras and other photographic equipment.

Our "Superfort" is the second in line. Its commander is Capt. Frederick C. Bock, 27, of 300 West Washington Street, Greenville, Mich. Its other officers are Second Lieut. Hugh C. Ferguson, 21, of 247 Windermere Avenue, Highland Park, Mich., pilot; Second Lieut. Leonard A. Godfrey, 24, of 72 Lincoln Street, Greenfield, Mass., navigator; and First Lieut. Charles Levy, 26, of 1954 Spencer Street, Philadelphia, bombardier.

The enlisted personnel of this "Superfort" are: T/Sgt. Roderick F. Arnold, 28, of 130 South Street, Rochester, Mich., flight engineer; Sgt. Ralph D. Curry, 20, of 1101 South Second Avenue, Hoopeston, Ill., radio operator; Sgt. William C. Barney, 22, of Columbia City, Ind., radar operator; Corp. Robert J. Stock, 21, of 415 Downing Street, Fort Wayne, Ind., assistant flight engineer, and Corp. Ralph D. Belanger, 19, of Thendara, N.Y., tail gunner.

The scientific personnel of our "Superfort" includes S/Sgt. Walter Goodman, 22, of 1956 Seventy-fourth Street, Brooklyn, N.Y., and Lawrence Johnson, graduate student at the University of California, whose home is at Hollywood, Calif.

The third "Superfort" is commanded by Maj. James Hopkins, 1311 North Queen Street, Palestine, Tex. His officers are Second Lieut. John E. Cantlon, 516 North Takima Street, Tacoma, Wash., pilot; Second Lieut. Stanley C. Steinke, 604 West Chestnut Street, West Chester, Pa., navigator; and Second Lieut. Myron Faryna, 16 Elgin Street, Rochester, N.Y., bombardier.

The crew are Tech. Sgt. George L. Brabenec, 9717 South Lawndale Avenue, Evergreen, Ill.; Sgt. Francis X. Dolan, 30-60 Warren Street, Elmhurst, Queens, N.Y.; Corp. Richard F. Cannon, 160 Carmel Road, Buffalo, N.Y.; Corp. Martin G. Murray, 7356 Dexter Street, Detroit, Mich., and Corp. Sidney J. Bellamy, 529 Johnston Avenue, Trenton, N.J.

On this "Superfort" are also two distinguished observers from Britain, whose scientists played an important role in the development of the atomic bomb. One of these is Group Capt. G. Leonard Cheshire, famous Royal Air Force pilot, who is now a member of the British military mission to the United States. The other is Dr. William G. Penney, Professor of Applied Mathematics, London University, one of the group of eminent British scientists that has been working at the "Y-Site" near Santa Fe, N.M., on the enormous problems involved in taming the atom.

Group Captain Cheshire, whose rank is the equivalent to that of colonel in the United States Army Air Forces, was designated as an observer of the atomic bomb in action by Winston Churchill when he was still Prime Minister. He is now the official representative of Prime Minister Clement R. Attlee.

We took off at 3:50 this morning and headed northwest on a straight line for the Empire. The night was cloudy and threatening, with only a few stars here and there breaking through the overcast. The weather report had predicted storms ahead part of the way but clear sailing for the final and climactic stages of our odyssey.

We were about an hour away from our base when the storm broke. Our great ship took some heavy dips through the abysmal darkness around us but it took these dips much more gracefully than a large commercial airliner, producing a sensation more in the nature of a glide than a "bump," like a great ocean liner riding the waves, except that in this case the air waves were much higher and the rhythmic tempo of the glide much faster.

I noticed a strange eerie light coming through the window high above the navigator's cabin and as I peered through the dark all around us I saw a startling phenomenon. The whirling giant propellers had somehow became great luminous disks of blue flame. The same luminous blue flame appeared on the plexiglass windows in the nose of the ship, and on the tips of the giant wings it looked as though we were riding the whirlwind through space on a chariot of blue fire.

It was, I surmised, a surcharge of static electricity that had accumulated on the tips of the propellers and on the dielectric material in the plastic windows. One's thoughts dwelt anxiously on the precious cargo in the invisible ship ahead of us. Was there any likelihood of danger that this heavy electric tension in the atmosphere all about us might set it off?

I expressed my fears to Captain Bock, who seems nonchalant and imperturbed at the controls. He quickly reassures me:

"It is a familiar phenomenon seen often on ships. I have seen it many times on bombing missions. It is known as St. Elmo's Fire."

On we went through the night. We soon rode out the storm and our ship was once again sailing on a smooth course straight ahead, on a direct line to the Empire.

Our altimeter showed that we were traveling through space at a height of 17,000 feet. The thermometer registered an outside temperature of 33 degrees below zero centigrade, about 30 below Fahrenheit. Inside our pressurized cabin the temperature was that of a comfortable air-conditioned room, and a pressure corresponding to an altitude of 8,000 feet. Captain Bock cautioned me, however, to keep my oxygen mask handy in case of emergency. This, he explained, might mean either something going wrong with the pressure equipment inside the ship or a hole through the cabin by flak.

The first signs of dawn came shortly after 5 o'clock. Sergeant Curry, who had been listening steadily on his earphones for radio reports, while maintaining a strict radio silence himself, greeted it by rising to his feet and gazing out the window.

"It's good to see the day," he told me. "I get a feeling of claustrophobia hemmed in in this cabin at night."

He is a typical American youth, looking even younger than his 20 years. It takes no mind-reader to read his thoughts.

"It's a long way from Hoopeston, Ill.," I find myself remarking.

"Yep," he replies, as he busies himself decoding a message from outer space.

"Think this atomic bomb will end the war?" he asks hopefully.

"There is a very good chance that this one may do the trick," I assure him, "but if not, then the next one or two surely will. Its power is such that no nation can stand up against it very long."

This was not my own view. I had heard it expressed all around a few hours earlier, before we took off. To anyone who had seen this man-made fireball in action, as I had less than a month ago in the desert of New Mexico, this view did not sound overoptimistic.

By 5:50 it was real light outside. We had lost our lead ship, but Lieutenant Godfrey, our navigator, informs me that we had arranged for that contingency. We have an assembly point in the sky above the little island of Yakoshima, southeast of Kyushu, at 9:10. We are to circle there and wait for the rest of our formation.

Our genial bombardier, Lieutenant Levy, comes over to invite me to take his front-row seat in the transparent nose of the ship and I accept eagerly. From that vantage point in space, 17,000 feet above the Pacific, one gets a view of hundreds of miles on all sides, horizontally and vertically. At that height the vast ocean below and the sky above seem to merge into one great sphere.

I was on the inside of that firmament, riding above the giant mountains of white cumulous clouds, letting myself be suspended in infinite space. One hears the whirl of the motors behind one, but it soon becomes insignificant against the immensity all around and is before long swallowed by it. There comes a point where space also swallows time and one lives through eternal moments filled with an oppressive loneliness, as though all life had suddenly vanished from the earth and you are the only one left, a lone survivor traveling endlessly through interplanetary space.

My mind soon returns to the mission I am on. Somewhere beyond these vast mountains of white clouds ahead of me there lies Japan, the land of our enemy. In about four hours from now one of its cities, making weapons of war for use against us, will be wiped off the map by the greatest weapon ever made by man. In one-tenth of a millionth of a second, a fraction of time immeasurable by any clock, a whirlwind from the skies will pulverize thousands of its buildings and tens of thousands of its inhabitants.

Our weather planes ahead of us are on their way to find out where the wind blows. Half an hour before target time we will know what the winds have decided.

Does one feel any pity or compassion for the poor devils about to die? Not when one thinks of Pearl Harbor and of the Death March on Bataan.

Captain Bock informs me that we are about to start our climb to bombing altitude.

He manipulates a few knobs on his control panel to the right of him and I alternately watch the white clouds and ocean below me and the altimeter on the bombardier's panel. We reached our altitude at 9 o'clock. We were then over Japanese waters, close to their mainland. Lieutenant Godfrey motioned to me to look through his radar scope. Before me was the outline of our assembly point. We shall soon meet our lead ship and proceed to the final stage of our journey.

We reached Yakoshima at 9:12 and there, about 4,000 feet ahead of us, was The Great Artiste with its precious load. I saw Lieutenant Godfrey and Sergeant Curry strap on their parachutes and I decided to do likewise.

We started circling. We saw little towns on the coastline,

heedless of our presence. We kept on circling, waiting for the third ship in our formation.

It was 9:56 when we began heading for the coastline. Our weather scouts had sent us code messages, deciphered by Sergeant Curry, informing us that both the primary target as well as the secondary were clearly visible.

The winds of destiny seemed to favor certain Japanese cities that must remain nameless. We circled about them again and again and found no opening in the thick umbrella of clouds that covered them. Destiny chose Nagasaki as the ultimate target.

We had been circling for some time when we noticed black puffs of smoke coming through the white clouds directly at us. There were fifteen bursts of flak in rapid succession, all too low. Captain Bock changed his course. There soon followed eight more bursts of flak, right up to our altitude, but by this time were too far to the left.

We flew southward down the channel and at 11:33 crossed the coastline and headed straight for Nagasaki about 100 miles to the west. Here again we circled until we found an opening in the clouds. It was 12:01 and the goal of our mission had arrived.

We heard the prearranged signal on our radio, put on our arc-welder's glasses and watched tensely the maneuverings of the strike ship about half a mile in front of us.

"There she goes!" someone said.

Out of the belly of The Great Artiste what looked like a black object went downward.

Captain Bock swung around to get out of range; but even though we were turning away in the opposite direction, and despite the fact that it was broad daylight in our cabin, all of us became aware of a giant flash that broke through the dark barrier of our arc-welder's lenses and flooded our cabin with intense light.

We removed our glasses after the first flash, but the light still lingered on, a bluish-green light that illuminated the entire sky all around. A tremendous blast wave struck our ship and made it tremble from nose to tail. This was followed by four more blasts in rapid succession, each resounding like the boom of cannon fire hitting our plane from all directions.

Observers in the tail of our ship saw a giant ball of fire rise as though from the bowels of the earth, belching forth enormous white smoke rings. Next they saw a giant pillar of purple fire, 10,000 feet high, shooting skyward with enormous speed.

By the time our ship had made another turn in the direction of the atomic explosion the pillar of purple fire had reached the level of our altitude. Only about forty-five seconds had passed. Awe-struck, we watched it shoot upward like a meteor coming from the earth instead of from outer space, becoming ever more alive as it climbed skyward through the white clouds. It was no longer smoke, or dust, or even a cloud of fire. It was a living thing, a new species of being, born right before our incredulous eyes.

At one stage of its evolution, covering millions of years in terms of seconds, the entity assumed the form of a giant square totem pole, with its base about three miles long, tapering off to about a mile at the top. Its bottom was brown, its center was amber, its top white. But it was a living totem pole, carved with many grotesque masks grimacing at the earth.

Then, just when it appeared as though the thing has settled down into a state of permanence, there came shooting out of the top a giant mushroom that increased the height of the pillar to a total of 45,000 feet. The mushroom top was even more alive than the pillar, seething and boiling in a white fury of creamy foam, sizzling upward and then descending earthward, a thousand Old Faithful geysers rolled into one.

It kept struggling in an elemental fury, like a creature in the act of breaking the bonds that held it down. In a few seconds it had freed itself from its gigantic stem and floated upward with tremendous speed, its momentum carrying into the stratosphere to a height of about 60,000 feet.

But no sooner did this happen when another mushroom, smaller in size than the first one, began emerging out of the pillar. It was as though the decapitated monster was growing a new head.

As the first mushroom floated off into the blue it changed its shape into a flowerlike form, its giant petal curving downward, creamy white outside, rose-colored inside. It still retained that shape when we last gazed at it from a distance of about 200 miles.

The New York Times, September 9, 1945

Japan Signs, Second World War Is Ended

by Homer Bigart

ABOARD U. S. S. MISSOURI, Tokyo Bay, Sept. 2 (Sunday). — Japan, paying for her desperate throw of the dice at Pearl Harbor, passed from the ranks of the major powers at 9:05 a.m. today when Foreign Minister Mamoru Shigemitsu signed the document of unconditional surrender.

If the memories of the bestialities of the Japanese prison camps were not so fresh in mind, one might have felt sorry for Shigemitsu as he hobbled on his wooden leg toward the green baize covered table where the papers lay waiting. He leaned heavily on his cane and had difficulty seating himself. The cane, which he rested against the table, dropped to the deck of this battleship as he signed.

No word passed between him and General Douglas MacArthur, who motioned curtly to the table when he had finished his opening remarks.

Lieutenant General Jonathan M. Wainwright, who surrendered Corregidor, haggard from his long imprisonment, and Lieutenant General A. E. Percival, who surrendered Singapore on another black day of the war, stood at MacArthur's side as the Allied Supreme Commander signed for all the powers warring against Japan.

Their presence was a sobering reminder of how desperately close to defeat our nation had fallen during the early months of 1942.

The Japanese delegation of eleven looked appropriately trim and sad. Shigemitsu was wearing morning clothes — frock coat, striped pants, silk hat and yellow gloves. None of the party exchanged a single word or salute while on board, except the foreign minister's aide, who had to be shown where to place the Japanese texts of the surrender documents.

Shigemitsu, however, doffed his silk hat as he reached the top of the starboard gangway and stepped aboard the broad deck of the Missouri.

New York *Herald Tribune*, September 2, 1945

A Month After the Atom Bomb: Hiroshima Still Can't Believe It

by Homer Bigart

HIROSHIMA, Japan, Sept. 3 (Delayed).—We walked today through Hiroshima, where survivors of the first atomic-bomb explosion four weeks ago are still dying at the rate of about one hundred daily from burns and infections which the Japanese doctors seem unable to cure.

The toll from the most terrible weapon ever devised now stands at 53,000 counted dead, 30,000 missing and presumed dead, 13,960 severely wounded and likely to die, and 43,000 wounded. The figures come from Hirokuni Dadai, who as "chief of thought control" of Hiroshima Prefecture is supposed to police subversive thinking.

On the morning of Aug. 6 the 340,000 inhabitants of Hiroshima were awakened by the familiar howl of air-raid sirens. The city had never been bombed—it had little industrial importance. The Kure naval base lay only twelve miles to the southeast and American bombers had often gone there to blast the remnants of the imperial navy, or had flown mine-laying or strafing missions over Shimonoseki Strait to the west. Almost daily enemy planes had flown over Hiroshima, but so far the city had been spared.

At 8 a.m. the "all clear" sounded. Crowds emerged from the shallow raid shelters in Military Park and hurried to their jobs in the score of tall, modern, earthquake-proof buildings along Hattchobori, the main business street of the city. Breakfast fires still smoldered in thousands of tiny ovens—presently they were to help to kindle a conflagration.

Very few persons saw the Superfortress when it first appeared more than five miles above the city. Some thought they saw a black object swinging down on a parachute from the plane, but for the most part Hiroshima never knew what hit it.

A Japanese naval officer, Vice-Admiral Masao Kanazawa, at the Kure base said the concussion from the blast twelve miles away was "like the great wind that made the trees sway." His aide, a senior lieutenant who was to accompany us into the city, volunteered that the flash was so bright even in Kure that he was awakened from his sleep. So loud was the explosion that many thought the bomb had landed within Kure.

When Lieutenant Taira Ake, a naval surgeon, reached the city at 2:30 p.m., he found hundreds of wounded still dying unattended in the wrecks and fields on the northern edge of the city. "They didn't look like human beings," he said. "The flesh was burned from their faces and hands, and many were blinded and deaf."

Dadai was standing in the doorway of his house nearly two miles from the center of impact. He had just returned from Tokyo.

"The first thing I saw was a brilliant flash," he said. "Then after a second or two came a shock like an earthquake. I knew immediately it was a new type of bomb. The house capsized on top of us and I was hit with falling timbers.

"I found my wife lying unconscious in the debris, and I dragged her to safety. My two children suffered cuts, and for the next hour or so I was too busy to think of what was happening in the city."

Doctors rushed from the Kure naval base—including Lieutenant Ake—were prevented from entering the city until six hours after the blast because of the searing heat of the explosion. City officials said that many indoors who were buried under collapsing walls and roofs subsequently were burned to death in the fires that broke out within a few minutes after the blast.

The first impression in the minds of the survivors was that a great fleet of Superfortresses flying at great height had somehow sneaked past the defenses and dropped thousands of fire bombs. Even today there are many who refuse to believe that a single bomb wiped out the city.

A party of newspaper men led by Colonel John McCrary was the first group of Americans to reach Hiroshima. We flew in today in a B-17, our pilot, Captain Mark Magnan, finding a hole in the clouds over Kure and setting the plane down on the tiny runway of the naval air base there with about seventy feet to spare.

The admiral in charge of the base, after telling us what he had seen and knew of the bombing, gave us two sedans and a truck, and we drove down a mountain, through ruined Kure and past the navy yard. A tall fence set up along the road to block the view of the yard had been removed, and we could see ten destroyers, two submarines and some gunboats anchored in the harbor.

Across the bay, beached on an island and listing to port so that the waves broke over her deck, was the battleship Haruna. Farther on we passed close to another beached warship, an old three-stacker that flaunted the silhouettes of ten American planes on her mid-stack. A four-engine bomber was among the planes the destroyer claimed to have shot down.

Several tunnels and deep cuts along the highway to Hiroshima were stacked with airplane motors and other vital equipment, leaving only a narrow lane for passage. Our driver, speeding at fifty miles an hour along the concrete highway, slammed into one crated engine and swerved across the road and struck another, shearing the rear fender.

Three miles outside Hiroshima we saw the first signs of blast damage—loose tiles torn from roofs and an occasional broken window. At the edge of town there were houses with roofs blown off, while the walls facing the center of the city had caved inward.

Finally we came to the river and saw the Island of Hiro, which holds, or rather held, the main districts of Hiroshima, which means "Hiro Island."

In the part of town east of the river the destruction had looked no different from a typical bomb-torn city in Europe. Many buildings were only partly demolished, and the streets were still choked with debris.

But across the river there was only flat, appalling desolation, the starkness accentuated by bare, blackened tree trunks and the occasional shell of a reinforced concrete building.

We drove to Military Park and made a walking tour of the ruins.

By all accounts the bomb seemed to have exploded directly

over Military Park. We saw no crater there. Apparently the full force of the explosion was expended laterally.

Aerial photographs had shown no evidence of rubble, leading to the belief that everything in the immediate area of impact had been literally pulverized into dust. But on the ground we saw this was not true. There was rubble everywhere, but much smaller in size than normal.

Approaching the Hattchobori, we passed what had been a block of small shops. We could tell that only because of office safes that lay at regular intervals on sites that retained little else except small bits of iron and tin. Sometimes the safes were blown in.

The steel door of a huge vault in the four-story Geibi Bank was flung open, and the management had installed a temporary padlocked door. All three banking houses—Geibi, Mitsubishi and the Bank of Japan—were conducting business in the sturdy concrete building of the Bank of Japan, which was less damaged than the rest.

Since the bank and the police station were the only buildings open for business, we asked our naval lieutenant guide if we could enter. He disappeared and was gone for several minutes.

We stood uneasily at the corner of the bank building, feeling very much like a youth walking down Main Street in his first long pants. There weren't many people abroad—a thin trickle of shabbily dressed men and women—but all of them stared at us.

There was hatred in some glances, but generally more curiosity than hatred. We were representatives of an enemy power that had employed a weapon far more terrible and deadly than poison gas, yet in the four hours we spent in Hiroshima none so much as spat at us, nor threw a stone.

We later asked the naval lieutenant, who once lived in Sacramento, to halt some pedestrians and obtain eyewitness accounts of the blast. He was very reluctant to do so.

"They may not want to talk to you," he said. But finally he stopped an old man, who bared his gold teeth in an apparent gesture of friendship.

"I am a Christian," said the old man, making the sign of the cross. He pointed to his ears, indicating deafness, and the lieutenant, after futile attempts to make him hear, told us that the old man, like many others, apparently had suffered permanent loss of his hearing when the crashing blast of the atomic bomb shattered his ear drums.

The lieutenant stopped a few more middle-aged civilians, but they backed off, bowing and grinning. They said they were not in Hiroshima on Aug. 6.

Two boys walking barefoot through the rubble displayed no fear of infection, although no doctor could say positively that the danger had ended. The boys said they had been brought in from the countryside to help clean up the city.

The cloying stench of death was still very noticeable in the street, and we were glad when the lieutenant finally motioned us inside the bank.

Except for broken windows and chipped cornices, the Bank of Japan presented an intact facade outside. Inside, however, we saw that the concussion had smashed the frail stalls and reduced the furnishings to matchwood. Under the lofty vaulted roof spaces had been roped off, and skeleton staffs of the three banking institutions sat behind crude wooden tables handing the government's new yen currency to waiting lines.

Several persons showed bad burns about their necks and faces, and nearly half the population seemed to be wearing gauze bandages over noses and mouths to protect them from germs.

Those who entered Hiroshima and stayed only a few hours appeared to suffer no ill effects, doctors said, but many who attempted to live in the ruins developed infections that reacted on the blood cells as destructively as leukemia, except that the white blood corpuscles and not the red were consumed. Victims became completely bald; they lost all appetite; they vomited blood.

A few of the main streets of Hiroshima have been cleared. Trolleys ran through the blighted areas down to the waterfront. But the public is forbidden to drink from wells, and water has to be brought in from the countryside.

Down one street was the ruined wall of a Christian church, and near it the site of the Japanese 2d Army headquarters. Hiroshima was an embarkation point for the invasion which threatened Kyushu, and the city had been filled with soldiers when the bomb fell. How many of them perished no one yet knows, for all records were destroyed by fire. Among the army staff members killed was the chief of military police.

The city and the prefectural (provincial) government had moved to a motorcycle plant in the outskirts of town, and there we met Dadai. He was introduced at first as "a high government official," but later admitted he was Chief of Thought Control.

Dadai's appearance fitted his role. He looked like a man who could not only suppress a thought, but could torture it. He wore a white bandage across his brow, tied in back of his head, and the face beneath it was sallow and repressive. His tight, grim mouth hardly opened as he answered questions put to him through the naval interpreter.

He told us that the wounded were doomed by the disintegrating effects of the uranium on the white blood corpuscles. This statement, however, was not substantiated by doctors, who said they knew so little about the strange disorders that it was useless to speculate on how high the death toll would run. They cited the case of the woman who suffered only a slight cut in the explosion, yet died eighteen days later.

Neither Dadai nor local correspondents who asked for an interview seemed to believe that the atomic bomb would end war. One of the first questions asked by Japanese newspaper men was: "What effect will the bomb have on future wars?" They also asked whether Hiroshima "would be dangerous for seventy years." We told them we didn't know.

New York *Herald Tribune*, September 5, 1945

Hiroshima

by John Hersey

I. A NOISELESS FLASH

AT EXACTLY fifteen minutes past eight in the morning, on August 6, 1945, Japanese time, at the moment when the atomic bomb flashed above Hiroshima, Miss Toshiko Sasaki, a clerk in the personnel department of the East Asia Tin Works, had just sat down at her place in the plant office and was turning her head to speak to the girl at the next desk. At that same moment, Dr. Masakazu Fujii was settling down cross-legged to read the Osaka *Asahi* on the porch of his private hospital, overhanging one of the seven deltaic rivers which divide Hiroshima; Mrs. Hatsuyo Nakamura, a tailor's widow, stood by the window of her kitchen, watching a neighbor tearing down his house because it lay in the path of an air-raid-defense fire lane; Father Wilhelm Kleinsorge, a German priest of the Society of Jesus, reclined in his underwear on a cot on the top floor of his order's three-story mission house, reading a Jesuit magazine, *Stimmen der Zeit*; Dr. Terufumi Sasaki, a young member of the surgical staff of the city's large, modern Red Cross Hospital, walked along one of the hospital corridors with a blood specimen for a Wassermann test in his hand; and the Reverend Mr. Kiyoshi Tanimoto, pastor of the Hiroshima Methodist Church, paused at the door of a rich man's house in Koi, the city's western suburb, and prepared to unload a handcart full of things he had evacuated from town in fear of the massive B-29 raid which everyone expected Hiroshima to suffer. A hundred thousand people were killed by the atomic bomb, and these six were among the survivors. They still wonder why they lived when so many others died. Each of them counts many small items of chance or volition—a step taken in time, a decision to go indoors, catching one streetcar instead of the next—that spared him. And now each knows that in the act of survival he lived a dozen lives and saw more death than he ever thought he would see. At the time, none of them knew anything.

The Reverend Mr. Tanimoto got up at five o'clock that morning. He was alone in the parsonage, because for some time his wife had been commuting with their year-old baby to spend nights with a friend in Ushida, a suburb to the north. Of all the important cities of Japan, only two, Kyoto and Hiroshima, had not been visited in strength by *B-san*, or Mr. B, as the Japanese, with a mixture of respect and unhappy familiarity, called the B-29; and Mr. Tanimoto, like all his neighbors and friends, was almost sick with anxiety. He had heard uncomfortably detailed accounts of mass raids on Kure, Iwakuni, Tokuyama, and other nearby towns; he was sure Hiroshima's turn would come soon. He had slept badly the night before, because there had been several air-raid warnings. Hiroshima had been getting such warnings almost every night for weeks, for at that time the B-29s were using Lake Biwa, northeast of Hiroshima, as a rendezvous point, and no matter what city the Americans planned to hit, the Superfortresses streamed in over the coast near Hiroshima. The frequency of the warnings and the continued abstinence of Mr. B with respect to Hiroshima had made its citizens jittery; a rumor was going around that the Americans were saving something special for the city.

Mr. Tanimoto is a small man, quick to talk, laugh, and cry. He wears his black hair parted in the middle and rather long; the prominence of the frontal bones just above his eyebrows and the smallness of his mustache, mouth, and chin give him a strange, old-young look, boyish and yet wise, weak and yet fiery. He moves nervously and fast, but with a restraint which suggests that he is a cautious, thoughtful man. He showed, indeed, just those qualities in the uneasy days before the bomb fell. Besides having his wife spend the nights in Ushida, Mr. Tanimoto had been carrying all the portable things from his church, in the close-packed residential district called Naga-ragawa, to a house that belonged to a rayon manufacturer in Koi, two miles from the center of town. The rayon man, a

Mr. Matsui, had opened his then unoccupied estate to a large number of his friends and acquaintances, so that they might evacuate whatever they wished to a safe distance from the probable target area. Mr. Tanimoto had had no difficulty in moving chairs, hymnals, Bibles, altar gear, and church records by pushcart himself, but the organ console and an upright piano required some aid. A friend of his named Matsuo had, the day before, helped him get the piano out to Koi; in return, he had promised this day to assist Mr. Matsuo in hauling out a daughter's belongings. That is why he had risen so early.

Mr. Tanimoto cooked his own breakfast. He felt awfully tired. The effort of moving the piano the day before, a sleepless night, weeks of worry and unbalanced diet, the cares of his parish—all combined to make him feel hardly adequate to the new day's work. There was another thing, too: Mr. Tanimoto had studied theology at Emory College, in Atlanta, Georgia; he had graduated in 1940; he spoke excellent English; he dressed in American clothes; he had corresponded with many American friends right up to the time the war began; and among a people obsessed with a fear of being spied upon—perhaps almost obsessed himself—he found himself growing increasingly uneasy. The police had questioned him several times, and just a few days before, he had heard that an influential acquaintance, a Mr. Tanaka, a retired officer of the Toyo Kisen Kaisha steamship line, an anti-Christian, a man famous in Hiroshima for his showy philanthropies and notorious for his personal tyrannies, had been telling people that Tanimoto should not be trusted. In compensation, to show himself publicly a good Japanese, Mr. Tanimoto had taken on the chairmanship of his local *tonarigumi*, or Neighborhood Association, and to his other duties and concerns this position had added the business of organizing air-raid defense for about twenty families.

Before six o'clock that morning, Mr. Tanimoto started for Mr. Matsuo's house. There he found that their burden was to be a *tansu*, a large Japanese cabinet, full of clothing and household goods. The two men set out. The morning was perfectly clear and so warm that the day promised to be uncomfortable. A few minutes after they started, the air-raid siren went off—a minute-long blast that warned of approaching planes but indicated to the people of Hiroshima only a slight degree of danger, since it sounded every morning at this time, when an American weather plane came over. The two men pulled and pushed the handcart through the city streets. Hiroshima was a fan-shaped city, lying mostly on the six islands formed by the seven estuarial rivers that branch out from the Ota River; its main commercial and residential districts, covering about four square miles in the center of the city, contained three-quarters of its population, which had been reduced by several evacuation programs from a wartime peak of 380,000 to about 245,000. Factories and other residential districts, or suburbs, lay compactly around the edges of the city. To the south were the docks, an airport, and the island-studded Inland Sea. A rim of mountains runs around the other three sides of the delta. Mr. Tanimoto and Mr. Matsuo took their way through the shopping center, already full of people, and across two of the rivers to the sloping streets of Koi, and up them to the outskirts and foothills. As they started up a valley away from the tight-ranked houses, the all-clear sounded. (The Japanese radar operators, detecting only three planes, supposed that they comprised a reconnaissance.) Pushing the handcart up to the rayon man's house was tiring, and the men, after they had maneuvered their load into the driveway and to the front steps, paused to rest awhile. They stood with a wing of the house between them and the city. Like most homes in this part of Japan, the house consisted of a wooden frame and wooden walls supporting a heavy tile roof. Its front hall, packed with rolls of bedding and clothing, looked like a cool cave full of fat cushions. Opposite the house, to the right of the front door, there was a large, finicky rock garden. There was no sound of planes. The morning was still; the place was cool and pleasant.

Then a tremendous flash of light cut across the sky. Mr. Tanimoto has a distinct recollection that it travelled from east to west, from the city toward the hills. It seemed a sheet of sun. Both he and Mr. Matsuo reacted in terror—and both had time to react (for they were 3,500 yards, or two miles, from the center of the explosion). Mr. Matsuo dashed up the front steps into the house and dived among the bedrolls and buried himself there. Mr. Tanimoto took four or five steps and threw himself between two big rocks in the garden. He bellied up very hard against one of them. As his face was against the stone, he did not see what happened. He felt a sudden pressure, and then splinters and pieces of board and fragments of tile fell on him. He heard no roar. (Almost no one in Hiroshima recalls hearing any noise of the bomb. But a fisherman in his sampan on the Inland Sea near Tsuzu, the man with whom Mr. Tanimoto's mother-in-law and sister-in-law were living, saw the flash and heard a tremendous explosion; he was nearly twenty miles from Hiroshima, but the thunder was greater than when the B-29s hit Iwakuni, only five miles away.)

When he dared, Mr. Tanimoto raised his head and saw that the rayon man's house had collapsed. He thought a bomb had fallen directly on it. Such clouds of dust had risen that there was a sort of twilight around. In panic, not thinking for the moment of Mr. Matsuo under the ruins, he dashed out into the street. He noticed as he ran that the concrete wall of the estate had fallen over—toward the house rather than away from it. In the street, the first thing he saw was a squad of soldiers who had been burrowing into the hillside opposite, making one of the thousands of dugouts in which the Japanese apparently intended to resist invasion, hill by hill, life for life; the soldiers were coming out of the hole, where they should have been safe, and blood was running from their heads, chests, and backs. They were silent and dazed.

Under what seemed to be a local dust cloud, the day grew darker and darker.

At nearly midnight, the night before the bomb was dropped, an announcer on the city's radio station said that about two hundred B-29s were approaching southern Honshu and advised the population of Hiroshima to evacuate to their designated "safe areas." Mrs. Hatsuyo Nakamura, the tailor's widow, who lived in the section called Nobori-cho and who had long had a habit of doing as she was told, got her three children—a ten-year-old boy, Toshio, an eight-year-old girl, Yaeko, and a five-year-old girl, Myeko—out of bed and dressed them and walked with them to the military area known as the East Parade Ground, on the northeast edge of the city. There she unrolled some mats and the children lay down on them. They slept until about two, when they were awakened by the roar of the planes going over Hiroshima.

As soon as the planes had passed, Mrs. Nakamura started back with her children. They reached home a little after two-thirty and she immediately turned on the radio, which, to her distress, was just then broadcasting a fresh warning. When she looked at the children and saw how tired they were, and when she thought of the number of trips they had made in past weeks, all to no purpose, to the East Parade Ground, she decided that in spite of the instructions on the radio, she simply could not face starting out all over again. She put the children in their bedrolls on the floor, lay down herself at three o'clock, and fell asleep at once, so soundly that when planes passed over later, she did not waken to their sound.

The siren jarred her awake at about seven. She arose, dressed quickly, and hurried to the house of Mr. Nakamoto, the head of her Neighborhood Association, and asked him what she should do. He said that she should remain at home unless an urgent warning—a series of intermittent blasts of the siren—was sounded. She returned home, lit the stove in the kitchen, set some rice to cook, and sat down to read that morning's Hiroshima *Chugoku*. To her relief, the all-clear sounded at eight o'clock. She heard the children stirring, so she went and gave each of them a handful of peanuts and told them to stay on their bedrolls, because they were tired from the night's walk. She had hoped that they would go back to sleep, but the man in the house directly to the south began to make a terrible hullabaloo of hammering, wedging, ripping, and splitting. The prefectural government, convinced, as everyone in Hiroshima was, that the city would be attacked soon, had begun to press with threats and warnings for the completion of wide fire lanes, which, it was hoped, might act in conjunction with the rivers to localize any fires started by an incendiary raid; and the neighbor was reluctantly sacrificing his home to the city's safety. Just the day before, the prefecture had ordered all able-bodied girls from the secondary schools to spend a few days helping to clear these lanes, and they started work soon after the all-clear sounded.

Mrs. Nakamura went back to the kitchen, looked at the rice, and began watching the man next door. At first, she was annoyed with him for making so much noise, but then she was moved almost to tears by pity. Her emotion was specifically directed toward her neighbor, tearing down his home, board by board, at a time when there was so much unavoidable destruction, but undoubtedly she also felt a generalized, community pity, to say nothing of self-pity. She had not had an easy time. Her husband, Isawa, had gone into the Army just after Myeko was born, and she had heard nothing from or of him for a long time, until, on March 5, 1942, she received a seven-word telegram: "Isawa died an honorable death at Singapore." She learned later that he had died on February 15th, the day Singapore fell, and that he had been a corporal. Isawa had been a not particularly prosperous tailor, and his only capital was a Sankoku sewing machine. After his death, when his allotments stopped coming, Mrs. Nakamura got out the machine and began to take in piecework herself, and since then had supported the children, but poorly, by sewing.

As Mrs. Nakamura stood watching her neighbor, everything flashed whiter than any white she had ever seen. She did not notice what happened to the man next door; the reflex of a mother set her in motion toward her children. She had taken a single step (the house was 1,350 yards, or three-quarters of a mile, from the center of the explosion) when something picked her up and she seemed to fly into the next room over the raised sleeping platform, pursued by parts of her house.

Timbers fell around her as she landed, and a shower of tiles pommelled her; everything became dark, for she was buried. The debris did not cover her deeply. She rose up and freed herself. She heard a child cry, "Mother, help me!," and saw her youngest—Myeko, the five-year-old—buried up to her breast and unable to move. As Mrs. Nakamura started frantically to claw her way toward the baby, she could see or hear nothing of her other children.

In the days right before the bombing, Dr. Masakazu Fujii, being prosperous, hedonistic, and, at the time, not too busy, had been allowing himself the luxury of sleeping until nine or nine-thirty, but fortunately he had to get up early the morning the bomb was dropped to see a house guest off on a train. He rose at six, and half an hour later walked with his friend to the station, not far away, across two of the rivers. He was back home by seven, just as the siren sounded its sustained warning. He ate breakfast and then, because the morning was already hot, undressed down to his underwear and went out on the porch to read the paper. This porch—in fact, the whole building—was curiously constructed. Dr. Fujii was the proprietor of a peculiarly Japanese institution, a private, single-doctor hospital. This building, perched beside and over the water of the Kyo River, and next to the bridge of the same name, contained thirty rooms for thirty patients and their kinfolk—for, according to Japanese custom, when a person falls sick and goes to a hospital, one or more members of his family go and live there with him, to cook for him, bathe, massage, and read to him, and to offer incessant familial sympathy, without which a Japanese patient would be miserable indeed. Dr. Fujii had no beds—only straw mats—for his patients. He did, however, have all sorts of modern equipment: an X-ray machine, diathermy apparatus, and a fine tiled laboratory. The structure rested two-thirds on the land, one-third on piles over the tidal waters of the Kyo. This overhang, the part of the building where Dr. Fujii lived, was queer-looking, but it was cool in summer and from the porch, which faced away from the center of the city, the prospect of the river, with pleasure boats drifting up and down it, was always refreshing. Dr. Fujii had occasionally had anxious moments when the Ota and its mouth branches rose to flood, but the piling was apparently firm enough and the house had always held.

Dr. Fujii had been relatively idle for about a month because in July, as the number of untouched cities in Japan dwindled and as Hiroshima seemed more and more inevitably a target, he began turning patients away, on the ground that in case of a fire raid he would not be able to evacuate them. Now he had only two patients left—a woman from Yano, injured in the shoulder, and a young man of twenty-five recovering from burns he had suffered when the steel factory near Hiroshima in which he worked had been hit. Dr. Fujii had six nurses to tend his patients. His wife and children were safe; his wife and one son were living outside Osaka, and another son and two daughters were in the country on Kyushu. A niece was living with him, and a maid and a manservant. He had little to do and did not mind, for he had saved some money. At fifty, he was healthy, convivial, and calm, and he was pleased to pass the evenings drinking whiskey with friends, always sensibly and for the sake of conversation. Before the war, he had affected brands imported from Scotland and America; now he was perfectly satisfied with the best Japanese brand, Suntory.

Dr. Fujii sat down cross-legged in his underwear on the spotless matting of the porch, put on his glasses, and started reading the Osaka *Asahi*. He liked to read the Osaka news because his wife was there. He saw the flash. To him—faced away from the center and looking at his paper—it seemed a brilliant yellow. Startled, he began to rise to his feet. In that moment (he was 1,550 yards from the center), the hospital leaned behind his rising and, with a terrible ripping noise, toppled into the river. The Doctor, still in the act of getting to his feet, was thrown forward and around and over; he was buffeted and gripped; he lost track of everything, because things were so speeded up; he felt the water.

Dr. Fujii hardly had time to think that he was dying before he realized that he was alive, squeezed tightly by two long timbers in a V across his chest, like a morsel suspended between two huge chopsticks—held upright, so that he could not move, with his head miraculously above water and his torso and legs in it. The remains of his hospital were all around him in a mad assortment of splintered lumber and materials for the relief of pain. His left shoulder hurt terribly. His glasses were gone.

Father Wilhelm Kleinsorge, of the Society of Jesus, was, on the morning of the explosion, in rather frail condition. The Japanese wartime diet had not sustained him, and he felt the strain of being a foreigner in an increasingly xenophobic Japan; even a German, since the defeat of the Fatherland, was unpopular. Father Kleinsorge had, at thirty-eight, the look of a boy growing too fast—thin in the face, with a prominent Adam's apple, a hollow chest, dangling hands, big feet. He walked clumsily, leaning forward a little. He was tired all the time. To make matters worse, he had suffered for two days, along with Father Cieslik, a fellow-priest, from a rather painful and urgent diarrhea, which they blamed on the beans and black ration bread they were obliged to eat. Two other priests then living in the mission compound, which was in the Nobori-cho section—Father Superior LaSalle and Father Schiffer—had happily escaped this affliction.

Father Kleinsorge woke up about six the morning the bomb was dropped, and half an hour later—he was a bit tardy because of his sickness—he began to read Mass in the mission chapel, a small Japanese-style wooden building which was without pews, since its worshippers knelt on the usual Japanese matted floor, facing an altar graced with splendid silks, brass, silver, and heavy embroideries. This morning, a Monday, the only worshippers were Mr. Takemoto, a theological student living in the mission house; Mr. Fukai, the secretary of the diocese; Mrs. Murata, the mission's devoutly Christian housekeeper; and his fellow-priests. After Mass, while Father Kleinsorge was reading the Prayers of Thanksgiving, the siren sounded. He stopped the service and the missionaries retired across the compound to the bigger building. There, in his room on the ground floor, to the right of the front door, Father Kleinsorge changed into a military uniform which he had acquired when he was teaching at the Rokko Middle School in Kobe and which he wore during air-raid alerts.

After an alarm, Father Kleinsorge always went out and scanned the sky, and this time, when he stepped outside, he was glad to see only the single weather plane that flew over Hiroshima each day about this time. Satisfied that nothing would happen, he went in and breakfasted with the other Fathers on substitute coffee and ration bread, which, under the circumstances, was especially repugnant to him. The Fathers sat and talked a while, until, at eight, they heard the all-clear. They went then to various parts of the building. Father Schiffer retired to his room to do some writing. Father Cieslik sat in his room in a straight chair with a pillow over his stomach to ease his pain, and read. Father Superior LaSalle stood at the window of his room, thinking. Father Kleinsorge went up to a room on the third floor, took off all his clothes except his underwear, and stretched out on his right side on a cot and began reading his *Stimmen der Zeit.*

After the terrible flash—which, Father Kleinsorge later realized, reminded him of something he had read as a boy about a large meteor colliding with the earth—he had time (since he was 1,400 yards from the center) for one thought: A bomb has fallen directly on us. Then, for a few seconds or minutes, he went out of his mind.

Father Kleinsorge never knew how he got out of the house. The next things he was conscious of were that he was wandering around in the mission's vegetable garden in his underwear, bleeding slightly from small cuts along his left flank; that all the buildings round about had fallen down except the Jesuits' mission house, which had long before been braced and double-braced by a priest named Gropper, who was terrified of earthquakes; that the day had turned dark; and that Murata-*san*, the housekeeper, was nearby, crying over and over, "*Shu Jesusu, awaremi tamai!* Our Lord Jesus, have pity on us!"

On the train on the way into Hiroshima from the country, where he lived with his mother, Dr. Terufumi Sasaki, the Red Cross Hospital surgeon, thought over an unpleasant nightmare he had had the night before. His mother's home was in Mukaihara, thirty miles from the city, and it took him two hours by train and tram to reach the hospital. He had slept uneasily all night and had wakened an hour earlier than usual, and, feeling sluggish and slightly feverish, had debated whether to go to the hospital at all; his sense of duty finally forced him to go, and he had started out on an earlier train than he took most mornings. The dream had particularly frightened him because it was so closely associated, on the surface at least, with a disturbing actuality. He was only twenty-five years old and had just completed his training at the Eastern Medical University, in Tsingtao, China. He was something of an idealist and was much distressed by the inadequacy of medical facilities in the country town where his mother lived. Quite on his own, and without a permit, he had begun visiting a few sick people out there in the evenings, after his eight hours at the hospital and four hours' commuting. He had recently learned that the penalty for practicing without a permit was severe; a fellow-doctor whom he had asked about it had given him a serious scolding. Nevertheless, he had continued to practice. In his dream, he had been at the bedside of a country patient when the police and the doctor he had consulted burst into the room, seized him, dragged him outside, and beat him up cruelly. On the train, he just about decided to give up the work in Mukaihara, since he felt it would be impossible to get a permit, because the authorities would hold that it would conflict with his duties at the Red Cross Hospital.

At the terminus, he caught a streetcar at once. (He later calculated that if he had taken his customary train that morning, and if he had had to wait a few minutes for the streetcar, as often happened, he would have been close to the center at the time of the explosion and would surely have perished.) He arrived at the hospital at seven-forty and reported to the chief surgeon. A few minutes later, he went to a room on the first floor and drew blood from the arm of a man in order to perform a Wassermann test. The laboratory containing the incubators for the test was on the third floor. With the blood specimen in his left hand, walking in a kind of distraction he had felt all morning, probably because of the dream and his restless night, he started along the main corridor on his way toward the stairs. He was one step beyond an open window when the light of the bomb was reflected, like a gigantic photographic flash, in the corridor. He ducked down on one knee and said to himself, as only a Japanese would, "Sasaki, *gambare!* Be brave!" Just then (the building was 1,650 yards from the center), the blast ripped through the hospital. The glasses he was wearing flew off his face; the bottle of blood crashed against one wall; his Japanese slippers zipped out from under his feet—but otherwise, thanks to where he stood, he was untouched.

Dr. Sasaki shouted the name of the chief surgeon and rushed around to the man's office and found him terribly cut by glass. The hospital was in horrible confusion: heavy partitions and ceilings had fallen on patients, beds had overturned, windows had blown in and cut people, blood was spattered on the walls and floors, instruments were everywhere, many of the patients were running about screaming, many more lay dead. (A colleague working in the laboratory to which Dr. Sasaki had been walking was dead; Dr. Sasaki's patient, whom he had just left and who a few moments before had been dreadfully afraid of syphilis, was also dead.) Dr. Sasaki found himself the only doctor in the hospital who was unhurt.

Dr. Sasaki, who believed that the enemy had hit only the building he was in, got bandages and began to bind the wounds of those inside the hospital; while outside, all over Hiroshima, maimed and dying citizens turned their unsteady steps toward the Red Cross Hospital to begin an invasion that was to make Dr. Sasaki forget his private nightmare for a long, long time.

Miss Toshiko Sasaki, the East Asia Tin Works clerk, who is not related to Dr. Sasaki, got up at three o'clock in the morning on the day the bomb fell. There was extra housework to do. Her eleven-month-old brother, Akio, had come down the day before with a serious stomach upset; her mother had taken him to the Tamura Pediatric Hospital and was staying there with him. Miss Sasaki, who was about twenty, had to cook breakfast for her father, a brother, a sister, and herself, and — since the hospital, because of the war, was unable to provide food — to prepare a whole day's meals for her mother and the baby, in time for her father, who worked in a factory making rubber earplugs for artillery crews, to take the food by on his way to the plant. When she had finished and had cleaned and put away the cooking things, it was nearly seven. The family lived in Koi, and she had a forty-five-minute trip to the tin works, in the section of town called Kannon-machi. She was in charge of the personnel records in the factory. She left Koi at seven, and as soon as she reached the plant, she went with some of the other girls from the personnel department to the factory auditorium. A prominent local Navy man, a former employee, had committed suicide the day before by throwing himself under a train — a death considered honorable enough to warrant a memorial service, which was to be held at the tin works at ten o'clock that morning. In the large hall, Miss Sasaki and the others made suitable preparations for the meeting. This work took about twenty minutes.

Miss Sasaki went back to her office and sat down at her desk. She was quite far from the windows, which were off to her left, and behind her were a couple of tall bookcases containing all the books of the factory library, which the personnel department had organized. She settled herself at her desk, put some things in a drawer, and shifted papers. She thought that before she began to make entries in her lists of new employees, discharges, and departures for the Army, she would chat for a moment with the girl at her right. Just as she turned her head away from the windows, the room was filled with a blinding light. She was paralyzed by fear, fixed still in her chair for a long moment (the plant was 1,600 yards from the center).

Everything fell, and Miss Sasaki lost consciousness. The ceiling dropped suddenly and the wooden floor above collapsed in splinters and the people up there came down and the roof above them gave way; but principally and first of all, the bookcases right behind her swooped forward and the contents threw her down, with her left leg horribly twisted and breaking underneath her. There, in the tin factory, in the first moment of the atomic age, a human being was crushed by books.

II. THE FIRE

Immediately after the explosion, the Reverend Mr. Kiyoshi Tanimoto, having run wildly out of the Matsui estate and having looked in wonderment at the bloody soldiers at the mouth of the dugout they had been digging, attached himself sympathetically to an old lady who was walking along in a daze, holding her head with her left hand, supporting a small boy of three or four on her back with her right, and crying, "I'm hurt! I'm hurt! I'm hurt!" Mr. Tanimoto transferred the child to his own back and led the woman by the hand down the street, which was darkened by what seemed to be a local column of dust. He took the woman to a grammar school not far away that had previously been designated for use as a temporary hospital in case of emergency. By this solicitous behavior, Mr. Tanimoto at once got rid of his terror. At the school, he was much surprised to see glass all over the floor and fifty or sixty injured people already waiting to be treated. He reflected that, although the all-clear had sounded and he had heard no planes, several bombs must have been dropped. He thought of a hillock in the rayon man's garden from which he could get a view of the whole of Koi—of the whole of Hiroshima, for that matter—and he ran back up to the estate.

From the mound, Mr. Tanimoto saw an astonishing panorama. Not just a patch of Koi, as he had expected, but as much of Hiroshima as he could see through the clouded air was giving off a thick, dreadful miasma. Clumps of smoke, near and far, had begun to push up through the general dust. He wondered how such extensive damage could have been dealt out of a silent sky; even a few planes, far up, would have been audible. Houses nearby were burning, and when huge drops of water the size of marbles began to fall, he half thought that they must be coming from the hoses of firemen fighting the blazes. (They were actually drops of condensed moisture falling from the turbulent tower of dust, heat, and fission fragments that had already risen miles into the sky above Hiroshima.)

Mr. Tanimoto turned away from the sight when he heard Mr. Matsuo call out to ask whether he was all right. Mr. Matsuo had been safely cushioned within the falling house by the bedding stored in the front hall and had worked his way out. Mr. Tanimoto scarcely answered. He had thought of his wife and baby, his church, his home, his parishioners, all of them down in that awful murk. Once more he began to run in fear—toward the city.

Mrs. Hatsuyo Nakamura, the tailor's widow, having struggled up from under the ruins of her house after the explosion, and seeing Myeko, the youngest of her three children, buried breast-deep and unable to move, crawled across the debris, hauled at timbers, and flung tiles aside, in a hurried effort to free the child. Then, from what seemed to be caverns far below, she heard two small voices crying, "*Tasukete! Tasukete!* Help! Help!"

She called the names of her ten-year-old son and eight-year-old daughter: "Toshio! Yaeko!"

The voices from below answered.

Mrs. Nakamura abandoned Myeko, who at least could breathe, and in a frenzy made the wreckage fly above the crying voices. The children had been sleeping nearly ten feet apart, but now their voices seemed to come from the same place. Toshio, the boy, apparently had some freedom to move, because she could feel him undermining the pile of wood and tiles as she worked from above. At last she saw his head, and she hastily pulled him out by it. A mosquito net was wound intricately, as if it had been carefully wrapped, around his feet. He said he had been blown right across the room and had been on top of his sister Yaeko under the wreckage. She now said, from underneath, that she could not move, because there was something on her legs. With a bit more digging, Mrs Nakamura cleared a hole above the child and began to pull her arm. "*Itai!* It hurts!" Yaeko cried. Mrs. Nakamura shouted, "There's no time now to say whether it hurts or not," and yanked her whimpering daughter up. Then she freed Myeko. The children were filthy and bruised, but none of them had a single cut or scratch.

Mrs. Nakamura took the children out into the street. They had nothing on but underpants, and although the day was very hot, she worried rather confusedly about their being cold, so she went back into the wreckage and burrowed underneath and found a bundle of clothes she had packed for an emergency, and she dressed them in pants, blouses, shoes, padded-cotton air-raid helmets called *bokuzuki*, and even, irrationally, overcoats. The children were silent, except for the five-year-old, Myeko, who kept asking questions: "Why is it night already? Why did our house fall down? What happened?" Mrs. Nakamura, who did not know what had happened (had not the all-clear sounded?), looked around and saw through the darkness that all the houses in her neighborhood had collapsed. The house next door, which its owner had been tearing down to make way for a fire lane, was now very thoroughly, if crudely, torn down; its owner, who had been sacrificing his home for the community's safety, lay dead. Mrs. Nakamoto, wife of the head of the local air-raid-defense Neighborhood Association, came across the street with her head all bloody, and said that her baby was badly cut; did Mrs. Nakamura have any bandage? Mrs. Nakamura did not, but she crawled into the remains of her house again and pulled out some white cloth that she had been using in her work as a seamstress, ripped it into strips, and gave it to Mrs. Nakamoto. While fetching the cloth, she noticed her sewing machine; she went back in for it and dragged it out. Obviously, she could not carry it with her, so she unthinkingly plunged her symbol of livelihood into the receptacle which for weeks had been her symbol of safety—the cement tank of water in front of her house, of the type every household had been ordered to construct against a possible fire raid.

A nervous neighbor, Mrs. Hataya, called to Mrs. Nakamura to run away with her to the woods in Asano Park—an estate, by the Kyo River not far off, belonging to the wealthy Asano family, who once owned the Toyo Kisen Kaisha steamship line. The park had been designated as an evacuation area for their neighborhood. Seeing fire breaking out in a nearby ruin (except at the very center, where the bomb itself ignited some fires, most of Hiroshima's citywide conflagration was caused by inflammable wreckage falling on cook-stoves and live wires), Mrs. Nakamura suggested going over to fight it. Mrs. Hataya said, "Don't be foolish. What if planes come and drop more bombs?" So Mrs. Nakamura started out for Asano Park with her children and Mrs. Hataya, and she carried her rucksack of emergency clothing, a blanket, an umbrella, and a suitcase of things she had cached in her air-raid shelter. Under many ruins, as they hurried along, they heard muffled screams for help. The only building they saw standing on their way to Asano Park was the Jesuit mission house, alongside the Catholic kindergarten to which Mrs. Nakamura had sent Myeko for a time. As they passed it, she saw Father Kleinsorge, in bloody underwear, running out of the house with a small suitcase in his hand.

Right after the explosion, while Father Wilhelm Kleinsorge, S. J., was wandering around in his underwear in the vegetable garden, Father Superior LaSalle came around the corner of the building in the darkness. His body, especially his back, was bloody; the flash had made him twist away from his window, and tiny pieces of glass had flown at him. Father Kleinsorge, still bewildered, managed to ask, "Where are the rest?" Just then, the two other priests living in the mission house appeared—Father Cieslik, unhurt, supporting Father Schiffer, who was covered with blood that spurted from a cut above his left ear and who was very pale. Father Cieslik was rather pleased with himself, for after the flash he had dived into a doorway, which he had previously reckoned to be the safest place inside the building, and when the blast came, he was not injured. Father LaSalle told Father Cieslik to take Father Schiffer to a doctor before he bled to death, and suggested either Dr. Kanda, who lived on the next corner, or Dr. Fujii, about six blocks away. The two men went out of the compound and up the street.

The daughter of Mr. Hoshijima, the mission catechist, ran up to Father Kleinsorge and said that her mother and sister were buried under the ruins of their house, which was at the back of the Jesuit compound, and at the same time the priests noticed that the house of the Catholic-kindergarten teacher at the front of the compound had collapsed on her. While Father LaSalle and Mrs. Murata, the mission housekeeper, dug the teacher out, Father Kleinsorge went to the catechist's fallen house and began lifting things off the top of the pile. There was not a sound underneath; he was sure the Hoshijima women had been killed. At last, under what had been a corner of the kitchen, he saw Mrs. Hoshijima's head. Believing her dead, he began to haul her out by the hair, but suddenly she screamed, "*Itai! Itai!* It hurts! It hurts!" He dug some more and lifted her out. He managed, too, to find her daughter in the rubble and free her. Neither was badly hurt.

A public bath next door to the mission house had caught fire, but since there the wind was southerly, the priests thought their house would be spared. Nevertheless, as a precaution, Father Kleinsorge went inside to fetch some things he wanted to save. He found his room in a state of weird and illogical confusion. A first-aid kit was hanging undisturbed on a hook on the wall, but his clothes, which had been on other hooks nearby, were nowhere to be seen. His desk was in splinters all over the room, but a mere papier-mâché suitcase, which he had hidden under the desk, stood handle-side up, without a scratch on it, in the doorway of the room, where he could not miss it. Father Kleinsorge later came to regard this as a bit of Providential interference, inasmuch as the suitcase contained his breviary, the account books for the whole diocese, and a considerable amount of paper money belonging to the mission, for which he was responsible. He ran out of the house and deposited the suitcase in the mission air-raid shelter.

At about this time, Father Cieslik and Father Schiffer, who was still spurting blood, came back and said that Dr. Kanda's house was ruined and that fire blocked them from getting out of what they supposed to be the local circle of destruction to Dr. Fujii's private hospital, on the bank of the Kyo River.

Dr. Masakazu Fujii's hospital was no longer on the bank of the Kyo River; it was in the river. After the overturn, Dr. Fujii was so stupefied and so tightly squeezed by the beams gripping his chest that he was unable to move at first, and he hung there about twenty minutes in the darkened morning. Then a thought which came to him—that soon the tide would be running in through the estuaries and his head would be submerged—inspired him to fearful activity; he wriggled and turned and exerted what strength he could (though his left arm, because of the pain in his shoulder, was useless), and before long he had freed himself from the vise. After a few moments' rest, he climbed onto the pile of timbers and, finding a long one that slanted up to the river-bank, he painfully shinnied up it.

Dr. Fujii, who was in his underwear, was now soaking and dirty. His undershirt was torn, and blood ran down it from bad cuts on his chin and back. In this disarray, he walked out onto Kyo Bridge, beside which his hospital had stood. The bridge had not collapsed. He could see only fuzzily without his glasses, but he could see enough to be amazed at the number of houses that were down all around. On the bridge, he encountered a friend, a doctor named Machii, and asked in bewilderment, "What do you think it was?"

Dr. Machii said, "It must have been a *Molotoffano hana-*

kago" — a Molotov flower basket, the delicate Japanese name for the "bread basket," or self-scattering cluster of bombs.

At first, Dr. Fujii could see only two fires, one across the river from his hospital site and one quite far to the south. But at the same time, he and his friend observed something that puzzled them, and which, as doctors, they discussed: although there were as yet very few fires, wounded people were hurrying across the bridge in an endless parade of misery, and many of them exhibited terrible burns on their faces and arms. "Why do you suppose it is?" Dr. Fujii asked. Even a theory was comforting that day, and Dr. Machii stuck to his. "Perhaps because it was a Molotov flower basket," he said.

There had been no breeze earlier in the morning when Dr. Fujii had walked to the railway station to see his friend off, but now brisk winds were blowing every which way; here on the bridge the wind was easterly. New fires were leaping up, and they spread quickly, and in a very short time terrible blasts of hot air and showers of cinders made it impossible to stand on the bridge any more. Dr. Machii ran to the far side of the river and along a still unkindled street. Dr. Fujii went down into the water under the bridge, where a score of people had already taken refuge, among them his servants, who had extricated themselves from the wreckage. From there, Dr. Fujii saw a nurse hanging in the timbers of his hospital by her legs, and then another painfully pinned across the breast. He enlisted the help of some of the others under the bridge and freed both of them. He thought he heard the voice of his niece for a moment, but he could not find her; he never saw her again. Four of his nurses and the two patients in the hospital died, too. Dr. Fujii went back into the water of the river and waited for the fire to subside.

The lot of Drs. Fujii, Kanda, and Machii right after the explosion — and, as these three were typical, that of the majority of the physicians and surgeons of Hiroshima — with their offices and hospitals destroyed, their equipment scattered, their own bodies incapacitated in varying degrees, explained why so many citizens who were hurt went untended and why so many who might have lived died. Of a hundred and fifty doctors in the city, sixty-five were already dead and most of the rest were wounded. Of 1,780 nurses, 1,654 were dead or too badly hurt to work. In the biggest hospital, that of the Red Cross, only six doctors out of thirty were able to function, and only ten nurses out of more than two hundred. The sole uninjured doctor on the Red Cross Hospital staff was Dr. Sasaki. After the explosion, he hurried to a storeroom to fetch bandages. This room, like everything he had seen as he ran through the hospital, was chaotic—bottles of medicines thrown off shelves and broken, salves spattered on the walls, instruments strewn everywhere. He grabbed up some bandages and an unbroken bottle of mercurochrome, hurried back to the chief surgeon, and bandaged his cuts. Then he went out into the corridor and began patching up the wounded patients and the doctors and nurses there. He blundered so without his glasses that he took a pair off the face of a wounded nurse, and although they only approximately compensated for the errors of his vision, they were better than nothing. (He was to depend on them for more than a month.)

Dr. Sasaki worked without method, taking those who were nearest him first, and he noticed soon that the corridor seemed to be getting more and more crowded. Mixed in with the abrasions and lacerations which most people in the hospital had suffered, he began to find dreadful burns. He realized then that casualties were pouring in from outdoors. There were so many that he began to pass up the lightly wounded; he decided that all he could hope to do was to stop people from bleeding to death. Before long, patients lay and crouched on the floors of the wards and the laboratories and all the other rooms, and in the corridors, and on the stairs, and in the front hall, and under the porte-cochère, and on the stone front steps, and in the driveway and courtyard, and for blocks each way in the streets outside. Wounded people supported maimed people; disfigured families leaned together. Many people were vomiting. A tremendous number of schoolgirls—some of those who had been taken from their classrooms to work outdoors, clearing fire lanes—crept into the hospital. In a city of two hundred and forty-five thousand, nearly a hundred thousand people had been killed or doomed at one blow; a hundred thousand more were hurt. At least ten thousand of the wounded made their way to the best hospital in town, which was altogether unequal to such a trampling, since it had only six hundred beds, and they had all been occupied. The people in the suffocating crowd inside the hospital wept and cried, for Dr. Sasaki to hear, "*Sensei! Doctor!,*" and the less seriously wounded came and pulled at his sleeve and begged him to come to the aid of the worse wounded. Tugged here and there in his stockinged feet, bewildered by the numbers, staggered by so much raw flesh, Dr. Sasaki lost all sense of profession and stopped working as a skillful surgeon and a sympathetic man; he became an automaton, mechanically wiping, daubing, winding, wiping, daubing, winding.

Some of the wounded in Hiroshima were unable to enjoy the questionable luxury of hospitalization. In what had been the personnel office of the East Asia Tin Works, Miss Sasaki lay doubled over, unconscious, under the tremendous pile of books and plaster and wood and corrugated iron. She was wholly unconscious (she later estimated) for about three hours. Her first sensation was of dreadful pain in her left leg. It was so black under the books and debris that the borderline between awareness and unconsciousness was fine; she apparently crossed it several times, for the pain seemed to come and go. At the moments when it was sharpest, she felt that her leg had been cut off somewhere below the knee. Later, she heard someone walking on top of the wreckage above her, and anguished voices spoke up, evidently from within the mess around her: "Please help! Get us out!"

Father Kleinsorge stemmed Father Schiffer's spurting cut as well as he could with some bandage that Dr. Fujii had given the priests a few days before. When he finished, he ran into the mission house again and found the jacket of his military uniform and an old pair of gray trousers. He put them on and went outside. A woman from next door ran up to him and shouted that her husband was buried under her house and the house was on fire; Father Kleinsorge must come and save him.

Father Kleinsorge, already growing apathetic and dazed in the presence of the cumulative distress, said, "We haven't much time." Houses all around were burning, and the wind was now blowing hard. "Do you know exactly which part of the house he is under?" he asked.

"Yes, yes," she said. "Come quickly."

They went around to the house, the remains of which blazed violently, but when they got there, it turned out that the woman had no idea where her husband was. Father Kleinsorge shouted several times, "Is anyone there?" There was no answer. Father Kleinsorge said to the woman, "We must get away or we will all die." He went back to the Catholic compound and told the Father Superior that the fire was coming closer on the wind, which had swung around and was now from the north; it was time for everybody to go.

Just then, the kindergarten teacher pointed out to the priests Mr. Fukai, the secretary of the diocese, who was standing in his window on the second floor of the mission house, facing in the direction of the explosion, weeping. Father Cieslik, because he thought the stairs unusable, ran around to the back of the mission house to look for a ladder. There he heard people crying for help under a nearby fallen roof. He called to passers-by running away in the street to help him lift it, but nobody paid any attention, and he had to leave the buried ones to die. Father Kleinsorge ran inside the mission house and scrambled up the stairs, which were awry and piled with plaster and lathing, and called to Mr. Fukai from the doorway of his room.

Mr. Fukai, a very short man of about fifty, turned around slowly, with a queer look, and said, "Leave me here."

Father Kleinsorge went into the room and took Mr. Fukai by the collar of his coat and said, "Come with me or you'll die."

Mr. Fukai said, "Leave me here to die."

Father Kleinsorge began to shove and haul Mr. Fukai out of the room. Then the theological student came up and grabbed Mr. Fukai's feet, and Father Kleinsorge took his shoulders, and together they carried him downstairs and outdoors. "I can't walk!" Mr. Fukai cried. "Leave me here!" Father Kleinsorge got his paper suitcase with the money in it

and took Mr. Fukai up pickaback, and the party started for
the East Parade Ground, their district's "safe area." As they
went out of the gate, Mr. Fukai, quite childlike now, beat on
Father Kleinsorge's shoulders and said, "I won't leave. I
won't leave." Irrelevantly, Father Kleinsorge turned to Father
LaSalle and said, "We have lost all our possessions but not our
sense of humor."

The street was cluttered with parts of houses that had slid
into it, and with fallen telephone poles and wires. From every
second or third house came the voices of people buried and
abandoned, who invariably screamed, with formal politeness,
"*Tasukete kure!* Help, if you please!" The priests recognized
several ruins from which these cries came as the homes of
friends, but because of the fire it was too late to help. All the
way, Mr. Fukai whimpered, "Let me stay." The party turned
right when they came to a block of fallen houses that was one
flame. At Sakai Bridge, which would take them across to the
East Parade Ground, they saw that the whole community on
the opposite side of the river was a sheet of fire; they dared
not cross and decided to take refuge in Asano Park, off to
their left. Father Kleinsorge, who had been weakened for a
couple of days by his bad case of diarrhea, began to stagger
under his protesting burden, and as he tried to climb up over
the wreckage of several houses that blocked their way to the
park, he stumbled, dropped Mr. Fukai, and plunged down,
head over heels, to the edge of the river. When he picked
himself up, he saw Mr. Fukai running away. Father Kleinsorge
shouted to a dozen soldiers, who were standing by the
bridge, to stop him. As Father Kleinsorge started back to get
Mr. Fukai, Father LaSalle called out, "Hurry! Don't waste
time!" So Father Kleinsorge just requested the soldiers to take
care of Mr. Fukai. They said they would, but the little, broken
man got away from them, and the last the priests could see of
him, he was running back toward the fire.

Mr. Tanimoto, fearful for his family and church, at first ran
toward them by the shortest route, along Koi Highway. He
was the only person making his way into the city; he met
hundreds and hundreds who were fleeing, and every one of
them seemed to be hurt in some way. The eyebrows of some

were burned off and skin hung from their faces and hands. Others, because of pain, held their arms up as if carrying something in both hands. Some were vomiting as they walked. Many were naked or in shreds of clothing. On some undressed bodies, the burns had made patterns—of undershirt straps and suspenders and, on the skin of some women (since white repelled the heat from the bomb and dark clothes absorbed it and conducted it to the skin), the shapes of flowers they had had on their kimonos. Many, although injured themselves, supported relatives who were worse off. Almost all had their heads bowed, looked straight ahead, were silent, and showed no expression whatever.

After crossing Koi Bridge and Kannon Bridge, having run the whole way, Mr. Tanimoto saw, as he approached the center, that all the houses had been crushed and many were afire. Here the trees were bare and their trunks were charred. He tried at several points to penetrate the ruins, but the flames always stopped him. Under many houses, people screamed for help, but no one helped; in general, survivors that day assisted only their relatives or immediate neighbors, for they could not comprehend or tolerate a wider circle of misery. The wounded limped past the screams, and Mr. Tanimoto ran past them. As a Christian he was filled with compassion for those who were trapped, and as a Japanese he was overwhelmed by the shame of being unhurt, and he prayed as he ran, "God help them and take them out of the fire."

He thought he would skirt the fire, to the left. He ran back to Kannon Bridge and followed for a distance one of the rivers. He tried several cross streets, but all were blocked, so he turned far left and ran out to Yokogawa, a station on a railroad line that detoured the city in a wide semicircle, and he followed the rails until he came to a burning train. So impressed was he by this time by the extent of the damage that he ran north two miles to Gion, a suburb in the foothills. All the way, he overtook dreadfully burned and lacerated people, and in his guilt he turned to right and left as he hurried and said to some of them, "Excuse me for having no burden like yours." Near Gion, he began to meet country people going toward the city to help, and when they saw him, several exclaimed, "Look! There is one who is not wounded." At Gion, he bore toward the right bank of the main river, the Ota, and ran down it until he reached fire again. There was no fire on the other side of the river, so he threw off his shirt and shoes and plunged into it. In midstream, where the current was fairly strong, exhaustion and fear finally caught up with him—he had run nearly seven miles—and he became limp and drifted in the water. He prayed, "Please, God, help me to cross. It would be nonsense for me to be drowned when I am the only uninjured one." He managed a few more strokes and fetched up on a spit downstream.

Mr. Tanimoto climbed up the bank and ran along it until, near a large Shinto shrine, he came to more fire, and as he turned left to get around it, he met, by incredible luck, his wife. She was carrying their infant son. Mr. Tanimoto was now so emotionally worn out that nothing could surprise him. He did not embrace his wife; he simply said, "Oh, you are safe." She told him that she had got home from her night in Ushida just in time for the explosion; she had been buried under the parsonage with the baby in her arms. She told how the wreckage had pressed down on her, how the baby had cried. She saw a chink of light, and by reaching up with a hand, she worked the hole bigger, bit by bit. After about half an hour, she heard the crackling noise of wood burning. At last the opening was big enough for her to push the baby out, and afterward she crawled out herself. She said she was now going out to Ushida again. Mr. Tanimoto said he wanted to see his church and take care of the people of his Neighborhood Association. They parted as casually—as bewildered—as they had met.

Mr. Tanimoto's way around the fire took him across the East Parade Ground, which, being an evacuation area, was now the scene of a gruesome review: rank on rank of the burned and bleeding. Those who were burned moaned, "*Mizu, mizu!* Water, water!" Mr. Tanimoto found a basin in a nearby street and located a water tap that still worked in the crushed shell of a house, and he began carrying water to the suffering strangers. When he had given drink to about thirty of them, he realized he was taking too much time. "Excuse me," he said loudly to those nearby who were reaching out their hands to him and crying their thirst. "I have many people to take care of." Then he ran away. He went to the river again, the basin in his hand, and jumped down onto a sandspit. There he saw hundreds of people so badly wounded that they could not get up to go farther from the burning city. When they saw a man erect and unhurt, the chant began again: *"Mizu, mizu, mizu."* Mr. Tanimoto could not resist them; he carried them water from the river—a mistake, since it was tidal and brackish. Two or three small boats were ferrying hurt people across the river from Asano Park, and when one touched the spit, Mr. Tanimoto again made his loud, apologetic speech and jumped into the boat. It took him across to the park. There, in the underbrush, he found some of his charges of the Neighborhood Association, who had come there by his previous instructions, and saw many acquaintances, among them Father Kleinsorge and the other Catholics. But he missed Fukai, who had been a close friend. "Where is Fukai-*san*?" he asked.

"He didn't want to come with us," Father Kleinsorge said. "He ran back."

When Miss Sasaki heard the voices of the people caught along with her in the dilapidation at the tin factory, she began speaking to them. Her nearest neighbor, she discovered, was a high-school girl who had been drafted for factory work, and who said her back was broken. Miss Sasaki replied, "I am lying here and I can't move. My left leg is cut off."

Some time later, she again heard somebody walk overhead and then move off to one side, and whoever it was began burrowing. The digger released several people, and when he had uncovered the high-school girl, she found that her back was not broken, after all, and she crawled out. Miss Sasaki spoke to the rescuer, and he worked toward her. He pulled away a great number of books, until he had made a tunnel to her. She could see his perspiring face as he said, "Come out, Miss." She tried. "I can't move," she said. The man excavated some more and told her to try with all her strength to get out. But books were heavy on her hips, and the man finally saw that a bookcase was leaning on the books and that a heavy beam pressed down on the bookcase. "Wait," he said. "I'll get a crowbar."

The man was gone a long time, and when he came back, he was ill-tempered, as if her plight were all her fault. "We have no men to help you!" he shouted in through the tunnel. "You'll have to get out by yourself."

"That's impossible," she said. "My left leg . . ." The man went away.

Much later, several men came and dragged Miss Sasaki out. Her left leg was not severed, but it was badly broken and cut and it hung askew below the knee. They took her out into a courtyard. It was raining. She sat on the ground in the rain. When the downpour increased, someone directed all the wounded people to take cover in the factory's air-raid shelters. "Come along," a torn-up woman said to her. "You can hop." But Miss Sasaki could not move, and she just waited in the rain. Then a man propped up a large sheet of corrugated iron as a kind of lean-to, and took her in his arms and carried her to it. She was grateful until he brought two horribly wounded people—a woman with a whole breast sheared off and a man whose face was all raw from a burn—to share the simple shed with her. No one came back. The rain cleared and the cloudy afternoon was hot; before nightfall the three grotesques under the slanting piece of twisted iron began to smell quite bad.

The former head of the Nobori-cho Neighborhood Association, to which the Catholic priests belonged, was an energetic man named Yoshida. He had boasted, when he was in charge of the district air-raid defenses, that fire might eat away all of Hiroshima but it would never come to Nobori-cho. The bomb blew down his house, and a joist pinned him by the legs, in full view of the Jesuit mission house across the way and of the people hurrying along the street. In their confusion as they hurried past, Mrs. Nakamura, with her children, and Father Kleinsorge, with Mr. Fukai on his back, hardly saw him; he was just part of the general blur of misery through which they moved. His cries for help brought no response from them; there were so many people shouting for help that they could not hear him separately. They and all the others went along. Nobori-cho became absolutely deserted, and the fire swept through it. Mr. Yoshida saw the wooden mission house—the only erect building in the area—go up in a lick of flame, and the heat was terrific on his face. Then flames came along his side of the street and entered his house. In a paroxysm of terrified strength, he freed himself and ran down the alleys of Nobori-cho, hemmed in by the fire he had said would never come. He began at once to behave like an old man; two months later his hair was white.

As Dr. Fujii stood in the river up to his neck to avoid the heat of the fire, the wind blew stronger and stronger, and soon, even though the expanse of water was small, the waves grew so high that the people under the bridge could no longer keep their footing. Dr. Fujii went close to the shore, crouched down, and embraced a large stone with his usable arm. Later it became possible to wade along the very edge of the river, and Dr. Fujii and his two surviving nurses moved about two hundred yards upstream, to a sandspit near Asano Park. Many wounded were lying on the sand. Dr. Machii was there with his family; his daughter, who had been outdoors when the bomb burst, was badly burned on her hands and legs but fortunately not on her face. Although Dr. Fujii's shoulder was by now terribly painful, he examined the girl's burns curiously. Then he lay down. In spite of the misery all around, he was ashamed of his appearance, and he remarked to Dr. Machii that he looked like a beggar, dressed as he was in nothing but torn and bloody underwear. Later in the afternoon, when the fire began to subside, he decided to go to his parental house, in the suburb of Nagatsuka. He asked Dr. Machii to join him, but the Doctor answered that he and his family were going to spend the night on the spit, because of his daughter's injuries. Dr. Fujii, together with his nurses, walked first to Ushida, where, in the partially damaged house of some relatives, he found first-aid materials he had stored there. The two nurses bandaged him and he them. They went on. Now not many people walked in the streets, but a great number sat and lay on the pavement, vomited, waited for death, and died. The number of corpses on the way to Nagatsuka was more and more puzzling. The Doctor wondered: Could a Molotov flower basket have done all this?

Dr. Fujii reached his family's house in the evening. It was

five miles from the center of town, but its roof had fallen in and the windows were all broken.

All day, people poured into Asano Park. This private estate was far enough away from the explosion so that its bamboos, pines, laurel, and maples were still alive, and the green place invited refugees—partly because they believed that if the Americans came back, they would bomb only buildings; partly because the foliage seemed a center of coolness and life, and the estate's exquisitely precise rock gardens, with their quiet pools and arching bridges, were very Japanese, normal, secure; and also partly (according to some who were there) because of an irresistible, atavistic urge to hide under leaves. Mrs. Nakamura and her children were among the first to arrive, and they settled in the bamboo grove near the river. They all felt terribly thirsty, and they drank from the river. At once they were nauseated and began vomiting, and they retched the whole day. Others were also nauseated; they all thought (probably because of the strong odor of ionization, an "electric smell" given off by the bomb's fission) that they were sick from a gas the Americans had dropped. When Father Kleinsorge and the other priests came into the park, nodding to their friends as they passed, the Nakamuras were all sick and prostrate. A woman named Iwasaki, who lived in the neighborhood of the mission and who was sitting near the Nakamuras, got up and asked the priests if she should stay where she was or go with them. Father Kleinsorge said, "I hardly know where the safest place is." She stayed there, and later in the day, though she had no visible wounds or burns, she died. The priests went farther along the river and settled down in some underbrush. Father LaSalle lay down and went right to sleep. The theological student, who was wearing slippers, had carried with him a bundle of clothes, in which he had packed two pairs of leather shoes. When he sat down with the others, he found that the bundle had broken open and a couple of shoes had fallen out and now he had only two lefts. He retraced his steps and found one right. When he rejoined the priests, he said, "It's funny, but things don't matter any more. Yesterday, my shoes were my most important possessions. Today, I don't care. One pair is enough."

Father Cieslik said, "I know. I started to bring my books along, and then I thought, 'This is no time for books.'"

When Mr. Tanimoto, with his basin still in his hand, reached the park, it was very crowded, and to distinguish the living from the dead was not easy, for most of the people lay still, with their eyes open. To Father Kleinsorge, an Occidental, the silence in the grove by the river, where hundreds of gruesomely wounded suffered together, was one of the most dreadful and awesome phenomena of his whole experience. The hurt ones were quiet; no one wept, much less screamed in pain; no one complained; none of the many who died did so noisily; not even the children cried; very few people even spoke. And when Father Kleinsorge gave water to some whose faces had been almost blotted out by flash burns, they took their share and then raised themselves a little and bowed to him, in thanks.

Mr. Tanimoto greeted the priests and then looked around for other friends. He saw Mrs. Matsumoto, wife of the director of the Methodist School, and asked her if she was thirsty. She was, so he went to one of the pools in the Asanos' rock gardens and got water for her in his basin. Then he decided to try to get back to his church. He went into Nobori-cho by the way the priests had taken as they escaped, but he did not get far; the fire along the streets was so fierce that he had to turn back. He walked to the riverbank and began to look for a boat in which he might carry some of the most severely injured across the river from Asano Park and away from the spreading fire. Soon he found a good-sized pleasure punt drawn up on the bank, but in and around it was an awful tableau—five dead men, nearly naked, badly burned, who must have expired more or less all at once, for they were in attitudes which suggested that they had been working together to push the boat down into the river. Mr. Tanimoto lifted them away from the boat, and as he did so, he experienced such horror at disturbing the dead—preventing them, he momentarily felt, from launching their craft and going on their ghostly way—that he said out loud, "Please forgive me for taking this boat. I must use it for others, who are alive." The punt was heavy, but he managed to slide it into the water. There were no oars, and all he could find for propulsion was a thick bamboo pole. He worked the boat upstream to the most crowded part of the park and began to ferry the wounded. He could pack ten or twelve into the boat for each crossing, but as the river was too deep in the center to pole his way across, he had to paddle with the bamboo, and consequently each trip took a very long time. He worked several hours that way.

Early in the afternoon, the fire swept into the woods of Asano Park. The first Mr. Tanimoto knew of it was when, returning in his boat, he saw that a great number of people had moved toward the riverside. On touching the bank, he went up to investigate, and when he saw the fire, he shouted, "All the young men who are not badly hurt come with me!" Father Kleinsorge moved Father Schiffer and Father LaSalle close to the edge of the river and asked people there to get them across if the fire came too near, and then joined Tanimoto's volunteers. Mr. Tanimoto sent some to look for buckets and basins and told others to beat the burning underbrush with their clothes; when utensils were at hand, he formed a bucket chain from one of the pools in the rock gardens. The team fought the fire for more than two hours, and gradually defeated the flames. As Mr. Tanimoto's men worked, the frightened people in the park pressed closer and closer to the river, and finally the mob began to force some of the unfortunates who were on the very bank into the water. Among those driven into the river and drowned were Mrs. Matsumoto, of the Methodist School, and her daughter.

When Father Kleinsorge got back after fighting the fire, he found Father Schiffer still bleeding and terribly pale. Some Japanese stood around and stared at him, and Father Schiffer whispered, with a weak smile, "It is as if I were already dead." "Not yet," Father Kleinsorge said. He had brought Dr. Fujii's first-aid kit with him, and he had noticed Dr. Kanda in the crowd, so he sought him out and asked him if he would dress Father Schiffer's bad cuts. Dr. Kanda had seen his wife and daughter dead in the ruins of his hospital; he sat now with his head in his hands. "I can't do anything," he said. Father Kleinsorge bound more bandage around Father Schiffer's head, moved him to a steep place, and settled him so that his head was high, and soon the bleeding diminished.

The roar of approaching planes was heard about this time. Someone in the crowd near the Nakamura family shouted, "It's some Grummans coming to strafe us!" A baker named Nakashima stood up and commanded, "Everyone who is wearing anything white, take it off." Mrs. Nakamura took the blouses off her children, and opened her umbrella and made them get under it. A great number of people, even badly burned ones, crawled into bushes and stayed there until the hum, evidently of a reconnaissance or weather run, died away.

It began to rain. Mrs. Nakamura kept her children under the umbrella. The drops grew abnormally large, and someone shouted, "The Americans are dropping gasoline. They're going to set fire to us!" (This alarm stemmed from one of the theories being passed through the park as to why so much of Hiroshima had burned: it was that a single plane had sprayed gasoline on the city and then somehow set fire to it in one flashing moment.) But the drops were palpably water, and as they fell, the wind grew stronger and stronger, and sud-denly—probably because of the tremendous convection set up by the blazing city—a whirlwind ripped through the park. Huge trees crashed down; small ones were uprooted and flew into the air. Higher, a wild array of flat things revolved in the twisting funnel—pieces of iron roofing, papers, doors, strips of matting. Father Kleinsorge put a piece of cloth over Father Schiffer's eyes, so that the feeble man would not think he was going crazy. The gale blew Mrs. Murata, the mission house-keeper, who was sitting close by the river, down the embank-ment at a shallow, rocky place, and she came out with her bare feet bloody. The vortex moved out onto the river, where it sucked up a waterspout and eventually spent itself.

After the storm, Mr. Tanimoto began ferrying people again, and Father Kleinsorge asked the theological student to go across and make his way out to the Jesuit Novitiate at Naga-tsuka, about three miles from the center of town, and to re-quest the priests there to come with help for Fathers Schiffer and LaSalle. The student got into Mr. Tanimoto's boat and went off with him. Father Kleinsorge asked Mrs. Nakamura if she would like to go out to Nagatsuka with the priests when they came. She said she had some luggage and her children were sick—they were still vomiting from time to time, and so, for that matter, was she—and therefore she feared she could not. He said he thought the fathers from the Novitiate could come back the next day with a pushcart to get her.

Late in the afternoon, when he went ashore for a while, Mr. Tanimoto, upon whose energy and initiative many had come to depend, heard people begging for food. He consulted Father Kleinsorge, and they decided to go back into town to get some rice from Mr. Tanimoto's Neighborhood Association shelter and from the mission shelter. Father Cieslik and two or three others went with them. At first, when they got among the rows of prostrate houses, they did not know where they were; the change was too sudden, from a busy city of two hundred and forty-five thousand that morning to a mere pattern of residue in the afternoon. The asphalt of the streets was still so soft and hot from the fires that walking was uncomfortable. They encountered only one person, a woman, who said to them as they passed, "My husband is in those ashes." At the mission, where Mr. Tanimoto left the party, Father Kleinsorge was dismayed to see the building razed. In the garden, on the way to the shelter, he noticed a pumpkin roasted on the vine. He and Father Cieslik tasted it and it was good. They were surprised at their hunger, and they ate quite a bit. They got out several bags of rice and gathered up several other cooked pumpkins and dug up some potatoes that were nicely baked under the ground, and started back. Mr. Tanimoto rejoined them on the way. One of the people with him had some cooking utensils. In the park, Mr. Tanimoto organized the lightly wounded women of his neighborhood to cook. Father Kleinsorge offered the Nakamura family some pumpkin, and they tried it, but they could not keep it on their stomachs. Altogether, the rice was enough to feed nearly a hundred people.

Just before dark, Mr. Tanimoto came across a twenty-year-old girl, Mrs. Kamai, the Tanimotos' next-door neighbor. She was crouching on the ground with the body of her infant daughter in her arms. The baby had evidently been dead all day. Mrs. Kamai jumped up when she saw Mr. Tanimoto and said, "Would you please try to locate my husband?"

Mr. Tanimoto knew that her husband had been inducted into the Army just the day before; he and Mrs. Tanimoto had entertained Mrs. Kamai in the afternoon, to make her forget. Kamai had reported to the Chugoku Regional Army Head-quarters—near the ancient castle in the middle of town—where some four thousand troops were stationed. Judging by the many maimed soldiers Mr. Tanimoto had seen during the day, he surmised that the barracks had been badly damaged by whatever it was that had hit Hiroshima. He knew he hadn't a chance of finding Mrs. Kamai's husband, even if he searched, but he wanted to humor her. "I'll try," he said.

"You've got to find him," she said. "He loved our baby so much. I want him to see her once more."

III. DETAILS ARE BEING INVESTIGATED

Early in the evening of the day the bomb exploded, a Japa-nese naval launch moved slowly up and down the seven rivers of Hiroshima. It stopped here and there to make an an-nouncement—alongside the crowded sandspits, on which hundreds of wounded lay; at the bridges, on which others were crowded; and eventually, as twilight fell, opposite Asano Park. A young officer stood up in the launch and shouted through a megaphone, "Be patient! A naval hospital ship is coming to take care of you!" The sight of the shipshape launch against the background of the havoc across the river; the unruffled young man in his neat uniform; above all, the promise of medical help—the first word of possible succor anyone had heard in nearly twelve awful hours—cheered the people in the park tremendously. Mrs. Nakamura settled her family for the night with the assurance that a doctor would come and stop their retching. Mr. Tanimoto resumed ferrying the wounded across the river. Father Kleinsorge lay down and said the Lord's Prayer and a Hail Mary to himself, and fell right asleep; but no sooner had he dropped off than Mrs. Murata, the conscientious mission housekeeper, shook him and said, "Father Kleinsorge! Did you remember to repeat your evening prayers?" He answered rather grumpily, "Of course," and he tried to go back to sleep but could not. This, apparently, was just what Mrs. Murata wanted. She began to chat with the exhausted priest. One of the questions she raised was when he thought the priests from the Novitiate, for whom he had sent a messenger in midafternoon, would arrive to evacuate Father Superior LaSalle and Father Schiffer.

The messenger Father Kleinsorge had sent—the theological student who had been living at the mission house—had arrived at the Novitiate, in the hills about three miles out, at half past four. The sixteen priests there had been doing rescue work in the outskirts; they had worried about their colleagues in the city but had not known how or where to look for them. Now they hastily made two litters out of poles and boards, and the student led half a dozen of them back into the devastated area. They worked their way along the Ota above the city; twice the heat of the fire forced them into the river. At Misasa Bridge, they encountered a long line of soldiers making a bizarre forced march away from the Chugoku Regional Army Headquarters in the center of the town. All were grotesquely burned, and they supported themselves with staves or leaned on one another. Sick, burned horses, hanging their heads, stood on the bridge. When the rescue party reached the park, it was after dark, and progress was made extremely difficult by the tangle of fallen trees of all sizes that had been knocked down by the whirlwind that afternoon. At last—not long after Mrs. Murata asked her question—they reached their friends, and gave them wine and strong tea.

The priests discussed how to get Father Schiffer and Father LaSalle out to the Novitiate. They were afraid that blundering through the park with them would jar them too much on the wooden litters, and that the wounded men would lose too much blood. Father Kleinsorge thought of Mr. Tanimoto and his boat, and called out to him on the river. When Mr. Tanimoto reached the bank, he said he would be glad to take the injured priests and their bearers upstream to where they could find a clear roadway. The rescuers put Father Schiffer onto one of the stretchers and lowered it into the boat, and two of them went aboard with it. Mr. Tanimoto, who still had no oars, poled the punt upstream.

About half an hour later, Mr. Tanimoto came back and excitedly asked the remaining priests to help him rescue two children he had seen standing up to their shoulders in the river. A group went out and picked them up—two young girls who had lost their family and were both badly burned. The priests stretched them on the ground next to Father Kleinsorge and then embarked Father LaSalle. Father Cieslik thought he could make it out to the Novitiate on foot, so he went aboard with the others. Father Kleinsorge was too feeble; he decided to wait in the park until the next day. He asked the men to come back with a handcart, so that they could take Mrs. Nakamura and her sick children to the Novitiate.

Mr. Tanimoto shoved off again. As the boatload of priests moved slowly upstream, they heard weak cries for help. A woman's voice stood out especially: "There are people here about to be drowned! Help us! The water is rising!" The sounds came from one of the sandspits, and those in the punt could see, in the reflected light of the still-burning fires, a number of wounded people lying at the edge of the river, already partly covered by the flooding tide. Mr. Tanimoto wanted to help them, but the priests were afraid that Father Schiffer would die if they didn't hurry, and they urged their ferryman along. He dropped them where he had put Father Schiffer down and then started back alone toward the sand-spit.

The night was hot, and it seemed even hotter because of the fires against the sky, but the younger of the two girls Mr. Tanimoto and the priests had rescued complained to Father Kleinsorge that she was cold. He covered her with his jacket. She and her older sister had been in the salt water of the river for a couple of hours before being rescued. The younger one had huge, raw flash burns on her body; the salt water must have been excruciatingly painful to her. She began to shiver heavily, and again said it was cold. Father Kleinsorge borrowed a blanket from someone nearby and wrapped her up, but she shook more and more, and said again, "I am so cold," and then she suddenly stopped shivering and was dead.

Mr. Tanimoto found about twenty men and women on the sandspit. He drove the boat onto the bank and urged them to get aboard. They did not move and he realized that they were too weak to lift themselves. He reached down and took a woman by the hands, but her skin slipped off in huge, glove-like pieces. He was so sickened by this that he had to sit down for a moment. Then he got out into the water and, though a small man, lifted several of the men and women, who were naked, into his boat. Their backs and breasts were clammy, and he remembered uneasily what the great burns he had seen during the day had been like: yellow at first, then red and swollen, with the skin sloughed off, and finally, in the evening, suppurated and smelly. With the tide risen, his bamboo pole was now too short and he had to paddle most of the way across with it. On the other side, at a higher spit, he lifted the slimy living bodies out and carried them up the slope away from the tide. He had to keep consciously re-peating to himself, "These are human beings." It took him three trips to get them all across the river. When he had fin-ished, he decided he had to have a rest, and he went back to the park.

As Mr. Tanimoto stepped up the dark bank, he tripped over someone, and someone else said angrily, "Look out! That's my hand." Mr. Tanimoto, ashamed of hurting wounded people, embarrassed at being able to walk upright, suddenly thought of the naval hospital ship, which had not come (it never did), and he had for a moment a feeling of blind, mur-derous rage at the crew of the ship, and then at all doctors. Why didn't they come to help these people?

Dr. Fujii lay in dreadful pain throughout the night on the floor of his family's roofless house on the edge of the city. By the light of a lantern, he had examined himself and found: left clavicle fractured; multiple abrasions and lacerations of face and body, including deep cuts on the chin, back, and legs; extensive contusions on chest and trunk; a couple of ribs pos-sibly fractured. Had he not been so badly hurt, he might have been at Asano Park, assisting the wounded.

By nightfall, ten thousand victims of the explosion had in-vaded the Red Cross Hospital, and Dr. Sasaki, worn out, was moving aimlessly and dully up and down the stinking corri-dors with wads of bandage and bottles of mercurochrome, still wearing the glasses he had taken from the wounded nurse, binding up the worst cuts as he came to them. Other doctors were putting compresses of saline solution on the worst burns. That was all they could do. After dark, they worked by the light of the city's fires and by candles the ten remaining nurses held for them. Dr. Sasaki had not looked outside the hospital all day; the scene inside was so terrible and so compelling that it had not occurred to him to ask any questions about what had happened beyond the windows and doors. Ceilings and partitions had fallen; plaster, dust, blood, and vomit were everywhere. Patients were dying by the hundreds, but there was nobody to carry away the corpses. Some of the hospital staff distributed biscuits and rice balls, but the charnel-house smell was so strong that few were hungry. By three o'clock the next morning, after nineteen straight hours of his gruesome work, Dr. Sasaki was incapable of dressing another wound. He and some other survivors of the hospital staff got straw mats and went outdoors—thousands of patients and hundreds of dead were in the yard and on the driveway—and hurried around behind the hospital and lay down in hiding to snatch some sleep. But within an hour wounded people had found them; a complaining circle formed around them: "Doctors! Help us! How can you sleep?" Dr. Sasaki got up again and went back to work. Early in the day, he thought for the first time of his mother, at their country home in Mukaihara, thirty miles from town. He usually went home every night. He was afraid she would think he was dead.

Near the spot upriver to which Mr. Tanimoto had transported the priests, there sat a large case of rice cakes which a rescue party had evidently brought for the wounded lying thereabouts but hadn't distributed. Before evacuating the wounded priests, the others passed the cakes around and helped themselves. A few minutes later, a band of soldiers came up, and an officer, hearing the priests speaking a foreign language, drew his sword and hysterically asked who they were. One of the priests calmed him down and explained that they were Germans—allies. The officer apologized and said that there were reports going around that American parachutists had landed.

The priests decided that they should take Father Schiffer first. As they prepared to leave, Father Superior LaSalle said he felt awfully cold. One of the Jesuits gave up his coat, another his shirt; they were glad to wear less in the muggy night. The stretcher bearers started out. The theological student led the way and tried to warn the others of obstacles, but one of the priests got a foot tangled in some telephone wire and tripped and dropped his corner of the litter. Father Schiffer rolled off, lost consciousness, came to, and then vomited. The bearers picked him up and went on with him to the edge of the city, where they had arranged to meet a relay of other priests, left him with them, and turned back and got the Father Superior.

The wooden litter must have been terribly painful for Father LaSalle, in whose back scores of tiny particles of window glass were embedded. Near the edge of town, the group had to walk around an automobile burned and squatting on the narrow road, and the bearers on one side, unable to see their way in the darkness, fell into a deep ditch. Father LaSalle was thrown onto the ground and the litter broke in two. One priest went ahead to get a handcart from the Novitiate, but he soon found one beside an empty house and wheeled it back. The priests lifted Father LaSalle into the cart and pushed him over the bumpy road the rest of the way. The rector of the Novitiate, who had been a doctor before he entered the religious order, cleaned the wounds of the two priests and put them to bed between clean sheets, and they thanked God for the care they had received.

Thousands of people had nobody to help them. Miss Sasaki was one of them. Abandoned and helpless, under the crude lean-to in the courtyard of the tin factory, beside the woman who had lost a breast and the man whose burned face was scarcely a face any more, she suffered awfully that night from the pain in her broken leg. She did not sleep at all; neither did she converse with her sleepless companions.

In the park, Mrs. Murata kept Father Kleinsorge awake all night by talking to him. None of the Nakamura family were able to sleep, either; the children, in spite of being very sick, were interested in everything that happened. They were delighted when one of the city's gas-storage tanks went up in a tremendous burst of flame. Toshio, the boy, shouted to the others to look at the reflection in the river. Mr. Tanimoto, after his long run and his many hours of rescue work, dozed uneasily. When he awoke, in the first light of dawn, he looked across the river and saw that he had not carried the festered, limp bodies high enough on the sandspit the night before. The tide had risen above where he had put them; they had not had the strength to move; they must have drowned. He saw a number of bodies floating in the river.

Early that day, August 7th, the Japanese radio broadcast for the first time a succinct announcement that very few, if any, of the people most concerned with its content, the survivors in Hiroshima, happened to hear: "Hiroshima suffered considerable damage as the result of an attack by a few B-29s. It is believed that a new type of bomb was used. The details are being investigated." Nor is it probable that any of the survivors happened to be tuned in on a short-wave rebroadcast of an extraordinary announcement by the President of the United States, which identified the new bomb as atomic: "That bomb had more power than twenty thousand tons of TNT. It had more than two thousand times the blast power of the British Grand Slam, which is the largest bomb ever yet used in the history of warfare." Those victims who were able to worry at all about what had happened thought of it and discussed it in more primitive, childish terms—gasoline sprinkled from an airplane, maybe, or some combustible gas, or a big cluster of incendiaries, or the work of parachutists; but, even if they had known the truth, most of them were too busy or too weary or too badly hurt to care that they were the objects of the first great experiment in the use of atomic power, which (as the voices on the short wave shouted) no country except the United States, with its industrial know-how, its willingness to throw two billion gold dollars into an important wartime gamble, could possibly have developed.

Mr. Tanimoto was still angry at doctors. He decided that he would personally bring one to Asano Park—by the scruff of the neck, if necessary. He crossed the river, went past the Shinto shrine where he had met his wife for a brief moment the day before, and walked to the East Parade Ground. Since this had long before been designated as an evacuation area, he thought he would find an aid station there. He did find one, operated by an Army medical unit, but he also saw that its doctors were hopelessly overburdened, with thousands of patients sprawled among corpses across the field in front of it. Nevertheless, he went up to one of the Army doctors and said, as reproachfully as he could, "Why have you not come to Asano Park? You are badly needed there."

Without even looking up from his work, the doctor said in a tired voice, "This is my station."

"But there are many dying on the riverbank over there."

"The first duty," the doctor said, "is to take care of the slightly wounded."

"Why—when there are many who are heavily wounded on the riverbank?"

The doctor moved to another patient. "In an emergency like this," he said, as if he were reciting from a manual, "the first task is to help as many as possible—to save as many lives as possible. There is no hope for the heavily wounded. They will die. We can't bother with them."

"That may be right from a medical standpoint—" Mr. Tanimoto began, but then he looked out across the field, where the many dead lay close and intimate with those who were still living, and he turned away without finishing his sentence, angry now with himself. He didn't know what to do; he had promised some of the dying people in the park that he would bring them medical aid. They might die feeling cheated. He saw a ration stand at one side of the field, and he went to it and begged some rice cakes and biscuits, and he took them back, in lieu of doctors, to the people in the park.

The morning, again, was hot. Father Kleinsorge went to fetch water for the wounded in a bottle and a teapot he had borrowed. He had heard that it was possible to get fresh tap water outside Asano Park. Going through the rock gardens, he had to climb over and crawl under the trunks of fallen pine trees; he found he was weak. There were many dead in the gardens. At a beautiful moon bridge, he passed a naked, living woman who seemed to have been burned from head to toe and was red all over. Near the entrance to the park, an Army doctor was working, but the only medicine he had was iodine, which he painted over cuts, bruises, slimy burns, everything—and by now everything that he painted had pus on it. Outside the gate of the park, Father Kleinsorge found a faucet that still worked—part of the plumbing of a vanished house—and he filled his vessels and returned. When he had given the wounded the water, he made a second trip. This time, the woman by the bridge was dead. On his way back with the water, he got lost on a detour around a fallen tree, and as he looked for his way through the woods, he heard a voice ask from the underbrush, "Have you anything to drink?" He saw a uniform. Thinking there was just one soldier, he approached with the water. When he had penetrated the bushes, he saw there were about twenty men, and they were all in exactly the same nightmarish state: their faces were wholly burned, their eyesockets were hollow, the fluid from their melted eyes had run down their cheeks. (They must have had their faces upturned when the bomb went off; perhaps they were anti-aircraft personnel.) Their mouths were mere swollen, pus-covered wounds, which they could not bear to stretch enough to admit the spout of the teapot. So Father Kleinsorge got a large piece of grass and drew out the stem so as to make a straw, and gave them all water to drink that way. One of them said, "I can't see anything." Father Kleinsorge answered, as cheerfully as he could, "There's a doctor at the entrance to the park. He's busy now, but he'll come soon and fix your eyes, I hope."

Since that day, Father Kleinsorge has thought back to how queasy he had once been at the sight of pain, how someone else's cut finger used to make him turn faint. Yet there in the park he was so benumbed that immediately after leaving this horrible sight he stopped on a path by one of the pools and discussed with a lightly wounded man whether it would be safe to eat the fat, two-foot carp that floated dead on the surface of the water. They decided, after some consideration, that it would be unwise.

Father Kleinsorge filled the containers a third time and

went back to the riverbank. There, amid the dead and dying, he saw a young woman with a needle and thread mending her kimono, which had been slightly torn. Father Kleinsorge joshed her. "My, but you're a dandy!" he said. She laughed.

He felt tired and lay down. He began to talk with two engaging children whose acquaintance he had made the afternoon before. He learned that their name was Kataoka; the girl was thirteen, the boy five. The girl had been just about to set out for a barbershop when the bomb fell. As the family started for Asano Park, their mother decided to turn back for some food and extra clothing; they became separated from her in the crowd of fleeing people, and they had not seen her since. Occasionally they stopped suddenly in their perfectly cheerful playing and began to cry for their mother.

It was difficult for all the children in the park to sustain the sense of tragedy. Toshio Nakamura got quite excited when he saw his friend Seichi Sato riding up the river in a boat with his family, and he ran to the bank and waved and shouted, "Sato! Sato!"

The boy turned his head and shouted, "Who's that?"

"Nakamura."

"Hello, Toshio!"

"Are you all safe?"

"Yes. What about you?"

"Yes, we're all right. My sisters are vomiting, but I'm fine."

Father Kleinsorge began to be thirsty in the dreadful heat, and he did not feel strong enough to go for water again. A little before noon, he saw a Japanese woman handing something out. Soon she came to him and said in a kindly voice, "These are tea leaves. Chew them, young man, and you won't feel thirsty." The woman's gentleness made Father Kleinsorge suddenly want to cry. For weeks, he had been feeling oppressed by the hatred of foreigners that the Japanese seemed increasingly to show, and he had been uneasy even with his Japanese friends. This stranger's gesture made him a little hysterical.

Around noon, the priests arrived from the Novitiate with the handcart. They had been to the site of the mission house in the city and had retrieved some suitcases that had been stored in the air-raid shelter and had also picked up the remains of melted holy vessels in the ashes of the chapel. They now packed Father Kleinsorge's papier-mâché suitcase and the things belonging to Mrs. Murata and the Nakamuras into the cart, put the two Nakamura girls aboard, and prepared to start out. Then one of the Jesuits who had a practical turn of mind remembered that they had been notified some time before that if they suffered property damage at the hands of the enemy, they could enter a claim for compensation with the prefectural police. The holy men discussed this matter there in the park, with the wounded as silent as the dead around them, and decided that Father Kleinsorge, as a former resident of the destroyed mission, was the one to enter the claim. So, as the others went off with the handcart, Father Kleinsorge said goodbye to the Kataoka children and trudged to a police station. Fresh, clean-uniformed policemen from another town were in charge, and a crowd of dirty and disarrayed citizens crowded around them, mostly asking after lost relatives. Father Kleinsorge filled out a claim form and started walking through the center of the town on his way to Nagatsuka. It was then that he first realized the extent of the damage; he passed block after block of ruins, and even after all he had seen in the park, his breath was taken away. By the time he reached the Novitiate, he was sick with exhaustion. The last thing he did as he fell into bed was request that someone go back for the motherless Kataoka children.

Altogether, Miss Sasaki was left two days and two nights under the piece of propped-up roofing with her crushed leg and her two unpleasant comrades. Her only diversion was when men came to the factory air-raid shelters, which she could see from under one corner of her shelter, and hauled corpses up out of them with ropes. Her leg became discolored, swollen, and putrid. All that time, she went without food and water. On the third day, August 8th, some friends who supposed she was dead came to look for her body and found her. They told her that her mother, father, and baby brother, who at the time of the explosion were in the Tamura Pediatric Hospital, where the baby was a patient, had all been given up as certainly dead, since the hospital was totally destroyed. Her friends then left her to think that piece of news over. Later, some men picked her up by the arms and legs and carried her quite a distance to a truck. For about an hour, the truck moved over a bumpy road, and Miss Sasaki, who had become convinced that she was dulled to pain, discovered that she was not. The men lifted her out at a relief station in the section of Inokuchi, where two Army doctors looked at her. The moment one of them touched her wound, she fainted. She came to in time to hear them discuss whether or not to cut off her leg; one said there was gas gangrene in the lips of the wound and predicted she would die unless they amputated, and the other said that was too bad, because they had no equipment with which to do the job. She fainted again. When she recovered consciousness, she was being carried somewhere on a stretcher. She was put aboard a launch, which went to the nearby island of Ninoshima, and she was taken to a military hospital there. Another doctor examined her and said that she did not have gas gangrene, though she did have a fairly ugly compound fracture. He said quite coldly that he was sorry, but this was a hospital for operative surgical cases only, and because she had no gangrene, she would have to return to Hiroshima that night. But then the doctor took her temperature, and what he saw on the thermometer made him decide to let her stay.

That day, August 8th, Father Cieslik went into the city to look for Mr. Fukai, the Japanese secretary of the diocese, who had ridden unwillingly out of the flaming city on Father Kleinsorge's back and then had run back crazily into it. Father Cieslik started hunting in the neighborhood of Sakai Bridge, where the Jesuits had last seen Mr. Fukai; he went to the East Parade Ground, the evacuation area to which the secretary might have gone, and looked for him among the wounded and dead there; he went to the prefectural police and made inquiries. He could not find any trace of the man. Back at the Novitiate that evening, the theological student, who had been rooming with Mr. Fukai at the mission house, told the priests that the secretary had remarked to him, during an air-raid alarm one day not long before the bombing, "Japan is dying. If there is a real air raid here in Hiroshima, I want to die with our country." The priests concluded that

Mr. Fukai had run back to immolate himself in the flames. They never saw him again.

At the Red Cross Hospital, Dr. Sasaki worked for three straight days with only one hour's sleep. On the second day, he began to sew up the worst cuts, and right through the following night and all the next day he stitched. Many of the wounds were festered. Fortunately, someone had found intact a supply of *narucopon*, a Japanese sedative, and he gave it to many who were in pain. Word went around among the staff that there must have been something peculiar about the great bomb, because on the second day the vice-chief of the hospital went down in the basement to the vault where the X-ray plates were stored and found the whole stock exposed as they lay. That day, a fresh doctor and ten nurses came in from the city of Yamaguchi with extra bandages and antiseptics, and the third day another physician and a dozen more nurses arrived from Matsue—yet there were still only eight doctors for ten thousand patients. In the afternoon of the third day, exhausted from his foul tailoring, Dr. Sasaki became obsessed with the idea that his mother thought he was dead. He got permission to go to Mukaihara. He walked out to the first suburbs, beyond which the electric train service was still functioning, and reached home late in the evening. His mother said she had known he was all right all along; a wounded nurse had stopped by to tell her. He went to bed and slept for seventeen hours.

Before dawn on August 8th, someone entered the room at the Novitiate where Father Kleinsorge was in bed, reached up to the hanging light bulb, and switched it on. The sudden flood of light, pouring in on Father Kleinsorge's half sleep, brought him leaping out of bed, braced for a new concussion. When he realized what had happened, he laughed confusedly and went back to bed. He stayed there all day.

On August 9th, Father Kleinsorge was still tired. The rector looked at his cuts and said they were not even worth dressing, and if Father Kleinsorge kept them clean, they would heal in three or four days. Father Kleinsorge felt uneasy; he could not yet comprehend what he had been through; as if he were guilty of something awful, he felt he had to go back to the scene of the violence he had experienced. He got up out of bed and walked into the city. He scratched for a while in the ruins of the mission house, but he found nothing. He went to the sites of a couple of schools and asked after people he knew. He looked for some of the city's Japanese Catholics, but he found only fallen houses. He walked back to the Novitiate, stupefied and without any new understanding.

At two minutes after eleven o'clock on the morning of August 9th, the second atomic bomb was dropped, on Nagasaki. It was several days before the survivors of Hiroshima knew they had company, because the Japanese radio and newspapers were being extremely cautious on the subject of the strange weapon.

On August 9th, Mr. Tanimoto was still working in the park. He went to the suburb of Ushida, where his wife was staying with friends, and got a tent which he had stored there before the bombing. He now took it to the park and set it up as a shelter for some of the wounded who could not move or be moved. Whatever he did in the park, he felt he was being watched by the twenty-year-old girl, Mrs. Kamai, his former neighbor, whom he had seen on the day the bomb exploded, with her dead baby daughter in her arms. She kept the small corpse in her arms for four days, even though it began smelling bad on the second day. Once, Mr. Tanimoto sat with her for a while, and she told him that the bomb had buried her under their house with the baby strapped to her back, and that when she had dug herself free, she had discovered that the baby was choking, its mouth full of dirt. With her little finger, she had carefully cleaned out the infant's mouth, and for a time the child had breathed normally and seemed all right; then suddenly it had died. Mrs. Kamai also talked about what a fine man her husband was, and again urged Mr. Tanimoto to search for him. Since Mr. Tanimoto had been all through the city the first day and had seen terribly burned soldiers from Kamai's post, the Chugoku Regional Army Headquarters, everywhere, he knew it would be impossible to find Kamai, even if he were living, but of course he didn't tell her that. Every time she saw Mr. Tanimoto, she asked whether he had found her husband. Once, he tried to suggest that perhaps it was time to cremate the baby, but Mrs. Kamai only held it tighter. He began to keep away from her, but whenever he looked at her, she was staring at him and her eyes asked the same question. He tried to escape her glance by keeping his back turned to her as much as possible.

The Jesuits took about fifty refugees into the exquisite chapel of the Novitiate. The rector gave them what medical care he could—mostly just the cleaning away of pus. Each of the Nakamuras was provided with a blanket and a mosquito net. Mrs. Nakamura and her younger daughter had no appetite and ate nothing; her son and other daughter ate, and lost, each meal they were offered. On August 10th, a friend, Mrs. Osaki, came to see them and told them that her son Hideo had been burned alive in the factory where he worked. This Hideo had been a kind of hero to Toshio, who had often gone to the plant to watch him run his machine. That night, Toshio woke up screaming. He had dreamed that he had seen Mrs. Osaki coming out of an opening in the ground with her family, and then he saw Hideo at his machine, a big one with a revolving belt, and he himself was standing beside Hideo, and for some reason this was terrifying.

On August 10th, Father Kleinsorge, having heard from someone that Dr. Fujii had been injured and that he had eventually gone to the summer house of a friend of his named Okuma, in the village of Fukawa, asked Father Cieslik if he would go and see how Dr. Fujii was. Father Cieslik went to Misasa station, outside Hiroshima, rode for twenty minutes on an electric train, and then walked for an hour and a half in a terribly hot sun to Mr. Okuma's house, which was beside the Ota River at the foot of a mountain. He found Dr. Fujii sitting in a chair in a kimono, applying compresses to his broken collarbone. The Doctor told Father Cieslik about having lost his glasses and said that his eyes bothered him. He showed the priest huge blue and green stripes where beams had bruised him. He offered the Jesuit first a cigarette and then whiskey, though it was only eleven in the morning. Father Cieslik thought it would please Dr. Fujii if he took a little, so he said yes. A servant brought some Suntory whiskey, and the Jesuit, the Doctor, and the host had a very pleasant chat. Mr. Okuma had lived in Hawaii, and he told some things about Americans. Dr. Fujii talked a bit about the disaster. He said that Mr. Okuma and a nurse had gone into the ruins of his hospital and brought back a small safe which he had moved into his air-raid shelter. This contained some surgical instruments, and Dr. Fujii gave Father Cieslik a few pairs of scissors and tweezers for the rector at the Novitiate. Father Cieslik was bursting with some inside dope he had, but he waited until the conversation turned naturally to the mystery of the bomb. Then he said he knew what kind of bomb it was; he had the secret on the best authority—that of a Japanese newspaperman who had dropped in at the Novitiate. The bomb was not a bomb at all; it was a kind of fine magnesium powder sprayed over the whole city by a single plane, and it exploded when it came into contact with the live wires of the city power system. "That means," said Dr. Fujii, perfectly satisfied, since after all the information came from a newspaperman, "that it can only be dropped on big cities and only in the daytime, when the tram lines and so forth are in operation."

After five days of ministering to the wounded in the park, Mr. Tanimoto returned, on August 11th, to his parsonage and dug around in the ruins. He retrieved some diaries and church records that had been kept in books and were only charred around the edges, as well as some cooking utensils and pottery. While he was at work, a Miss Tanaka came and said that her father had been asking for him. Mr. Tanimoto had reason to hate her father, the retired shipping-company official who, though he made a great show of his charity, was notoriously selfish and cruel, and who, just a few days before the bombing, had said openly to several people that Mr. Tanimoto was a spy for the Americans. Several times he had derided Christianity and called it un-Japanese. At the moment of the bombing, Mr. Tanaka had been walking in the street in front of the city's radio station. He received serious flash burns, but he was able to walk home. He took refuge in his Neighborhood Association shelter and from there tried hard to get medical aid. He expected all the doctors of Hiroshima to come to him, because he was so rich and so famous for giving his money away. When none of them came, he angrily set out to look for them; leaning on his daughter's arm, he walked from private hospital to private hospital, but all were in ruins, and he went back and lay down in the shelter again. Now he was very weak and knew he was going to die. He was willing to be comforted by any religion.

Mr. Tanimoto went to help him. He descended into the tomblike shelter and, when his eyes were adjusted to the darkness, saw Mr. Tanaka, his face and arms puffed up and covered with pus and blood, and his eyes swollen shut. The old man smelled very bad, and he moaned constantly. He seemed to recognize Mr. Tanimoto's voice. Standing at the shelter stairway to get light, Mr. Tanimoto read loudly from a Japanese-language pocket Bible: "For a thousand years in Thy sight are but as yesterday when it is past, and as a watch in the night. Thou carriest the children of men away as with a flood; they are as a sleep; in the morning they are like grass which groweth up. In the morning it flourisheth and groweth up; in the evening it is cut down, and withereth. For we are consumed by Thine anger and by Thy wrath are we troubled. Thou hast set our iniquities before Thee, our secret sins in the light of Thy countenance. For all our days are passed away in Thy wrath: we spend our years as a tale that is told. . . ."

Mr. Tanaka died as Mr. Tanimoto read the psalm.

On August 11th, word came to the Ninoshima Military Hospital that a large number of military casualties from the Chugoku Regional Army Headquarters were to arrive on the island that day, and it was deemed necessary to evacuate all civilian patients. Miss Sasaki, still running an alarmingly high fever, was put on a large ship. She lay out on deck, with a pillow under her leg. There were awnings over the deck, but the vessel's course put her in the sunlight. She felt as if she were under a magnifying glass in the sun. Pus oozed out of her wound, and soon the whole pillow was covered with it. She was taken ashore at Hatsukaichi, a town several miles to the southwest of Hiroshima, and put in the Goddess of Mercy

Primary School, which had been turned into a hospital. She lay there for several days before a specialist on fractures came from Kobe. By then her leg was red and swollen up to her hip. The doctor decided he could not set the breaks. He made an incision and put in a rubber pipe to drain off the putrescence.

At the Novitiate, the motherless Kataoka children were inconsolable. Father Cieslik worked hard to keep them distracted. He put riddles to them. He asked, "What is the cleverest animal in the world?," and after the thirteen-year-old girl had guessed the ape, the elephant, the horse, he said, "No, it must be the hippopotamus," because in Japanese that animal is *kaba*, the reverse of *baka*, stupid. He told Bible stories, beginning, in the order of things, with the Creation. He showed them a scrapbook of snapshots taken in Europe. Nevertheless, they cried most of the time for their mother.

Several days later, Father Cieslik started hunting for the children's family. First, he learned through the police that an uncle had been to the authorities in Kure, a city not far away, to inquire for the children. After that, he heard that an older brother had been trying to trace them through the post office in Ujina, a suburb of Hiroshima. Still later, he heard that the mother was alive and was on Goto Island, off Nagasaki. And at last, by keeping a check on the Ujina post office, he got in touch with the brother and returned the children to their mother.

About a week after the bomb dropped, a vague, incomprehensible rumor reached Hiroshima—that the city had been destroyed by the energy released when atoms were somehow split in two. The weapon was referred to in this word-of-mouth report as *genshi bakudan*—the root characters of which can be translated as "original child bomb." No one understood the idea or put any more credence in it than in the powdered magnesium and such things. Newspapers were being brought in from other cities, but they were still confining themselves to extremely general statements, such as Domei's assertion on August 12th: "There is nothing to do but admit the tremendous power of this inhuman bomb."

Already, Japanese physicists had entered the city with Lauritsen electroscopes and Neher electrometers; they understood the idea all too well.

On August 12th, the Nakamuras, all of them still rather sick, went to the nearby town of Kabe and moved in with Mrs. Nakamura's sister-in-law. The next day, Mrs. Nakamura, although she was too ill to walk much, returned to Hiroshima alone, by electric car to the outskirts, by foot from there. All week, at the Novitiate, she had worried about her mother, brother, and older sister, who had lived in the part of town called Fukuro, and besides, she felt drawn by some fascination, just as Father Kleinsorge had been. She discovered that her family were all dead. She went back to Kabe so amazed and depressed by what she had seen and learned in the city that she could not speak that evening.

A comparative orderliness, at least, began to be established at the Red Cross Hospital. Dr. Sasaki, back from his rest, undertook to classify his patients (who were still scattered everywhere, even on the stairways). The staff gradually swept up the debris. Best of all, the nurses and attendants started to remove the corpses. Disposal of the dead, by decent cremation and enshrinement, is a greater moral responsibility to the Japanese than adequate care of the living. Relatives identified most of the first day's dead in and around the hospital. Beginning on the second day, whenever a patient appeared to be moribund, a piece of paper with his name on it was fastened to his clothing. The corpse detail carried the bodies to a clearing outside, placed them on pyres of wood from ruined houses, burned them, put some of the ashes in envelopes intended for exposed X-ray plates, marked the envelopes with the names of the deceased, and piled them, neatly and respectfully, in stacks in the main office. In a few days, the envelopes filled one whole side of the impromptu shrine.

In Kabe, on the morning of August 15th, ten-year-old Toshio Nakamura heard an airplane overhead. He ran outdoors and identified it with a professional eye as a B-29. "There goes Mr. B!" he shouted.

One of his relatives called out to him, "Haven't you had enough of Mr. B?"

The question had a kind of symbolism. At almost that very moment, the dull, dispirited voice of Hirohito, the Emperor Tenno, was speaking for the first time in history over the radio: "After pondering deeply the general trends of the world and the actual conditions obtaining in Our Empire today, We have decided to effect a settlement of the present situation by resorting to an extraordinary measure. . . ."

Mrs. Nakamura had gone to the city again, to dig up some rice she had buried in her Neighborhood Association air-raid shelter. She got it and started back for Kabe. On the electric car, quite by chance, she ran into her younger sister, who had not been in Hiroshima the day of the bombing. "Have you heard the news?" her sister asked.

"What news?"

"The war is over."

"Don't say such a foolish thing, sister."

"But I heard it over the radio myself." And then, in a whisper, "It was the Emperor's voice."

"Oh," Mrs. Nakamura said (she needed nothing more to make her give up thinking, in spite of the atomic bomb, that Japan still had a chance to win the war), "in that case . . ."

Some time later, in a letter to an American, Mr. Tanimoto described the events of that morning. "At the time of the Post-War, the marvelous thing in our history happened. Our Emperor broadcasted his own voice through radio directly to us, common people of Japan. Aug. 15th we were told that some news of great importance could be heard & all of us should hear it. So I went to Hiroshima railway station. There set a loud-speaker in the ruins of the station. Many civilians, all of them were in boundage, some being helped by shoulder of their daughters, some sustaining their injured feet by sticks, they listened to the broadcast and when they came to realize the fact that it was the Emperor, they cried with full tears in their eyes, 'What a wonderful blessing it is that Tenno himself call on us and we can hear his own voice in person. We are thoroughly satisfied in such a great sacrifice.' When they came to know the war was ended—that is, Japan was defeated, they, of course, were deeply disappointed, but followed after their Emperor's commandment in calm spirit, making whole-hearted sacrifice for the everlasting peace of the world—and Japan started her new way."

IV. PANIC GRASS AND FEVERFEW

On August 18th, twelve days after the bomb burst, Father Kleinsorge set out on foot for Hiroshima from the Novitiate with his papier-mâché suitcase in his hand. He had begun to think that this bag, in which he kept his valuables, had a talismanic quality, because of the way he had found it after the explosion, standing handle-side up in the doorway of his room, while the desk under which he had previously hidden it was in splinters all over the floor. Now he was using it to carry the yen belonging to the Society of Jesus to the Hiroshima branch of the Yokohama Specie Bank, already reopened in its half-ruined building. On the whole, he felt quite well that morning. It is true that the minor cuts he had received had not healed in three or four days, as the rector of the Novitiate, who had examined them, had positively promised they would, but Father Kleinsorge had rested well for a week and considered that he was again ready for hard work. By now he was accustomed to the terrible scene through which he walked on his way into the city: the large rice field near the Novitiate, streaked with brown; the houses on the outskirts of the city, standing but decrepit, with broken windows and di-shevelled tiles; and then, quite suddenly, the beginning of the four square miles of reddish-brown scar, where nearly every-thing had been buffeted down and burned; range on range of collapsed city blocks, with here and there a crude sign erected on a pile of ashes and tiles ("Sister, where are you?" or "All safe and we live at Toyosaka"); naked trees and canted tele-phone poles; the few standing, gutted buildings only accentu-ating the horizontality of everything else (the Museum of Science and Industry, with its dome stripped to its steel frame, as if for an autopsy; the modern Chamber of Com-merce Building, its tower as cold, rigid, and unassailable after the blow as before; the huge, low-lying, camouflaged city hall; the row of dowdy banks, caricaturing a shaken economic system); and in the streets a macabre traffic—hundreds of crumpled bicycles, shells of streetcars and automobiles, all halted in mid-motion. The whole way, Father Kleinsorge was oppressed by the thought that all the damage he saw had been done in one instant by one bomb. By the time he reached the center of town, the day had become very hot. He walked to the Yokohama Bank, which was doing business in a temporary wooden stall on the ground floor of its building, deposited the money, went by the mission compound just to have another look at the wreckage, and then started back to the Novitiate. About halfway there, he began to have peculiar sensations. The more or less magical suitcase, now empty, suddenly seemed terribly heavy. His knees grew weak. He felt excruciatingly tired. With a considerable expenditure of spirit, he managed to reach the Novitiate. He did not think his weakness was worth mentioning to the other Jesuits. But a couple of days later, while attempting to say Mass, he had an onset of faintness and even after three attempts was unable to go through with the service, and the next morning the rector, who had examined Father Kleinsorge's apparently negligible but unhealed cuts daily, asked in surprise, "What have you done to your wounds?" They had suddenly opened wider and were swollen and inflamed.

As she dressed on the morning of August 20th, in the home of her sister-in-law in Kabe, not far from Nagatsuka, Mrs. Nakamura, who had suffered no cuts or burns at all, though she had been rather nauseated all through the week she and her children had spent as guests of Father Kleinsorge and the other Catholics at the Novitiate, began fixing her hair and noticed, after one stroke, that her comb carried with it a whole handful of hair; the second time, the same thing happened, so she stopped combing at once. But in the next three or four days, her hair kept falling out of its own accord, until she was quite bald. She began living indoors, practically in hiding. On August 26th, both she and her younger daughter, Myeko, woke up feeling extremely weak and tired, and they stayed on their bedrolls. Her son and other daughter, who had shared every experience with her during and after the bombing, felt fine.

At about the same time—he lost track of the days, so hard

was he working to set up a temporary place of worship in a private house he had rented in the outskirts — Mr. Tanimoto fell suddenly ill with a general malaise, weariness, and feverishness, and he, too, took to his bedroll on the floor of the half-wrecked house of a friend in the suburb of Ushida.

These four did not realize it, but they were coming down with the strange, capricious disease which came later to be known as radiation sickness.

Miss Sasaki lay in steady pain in the Goddess of Mercy Primary School, at Hatsukaichi, the fourth station to the southwest of Hiroshima on the electric train. An internal infection still prevented the proper setting of the compound fracture of her lower left leg. A young man who was in the same hospital and who seemed to have grown fond of her in spite of her unremitting preoccupation with her suffering, or else just pitied her because of it, lent her a Japanese translation of de Maupassant, and she tried to read the stories, but she could concentrate for only four or five minutes at a time.

The hospitals and aid stations around Hiroshima were so crowded in the first weeks after the bombing, and their staffs were so variable, depending on their health and on the unpredictable arrival of outside help, that patients had to be constantly shifted from place to place. Miss Sasaki, who had already been moved three times, twice by ship, was taken at the end of August to an engineering school, also at Hatsukaichi. Because her leg did not improve but swelled more and more, the doctors at the school bound it with crude splints and took her by car, on September 9th, to the Red Cross Hospital in Hiroshima. This was the first chance she had had to look at the ruins of Hiroshima; the last time she had been carried through the city's streets, she had been hovering on the edge of unconsciousness. Even though the wreckage had been described to her, and though she was still in pain, the sight horrified and amazed her, and there was something she noticed about it that particularly gave her the creeps. Over everything — up through the wreckage of the city, in gutters, along the riverbanks, tangled among tiles and tin roofing, climbing on charred tree trunks — was a blanket of fresh, vivid, lush, optimistic green; the verdancy rose even from the foundations of ruined houses. Weeds already hid the ashes, and wild flowers were in bloom among the city's bones. The bomb had not only left the underground organs of plants intact; it had stimulated them. Everywhere were bluets and Spanish bayonets, goosefoot, morning glories and day lilies, the hairy-fruited bean, purslane and clotbur and sesame and panic grass and feverfew. Especially in a circle at the center, sickle senna grew in extraordinary regeneration, not only standing among the charred remnants of the same plant but pushing up in new places, among bricks and through cracks in the asphalt. It actually seemed as if a load of sickle-senna seed had been dropped along with the bomb.

At the Red Cross Hospital, Miss Sasaki was put under the care of Dr. Sasaki. Now, a month after the explosion, something like order had been reëstablished in the hospital; which is to say that the patients who still lay in the corridors at least had mats to sleep on and that the supply of medicines, which had given out in the first few days, had been replaced, though inadequately, by contributions from other cities. Dr. Sasaki, who had had one seventeen-hour sleep at his home on the third night, had ever since then rested only about six hours a night, on a mat at the hospital; he had lost twenty pounds from his very small body; he still wore the ill-fitting glasses he had borrowed from an injured nurse.

Since Miss Sasaki was a woman and was so sick (and perhaps, he afterward admitted, just a little bit because she was named Sasaki), Dr. Sasaki put her on a mat in a semi-private room, which at that time had only eight people in it. He questioned her and put down on her record card, in the correct, scrunched-up German in which he wrote all his records: "*Mittelgrosse Patientin in gutem Ernährungszustand. Fraktur am linken Unterschenkelknochen mit Wunde; Anschwellung in der linken Unterschenkelgegend. Haut und sichtbare Schleimhäute mässig durchblutet und kein Oedema,*" noting that she was a medium-sized female patient in good general health; that she had a compound fracture of the left tibia, with swelling of the left lower leg; that her skin and visible mucous membranes were heavily spotted with *petechiae*, which are hemorrhages about the size of grains of rice, or even as big as soybeans; and, in addition, that her head, eyes, throat, lungs, and heart were apparently normal; and that she had a fever. He wanted to set her fracture and put her leg in a cast, but he had run out of plaster of Paris long since, so he just stretched her out on a mat and prescribed aspirin for her fever, and glucose intravenously and diastase orally for her undernourishment (which he had not entered on her record because everyone suffered from it). She exhibited only one of the queer symptoms so many of his patients were just then beginning to show—the spot hemorrhages.

Dr. Fujii was still pursued by bad luck, which still was connected with rivers. Now he was living in the summer house of Mr. Okuma, in Fukawa. This house clung to the steep banks of the Ota River. Here his injuries seemed to make good progress, and he even began to treat refugees who came to him from the neighborhood, using medical supplies he had retrieved from a cache in the suburbs. He noticed in some of his patients a curious syndrome of symptoms that cropped out in the third and fourth weeks, but he was not able to do much more than swathe cuts and burns. Early in September, it began to rain, steadily and heavily. The river rose. On September 17th, there came a cloudburst and then a typhoon, and the water crept higher and higher up the bank. Mr. Okuma and Dr. Fujii became alarmed and scrambled up the mountain to a peasant's house. (Down in Hiroshima, the flood took up where the bomb had left off—swept away bridges that had survived the blast, washed out streets, undermined foundations of buildings that still stood—and ten miles to the west, the Ono Army Hospital, where a team of experts from Kyoto Imperial University was studying the delayed affliction of the patients, suddenly slid down a beautiful, pine-dark mountainside into the Inland Sea and drowned most of the investigators and their mysteriously diseased patients alike.) After the storm, Dr. Fujii and Mr. Okuma went down to the river and found that the Okuma house had been washed altogether away.

Because so many people were suddenly feeling sick nearly a month after the atomic bomb was dropped, an unpleasant rumor began to move around, and eventually it made its way to the house in Kabe where Mrs. Nakamura lay bald and ill. It was that the atomic bomb had deposited some sort of poison on Hiroshima which would give off deadly emanations for seven years; nobody could go there all that time. This especially upset Mrs. Nakamura, who remembered that in a moment of confusion on the morning of the explosion she had literally sunk her entire means of livelihood, her Sankoku sewing machine, in the small cement water tank in front of what was left of her house; now no one would be able to go and fish it out. Up to this time, Mrs. Nakamura and her relatives had been quite resigned and passive about the moral issue of the atomic bomb, but this rumor suddenly aroused them to more hatred and resentment of America than they had felt all through the war.

Japanese physicists, who knew a great deal about atomic fission (one of them owned a cyclotron), worried about lingering radiation at Hiroshima, and in mid-August, not many days after President Truman's disclosure of the type of bomb that had been dropped, they entered the city to make investigations. The first thing they did was roughly to determine a center by observing the side on which telephone poles all around the heart of the town were scorched; they settled on the torii gateway of the Gokoku Shrine, right next to the parade ground of the Chugoku Regional Army Headquarters. From there, they worked north and south with Lauritsen electroscopes, which are sensitive to both beta rays and gamma rays. These indicated that the highest intensity of radioactivity, near the torii, was 4.2 times the average natural "leak" of ultra-short waves for the earth of that area. The scientists noticed that the flash of the bomb had discolored concrete to a light reddish tint, had scaled off the surface of granite, and had scorched certain other types of building material, and that consequently the bomb had, in some places, left prints of the shadows that had been cast by its light. The experts found, for instance, a permanent shadow thrown on the roof of the Chamber of Commerce Building (220 yards from the rough center) by the structure's rectangular tower; several others in the lookout post on top of the Hypothec Bank (2,050 yards); another in the tower of the Chugoku Electric Supply Building (800 yards); another projected by the handle of a gas pump (2,630 yards); and several on granite tombstones in the Gokoku Shrine (385 yards). By triangulating these and other such shadows with the objects that formed them, the scientists determined that the exact center was a spot a hundred and fifty yards south of the torii and a few yards southeast of the pile of ruins that had once been the Shima Hospital. (A few vague human silhouettes were found, and these gave rise to stories that eventually included fancy and precise details. One story told how a painter on a ladder was monumentalized in a kind of bas-relief on the stone façade of a bank building on which he was at work, in the act of dipping his brush into his paint can; another, how a man and his cart on the bridge near the Museum of Science and Industry, almost under the center of the explosion, were cast down in an embossed shadow which made it clear that the man was about to whip his horse.) Starting east and west from the actual center, the scientists, in early September, made new measurements, and the highest radiation they found this time was 3.9 times the natural "leak." Since radiation of at least a thousand times the natural "leak" would be required to cause serious effects on the human body, the scientists announced that people could enter Hiroshima without any peril at all.

As soon as this reassurance reached the household in which Mrs. Nakamura was concealing herself—or, at any rate, within a short time after her hair had started growing back again—her whole family relaxed their extreme hatred of America, and Mrs. Nakamura sent her brother-in-law to look for the sewing machine. It was still submerged in the water tank, and when he brought it home, she saw, to her dismay, that it was all rusted and useless.

By the end of the first week in September, Father Kleinsorge was in bed at the Novitiate with a fever of 102.2, and since he seemed to be getting worse, his colleagues decided to send him to the Catholic International Hospital in Tokyo. Father Cieslik and the rector took him as far as Kobe and a Jesuit from that city took him the rest of the way, with a message from a Kobe doctor to the Mother Superior of the International Hospital: "Think twice before you give this man blood transfusions, because with atomic-bomb patients we aren't at all sure that if you stick needles in them, they'll stop bleeding."

When Father Kleinsorge arrived at the hospital, he was terribly pale and very shaky. He complained that the bomb had upset his digestion and given him abdominal pains. His white blood count was three thousand (five to seven thousand is normal), he was seriously anemic, and his temperature was 104. A doctor who did not know much about these strange manifestations—Father Kleinsorge was one of a handful of atomic patients who had reached Tokyo—came to see him, and to the patient's face he was most encouraging. "You'll be out of here in two weeks," he said. But when the doctor got out in the corridor, he said to the Mother Superior, "He'll die. All these bomb people die—you'll see. They go along for a couple of weeks and then they die."

The doctor prescribed suralimentation for Father Kleinsorge. Every three hours, they forced some eggs or beef juice into him, and they fed him all the sugar he could stand. They gave him vitamins, and iron pills and arsenic (in Fowler's solution) for his anemia. He confounded both the doctor's predictions; he neither died nor got up in a fortnight. Despite the fact that the message from the Kobe doctor deprived him of transfusions, which would have been the most useful therapy of all, his fever and his digestive troubles cleared up fairly quickly. His white count went up for a while, but early in October it dropped again, to 3,600; then, in ten days, it suddenly climbed above normal, to 8,800; and it finally settled at 5,800. His ridiculous scratches puzzled everyone. For a few days, they would mend, and then, when he moved around, they would open up again. As soon as he began to feel well, he enjoyed himself tremendously. In Hiroshima he had been one of thousands of sufferers; in Tokyo he was a curiosity. American Army doctors came by the dozen to observe him. Japanese experts questioned him. A newspaper interviewed him. And once, the confused doctor came and shook his head and said, "Baffling cases, these atomic-bomb people."

Mrs. Nakamura lay indoors with Myeko. They both continued sick, and though Mrs. Nakamura vaguely sensed that

their trouble was caused by the bomb, she was too poor to
see a doctor and so never knew exactly what the matter was.
Without any treatment at all, but merely resting, they began
gradually to feel better. Some of Myeko's hair fell out, and
she had a tiny burn on her arm which took months to heal.
The boy, Toshio, and the older girl, Yaeko, seemed well
enough, though they, too, lost some hair and occasionally
had bad headaches. Toshio was still having nightmares, always
about the nineteen-year-old mechanic, Hideo Osaki, his hero,
who had been killed by the bomb.

On his back with a fever of 104, Mr. Tanimoto worried about
all the funerals he ought to be conducting for the deceased of
his church. He thought he was just overtired from the hard
work he had done since the bombing, but after the fever had
persisted for a few days, he sent for a doctor. The doctor was
too busy to visit him in Ushida, but he dispatched a nurse,
who recognized his symptoms as those of mild radiation disease and came back from time to time to give him injections
of Vitamin B_1. A Buddhist priest with whom Mr. Tanimoto
was acquainted called on him and suggested that moxibustion
might give him relief; the priest showed the pastor how to
give himself the ancient Japanese treatment, by setting fire to
a twist of the stimulant herb moxa placed on the wrist pulse.
Mr. Tanimoto found that each moxa treatment temporarily
reduced his fever one degree. The nurse had told him to eat
as much as possible, and every few days his mother-in-law
brought him vegetables and fish from Tsuzu, twenty miles
away, where she lived. He spent a month in bed, and then
went ten hours by train to his father's home in Shikoku.
There he rested another month.

Dr. Sasaki and his colleagues at the Red Cross Hospital
watched the unprecedented disease unfold and at last evolved
a theory about its nature. It had, they decided, three stages.
The first stage had been all over before the doctors even knew
they were dealing with a new sickness; it was the direct reaction to the bombardment of the body, at the moment when
the bomb went off, by neutrons, beta particles, and gamma
rays. The apparently uninjured people who had died so mys-

teriously in the first few hours or days had succumbed in this first stage. It killed ninety-five per cent of the people within a half mile of the center, and many thousands who were farther away. The doctors realized in retrospect that even though most of these dead had also suffered from burns and blast effects, they had absorbed enough radiation to kill them. The rays simply destroyed body cells—caused their nuclei to degenerate and broke their walls. Many people who did not die right away came down with nausea, headache, diarrhea, malaise, and fever, which lasted several days. Doctors could not be certain whether some of these symptoms were the result of radiation or nervous shock. The second stage set in ten or fifteen days after the bombing. The main symptom was falling hair. Diarrhea and fever, which in some cases went as high as 106, came next. Twenty-five to thirty days after the explosion, blood disorders appeared: gums bled, the white-blood-cell count dropped sharply, and *petechiae* appeared on the skin and mucous membranes. The drop in the number of white blood corpuscles reduced the patient's capacity to resist infection, so open wounds were unusually slow in healing and many of the sick developed sore throats and mouths. The two key symptoms, on which the doctors came to base their prognosis, were fever and the lowered white-corpuscle count. If fever remained steady and high, the patient's chances for survival were poor. The white count almost always dropped below four thousand; a patient whose count fell below one thousand had little hope of living. Toward the end of the second stage, if the patient survived, anemia, or a drop in the red blood count, also set in. The third stage was the reaction that came when the body struggled to compensate for its ills—when, for instance, the white count not only returned to normal but increased to much higher than normal levels. In this stage, many patients died of complications, such as infections in the chest cavity. Most burns healed with deep layers of pink, rubbery scar tissue, known as keloid tumors. The duration of the disease varied, depending on the patient's constitution and the amount of radiation he had received. Some victims recovered in a week; with others the disease dragged on for months.

As the symptoms revealed themselves, it became clear that

many of them resembled the effects of overdoses of X-ray, and the doctors based their therapy on that likeness. They gave victims liver extract, blood transfusions, and vitamins, especially B_1. The shortage of supplies and instruments hampered them. Allied doctors who came in after the surrender found plasma and penicillin very effective. Since the blood disorders were, in the long run, the predominant factor in the disease, some of the Japanese doctors evolved a theory as to the seat of the delayed sickness. They thought that perhaps gamma rays, entering the body at the time of the explosion, made the phosphorus in the victims' bones radioactive, and that they in turn emitted beta particles, which, though they could not penetrate far through flesh, could enter the bone marrow, where blood is manufactured, and gradually tear it down. Whatever its source, the disease had some baffling quirks. Not all the patients exhibited all the main symptoms. People who suffered flash burns were protected, to a considerable extent, from radiation sickness. Those who had lain quietly for days or even hours after the bombing were much less liable to get sick than those who had been active. Gray hair seldom fell out. And, as if nature were protecting man against his own ingenuity, the reproductive processes were affected for a time; men became sterile, women had miscarriages, menstruation stopped.

For ten days after the flood, Dr. Fujii lived in the peasant's house on the mountain above the Ota. Then he heard about a vacant private clinic in Kaitaichi, a suburb to the east of Hiroshima. He bought it at once, moved there, and hung out a sign inscribed in English, in honor of the conquerors:

M. FUJII, M.D.
MEDICAL & VENEREAL

Quite recovered from his wounds, he soon built up a strong practice, and he was delighted, in the evenings, to receive members of the occupying forces, on whom he lavished whiskey and practiced English.

Giving Miss Sasaki a local anaesthetic of procaine, Dr. Sasaki made an incision in her leg on October 23rd, to drain the infection, which still lingered on eleven weeks after the injury. In the following days, so much pus formed that he had to dress the opening each morning and evening. A week later, she complained of great pain, so he made another incision; he cut still a third, on November 9th, and enlarged it on the twenty-sixth. All this time, Miss Sasaki grew weaker and weaker, and her spirits fell low. One day, the young man who had lent her his translation of de Maupassant at Hatsukaichi came to visit her; he told her that he was going to Kyushu but that when he came back, he would like to see her again. She didn't care. Her leg had been so swollen and painful all along that the doctor had not even tried to set the fractures, and though an X-ray taken in November showed that the bones were mending, she could see under the sheet that her left leg was nearly three inches shorter than her right and that her left foot was turning inward. She thought often of the man to whom she had been engaged. Someone told her he was back from overseas. She wondered what he had heard about her injuries that made him stay away.

Father Kleinsorge was discharged from the hospital in Tokyo on December 19th and took a train home. On the way, two days later, at Yokogawa, a stop just before Hiroshima, Dr. Fujii boarded the train. It was the first time the two men had met since before the bombing. They sat together. Dr. Fujii said he was going to the annual gathering of his family, on the anniversary of his father's death. When they started talking about their experiences, the Doctor was quite entertaining as he told how his places of residence kept falling into rivers. Then he asked Father Kleinsorge how he was, and the Jesuit talked about his stay in the hospital. "The doctors told me to be cautious," he said. "They ordered me to have a two-hour nap every afternoon."

Dr. Fujii said, "It's hard to be cautious in Hiroshima these days. Everyone seems to be so busy."

A new municipal government, set up under Allied Military Government direction, had gone to work at last in the city hall. Citizens who had recovered from various degrees of radiation sickness were coming back by the thousand—by

November 1st, the population, mostly crowded into the outskirts, was already 137,000, more than a third of the wartime peak—and the government set in motion all kinds of projects to put them to work rebuilding the city. It hired men to clear the streets, and others to gather scrap iron, which they sorted and piled in mountains opposite the city hall. Some returning residents were putting up their own shanties and huts, and planting small squares of winter wheat beside them, but the city also authorized and built four hundred one-family "barracks." Utilities were repaired—electric lights shone again, trams started running, and employees of the waterworks fixed seventy thousand leaks in mains and plumbing. A Planning Conference, with an enthusiastic young Military Government officer, Lieutenant John D. Montgomery, of Kalamazoo, as its adviser, began to consider what sort of city the new Hiroshima should be. The ruined city had flourished—and had been an inviting target—mainly because it had been one of the most important military-command and communications centers in Japan, and would have become the Imperial headquarters had the islands been invaded and Tokyo been captured. Now there would be no huge military establishments to help revive the city. The Planning Conference, at a loss as to just what importance Hiroshima could have, fell back on rather vague cultural and paving projects. It drew maps with avenues a hundred yards wide and thought seriously of preserving the half-ruined Museum of Science and Industry more or less as it was, as a monument to the disaster, and naming it the Institute of International Amity. Statistical workers gathered what figures they could on the effects of the bomb. They reported that 78,150 people had been killed, 13,983 were missing, and 37,425 had been injured. No one in the city government pretended that these figures were accurate—though the Americans accepted them as official—and as the months went by and more and more hundreds of corpses were dug up from the ruins, and as the number of unclaimed urns of ashes at the Zempoji Temple in Koi rose into the thousands, the statisticians began to say that at least a hundred thousand people had lost their lives in the bombing. Since many people died of a combination of causes, it was impossible to figure exactly how many were killed by each cause, but the statisticians calculated that about twenty-five per cent had died of direct burns from the bomb, about fifty per cent from other injuries, and about twenty per cent as a result of radiation effects. The statisticians' figures on property damage were more reliable: sixty-two thousand out of ninety thousand buildings destroyed, and six thousand more damaged beyond repair. In the heart of the city, they found only five modern buildings that could be used again without major repairs. This small number was by no means the fault of flimsy Japanese construction. In fact, since the 1923 earthquake, Japanese building regulations had required that the roof of each large building be able to bear a minimum load of seventy pounds per square foot, whereas American regulations do not normally specify more than forty pounds per square foot.

Scientists swarmed into the city. Some of them measured the force that had been necessary to shift marble gravestones in the cemeteries, to knock over twenty-two of the forty-seven railroad cars in the yards at Hiroshima station, to lift and move the concrete roadway on one of the bridges, and to perform other noteworthy acts of strength, and concluded that the pressure exerted by the explosion varied from 5.3 to 8.0 tons per square yard. Others found that mica, of which the melting point is 900° C., had fused on granite gravestones three hundred and eighty yards from the center; that telephone poles of *Cryptomeria japonica*, whose carbonization temperature is 240° C., had been charred at forty-four hundred yards from the center; and that the surface of gray clay tiles of the type used in Hiroshima, whose melting point is 1,300° C., had dissolved at six hundred yards; and, after examining other significant ashes and melted bits, they concluded that the bomb's heat on the ground at the center must have been 6,000° C. And from further measurements of radiation, which involved, among other things, the scraping up of fission fragments from roof troughs and drainpipes as far away as the suburb of Takasu, thirty-three hundred yards from the center, they learned some far more important facts about the nature of the bomb. General MacArthur's headquarters systematically censored all mention of the bomb in Japanese scientific publications, but soon the fruit of the scientists' calculations became common knowledge among Japanese physicists, doctors, chemists, journalists, professors, and, no doubt, those statesmen and military men who were still in circulation. Long before the American public had been told, most of the scientists and lots of non-scientists in Japan knew—from the calculations of Japanese nuclear physicists—that a uranium bomb had exploded at Hiroshima and a more powerful one, of plutonium, at Nagasaki. They also knew that theoretically one ten times as powerful—or twenty—could be developed. The Japanese scientists thought they knew the exact height at which the bomb at Hiroshima was exploded and the approximate weight of the uranium used. They estimated that, even with the primitive bomb used at Hiroshima, it would require a shelter of concrete fifty inches thick to protect a human being entirely from radiation sickness. The scientists had these and other details which remained subject to security in the United States printed and mimeographed and bound into little books. The Americans knew of the existence of these, but tracing them and seeing that they did not fall into the wrong hands would have obliged the occupying authorities to set up, for this one purpose alone, an enormous police system in Japan. Altogether, the Japanese scientists were somewhat amused at the efforts of their conquerors to keep security on atomic fission.

Late in February, 1946, a friend of Miss Sasaki's called on Father Kleinsorge and asked him to visit her in the hospital. She had been growing more and more depressed and morbid; she seemed little interested in living. Father Kleinsorge went to see her several times. On his first visit, he kept the conversation general, formal, and yet vaguely sympathetic, and did not mention religion. Miss Sasaki herself brought it up the second time he dropped in on her. Evidently she had had some talks with a Catholic. She asked bluntly, "If your God is so good and kind, how can he let people suffer like this?" She made a gesture which took in her shrunken leg, the other patients in her room, and Hiroshima as a whole.

"My child," Father Kleinsorge said, "man is not now in the condition God intended. He has fallen from grace through sin." And he went on to explain all the reasons for everything.

*　　*　　*

It came to Mrs. Nakamura's attention that a carpenter
from Kabe was building a number of wooden shanties in Hiroshima which he rented for fifty yen a month—$3.33, at the
fixed rate of exchange. Mrs. Nakamura had lost the certifi-
cates for her bonds and other wartime savings, but fortunately
she had copied off all the numbers just a few days before the
bombing and had taken the list to Kabe, and so, when her
hair had grown in enough for her to be presentable, she went
to her bank in Hiroshima, and a clerk there told her that after
checking her numbers against the records the bank would
give her her money. As soon as she got it, she rented one of
the carpenter's shacks. It was in Nobori-cho, near the site of
her former house, and though its floor was dirt and it was
dark inside, it was at least a home in Hiroshima, and she was
no longer dependent on the charity of her in-laws. During the
spring, she cleared away some nearby wreckage and planted a
vegetable garden. She cooked with utensils and ate off plates
she scavenged from the debris. She sent Myeko to the kindergarten which the Jesuits reopened, and the two older children
attended Nobori-cho Primary School, which, for want of
buildings, held classes out of doors. Toshio wanted to study
to be a mechanic, like his hero, Hideo Osaki. Prices were
high; by midsummer Mrs. Nakamura's savings were gone.
She sold some of her clothes to get food. She had once had
several expensive kimonos, but during the war one had been
stolen, she had given one to a sister who had been bombed
out in Tokuyama, she had lost a couple in the Hiroshima
bombing, and now she sold her last one. It brought only a
hundred yen, which did not last long. In June, she went to
Father Kleinsorge for advice about how to get along, and in
early August, she was still considering the two alternatives he
suggested—taking work as a domestic for some of the Allied
occupation forces, or borrowing from her relatives enough
money, about five hundred yen, or a bit more than thirty
dollars, to repair her rusty sewing machine and resume the
work of a seamstress.

When Mr. Tanimoto returned from Shikoku, he draped a tent
he owned over the roof of the badly damaged house he had
rented in Ushida. The roof still leaked, but he conducted ser-

vices in the damp living room. He began thinking about raising money to restore his church in the city. He became quite friendly with Father Kleinsorge and saw the Jesuits often. He envied them their Church's wealth; they seemed to be able to do anything they wanted. He had nothing to work with except his own energy, and that was not what it had been.

The Society of Jesus had been the first institution to build a relatively permanent shanty in the ruins of Hiroshima. That had been while Father Kleinsorge was in the hospital. As soon as he got back, he began living in the shack, and he and another priest, Father Laderman, who had joined him in the mission, arranged for the purchase of three of the standardized "barracks," which the city was selling at seven thousand yen apiece. They put two together, end to end, and made a pretty chapel of them; they ate in the third. When materials were available, they commissioned a contractor to build a three-story mission house exactly like the one that had been destroyed in the fire. In the compound, carpenters cut timbers, gouged mortises, shaped tenons, whittled scores of wooden pegs and bored holes for them, until all the parts for the house were in a neat pile; then, in three days, they put the whole thing together, like an Oriental puzzle, without any nails at all. Father Kleinsorge was finding it hard, as Dr. Fujii had suggested he would, to be cautious and to take his naps. He went out every day on foot to call on Japanese Catholics and prospective converts. As the months went by, he grew more and more tired. In June, he read an article in the Hiroshima *Chugoku* warning survivors against working too hard—but what could he do? By July, he was worn out, and early in August, almost exactly on the anniversary of the bombing, he went back to the Catholic International Hospital, in Tokyo, for a month's rest.

Whether or not Father Kleinsorge's answers to Miss Sasaki's questions about life were final and absolute truths, she seemed quickly to draw physical strength from them. Dr. Sasaki noticed it and congratulated Father Kleinsorge. By April 15th, her temperature and white count were normal and the infection in the wound was beginning to clear up. On the twentieth, there was almost no pus, and for the first time she jerked along a corridor on crutches. Five days later, the wound had begun to heal, and on the last day of the month she was discharged.

During the early summer, she prepared herself for conversion to Catholicism. In that period she had ups and downs. Her depressions were deep. She knew she would always be a cripple. Her fiancé never came to see her. There was nothing for her to do except read and look out, from her house on a hillside in Koi, across the ruins of the city where her parents and brother died. She was nervous, and any sudden noise made her put her hands quickly to her throat. Her leg still hurt; she rubbed it often and patted it, as if to console it.

It took six months for the Red Cross Hospital, and even longer for Dr. Sasaki, to get back to normal. Until the city restored electric power, the hospital had to limp along with the aid of a Japanese Army generator in its back yard. Operating tables, X-ray machines, dentist chairs, everything complicated and essential came in a trickle of charity from other cities. In Japan, face is important even to institutions, and long before the Red Cross Hospital was back to par on basic medical equipment, its directors put up a new yellow brick veneer façade, so the hospital became the handsomest building in Hiroshima—from the street. For the first four months, Dr. Sasaki was the only surgeon on the staff and he almost never left the building; then, gradually, he began to take an interest in his own life again. He got married in March. He gained back some of the weight he lost, but his appetite remained only fair; before the bombing, he used to eat four rice balls at every meal, but a year after it he could manage only two. He felt tired all the time. "But I have to realize," he said, "that the whole community is tired."

A year after the bomb was dropped, Miss Sasaki was a cripple; Mrs. Nakamura was destitute; Father Kleinsorge was back in the hospital; Dr. Sasaki was not capable of the work he once could do; Dr. Fujii had lost the thirty-room hospital it took him many years to acquire, and had no prospects of rebuilding it; Mr. Tanimoto's church had been ruined and he no longer had his exceptional vitality. The lives of these six people, who were among the luckiest in Hiroshima, would never be the same. What they thought of their experiences and of the use of the atomic bomb was, of course, not unanimous. One feeling they did seem to share, however, was a curious kind of elated community spirit, something like that of the Londoners after their blitz—a pride in the way they and their fellow-survivors had stood up to a dreadful ordeal. Just before the anniversary, Mr. Tanimoto wrote in a letter to an American some words which expressed this feeling: "What a heartbreaking scene this was the first night! About midnight I landed on the riverbank. So many injured people lied on the ground that I made my way by striding over them. Repeating 'Excuse me,' I forwarded and carried a tub of water with me and gave a cup of water to each one of them. They raised their upper bodies slowly and accepted a cup of water with a bow and drunk quietly and, spilling any remnant, gave back a cup with hearty expression of their thankfulness, and said, 'I couldn't help my sister, who was buried under the house, because I had to take care of my mother who got a deep wound on her eye and our house soon set fire and we hardly escaped. Look, I lost my home, my family, and at last my-self bitterly injured. But now I have gotted my mind to dedicate what I have and to complete the war for our country's sake.' Thus they pledged to me, even women and children did the same. Being entirely tired I lied down on the ground among them, but couldn't sleep at all. Next morning I found many men and women dead, whom I gave water last night. But, to my great surprise, I never heard any one cried in disorder, even though they suffered in great agony. They died in silence, with no grudge, setting their teeth to bear it. All for the country!

"Dr. Y. Hiraiwa, professor of Hiroshima University of Literature and Science, and one of my church members, was buried by the bomb under the two storied house with his son, a student of Tokyo University. Both of them could not move an inch under tremendously heavy pressure. And the house already caught fire. His son said, 'Father, we can do nothing except make our mind up to consecrate our lives for the country. Let us give *Banzai* to our Emperor.' Then the father followed after his son, *'Tenno-heika, Banzai, Banzai, Banzai!'* In the result, Dr. Hiraiwa said, 'Strange to say, I felt calm and bright and peaceful spirit in my heart, when I chanted *Banzai* to Tenno.' Afterward his son got out and digged down and pulled out his father and thus they were saved. In thinking of their experience of that time Dr. Hiraiwa repeated, 'What a fortunate that we are Japanese! It was my first time I ever tasted such a beautiful spirit when I decided to die for our Emperor.'

"Miss Kayoko Nobutoki, a student of girl's high school, Hiroshima Jazabuin, and a daughter of my church member, was taking rest with her friends beside the heavy fence of the Buddhist Temple. At the moment the atomic bomb was dropped, the fence fell upon them. They could not move a bit under such a heavy fence and then smoke entered into even a crack and choked their breath. One of the girls begun to sing *Kimi ga yo*, national anthem, and others followed in chorus and died. Meanwhile one of them found a crack and struggled hard to get out. When she was taken in the Red Cross Hospital she told how her friends died, tracing back in her memory to singing in chorus our national anthem. They were just 13 years old.

"Yes, people of Hiroshima died manly in the atomic bombing, believing that it was for Emperor's sake."

A surprising number of the people of Hiroshima remained more or less indifferent about the ethics of using the bomb. Possibly they were too terrified by it to want to think about it at all. Not many of them even bothered to find out much about what it was like. Mrs. Nakamura's conception of it—and awe of it—was typical. "The atom bomb," she would say when asked about it, "is the size of a matchbox. The heat of it is six thousand times that of the sun. It exploded in the air. There is some radium in it. I don't know just how it works, but when the radium is put together, it explodes." As for the use of the bomb, she would say, "It was war and we had to expect it." And then she would add, *"Shikata ga nai,"* a Japanese expression as common as, and corresponding to, the Russian word *"nichevo"*: "It can't be helped. Oh, well. Too bad." Dr. Fujii said approximately the same thing about the use of the bomb to Father Kleinsorge one evening, in German: "*Da ist nichts zu machen.* There's nothing to be done about it."

Many citizens of Hiroshima, however, continued to feel a hatred for Americans which nothing could possibly erase. "I see," Dr. Sasaki once said, "that they are holding a trial for war criminals in Tokyo just now. I think they ought to try the men who decided to use the bomb and they should hang them all."

Father Kleinsorge and the other German Jesuit priests, who, as foreigners, could be expected to take a relatively detached view, often discussed the ethics of using the bomb. One of them, Father Siemes, who was out at Nagatsuka at the time of the attack, wrote in a report to the Holy See in Rome, "Some of us consider the bomb in the same category as poison gas and were against its use on a civilian population. Others were of the opinion that in total war, as carried on in Japan, there was no difference between civilians and soldiers, and that the bomb itself was an effective force tending to end the bloodshed, warning Japan to surrender and thus to avoid total destruction. It seems logical that he who supports total war in principal cannot complain of a war against civilians. The crux of the matter is whether total war in its present form is justifiable, even when it serves a just purpose. Does it not have material and spiritual evil as its consequences which far exceed whatever good might result? When will our moralists give us a clear answer to this question?"

It would be impossible to say what horrors were embedded in the minds of the children who lived through the day of the bombing in Hiroshima. On the surface their recollections, months after the disaster, were of an exhilarating adventure. Toshio Nakamura, who was ten at the time of the bombing, was soon able to talk freely, even gaily, about the experience, and a few weeks before the anniversary he wrote the following matter-of-fact essay for his teacher at Nobori-cho Primary School: "The day before the bomb, I went for a swim. In the morning, I was eating peanuts. I saw a light. I was knocked to little sister's sleeping place. When we were saved, I could only see as far as the tram. My mother and I started to pack our things. The neighbors were walking around burned and bleeding. Hataya-*san* told me to run away with her. I said I wanted to wait for my mother. We went to the park. A whirlwind came. At night a gas tank burned and I saw the reflection in the river. We stayed in the park one night. Next day I went to Taiko Bridge and met my girl friends Kikuki and Murakami. They were looking for their mothers. But Kikuki's mother was wounded and Murakami's mother, alas, was dead."

The New Yorker, August 31, 1946

Chronology, 1933–1945

Adolf Hitler, leader since 1921 of the National Socialist German Workers' (Nazi) Party, is named chancellor of Germany by President Paul von Hindenburg on January 30, heading cabinet with only two other Nazi members. (Appointment is result of agreement between Hitler and small group of right-wing politicians and military leaders, who hope that Nazis will provide popular support for an authoritarian government dominated by traditional conservatives and the army.) Hitler dissolves Reichstag (parliament), in which Nazis hold almost 34 percent of the seats, and calls for new election. Using emergency decree powers of the 1919 Weimar constitution and exploiting their control of the Prussian state police, Nazis begin campaign of violence and intimidation directed against Communists and Social Democrats. Following destruction of Reichstag chamber by arson on February 27, emergency decree is issued suspending all civil liberties and allowing indefinite detention without trial. In election on March 5, Nazis win 44 percent of Reichstag seats. On March 23 Reichstag approves, 441–94, enabling act that allows Hitler unilaterally to alter the constitution and enact legislation (dissenting votes are from Social Democrats; all of the Communist deputies have been arrested). Nazis begin purging civil service and educational institutions of Jews and political opponents and take control of trade unions, civil organizations, and local and state governments throughout Germany. Decree issued July 14 makes Nazis only legal party in Germany. Germany withdraws from League of Nations and Geneva Disarmament Conference on October 14. Hitler continues policy, begun by military in early 1920s, of clandestinely circumventing 1919 Versailles Peace Treaty, which limited German army to 100,000 men and prohibited it from possessing tanks or aircraft.

1934 Tensions increase between Hitler and leadership of the SA ("Storm Detachment," Nazi party paramilitary force), who seek greater share of power and more radical social and economic change. With support from the army, Hitler has SA leaders and several other political opponents shot without trial, June 30–July 2. Hindenburg dies on August 1 and Hitler is proclaimed Führer ("Leader") of Germany; military and civil service personnel swear personal oath of allegiance to him on August 2. Purge of SA makes the SS ("Protection Detachment," originally Hitler's Nazi party bodyguard) the main instrument of terror in Germany (in 1936 SS is given control of all German police).

1935   Hitler reintroduces military conscription on March 16 and announces that Germany will no longer honor military restrictions of Versailles Treaty. Britain and Germany conclude naval pact on June 18 that allows Germany to contravene Versailles Treaty by building surface ships over 10,000 tons and U-boats (submarines). "Nuremberg laws" enacted in September deprive German Jews of their remaining citizenship rights and make marriages between Jews and non-Jews a criminal offense.

Italy, ruled by Fascist dictator Benito Mussolini since 1922, invades Ethiopia on October 3. League of Nations votes limited economic sanctions against Italy in October but does not impose oil embargo.

1936   Ultranationalist Japanese army officers stage coup attempt in Tokyo, February 26, that is quickly suppressed by army high command. Incident weakens civilian government in Japan and strengthens influence of generals favoring further expansion in China (Japanese had seized Manchuria in 1931 and part of northeast China in 1933).

Hitler reoccupies German Rhineland, an area demilitarized under the Versailles Treaty, on March 7; France and Britain take no action.

Italian army completes conquest of Ethiopia on May 6. League of Nations votes July 4 to lift sanctions against Italy.

Civil war begins in Spain on July 17 with army rebellion against elected left-wing Republican government. Italy and Germany move quickly to support insurgents with arms, transport, and troops (at their peak Italian forces in Spain number 50,000; German forces reach 10,000, including strong air force contingent that gains valuable experience). Soviet Union begins supplying arms and military specialists to the Republican government in autumn, and directs Communist parties to organize International Brigades of foreign volunteers. Britain, France, and the United States adopt policy of nonintervention.

1937   Eight prominent generals are executed in Moscow on June 12 on false charges of treason as Joseph Stalin, general secretary of the Soviet Communist party since 1922, begins purge of Soviet military (by late 1938 over 80 percent of the senior commanders in the Soviet army will have been shot or imprisoned; victims include many key proponents of modern mechanized warfare).

Fighting breaks out near Peking on July 7 between Chinese troops and Japanese legation garrison, and by the end of July Japanese troops control the Peking-Tientsin region. Chinese Nationalist leader Chiang Kai-shek orders attack on Japanese zone in Shanghai on August 14, leading to full-scale Sino-Japanese war.

Japanese army breaks through Chinese lines at Shanghai in November and enters Nanking, Chinese Nationalist capital, on December 13; its capture is followed by weeks of widespread killing, rape, and looting in which at least 40,000 Chinese die.

1938   German army occupies Austria without opposition on March 12, and on March 13 Germany annexes Austria in violation of the Versailles Treaty. Britain and France take no action. Hitler begins planning invasion of Czechoslovakia and launches propaganda campaign protesting alleged persecution of Germans in the Sudetenland (border regions of Bohemia and Moravia, which contain frontier fortifications essential to Czech defense). Neville Chamberlain, Conservative prime minister of Great Britain since May 1937 and leading proponent of conciliatory "appeasement" policy toward Germany, presses Czech government to make concessions to Sudeten Germans while declaring that Britain and France will fight Germany if it attacks Czechoslovakia (France has treaty of alliance with Czechoslovakia; Soviet Union is committed to assisting Czechoslovakia once France takes military action). Hitler escalates threats against Czechoslovakia in September. Chamberlain goes to Germany twice to negotiate with Hitler, while French and Soviet governments are unable to agree on response to crisis. French army and British navy begin partial mobilization, September 24-27, as German military prepares to attack Czechoslovakia on September 30. Chamberlain, French premier Édouard Daladier, Mussolini, and Hitler meet in Munich, September 29-30, and agree that Czechoslovakia will cede Sudetenland to Germany; Hitler and Chamberlain also sign declaration of Anglo-German friendship. Chamberlain returns to England and declares that agreement will bring "peace in our time." German army enters Sudetenland on October 1. Britain and Germany accelerate rearmament efforts, and Hitler plans invasion of remainder of Czechoslovakia.

After five-month battle, Japanese capture Wuhan in central China on October 25; by end of year Sino-Japanese war approaches stalemate as Japanese consolidate their conquests.

Nazi party carries out pogrom throughout Germany, November 9-10, in which 91 German Jews are killed; in its aftermath, 26,000 Jews are sent to concentration camps, and expropriation of Jewish property is intensified (pogrom becomes known as "Kristallnacht," from the broken glass of Jewish-owned shop windows).

1939   German army occupies Czechoslovakia on March 15 in violation of Munich Pact. Bohemia and Moravia become German protectorate, Slovakia a German satellite state; Hungary annexes

Ruthenia. Under threat of attack, Lithuania cedes city of Memel to Germany on March 23. Spanish civil war ends March 29 with victory of insurgent Nationalist regime led by General Francisco Franco. Chamberlain abandons appeasement policy after seizure of Czechoslovakia, and on March 31 declares that Britain and France will defend Poland against aggression.

Apr.–May   Hitler orders preparations for attack on Poland completed by September 1. Italy occupies Albania on April 7. Germany and Italy sign military alliance on May 22. Soviet and Japanese troops clash in disputed Khalkhin Gol region along Mongolian-Manchurian border in late May; both sides send reinforcements, and fighting continues for three months.

June–Aug.   Britain, France, and the Soviet Union are unable to agree on terms for an alliance. Soviet offensive in late August drives Japanese from Khalkhin Gol region (cease-fire is declared September 16; Soviet victory will contribute to Japanese decision not to attack Soviet Union in summer 1941). Germany and Soviet Union sign nonaggression pact on August 23 containing secret protocol partitioning Poland and establishing spheres of influence in eastern Europe.

Sept.   Germany invades Poland September 1. Italy declares neutrality despite alliance with Germany. Britain, Australia, New Zealand, and France declare war on Germany September 3 (South Africa and Canada declare war by September 10). Winston Churchill, severest critic of Chamberlain appeasement policy, joins British cabinet as First Lord of the Admiralty. Britain begins naval blockade of Germany. President Franklin D. Roosevelt signs American neutrality proclamation on September 5 after expressing sympathy for Allied cause in radio address. Luftwaffe (German air force) achieves air superiority over Poland, and German army advances rapidly despite determined Polish resistance. Soviets invade eastern Poland on September 17. Warsaw falls to Germans September 27, and fighting in Poland ends October 6. (New Polish government is formed in exile; its air, land, and naval forces will fight with Allies until end of the war.) SS units in Poland begin committing widespread atrocities. Allies do not attack into western Germany, fearing that assault against frontier fortifications would be repulsed with heavy losses and hoping that blockade will eventually cause German economic collapse. Numerically weaker German navy does not attempt to break blockade, but begins attacking British commerce (although Germans begin war with less than 30 U-boats capable of operating in the Atlantic, Allies will lose over 2 million tons of merchant shipping to U-boats, surface ships, mines, and aircraft by end of June 1940; Germans lose 24 U-boats in first ten months of war). Hitler orders planning for attack in western Europe.

General George C. Marshall, new U.S. Army Chief of Staff, begins planning expansion and modernization of the army, which has less than 200,000 men on active service (German army has mobilized over 2,700,000).

Oct.   Hitler orders killing of mentally and physically handicapped Germans (over 100,000 such persons will be systematically murdered before killings are suspended in August 1941). Soviets press Finnish government to make territorial concessions. British codebreakers continue work begun by Poles in 1930s on Enigma machine used by German armed forces to cipher radio messages (by late May 1940 British are able to break some Luftwaffe Enigma ciphers on daily basis).

Nov.–Dec.   U.S. neutrality law is modified on November 4 to allow Britain and France to purchase munitions and transport them in their own shipping. Soviet Union invades Finland November 30. Initial Soviet attacks are unsuccessful due to poor training, tactics, and leadership, and Finnish superiority at winter warfare.

1940   Reinforced and reorganized Soviet forces launch successful offensive against Finns in February. Finland signs armistice, March 13, yielding border territory to Soviets. Paul Reynaud succeeds Daladier as premier of France on March 21.

April   Germans invade Denmark and Norway (both neutral countries) April 9, beginning campaign designed to obtain northern naval bases and safeguard shipments of Swedish iron ore along Norwegian coast. Denmark is occupied without resistance. Attacks by sea and air against Norwegian ports and airfields achieve surprise, but despite initial confusion and loss of Oslo, Norwegian forces resist. British navy and air force attack German ships, and British troops begin landing in Norway April 14 (later joined by French and Polish forces). Germans win air superiority and Allies are unable to prevent German capture of key objectives.

Germans begin confining Polish Jews in ghettos.

May   British and French troops are evacuated from central Norway in early May; fighting continues in the north. After bitter parliamentary debate over Norwegian campaign, Chamberlain resigns May 10 and is replaced as prime minister by Churchill, who forms coalition government with opposition Labour party. Germans invade the Netherlands, Belgium, and Luxembourg (all neutral countries) on May 10 and launch heavy air attacks against France. British and French send strong forces into Belgium and the Netherlands, where they take up defensive positions. Allies fail to detect movement of concentrated German armor through the Ardennes, and Germans break through French positions along the Meuse River at Sedan on May 13.

Dutch army capitulates, May 15, after heavy German bombing of Rotterdam. German armored formations rapidly advance across northeastern France with close support from the Luftwaffe, which has achieved air superiority. French army, which has dispersed most of its tanks along the front in small units, is unable to mount effective counterattacks. Germans reach English Channel near Abbeville on May 20, completing encirclement of British and French armies in Belgium. After attempts to break encirclement fail, British begin evacuating troops from Dunkirk on May 27. Belgian army capitulates May 28 as Germans continue attacks on trapped Allied forces (Belgian and Dutch governments have gone into exile in Britain).

June
Dunkirk evacuation ends June 4 after approximately 225,000 British and 110,000 French troops are rescued; all of their heavy weapons and equipment are abandoned. Germans launch new offensive June 5 and break through French defensive line along Somme and Aisne rivers. Allies evacuate remaining troops from northern Norway June 8, and Norwegian government-in-exile orders its army to cease fighting on June 9. Italy declares war on France and Britain June 10. German army enters Paris on June 14. New French government headed by Marshal Philippe Pétain asks for armistice on June 17. Brigadier General Charles de Gaulle flies to England and organizes Free French movement. Armistice between France and Germany is signed June 22. Germans occupy northern France and Atlantic coast; Pétain establishes collaborationist regime (known as "Vichy," after its capital) with authority over unoccupied southern zone, North Africa, and other French colonies overseas.

Soviets occupy Lithuania on June 15 and force Romania to cede Bessarabia and northern Bukovina on June 27 (Soviet annexation of Lithuania, Latvia, and Estonia is completed by August 3, 1940).

Churchill government moves toward full mobilization of British society and economy for prolonged war and maximum military production, while Hitler directs that German economy continue to give high priority to production of goods for civilian consumption; German war production also suffers from confused planning and expectation that war will not be prolonged. (In 1940–41 Britain produces 6,200 tanks and self-propelled guns and 35,000 military aircraft, while Germany manufactures 5,400 tanks and self-propelled guns and 22,000 military aircraft.)

U.S. Congress approves major expansion of armed forces in response to German victories, but public opinion remains divided over extent to which U.S. should aid Britain. American arms production increases rapidly to fill orders from Britain and U.S. military.

July   British demand on July 3 that French fleet based at Mers-el-Kebir in Algeria take immediate action to ensure that its ships will not fall under German control. When French commander obeys order from Vichy to reject ultimatum, British ships open fire, destroying or damaging three battleships and killing over 1,200 French sailors. British and Italians begin prolonged naval struggle for control of Mediterranean.

Heavy air fighting begins between Luftwaffe and Royal Air Force (RAF) in early July as Germans attack Channel ports and convoys. Germans begin planning invasion of England; weakness of German navy, increased by serious losses in Norwegian campaign, makes achievement of air superiority over southern England essential. RAF and Luftwaffe fighter planes are roughly equal in number and performance, and British fighter production is higher; although Luftwaffe has more trained pilots, their fighters have limited range that allows them to escort bombers only over southern England. Revolutionary RAF air defense system allows commanders to control interception of enemy formations using information from radar (invented in Britain in 1935 and still secret in 1940) and ground observers.

Germans use naval and air bases along French coast to renew offensive against British commerce in the Atlantic, sinking over 5 million tons between July 1940 and June 1941 while losing only 20 U-boats. Loss of merchant shipping poses serious threat to British ability to wage war.

British form commando units for conducting coastal raids and begin working with exile governments to organize and supply resistance movements in occupied Europe (resistance movements will engage in espionage, sabotage, propaganda, and occasionally partisan warfare; Germans respond with indiscriminate reprisals).

In late July Hitler directs planning to begin for invasion of Soviet Union in 1941, intending to deprive Britain of possible ally and fulfill long-standing ambition of conquering "living space" (*Lebensraum*) for Germany in the east. Soviets continue supplying large amounts of raw materials to Germany while consolidating control over newly acquired territory.

Konoye Fumimaro becomes prime minister of Japan on July 17. New cabinet, which includes General Tojo Hideki as war minister, decides to seek alliance with Germany and Italy, isolate Nationalist China from foreign supplies, and pursue aggressive policy against vulnerable French and Dutch colonies in Southeast Asia in order to secure sources of oil, rubber, tin, and other raw materials.

Aug.   Luftwaffe begins offensive against RAF fighter airfields and air defense headquarters on August 13. Although German aircraft losses are higher than British, by end of August damage to airfields and attrition of fighter pilots places severe strain on RAF.

Sept.   In attempt to damage British morale and draw out remaining RAF fighters, Luftwaffe begins heavy bombing of London on September 7; switch in targets gives respite to RAF airfields. Battle of Britain reaches climax on September 15, when British destroy 60 aircraft while losing 26. Hitler indefinitely postpones invasion on September 17.

Under executive agreement concluded September 2, U.S. sends 50 old destroyers to Britain in return for bases in British territories in the Western Hemisphere (British are in severe need of escort vessels for convoys). Roosevelt signs act on September 16 establishing first peacetime draft in American history; law requires draftees to serve for only one year.

Italian army in Libya invades Egypt on September 13 and advances 60 miles before halting.

Under Japanese pressure, Vichy French agree on September 22 to allow Japan to station troops and aircraft in northern Indochina. U.S. responds with embargo of iron and steel scrap exports to Japan. Germany, Italy, and Japan sign Tripartite Pact, designed to deter the U.S. from entering the war in Europe or Asia, on September 27.

Oct.–Nov.   Germans gradually end daylight raids and begin intensive night bombing of London and other cities in campaign ("The Blitz") that continues into May 1941. Luftwaffe loses over 1,700 aircraft in Battle of Britain, July 10–October 31, 1940, the RAF over 900. RAF engages in limited night bombing of Germany. Hitler and Franco meet on October 23 and are unable to agree on terms for Spain to enter the war against Britain. Italy invades Greece October 28. Greek army repels attack and advances into Albania by the end of 1940. British carrier aircraft destroy or damage three Italian battleships in night raid on Taranto harbor, November 11–12.

Roosevelt is reelected for unprecedented third term on November 5.

Dec.   British and Indian troops in Egypt begin successful offensive against Italians on December 9 (Indian, Australian, New Zealand, South African, and Canadian troops comprise major portion of forces under British command throughout campaigns in the Mediterranean).

Hitler issues directive on December 18 for German invasion of Soviet Union in late spring 1941, with objective of capturing Leningrad, Moscow, and Kiev by early autumn. Encouraged by Stalin's 1937–38 purge of the army and poor Soviet performance in Finnish war, German high command expects to destroy

Soviet army during summer in series of encirclement battles near frontier.

1941   British begin series of offensives against Italians in Ethiopia and Somalia on January 19 (last Italian garrison in Ethiopia surrenders November 28, 1941).

British advance in North Africa stops at El Agheila in Libya on February 9 after capturing 130,000 Italian prisoners in two months; British, Indian, and Australian troops in campaign never total more than about 30,000. German forces land in Libya as British send troops and aircraft from North Africa to Greece.

In response to worsening British financial crisis, Roosevelt administration proposes Lend-Lease bill, which authorizes U.S. government to purchase war materials and then "lend" or "lease" them to Allied nations. House of Representatives passes bill by 260–165 vote on February 8.

March   After Senate passes Lend-Lease by 60–31, Roosevelt signs bill into law on March 11 (most Lend-Lease aid is never repaid in any form).

British sink three Italian cruisers and two destroyers off Greece in Battle of Cape Matapan, March 28–29, and achieve ascendancy over Italian navy in the Mediterranean. Germans and Italians (Axis) launch offensive in Libya on March 31 and drive British back to Egyptian border.

April   Coup in Iraq brings pro-German government to power (new regime is ousted by Allied military intervention, May 30, as British act to protect Persian Gulf oil fields). Germans invade Yugoslavia and Greece April 6. Yugoslavia surrenders April 17 and is partitioned into German, Italian, Hungarian, and Bulgarian zones; Germans also establish Serbian and Croatian puppet regimes. (Two rival resistance movements, the Serbian nationalist Chetniks and the Partisans, formed by Communist leader Tito, begin fighting Axis forces and each other in 1941.) Germans achieve air superiority in Greece and advance rapidly. British begin evacuating troops April 24. Germans capture Athens April 27, and country is occupied by Germans, Italians, and Bulgarians.

Stalin receives warnings of impending German attack from Soviet, British, and American sources, but dismisses them as British "provocations" designed to involve Soviets in war with Germany.

Roosevelt orders U.S. navy on April 10 to patrol into mid-Atlantic and report sightings of German ships to Allies.

U.S. and Japanese diplomats begin informal talks in Washington. Japan and Soviet Union sign neutrality pact on April 13. Roosevelt signs executive order on April 15 permitting pilots to resign from the U.S. armed forces and volunteer for combat service in China (American Volunteer Group, later known as the

"Flying Tigers," begins operations in late December 1941 and becomes part of U.S. army air forces in summer 1942).

May   Intensive bombing of Britain ends as Luftwaffe redeploys to the eastern front; British civilian deaths from bombing exceed 40,000.

Germans begin airborne invasion of Crete on May 20 and win battle for island June 1 after intense fighting. British are able to evacuate most of their troops despite heavy German air attacks. (German aircraft and U-boats inflict serious losses on British navy in Mediterranean in 1941–42.)

Sinking of German battleship *Bismarck* by the Royal Navy on May 27 ends Atlantic commerce raiding by large surface ships (in 1942 all large German warships are withdrawn to Germany or Norway, where they operate against convoys to Soviet Union with little success; limited raiding by armed merchant ships continues until autumn 1943).

U.S. begins sending Lend-Lease supplies to Nationalist China.

June   British invade Vichy-controlled Syria and Lebanon on June 8 (Vichy forces surrender July 11).

Germans invade Soviet Union on June 22, attacking with 3 million men (Soviet army has about 5 million men overall, with 3 million serving in western districts). Attack achieves complete surprise. Britain and United States pledge aid to Soviets. Romania, Italy, Hungary, Slovakia, and Finland declare war on Soviet Union. Luftwaffe destroys 4,000 Soviet aircraft in first week of fighting and wins control of air. German armor advances rapidly and Soviets suffer huge losses of men and matériel in series of encirclements.

Special SS and police units (*Einsatzgruppen*) begin systematically murdering Jewish population in conquered Soviet territory with assistance of German army and local collaborators; over 500,000 Jews are killed by December 1941. (Although no written orders survive, evidence strongly indicates that by spring 1941 Hitler had directed SS leaders to plan and carry out extermination of European Jews.) Hitler also orders mass murder of Roma and Sinti (Gypsies), which results in at least 250,000 deaths by 1945, and merciless treatment of Soviet prisoners; by early 1942 over two-thirds of the 3 million Soviet soldiers captured in 1941 have been shot, or have died from hunger, disease, and exposure.

British break Enigma machine cipher used by German navy and begin reading U-boat radio signals. Tracking of U-boat movements allows Royal Navy to engage in evasive convoy routing, and U-boat sinkings, July–December 1941, fall to about 700,000 tons, while U-boat losses in this period rise to 23 as number and effectiveness of British and Canadian escort vessels increase.

Japanese government debates whether to join attack on Soviet Union.

July–Aug.   Germans capture Smolensk, 400 miles east of frontier and 250 miles west of Moscow, on July 16. Supply difficulties, mechanical wear on vehicles, heavy casualties, and fierce Soviet resistance begin to slow German advance. Hitler orders halt in attack on Moscow in August and shifts armored forces from central front to offensives against Leningrad and the Ukraine. Soviets begin organizing partisan warfare behind German lines.

U.S. troops land in Iceland in July, relieving British forces for use elsewhere (British occupied island in May 1940). Churchill and Roosevelt meet off Newfoundland, August 9–12, to discuss strategy (first of their 12 wartime conferences). U.S. House of Representatives votes 203–202 to extend required service of draftees beyond one year; vote allows expansion of armed forces to continue.

British and Soviets occupy Iran on August 25 and begin opening overland supply route into Soviet Union; British also send convoys to Russian Arctic ports of Murmansk and Archangel, despite increasingly heavy losses to U-boat and aircraft attack. (U.S. later opens major shipping route across North Pacific to Siberia, and supplies most of the aid sent to Soviets, including extremely valuable railroad and telephone equipment, large amounts of food, and over 400,000 trucks.)

Japanese government formally decides on July 2 to remain neutral in German-Soviet war unless the Soviet Union collapses, to occupy southern Indochina, and to prepare for war with Britain and the United States. Vichy French sign agreement on July 21 giving Japanese military control of southern Indochina, including air and naval bases that can be used to attack Malaya, the Dutch East Indies, and the Philippines. Roosevelt responds on July 26 by freezing Japanese assets in the U.S. (implementation of policy results in total embargo of oil exports to Japan, although Roosevelt intended only to sharply reduce them; U.S. is the source of 80 percent of Japanese oil imports).

Sept.   Germans begin siege of Leningrad (some supplies continue to reach city across Lake Lagoda). Kiev falls to Germans, September 19, during encirclement battle in which they capture over 500,000 prisoners.

Following U-boat attack on U.S. destroyer, September 4, Roosevelt orders navy to escort convoys between the U.S. and Iceland and to destroy Axis naval vessels operating in this zone.

As negotiations in Washington continue, Japanese leadership decides on September 3 to go to war with the United States unless the U.S. accepts Japanese domination of China and Southeast Asia.

Oct.   Germans begin attack on Moscow October 2 and capture over 600,000 prisoners before advance is halted October 30 by autumn rain and mud. Soviet defense is strengthened by increasing production of T-34 tanks (until 1943 T-34 is superior to all German tanks, and is equal to new German models introduced in 1943). Relocation of factories to Urals region allows Soviet arms production to increase in 1942 despite German occupation of many key industrial centers.

Roosevelt orders intensification of U.S. research into atomic weapons on October 9 after receiving British report concluding that atomic bomb could be built within three years.

U-boat sinks U.S. destroyer on convoy duty in Atlantic, October 31, killing 115 men.

Konoye resigns as Japanese prime minister on October 16 and is succeeded by Tojo. Navy staff approves, October 20, proposal by fleet commander Admiral Yamamoto Isoroku to begin war with surprise air attack against U.S. naval base at Pearl Harbor in Hawaii (Yamamoto had begun planning for attack in December 1940).

Nov.   Attack on Moscow resumes November 15 after ground freezes. Germans continue offensive in blizzards and subzero temperatures despite lack of winter clothing and equipment and reach within 15 miles of Moscow by end of November.

British begin successful offensive into Libya on November 18.

Japanese government formally decides on November 5 to begin war in early December. War plan calls for conquering the Philippines, Malaya, Dutch East Indies, Burma, and the American islands in the western Pacific within six months, creating an extended defensive perimeter; Japanese hope that the U.S. will negotiate peace rather than fight a long and costly war. Task force of six aircraft carriers and 24 supporting ships sails from northern Japan on November 26 and begins crossing Pacific, avoiding normal shipping routes and maintaining complete radio silence.

Dec.   Soviets surprise Germans by launching major counteroffensive around Moscow on December 5, using recently mobilized reservists and troops brought from Siberia during autumn. Germans are driven back and their central front is threatened with disintegration.

Deciphered Japanese diplomatic messages alert Roosevelt and his senior advisers that Japanese have decided to go to war, but do not indicate that Pearl Harbor will be attacked. Administration anticipates that hostilities will begin in Malaya and East Indies, and army and navy commanders in Hawaii fail to act on general warnings of war and do not detect approaching task force. Japanese carriers approach to within 200 miles of Oahu on morning of December 7 and launch 350 aircraft in two waves. At 7:55 A.M. (Honolulu time) attack on Pearl Harbor and nearby airfields begins, achieving complete surprise. Attack sinks or damages eight battleships, three cruisers, three destroyers, and four auxiliary vessels, destroys 188 aircraft, and kills 2,335 servicemen. (Two battleships and one auxiliary vessel are permanently lost; all of the other ships are eventually repaired and see service during the war.) Japanese lose only 29 aircraft, but fail to launch second strike against oil storage tanks and repair facilities, allowing Pearl Harbor to continue serving as fleet base. All three U.S. carriers in the Pacific are at sea and escape damage (Japan has total of 10 carriers, the U.S. seven).

Japanese begin offensive across Southeast Asia, attacking Hong Kong, occupying Thailand, landing in northern Malaya, and bombing the Philippines on December 8 (December 7 in U.S.). In the Philippines more than 100 U.S. aircraft are destroyed on the ground nine hours after General Douglas MacArthur and other commanders learn of Pearl Harbor attack. United States, Britain, and Commonwealth nations declare war on Japan on December 8. Japanese capture Guam and land advance forces on main Philippine island of Luzon on December 10. Sinking of British battleship and battle cruiser by aircraft off Malaya on December 10 gives Japanese control of South China Sea, and long range and superior performance of their Zero fighters give Japanese control of the air in Malaya and over Luzon. Attempted landing on Wake Island is repulsed by U.S. marines on December 11.

Germany and Italy declare war on the United States on December 11 and the U.S. immediately responds with its own declarations. Hitler assumes direct operational control of German army, dismisses many senior commanders, and forbids general retreat on eastern front.

Roosevelt and Churchill begin conference in Washington, December 22, which confirms strategy, agreed upon in earlier Anglo-American consultations, of defeating Germany before Japan (Germany is considered by both American and British leaders to be the more dangerous enemy).

Main Japanese force of 43,000 men lands on Luzon in the Philippines on December 22. Japanese capture Wake Island on December 23. About 15,000 American and 65,000 Filipino troops on Luzon retreat to Bataan peninsula, where they suffer from severe shortages of food and medicine. British garrison surrenders at Hong Kong on December 25. U.S. submarines begin operations in Pacific, but achieve little success at first due to poor tactics, inexperienced leadership, defective torpedoes, and doctrine that emphasizes attacks on well-defended warships.

1942   Japanese forces begin offensive on Bataan, January 9, land in Dutch East Indies, January 11, advance into southern Burma, January 15, and seize Rabaul on New Britain on January 23. British, Indian, and Australian forces retreat from southern Malaya to Singapore on January 31, ending campaign in which 35,000 Japanese with superior training, equipment, and leadership defeat 60,000 Allied troops.

Stalin orders general offensive along entire front against advice of senior army commanders, who favor concentrating Soviet forces to achieve destruction of Germans outside of Moscow. Resulting dispersion of reserves, heavy losses since June 1941, and strength of German defensive positions prevent Soviets from winning decisive victory (Soviets will drive Germans back 80 miles from Moscow but fail to relieve Leningrad or regain major ground on southern front before thaw in April brings reduction in fighting).

Germans and Italians end their retreat in Libya at El Algheila. Reinforcement of Luftwaffe in Mediterranean allows more Axis supply ships to reach North Africa. Axis counterattack on January 21 reaches Gazala on February 7 before halting.

U-boats open offensive along U.S. Atlantic coast in January (later extended to Gulf of Mexico and Caribbean). Refusal of U.S. navy to organize coastal convoys until late spring and delay in instituting coastal blackout result in heavy losses, especially of tankers.

SS leaders meet with other German officials in Berlin district of Wannsee on January 20 to coordinate plans for deportation and murder of European Jews. *Einsatzgruppen* continue mass killings in eastern Europe in 1942, while from December 1941 to November 1942 SS establishes killing centers in Poland at Chelmno, Belzec, Auschwitz-Birkenau, Sobibor, Treblinka, and Majdanek, where Jews are brought by train from throughout Europe to be gassed. Genocide campaign eventually involves thousands of German officials and European collaborators and continues until the end of the war.

Feb.–Mar.   New Enigma cipher, introduced February 1, ends British reading of U-boat signals, while German navy begins breaking British code used to control convoy movements. Germans sink over 3 million tons of shipping, January–June 1942, while losing only 21 U-boats.

RAF abandons attempts to bomb precise targets at night and begins "area bombing" offensive designed to break morale of German industrial workers by destroying their housing (British will not have sufficient aircraft to begin sustained bombing offensive until 1943).

Germans begin economic mobilization for prolonged war and,

despite Allied bombing, are able to increase weapons production in 1942–44 by reducing civilian production, improving their economic planning and administration, and exploiting slave labor from occupied countries. (In 1942–44 Germany produces 37,000 tanks and self-propelled guns, while Britain manufactures 20,000; the Soviet Union, 77,000; and the U.S., 72,000. Germany produces 80,000 military aircraft in 1942–44, while Japan manufactures 53,500; Britain, 76,000; the Soviet Union, 100,000; and the U.S., 230,000.)

Japanese halt offensive on Bataan, February 8, and wait for reinforcements after suffering heavy losses in combat and from disease. Strength of Japanese air and naval forces in Pacific prevents any U.S. attempt to relieve or evacuate Philippines. Japanese attack Singapore on February 8. Singapore garrison surrenders on February 15 in worst British defeat of the war (Japanese capture 130,000 prisoners in Malaya and Singapore). Dutch, British, Australian, and U.S. navies lose five cruisers and six destroyers in surface actions in East Indies, February 27–March 1. Japanese capture Rangoon on March 8 and continue their advance into Burma, severing Allied supply route into China. MacArthur leaves the Philippines. Last Allied forces on Java surrender, March 12, completing Japanese conquest of Dutch East Indies.

Roosevelt signs executive order on February 19 that results by September 1942 in internment without trial or hearing of over 120,000 Japanese-Americans and Japanese resident aliens living on the West Coast. (Japanese-Americans are eventually permitted to join the military, and over 17,000 serve in the infantry in Europe and in front-line intelligence units in Asia and the Pacific.)

April   Japanese launch new offensive on Bataan on April 3. Campaign ends April 9 with surrender of 12,000 U.S. and 63,000 Filipino troops, who are forced to make 65-mile "Death March" on which thousands are murdered or die from disease. (Less than 60 percent of the 20,000 Americans captured in the Philippines survive the war.) Japanese carriers raid into the Indian Ocean in early April, bombing Ceylon and sinking a British light carrier and two cruisers. In raid designed to raise American morale, 16 twin-engine B-25 bombers take off from aircraft carrier 650 miles from Japan on April 18 and bomb Tokyo and four other cities before flying on to China. Raid causes very little damage, but shames Japanese commanders and results in final approval of proposal by Yamamoto to capture Midway Island and draw U.S. carriers into decisive battle. U.S. navy learns from Japanese radio signals of planned landing at Port Moresby in southeastern New Guinea, first in series of operations designed to sever

U.S.–Australia supply routes. Admiral Chester Nimitz, commander of U.S. Pacific fleet, sends two carriers to Coral Sea to block invasion.

May   Japanese capture of Corregidor on May 6 ends major resistance in the Philippines (Filipino guerrillas will fight throughout Japanese occupation). In Battle of the Coral Sea, May 7–8, U.S. navy turns back Port Moresby invasion force, losing one carrier and two smaller ships while sinking a Japanese light carrier and inflicting damage and aircraft losses that prevent two other Japanese carriers from participating in subsequent Midway operation. Battle is first in naval history fought between opposing carrier forces, and in which opposing ships never come into sight of one another. Japanese complete conquest of Burma in mid-May. U.S. navy codebreakers provide detailed information concerning Midway operation and simultaneous diversionary attack on Aleutian Islands. Nimitz commits the three remaining carriers in Pacific fleet to battle in hopes of taking Japanese by surprise (Yamamoto anticipates that U.S. carriers will be in harbor when Midway invasion begins).

British invade Vichy-controlled island of Madagascar on May 5 to prevent its possible use as naval base by Axis (campaign continues until Vichy forces surrender on November 5, 1942).

Soviet offensive against Kharkov in eastern Ukraine is defeated, May 12–29, with loss of over 200,000 prisoners.

Axis begins new offensive in Libya on May 26.

June   In Battle of Midway, June 3–6, U.S. carrier aircraft sink four Japanese carriers and one cruiser, while the U.S. loses one carrier and one destroyer to air and submarine attack. Japanese navy also loses many of its most experienced pilots, and abandons planned invasion of Midway. Victory allows U.S. to take the initiative in the Pacific war.

Japanese occupy Kiska and Attu, uninhabited islands at western end of the Aleutians, June 6–7.

Roosevelt authorizes full-scale U.S. effort to build atomic weapons on June 17.

Germans capture 30,000 Allied prisoners in Libyan port of Tobruk on June 21 and then advance into Egypt.

Germans launch general offensive in southern Russia and eastern Ukraine on June 28 with objective of capturing Caucasian oil fields (Germans no longer have enough men, vehicles, or draft horses to attack along entire front as in 1941; though heavy fighting will occur on central and northern fronts in 1942, neither side will gain or lose much territory).

July   British halt Axis advance in Egypt near El Alamein, only 60 miles from Alexandria, in heavy fighting July 1–22. Defense is aided by recent breaking of German army Enigma ciphers. (Allies will intermittently gain valuable intelligence from German army signals for remainder of war.)

German attack in southern Russia rapidly gains ground, but Soviets are generally able to retreat and avoid major encirclements. Hitler issues directive on July 23 calling for simultaneous advances southward into the Caucasus and eastward toward Stalingrad, industrial and transportation center on Volga River; order results in serious overextension of German forces.

U-boats end American coastal offensive and return in strength to Atlantic convoy routes, sinking over 3 million tons of shipping, July–December 1942; although Germans lose 65 U-boats in this period, increased production replaces these losses and allows Germany to begin 1943 with over 200 operational U-boats. Allied convoys lose most heavily in "air gap," mid-Atlantic region beyond the range of land-based air patrols (U-boats have limited underwater speed and endurance; to effectively pursue convoys, they must cruise on the surface and risk air attack). Although new American construction promises to eventually replace losses, rate of sinking threatens ability of Allies to move men and supplies overseas and launch offensives against the Axis.

U.S. transport aircraft based in northeastern India begin flying supplies across mountains ("The Hump") into China.

Japanese land at Buna on northern coast of eastern New Guinea (Papua), July 21, and begin overland advance toward Port Moresby. Americans prepare for landing on Guadalcanal, first stage of planned counteroffensive in the Solomon Islands and New Guinea with ultimate objective of capturing Rabaul, key Japanese naval and air base in the southwest Pacific.

Aug. Marines land on Guadalcanal and nearby islands of Tulagi and Gavutu, August 7, and capture partially constructed airfield on northern Guadalcanal; surviving Japanese retreat inland. Night attack by Japanese cruiser force early on August 9 sinks one Australian and three U.S. cruisers in Battle of Savo Island. (For most of Guadalcanal campaign superior training, tactics, equipment, and torpedoes give Japanese navy advantage in night surface engagements.) Allied transport ships are withdrawn on August 9 before they are fully unloaded, leaving 17,000 marines onshore short of supplies and equipment. Marines establish defensive perimeter around airfield (Henderson Field) and complete its construction. Japanese begin landing reinforcements on Guadalcanal. First aircraft land at Henderson Field on August 20. U.S. achieves control of air during day, but Japanese navy is able to land supplies and troops and bombard American positions at night. Japanese lose one light carrier in Battle of the Eastern Solomons on August 24. In Papua Japanese continue advance across Owen Stanley mountains toward Port Moresby, and on

August 25 land troops at Milne Bay on eastern end of New Guinea.

Germans advance into northern Caucasus. Allied raid against French port of Dieppe on August 19 is repulsed with loss of over 3,000 men killed or captured, almost all of them Canadian; disaster causes Allied planners to avoid direct assaults on well-defended ports in future amphibious landings.

Renewed Axis offensive in Egypt is defeated in battle of Alam Halfa, August 30–September 5. British receive emergency shipment of American tanks and prepare for major counteroffensive in Egypt.

Sept. Germans reach outskirts of Stalingrad in early September. Stalin agrees to proposal by generals Georgi Zhukov and Alexander Vasilevsky to hold city with minimum of forces possible while building large reserves of men, tanks, and artillery for counteroffensive against German flanks in open country outside Stalingrad. House-to-house fighting begins in city.

Australian defenders repulse Milne Bay landing in New Guinea, and surviving Japanese are evacuated on September 7. Major Japanese attack on Henderson Field on Guadalcanal is defeated in heavy fighting, September 12–14. Air and sea engagements in Solomons continue as both sides struggle to send men and supplies to Guadalcanal. Australians halt Japanese advance 30 miles from Port Moresby, September 16, then take the offensive (both sides in Papua fighting suffer from extreme terrain and climate conditions).

Oct.–Nov. British offensive at El Alamein begins October 23 and achieves decisive victory. Axis forces begin retreating toward Libya on November 4. U.S. and British forces land in Morocco and Algeria on November 8. Fighting between Allied and Vichy French troops ends November 11. Germans occupy southern France and begin moving troops and aircraft into Tunisia. British troops enter Tunisia November 16 and encounter strong German resistance. Vichy French navy scuttles remainder of its Mediterranean fleet to prevent its falling under German control.

Soviet positions in Stalingrad are reduced by mid-November to series of strongholds in ruins along Volga. Soviet counteroffensive outside Stalingrad begins November 19, and on November 23 Soviets complete encirclement of 250,000 German troops. Hitler forbids trapped German forces from attempting to break out of encirclement.

Two Japanese battleships bombard Henderson Field early on October 14, destroying about half the aircraft on Guadalcanal. Japanese land several thousand reinforcements and attack Henderson Field perimeter, October 23–26, but are repulsed in intense fighting and lose over 2,000 dead. U.S. loses aircraft carrier in Battle of Santa Cruz Islands, October 26; Japanese have two carriers damaged, and suffer severe aircraft losses (U.S. now has only two carriers in Pacific, both of which are undergoing repair for battle damage). Australians advance over Owen Stanley mountains in Papua.

In series of air attacks, submarine attacks, and two night surface engagements fought November 13–15 and later known as Naval Battle of Guadalcanal, U.S. loses two cruisers and seven destroyers while sinking two Japanese battleships, one cruiser, and three destroyers, and destroying large convoy carrying reinforcements and supplies. Increasing numbers of Japanese troops on Guadalcanal die from hunger and disease as U.S. gains control of waters around island.

Australians force Japanese in Papua to retreat into fortified Buna-Gona coastal area. American troops are flown into improvised landing strips and join attack on Buna-Gona position.

Dec.   German offensive designed to break into Stalingrad encirclement fails. Soviets launch new offensive on December 16 that threatens to reach Rostov-on-Don and cut off German forces in the Caucasus.

Tunisian fighting stalemates as winter rains make road movement extremely difficult. Axis forces continue retreat across Libya.

British break U-boat Enigma cipher system introduced in February 1942 and begin intermittently reading U-boat signals (Enigma cipher keys change daily; some keys are never broken, while others are broken only after considerable delay).

First self-sustaining nuclear chain reaction is achieved on December 2 at University of Chicago.

U.S. forces on Guadalcanal begin series of attacks against Japanese positions on jungle-covered ridges overlooking Henderson Field. Allies suffer high casualties in offensive against Buna-Gona in Papua, but use air attacks to keep supplies from reaching Japanese defenders. Concerned by Allied gains in Papua, Japanese command decides on December 26 to evacuate Guadalcanal.

British and Indian troops begin limited offensive in Burma in Arakan region along coast.

1943   Germans begin retreating from Caucasus. Soviets continue offensives in southern Russia and, in northwestern Russia, open narrow land corridor into Leningrad on January 18.

Roosevelt announces and Churchill endorses demand for "unconditional surrender" of Germany, Italy, and Japan at close of their conference in Casablanca, January 24. American bombers based in England attack Germany for first time on January 27. (American air strategy calls for daylight precision bombing of key industrial targets by aircraft flying beyond the range of fighter escort; U.S. commanders believe that close-formation flying and heavy defensive armament will sufficiently protect bombers against fighter attack.)

Americans begin major offensive on Guadalcanal. Allies complete capture of Buna-Gona position on January 22, ending six-month campaign in Papua costing about 3,000 U.S. and Australian and 7,000 Japanese lives.

Feb.–Mar.   Last German troops in Stalingrad surrender on February 2. Soviets capture Kharkov February 16 as their advance threatens destruction of entire German southern front. Germans open counteroffensive against overextended Soviet forces on February 20, and recapture Kharkov March 14. Front stabilizes as thaw in late March brings lull in fighting.

British forces advance from Libya into southeastern Tunisia. Germans begin counteroffensive against U.S. troops in Tunisia, February 14, and capture Kasserine Pass before being halted by British and American forces on February 22. British drive Axis forces from Mareth Line, defensive position in southeastern Tunisia, March 20–28.

RAF begins sustained night area bombing offensive against Germany on March 5, repeatedly attacking cities in the Ruhr and elsewhere with hundreds of bombers; by July 1943 campaign exceeds intensity of 1940–41 "Blitz" of Britain.

U-boats sink nearly 1.2 million tons of shipping, January–March 1943; Allies sink 40 U-boats, but grow increasingly concerned about safety of North Atlantic convoy routes.

Japanese complete evacuation of Guadalcanal on February 8, ending air, sea, and land campaign in which 7,000 Americans and 30,000 Japanese die (over 4,700 U.S. deaths are at sea). Allies begin logistical preparations for further operations in New Guinea and the Solomons with eventual objective of capturing Rabaul. (All Allied plans for amphibious operations are constrained by worldwide shortages of shipping and landing craft, and operations in the Pacific are generally given lower priority than those in Europe in accordance with "Germany First" strategy.) Losses at Midway, Guadalcanal, and Papua force Japanese to go on defensive throughout Pacific. In Battle of the Bismarck Sea, March 2–4, U.S. and Australian aircraft destroy convoy bringing reinforcements to Lae in eastern New Guinea, killing over 3,000 Japanese troops at sea. American air strength in Southwest Pacific increases as U.S. begins to produce land-based fighter aircraft equal in performance to the Japanese Zero.

Japanese begin series of counterattacks in Burma against Allied advance in the Arakan.

April   Germans begin planning offensive to destroy Soviet forces in large salient around Kursk. Soviets anticipate attack and begin building anti-tank defenses and accumulating armored reserves.

Axis forces retreat into northern Tunisia as Allied air attacks sharply reduce supplies reaching them from across the Mediterranean.

Jewish resistance organizations in Warsaw ghetto begin uprising on April 19 as SS prepares to send remaining inhabitants to Treblinka extermination camp.

Secret scientific laboratory at Los Alamos, New Mexico, begins work on design and manufacture of fission atomic weapons (construction of industrial facility for separating uranium-235 from uranium ore began in November 1942 at Oak Ridge, Tennessee; in August 1943 construction begins at Hanford, Washington, for reactor and processing plant for production of plutonium-239).

May–June   Allies break through Axis lines in northern Tunisia after heavy fighting, May 6–7. North African campaign ends May 13 with capture of 125,000 German and 115,000 Italian troops.

Fighting in Warsaw ends May 15. Ghetto is destroyed by SS, and 56,000 Jews are killed either in Warsaw or at Treblinka; several thousand survivors hide among Polish population.

Allies gain decisive advantage in Battle of the Atlantic as increasing numbers of long-range land-based aircraft and small escort aircraft carriers close mid-Atlantic "air gap." Improved airborne and ship radar, growing number of escort vessels with high-frequency direction-finding equipment (used to locate U-boats making radio transmissions), improved tactics and weapons, and increasing success in reading U-boat ciphers also contribute to sinking of 15 U-boats in April 1943 and 41 in May. On May 24 German navy orders U-boats to withdraw from main North Atlantic convoy routes. Allies adopt secure cipher for convoy signals in June.

Roosevelt, Churchill, and their staffs meet in Washington in May and set May 1, 1944, as date (D-Day) for cross-Channel invasion of France and opening of major land campaign against Germans in northwest Europe.

U.S. forces land on Attu in Aleutians on May 11 and kill last defenders on May 30 as Japanese garrison fights until it is annihilated; over 2,300 Japanese and 600 Americans die in battle (Japanese will evacuate Kiska in July).

British and Indian troops in Burma retreat from the Arakan.

Allies launch major offensive in Southwest Pacific on June 30, with U.S. and Australian troops attacking in New Guinea and U.S. forces landing on New Georgia in the Solomons.

July   Germans launch offensive against Kursk salient July 5, beginning largest tank battle of the war. British and Americans invade

Sicily July 10. Germans are unable to break through Soviet defenses and suffer heavy tank losses. Concerned about possible Italian collapse, Hitler orders Kursk offensive abandoned on July 13 and begins shifting troops to Italy. Mussolini is overthrown by coup in Rome, July 25, and new Italian government begins secret talks with Allies on surrender. (New regime imprisons Mussolini, but he is freed by Germans on September 12 and establishes a fascist government in northern Italy.)

RAF night raid on Hamburg on July 28 kills 40,000 civilians when unusually dense concentration of incendiary bombs create intense fires.

Aug.   Soviets begin series of major offensives on southern and central fronts on August 3 and capture Kharkov on August 23.

Allies enter Messina August 17, ending Sicilian campaign; most German troops escape to southern Italy.

American bombers attack Regensburg and Schweinfurt, August 17, in their deepest raid yet into Germany, losing 60 out of 376 aircraft. RAF continues area offensive against German cities.

Anglo-American chiefs of staff approve choice of Caen-Bayeux area of Normandy for invasion (landing area is later extended westward onto shore of Cotentin peninsula).

Americans capture Munda airfield, key objective on New Georgia, on August 5 after heavy fighting. U.S. destroyers sink three Japanese destroyers bringing reinforcements to New Georgia on August 6 as effective use of radar gives U.S. navy increasing advantage in night surface engagements. Japanese resistance on New Georgia ends in late August.

Sept.   British troops cross Straits of Messina on September 3 and land in southern Italy. Italian surrender is announced September 8. U.S. and British forces land at Salerno on September 9. Germans occupy Italy and launch counterattacks at Salerno, September 12–16, that threaten beachhead before they are repulsed with aid of heavy naval gunfire. Allied advance northward is slowed by mountainous terrain, poor roads, and extensive German demolitions.

Soviets capture Smolensk September 25 and begin establishing bridgeheads along western bank of Dnieper River. Recovery of agricultural and industrial resources of eastern Ukraine eases strain on Soviet economy.

U-boats return to North Atlantic convoy routes, hoping to regain initiative by using new acoustic homing torpedoes against escorts, but Allies quickly adopt effective countermeasures. Sinkings by U-boats, April–December 1943, total 1.4 million tons, while Allies sink 197 U-boats in this period.

U.S. and Australian forces land in New Guinea near Lae, September 4, and capture village on September 16. Allies continue offensive westward along northern New Guinea coast in series of overland advances and amphibious landings. U.S. submarine operations become increasingly effective as reliability of American torpedoes improves and more submarines are equipped with search radar. Submarine campaign now concentrates on destruction of merchant ships transporting oil and raw materials from Southeast Asia to Japan, and is aided by intelligence derived from decoded Japanese signals. Japanese lose 2.8 million tons of shipping from December 1941 to December 1943, almost 80 percent sunk by submarines; in this period 22 U.S. submarines are lost on Pacific patrols. (Japanese use their submarines for attacks on warships and for transporting supplies to isolated island garrisons, and lose 130 during the war.)

Oct.   Allies enter Naples October 1 and attack across Volturno River in mid-October. New Italian government declares war on Germany October 13.

Soviets attack across Dnieper into western Ukraine, preventing the Germans from using the river as winter defensive line. (Summer and autumn Soviet offensives in 1943 are aided by growing strength of their air force in close support of ground operations, and by increasing mobility given to their army by American trucks; most of German army still relies upon horse-drawn transport.)

U.S. loses 148 bombers over Germany in seven days, including 60 out of 291 sent October 14 on second raid against Schweinfurt ball-bearing plants. Losses force suspension of raids beyond range of fighter escort, which extends only over northwestern Germany.

Allies begin series of intensive air attacks on Rabaul; new plan calls for Rabaul to be heavily bombed and blockaded, but rejects land assault as unnecessary and highly costly.

Nov.–Dec.   Germans reinforce troops in France and begin strengthening coastal fortifications in anticipation of Allied invasion in 1944 (majority of German army will continue to fight Soviets for remainder of war).

Soviets capture Kiev November 6. Series of Soviet offensives in south during winter results in heavy German casualties and recovery by early 1944 of almost all Ukrainian territory lost in 1941.

In Italy, Allies attack across Sangro River in late November and reach Garigliano River in December. Heavy infantry casualties, difficult terrain, bad weather, and skillful defense slow Allied advance as Germans fight to hold southern Italy for as long as possible. (Hitler fears that Allies will use central and northern Italy to invade the Balkans, depriving Germany of important raw materials.)

RAF attacks Berlin November 18, beginning unsuccessful attempt to repeat devastation caused in Hamburg; British lose over 500 bombers in 16 raids through late March 1944.

Roosevelt, Churchill, and Stalin meet in Teheran, November 28–December 1. Stalin promises to enter war against Japan after defeat of Germany, and Roosevelt and Churchill agree in principle to major shifts in Polish borders (Poland eventually loses 70,000 square miles of its pre-war territory to the Soviet Union and is compensated with 40,000 square miles of eastern Germany, from which several million Germans are expelled in 1945–46). General Dwight Eisenhower is appointed as supreme allied commander for invasion of France with orders to "undertake operations aimed at the heart of Germany" and the destruction of its armed forces.

U.S. troops land on November 1 on Bougainville in the Solomons, where they establish defensive perimeter and begin constructing airfield. Japanese concentrate aircraft and warships at Rabaul to oppose Bougainville landing, but abandon counteroffensive after damaging raids by U.S. carrier aircraft in early November (in early 1944 Japanese withdraw remaining aircraft from Rabaul).

Growing number of U.S. aircraft carriers and support ships allows launching of series of offensives against Japanese-held Gilbert, Marshall, and Caroline island chains in central Pacific. (In 1942–45, Japanese bring into service 14 carriers of all sizes, many of them inadequate conversions of existing ships, while the U.S. commissions 17 large fleet carriers, nine light carriers, and 77 small escort carriers.) American forces land on Tarawa and Makin atolls in the Gilberts on November 20. Battle on Tarawa ends on November 23 after 1,000 Americans and 4,800 Japanese are killed. Fighting on Makin ends on November 23 with destruction of smaller Japanese garrison. U.S. marines land on Cape Gloucester at western end of New Britain on December 26.

1944   Soviet offensive, January 14–27, drives Germans away from Leningrad and brings final end to siege in which 800,000–1,000,000 Soviet civilians died of starvation and disease.

Allies launch major offensive against Gustav Line, main German defensive position south of Rome, on January 17. British and American troops land at Anzio, 30 miles south of Rome and 60 miles behind Gustav Line, on January 22. Germans send troops to contain beachhead as Allied forces consolidate their position near the coast. Heavy fighting continues along Gustav Line, especially in mountains around Cassino, town commanding main highway to Rome.

Marines capture airfield on Cape Gloucester and repulse Japanese counterattacks. After preliminary carrier raids and shore bombardment, U.S. forces begin landing on Kwajalein atoll in the Marshalls on January 31.

Feb.–Mar.   Attacks by British, Indian, and New Zealand troops, February 15–18 and March 15–23, fail to drive Germans from Cassino. German counteroffensive at Anzio is repulsed in intense fighting, February 16–18, but Allies are unable to subsequently advance from beachhead.

Increasing numbers of P-51B long-range fighter aircraft allow U.S. to resume daylight raids deep into Germany in series of raids against aircraft factories, February 20–25 ("Big Week"). Escorted U.S. bombers attack Berlin on March 6 as daylight air battle continues over Germany with heavy losses on both sides. RAF suspends deep raids into Germany and begins major bombing campaign against French and Belgian railway system in preparation for invasion.

Using dummy landing craft, false radio signals, and their complete control of the German espionage network in Britain, Allies begin successful deception operation designed to lead Germans to suspect invasion will occur not in Normandy but in the Pas de Calais, northeastern region of France that is closer to Germany.

Fighting on Kwajalein ends February 4. U.S. launches highly successful carrier raid against Truk, major Japanese air and naval base in the Carolines (after further raids against Truk in April, Carolines are bypassed for remainder of war). Landings begin on Eniwetok atoll in the Marshalls, February 17, and fighting continues until February 23. U.S. casualties in Marshalls are lower than on Tarawa; Japanese garrisons are almost completely annihilated.

British and Indian troops advance in Burma in renewed offensive in the Arakan. Japanese counterattack and succeed in encircling several Allied positions, but surrounded troops receive supplies by parachute drop and hold their positions (in previous jungle battles in Southeast Asia, Allied troops usually retreated when the Japanese launched infiltration attacks against their supply lines). Small American infantry force joins U.S.-trained and -equipped Chinese troops in offensive in northern Burma intended to increase flow of supplies into China.

U.S. troops land in Admiralty Islands north of New Britain on February 29, and Japanese resistance on islands ends March 18. Japanese counteroffensive on Bougainville in March is defeated in heavy fighting. Securing of bases on Bougainville, New Britain, and Admiralties completes the containment of Japanese at Rabaul. (Australian troops relieve U.S. forces on New Britain and Bougainville in autumn 1944, and fighting continues on both islands until the end of the war, when over 90,000 Japanese troops surrender.)

Japanese launch major offensive into northeastern India on March 8 with objective of capturing Allied bases at Imphal and Kohima. British and Indian troops withdraw into perimeter around Imphal airfields as siege begins on March 29.

April

Soviets approach Hungarian border and cross into northern Romania before end of their spring offensive.

British garrison at Kohima is besieged, April 5–18, but is supplied by parachute drops during intense close-range battle. Heavy fighting continues at Kohima, Imphal, and in the Arakan throughout spring.

Japanese begin series of major offensives in central and southern China on April 17 that continue into autumn and inflict severe losses on Nationalist Chinese forces.

U.S. forces land at Aitape and Hollandia in northern New Guinea on April 22, bypassing Japanese position at Wewak in westward advance designed to secure bases for invasion of the Philippines.

May

Allies launch major offensive in Italy against Gustav Line on May 11. French and North African troops break through and force German withdrawal. Polish troops capture monastery at Cassino, May 18. Allies break out of Anzio beachhead, May 23, but are unable to trap retreating Germans, who begin pulling back in stages to Gothic Line, defensive position extending across northern Italy from Pisa to Rimini.

Allies win air superiority over western Europe as Luftwaffe is crippled by heavy losses in battles with U.S. fighters over Germany and increasing shortages of fuel and adequately trained pilots. U.S. begins bombing synthetic oil plants.

Heavy fighting continues in northwestern New Guinea as U.S. forces begin offensive in Wakde-Sarmi area, May 17, and land on Biak island, May 27, where they meet strong resistance from Japanese dug into hillside caves and bunkers (fighting continues on Biak until end of July).

U.S. and Chinese troops capture Myitkyina airfield in northern Burma on May 17 and begin battle for nearby town.

June

Allies enter Rome June 4. Eisenhower postpones D-Day, which had been rescheduled for June 5, because of adverse weather forecast, then decides to invade on June 6. British and American parachute and glider troops begin airborne assault on Normandy during night of June 5–6 and secure key positions on western and eastern flanks of invasion area. American, British, and Canadian troops begin landing on five Normandy beaches on morning of June 6 in largest amphibious operation in history. Resistance is heaviest on Omaha Beach, where U.S. infantry suffers heavy casualties before capturing high ground overlooking shore. German commanders are surprised by timing and location of invasion and respond slowly. By night of June 6 Allies have landed over 150,000 men at cost of about 10,000 men killed, wounded, or captured. Initial German counterattacks fail, and individual beachheads are joined into single continuous front by June 12. Allied control of air and sea allows rapid buildup of men and matériel in Normandy, while German reinforcements are delayed by Allied air attack, sabotage and ambushes by the French resistance, and belief by German commanders that Allies will launch second invasion in the Pas de Calais. Germans concentrate majority of their armored forces at eastern end of front to defend Caen from British and Canadian attacks. (Open country southeast of Caen is suitable for rapid armored advance; Germans hope to keep Allies confined in hedgerow country near coast, well-suited to their defensive tactics.)

Germans begin attacking London with V-1 unmanned jet aircraft on June 13.

Soviets concentrate massive numbers of men, tanks, artillery, and aircraft in Belorussia and on June 22 launch offensive that destroys center of German eastern front (Soviet deception plan has led Germans to send their reserves to northern Ukraine in anticipation of a renewed attack there).

British and Canadians continue attacks in Caen sector. Americans capture port of Cherbourg June 27.

U.S. troops invade Saipan in the Marianas on June 15, beginning campaign designed to secure bases for long-range bombing of Japan. Japanese navy responds in hopes of winning decisive victory, leading to first carrier engagement in Pacific since October 1942. In Battle of the Philippine Sea, June 19–20, Japanese lose three carriers (two of which are sunk by U.S. submarines) and over 400 aircraft; U.S. loses about 50 aircraft in combat. (U.S. navy fighter pilots are now better trained than Japanese, and fly new Hellcat fighters superior to the Zero; effectiveness of anti-aircraft fire from U.S. ships is significantly increased by use of radar proximity fuses. Increasing shortage of fuel prevents Japanese from adequately training pilots to replace those lost in Philippine Sea.) Heavy fighting continues on Saipan, where Japanese defenders make extensive use of caves in jungle-covered hills.

U.S. begins bombing Japan from Chinese airfields on June 15, but is unable to mount major attacks due to supply difficulties in China.

Allied forces in India end siege of Imphal on June 22.

July   Soviets capture Minsk in Belorussia on July 3 and begin offensive into the Baltic states. By mid-July German losses in Belorussia total 350,000 men, mostly killed or captured. Soviets launch offensive in northern Ukraine and advance into Poland.

Americans capture key crossroads at St. Lô in western Normandy on July 18 after weeks of costly fighting. British offensive southeast of Caen, July 18–20, fails to break through but causes further attrition of German armor.

Hitler is slightly wounded when bomb planted by anti-Nazi military officers explodes at his East Prussian headquarters on July 20. Coup attempt in Berlin fails when his survival becomes known (over 200 people are executed for involvement in the plot). Americans launch major offensive west of St. Lô on July 25 that breaks through German lines and allows U.S. armor to reach open country.

Soviets establish bridgeheads across Vistula River and begin fighting in eastern suburbs of Warsaw.

Fighting ends on Saipan on July 9. Over 8,000 Japanese civilians living on the island commit suicide rather than surrender. Tojo resigns on July 18 and is replaced as prime minister by General Koiso Kuniaki. Marianas campaign continues with landings on Guam, July 21, and Tinian, July 24.

Japanese abandon Imphal offensive on July 9 and retreat through mountains into Burma; 30,000–50,000 Japanese die in Imphal-Kohima battles, many from hunger and disease. British prepare for offensive into Burma at end of monsoon season.

U.S. forces reach northwestern end of New Guinea on July 30. (Fighting continues in New Guinea until end of war, especially between Australians and Japanese in Aitape-Wewak area.)

Aug.   Polish Home Army, anti-communist resistance movement, begins uprising against Germans in Warsaw on August 1. Soviets obstruct Western attempts to parachute aid to insurgents. Soviet offensive in Poland is slowed by shortage of supplies and increasing German resistance.

U.S. forces advance rapidly into Brittany and northeastern France as British and Canadians attack south from Caen. German counteroffensive intended to cut off American advance is defeated, August 7–10. U.S. and French troops land in southern France west of Cannes on August 15. Refusal of Hitler to authorize retreat in Normandy results in severe German losses of men and equipment in "pocket" near Falaise, closed by U.S., Canadian, and Polish troops, August 19–21. Paris is liberated by French troops on August 25 as Germans retreat across France. Losses in Normandy campaign in men killed, wounded, or captured are 450,000 for Germans and over 200,000 for Allies.

Soviets launch offensive into Romania August 20. New Romanian government signs armistice with Soviets August 23, then declares war on Hungary and Germany. Germans lose almost 200,000 men killed or captured in collapse of Romanian front.

Allies begin offensive along Adriatic coast of Italy against Gothic Line on August 25.

U-boats are forced to leave French Atlantic ports and retreat to Norwegian and German bases. Use of *Schnorchel* underwater breathing apparatus allows increasing number of U-boats to re-charge their batteries without surfacing, but their effectiveness is severely limited by slow underwater speed. German development of new class of U-boats capable of high underwater speeds worries Allies, but production difficulties and Allied bombing prevents them from becoming operational before the end of the war. U-boats sink 1 million tons of shipping, January 1944–May 1945; Allies sink 393 U-boats (27,500 U-boat crewmen are killed, 1939–45).

Effective Japanese resistance ends on Tinian and Guam in early August; over 5,000 Americans and about 50,000 Japanese are killed in Marianas campaign, mostly on Saipan.

Allied forces capture town of Myitkyina on August 3 as engineers work on Ledo Road, new overland route from India through north Burma into China.

Sept.   Finland signs armistice with Soviet Union on September 4. Bulgaria declares war on Germany September 8 as Soviet army enters the country.

British troops liberate Brussels, September 3, and Antwerp on September 4. Germans begin attacking London with V-2 ballistic missiles on September 8. U.S. forces advancing from northern and southern France meet near Dijon and American patrols cross German frontier near Aachen, September 11. Allied advance is slowed by difficulty in bringing gasoline and other supplies forward from Normandy and the Mediterranean coast (Germans still control Scheldt estuary leading to Antwerp and have left garrisons in many Channel and Brittany ports). Hitler begins planning late autumn counteroffensive in the Ardennes designed to split the Allied front and recapture Antwerp. American and British airborne troops land near Dutch towns of Eindhoven, Nijmegen, and Arnhem on September 17 as British armored forces attack northward in operation designed to seize bridges across Waal, Maas, and lower Rhine rivers. Attack is halted south of Rhine, and on September 26 surviving British airborne troops at Arnhem are either evacuated across river or taken prisoner; total Allied casualties in operation are over 17,000 men killed, wounded, or captured.

Attacks on Gothic Line continue on both Adriatic and Mediterranean sides of the Apennines.

Loss of Romanian oil fields and continued U.S. bombing of synthetic oil plants causes fuel shortage that cripples Luftwaffe training and operations and severely affects motorized forces of German army.

Soviets attack into Hungary in late September.

Americans begin campaign in Palau Islands with landings on

Peleliu, September 15, and Anguar, September 17. Resistance on Peleliu is unexpectedly intense, and U.S. troops begin protracted struggle to kill Japanese defenders fighting from fortified caves in steep coral ridges.

Oct.   Warsaw uprising ends October 2; over 200,000 Poles are killed during revolt and the city is almost completely destroyed. Soviet advance into Romania and Bulgaria forces Germans to begin evacuating Greece, Albania, and southern Yugoslavia.

Canadian troops begin offensive to clear Scheldt estuary on October 6. Germans begin bombarding Antwerp with V-1s and V-2s on October 13 (attacks are extended to other Belgian cities during winter; V-weapons kill over 12,000 people in England and Belgium by spring 1945 and cause considerable destruction, but are too inaccurate to be militarily effective).

Luftwaffe begins limited operational use of Me-262 jet fighter, with top speed 100 miles per hour faster than American P-51B, but is unable to regain control of the air because of difficulty of mass-producing jet engines, crippling lack of fuel, severe shortage of trained pilots, and overwhelming Allied numerical superiority. German war production begins to decline as intensive bombing of transportation system disrupts the movement of coal and other industrial materials.

Soviets reach Baltic coast of Lithuania on October 9. German coup installs fascist puppet regime in Hungary on October 16, preventing Hungarian armistice with Soviets. Soviet troops and Titoist Partisans capture Belgrade on October 20. U.S. troops capture Aachen, first German city to fall to Allies, on October 21. Continuing Allied attacks in the Netherlands, Aachen region, Lorraine, and Alsace gain ground slowly in face of determined German resistance, bad weather, difficult terrain, and shortages of supplies and infantry replacements. Germans build armored reserves for Ardennes counteroffensive. Heavy rain and flooded rivers make Allied operations in Italy increasingly difficult.

U.S. troops begin invasion of Philippines with landing on island of Leyte on October 20. Japanese navy commits most of its remaining ships to battle in attempt to destroy supply ships for invasion force. In the Battle of Leyte Gulf, complex series of air, submarine, and night and day surface engagements fought around northern and central Philippine islands, October 23–27, Japanese lose four carriers, three battleships, nine cruisers, and nine destroyers; U.S. losses are one light carrier, two escort carriers, and three destroyers (battle is largest naval engagement in history). Defeat leaves Japanese incapable of mounting major naval operations. An escort carrier sunk on October 25 is victim of first mass suicide attack ("kamikaze") by Japanese aircraft. Suicide attacks against ships continue as Japanese attempt to break American morale; kamikaze tactics also allow minimally trained pilots to cause greater damage than they would in conventional attacks.

Nov. Roosevelt is reelected for fourth term on November 6. Scheldt estuary is cleared of German troops on November 8 (minesweeping delays arrival of first supply ships in Antwerp until November 28). Major American offensive launched near Aachen on November 16 reaches Roer River by end of November but is unable to advance further.

Heavy fighting continues on Leyte as Japanese reinforce island with troops from Luzon. Japanese resistance ends on Peleliu in late November; over 1,200 Americans and 11,000 Japanese are killed in Palaus, mostly on Peleliu. U.S. begins bombing Japan from bases in the Marianas on November 24, attacking industrial targets in daylight from high altitude, although high winds and dense clouds over targets make accurate bombing extremely difficult.

Japanese begin consolidating gains from 1944 offensives in southern China (in 1945 some conquered territory is abandoned in order to free troops for use elsewhere).

Dec. Winter halts major Allied offensive operations in Italy. Germans attack thinly held American front in the Ardennes on December 16. After initial surprise and confusion, U.S. commanders begin sending reinforcements and planning counterattacks. Bad weather prevents air attacks on advancing Germans. Outnumbered American troops delay or prevent German capture of key road junctions, and offensive quickly falls behind schedule. German advance is halted east of the Meuse River on December 24 and U.S. counteroffensive against southern flank of German salient ("the Bulge") begins December 25. Allied fighter-bombers attack as weather improves.

British, Indian, and African troops begin advancing across Chindwin River in northern Burma. U.S. troops in Philippines land on island of Mindoro on December 15. Major Japanese resistance on Leyte ends on December 31.

Japanese merchant fleet is crippled by loss of 3.9 million tons of shipping in 1944 (U.S. submarines sink 70 percent of total tonnage, with carrier aircraft destroying most of remainder). Land-based aircraft begin using bases on Mindoro for attacks on shipping in South China Sea.

1945 Germans launch counteroffensive against Americans in Alsace on January 1 that threatens Strasbourg before it is halted in late January. By January 16 heavy fighting has regained Allies almost all ground lost in December; Ardennes battle costs U.S. 19,000 men killed, 47,000 wounded, and 15,000 captured; Germans lose 80,000-100,000 men killed, wounded, or captured.

Soviets launch offensive in Poland January 12, attacking out of Vistula bridgeheads with overwhelming superiority in men and weapons, and capture Warsaw January 17 (German forces in Poland have been weakened by priority given by Hitler to Ardennes offensive and defense of Hungarian oil fields). German front disintegrates, and millions of refugees flee as Soviet troops advance into eastern Germany, where they commit widespread murder and rape against civilian population. Soviets reach Oder River, 50 miles east of Berlin, on January 31.

U.S. invasion force sailing from Leyte to Luzon comes under heavy kamikaze attack. Troops begin landing at Lingayen Gulf on January 9. Japanese do not defend invasion beaches and withdraw into Luzon mountains. American forces encounter increasing resistance as they advance inland.

British forces in Burma begin series of crossings of Irrawaddy River. U.S. and Chinese troops open Ledo Road into China.

Feb.
Roosevelt, Churchill, and Stalin meet at Yalta in the Crimea, February 4–11, and reach agreements on occupation of Germany, organization of the United Nations, terms for Soviet entry into war against Japan, and holding of free elections in Poland (Soviets will fail to honor agreement on Poland).

Allies begin series of attacks into the German Rhineland on February 8. Soviet advance on Berlin is halted along Oder by supply difficulties and concern about remaining German forces in East Prussia and Silesia; Soviets shift forces to complete conquest of both regions. German resistance in Budapest ends February 13 after seven-week battle in city (intense fighting continues in Hungary until early April). RAF bombing of Dresden on February 13–14 kills approximately 35,000 civilians and destroys much of city. Allies advance toward Rhine in heavy fighting.

U.S. troops reach northern suburbs of Manila on February 3, then begin house-to-house battle for city. American carrier aircraft attack Japan on February 16 in first in series of raids. U.S. troops land on Palawan as operations begin to free central and southern Philippines from Japanese.

Marines land on Iwo Jima, volcanic island 760 miles south of Tokyo, on February 19 in attack aimed at capturing airfields for use as refueling and emergency landing strips by bombers based in the Marianas. Island is defended by over 21,000 Japanese fighting from extensive network of tunnels, bunkers, and caves. Marines capture summit of Mount Suribachi at southern end of Iwo Jima on February 23 (photograph of second flag raising on Suribachi becomes famous). Intense fighting continues as marines slowly advance northward.

British and Indian troops in Burma continue offensive across

Irrawaddy, receiving supplies by air and successfully using tanks in open country east of the river.

March Americans capture bridge across Rhine at Remagen on March 7. Allies make series of assault crossings of the Rhine, March 22–24. Heavy losses in Ardennes and Rhineland battles leave Germans incapable of mounting continuous defense east of the Rhine, and U.S. troops begin rapid advance across northern Germany.

Battle for Manila ends on March 3 after most of the city is destroyed; about 1,000 Americans and 20,000 Japanese die in the fighting, while as many as 100,000 Filipino civilians are killed by artillery fire or are massacred by Japanese troops. Fighting continues in Luzon mountains.

U.S. abandons high-altitude daylight precision bombing of Japan and begins low-altitude night area attacks. In first major raid using new tactics, 334 B-29 bombers attack Tokyo with napalm on night of March 9–10, killing at least 84,000 civilians. (Incendiary bombing of Japanese cities continues until end of war, killing over 180,000 people and causing immense devastation.)

Major fighting on Iwo Jima ends on March 26 as marines overrun Japanese positions on northern end of the island. Battle costs lives of over 6,800 Americans and 20,000 Japanese.

Allies capture Meiktila, key Burmese transportation center, March 3, and successfully defend it against counterattacks.

April U.S. forces encircle over 300,000 German troops in the Ruhr on April 1 and advance rapidly across northern Germany toward the Elbe River. Allies open spring offensive in Italy on April 9. American troops reach the Elbe near Magdeburg, about 60 miles west of Berlin, on April 11. Roosevelt dies of cerebral hemorrhage on April 12, and Vice-President Harry S. Truman becomes president. Eisenhower halts advance toward Berlin and directs Allied commanders to concentrate instead on destruction of remaining German forces west of the Elbe, an objective he considers to be of greater military importance. Soviets launch massive offensive across Oder and Neisse rivers toward Berlin on April 16. U.S. and Soviet troops meet on Elbe at Torgau, east of Leipzig, on April 25, cutting Germany in half. Soviets begin assault on center of Berlin on April 26. Mussolini is summarily shot by Italian partisans near Milan on April 28 as Allies advance rapidly northward. Hitler appoints Admiral Karl Dönitz, commander of the German navy, as his successor, then commits suicide in his Berlin bunker on April 30, with attacking Soviet troops only a quarter of a mile away.

U.S. forces invade Okinawa, densely populated island 350 miles southwest of Japan, on April 1 in largest amphibious operation of Pacific war. Japanese do not defend landing beaches, concentrating troops instead in caves, bunkers, and tunnels dug into series of steep ridges on southern end of island. U.S. troops quickly capture airfields in center of island and begin advancing north and south. Prime Minister Koiso resigns on April 5 and is succeeded by retired admiral Suzuki Kantaro. Japanese begin series of mass air attacks against Okinawa invasion fleet, using both conventional and kamikaze tactics. Major Japanese resistance in northern Okinawa ends in late April, but intense fighting continues in south.

Allied forces in central Burma begin mechanized advance southward toward Rangoon.

May   German forces in Italy surrender, May 2. (Losses of men killed, wounded, or captured in Italian campaign are 312,000 for the Allies, 435,000 for the Germans.) Berlin garrison surrenders on May 2. British troops reach the Baltic and U.S. forces advance into Bavaria and Austria as organized German resistance on the western front collapses. U.S. troops reach Mauthausen, last in series of concentration camps liberated by Americans in spring 1945, on May 5. After their offer to surrender only in the west is summarily rejected, representatives of German high command sign unconditional surrender on all fronts at Reims, France, on May 7, effective May 8; at Soviet insistence, surrender is again signed in Berlin on May 9.

Australian troops land in Borneo on May 1, beginning campaign that continues until the end of the war. Indian troops occupy Rangoon on May 3 before monsoon brings halt to major Allied operations in Southeast Asia.

Intense kamikaze raids continue on U.S. and British ships off Okinawa, with especially heavy attacks directed at destroyers and other escort vessels serving as radar pickets. U.S. army troops and marines attack Shuri Line, main defensive position in southern Okinawa, despite heavy rain, thick mud, and most intense Japanese artillery fire of Pacific war. Loss of key hill positions forces Japanese withdrawal from Shuri Line in late May.

June   Major fighting on Okinawa ends on June 21 after final Japanese defensive line is overrun. Americans lose 7,600 dead in land fighting; 4,900 men are killed in Okinawa naval campaign, mostly by kamikazes. Over 100,000 Japanese and Okinawan soldiers and between 70,000 and 150,000 Okinawan civilians are killed. U.S. invasion of Kyushu, southernmost of Japanese home islands, is scheduled for November 1, 1945.

July   Blockade of Japan intensifies as U.S. bombers lay thousands of mines in ports and straits of Japanese home islands, drastically reducing coastal shipping essential to Japanese economy. Continued U.S. air and submarine attacks reduce Japanese merchant fleet to one-sixth of its 1941 size and effectively end importation of oil, food, and raw materials into Japan. (During Pacific war U.S. submarines also sink eight Japanese carriers and one battleship; 52 boats and 3,500 men are lost in wartime submarine operations.)

Liberation of Philippines is proclaimed on July 5, but U.S. and Filipino troops continue fighting on Luzon and Mindanao until end of war, when over 110,000 surviving Japanese surrender. U.S. loses 14,000 men killed in Philippines land fighting, October 1944–August 1945, while over 300,000 Japanese either are killed or die from starvation and disease. (Philippines campaign engages more U.S. troops than any other operation in Pacific war.)

Japanese begin diplomatic effort to enlist Soviets in mediating end to the Pacific war. U.S. learns from reading coded messages between Tokyo and Japanese ambassador in Moscow that Japanese government considers unconditional surrender unacceptable, but is unable to agree on acceptable peace terms.

Los Alamos scientists test implosion design for atomic bomb using plutonium in desert 60 miles northwest of Alamogordo, New Mexico, on July 16, detonating device with explosive force equivalent to 18,000 tons of TNT. (Design for "gun assembly" bomb using uranium-235 is judged not to require explosive testing.) At conference in Potsdam, Germany, Stalin promises Truman that Soviet Union will enter war against Japan on August 15. Truman and senior advisers agree to use atomic bombs if Japanese reject ultimatum demanding their surrender, and order is transmitted on July 25. United States, Britain, and China issue Potsdam Declaration on July 26, calling for unconditional surrender of Japanese armed forces and warning that the "alternative for Japan is prompt and utter destruction." Declaration does not mention Japanese emperor, but promises eventual establishment of a "peacefully inclined and responsible" Japanese government "in accordance with the freely expressed will of the Japanese people." Japanese government rejects Potsdam ultimatum on July 28.

Aug.   B-29 flying from Tinian drops uranium bomb over Hiroshima on August 6. Weapon explodes 1,900 feet above city at 8:16 A.M. with force equivalent to about 13,000 tons of TNT, killing at least 80,000 people. Soviet Union declares war on Japan on August 8 and launches massive invasion of Manchuria on August 9. Plutonium bomb is dropped by B-29 over Nagasaki on August 9, and explodes 1,650 feet above city at 11:02 A.M. with force equivalent to 22,000 tons of TNT, killing at least 35,000 people (hills shield part of Nagasaki from blast and heat of bomb). Japanese supreme council divides over issue of surrender, with prime minister, foreign minister, and navy minister favoring immediate acceptance of Potsdam Declaration on condition that the Allies preserve the sovereignty of the emperor; army minister and army and navy chiefs of staff advocate continuing the war in hopes of obtaining better terms. Emperor Hirohito makes unprecedented intervention on August 10 by expressing support for immediate conditional acceptance of Potsdam Declaration. Conditional surrender offer is communicated to Allies on August 10 as U.S. continues large-scale conventional air attacks on Japan. American reply on August 11 states that the authority of the Emperor "to rule the state" after the surrender "shall be subject" to the decisions of the Allied occupation commander. Hirohito decides on August 14 to accept terms of U.S. reply. Truman announces Japanese surrender on August 14. Coup attempt by army officers in Tokyo fails to prevent unprecedented radio broadcast by Emperor on August 15 announcing surrender to Japanese people.

Sept.   Surrender is formally signed onboard American battleship in Tokyo Bay on September 2.

Over 293,000 Americans died in battle, from battle wounds, or as prisoners of war from 1941 to 1945, while another 115,000 Americans died from non-combat causes while serving in the armed forces during World War II. Over 107,000 died in battle in the war against Japan, and over 185,000 were killed in the war against Italy and Germany, mostly in the 1944–45 campaign in northwest Europe. Battle deaths by service were approximately 180,000 in the army, 55,000 in the army air forces, 38,000 in the navy, and 20,000 in the marines.

Britain lost 400,000 dead in the war, including over 60,000 civilians killed by air attacks and over 30,000 merchant seamen killed by enemy action. Canada lost over 39,000 military dead; India, 36,000; Australia, 27,000; and New Zealand, over 11,000. France lost about 200,000 military and at least 400,000 civilian dead, and there were more than 300,000 military and civilian dead in Italy. Over 1 million people died in Yugoslavia. Japan lost at least 1,500,000 military and 400,000 civilian dead in 1941–45, as well as 185,000 soldiers killed in China, 1937–41. Germany lost at least 3,300,000 military dead; over 500,000 German civilians were killed in air raids and another 1 million civilians died during the Soviet conquest of eastern Germany in 1945. At least 5,400,000 people died in Poland, almost all of them as the result of German atrocities. About 3 million of the Polish dead were Jews, and throughout Europe at least 5,750,000 Jews were murdered. Chinese deaths from 1937 to 1945 are estimated at between 10 and 15 million, mostly from famine. The Soviet Union lost at least 20 million military and civilian dead, and perhaps as many as 27 million. It is estimated that between 50 and 60 million people died in World War II.

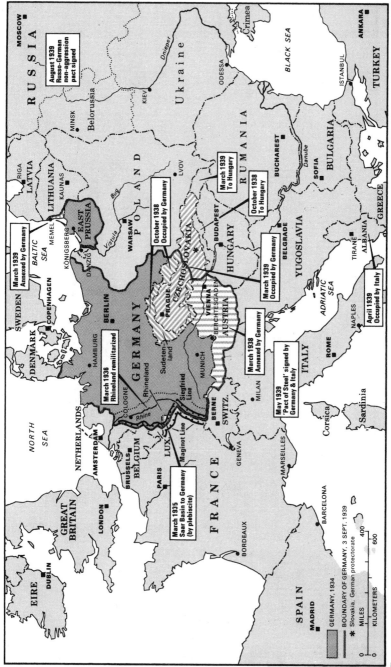

Europe, 1934–39

RUSSIA

August 1939
Russo-German
non-aggression
pact signed

MOSCOW

Dnieper

Crimea

BLACK SEA

ANKARA

TURKEY

ISTANBUL

Ukraine

ODESSA

KIEV

Belorussia

MINSK

RUMANIA

BUCHAREST

Danube

SOFIA

BULGARIA

GREECE

RIGA

LATVIA

LITHUANIA

KAUNAS

Bug

March 1939
To Hungary

LVOV

October 1938
To Hungary

March 1939
Annexed by Germany

EAST PRUSSIA

MEMEL

KÖNIGSBERG

BALTIC SEA

Vistula

DANZIG

POLAND

WARSAW

October 1938
Occupied by Germany

CZECHOSLOVAKIA

PRAGUE

BUDAPEST

HUNGARY

March 1939
Occupied by Germany

BELGRADE

YUGOSLAVIA

TIRANE

ALBANIA

April 1939
Occupied by Italy

ADRIATIC SEA

SWEDEN

COPENHAGEN

DENMARK

BERLIN

HAMBURG

GERMANY

March 1936
Rhineland remilitarized

Rhineland

Sudetenland

BERCHTESGADEN

VIENNA

AUSTRIA

March 1938
Annexed by Germany

MUNICH

Siegfried Line

May 1939
'Pact of Steel' signed by
Germany & Italy

NAPLES

ROME

ITALY

MILAN

COLOGNE

Rhine

BERNE

SWITZ.

GENEVA

MARSEILLES

Corsica

Sardinia

NORTH SEA

NETHERLANDS

AMSTERDAM

BELGIUM

BRUSSELS

LUX.

Maginot Line

March 1935
Saar Basin to Germany
(by plebiscite)

PARIS

FRANCE

BORDEAUX

SPAIN

MADRID

BARCELONA

GREAT BRITAIN

LONDON

EIRE

DUBLIN

GERMANY, 1934

BOUNDARY OF GERMANY, 3 SEPT. 1939

* Slovakia, German protectorate

MILES

0   400   600

KILOMETERS

0

ARCTIC OCEAN

REYKJAVIK ICELAND

PET

NARVIK

SUOM

TRONDHEIM

FI

HELS

BERGEN OSLO STOCKHOLM TALLIN

3 Sept 1939
Britain & France
declare war on
Germany

9 April 1940
Germany invades
Norway & Denmark

Baltic
Sea

E

NORTH
SEA

DENMARK
COPENHAGEN

1 Sept 1939
Germany invades
Poland

LI

KONI
E.PRUSS.

DANZIG

EDINBURGH

GREAT

EIRE

DUBLIN LIVERPOOL

BRITAIN

HAMBURG

BERLIN

Vistula

PO

AMSTERDAM

NETH.

LONDON

W

DUNKIRK

COLOGNE

GERMANY

PRAGUE

BRUSSELS BELG.

SLOVAKIA

10 May 1940
Germany invades
the Low Countries
and France

4 June 1940

Rhine

LUX.

PARIS

FRANCE

Danube

MUNICH

VIENNA

BUDAP

Bay of
Biscay

VICHY BERNE

SWITZ.

HUNGARY

25 June 1940
BORDEAUX
(Vichy France)

MILAN

BELGRADE

MARSEILLES

TURIN

VENICE

YUGOSLAV

FLORENCE

Adriatic Sea

LISBON

MADRID

10 June 1940
Italy declares war
on Britain and France

ROME

ALBANIA

PORTUGAL

SPAIN

NAPLES

Sardinia

M
E
D
I
T
E
R
R
A
N
E

PALERMO

28 Oct 1940
Italy invades
Greece

GIBRALTAR (Br)

Sicily

SP.MOR.

ALGIERS

TUNIS

MALTA (Br)

CASABLANCA

ORAN

MOROCCO
(Fr)

ALGERIA
(Fr)

TUNISIA
(Fr)

TRIPOLI

SIRTE

EL A

L
I
B
Y

(Italian)

Ceded Rumanian territories:
1. Bessarabia & N. Bukovina to Russia, June 1940
2. S. Dobruja to Bulgaria, August 1940
3. Transylvania to Hungary, September 1940

ATLANTIC

OCEAN

Barents Sea

SAMO

MURMANSK

White Sea

ARCHANGEL

USSALMI

Ceded to Russia, 1940

NLAND

**30 Nov 1939-1 March 1940
Russo-Finnish War**

VIIPURI

INKI

L.Ladoga

LENINGRAD

STONIA

**June 1940
Annexed by Russia**

RIGA

LATVIA

THUANIA

KAUNAS

GSBERG

IA

MINSK

MOSCOW

R U S S I A

SMOLENSK

VORONEZH

Volga

**17 Sept 1939
Russia invades
Poland**

STALINGRAD

ARSAW

LAND

KIEV

Dnieper

KHARKOV

Don

LVOV

ROSTOV

*Caspian
Sea*

EST

3

ODESSA

1

RUMANIA

SEVASTOPOL

TIFLIS

BUCHAREST

Danube

2

BLACK SEA

IA

BULGARIA

SOFIA

IRAN

ISTANBUL

ANKARA

T U R K E Y

GREECE

IRAQ
(Br)

ATHENS

SYRIA
(Fr)

Dodecanese
(Italian)

Cyprus
(Br)

DAMASCUS

Crete

A

N

S

E

A

PALESTINE
(Br)

AMMAN

JERUSALEM

TRANSJORDAN
(Br)

TOBRUK

ALEXANDRIA

*Suez
Canal*

BENGHAZI

Nile

CAIRO

**SAUDI
ARABIA**

GHEILA

A

EGYPT
(Br protectorate)

AXIS PARTNERS: 1939

GERMANY | | | | ITALY

GERMAN SATELLITE

GERMAN OCCUPIED, 27 SEPT 1939

GERMAN OCCUPIED, 23 JUNE 1940

GERMAN FRONT LINES AT
DATES SHOWN

MILES   500

0

KILOMETERS   800

0

The War in Europe
and North Africa,
1941–42

GERMAN OCCUPIED, 1 JAN 1941
ALLIED WITH AXIS
GERMAN OCCUPIED, 1 JAN – 29 MAY 1941
22 JUNE 1941 – 19 NOV 1942

GERMAN FRONT LINES
— — — 16 JULY 1941
– – – – 5 DECEMBER 1941
—·—·— END-APRIL 1942
—··—··— 19 NOVEMBER 1942

MILES 0 — 500
KILOMETERS 0 — 800

Barents Sea

MURMANSK

White Sea

ARCHANGEL

AND

PETROZAVODSK

L.Ladoga

**15 Sept 1941
Seige of Leningrad
begins**

LENINGRAD

DEMYANSK

**5/6 Dec 1941-end April 1942
Russian counteroffensive
on Moscow axis**

PSKOV

MOSCOW

RIGA

R U S S I A

KAUNAS

RG

SMOLENSK

TULA

Volga

MINSK

VORONEZH

**19 Nov 1942
High-tide of German expansion.
Russian counteroffensive begins**

W

KIEV

KHARKOV

STALINGRAD

Dnieper

Don

LVOV

ZAPOROZHYE

ROSTOV

*Caspian
Sea*

ODESSA

GROZNY

NOVOROSSIISK

UMANIA

SEVASTOPOL

TIFLIS

UCHAREST

Danube

BLACK SEA

BULGARIA

SOFIA

IRAN

ISTANBUL

ANKARA

T U R K E Y

EECE

SYRIA
(Free French)

IRAQ
(Br)

ATHENS

*Dodecanese
(Italian)*

Cyprus
(Br)

DAMASCUS

**1941
ded**

Crete

PALESTINE
(Br)
JERUSALEM

AMMAN

TRANSJORDAN
(Br)

S E A

**Brit Eighth Army
:tles across the desert**

ALEXANDRIA

*Suez
Canal*

**SAUDI
ARABIA**

TRIPOLI

EL ALAMEIN

Nile

CAIRO

LA

**23 Oct-4 Nov 1942
Battle of El Alamein**

A

E G Y P T

The War in Europe,
and North Africa,
1943–44

The Defeat of Germany, 1944–45

LIBERATED/OCCUPIED BY ALLIES
23 JUNE –15 DECEMBER 1944 *
15 DECEMBER 1944 – 7 MAY 1945

ALLIED FRONT LINES
25 AUGUST 1944
15 DECEMBER 1944
21 MARCH 1945
7 MAY 1945

* German forces withdrew from Greece, Albania and Yugoslavia in face of partisan attacks

0   MILES   500
0   KILOMETERS   800

Barents Sea

MURMANSK

White Sea

ARCHANGEL

NLAND

VIIPURI
INKI

L.Ladoga

LENINGRAD

PSKOV

RIGA

R U S S I A

MOSCOW

KAUNAS
SBERG

SMOLENSK

MINSK

VORONEZH

Volga

RSAW

D

KIEV

Dnieper

KHARKOV

STALINGRAD

LVOV

ROSTOV

Don

Caspian Sea

EST

ODESSA

RUMANIA
BUCHAREST

SEVASTOPOL

• TIFLIS

A

Danube

25 Aug 1944
Rumania and
8 Dec 1944
Bulgaria declare
war on Germany

BLACK SEA

BULGARIA
■ SOFIA

IRAN

ISTANBUL

ANKARA

T U R K E Y

GREECE

SYRIA
(Free Fr)

IRAQ
(Br)

■ ATHENS

Dodecanese

Cyprus
(Br)

DAMASCUS

Crete

A   N   S   E   A

PALESTINE
(Br)
JERUSALEM

AMMAN
TRANSJORDAN
(Br)

TOBRUK

ALEXANDRIA

Suez Canal

BENGHAZI

EL ALAMEIN

Nile

CAIRO

SAUDI
ARABIA

A

E G Y P T
(Br prot)

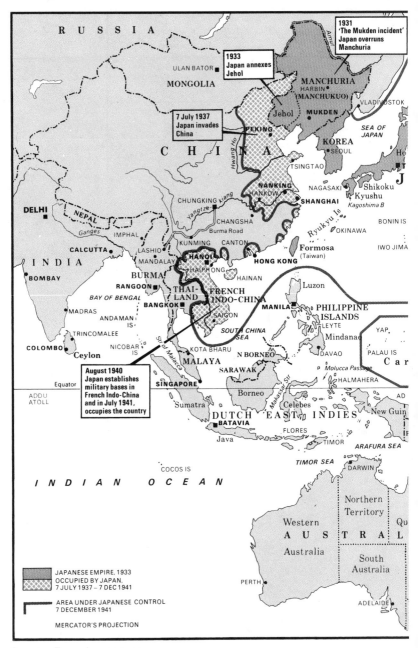

Japanese Expansion, 1931–41

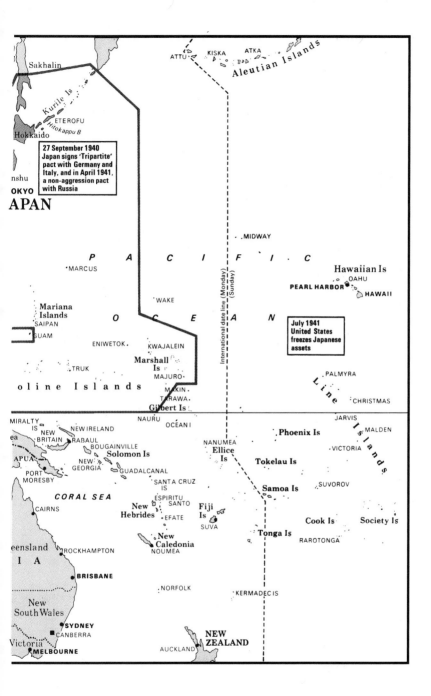

Sakhalin

Kurile Is

ETEROFU
Hitokappu B
Hokkaido

nshu

OKYO
APAN

27 September 1940
Japan signs 'Tripartite'
pact with Germany and
Italy, and in April 1941,
a non-aggression pact
with Russia

ATTU   KISKA   ATKA   Aleutian Islands

•MIDWAY

P   A   C   I   F   I   •   C

•MARCUS

•WAKE

Mariana
Islands
SAIPAN

GUAM

ENIWETOK•

KWAJALEIN

**Marshall
Is**
MAJURO•

oline Islands

MAKIN•
TARAWA•
Gilbert Is

O   C   E   A   N

International date line (Monday)
(Sunday)

**July 1941
United States
freezes Japanese
assets**

Hawaiian Is
OAHU
PEARL HARBOR
HAWAII

PALMYRA

Line Islands

•CHRISTMAS

JARVIS

NAURU•   OCEAN I

MIRALTY
IS
NEW   NEW IRELAND
ea   BRITAIN RABAUL
APUA   BOUGAINVILLE   **Solomon Is**
NEW
PORT   GEORGIA   GUADALCANAL
MORESBY
SANTA CRUZ
IS
CORAL SEA   ESPIRITU
CAIRNS   SANTO
New   •EFATE
Hebrides

ROCKHAMPTON

eensland
I   A

•BRISBANE

New
South Wales

SYDNEY
CANBERRA
Victoria
•MELBOURNE

NANUMEA
**Ellice
Is**

•NORFOLK

AUCKLAND

•MALDEN
•Phoenix Is
•VICTORIA

Tokelau Is

Samoa Is   •SUVOROV

Fiji
Is
SUVA

•Tonga Is

Cook Is   Society Is

RAROTONGA

•KERMADEC IS

**NEW
ZEALAND**

New
Caledonia
NOUMEA

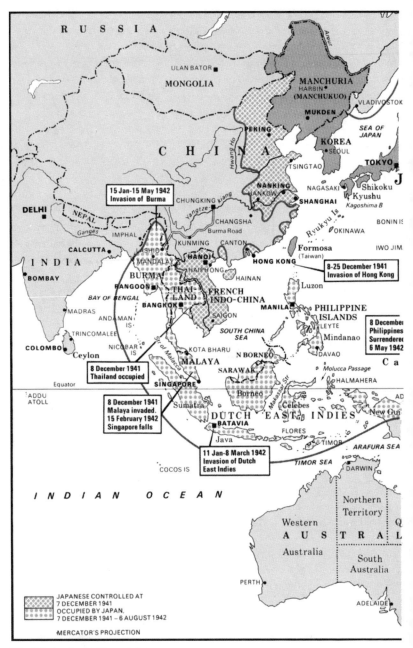

The War in the Pacific and Asia, 1941–42

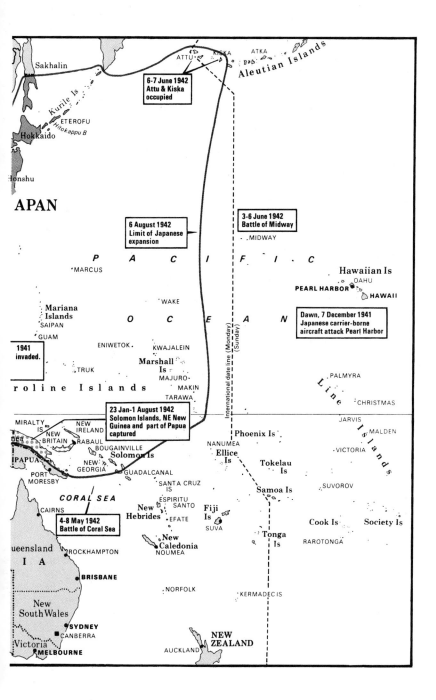

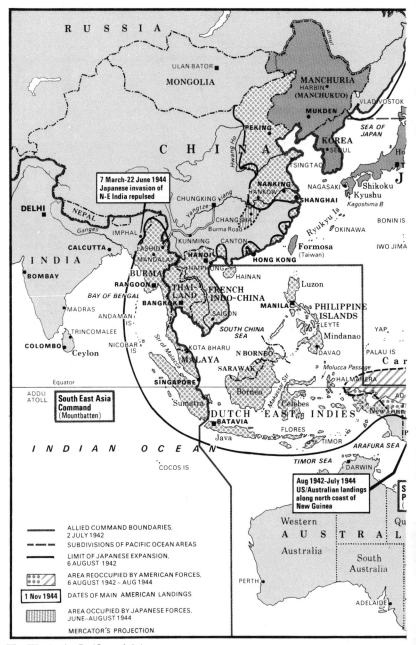

The War in the Pacific and Asia, 1942–44

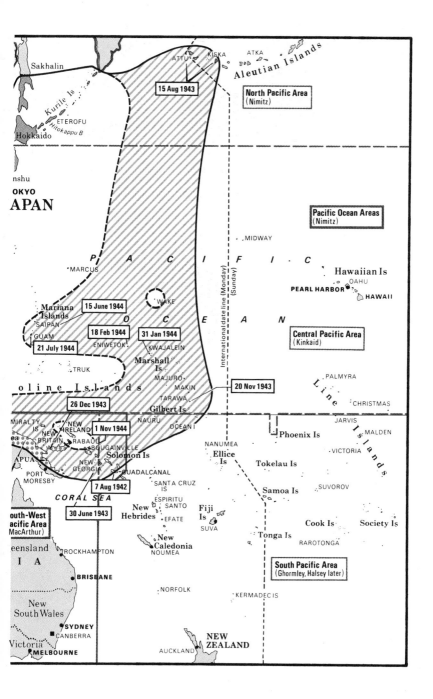

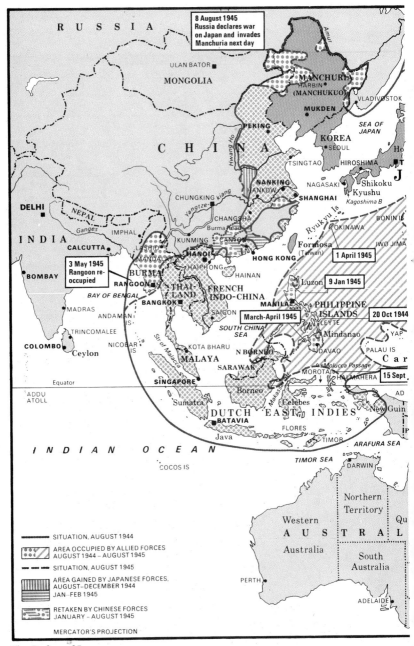

The Defeat of Japan, 1944–45

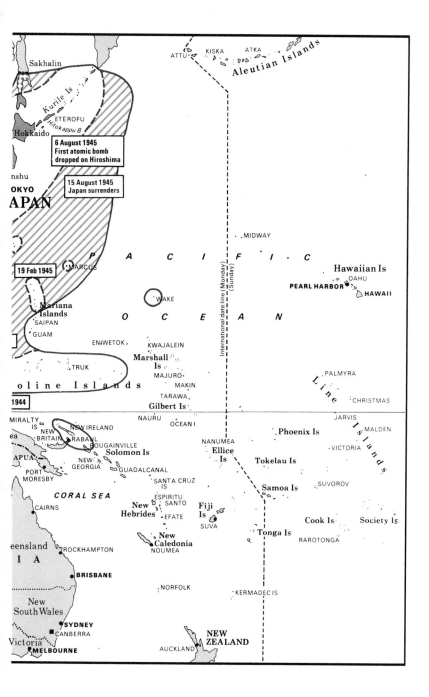

Biographical Notes

PHELPS ADAMS (December 14, 1902–January 13, 1991) Born in Boston, Massachusetts. Educated at University of Colorado, Columbia School of Journalism, London School of Economics, and the Sorbonne. Worked briefly for New York *Herald* before joining staff of New York *Sun*, becoming a reporter in 1926 and serving as Washington correspondent from 1928 to 1950. War correspondent aboard U.S.S. *Enterprise*, April–May 1945. Worked as public relations executive for U.S. Steel Corporation, 1950–67.

JAMES AGEE (November 27, 1909–May 15, 1955) Born in Knoxville, Tennessee. Educated at Harvard. Staff writer for *Fortune*, 1932–37. Published *Permit Me Voyage* (1934), a poetry collection, and *Let Us Now Praise Famous Men* (1941), report on Alabama sharecroppers with photographs by Walker Evans. Wrote book and film reviews and feature articles for *Time* and film reviews for *The Nation*. Wrote screenplays for *The Quiet One* (1949), *The African Queen* (1951), and *The Night of the Hunter* (1955); published novella *The Morning Watch* (1951). His novel *A Death in the Family*, published posthumously in 1957, won the Pulitzer Prize. Film reviews and screenplays collected in *Agee on Film* (1958–60), and correspondence in *The Letters of James Agee to Father Flye* (1962).

SUSAN B. ANTHONY II (July 26, 1916–July 8, 1991) Born in Easton, Pennsylvania (great-niece of suffragist Susan B. Anthony). Educated at University of Rochester and American University. Reporter for *Washington Star*, 1942–43. Published *Out of the Kitchen—Into the War: Women's Winning Role in the Nation's Drama* in 1943, followed by *Women During the War and After* (1945). Wrote for *Key West Citizen* (1950–53) and *Jamaica Gleaner* (1956–60). In later years, active in organizing alcoholism treatment programs; converted to Roman Catholicism and served as Eucharistic minister in Deerfield Beach, Florida. Her autobiography, *The Ghost in My Life*, appeared in 1971.

JACK BELDEN (1910–89) Born in Brooklyn, New York. Educated at Adelphi Academy and Colgate University. Following graduation lived in China for ten years, eventually becoming correspondent for United Press, International News Service, and *Time*; published *New Fourth Army* (1938). Accompanied General Joseph Stilwell on retreat from Burma in May 1942, described in *Retreat with Stilwell* (1943). Wounded at Salerno, Italy, in September 1943; after months of rehabilitation, returned to Europe to cover the final phases of the war. *Still Time to Die*, a collection of war pieces, published in 1944. Returned to China in 1946 to cover civil war; published *China Shakes the World* (1949). Spent last decades of his life in Paris.

WALTER BERNSTEIN (August 20, 1919–) Born in Brooklyn, New York. Educated at Dartmouth. Wrote for *The New Yorker* and *Yank*, publishing accounts of army training camps and later covering the war in Italy; in Yugoslavia in early 1944 met and interviewed Tito. In Hollywood, worked on screenplay of *Kiss the Blood Off My Hands* (1948); active in writing scripts for live television; blacklisted during 1950s. Later screenwriting credits include *That Kind of Woman* (1959), *Heller in Pink Tights* (1960), *Paris Blues* (1961), *Fail Safe* (1964), *The Train* (1964), *The Money Trap* (1966), *The Molly Maguires* (1970), *The Front* (1976), *Semi-Tough* (1977), *Yanks* (1978), and *The House on Carroll Street* (1988). Most recently he has written *Inside Out: A Memoir of the Blacklist* (1996).

HOMER BIGART (October 25, 1907–April 16, 1991) Born in Hawley, Pennsylvania. Educated Carnegie Institute of Technology and New York University. Began to work for New York *Herald Tribune* as copyboy in 1929; became reporter in 1933. Traveled to Europe as war correspondent in 1942, moving to Pacific theater in autumn 1944. Won Pulitzer Prize in 1951 for coverage of Korean War (in Korea, intense professional rivalry with fellow *Tribune* correspondent Marguerite Higgins became famous among journalists). Left *Tribune* for *The New York Times* in 1955. In later years covered the Middle East, the trial of Nazi war criminal Adolf Eichmann, and the Vietnam War. Writings collected posthumously in *Forward Positions: The War Correspondence of Homer Bigart* (1992).

MARGARET BOURKE-WHITE (June 14, 1904–August 27, 1971) Born in the Bronx, New York. Educated at Columbia, where she studied photography with Clarence H. White, University of Michigan, and Cornell. Acquired reputation as industrial photographer and in 1929 went to work for *Fortune*. Traveled often to Soviet Union in early 1930s and made documentary films there. Became staff photographer for *Life* from its inception in 1936. With novelist Erskine Caldwell, produced collaborative works about southern sharecroppers (*You Have Seen Their Faces*, 1937), Central Europe (*North of the Danube*, 1939), and everyday life in America (*Say, is this the U.S.A.*, 1941); married to Caldwell 1939–42. Traveled in Soviet Union with Caldwell in 1941 and the following year published *Russia at War* (text by Caldwell) and *Shooting the Russian War* (text by Bourke-White). Covered war in North Africa and Italy; Italian experiences described in *They Called It "Purple Heart Valley"* (1944). In Germany in spring 1945 covered advance of American army; photographed Buchenwald concentration camp immediately after its liberation; published book on Germany, *"Dear Fatherland, Rest Quietly."* In later years, traveled in India (about which she wrote *Halfway to Freedom*, 1949), South Africa, and Korea. Career as photographer cut short by Parkinson's disease. An autobiography, *Portrait of Myself*, appeared in 1963.

HOWARD BRODIE (November 28, 1915–) Born in Oakland, California. Educated at Art Institute of San Francisco, Art Students League, New York, and University of Ghana (Accra). Staff artist for *Life*, *Yank*, *Collier's*, Associated Press, and (from 1969 to 1989) for CBS News. As sketch artist, covered World War II, the Korean War, the Vietnam War, and many important trials and public hearings, including those of Jack Ruby, James Earl Ray, Sirhan Sirhan, Lt. William Calley, Charles Manson, the Chicago Seven, and the Watergate conspirators. A portfolio of his art, *Howard Brodie's War Drawings*, was published in 1963. *Drawing Fire: A Combat Artist at War* appeared in 1996.

CECIL BROWN (September 14, 1907–October 25, 1987) Born in New Brighton, Pennsylvania. Educated Western Reserve University and Ohio State University. Worked as reporter for United Press, Los Angeles, 1931–32; edited Prescott (Arizona) *Journal-Miner*, 1933; on staff of *Pittsburgh Press*, 1934–36, and *Newark Ledger*, 1936–37. In late 1930s freelanced in Europe and North Africa and worked for International News Service. Broadcaster for CBS in Rome (1940–41), until expelled by Mussolini government for "hostile attitude," and in Yugoslavia, Cairo, and Singapore (1941–42); resigned from CBS in 1942, charging network with censorship of controversial opinion. Published *Suez to Singapore* in 1942. News commentator for Mutual Broadcasting System (1944–57) and ABC (1957–58) and Tokyo bureau chief for NBC from 1958 to 1962. He was later a television and radio news commentator in Los Angeles and taught at California State Polytechnic University.

VIRGINIA COWLES (August 24, 1910–September 17, 1983) Born in Brattleboro, Vermont. Traveled with family to England in 1917; educated privately. Contributed column to the Boston *Breeze* in the early 1930s. Foreign correspondent for *Sunday Times* (London), *London Daily Telegraph*, and Hearst newspapers. Covered Spanish Civil War; later reported from Russia, Germany, Czechoslovakia, Finland, and France; returned to England in 1940 after fall of France. Published *Looking for Trouble* in 1941. Special assistant to American ambassador to London, 1942–43; reported from Italy and France in 1944. Remained in London after the war; married Aidan Crawley (later British cabinet official and member of Parliament) in 1945. *No Cause for Alarm*, study of British society, published in 1949. Published many biographies and popular histories, including *Winston Churchill: The Era and the Man* (1953), *Edward VII and His Circle* (1956), *The Phantom Major: The Story of David Stirling and His Desert Command* (1958), *1913: The Defiant Swan Song* (1967), *The Russian Dagger: Cold War in the Days of the Czars* (1969), *The Romanovs* (1971), *The Rothschilds* (1973), *The Astors* (1979), and *The Great Marlborough and His Duchess* (1983).

JOHN H. CRIDER (February 26, 1906–July 7, 1966) Born in Mount Vernon, New York. Educated at Columbia School of Journalism. After graduation worked for *The New York Times*. Worked briefly as economic correspondent for *Time* in 1942 before rejoining the *Times*. Published *The Bureaucrat* (1944). In 1946, appointed editor-in-chief of *Boston Herald*; received Pulitizer Prize in 1949 for economic reporting. Dismissed in 1951 after internal dispute over his editorial attacks on Senator Robert A. Taft. Later worked for CBS, *Life*, and *Barron's Weekly*, as diplomatic correspondent in London for International News Service, for Committee for Economic Development, and for Morgan Guaranty Trust Company (1964–66).

JANET FLANNER (March 13, 1892–November 7, 1978) Born in Indianapolis, Indiana. Studied for two years at University of Chicago (dismissed for exerting "rebellious influence"). Served as film critic for *Indianapolis Star*, active in support of woman suffrage; worked at girls' reformatory in Pennsylvania. Settled in Paris in 1922, living for 18 years at Hotel Saint-Germain-des-Prés; under pen name "Genêt," became Paris correspondent of *The New Yorker* from its founding in 1925. *The Cubical City*, a novel, appeared in 1926. Returned to U.S. in October 1939. *New Yorker* pieces collected in *An American in Paris* (1940) and *Pétain: The Old Man of France* (1944); translated two novels by Colette, *Chéri* (1929) and *Claudine at School* (1930). Returned to Paris in November 1944; went to Germany, reporting from Cologne and Buchenwald. Continued "Letter from Paris" for *The New Yorker* for 30 years. Writings collected in *Men and Monuments* (1957), *Paris Journal: 1944–1965* (1965), *Paris Journal: 1965–1971* (1971), *Paris Was Yesterday, 1925–1930* (1971), and *London Was Yesterday, 1934–1939* (1975), along with the posthumous volumes *Janet Flanner's World: Uncollected Writings, 1932–1975* (1979) and *Darlinghissima: Letters to a Friend* (1985). Died in New York.

MARTHA GELLHORN (November 1908–February 15, 1998) Born in St. Louis, Missouri. Educated at Bryn Mawr. Worked in New York for *The New Republic* and in Albany as a reporter for *Times Union*. Traveled in Europe and around the U.S. in early 1930s, often with French writer Bertrand de Jouvenel. First novel, *What Mad Pursuit*, published 1934. Worked as field investigator for Federal Emergency Relief Administration; dined at White House with the Roosevelts, forming lifelong friendship with Eleanor Roosevelt. *The Trouble I've Seen*, collection of short stories based on relief work, published 1936. On trip to Key West in December 1936 met Ernest Hemingway and traveled with him in Spain, March–May 1937; worked in field hospitals and visited Loyalist fronts; account of fighting published in *Collier's*, to which she became a regular contributor. Returned three more times to Spain in 1938, and also reported from England and Czechoslovakia. Lived with Hemingway in Cuba for much of 1939–40, writing novel *A Stricken Field* (1940) and story collection *The Heart of Another* (1941). Covered Soviet-Finnish War, November–December 1939. Married Hemingway in November 1940, and traveled to Asia in February 1941, spending several months in China with him and traveling on alone to Java and Singapore. Covered war in Europe, October 1943–February 1944 and May 1944–May 1945. Published novel *Liana* (1944). Marriage to Hemingway ended in 1945. Collaborated with Virginia Cowles on play *Love Goes to Press* (1946), comedy about war correspondents. Reported on Indonesian rebellion against the Dutch and on

Nuremberg war crimes trials. In 1947 launched attack on House Un-American Activities Committee. Published novels *The Wine of Astonishment* (1948; republished as *Point of No Return*), *His Own Man* (1961), and *The Lowest Trees Have Tops* (1967), story collections *The Honeyed Peace* (1953), *Two by Two* (1958), *Pretty Tales for Tired People* (1965), and *The Weather in Africa* (1981), and memoir *Travels with Myself and Another* (1978). Married to T. S. Matthews, 1954–63. Settled in England. War reporting collected in *The Face of War* (1959; revised edition, 1987). Reported on Eastern Europe and the Middle East; traveled to Vietnam as correspondent for *The Guardian* in 1966, and to Israel in 1967 during Six-Day War; reported on El Salvador and Nicaragua during 1980s. Her last book, *Novellas*, was published in 1993.

BRENDAN GILL (October 4, 1914–December 27, 1997) Born in Hartford, Connecticut. Educated at Yale. Contributor to *The New Yorker* since 1936, writing frequently on film and theater. During World War II wrote on aspects of the American home front. In later years active in campaign to preserve urban landmarks in New York City. Books include *The Trouble of One House* (1950), *The Day the Money Stopped* (1957), *Tallulah* (1972), *Ways of Loving* (1974), *Here at The New Yorker* (1978), *A Fair Land to Build In* (1984), *Many Masks: A Life of Frank Lloyd Wright* (1987), and *A New York Life* (1990).

FOSTER HAILEY (August 13, 1899–August 13, 1966) Born in Meredosia, Illinois. Educated University of Missouri. Served in navy for two years during World War I. After the war worked as reporter for *New Orleans Item-Tribune*, *Miami Daily Tab*, *Tampa Sun*, and *Des Moines Tribune*. Staff member of Associated Press, 1927–37; joined *The New York Times* in 1937. Spent two years in the Pacific during World War II before being invalided home with malaria in September 1943; *Pacific Battle Line*, a memoir, published 1944. Continued to work for the *Times* on a variety of assignments, traveling extensively in Asia and Latin America. Published *Half of One World*, study of Asian nationalism, in 1947. After five years as member of the *Times* editorial board, resigned in 1948 because of dispute over the paper's coverage of Indonesia; continued to work for the *Times* as reporter and editorial writer until 1965. Co-author with Milton Lancelot of *Clear for Action: The Photographic Story of Modern Naval Combat, 1898–1964*.

JOHN HERSEY (June 17, 1914–March 24, 1993) Born in Tientsin, China, son of American missionaries; spent first ten years of life in China. Educated at Yale and Cambridge. Worked for Sinclair Lewis as secretary in 1937. Began to work for *Time* in 1937; traveled to Asia as correspondent in 1939; went to England in 1942 to cover war. Reported from Southwest Pacific and Italy for *Time* and *Life*, and published three nonfiction books about the war: *Men on Bataan* (1942), *Into the Valley* (1943), and *Hiroshima* (1946). His novel *A Bell for Adano*, about American occupation of Sicily, won Pulitzer Prize for 1944. Master of Pierson College at Yale, 1965–70. Later novels include *The Wall*

(1950), *The Marmot Drive* (1953), *A Single Pebble* (1956), *The War Lover* (1959), *The Child Buyer* (1960), *Too Far to Walk* (1966), *Under the Eye of the Storm* (1967), and *The Call* (1985); also published nonfiction including *The Algiers Motel Incident* (1968), *Letter to the Alumni* (1970), and *The President* (1975).

VIRGINIA IRWIN (June 29, 1908–August 19, 1980) Born in Quincy, Illinois. Educated at Lindenwood College (St. Charles, Missouri) and Gem City Business College (Quincy, Illinois). Began working for St. Louis *Post-Dispatch* in 1932, becoming feature writer for the paper's magazine supplement. After outbreak of World War II, focused on home front, including II-part series on women in war industries; denied assignment as war correspondent, went to Europe to work for Red Cross. Received accreditation from War Department just before D-Day, and arrived in France in July 1944; covered war in France, Belgium, Holland, Luxembourg, and Germany. In late April 1945, without official permission, drove to Berlin with Boston *Traveler* correspondent Andrew Tully, witnessing final days of fighting; military authorities delayed publication of story and stripped her of credentials as war correspondent. Worked at New York bureau of *Post-Dispatch*, 1946–60.

ANNALEE JACOBY (May 27, 1916–) Born Annalee Whitmore in Price, Utah; grew up in California. Educated at Stanford. Screenwriter for MGM. Worked in Chungking for United China Relief, 1941; married Melville Jacoby in Manila two weeks before Japanese invasion. With husband, escaped to Australia in March 1942. Co-author, with Theodore H. White, of *Thunder Out of China* (1946). Later married Clifton Fadiman in 1950.

MELVILLE JACOBY (1916–42) Born in Los Angeles, California. Educated at Stanford; spent junior year in China as exchange student; returned to Asia after completing master's degree. Worked for Chinese government information bureau in Chungking, then worked in Indochina as United Press correspondent for six months. Became head of *Time*'s Far East bureau in Manila in 1941; married Annalee Whitmore on November 24th of that year. Escaped from Philippines in March 1942 to Australia, where he was killed in airplane accident a month later.

EDWARD KENNEDY (1905–63) Born in Brooklyn, New York. Studied architecture at Carnegie Tech. Worked for Canonsburg (Pennsylvania) *Daily Notes* and on newspapers in New York, New Jersey, and Washington, D.C. Became staff member of Paris edition of *Herald Tribune* in 1931. Subsequently returned to U.S. and worked for *Newark Ledger*. Joined Associated Press in 1932; assigned to Paris bureau, 1934. Covered Spanish Civil War and developments in Balkans and Middle East. Accompanied General Archibald Wavell to Crete in 1940; was only American to cover British capture of Tobruk; subsequently reported on Italian campaign, including Anzio. After breaking a pledge to delay reporting the German surrender for 24 hours, stripped of credentials as war correspondent and dismissed by Associated Press. Became managing editor of Santa Barbara (California) *Press* in 1946, and in 1949 joined *Monterey Peninsula Herald.*

HELEN KIRKPATRICK (1909–1997) Born in Rochester, New York. Educated at Smith College and University of Geneva. Worked for Foreign Policy Association in Geneva as editor and writer for *Geneva Research Bulletin.* Wrote for British publications including *Manchester Guardian, London News Chronicle, London Daily Telegraph;* edited *Whitehall News;* foreign correspondent in Geneva for New York *Herald Tribune.* Published *This Terrible Peace* (1938) and *Under the British Umbrella: What the English Are and How They Go to War* (1939). Foreign correspondent for *Chicago Daily News* in London, 1939-44. Traveled with Free French forces; covered Normandy advance and liberation of Paris, then became *Daily News* Paris bureau chief before going into Germany in April 1945. In 1946 became foreign correspondent for New York *Post.* As head of information division of Economical Cooperation Administration in Paris, 1949–51, involved in implementation of Marshall Plan. Later served as adviser to Dean Acheson in State Department's European Affairs Bureau and as assistant to the president of Smith College, 1953–55.

WILLIAM L. LAURENCE (March 7, 1888–March 19, 1977) Born in Salantai, Lithuania, son of Lipman and Sarah Siew. Came to U.S. in 1905, adopting name Laurence; studied at Harvard and Boston University. Became U.S. citizen in 1913; after serving in World War I studied at University of Besançon in France. Wrote for New York *World* from 1926, and in 1930 moved to *The New York Times,* specializing in science reporting. Won Pulitzer Prize for 1936. In front-page story published in the *Times* in May 1940, predicted development of atomic energy. Attached to the Manhattan Project, witnessed secret Alamogordo atomic test explosion on July 16, 1945, and accompanied bombing mission over Nagasaki, winning a second Pulitzer Prize in 1946. Science editor of the *Times,* 1956–64. Author of *Dawn Over Zero: The Story of the Atomic Bomb* (1946), *The Hell Bomb* (1951), and *Men and Atoms* (1959). Died in Majorca.

HELEN LAWRENSON (1907–82) Born Helen Brown in LaFargeville, New York. Educated at Vassar. Worked for *Syracuse Herald,* 1926–30; editor at *Vanity Fair,* 1932–35; later wrote frequently for *Esquire.* Early journalism collected in *The Hussy's Handbook, Including Latins Are Lousy Lovers and Others* (1937). Married to Jack Lawrenson, leading figure in National Maritime Union, 1939–57. Published two volumes of memoirs, *Stranger at the Party* (1975) and *Whistling Girl* (1978), as well as *Latins Are Still Lousy Lovers* (1968) and a novel, *Dance of the Scorpions,* which appeared posthumously in 1982.

BEIRNE LAY, JR. (September 1, 1909–May 26, 1982) Born in Berkeley Springs, West Virginia. Educated at Yale. Entered Army Air Corps in 1932.

Published *I Wanted Wings* in 1937 (collaborated on screenplay of 1941 film version). As lieutenant colonel, commanded a B-24 bomber group in the 8th Air Force during World War II. Shot down over France in May 1944, he evaded capture with the aid of members of the French resistance; experience recounted in *I've Had It: The Survival of a Bomb Group Commander* (1945). With Sy Bartlett, wrote novel *Twelve O'Clock High* (1947) and was nominated for Academy Award for screenplay of 1949 film based on the book. Later screenwriting credits include *Above and Beyond* (1952), *Strategic Air Command* (1955), *Toward the Unknown* (1956), and *The Gallant Hours* (1960). Published *Earthbound Astronauts* in 1971.

TOM LEA (July 11, 1907–) Born in El Paso, Texas. Studied at Art Institute of Chicago. Worked as mural painter and commercial artist in Chicago (1926–33), New Mexico (1933–35), and El Paso from 1936. War correspondent for *Life*, 1941–46; combat experiences recounted in *A Grizzly from the Coral Sea* (1944) and *Peleliu Landing* (1945). Author of *The Brave Bulls* (1949), *The Wonderful Country* (1952), *The King Ranch* (1957), *The Primal Yoke* (1960), *The Hands of Cantu* (1964), *A Picture Gallery* (1968), *In the Crucible of the Sun* (1974), and *The Southwest: It's Where I Live* (1992).

LARRY LESUEUR (June 10, 1909–) Born in New York City. Educated at New York University. Worked as reporter for *Women's Wear Daily*; joined United Press 1931. Radio commentator for CBS in Europe from 1939; after French surrender became assistant to Edward R. Murrow in London. Went to Soviet Union in fall of 1941; published *Twelve Months That Changed the World* (1943) and broadcast weekly radio series "An American in Russia." Later traveled in Middle East and Africa. From 1963, worked for United States Information Agency as a writer, correspondent, and information specialist.

A. J. LIEBLING (October 18, 1904–December 21, 1963) Born Abbott Joseph Liebling in New York City. Educated at Dartmouth and Columbia School of Journalism. Worked for *The New York Times* as copyreader, 1925–26, and briefly for Providence (R.I.) *Journal* as reporter. Sailed to Europe in summer 1926; studied French medieval literature at Sorbonne. Returned to Providence in autumn 1927, continuing to write for *Journal*. Moved to New York and wrote for New York *World*, 1930–31, and *World-Telegram*, 1931–35. Married Ann Quinn in 1934, despite knowing that she was schizophrenic (in the course of their marriage she was hospitalized many times). Joined staff of *The New Yorker* in 1935; early pieces collected in *Back Where I Came From* (1938) and *The Telephone Booth Indian* (1942). Flew to Europe in October 1939 to cover war; remained in Paris until June 10, 1940; returned to U.S. by way of Lisbon. Flew to Britain in July 1941 to cover war; after briefly returning to U.S. in early 1942, sailed to Algeria in November. Followed war on Tunisian front, January–May 1943. Early war pieces collected in *The Road Back to Paris* (1944). Covered D-Day invasion and afterwards spent two months in Normandy and Brittany, June–August, before returning to U.S. Began writing column "The Wayward Press" in 1945. Collected material from French resistance newspapers for *La République du Silence* (1946). Criticized House Un-American Activities Committee and became friend of Alger Hiss. Divorced from Ann Quinn; married Lucille Spectorsky in 1949; following dissolution of second marriage, married novelist Jean Stafford in 1959. Later books include *The Wayward Pressman* (1947), *Mink and Red Herring: The Wayward Pressman's Casebook* (1949), *Chicago: The Second City* (1952), *The Honest Rainmaker: The Life and Times of Colonel John R. Stingo* (1953), *The Sweet Science* (1956), *Normandy Revisited* (1958), *The Press* (1961), *The Earl of Louisiana* (1961), and *Between Meals: An Appetite for Paris* (1962). Wartime articles collected posthumously in *Mollie and Other War Pieces* (1964).

BILL MAULDIN (October 29, 1921–) Born in Mountain Park, New Mexico. Attended high school in Phoenix, Arizona; studied at Chicago Academy of Fine Arts. Served with 45th Infantry Division and as staff cartoonist for *Stars and Stripes*, 1940–45; participated in campaigns in Italy and France. Cartoons collected in *Star Spangled Banter* (1941), *Sicily Sketch Book* (1943), *Mud, Mules and Mountains* (1943), and *This Damn Tree Leaks* (1945); won Pulitzer Prize as cartoonist in 1945. *Up Front*, collection of cartoons with linking text, became a bestseller in 1945. After the war, cartoonist for St. Louis *Post-Dispatch* until 1962, and thereafter for *Chicago Sun-Times*. Appeared as actor in films *Teresa* (1950) and *The Red Badge of Courage* (1950). Received second Pulitzer Prize in 1959. Later publications include *Back Home* (1945), *A Sort of a Saga* (1949), *Bill Mauldin's Army* (1951), *Bill Mauldin in Korea* (1952), *What's Got Your Back Up?* (1961), *I've Decided I Want My Seat Back* (1965), *Mud and Guts* (1978), and *Let's Declare Ourselves Winners and Get the Hell Out* (1985); *The Brass Ring*, an autobiography, appeared in 1971.

LEE MILLER (April 23, 1907–July 27, 1977) Born Elizabeth Miller in Poughkeepsie, New York. Studied at theater school in Paris, 1925–26. In 1927 met Condé Nast and became model for *Vogue*; worked as model for photographers including Edward Steichen and Arnold Genthe. Studied at Art Students League in New York. Returned to France in 1929 and lived with Surrealist artist and photographer Man Ray; established her own photography studio; starred in Jean Cocteau's film *Le Sang d'un poète* (*The Blood of a Poet*, 1930). Opened studio in New York in 1932 and took portraits of many artists and celebrities including Virgil Thomson, Joseph Cornell, and Gertrude Lawrence. Married wealthy Egyptian Aziz Eloui in 1934; lived with him for three years in Cairo and Alexandria. Returned to Paris in summer of 1937; met Roland Penrose, English painter and writer, and traveled with him throughout Europe. Settled with Penrose in London after outbreak of war in 1939. Joined staff of *Vogue*; in addition to fashion photography, took pictures of London Blitz and British war effort; photographs collected in *Grim Glory: Pictures of Britain Under Fire* (1940) and *Wrens in Camera* (1942). In June 1944 traveled to Normandy as war correspondent for *Vogue*; was present at siege of St. Malo and liberation of Paris; covered fighting in Luxembourg and Alsace and advance of Allies into Germany. Married Ronald Penrose in 1947. Photographs included in exhibit *The Family of Man* in 1955.

MACK MORRISS (November 11, 1919–February 18, 1976) Born in Baltimore, Maryland; lifelong resident of Elizabethton, Tennessee. Staff writer for *Yank*, May 1942–July 1945; covered campaigns on Guadalcanal and New Georgia in the Solomons, Siegfried Line and Huertgen Forest in the European theater, and was among first American correspondents to enter Berlin after its fall in May 1945 in defiance of ban by Allied authorities. After the war worked briefly for *Life* and as freelance writer, 1946–51; published war novel *The Proving Ground* (1951). Editor, Elizabethton *Star*, 1951–55; newscaster and later manager of radio station WBEJ, 1956–76. Mayor of Elizabethton, 1966–69.

EDWARD R. MURROW (April 25, 1908–April 27, 1965) Born Egbert Roscoe Murrow in Greensboro, North Carolina. Educated at Washington State College. President of National Student Federation of America (1930–31); as assistant director of Institute of International Education, 1932–34, participated in resettlement of German scholars fleeing Nazism. Became director of talks and educational programs for CBS in 1935, and in 1937 became head of CBS European bureau in London; assembled staff that eventually included William L. Shirer, Howard K. Smith, Charles Collingwood, Larry Lesueur, Richard C. Hottelet, and Cecil Brown. Became well known for broadcasts during London Blitz; broadcasts collected in *This Is London* (1941). Continued to report on war from Europe and North Africa. Became CBS vice-president for news programs in 1946. Produced radio program *Hear It Now*, which moved to television as *See It Now* (1951–58); also developed interview program *Person-to-Person* (1953–59). Critical television report on Senator Joseph McCarthy in 1954 played significant role in undermining McCarthy's influence. Became head of U.S. Information Agency in 1961, resigning in 1964 due to illness.

TED NAKASHIMA (August 19, 1911–September 14, 1980) Born Seattle. Degree in architecture from University of Washington. While interned as Japanese-American during the war, employed by federal government as architect in defense housing program. After a period as a chicken farmer in Spokane, worked in later years as director of facilities planning at school districts in Kirkland and Silverdale, Washington.

MINÉ OKUBO (June 27, 1912–) Born in Riverdale, California. Educated at Riverside Junior College and University of California at Berkeley. Received art fellowship and traveled in Europe, 1938–39. Worked as artist for

Federal Arts Program; received prizes and exhibited work in San Francisco in 1940 and 1941. Interned in 1942 at Tanforan Relocation Camp in San Bruno, California; transferred later to Central Utah Relocation Camp, Topaz, Utah; helped found literary magazine *Trek* with other internees. Released from camp in March 1944 to accept job offer from *Fortune* in New York to illustrate special issue on Japan; remained in New York, working as illustrator and freelance graphic artist. Participated in 1945 in exhibit of drawings and paintings of Japanese relocation camps; published *Citizen 13660*, memoir of internment camps, in 1946. Testified in 1981 before government commission on wartime relocation. Major retrospectives of her work were held in Oakland in 1974, in New York in 1985, and in Boston in 1993.

ROI OTTLEY   (August 2, 1906–October 1, 1960)   Born in New York City. Educated at St. Bonaventure College (Olean, New York), University of Michigan, and St. John's Law School (Brooklyn, New York). Worked for *New York Amsterdam News* as reporter, columnist, and editor, 1931–37. Joined New York City Writers' Project as editor in 1937. Published *New World A-Coming: Inside Black America* in 1943; it became a bestseller and was adapted into a series of radio programs. Worked as war correspondent for *PM*, *Pittsburgh Courier*, and *Liberty*; publicity director of National CIO War Relief Committee in 1943. Other books include *Black Odyssey: The Story of the Negro in America* (1948), *No Green Pastures* (1951), *The Lonely Warrior: The Life and Times of Robert S. Abbott* (1955), *White Marble Lady* (1965), a novel, and *The Negro in New York: An Informal Social History, 1626–1940* (1967, with William J. Weatherby).

ERNIE PYLE   (August 3, 1900–April 18, 1945)   Born Ernest Taylor Pyle on farm near Dana, Indiana. Attended Indiana University but did not complete journalism degree. Worked briefly in early 1923 as reporter for a local paper, *The La Porte Herald*, then joined the Scripps-Howard *Washington Daily News*. In 1926, with wife, Geraldine Siebolds, traveled around the U.S.; worked for a short time in New York for the *Evening World* before returning to *Washington Daily News* in 1927 as telegraph editor. Wrote aviation column and became aviation editor for Scripps-Howard chain, 1928–32. Managing editor of *Daily News*, 1932–35. In 1935 began six-day-a-week human interest column based on regular travels across U.S. and to Alaska, Hawaii, and Central and South America (prewar columns collected posthumously in *Home Country*, 1947). Went to England in November 1940 for three-month stay; English columns collected in *Ernie Pyle in England* (1941). Divorced in July 1942; Geraldine committed to sanitarium shortly afterward for six-month stay. Flew to England in June 1942 to cover training of American troops. Accompanied Allied troops to Algeria in November 1942; went to Tunisian front in January 1943. Remarried to Geraldine by proxy in March 1943. Covered Tunisian war with 1st Infantry Division until campaign's end in mid-May; Tunisian dispatches collected in *Here Is Your War* (1943). Covered Sicilian campaign (July–August 1943) and returned to U.S. in September;

Geraldine hospitalized again at end of visit. Returned to Italy in November; at Anzio in March 1944, narrowly escaped death from a German bomb. Won Pulitzer Prize in 1943. Went to France immediately after D-Day invasion. Featured in *Time* cover story in July. Caught in accidental bombing of U.S. troops by American aircraft in Normandy on July 25. *Brave Men*, another compilation of columns, published 1944. Returned to U.S. in September and was hailed by press and public. Geraldine made suicide attempt during visit. Involved in discussions with makers of *The Story of G.I. Joe*, film based on his columns. In January 1945 sailed to Hawaii to cover Pacific theater; boarded aircraft carrier U.S.S. *Cabot*, sailing to Marianas and then proceeding to Okinawa with 1st Marine Division. Killed by Japanese sniper on Ie Shima, small island near Okinawa. Final columns collected in *Last Chapter* (1946).

ROBERT ST. JOHN (March 9, 1902–) Born in Chicago, Illinois. Studied at Trinity College (Connecticut). Reporter for *Hartford Courant*, *Chicago American*, and *Chicago Daily News*, 1922–23. With brother owned and operated *Cicero Tribune*, *Berwyn Tribune*, and *Riverside Times* in Illinois, 1923–35; was badly beaten by members of the Capone mob after writing an exposé about one of its brothels. Editor, 1927–31, at Rutland (Vermont) *News*, *Rutland Herald*, Camden (New Jersey) *Courier*, and *Philadelphia Record*. Balkan correspondent for Associated Press, 1939–41; experiences in Yugoslavia and Greece recounted in *The Land of Silent People* (1942). NBC news commentator from London, Washington, and New York, 1942–46; subsequently correspondent for NBC-Monitor (1959–60) and Syndicated Broadcast Features (1960–70). Later books include *It's Always Tomorrow* (1944), *The Silent People Speak* (1948), *Shalom Means Peace* (1949), *Tongue of the Prophets* (1952), *This Was My World* (1953), *Through Malan's Africa* (1954), *Foreign Correspondent* (1957), *Ben-Gurion* (1959), *The Boss: The Biography of Nasser* (1960), *Builder of Israel* (1961), *They Came From Everywhere* (1962), *Roll Jordan Roll: The Story of a River and Its People* (1965), *Encyclopedia of Broadcasting* (1967), *Jews, Justice, and Judaism* (1969), *South America More or Less* (1970), and *Eban* (1972).

VINCENT SHEEAN (December 5, 1899–March 15, 1975) Born James Vincent Sheean in Pana, Illinois. Educated at University of Chicago. Worked for *Chicago Daily News* and *New York Daily News*. Went to Paris in 1922 and became correspondent for *Chicago Tribune*. Covered Riff rebellion in Morocco in 1925, publishing *An American Among the Riffs* (1926). Worked thereafter as freelancer; during coverage of Chinese revolution in 1927, met American Communist Rayna Prohme, whom he credited with steering him toward an activist approach to journalism. Covered Jerusalem riots of 1929, Italian invasion of Ethiopia, and German reoccupation of the Rhineland. Memoir *Personal History* (1935) became bestseller. Covered Spanish Civil War for New York *Herald Tribune*. During World War II, joined U.S. Army Air Force and participated in invasion of Italy. Traveled to India to interview Mahatma Gandhi and witnessed Gandhi's assassination in

1948. Other books include *The New Persia* (1927); *Not Peace But a Sword* (1939); *Between the Thunder and the Sun* (1943); *This House Against This House* (1946); *Lead Kindly, Light* (1949), study of Gandhi; *The Indigo Bunting* (1950), memoir of Edna St. Vincent Millay; *Mahatma Gandhi* (1955); *Oscar Hammerstein I* (1956); *Orpheus at Eighty* (1958), biography of Verdi; *Nehru: Ten Years of Power* (1959); *Dorothy and Red* (1963), memoir of Dorothy Thompson and Sinclair Lewis; and *Faisal: The King and His Kingdom* (1975). Also published eight novels. Died at his home in Arolo, Italy.

ROBERT SHERROD   (February 8, 1909–February 14, 1994)   Born Thomas County, Georgia. Educated University of Georgia. Worked as reporter for *Atlanta Constitution*, Palm Beach (Fla.) *Daily News*, and other newspapers (1929–35). Correspondent and editor for *Time* and *Life* (1935–52). Began covering U.S. military in mid-1941; traveled with first convoys to Australia in February 1942, and covered Marine landings on Tarawa, Saipan, and Iwo Jima. Far East correspondent (1952–55) and editor (1955–64) at *The Saturday Evening Post*; vice-president of Curtis Publishing (1965–66). Author of *Tarawa: The Story of a Battle* (1944), *On to Westward: War in the Central Pacific* (1945), and *History of Marine Corps Aviation in World War II* (1952); contributed to *Life's Picture History of World War II* (1950) and *Apollo Expeditions to the Moon* (1975).

WILLIAM L. SHIRER   (February 23, 1904–December 28, 1993)   Born in Chicago, Illinois; from age of nine grew up in Cedar Rapids, Iowa. Educated at Coe College. Worked for Paris edition of *Chicago Tribune*, 1925–27; foreign correspondent for *Tribune*, 1927–30, reporting from Paris, London, Rome, and Vienna; traveled to Afghanistan, India, and Middle East, 1930–31. Worked on Paris edition of New York *Herald*, 1934; went to Berlin in August 1934 as correspondent for Universal News Service. Joined CBS in 1937, broadcasting from Vienna, London, Prague, Berlin, and Paris. Witnessed French surrender at Compiègne in June 1940. Left Berlin in December 1940 after being warned that he might soon be arrested on charges of espionage; after return to U.S. published *Berlin Diary* (1941), which became bestseller. Left CBS in 1947 following public dispute with management, whom he accused of forcing him out because of his liberal views, a charge denied by Edward R. Murrow as network spokesman. Columnist for New York *Herald Tribune* (1942–48); news broadcaster for Mutual Broadcasting System (1947–49); after being cited in anti-Communist publication *Red Channels*, blacklisted from broadcasting during 1950s. Awarded National Book Award for *The Rise and Fall of the Third Reich* (1960). Other books include *End of a Berlin Diary* (1947), *Midcentury Journey* (1952), *The Sinking of the Bismarck* (1962), *The Collapse of the Third Republic* (1969), *20th Century Journey* (1976), *Gandhi: A Memoir* (1979), *The Nightmare Years* (1984), and *A Native's Return* (1990). Also published novels *The Traitor* (1950), *Stranger Come Home* (1954), and *The Consul's Wife* (1956).

HOWARD K. SMITH (May 12, 1914–) Born in Ferriday, Louisiana. Educated at Tulane University. Traveled to Europe in 1936 following graduation. Worked for *New Orleans Item-Tribune* before attending Oxford as Rhodes scholar. In 1939 served as London and Copenhagen correspondent for United Press; subsequently stationed in Germany. In 1941 worked as assistant to Harry Flannery, CBS radio correspondent, and became sole Berlin correspondent for CBS following Flannery's return to U.S. Left Berlin on December 7, 1941, and continued to broadcast from Berne, Switzerland. Published *Last Train from Berlin* (1942). Succeeded Edward R. Murrow in 1946, reporting on European and Middle Eastern affairs from London. After returning to the U.S., was a reporter and commentator for television shows including *CBS Reports, Face the Nation,* and *Eyewitness to History.* Later books include *The State of Europe* (1949) and *The Story of Our Nation's Capital* (1967). Became CBS Washington correspondent in 1957, resigning in 1961 because of policy disagreements; joined ABC as anchorman and commentator for the *ABC Evening News.* His autobiography, *Events Leading up to My Death: The Life of a Twentieth-Century Reporter,* was published in 1996.

JOHN STEINBECK (February 27, 1902–December 20, 1968) Born in Salinas, California. Studied at Stanford University. Published fiction including *The Pastures of Heaven* (1932) and *To a God Unknown* (1933) before achieving wider readership with *Tortilla Flat* (1935), *In Dubious Battle* (1936), and *Of Mice and Men* (1937). *The Grapes of Wrath* (1939) became a bestseller. Worked as writer for Foreign Information Service under Robert E. Sherwood, 1941–42. *The Moon Is Down,* novel about the Nazi occupation of Norway, published in 1942. Visited air bases across U.S. to write *Bombs Away: The Story of a Bomber Team* (1942) for army air force. Served as war correspondent in England, North Africa, and Italy for New York *Herald Tribune,* June–October 1943, participating in naval commando raids as part of special operations unit in Mediterranean. Later novels included *Cannery Row* (1945), *The Wayward Bus* (1947), *The Pearl* (1947), *East of Eden* (1952), and *The Winter of Our Discontent* (1961). Traveled to Vietnam as war correspondent for New York *Newsday,* 1966–67.

OTTO D. TOLISCHUS (November 20, 1890–February 24, 1967) Born in Germany near Memel (now part of Lithuania). Renounced German citizenship in 1907 and went to U.S.; worked in factories in Syracuse, New York, and Trenton, New Jersey. Studied at Columbia School of Journalism. Joined staff of *Cleveland Press* in 1916. Returning to Europe in 1923, worked for Hearst's Universal Service in Berlin, 1923–31, and for International News Service in London, 1931–32. Returned to Berlin as correspondent for *The New York Times* in 1933; expelled by Nazis in 1940, receiving Pulitzer Prize the same year. Went to Tokyo in January 1941 to replace Hugh Byas as bureau chief. Imprisoned by Japanese following Pearl Harbor; subjected to harsh conditions including torture; repatriated on *Gripsholm* in July 1942. Author of *They Wanted War* (1940), *Tokyo Record* (1943), and *Through Japanese Eyes* (1945). After the war, member of the editorial board of the *Times*.

RICHARD TREGASKIS (November 28, 1916–August 15, 1973) Born in Elizabeth, New Jersey. Educated at Harvard; an editor of *Harvard Crimson*. While still at Harvard began to write for *Boston American* where he subsequently joined editorial staff. Later joined cable department of International News Service. Accompanied Marines on invasion of Guadalcanal; *Guadalcanal Diary* (1943) became bestseller. Severely wounded in Italy in November 1943; Italian experiences recounted in *Invasion Diary* (1944). After intensive rehabilitation accompanied U.S. First Army from Normandy to Aachen. Flew five missions with B-29 crew in Pacific and with torpedo squadron. Published *Stronger Than Fear*, a war novel, in 1945. After the war, wrote for *The Saturday Evening Post* and other periodicals. Later books include *Seven Leagues to Paradise* (1951), *X-15 Diary* (1961), *John F. Kennedy and PT 109* (1962), *Vietnam Diary* (1963), and *China Bomb* (1967).

VINCENT TUBBS (September 25, 1915–February 1989) Born in Dallas, Texas. Educated at Morehouse College and Atlanta University. Editor and publisher of *Macon Broadcast*, 1940–41; news editor, *Norfolk Journal and Guide*, 1942–43. From 1943 to 1947 he was foreign and war correspondent for *Baltimore Afro-American*, and was an editor of the paper until 1954. Subsequently worked as editor for *Ebony* (1954–55) and *Jet* (1955–59), before establishing successful career in Hollywood as film publicist. Elected president of Hollywood Publicists' Guild in 1967; press director for community relations at Warner Brothers, 1971–80.

MARY HEATON VORSE (October 9, 1874–June 14, 1966) Born Mary Heaton in New York City. Married writer and explorer Albert White Vorse in 1898 (he died in 1910). Lived in Provincetown, Massachusetts, from 1907; associated there with writers including Eugene O'Neill, Edna St. Vincent Millay, Susan Glaspell, and Max Eastman; involved in founding of Provincetown Players. Following husband's death, turned to writing to support family; early books included *The Very Little Person*, *The Heart's Country*, *The Ninth Man*, *The Prestons*, *I've Come to Stay*, and *Growing Up: The Autobiography of an Elderly Woman*, about her mother's life, published in 1911. As journalist, covered Lawrence, Massachusetts, textile strike of 1912; married radical journalist Joseph O'Brien in the spring of that year (he died in 1915). Reported on famine in Soviet Union, 1921–22, for Hearst papers. As labor activist, addressed striking textile workers in Passaic, New Jersey, in 1926, and textile union rally in Gastonia, North Carolina, in 1930 at which violence broke out. Wounded in 1937 by vigilante gunfire during steel strike in Youngstown, Ohio. Went to Europe in 1939 and covered German occupation of Czechoslovakia, invasion of Poland, and French preparations for war. Author of *Men and Steel* (1920), *Passaic* (1926), *Second Cabin* (1928), *Strike!: A*

Novel of Gastonia (1930), *Footnote to Folly* (1935), *Labor's New Millions* (1938), and *Time and the Town* (1942). Traveled in Europe on behalf of United Nations Relief and Rehabilitation Administration, 1945–47.

WILLIAM WALTON (1909–94) Born in Jacksonville, Illinois. Educated at Illinois College and University of Wisconsin. Worked for Associated Press in Chicago and New York from 1935 to 1940. Covered war news for *PM* (1940–42) and for *Time* and *Life* (1942–46); parachuted into Normandy at beginning of D-Day invasion, June 1944. Washington editor of *The New Republic*, 1946–49. Later worked as painter and freelance writer; served as chairman of Fine Arts Commission, 1963–71. Author of *The Evidence of Washington* (1968) and editor of *A Civil War Courtship: The Letters of Edwin Weller From Antietam to Atlanta* (1980).

E. B. WHITE (July 11, 1899–October 1, 1985) Born Elwyn Brooks White in Mount Vernon, New York. Educated at Cornell University. Worked from 1921 as reporter and editor for the *Cornell Sun*, the United Press, and the *Seattle Times*; also worked as advertising copywriter. Became contributor and editor at *The New Yorker*, largely responsible for "The Talk of the Town." Wrote monthly column "One Man's Meat" for *Harper's Magazine*, 1938–43. Lived with his wife Katharine on farm in Maine from 1938. Books include *Is Sex Necessary?* (with James Thurber, 1929), *Every Day Is Saturday* (1934), *The Fox of Peapack* (1938), *Quo Vadimus?* (1939), *One Man's Meat* (1942), *Stuart Little* (1945), *The Wild Flag* (1946), *Here Is New York* (1949), *Charlotte's Web* (1952), *The Second Tree from the Corner* (1953), *The Points of My Compass* (1962), and *The Trumpet of the Swan* (1970); co-edited *A Subtreasury of American Humor* (1941). Awarded Presidential Medal of Freedom in 1963 and Pulitzer Prize special citation in 1978.

EVAN WYLIE (December 9, 1916–) Born Evan McLeod Wylie in Dunellen, New Jersey. Educated University of Virginia. Staff editor for *Newsweek*, 1941–42. Staff writer for *Yank*, 1944–45. After war, contributed frequently to periodicals including *The Saturday Evening Post*, *Holiday*, *Collier's*, *Life*, and *The Reader's Digest*. Co-authored *Movin' On Up* (1966), autobiography of Mahalia Jackson; other books include *The Nine Months* (1971), a novel, and *A Guide to Voluntary Sterilization: The New Birth Control* (1972). With Jack Ruge, wrote play later adapted into film *Joe Butterfly* (1957); also wrote screenplays and television scripts. Contributing editor to *Yankee* since 1980.

Note on the Texts

This volume collects newspaper and magazine articles, transcripts of radio broadcasts, and excerpts from books by American writers and reporters written between 1938 and 1946, and dealing with events connected with World War II and its aftermath in the period between October 1938 and August 1946. The texts chosen are the first published versions.

The following is a list of the sources of the texts included in this volume, listed alphabetically by author. For untitled pieces and book excerpts, a phrase selected from the text has been enclosed in quotation marks and used as a title. (In the case of articles from *Yank* and some newspaper articles, variant versions may exist in different editions.)

Phelps Adams. Attack on Carrier Bunker Hill: *The New York Sun*, June 28, 1945.

James Agee. "These Terrible Records of War": *The Nation*, March 24, 1945.

Susan B. Anthony II. Working at the Navy Yard: *The New Republic*, May 1, 1944.

Jack Belden. Flight Through the Jungle: Belden, *Retreat with Stilwell* (New York: Alfred A. Knopf, 1943), pp. 289–304.

Walter Bernstein. Search for a Battle: *The New Yorker*, September 23, 1944.

Homer Bigart. San Pietro a Village of the Dead; Victory Cost Americans Dearly: New York *Herald Tribune*, December 20, 1943. Japan Signs, Second World War Is Ended: New York *Herald Tribune*, September 2, 1945. A Month After the Atom Bomb: Hiroshima Still Can't Believe It: New York *Herald Tribune*, September 5, 1945.

Margaret Bourke-White. Over the Lines: Bourke-White, *They Called It "Purple Heart Valley": A Combat Chronicle of the War in Italy* (New York: Simon & Schuster, 1944), pp. 3–11.

Howard Brodie. Jump-Off: *Yank*, March 11, 1945 (Continental Edition); drawings from *Yank*, April 13, 1945.

Cecil Brown. "Prepare to Abandon Ship": Columbia Broadcasting System, *From Pearl Harbor Into Tokyo: The Story as Told by War Correspondents on the Air* (New York: Columbia Broadcasting System, 1945).

Virginia Cowles. The Beginning of the End: Cowles, *Looking for Trouble* (New York and London: Harper & Brothers, 1941), pp. 375–383.

John H. Crider. U.S. Board Bares Atrocity Details Told by Witnesses at Polish Camps: *The New York Times*, November 26, 1944.

Janet Flanner (Genêt). Letter from Cologne: *The New Yorker*, March 31, 1945.

Fortune. Issei, Nisei, Kibei: *Fortune*, April 1944. Drawings by Miné Okubo.

Martha Gellhorn. The Battle of the Bulge: Gellhorn, *The Face of War* (New

York: Simon & Schuster, 1959). Das Deutsches Volk (originally published as "We Were Never Nazis"): *Collier's*, May 26, 1945.

Brendan Gill. Young Man Behind Plexiglass: *The New Yorker*, August 12, 1944.

Robert Hagy. "The Worst News That I Have Encountered in the Last 20 Years": *Time-Life-Fortune* News Bureau, *War Comes to the U.S.—Dec. 7th, 1941: The First 30 Hours* (New York: Time-Life-Fortune, 1942).

Foster Hailey. The Battle of Midway: Hailey, *Pacific Battle Line* (New York: The Macmillan Company, 1944), pp. 170–178.

John Hersey. Hiroshima: *The New Yorker*, August 31, 1946.

Virginia Irwin. "A Giant Whirlpool of Destruction": *St. Louis Post-Dispatch*, May 9, May 10, and May 11, 1945.

Annalee Jacoby. Bataan Nurses: *Life*, June 15, 1942.

Melville Jacoby. War Hits Manila: Gordon Carroll (ed.), *History in the Writing* (New York: Duell, Sloan and Pearce, 1945), pp. 45–50.

Edward Kennedy. The War in Europe Is Ended!: *The New York Times*, May 8, 1945.

Helen Kirkpatrick. Daily News Writer Sees Man Slain at Her Side in Hail of Lead: *The Chicago Daily News*, August 26, 1944.

William L. Laurence. Atomic Bombing of Nagasaki Told By Flight Member: *The New York Times*, September 9, 1945.

Helen Lawrenson. "Damn the Torpedoes!": *Harper's Magazine*, July 1942.

Beirne Lay, Jr. I Saw Regensburg Destroyed: *The Saturday Evening Post*, November 6, 1943.

Tom Lea. Peleliu Landing: Lea, *Peleliu Landing* (El Paso: Carl Hertzog, 1945).

Larry Lesueur. "Tanks and Cannons Standing Starkly in the Snow": Lesueur, *Twelve Months That Changed the World* (New York: Alfred A. Knopf, 1943), pp. 85–99.

A. J. Liebling. Paris Postscript: *The New Yorker*, August 3, 1940. The Foamy Fields: *The New Yorker*, March 20, April 3, April 10, and April 17, 1943. The A.P. Surrender: *The New Yorker*, May 19, 1945.

Bill Mauldin. from *Up Front*: Mauldin, *Up Front* (New York: Henry Holt and Company, 1945).

Lee Miller. The Siege of St. Malo: *Vogue*, October 1944. Photographs by Lee Miller.

Mack Morriss. War in the Huertgen Forest: *Yank*, January 5, 1945.

Edward R. Murrow. Can They Take It?: Murrow, *This Is London* (New York: Simon & Schuster, 1941), pp. 157–191. "The Target Was To Be the Big City": Edward Bliss, Jr. (ed.), *In Search of Light: The Broadcasts of Edward R. Murrow, 1938–1961* (New York: Alfred A. Knopf, 1967), pp. 70–76. "For Most of It I Have No Words": *In Search of Light: The Broadcasts of Edward R. Murrow, 1938–1961*, pp. 90–95.

Ted Nakashima. Concentration Camp, U.S. Style: *The New Republic*, June 15, 1942.

New York *Herald Tribune*. President's War Message: New York *Herald Tribune*, December 9, 1941.

The New York Times. 1,000,000 Jews Slain by Nazis, Report Says: *The New York Times,* June 30, 1942. Allies Are Urged to Execute Nazis: *The New York Times,* July 2, 1942.

Roi Ottley. Negroes Are Saying . . . : Ottley, *'New World A-Coming'* (Boston: Houghton Mifflin Company, 1943), pp. 306–326.

Ernie Pyle. "This Dreadful Masterpiece": Scripps-Howard wire copy, December 30, 1940. "Only Slightly Above the Caveman Stage": Scripps-Howard, February 19, 1943. "What a Tank Battle Looks Like": Scripps-Howard, March 1, 1943. "The Fantastic Surge of Caterpillar Metal": Scripps-Howard, March 2, 1943. "Into the Thick of the Battle": Scripps-Howard, March 3, 1943. "Brave Men. Brave Men!": Scripps-Howard, April 22, 1943. "Little Boys Again, Lost in the Dark": Scripps-Howard, April 27, 1943. "The Greatest Damage Is Psychological": Scripps-Howard, May 1, 1943. "The God-Damned Infantry": Scripps-Howard, May 2, 1943. "This One Is Captain Waskow": Scripps-Howard, January 10, 1944. "And Yet We Got On": Scripps-Howard, June 12, 1944. "The Wreckage Was Vast and Startling": Scripps-Howard, June 16, 1944. "This Long Thin Line of Personal Anguish": Scripps-Howard, June 17, 1944. "A Ghastly Relentlessness": Scripps-Howard, August 8, 1944. "The Universe Became Filled with a Gigantic Rattling": August 9, 1944. "Anybody Makes Mistakes": Scripps-Howard, August 10, 1944. "This Weird Hedgerow Fighting": Scripps-Howard, August 11, 1944.

Robert St. John. Under Fire: St. John, *From the Land of Silent People* (New York: Doubleday, Doran and Co., 1942), pp. 242–258.

Vincent Sheean. Aufenthalt in Rosenheim: *The New Republic,* December 7, 1938.

Robert Sherrod. "I Didn't Know Whether We Had the Heart to Fight a War": Sherrod, *Tarawa: The Story of a Battle* (New York: Duell, Sloan and Pearce, 1944), pp. 30–35. View of the Carnage: *Tarawa,* pp. 123–146. "The Hard Facts of War": *Tarawa,* pp. 147–151. The First Three Days: *Life,* March 5, 1945.

William L. Shirer. "It's All Over": Shirer, *Berlin Diary* (New York: Alfred A. Knopf, 1941), pp. 144–147. "Revengeful, Triumphant Hate": *Berlin Diary,* pp. 419–425.

Howard K. Smith. Valhalla in Transition: Smith, *Last Train from Berlin* (New York: Alfred A. Knopf, 1942), pp. 143–174.

John Steinbeck. Fear of Death as Green Troops Sail to Invasion: New York *Herald Tribune,* October 3, 1943.

Otto D. Tolischus. Last Warsaw Fort Yields to Germans: *The New York Times,* September 29, 1939. The Way of Subjects: Tolischus, *Tokyo Record* (New York: Reynald and Hitchcock, 1943), pp. 186–191.

Richard Tregaskis. Battle of the Ridge: Tregaskis, *Guadalcanal Diary* (New York: Random House, 1943), pp. 204–251. "Then I Got It": *Invasion Diary* (New York: Random House, 1944), pp. 203–214.

Rupert Trimmingham and others. Democracy?: *Yank,* April 28, June 9, and July 28, 1944.

Vincent Tubbs. No Picturesque Battle Scenes in SWP War: *Baltimore Afro-American*, February 12, 1944. Homesick Joe in Pacific: *Baltimore Afro-American*, February 26, 1944. Men Can't Sleep; They Talk, Dream of Home: *Baltimore Afro-American*, March 18, 1944.

Mary Heaton Vorse. The Girls of Elkton, Maryland: *Harper's Magazine*, March 1943.

William Walton. Now the Germans Are the Refugees: *Life*, November 6, 1944.

E. B. White. Bond Rally: "One Man's Meat," *Harper's Magazine*, December 1942.

Evan Wylie. Ernie Pyle: *Yank*, May 18, 1945.

ACKNOWLEDGMENTS

Great care has been taken to trace all owners of copyright material included in this book. If any have been inadvertently omitted or overlooked, acknowledgment will gladly be made in future printings.

James Agee. "These Terrible Records of War": Reprinted with permission from the March 24, 1945, issue of *The Nation*; © The Nation Company, Inc. "A Soldier Died Today": © 1945 Time Inc. Reprinted by permission.

Susan B. Anthony II. Working at the Navy Yard: Originally appeared in *The New Republic*.

Walter Bernstein. Search for a Battle: Published in *Keep Your Head Down* by Walter Bernstein. Copyright © 1945. Used by permission of Walter Bernstein. Originally published in *The New Yorker*.

Homer Bigart. San Pietro a Village of the Dead; Victory Cost Americans Dearly: From New York *Herald Tribune*, December 20, 1943. © 1943, New York Herald Tribune Inc.; all rights reserved, reprinted by permission. Japan Signs, Second World War Is Ended: From the New York *Herald Tribune*, September 2, 1945. © 1945, New York Herald Tribune Inc.; all rights reserved; reprinted by permission. A Month After the Atom Bomb: Hiroshima Still Can't Believe It: From the New York *Herald Tribune*, September 5, 1945. © 1945, New York Herald Tribune Inc.; all rights reserved; reprinted by permission.

Margaret Bourke-White. Over the Lines: Reprinted by permission of the Estate of Margaret Bourke-White.

Cecil Brown. "Prepare to Abandon Ship": CBS Radio Network broadcast. Printed with permission.

Virginia Cowles. The Beginning of the End: From *Looking for Trouble* by Virginia Cowles. Copyright 1941 by Virginia Cowles, copyright renewed 1969 by Virginia Cowles. Reprinted by permission of HarperCollins Publishers, Inc.

John H. Crider. U.S. Board Bares Atrocity Details Told by Witnesses at Polish Camps: Copyright © 1944, 2000 by The New York Times Company; reprinted by permission.

Janet Flanner (Genêt). Letter from Cologne: First published in *The New Yorker*, March 31, 1945. Reprinted by permission of William Murray.

Fortune. Issei, Nisei, Kibei: © 1944 Time, Inc. Reprinted by permission.

Martha Gellhorn. The Battle of the Bulge; Das Deutsches Volk: From *The Face of War*, copyright © 1988, reprinted by permission of Grove/Atlantic, Inc., and Dr. Alexander Matthews.

Brendan Gill. Young Man Behind Plexiglass: From *The New Yorker Book of War Pieces* (Schocken Books). © 1944, 1972 The New Yorker Magazine, Inc. Reprinted by permission of The Estate of Brendan Gill.

Foster Hailey. The Battle of Midway: Copyright © 1944 by Foster Hailey, renewed.

John Hersey. Hiroshima: *Hiroshima* by John Hersey. Copyright 1946 and renewed 1974 by John Hersey. Used by permission of Alfred A. Knopf, a division of Random House, Inc.

Virginia Irwin. "A Giant Whirlpool of Destruction": Reprinted with the permission of *St. Louis Post-Dispatch*, © 1945.

Annalee Jacoby. Bataan Nurses: Reprinted by permission of the author.

Edward Kennedy. The War in Europe Is Ended!: Copyright © 1945 by The New York Times Company; reprinted by permission of The Associated Press.

Helen Kirkpatrick. Daily News Writer Sees Man Slain at Her Side in Hail of Lead: Reprinted by permission of the Sophia Smith Collection, Smith College.

William L. Laurence. Atomic Bombing of Nagasaki Told By Flight Member: Copyright © 1945, 2000 by The New York Times Company; reprinted by permission.

Beirne Lay, Jr. I Saw Regensburg Destroyed: Reprinted from *The Saturday Evening Post*, © 1943.

Tom Lea. Peleliu Landing: Reprinted by permission of the author and The Still Point Press. Drawings reprinted by permission of the Harry Ransom Humanities Research Center of The University of Texas at Austin and Tom Lea.

Larry Lesueur. "Tanks and Cannons Standing Starkly in the Snow": From *Twelve Months That Changed the World* by Larry Lesueur. Copyright 1943 by Larry Lesueur; used by permission of Alfred A. Knopf, a division of Random House, Inc.

A. J. Liebling. Paris Postscript: *New Yorker*, August 3, 1940. © 1940 by A. J. Liebling, copyright renewed 1968 by Jean Stafford. Reprinted by permission of Russell & Volkening as agents for the author. The Foamy Fields: *New Yorker*, March 20, April 3, April 10, and April 17, 1943. © 1964 by Jean Stafford, renewed in 1992 by Norma Stonehill. Reprinted by permission of Russell & Volkening as agents for the author. The A.P. Surrender: *The New Yorker*, May 19, 1945. © copyright 1945 by A. J. Liebling, copyright renewed 1973 by Jean Stafford. Reprinted by permission of Russell & Volkening as agents for the author.

Bill Mauldin. *Up Front*: Published by permission of Bill Mauldin and The Watkins/Loomis Agency.

Lee Miller. The Siege of St. Malo: Reprinted from *Lee Miller's War* by Anthony Penrose. © 1992 by The Lee Miller Archives; by permission of Little, Brown and Company, Inc., and Ebury Press.

Edward R. Murrow. Can They Take It?: © 1941 by Edward R. Murrow; copyright renewed 1969 by Janet H. B. Murrow and Charles Casey Murrow. Reprinted with permission of Casey Murrow on behalf of the Estates of Edward R. Murrow and Janet H. B. Murrow. "The Target Was To Be the Big City": © 1943 by Edward R. Murrow; copyright renewed 1969 by Janet H. B. Murrow and Charles Casey Murrow. Reprinted with permission of Casey Murrow on behalf of the Estates of Edward R. Murrow and Janet H. B. Murrow. "For Most of It I Have No Words": Edward Bliss, Jr. (ed.), *In Search of Light: The Broadcasts of Edward R. Murrow, 1938–1961.* © by Edward R. Murrow; copyright renewed 1969 by Janet H. B. Murrow and Charles Casey Murrow.

Ted Nakashima. Concentration Camp, U.S. Style: Originally in *The New Republic*.

New York *Herald Tribune*. President's War Message: From New York *Herald Tribune*, December 9, 1941. © 1941, New York Herald Tribune Inc.; all rights reserved; reprinted by permission.

The New York Times. 1,000,000 Jews Slain by Nazis, Report Says: Copyright © 1942 by The New York Times Company; reprinted by permission. Allies Are Urged to Execute Nazis: Copyright © 1942 by The New York Times Company; reprinted by permission.

Roi Ottley. Negroes Are Saying . . . : Reprinted with permission of Lynne Ottley Ware.

Ernie Pyle. All Ernie Pyle pieces reprinted by permission of the Scripps Howard Foundation. The assistance of Weil Journalism Library, Indiana University, is gratefully acknowledged.

Robert St. John. Under Fire: Copyright © 1942, © renewed 1969 by Robert St. John. Reprinted by permission of Harold Matson Co., Inc.

Vincent Sheean. Aufenthalt in Rosenheim: Originally appeared in *The New Republic*.

Robert Sherrod. "I Didn't Know Whether We Had the Heart to Fight a War"; View of the Carnage; "The Hard Facts of War": Reprinted by permission of The Admiral Nimitz Foundation. The First Three Days: © 1945 Time, Inc.

William L. Shirer. "It's All Over"; "Revengeful, Triumphant Hate": Reprinted by permission of William L Shirer Literary Trust.

Howard K. Smith. Valhalla in Transition: From *Last Train from Berlin* by Howard K. Smith. Copyright © 1942 and renewed 1970 by Howard K. Smith.

John Steinbeck. Fear of Death as Green Troops Sail to Invasion: From *Once There Was a War* by John Steinbeck. Copyright 1943, 1958 by John Steinbeck; renewed © 1971 by Elaine Steinbeck, John Steinbeck IV, and Thomas Steinbeck. Used by permission of Viking-Penguin, a division of Penguin Putnam, Inc.

Otto D. Tolischus. Last Warsaw Fort Yields to Germans: Copyright © 1939, 2000 by The New York Times Company; reprinted by permission.

Richard Tregaskis. Battle of the Ridge: From *Guadalcanal Diary* by Richard Tregaskis. Copyright © 1943 by Random House, Inc., and renewed 1971 by Richard Tregaskis; copyright 1955 by Richard Tregaskis; reprinted by permission of Random House, Inc. "Then I Got It": From *Invasion Diary* by Richard Tregaskis. Copyright © 1944 by Random House, Inc.; reprinted by permission of Random House, Inc.

Vincent Tubbs. All Vincent Tubbs pieces reprinted by permission of the Afro-American Newspapers Archives and Research Center.

Mary Heaton Vorse. The Girls of Elkton, Maryland: Copyright © 1943 by Harper's Magazine; all rights reserved; reprinted from the March number by special permission.

E. B. White. Bond Rally: Copyright © 1942 by Harper's Magazine; all rights reserved; reproduced from the December number by special permission.

Notes

In the notes below, the reference numbers denote page and line of this volume (the line count includes headings and captions). No note is made for information that can be found in common desk-reference books such as *Webster's Collegiate* and *Webster's Biographical* dictionaries. Footnotes and bracketed editorial notes within the text were in the originals. For historical background see Chronology in this volume. For weapons and military terms not identified in the notes, see Glossary in this volume. For further historical background and references to other studies, see Gerhard L. Weinberg, *A World at Arms: A Global History of World War II* (Cambridge: Cambridge University Press, 1994). For further background on wartime journalists and journalism, see Frederick S. Voss, *Reporting the War: The Journalistic Coverage of World War II* (Washington, D.C.: Smithsonian Institution Press for the National Portrait Gallery, 1994), and *Ernie's War: The Best of Ernie Pyle's World War II Dispatches*, ed. David Nichols (New York: Touchstone, 1987). For more detailed maps, see *The Times Atlas of the Second World War*, ed. John Keegan (New York: Harper & Row, 1989), and Richard Natkiel, *Atlas of World War II* (New York: Military Press, 1985).

1.7   Sudetenland] German-speaking border regions of Bohemia and Moravia that were included in Czechoslovakia under the terms of the 1919 Versailles Treaty. Under the Munich Pact Czechoslovakia ceded to Germany almost 11,000 square miles of land and 3,600,000 people, of whom 2,800,000 were German-speaking. The ceded territory included frontier fortifications vital to the defense of the remainder of Czechoslovakia. After the war almost the entire German-speaking population of Czechoslovakia was expelled into Germany.

1.10–11   Sportpalast boast] Hitler made his speech in the Berlin Sportpalast on September 26, 1938.

1.29–30   Dr. Masaryk] Hubert Masarik.

2.28–29   Wiegand] Karl H. von Wiegand, foreign correspondent for the Hearst papers.

2.29–30   Sir Horace Wilson] Neville Chamberlain's confidential adviser; Wilson previously accompanied the prime minister in negotiations with Hitler on the Sudetenland, September 16–17 and 22–23, 1938, and served as his special emissary in further negotiations, September 26–27.

2.37   Demaree Bess] Associate editor of *The Saturday Evening Post*.

3.25–26   Halfeld . . . *Nachtausgabe*] Adolf Halfeld and Kriegk were editors of the respective newspapers.

7.16–18   Prince Bülow . . . memoirs] Bernhard Furst von Bülow (1849–1929), German imperial chancellor under Kaiser Wilhelm II, 1900–9. His memoirs were published posthumously in 1930.

8.5   Reichswehr] Name for the German armed forces, 1919–35; from 1935 to 1945 they were known as the Wehrmacht.

8.6   "third zone"] The Munich Pact divided the ceded territory of the Sudetenland into four zones and established a timetable for their occupation by German troops between October 1 and October 10, 1938.

8.29–31   Goethe's . . . *versöhnt.*] "Prelude in the Theater," *Faust*, Part I (1808), line 43.

10.6   General Werner von Fritsch] Werner Freiherr von Fritsch (1880–1939) became commander of the German army in February 1934. At a secret conference with Hitler on November 5, 1937, Fritsch opposed pursuing an aggressive policy against Czechoslovakia and warned that Germany was unprepared for a general European war. In January 1938 Fritsch was removed from his post by Hitler after being falsely accused of homosexual conduct by Heinrich Himmler, head of the SS. Fritsch was cleared by an honor court of officers and allowed to serve as commander of an artillery regiment. In a letter to a friend in August 1939, Fritsch wrote that he would accompany his regiment in the Polish campaign "only as a target."

12.20–21   Russian occupation . . . Poland] Soviet troops invaded Poland on September 17, 1939, and quickly overran the eastern area of the country.

12.38   General Rommel] Polish Major General Juliusz Rommel.

15.10   Albert Canal] Canal in northern Belgium running from Liège to Antwerp. Eben Emael, the strongest fortress in Belgium, was built north of Liège to guard the canal. German combat engineers landed in gliders on Eben Emael on May 10, 1940, and destroyed its gun turrets with explosive charges while other glider troops captured two nearby bridges over the canal. On May 11 the garrison surrendered as German troops advanced in strength across the canal.

15.14   Maginot Line] Series of underground fortresses built 1929–34 along the eastern border of France from the Swiss frontier to Longwy. For financial and diplomatic reasons the Maginot Line stopped short of the Belgian border.

15.17   "They . . . pass"] Although often attributed to Pétain, the first recorded use of the phrase during the Battle of Verdun is in French General Robert Nivelle's Order of the Day to his troops, June 23, 1916: "You will not let them pass!"

15.23   break-through at Sedan] See Chronology for May 1940.

17.21–22   deep incision . . . Allied armies.] See Chronology for May 1940.

25.25   Tom] Tom Healy, correspondent for London *Daily Mirror*.

29.36–37   *"Ne dites. . . espèrer."*] "Don't talk like that. One must hope."

30.29   Knickerbocker] H. R. (Hubert Renfro) Knickerbocker was chief foreign correspondent for the New York *Post* and Philadelphia *Public Ledger* and traveling correspondent for the International News Service.

31.37   Harold King] Foreign correspondent for Reuters News Service.

32.30   *"Nous . . . Boches!"*] "We've seen the *Boches!*" *Boches* is a pejorative term for Germans.

35.30   Kerker] William Kerker was foreign correspondent for NBC.

39.31   *Horst Wessel* song] Nazi party song that became the second national anthem of the Third Reich. Wessel (1907–30) was a Berlin SA (Storm Detachment) leader who, while living with a prostitute, was tracked down by a pimp and several Communist militants and fatally shot. Propaganda chief Joseph Goebbels made Wessel into a Nazi martyr and his poem "Up With The Flag" was set to the melody of a German sailors' song.

41.22   *The Damnation of Faust*] Dramatic cantata (1846) by Hector Berlioz.

45.18   * * *] These asterisks, and all others in pieces by Pyle printed in this volume, appear in the copy originally submitted to Scripps-Howard.

49.13   Shorty's] Engineer of the schooner *Spiradon Piraeus*, Greek army supply ship on which St. John had just sailed from Corfu to Patras.

49.25   *État Major*] Military Staff.

51.13–14   Mike and White and Atherton] Milan "Mike" Francisikovicz was a Yugoslav who navigated the fishing boat *Makedonka* on which St. John and his companions had escaped to Corfu. Leigh White of the New York *Post*, Terence Atherton of London *Daily Mail*, and Francisikovicz continued on from Corfu aboard the fishing boat.

62.9–10   King Peter's] Peter II (1923–70), king of Yugoslavia.

63.9   *The Way of Subjects*] In Japanese, *Shinmin no Michi*; it was published by the Ministry of Education in August 1941.

63.28–30   Sun . . . Jimmu] Jimmu (711–585 B.C.), legendary first emperor of Japan and founder of its dynasty, is considered the direct descendant of sun goddess Amaterasu Omikami.

63.31   Hakko Ichiu] "The eight directions under one roof"; "Eight corners of the world under one roof."

64.2   Imperial Rescript] Issued on the occasion of the signing of the Tripartite Alliance on September 27, 1940.

64.14   "Manchurian Affair,"]   On September 18, 1931, Japanese army officers in Manchuria provoked a clash between Japanese and Chinese troops by blowing up a stretch of railway line near Mukden. By the end of 1931 the Japanese had gained complete control of Manchuria, and in March 1932 they established a puppet Manchurian government under the former Manchu emperor Puyi.

64.32   Yamato]   Name of the Japanese state founded by Jimmu.

64.33   Tanaka memorial]   Document published in China in 1931 that presented a plan for Japanese world conquest allegedly left by emperor Meiji and submitted to Hirohito in 1927 by Prime Minister Tanaka Giichi (1863–1929). Its authenticity was disputed at the time of its publication, and most scholars consider it an anti-Japanese hoax.

65.31   "Showa]   "Enlightened Peace," the reign name of Hirohito (1901–89; regent, 1921–26; emperor from 1926).

65.33   Meiji's hapless grandson]   Meiji ("Enlightened Rule") was the reign name of Mutsuhito (1852–1912; emperor from 1867), grandfather of Hirohito.

66.7–8   Imperial . . . Education]   Edict issued in 1890, the year after the constitution was completed, to ensure that Japan's educational system would promote loyalty and obedience to the emperor.

66.27–28   "turning . . . world,"]   Tolischus had written earlier in *Tokyo Record* that Japanese militarists were hailing the "Manchuria Incident" as the start of the creation of a new order in the world.

67.34   Joseph Warren Teets Mason]   United Press foreign correspondent, columnist, and author J.W.T. Mason (1879–1941); among his books are *The Creative East* (1928), *The Meaning of Shinto* (1935), and *The Spirit of Shinto Mythology* (1939).

68.1–2   Sakaki . . . *Nichi Nichi*]   The Sakaki tree (*Cleyera japonica*) is an ornamental Japanese evergreen shrub. *Nichi Nichi* was a leading pro-militarist Tokyo newspaper.

69.16   Alois . . . restaurant]   Adolf Hitler's half-brother ran the Alois restaurant on Wittenberg Platz.

72.28   Jack Fleischer's]   United Press correspondent who shared an apartment with Smith in Berlin.

72.31–36   Udet . . . Todt]   Colonel General Ernst Udet (1896–1941), director of the Luftwaffe ordnance department and a leading World War I fighter ace, shot himself on November 17, 1941. For morale reasons, his death was falsely announced as having occurred while testing a new type of aircraft. Udet's poor management of aircraft production caused the Luftwaffe severe difficulty in replacing losses suffered during the Battle of Britain and the campaign in the Soviet Union, and by late 1941 he had lost the confidence of

Hitler and Hermann Göring and become despondent. Fighter pilot Colonel Werner Mölders (1913–41) shot down 14 aircraft during the Spanish Civil War and 101 during World War II, and developed the four-plane Luftwaffe tactical fighter formation later adopted by Allied pilots. Mölders was killed in an airplane crash in Germany on November 22, 1941, while flying as a passenger to Berlin in order to serve as a pallbearer at Udet's state funeral. At the time of his death, he had more aerial victories than any other fighter pilot in the war. Field Marshal Walter von Reichenau (1884–1942), an ardent Nazi, died from a stroke on January 17, 1942, while commanding Army Group South in the Ukraine. Fritz Todt (1891–1942) directed autobahn construction in the 1930s and became minister of armaments and munitions in March 1940. He was killed in an airplane crash on February 7, 1942, and was succeeded as armaments minister by Albert Speer.

73.27   Rostov]   German troops captured Rostov-on-Don on November 20, 1941, but were driven out of the city by a Soviet counteroffensive on November 29 in one of the earliest German defeats of the Russian campaign. The Soviets again lost Rostov to the Germans on July 23, 1942, but regained the city on February 14, 1943, following their victory at Stalingrad.

73.28   *Attrapen.*]   Dummies.

73.40   *buergerliche*]   Bourgeois; plain.

75.37   *elegante Viertel*]   Elegant, or smart, quarter.

78.26   Gestapo]   The State Secret Police (*Geheime Staatspolizei*) was founded by Hermann Göring in 1933 and came under the control of the SS in 1934.

79.18   P. G. Wodehouse]   English humorist Wodehouse (1881–1975) had been captured by the Germans at his home in France in May 1940 and was eventually coerced into making several broadcasts from Berlin, in which he spoke humorously about his arrest and internment. He was released in October 1941 but not allowed to leave Germany. In 1955 he became a U.S. citizen.

79.30   Hess . . . Scotland]   Rudolph Hess (1894–1987), the deputy leader of the Nazi party, flew alone to Scotland on May 10, 1941, in an unauthorized personal attempt to negotiate Britain's surrender. Hess was imprisoned in Britain during the war and sentenced to life imprisonment by the international war crimes tribunal at Nuremberg in 1946. He committed suicide in Spandau prison, Berlin, on August 17, 1987.

82.2   big "ear"]   A large radar antenna.

94.20–21   Irene . . . dancer killed]   Ballroom dancers Irene (1893–1969) and Vernon (1887–1918) Castle introduced dances including the turkey trot, one-step, and Castle walk, and initiated a "dancing craze" in the United States; Vernon, an Englishman, joined the Royal Flying Corps in 1916 and was killed in a training accident. Irene's third husband was Frederick

McLaughlin. *The Story of Vernon and Irene Castle*, a film based on her memoirs and starring Fred Astaire and Ginger Rogers, was released in 1939.

94.28–29 *Greer* incident] U.S. Marines landed in Iceland in early July 1941 with the permission of the Icelandic government. On September 4, 1941, the U.S. destroyer *Greer* was carrying mail to American troops in Iceland when a British patrol aircraft alerted it that a submerged German U-boat lay 10 miles ahead. Following orders then in effect, the *Greer* used sonar to track the U-boat and reported its position to the British airplane, but did not attempt to attack the submarine. After the British plane dropped several depth bombs, the U-boat fired a torpedo at the *Greer*, apparently without knowing the nationality of its target. The torpedo missed, and the *Greer* then depth-bombed the U-boat, which fired a second torpedo that also missed; the *Greer* then lost sonar contact and proceeded to Iceland. In a national radio address on September 11, President Roosevelt did not mention the role of the British aircraft in the incident, accused the Germans of having "fired first . . . without warning," and described the attack as "piracy legally and morally." On September 13 Roosevelt ordered the navy to escort Allied convoys to Iceland and to destroy any Axis submarines or surface raiders it encountered between the U.S. and Iceland. By October 1, 1941, a full account of the *Greer* incident had been made public as the result of congressional inquiries.

96.20 50 ships] In September 1940 Roosevelt sent 50 destroyers to Britain in exchange for the right to use British bases in the Western Hemisphere.

99.15–16 Japanese Ambassador . . . colleague] Ambassador Nomura Kichisaburo (1887–1964) and special envoy Kurusu Saburo (1888–1954).

99.17–18 recent American message] On November 26, 1941, Secretary of State Hull presented a note to Nomura and Kurusu outlining the basis for an agreement between Japan and the United States. The document called for Japan to withdraw its troops from China and Indochina and to recognize the Chinese Nationalist government in return for the lifting of the embargo on U.S. exports to Japan.

99.30–31 American ships . . . Honolulu] These reports were incorrect.

101.29 Davao bombing] Davao, on the Philippine island of Mindanao, was raided by Japanese carrier aircraft on December 8, 1941.

109.1–2 REPULSE . . . WALES] The British battle cruiser *Repulse* and battleship *Prince of Wales* sailed from Singapore on December 8 in an attempt to intercept Japanese troop convoys headed for Malaya.

109.5 DECEMBER 11, 5:00:16 a.m.] The text printed here is of a dispatch that Brown wrote and cabled to CBS as soon as he returned to Singapore.

113.29–30 Captain Leech] John C. Leach.

114.3   Phillips and Leech] Rear Admiral Phillips and Captain Leach were lost; Captain Tennant of the *Repulse* was rescued.

114.21–23   *Wales. . .* ratings.] There were 1,285 survivors from the crew of 1,612 men on the *Prince of Wales*, and 796 survivors from the crew of 1,306 men on the *Repulse*.

116.9   Battle of Moscow] See Chronology, October–December 1941.

118.26–27   Solnetchnogorsk] The town, about 25 miles north of Moscow, was captured by the Germans on November 24, 1941, and recaptured by the Soviets on December 12.

122.15–16   Japanese border war] See Chronology, May–August 1939.

123.23   General Vlasov] Andrei A. Vlasov (1900–46) successfully commanded the 20th Army in the fighting around Moscow, November 1941–March 1942, and was promoted to lieutenant general in January 1942. On March 21, 1942, he assumed command of the 2nd Shock Army, which had been encircled in northern Russia during a failed attempt to break the German siege of Leningrad. After months of fighting, the trapped 2nd Shock Army disintegrated and Vlasov was captured on July 12, 1942. Disillusioned with Stalin and the Communist regime, in September 1942 Vlasov became the most prominent Soviet officer to collaborate with the German military in propaganda efforts aimed at enlisting Soviet prisoners-of-war in the German army. Although Vlasov hoped to form an independent anti-Communist "Russian Liberation Army" under Russian leadership, Hitler refused to authorize such a force. In January 1945 Vlasov was finally permitted to become commander of approximately 20,000–30,000 troops. He was captured by the Soviet army in Czechoslovakia on May 12, 1945, and hanged for treason in Moscow on August 1, 1946.

126.36   capture Volokolomsk] The Soviets recaptured the city on December 20, 1941.

126.37   Von Strauss] Colonel General Adolf Strauss, commander of the German Ninth Army.

134.6   Gloucesters] British infantrymen from the 1st Battalion of the Gloucestershire Regiment.

135.34   Seagrave nurses] Burmese nurses working with Dr. Gordon Seagrave, an American medical missionary.

153.5–6   striking force . . . Hiryu] The aircraft carrier *Hiryu* was part of the Midway striking force, along with the carriers *Akagi*, *Kaga*, and *Soryu*. All four ships had participated in the attack on Pearl Harbor.

157.2   Akagi] The *Yorktown* dive bombers attacked the *Soryu*; *Akagi* and *Kaga* were hit by dive bombers from the *Enterprise*. The three carriers were fatally damaged between 10:25 and 10:30 A.M. on June 4, 1942, as they were launching an air strike against the U.S. fleet.

158.5–6   Hiryu . . . Enterprise] Dive bombers from the *Enterprise* fatally damaged the *Hiryu* late on the afternoon of June 4.

159.17   die . . . Solomons] The cruiser *Astoria* was sunk on August 9, 1942, in the Battle of Savo Island; 235 of her crew were killed.

160.14–15   Yorktown] Despite its battle damage, the *Yorktown* remained afloat until the morning of June 7, 1942, when it was torpedoed and sunk by a Japanese submarine.

161.33   "Camp Harmony."] A holding center for internees from the Seattle area, located in Puyallup, Washington, on the site of fairgrounds; those held there were later relocated to Idaho.

164.4   *1,000,000 . . . Says*] This story and the one printed on pp. 165–67 in this volume originally ran on inside pages of *The New York Times*.

164.8   spokesmen . . . Congress] Ignacy Schwartzbart, member of the Polish National Council in London, Sidney Silverman, Labour member of Parliament, and Ernst Frischer, member of the Czechoslovak State Council in London, appeared at a press conference sponsored by the World Jewish Congress, an international association of Jewish organizations formed in 1936.

164.21   Polish Government in London] The Polish government-in-exile was formed in Paris upon the resignation of President Ignacy Mościcki, September 30, 1939, and moved to London in 1940. Wladislaw Raczkiewicz (1885–1947) served as president and General Wladislaw Sikorski (1881–1943) as prime minister.

165.23–24   Szmul Zygelbojm] Zygielbojm was representative of the Jewish Labour *Bund* on the Polish National Council in exile; he committed suicide on May 12, 1943, to protest world indifference to the fate of Polish Jews.

166.32–33   Gouvernement General] In 1939 approximately half of German-occupied Poland was annexed into the Reich, while the General-Government of Poland was established in Cracow to rule the remainder.

167.2   Hitler's threat] In a speech to the Reichstag on January 30, 1939, Hitler said that if "international finance Jewry within Europe and abroad should succeed once more in plunging the peoples into a world war, then the consequence will be not the Bolshevization of the world and therewith a victory of Jewry, but on the contrary, the destruction of the Jewish race in Europe."

168.1   DOROTHY LAMOUR] Hollywood actress (1914–96) whose films included *Her Jungle Love* (1938), *Tropic Holiday* (1938), *Moon Over Burma* (1940), *The Road to Singapore* (1940), *Aloma of the South Seas* (1941), and *Star Spangled Rhythm* (1942).

174.5   Col. Edson] Merritt A. Edson, commanding officer of the First Raider Battalion.

174.11   Col. Griffith] Lieutenant Colonel Samuel B. Griffith, executive officer of the First Raider Battalion.

176.24   Pursuits] Single-engine, single-seat P-39 Airacobra fighter planes.

181.31   cross the Tenaru] More than 750 Japanese soldiers were killed on August 21, 1942, in an unsuccessful attack against Marine positions west of the Tenaru River on Guadalcanal.

182.7   Tulagi] Small island about 20 miles north of Guadalcanal, captured by the Marines, August 7–9, 1942.

184.19   Commissioner, Martin Clemens] British district officer on Guadalcanal and coast watcher for the Australian navy. After the Marines landed, Clemens organized several companies of Melanesian scouts who served as jungle guides and provided intelligence on Japanese troop movements.

186.18   Gizo] Island in the New Georgia group of the Solomons, about 240 miles northwest of Guadalcanal.

195.29   "Banzai"] Japanese war cry, from *Tenno heika banzai*: "May the Son of Heaven live ten thousand years!" (The emperor was called "Son of Heaven.")

205.25   *Wasp*] The aircraft carrier was sunk on September 15, 1942.

206.24   battle of Savo Island] See Chronology, August 1942.

210.25   Maj. Bailey] Major Bailey was posthumously awarded the Congressional Medal of Honor for his actions on the night of September 13–14, 1942. Edson also received the Medal of Honor for his leadership in the "Battle of the Ridge"; he survived the war.

211.13   Pittsburgh *Courier*] African-American newspaper founded in 1910 and edited and published by Robert L. Vann (1879–1940); in 1940 his widow, Jesse Matthews Vann, became publisher and P. L. Prattis, executive editor. It was later called the *New Courier*.

212.6   Harlem's *People's Voice*] Weekly New York tabloid (1942–47) founded and edited by Adam Clayton Powell Jr. (1908–72).

212.32   Joe Louis bought!] The heavyweight champion had donated his share of the purse from a January 1942 title defense to the Navy Relief Fund, and later helped raise contributions for the Fund.

218.30–31   Hastie . . . War] William Hastie (1904–76) in 1940 took a leave from his position as dean of the School of Law at Howard University to serve as civilian aide to Secretary of War Henry L. Stimson; he resigned in 1943 to protest continued segregation in the armed services. He was judge of the U.S. District Court for the Virgin Islands, 1937–39, and of the U.S. Circuit Court of Appeals, Third Circuit, 1949–71.

219.3–6   Du Bois . . . statement]   In an editorial in *The Crisis*, July 1918.

219.35   *The Crisis*]   Magazine founded in 1910 by W.E.B. Du Bois, its first editor, and published by the National Association for the Advancement of Colored People; Roy Wilkins was editor, 1935–50.

222.36–38   battle . . . Homes]   On February 28, 1942, local police stood by as a white mob prevented black families from moving into the Sojourner Truth Homes. Under National Guard and state police protection, several black families moved into the project on April 30, 1942.

224.32   Marcus Garvey's Black Star Line]   Garvey (1887–1940) was a Jamaican-born leader whose United Negro Improvement Association advocated the resettlement of African-Americans in Africa and attracted widespread support from blacks in the 1920s. The Black Star Line, a steamship company, was established by the UNIA in 1919 to facilitate resettlement.

224.36–37   Anderson . . . 'Rochester,']   Comedian Eddie (Edmund Lincoln) Anderson (1906–77), famous for his portrayal of "Rochester" on the Jack Benny radio and television shows, was also featured in films, including *Star Spangled Rhythm*, *Cabin in the Sky*, and *The Green Pastures*.

224.40   Andy Razaf]   Razaf (1895–1973) wrote the lyrics for more than 1,000 songs by composers including Eubie Blake (1883–1983), J. C. Johnson (1896–1981), and Fats Waller (1904–43); his librettos included *Keep Shufflin'* (1928), *Hot Chocolates* (1929), and the 1930 *Blackbirds*. After retiring as a lyricist he became a newspaper reporter.

228.11   Vito Marcantonio]   Marcantonio (1902–54) was a left-wing congressman from New York City, 1934–36 and 1938–50.

235.18   Paul McNutt]   Former governor of Indiana and chairman of the War Manpower Commission.

246.22–23   B-26 . . . there?"]   When Liebling prepared "The Foamy Fields" for publication in his collection *Mollie & Other War Pieces* (1964), he added the footnote: "The B-26 was Lieutenant-General James Doolittle's personal plane. He was on a tour of inspection, and the three soldiers were members of his crew."

249.37   landscape . . . Technicolor.]   Liebling noted in *Mollie*: "This use of the familiar false as touchstone of the unfamiliar real recurred often both in writing and conversation during World War II. 'Just like a movie!' was a standard reaction. It assured the speaker of the authenticity of what he had just experienced."

251.24   Larry Adler . . . player]   American harmonica virtuoso.

255.22–24   ground fire . . . killed."]   Liebling noted in *Mollie*: "Normal confusion."

256.13   an airfield] Liebling noted in *Mollie*: "This time it was Thélepte, in Tunisia."

257.10–11   Sam Spewack . . . Bella] The Spewacks were collaborative dramatists whose numerous Broadway plays and musicals included *Clear All Wires* (1932), *Boy Meets Girl* (1935), *Leave It to Me!* (1938), and later *Kiss Me Kate* (1948). Both were originally journalists.

258.23   Luna Park!"] An amusement park at Coney Island, Brooklyn, that featured nightly fireworks.

258.36   Major ——] In *Mollie* Liebling noted: "We were not allowed by the censor to mention names of casualties until they had appeared in the lists published at home. Now I cannot fill in this blank, because I forget the poor gentleman's name."

259.23–27   "I guess . . . for home.] In a footnote in *Mollie* Liebling cited this passage as another example of "confusion."

260.16   'Journey's End.'] Play (1929) by R. C. Sherriff about the British army fighting in the trenches in World War I; it was made into a film in 1930.

260.24   Léon] Liebling noted in *Mollie* that he had suppressed Léon Caplan's last name in case he had relatives living in France, and that after the war Caplan became the "number two man in the French Shell Oil Company—a *potentat pétrolier*."

260.31   Norgaard] In *Mollie* Liebling dedicated "The Foamy Fields" and "Gafsa," another article describing his travels in Tunisia with Norgaard, to "Boots Norgaard."

261.38–39   Kostia Rozanoff] Liebling included "P.S. on Rozanoff in 1954" in *Mollie*; in it he wrote that Constantin Rozanoff became a leading French test pilot after the war and was killed in 1954, aged 49, while flying the new Mystère IV jet fighter.

261.39   Lafayette Escadrille] Free French unit named after the squadron of American pilots who flew in the French service before the United States entered World War I.

275.2–6   C-rations . . . P-40.] Liebling noted in *Mollie*: "I was back in 1956, but even the C-ration cans are gone. The natives of those parts are extremely poor, and may have thought even tin cans worth salvaging."

282.33–36   Horse . . . dead.] Liebling noted in *Mollie*: "Horse's square name was Alton B. Watkins, but hardly anybody at Thélepte knew. Father McCreedy buried him under a metal plate marked 'Horace.'"

283.40–384.1   radio . . . detectors] Radar.

285.5–7   Boone . . . planes."] Liebling noted in *Mollie*: "His luck did not last. He was killed a couple of weeks later."

286.34–35   Freddie Bartholomew]   Child actor who starred in films including *David Copperfield* (1935), *Little Lord Fauntleroy* (1936), and *Captains Courageous* (1937).

290.26   Sidi Bou Zid]   The German offensive in Tunisia began on February 14, 1943, with an attack through the Faïd Pass at the town of Sidi Bou Zid, about 125 miles southeast of Tunis. The offensive was halted on February 22, 1943.

308.29   Tokyo tanks]   So-called because it was hoped that they would eventually be used by B-17s bombing Tokyo.

309.14–15   Col. Curtis E. Le May]   In March 1945 LeMay, then a major-general commanding the B-29 force based in the Marianas, began low-level incendiary raids against Japan (see Chronology). He later commanded the Strategic Air Command, 1948–57, and was Chief of Staff of the U.S. Air Force, 1961–65.

309.32   RDF]   Radio direction finding; radar.

313.4   *Staffeln*]   A *Staffel* was a Luftwaffe unit of 10 to 12 aircraft.

323.39   Col. Darby . . . Ranger]   William O. Darby was commander of the Ranger Force, made up of three Ranger battalions. The Rangers were elite troops, formed in 1942 as the American counterpart of the British Commandos. Darby was killed April 30, 1945, just before the German surrender in Italy, and was posthumously promoted to the rank of brigadier general.

337.1   *Blue Fox*]   Pseudonym given by Sherrod to the transport *Zeilin* for security reasons.

337.12   Betio . . . fourth day]   Betio is the main island of Tarawa atoll. The Marines landed on November 20, 1943, and the island was declared secure on November 23.

338.16   Dick Johnston]   Richard Johnston, a United Press correspondent.

342.28   3/2]   Third Battalion, Second Marine Regiment.

347.32–36   Makin . . . killed]   See Chronology, November 1943.

349.15–17   Hawkins . . . Honor]   First Lieutenant William D. Hawkins, commander of the Scout and Sniper platoon of the Second Marine Regiment, was mortally wounded on November 21. He was posthumously awarded the Medal of Honor.

355.1   Burns Philp]   Burns Philp & Co., a South Seas trading firm.

358.19–20   1,026 . . . wounded]   Sherrod wrote in his preface to the 1954 edition of *Tarawa* that the final Marine Corps compilation for casualties in the battle showed 990 men killed and 2,296 wounded.

363.14   Jock . . . commander]   Wing Commander William Abercromby, commanding officer of 619 Squadron (wing commander is an RAF rank equivalent to lieutenant colonel). Abercromby was shot down and killed on January 2, 1944, while flying to Berlin with a different squadron.

363.15–16   Pathfinders] Pathfinder aircraft used radio and radar navigational aids to locate targets, then marked them with colored parachute flares and slow-burning incendiary bombs known as "target indicators."

363.29   *Star Spangled Rhythm*] Film (1942) written by Harry Turgend and directed by George Marshall; its all-star cast included Betty Hutton, Eddie Bracken, Victor Moore, and Walter Abel.

365.28   kite] RAF slang for an airplane.

365.32–33   "Target indicators] See note 363.15–16.

369.9   Mule Bag] Radio code for an airfield.

369.19–20   Stockton . . . Bennett] Stockton was killed; Bennett safely parachuted and was a prisoner of war until May 1945.

369.39–370.2   Berlin . . . blitz] RAF Bomber Command sent 458 aircraft to Berlin on the night of December 2–3, 1943. Strong winds and mistakes in identifying navigational landmarks by radar resulted in the Pathfinders marking a point 15 miles south of the intended target area inside Berlin. About three-quarters of the bombs dropped fell in open country outside the city, and those that fell on Berlin were widely scattered. Between 100 and 150 people were killed by the bombing, while the RAF lost 40 aircraft and 228 men killed; another 60 aircrew were captured.

374.25   15th Panzer Grenadiers] German motorized infantry division.

375.22   "Voelkischer Beobachter"] The official newspaper of the Nazi party after 1920. Its name may be translated "National Observer" or "Racialist Observer."

375.39   Volturno crossing] U.S. troops crossed the Volturno River, October 12–13, 1943.

385.15   hows] Howitzers.

387.34–35   Benedictine . . . intact] The monastery was destroyed by Allied bombing on February 15, 1944.

397.6   Cape Gloucester] At the western end of New Britain Island.

397.27–28   Enoc Waters . . . Defender] War correspondent for the *Chicago Defender,* an African-American newspaper. In 1957 Waters became editor of Associated Negro Press news service and later published *American Diary: A Personal History of the Black Press* (1987).

400.37–38   belt . . . stitches] In Japanese, *senninbari.* See also page 558.18–23 in this volume.

401.37–38   General Rupertus] Major General William H. Rupertus, commander of the First Marine Division.

407.12   Salerno] See Chronology, September 1943.

421.5–6   Japanese . . . Bataan] See Chronology, April 1942. William Dyess, an air force officer who had survived the Bataan "Death March," escaped from the Philippines to Australia in 1943 and provided the U.S. government with its first eyewitness account of the Bataan atrocities. The government made information based on his report public on January 28, 1944.

422.37   Terminal Island] In 1942 a Japanese community of some 2,100 fishermen, of whom 800 were aliens, lived on Terminal Island, where ten fish canneries were located.

423.5–6   Attorney General Warren] Earl Warren (1891–1974), later Chief Justice of the U.S. Supreme Court, 1953–69.

424.31–32   Japanese . . . Santa Barbara] The shelling was aimed at an oilfield west of Santa Barbara, California, and caused no significant damage.

428.2   Dies Committee] The House Committee to Investigate Un-American Activities, founded in 1938 and chaired by Martin Dies Jr. (1901–72), Democratic Representative from Texas.

434.36   combat unit] The 442nd Regimental Combat Team, a rein-forced infantry regiment, fought in Italy and France in 1944–45. It became the most decorated unit of its size in the U.S. army.

437.38   *Gripsholm*] Swedish vessel used in the exchange of Japanese interned in the U.S. and Americans interned by the Japanese.

440.38   all-Japanese-American battalion] The 100th Battalion, drawn from Nisei members of the Hawaii National Guard, began fighting in Italy in the autumn of 1943. It became part of the 442nd Regimental Combat Team in the summer of 1944.

441.25–27   cases . . . higher courts] In *Korematsu* v. *United States,* decided on December 18, 1944, the U.S. Supreme Court upheld by a 6 to 3 vote the conviction of a Japanese-American citizen for violating the 1942 military order excluding people of Japanese ancestry from the Pacific Coast. The majority opinion, written by Justice Hugo Black, accepted "the finding of the military authorities" that military necessity made it "impossible to bring about an immediate segregation of the disloyal from the loyal. . . ." Justice Frank Murphy, in dissent, described the decision as a "legalization of racism."

441.38   Hickam Field] Air base near Pearl Harbor, attacked on December 7, 1941.

442.17   Stimson . . . Knox] Henry Lewis Stimson, secretary of war, 1940–45; Frank Knox, secretary of the navy, 1940–44.

455.24   permitted . . . units] Identified by Pyle in his collection *Brave Men* (1944) as "the First and Twenty-ninth Divisions."

468.2–3   killed . . . American troops]   The "short" bombing on July 25, 1944, killed 111 Americans and wounded 490. Among the dead was Lieutenant General Lesley McNair, the highest-ranking American officer killed in action during the war. McNair, who from 1942 to 1944 directed the organization and training of U.S. army ground forces, had gone to Normandy to observe the troops in action.

472.20   haircutting]   In many liberated French towns, women accused of having had intimate relations with German soldiers were forced to have their heads shaved.

472.40   CIC]   Counter-Intelligence Corps.

475.39   *digue*]   Embankment.

481.2   oil bombs]   Napalm.

486.12   Koenig, Leclerc and Juin]   General Marie Pierre Joseph Koenig (1898–1970) commanded the French Forces of the Interior and became military governor of Paris after its liberation. The prolonged defense of Bir Hakeim, Libya, from May 27 to June 11, 1942, by Free French forces under his command helped restore French military prestige in Britain and the U.S. General Leclerc (nom de guerre of Vicomte Jacques-Philippe de Hauteclogne, 1902–47) fought with the Free French in North Africa, 1941–43, before becoming commander of the French 2nd Armored Division. The division landed in Normandy on August 1, 1944, and entered Paris on August 25. General Alphonse Juin (1888–1967) commanded the French army in North Africa under Vichy from 1940 to 1942, then joined the Allies after they landed in Morocco and Algeria in November 1942. In December 1943 he assumed command of the French Expeditionary Corps in Italy and played a major role in the breaking of the Gustav Line in May 1944.

487.40   the militia]   The *Milice,* formed by Vichy in 1943, fought the French resistance and assisted the SS in arresting and deporting Jews.

506.32   potato-masher grenade]   Grenade with cylindrical explosive charge attached to a wooden throwing stick.

515.32–33   League of Nations . . . Ethiopian grab]   See Chronology, 1935–36.

516.2   Senator Nye]   Gerald P. Nye, Republican of North Dakota, was a leading isolationist.

516.34–35   André Kostelanetz]   Russian-born American conductor (1901–80) known for his arrangements of light music.

518.18   Fred Perry]   British tennis player Frederick J. Perry (1909–95) was the champion at Wimbledon, 1934–36, and held the U.S. Open title, 1933–34 and 1936.

523.23   Stalag Luft]   German prisoner-of-war camp administered by the Luftwaffe.

526.33 Eaker and Doolittle] The Eighth Air Force, whose four-engine bombers raided Germany from bases in England, was commanded by Major General Ira Eaker from December 1942 to January 1944, and by Lieutenant General James Doolittle from January 1944 to May 1945.

529.9 *Peleliu Island*] See Chronology, September and November 1944.

529.27 kingposts] Short masts used to support cargo booms.

547.27 the Fifth] The Fifth Marine Regiment.

551.4 *Banzai*] See note 195.29.

570.10 Birkenau] The camp at Birkenau (Brzezinka), also known as Auschwitz II, was located a mile west of the main Auschwitz camp. Construction of the Birkenau camp began in October 1941.

570.11–13 horrors . . . Lublin 1,500,000] In July 1944 the Soviet army liberated Majdanek concentration camp outside of Lublin, Poland, and in August 1944 a group of Western correspondents toured the camp. It is estimated that between 200,000 and 360,000 persons died at Majdanek.

570.14 1,500,000 to 1,765,000] It is now estimated that 1,100,000 people died at Auschwitz-Birkenau between June 1940, when Auschwitz was established as a concentration camp for Polish political prisoners, and January 27, 1945, when the Soviet army liberated Auschwitz-Birkenau. About 90 percent of the victims were Jews from throughout occupied Europe. The gassing of Jews at Auschwitz-Birkenau began in February 1942 and continued until late November 1944, when Himmler ordered the SS to dismantle and destroy the gas chambers and crematoria.

571.6 two . . . Jews] Walter Rosenberg and Alfred Wetzler, who both survived the war (Rosenberg subsequently adopted the name Rudolf Vrba, which was the name on the false identity papers he used in Slovakia after his escape from the camp). Their 30-page report, based on information collected by dozens of Auschwitz prisoners, was sent to Jaromir Kopecky, the diplomatic representative in Switzerland of the Czechoslovak government-in-exile, in May 1944, and summaries of the report were given to Allied governments by early July. The full text reached the War Refugee Board in the United States in mid-October 1944.

571.8 Polish major] Jerzy Tabeau, a Polish medical student who escaped from Birkenau on November 19, 1943. His account of the camp was circulated by the Polish resistance as "The Report of a Polish Major." Tabeau joined a partisan unit of the Polish Socialist Party and survived the war.

571.9–10 Bergson . . . Liberation] Peter H. Bergson was the pseudonym of Hillel Kook, the leader of a group of young Jews who came to the United States from Palestine in 1939–40 to raise money for the militant underground group Irgun Zvai Leumi. In July 1943 Bergson helped organize the Emergency Committee to Save the Jewish People of Europe, which vigorously criticized the Roosevelt administration for its failure to help Jewish refugees. The Hebrew Committee of National Liberation, founded in May 1944, was intended to serve as a government-in-exile for the Jews of Palestine.

576.14–15   brother of Léon Blum] René Blum, former director of the Ballet de Monte Carlo, was arrested by the Gestapo in December 1941 and deported to Auschwitz in September 1942.

577.3   HUERTGEN FOREST] American name for forested area in Germany southeast of Aachen and west of the Roer River. U.S. troops first entered the forest on September 14, 1944, and heavy fighting continued in the region until early December. Over 23,000 Americans were killed, wounded, or captured in the Huertgen Forest, and another 8,000 became casualties from trench foot, exposure, and combat exhaustion. The area was finally cleared of German forces in February 1945.

577.15   Grosshau] Captured by the 4th Infantry Division on November 30, 1944.

577.29   New Georgia] See Chronology, June and August 1943.

579.20–21   Fourth . . . divisions] One regiment of the 4th Division, the 12th Infantry, began fighting in the Huertgen Forest on November 6, 1944. The 8th and 22nd Infantry Regiments began their attack on November 16, and the entire division was relieved between December 3 and 11, after having achieved a maximum advance of over three miles. During the Huertgen battle the 4th Infantry Division lost over 4,000 men killed, wounded, or captured, and suffered another 2,000 casualties from combat exhaustion, trench foot, and other "nonbattle" causes. The 1st, 8th, 9th, and 28th Infantry Divisions also fought in the Huertgen Forest, September–December 1944.

580.23   primacord] Detonating cord.

581.14   assault guns] Turretless tanks, used to provide close artillery support for infantry.

583.23   Bastogne] A key road junction in the southern Ardennes, Bastogne was surrounded by the Germans from December 21 to 26, 1944.

591.18–19   Vice Admiral Richmond Kelly Turner] Turner (1885–1961) was amphibious forces commander during the landings on Guadalcanal, New Georgia, the Gilberts, the Marshalls, and the Marianas.

594.35–38   They died . . . body.] This passage also appeared in a story by Sherrod about Iwo Jima printed in *Time* on March 5, 1945. In the *Time* version, Sherrod added: "Only the legs were easy to identify—Japanese if wrapped in khaki puttees, American if covered by canvas leggings."

600.22   T/Sgt] Technical Sergeant.

600.27   S/Sgt]   Staff Sergeant.

606.18–19   "The Crazy Ray."]   English title of Clair's experimental short film *Paris qui dort* (1923).

608.28   First Army's . . . city.]   Cologne was captured by U.S. troops March 5–7, 1945.

613.35   French Armed Elite Guard]   A Waffen SS division composed of French volunteers, the "Charlemagne," was formed in late 1944. It was virtually annihilated fighting on the eastern front in 1945.

615.13   *Schweinhunde*]   Dirty pig.

619.30   Oradour]   Troops of the 2nd SS Panzer Division murdered 642 people in Oradour-sur-Glane, about ten miles northwest of Limoges, on June 10, 1944. After shooting the men of the village inside several barns and garages, the SS set the church on fire and then shot at the women and children as they tried to escape. The massacre was committed in reprisal for recent attacks made by the French resistance in the region.

624.14   Whitman's great threnody]   "When Lilacs Last in the Dooryard Bloom'd" (1865–66), on the death of President Lincoln.

630.5   D-Day]   Okinawa was invaded on April 1, 1945; American troops landed on Ie Shima on April 16. ("D-Day" was a term used by military planners to designate the day an operation would begin.)

636.10–11   Capt. . . . Erween]   War correspondents accredited with the U.S. army wore military uniform.

641.21   "Sonny Boy."]   Al Jolson's theme song, written by Jolson, B. G. DeSylva, Lew Brown, and Ray Henderson, was first featured in the film musical *The Singing Fool* (1928).

642.40   Grover Whalen]   New York city police commissioner, known for his role in organizing public ceremonies, including homecoming parades after World War I.

646.12   SHAEF]   Supreme Headquarters Allied Expeditionary Force, the supreme Allied command for western Europe, headed by Eisenhower.

647.27   Shubert pass]   Revocable reviewer's pass provided by the Shubert theaters in New York City.

649.25   Dieppe]   See Chronology, August 1942.

656.7–8   Admiral Marc A. Mitscher]   Mitscher (1887–1947) commanded Task Force 58, the fast carrier task force of the Pacific fleet, from January to November 1944 and February to May 1945.

656.24   Franklin]   The *Franklin* was hit by two bombs off the Japanese coast on March 19, 1945, while preparing to launch an air strike; 724 men were killed.

662.16   Yamato] The *Yamato* was sunk by American carrier aircraft on April 7, 1945, while sailing toward Okinawa. *Yamato* and its sister ship, *Musashi,* were the largest battleships ever built. (*Musashi* was sunk by U.S. carrier aircraft on October 24, 1944, during the Battle of Leyte Gulf.)

663.29–30   different . . . Hiroshima] See Chronology, July–August 1945.

664.11   Dumbos and Superdumbos] Airplanes used for rescue missions.

664.28   The Great Artiste] Sweeney had flown *The Great Artiste* as the instrument plane on the Hiroshima mission. Piloted by Captain Frederick Bock, *The Great Artiste* was also used as the instrument plane on the Nagasaki mission, and was the aircraft on which Laurence flew. Sweeney flew the Nagasaki mission in a B-29 named *Bock's Car,* which carried the atomic bomb.

666.23   Cheshire . . . pilot] Cheshire had flown 100 missions as a bomber pilot in the war against Germany and been awarded the Victoria Cross. As commander of the elite 617 Squadron in 1944, he had pioneered the use of low-level target marking in both day and night precision bombing attacks.

666.25   William G. Penney] Penney later directed the development of the British atomic bomb. The first British bomb, exploded off the Australian coast in October 1952, was a plutonium implosion design very similar to that of the Nagasaki weapon.

666.28   "Y-Site"] The laboratory at Los Alamos, New Mexico.

670.5–6   primary . . . secondary] The primary target for the mission was the industrial city of Kokura, but when the bombardier on *Bock's Car* was unable to locate his visual aiming point through the smoke and haze obscuring the city, Ashworth, the Manhattan Project "weaponeer" in charge of arming the bomb, and Sweeney decided to fly to the secondary target, Nagasaki.

713.3   Grummans] Manufacturer of U.S. naval aircraft, including the F6F Hellcat fighter and the TBF Avenger bomber.

721.24   Grand Slam] A 22,000 pound bomb, used in March and April 1945 to destroy German railway viaducts and bridges.

734.4–5   Hirohito . . . Tenno] In Japan the reigning emperor was referred to as Tenno or Tenno Heika (Son of Heaven) rather than by his personal name.

740.23   torii] A simple gateway at the entrance to the grounds of a Shinto shrine.

748.25   *Cryptomeria japonica*] Japanese cedar.

Glossary of Military Terms

Notes on U.S. Army organization appear at the end of the Glossary

A-20] Twin-engine U.S. bomber. The "Havoc" had a three-man crew and a top speed of over 300 mph and was armed with at least seven machine guns; different versions carried between 2,000 and 4,000 pounds of bombs.

Amphtrack] Amphibious tractor. See LVT.

B-17] Four-engine U.S. heavy bomber. The "Flying Fortress" had a ten-man crew, a cruising speed of about 215 mph, was armed with 12 or 13 machine guns, and normally carried 4,000–6,000 pounds of bombs.

B-24] Four-engine U.S. heavy bomber. The "Liberator" had a crew of ten, a top speed of 290 mph, normally carried 5,000 pounds of bombs, and was armed with ten machine guns.

B-25] Twin-engine U.S. medium bomber. The "Mitchell" had a six-man crew, a top speed of about 275 mph, carried 3,000 pounds of bombs, and was armed with at least seven machine guns.

B-26] Twin-engine U.S. medium bomber. The "Marauder" had a six-man crew, a top speed of about 280 mph, carried 4,000 pounds of bombs, and was armed with up to 12 machine guns.

B-29] Four-engine U.S. heavy bomber, used in the Pacific and Asia in 1944–45. The "Superfortress" had an 11-man crew, a cruising speed of 290 mph, and normally carried 12,000 pounds of bombs (20,000 pounds was the maximum load). It was armed with ten machine guns and a rapid-firing 20 mm. cannon, although in 1945 many B-29s had their machine-gun turrets removed to increase speed and bomb load.

BAR] Browning automatic rifle. American rifle capable of full automatic fire, used as a light machine gun by army and marine infantry. It fired a .30 caliber bullet (i.e., a bullet 30/100 of an inch in diameter), was fed from a 20-round magazine, had an effective range of over 600 yards, and weighed 19 pounds.

Baugeki '97] Japanese single-engine dive bomber commonly known in the U.S. by its American code name "Val." It had a two-man crew, a top speed of 240 mph, and was armed with three machine guns and a 550-pound bomb.

Beaufighter] Twin-engine radar-equipped British night-fighter, with a two-man crew, top speed of 320 mph, and main armament of four rapid-firing 20 mm. cannon (i.e., cannon firing shells 20 mm. in diameter).

Bofors gun]   Rapid-firing 40 mm. anti-aircraft gun, effective against airplanes flying below 11,000 feet.

Butterfly bomb]   Small German anti-personnel bomb.

Carbine]   A short rifle. The American M-1 carbine was a semiautomatic weapon with a 15-round magazine; it fired a .30 caliber bullet, had an effective range of 300 yards, and weighed six pounds.

C ration]   American canned field rations that could be eaten hot or cold.

Dornier]   Twin-engine German bomber. The Dornier 17, in service from 1939 to 1942, had a four-man crew, a top speed of 255 mph, and was armed with six machine guns and 2,200 pounds of bombs.

Douglas transport]   Twin-engine C-47 transport, the military version of the DC-3 passenger plane.

Duck]   Six-wheeled American amphibious truck equipped with a propeller and rudder that could carry 25 men or 5,000 pounds of cargo. Also known as the DUKW, after the code name under which it was developed.

88]   German artillery gun firing shells or armor-piercing solid shot 88 mm. in diameter. Originally produced as an anti-aircraft gun, its high velocity and flat trajectory made it an extremely effective anti-tank gun, and it was also used as field artillery, often firing shells fused to burst in the air above Allied troops. As an anti-tank gun, it was effective at ranges up to 2,000 yards; as artillery, it could fire a 20-pound shell almost ten miles (17,500 yards).

F6F]   Single-engine, single-seat U.S. naval fighter. Developed in response to the Japanese Zero, it entered carrier service in September 1943. The "Hellcat" had a top speed of 375 mph and was armed with six machine guns.

F.F.I.]   *Forces Françaises de l'Intérieur*, name given in spring 1944 to all armed members of the French resistance under the control of the De Gaulle government (the Communist-led *Francs-Tireurs et Partisans* were officially under the command of the F.F.I. leadership, but often acted independently).

Focke-Wulf 190]   Single-engine, single-seat German fighter that entered service in late 1941. The FW-190 had a top speed of 395 mph (increased to 408 mph in some 1943 models) and was armed with four 20 mm. rapid-fire cannon and two machine guns.

Fortress]   See B-17.

4.2 inch mortar]   U.S. mortar that fired a 24-pound shell 4.2 inches in diameter, with a maximum range of over 2.5 miles (4,500 yards).

Garand]   See M-1 rifle.

Higgins boat]   See LCVP.

Howitzer]   An artillery gun capable of being elevated past 45°.

Judy]   American code name for single-engine Japanese dive bomber that entered service in 1943. It had a two-man crew, a top speed of 343 mph, carried 1,100 pounds of bombs, and was armed with three machine guns.

Junkers 52]   Three-engine German transport plane.

Junkers 86]   Twin-engine German aircraft, capable of flying at altitudes of over 39,000 feet and used mostly for photo-reconnaissance missions.

Junkers 88]   Twin-engine German bomber. It had a four-man crew, a top speed of 286 mph, carried 4,000 pounds of bombs, and was armed with several machine guns.

Kogekiki '97]   Japanese single-engine torpedo bomber commonly known in the U.S. by its American code name "Kate." It had a three-man crew, a top speed of 235 mph, and was armed with a single torpedo and one machine gun.

K ration]   American canned and packaged field rations, usually eaten cold in forward areas.

Lancaster]   Four-engine British bomber, in service 1942–45. The Lancaster had a seven-man crew, a cruising speed of 216 mph, and was armed with eight machine guns. It carried between 8,000 and 14,000 pounds of bombs.

LCI]   Landing Craft Infantry, a sea-going vessel that could land 200 men directly onto a beach. Some LCIs were armed with 40 mm. cannon and rockets and used to provide close-range fire support in amphibious landings.

LCT]   Landing Craft, Tank. The LCT could carry five tanks, nine trucks, or 150 tons of cargo.

LCVP]   Landing Craft, Vehicle and Personnel, designed by New Orleans boatbuilder Andrew J. Higgins. The LCVP was 36 feet long and could carry 36 men or a 2.5 ton truck. Over 23,000 were made during the war.

LST]   Landing Ship Tank, sea-going vessel capable of unloading 18 tanks or 500 tons of cargo directly onto a beach.

LVT]   Landing Vehicle, Tracked. American amphibious tractor that used specially shaped tracks to travel through water and over land. It could carry up to 20 men or two tons of cargo.

LVTA]   An LVT armed with a turret-mounted 75 mm. howitzer, used to provide close fire support in amphibious landings.

Liberator]   See B-24.

Long Tom]   American artillery gun with a maximum range of over 14.5 miles (25,700 yards). It fired a 95-pound shell 155 mm. in diameter.

M-1 rifle] Standard U.S. infantry rifle of World War II, often called the "Garand" after its inventor, John C. Garand. A semiautomatic weapon, it fired a .30 caliber bullet, held eight rounds in its magazine, had an effective range of 550 yards, and weighed over nine pounds.

Macchi C. 202] Single-engine, single-seat Italian fighter. It had a top speed of 369 mph and was armed with four machine guns.

Machine pistol] German submachine gun. The widely-used MP 40 fired a 9 mm. bullet, had a 32-round magazine, weighed about 10 pounds, and had an effective range of over 100 yards. (Submachine guns fire pistol ammunition, hence the German term *Maschinen Pistole.*)

Mark IV tank] German medium tank. It weighed 25 tons, had a five-man crew, a maximum speed of 25 mph, armor 80 mm. thick in the front and 30 mm. thick on the side, and was armed with a high-velocity 75 mm. gun. More than 7,000 were produced between 1942 and 1945.

Mark VI tank] German heavy tank that entered service in late 1942 and was first encountered by U.S. troops in Tunisia in 1943. The "Tiger" weighed 56 tons, had a five-man crew, very thick (100 mm.) frontal and turret armor, and was armed with a high-velocity 88 mm. gun. Highly effective in defensive fighting, the Tiger lacked mobility and mechanical reliability. Only 1,350 were made.

Me-109] Messerschmitt Bf 109, single-engine, single-seat German fighter. The Bf 109E, in service 1939–41, had a maximum speed of 354 mph and was armed with two 20 mm. cannon and two machine guns; the Bf 109G, the main Luftwaffe fighter from 1942 to 1945, had a top speed of 387 mph and was armed with one (sometimes three) 20 mm. cannon and two machine guns.

Me-110] Messerschmitt Bf 110, twin-engine German fighter with two-man crew. It had a top speed of 340 mph and was armed with two 20 mm. cannon and five machine guns.

Mitsubishi 97] Twin-engine Japanese bomber commonly known in the U.S. by its American code name "Betty." It had a seven-man crew, a top speed of about 270 mph, was armed with one 20 mm. cannon and three machine guns, and could carry up to 2,200 pounds of bombs.

MLR] Main line of resistance.

Mustang] See P-51.

Nambu] American term for Japanese 6.5 mm. and 7.7 mm. light machine guns.

Nebelwerfer] Literally, "smoke thrower"; German multi-barreled rocket launcher. The most common version was a six-barreled weapon that fired a

75-pound rocket 150 mm. in diameter. It had a range of over four miles (7,300 yards). Allied troops called the *Nebelwerfer* the "screaming meemie" from the sound its rockets (which were fitted with sirens) made in flight.

Norden bomb sight] American bomb sight that was linked to the aircraft autopilot, allowing the bombardier to control the plane's course during the final approach to the target.

105] Standard American field artillery gun of World War II. It fired a 33-pound shell 105 mm. in diameter and had a maximum range of almost seven miles (12,200 yards).

109] See Me-109

190] See Focke-Wulf 190

P-38] Twin-engine, single-seat U.S. fighter with distinctive twin-boomed airframe. The "Lightning" entered service in late 1942, had a top speed of 395 mph, and was armed with a 20 mm. cannon and four machine guns. P-38s achieved their greatest success in aerial combat against the Japanese, and were also used as photo-reconnaissance and fighter-bomber aircraft.

P-39] Single-engine, single-seat U.S. fighter. The "Airacobra" had a maximum speed of 355 mph and was armed with a 37 mm. cannon and four machines guns. It proved unsatisfactory as a fighter and saw limited service as a ground-attack aircraft.

P-40] Single-engine, single-seat U.S. fighter. Various models of the "Warhawk" had top speeds of 345 to 364 mph, and were armed with six machine guns.

P-47] Single-engine, single-seat U.S. fighter. Introduced into service in 1943, the "Thunderbolt" had a maximum speed of 406 mph (increased to 429 mph in 1944 models) and was armed with eight machine guns. Used as a fighter-bomber, it could carry eight air-to-ground rockets or 2,000 pounds of bombs.

P-51] Single-engine, single-seat U.S. fighter with the range to escort bombers deep into Germany while flying from British bases. The P-51B "Mustang" entered service in late 1943, had a maximum speed of 445 mph, and was armed with four machine guns.

Panzer grenadier] German motorized infantry. Panzer grenadier divisions, and the panzer grenadier regiments in panzer (armored) divisions, were equipped with sufficient trucks and half-tracks to move the formation's personnel, weapons, and equipment. (Most German infantry divisions relied on horse-drawn transport and artillery, and their men had to march cross-country when rail transport was unavailable.)

PB2Y] Four-engine flying boat used by U.S. navy as transport, and for air-sea rescue and ocean patrol missions.

Rifle grenade] Grenade fired from the muzzle of a rifle, using a special attachment and blank propellant cartridge.

S-3] U.S. army term for the staff section for operations at battalion or regimental level, used to refer to both the section itself and to the staff officer who headed it.

S mine] German anti-personnel mine containing over 300 ball bearings packed around an explosive charge, usually connected to a trip wire. When triggered, a propellant charge would lift the mine several feet into the air, where it would then explode.

SS] Schutzstaffel ("Protection Detachment"). Originally Hitler's Nazi party bodyguard, after 1933 the SS became the main instrument of state terror in Germany, with control over the police, the security service, and the concentration camps. The SS also had its own military force, known after 1940 as the Waffen (Armed) SS. Numbering 28,000 men at the start of the war, by 1944 the Waffen SS had over 500,000 men in its ranks and included seven well-equipped panzer (armored) divisions.

75 mm. howitzer] American field artillery gun that could be broken down into sections for easier transport. It fired a 14.6 pound shell 75 mm. in diameter and had a range of over 5.5 miles (9,750 yards). A similar weapon was used by the Japanese.

Sherman tank] American medium tank. About 49,000 Shermans were manufactured between 1942 and 1945, and it became the standard tank used by the western Allies. The Sherman weighed 33 tons, had a five-man crew, a maximum speed of 25 mph, armor ranging in thickness from 25 to 75 mm., and was armed with a 75 mm. gun.

Shoe mine] *Schü* mine (from *Schützenmine*, "rifleman's mine"), German anti-personnel mine with explosive charge of about seven ounces. The explosive was placed inside a wooden box instead of a metal casing to prevent detection by metal mine detectors.

60 mm. mortar] U.S. mortar firing 60 mm. shell weighing 3.1 pounds, with a maximum range of over one mile (1,985 yards).

Spandau] Allied name for 7.92 mm. light machine guns used by German infantry.

Spitfire] Single-engine, single-seat British fighter aircraft in operational service from 1939 to 1945. The Spitfire V, in service 1941–43, had a maximum speed of 374 mph and was armed with two 20 mm. cannon and four machine guns.

Stuka] Junkers 87, single-engine German dive bomber designed to give close support to ground troops. The "Stuka" (from *Sturzkampfflugzueg*— "dive bomber") had a two-man crew, a top speed of 242 mph, and was usually armed with three machine guns and a single 1,100 pound bomb carried under the fuselage.

T-5]   Rank of corporal in the U.S. army technical services.

TBF]   Single-engine U.S. torpedo bomber that entered carrier service in 1942. The "Avenger" had a crew of three, a top speed of 257 mph, and was armed with up to five machine guns and either one torpedo or 2,000 pounds of bombs; some aircraft were equipped to fire air-to-ground rockets.

Teller mine]   German anti-tank mine containing 9–12 pounds of high explosives.

Thunderbolt]   See P-47.

Tiger tank]   See Mark VI tank.

Time-fire]   Artillery shells fused to explode in the air in order to disperse fragments over a wider area.

V-1]   Unmanned German jet aircraft used to bombard Britain and Belgium in 1944–45. The V-1 (*Vergeltungswaffe*, "reprisal weapon") was guided by a gyroscope, had a speed of 350 mph, and carried 1,870 pounds of explosives in its warhead. About 40 percent of the V-1s launched were destroyed by Allied fighters or anti-aircraft fire. (The V-2, also used by the Germans in 1944–45, was a liquid-fueled ballistic missile with a 2,000 pound warhead. It traveled at supersonic speeds and could not be intercepted.)

Wehrmacht]   Name for the German armed forces, 1935–45.

Wildcat]   Name for the F4F, American single-engine, single-seat naval fighter. The "Wildcat" had a maximum speed of 318 mph and was armed with six machine guns. It was replaced as the standard carrier-based fighter by the F6F in 1943.

Zero]   Single-engine, single-seat Japanese naval fighter whose superior performance took the Allies by surprise in 1941. Highly maneuverable, it had a maximum speed of 316 mph (increased to 336 mph in 1942 models) and was armed with two 20 mm. cannon and two machine guns.

U.S. ARMY ORGANIZATION

Unit and formation strengths given below are those established by the U.S. Army for its infantry in 1943; equivalent units and formations in the U.S. Marines were similar in size.

Platoon]   Unit of about 40 men, commanded by a second lieutenant.

Company]   Unit made up of three rifle platoons, one weapons platoon, and other troops, with 193 men at full strength; usually commanded by a captain.

Battalion] Unit made up of three rifle companies, one weapons company, and a headquarters company, with 871 men at full strength; usually commanded by a lieutenant colonel.

Regiment] Formation made up of three battalions plus supporting troops, including artillery. It had 3,118 men at full strength and was commanded by a colonel.

Division] Formation made up of three regiments plus supporting troops, including artillery and combat engineers. It had 14,253 men at full strength and was commanded by a major general. The U.S. Army raised 89 divisions during World War II (67 infantry, 16 armored, five airborne, and one cavalry), and the Marine Corps raised six.

Index

Library of Congress Cataloging-in-Publication Data

Reporting World War II: American journalism, 1938–1946 /
    introduction by Stephen E. Ambrose.
        p.   cm.
    Originally published in a two-volume set in 1995.
    Includes index.
    ISBN 1–931082–05–7
    1. Journalism—United States—History—20th century.
2. World War, 1939–1945—Press coverage—United States.
I. Title: Reporting World War Two.   II. Title:
Reporting World War 2.

PN4867.R47   2001
070.4'4994053—dc21

                                        00–067284